D1301007

CCNA® Cisco® Certified Network Associate Routing and Switching Study Guide with Boson® NetSim®
Limited Edition

(Exam 200-101, ICND2)

Richard Deal

New York   Chicago   San Francisco
Athens   London   Madrid   Mexico City
Milan   New Delhi   Singapore   Sydney   Toronto

Cataloging-in-Publication Data is on file with the Library of Congress

McGraw-Hill Education books are available at special quantity discounts to use as premiums and sales promotions, or for use in corporate training programs. To contact a representative, please visit the Contact Us pages at www.mhprofessional.com.

CCNA° Cisco° Certified Network Associate Routing and Switching Study Guide (Exam 200-101, ICND2) with Boson° NetSim° Limited Edition

1234567890 DOC/DOC 1098765

ISBN: Book p/n 978-0-07-183228-1 and CD p/n 978-0-07-183229-8
of set 978-0-07-183234-2

MHID: Book p/n 0-07-183228-9 and CD p/n 0-07-183229-7
of set 0-07-183234-2

Sponsoring Editor	**Technical Editor**	**Production Supervisor**
Timothy Green	Desiree Lindfield	James Kussow
Editorial Supervisor	**Copy Editor**	**Composition**
Janet Walden	Bill McManus	Cenveo° Publisher Services
Project Editor	**Proofreader**	**Illustration**
LeeAnn Pickrell	Lisa McCoy	Cenveo Publisher Services
Acquisitions Coordinators	**Indexer**	**Art Director, Cover**
Mary Demery, Amy Stonebraker	Jack Lewis	Jeff Weeks

Boson° and the Boson logo, ExSim-Max™, and NetSim° Network Simulator° are trademarks of Boson Holdings, LLC.

To my two children, Alina and Nika.

For more than 20 years, **Richard Deal** has operated his own company, The Deal Group, Inc., in Oviedo, Florida, east of Orlando. Richard has more than 25 years of experience in the computing and networking industry, including networking, training, systems administration, and programming. In addition to earning a B.S. in mathematics from Grove City College, he holds many certifications from Cisco and has taught many beginning and advanced Cisco classes. Richard is the author of *Cisco ASA Configuration*, an in-depth book on Cisco's ASA firewall appliances and their implementation, published by McGraw-Hill Professional. Richard is also the author of two books with Cisco Press: *The Complete Cisco VPN Configuration Guide* and *Cisco Router Firewall Security*; both books made it to Cisco's CCIE Security recommended reading list.

About the Technical Editor

Desiree Lindfield is a Cisco Certified Systems Instructor (CCSI) and provides official Cisco training for Boson and Global Knowledge. She has delivered technical training for numerous vendors and technologies for teams located around the globe. In addition to training, Desiree serves on a team of consultants providing design, installation, and troubleshooting services. Recent implementations include Nexus 7000 switches and Cisco's Unified Computing System. Desiree is a regular attendee of Cisco Live, B-Sides, and DEF CON annual conferences.

CONTENTS AT A GLANCE

CONTENTS

Part II
Cisco Routers and LANs

Part III
Routing

Part IV
Cisco Routers and WANs

From Boson Software®

The Cisco CCNA certification requires that you learn and master a number of skills. As you study this book, incorporating Boson NetSim® into your learning process will help you successfully complete the CCNA certification by passing the ICND2 exam. The Boson NetSim Limited Edition (LE) included with this book will get you started on your way, and additional capability from the full edition is available after purchasing an upgrade.

The Boson NetSim Network Simulator® is an application that will help you with the practical, hands-on portion of your education. NetSim will ensure that you understand the concepts of routing and switching by challenging you to apply those concepts on Cisco devices. Once you feel that you have mastered both the theory and the practical labs, you can test your knowledge using the exams included with this book and the accompanying digital resources. You may also purchase ExSim-Max™ practice exams from Boson, available at www.boson .com. ExSim-Max practice exams are designed to simulate the complete exam experience, including topics covered, question types, question difficulty, and time allowed. With ExSim-Max, you can be sure you are ready to pass the real exam— guaranteed (www.boson.com/guarantee).

Boson NetSim provides more versatility and support than any other network simulation software on the market. Boson NetSim will not only help you become CCNA certified, it will actually help you learn and understand how to configure routers, switches, and networks.

The Boson NetSim LE can be upgraded to the full edition for CCNA at http://www.boson.com/netsim-cisco-network-simulator (a valid activation code from your qualifying McGraw-Hill Education book is required). Upgrading enables all other Boson NetSim labs, commands, and advanced features. Don't forget to complete your study with ExSim-Max practice exams.

Best wishes in your future studies!

PREFACE

The primary objective of this book is to help you achieve the Cisco Certified Network Associate (CCNA) certification so that you can enhance your career. I believe that the only way you can increase your knowledge is through theoretical and practical learning. In other words, this book provides the book learning as well as basic hands-on experience that you'll need to pass the exam. However, once you pass the CCNA exam, your journey is just beginning: you'll need to enhance your newly acquired skills with additional reading and a lot of hands-on experience.

You can achieve CCNA certification in two ways:

- Pass the CCNA (200-120) exam.
- Pass both the ICND1 (100-101) and ICND2 (200-101) exams.

The CCNA 200-120 exam includes the same topics covered by the ICND1 100-101 and ICND2 200-101 exams. Cisco developed the second approach particularly for individuals who are just beginning their journey into networking, especially for people taking the CCNA curriculum at a Cisco Network Academy. The two-test approach is better suited for this environment since it takes a year to two to go through Cisco's CCNA curriculum at the Network Academies. With this approach, you take the ICND1 100-101 exam halfway through the curriculum and the ICND2 200-101 exam at the end of the curriculum.

Another advantage of taking and passing the ICND1 exam is that you have achieved Cisco's newest entry-level certification: CCENT (Cisco Certified Entry Networking Technician). In August 2007, Cisco introduced this certification based on customer and employer demand for a lower-level certification demonstrating basic networking and hands-on skills with IOS devices such as routers and switches.

If you already have networking experience, especially if that experience includes configuring Cisco devices, you are better off taking the single CCNA 200-120 exam. The main advantage of this approach is that you have to pay for only one exam. Costs vary depending upon where you live in the world. Currently, the US exam cost of the ICND1 and ICND2 exams is $150 US each, while the CCNA 200-120 exam is $295 US (at the time of the printing of this book), but Cisco has changed its pricing scheme in the past and can do so in the future.

This book was primarily written for those individuals wishing to pass the ICND 200-101 exam. If you're thinking of taking the combination CCNA 200-120 exam, you should purchase my book *CCNA® Cisco® Certified Network Associate Routing and Switching Study Guide (Exam 200-120, ICND1 & ICND2) with Boson® NetSim® Limited Edition* from McGraw-Hill Education, which covers the topic thoroughly.

In This Book

This book covers all the exam objectives posted on Cisco's web site concerning the ICND2 200-101 exam. Each chapter covers one or more of the main objectives in this list, especially as it relates to how things work and how to configure them on Cisco's routers and switches. Appendix A has a breakdown of Cisco's objectives for the ICND2 200-101 and indicates which chapter in this book covers each of those objectives.

In Every Chapter

I've created a set of chapter components that call your attention to important items, reinforce important points, and provide helpful exam-taking hints. Take a look at what you'll find in almost every chapter:

■ Every chapter begins with the **Certification Objectives**—what you need to know to pass the section on the exam dealing with the chapter topic. The objective headings identify the objectives within the chapter, so you'll always know an objective when you see it!

■ **Practice Exercises** are interspersed throughout the chapters. These are step-by-step exercises that allow you to get the hands-on experience you need to pass the exams. They help you master skills that are likely to be an area of focus on the exams. Don't just read through the exercises; they are hands-on practice that you should be comfortable completing. Learning by doing is an effective way to increase your competency with a product. These exercises are directly tied to the McGraw-Hill Education NetSim Learning Edition simulator, produced by Boson Software and included in the digital resources that accompany this book. These exercises will always work with the simulator product. Please note that Cisco's real exams contain simulation questions, so it is very important that you practice your skills with either this simulator or with real routers and switches.

- **On the Job** notes describe the issues that come up most often in real-world settings. They provide a valuable perspective on certification- and product-related topics. They point out common mistakes and address questions that have arisen from on-the-job discussions and experience.

- **Exam Watch** notes point out important information you should learn when preparing for your exam.

The encapsulation ppp *command can be applied only to asynchronous or synchronous serial* interfaces on a router, and thus PPP's authentication is applicable only on serial interfaces.

- **Multimedia demonstrations**, in the form of videos, are included with the digital resources that accompany this book. If you want to see *actual* configurations of Cisco routers and switches in action, you can view these multimedia demonstrations. Throughout each chapter involving configurations are multiple multimedia demonstrations with a pointer to which video you can view. You will need to *read the instructions* included with the digital resources to run the multimedia demonstrations.

- The **Inside the Exam** element appears at the end of each chapter and focuses on important topics mentioned in the chapter, covering procedures you should take to ready yourself for the exam with the information discussed in the chapter. Many tips and tricks are pointed out here to help you pass your exam with confidence.

- The **Two-Minute Drill** at the end of every chapter offers a checklist of the main points of the chapter. It can be used for last-minute review.

Q&A
- The **Self Test** section at the end of each chapter offers questions similar to those found on the certification exams. The answers to these questions, as well as explanations of the answers, can be found in the final section of each chapter. By taking the practice exams after completing each chapter, you'll reinforce what you've learned from that chapter while becoming familiar with the structure of the exam questions.

■ The **Exam Readiness Checklist** in Appendix A is a list of the official ICND2 200-101 exam objectives, presented exactly as the vendor specifies them, cross-listed with the exam objectives as they are presented in the book and chapter references. You should work with this list as you study, noting your familiarity with the objectives by checking off the appropriate box before you review each chapter.

Some Pointers

Once you've finished reading this book, set aside some time to do a *thorough* review. You might want to return to the book several times and make use of all the methods it offers for reviewing the material:

1. *Re-read all the Two-Minute Drills,* or have someone quiz you. You also can use the drills as a way to do a quick cram before the exam.

2. *Re-read all the Exam Watch notes.* These are important items you should know for the exam. In other words, don't be surprised to see these topics appear on the real exam.

3. *Re-take the Self Test sections at the back of each chapter.* Taking the tests right after you've read the chapter is a good idea, because the questions help reinforce what you've just learned. However, it's an even better idea to return later and go through all the questions in the book in one sitting. Pretend that you're taking the live exam. (When you go through the questions the first time, you should mark your answers on a separate piece of paper. That way, you can run through the questions as many times as you need to until you feel comfortable with the material.)

4. *Use the exam test engine included in the digital resources that accompany this book.* Did you use the test engine to test your knowledge? The 100 questions in the test engine cover all the topics in the book. You can also purchase additional tests from Boson Software at its web site (www.boson.com).

5. *Do all the practice exercises in each of the chapters.* Some simulation questions appear on the actual CCNA exams. In the simulation questions, you'll be required to perform basic configuration *and* troubleshooting

tasks on a Cisco router and/or switch. Therefore, it is important that you have good configuration skills. Use the practice exercises to hone your configuration skills. I have developed two types of simulation questions in this book. All of them have to do with configuring Cisco routers and Catalyst switches; however, some of them also have you troubleshoot networking problems, where two or three configuration errors are introduced into the network and it is your job to track down these configuration errors, using the tools you learned about throughout this book, and fix them.

Practice Exams and the Simulator

As I mentioned earlier, it is important that you have hands-on experience not only for the exam, but also to prepare for working with Cisco equipment in a real network. A lot of time and effort have been devoted in the creation of the practice exercises in this book. I have developed Figures 1 and 2 that display the network topology used with the simulator.

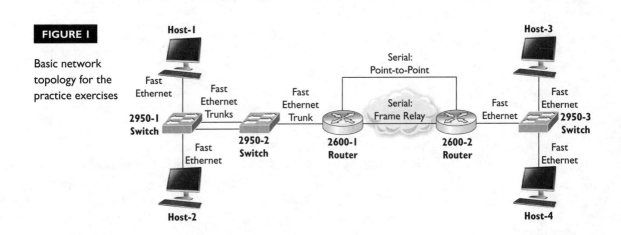

FIGURE 1

Basic network topology for the practice exercises

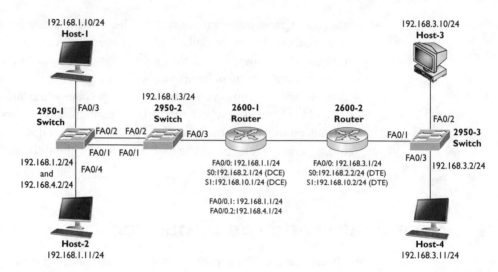

FIGURE 2

Addressing for the network topology used for the practice exercises

These figures show four PCs, two routers (both 2600s), and three Catalyst 2950 switches. Chapters that have practice exercises will refer you to these figures for the layout of the network topology and the addressing assigned to the devices in the topology. Refer to these figures when performing the exercises.

ACKNOWLEDGMENTS

I would like to thank the following people:

- This book would not have been possible without the support of my two kids, Alina and Nika. A book of this size is very time consuming, especially when you have to balance a book, a job, and, most importantly, a family. My kids provided endless encouragement to keep me writing when I was pressed to meet deadlines for the book.

- A special thanks to Desiree Lindfield for providing excellent feedback and encouragement on the technical content of this book. She provided many practical insights for the On the Job notes throughout the book. I would also like to thank Martin Frank, Jon Oden, Kelly Mansfield, and Matthew Woodruff from Boson Software for their assistance in setting up and using the router simulator product and test engine included with the digital media.

- The team at McGraw-Hill Professional, especially Tim Green, Mary Demery, Amy Stonebraker, and LeeAnn Pickrell. I owe a debt of gratitude to this team, especially in pulling all of the pieces together for the digital material and the final proofing—thanks for your help!

Best wishes to all! And cheers!

Richard A. Deal

How to Take a Cisco Certification Examination

This introduction covers the importance of your CCNA certification and prepares you for taking the actual examination. It gives you a few pointers on methods of preparing for the exam, including how to study and register, what to expect, and what to do on exam day.

Catch the Wave!

Congratulations on your pursuit of Cisco certification! In this fast-paced world of networking, few certification programs are as valuable as the one offered by Cisco.

The networking industry has virtually exploded in recent years, accelerated by nonstop innovation and the Internet's popularity. Cisco has stayed at the forefront of this tidal wave, maintaining a dominant role in the industry.

The networking industry is highly competitive, and evolving technology only increases in its complexity. The rapid growth of the networking industry has created a vacuum of qualified people: there simply aren't enough skilled networking people to meet the demand. Even the most experienced professionals must keep current with the latest technology in order to provide the skills that the industry demands. Cisco certification programs can help networking professionals succeed as they pursue their careers.

Cisco started its certification program many years ago, offering only the designation Cisco Certified Internetwork Expert (CCIE). Through the CCIE program, Cisco provided a means to meet the growing demand for experts in the field of networking. However, the CCIE tests are brutal, with a failure rate greater than 80 percent, and fewer than 5 percent of candidates pass on their first attempt! As you might imagine, few people attain CCIE status.

In early 1998, Cisco recognized the need for intermediate certifications, and several new programs were created. Four intermediate certifications were added: CCNA (Cisco Certified Network Associate), CCNP (Cisco Certified Network Professional), CCDA (Cisco Certified Design Associate), and CCDP (Cisco Certified Design Professional). In addition, several specialties were added to the professional and CCIE certification levels since then. Today, Cisco also has Professional and CCIE certifications in many areas, including security and voice, to name a couple.

Why Vendor Certification?

Over the years, vendors have created their own certification programs because of industry demand. This demand arises when the marketplace needs skilled professionals and an easy way to identify them. Vendors benefit because it promotes people skilled in managing their products. Professionals benefit because it boosts their careers. Employers benefit because it helps them identify qualified people.

In the networking industry, technology changes too often and too quickly to rely on traditional means of certification, such as universities and trade associations. Because of the investment and effort required to keep network certification programs current, vendors are the only organizations suited to keep pace with the changes. In general, such vendor certification programs are excellent, with most of them requiring a solid foundation in the essentials as well as their particular product line.

Corporate America has come to appreciate these vendor certification programs and the value they provide. Employers recognize that certifications, like university degrees, do not guarantee a level of knowledge, experience, or performance; rather, they establish a baseline for comparison. By seeking to hire vendor-certified employees, a company can be assured that not only has it found a person skilled in networking, but it has also hired a person skilled in the specific products the company uses.

Technical professionals have also begun to recognize the value of certification and the impact it can have on their careers. By completing a certification program, professionals gain an endorsement of their skills from a major industry source. This endorsement can boost their current position, and it makes finding the next job even easier. Often a certification determines whether a first interview is even granted.

Today a certification may place you ahead of the pack. Tomorrow it will be a necessity to keep from being left in the dust.

e x a m

ⓦ **a t c h** *Signing up for an exam has become easier with a web-based test registration system. To sign up for the CCNA exams, access VUE's site (www .VUE.com) and register for the Cisco Career Certification path. You will need to get an Internet account and password, if you do not already have one, for these sites. Just select the option for first-time registration, and the web site will walk you through that process. The registration wizard even provides maps to the testing centers, something that is not available when you call VUE on the telephone. As of 2007, Cisco no longer offers testing through Prometric.*

Cisco's Certification Program

Cisco now has a number of certifications for the Routing and Switching career track. While Cisco recommends a series of courses for each of these certifications, they are not required. Ultimately, certification is dependent upon a candidate's passing a series of exams. With the right experience and study materials, you can pass each of these exams without taking the associated class.

Cisco is constantly changing and updating its certification requirements. For more information about Cisco certifications and exams, visit Cisco on the Web at www.cisco.com/web/learning/index.html.

e x a m

ⓦ **a t c h** *In addition to the technical objectives that are being tested for each exam, you will find much more useful information on Cisco's web site at www .cisco.com. You will find information on becoming certified, exam-specific information, sample test questions, demonstration tutorial videos, and the latest news on Cisco certification. This is the most important site you will find on your journey to becoming Cisco certified. The Career and Certification sections of the web site change periodically, so be sure to check for updates regularly!*

Computer-Based Testing

In a perfect world, you would be assessed for your true knowledge of a subject, not simply how you respond to a series of test questions. But life isn't perfect, and it just isn't practical to evaluate everyone's knowledge on a one-to-one basis. (Cisco actually does have a one-to-one evaluation, but it's reserved for the CCIE Laboratory exam.)

For the majority of its certifications, Cisco evaluates candidates using a computer-based testing service operated by VUE. This form of testing service is quite popular in the industry, and it is used for a number of vendor certification programs. Thanks to VUE's large number of facilities, exams can be administered worldwide, and generally in the same town as a prospective candidate.

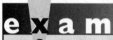

Cisco no longer allows you to mark questions for later review—once you answer a question, you cannot go back and change your answer.

For the most part, VUE exams work similarly from vendor to vendor. However, there is an important fact to know about Cisco's exams: They use the traditional test format, not the newer adaptive format. This allows Cisco to choose an appropriate number of questions on each objective in order to test your knowledge.

To discourage simple memorization, Cisco exams present a different set of questions every time the exam is administered. In the development of the exam, hundreds of questions are compiled and refined using beta testers. From this large collection, a random sampling is drawn for each test. Plus, Cisco has developed simulation questions that require you to place basic configurations on Cisco devices and troubleshoot an existing network topology. These types of questions require a candidate to have hands-on, not just book-learning, experience.

Each Cisco exam has a specific number of questions and test duration. Testing time is typically generous (75 to 90 minutes), and the time remaining is always displayed in the corner of the testing screen, along with the number of remaining questions. If time expires during an exam, the test terminates and incomplete answers are counted as incorrect.

At the end of the exam, your test is immediately graded and the results are displayed on the screen. Scores for each subject area are also provided, but the system will not indicate which specific questions were missed. A report is automatically printed at the proctor's desk for your files. The test score is electronically transmitted back to Cisco.

In the end, this computer-based system of evaluation is reasonably fair. You might think that one or two questions were poorly worded; this can certainly happen, but you shouldn't worry too much. Ultimately, it's all factored into the required passing score.

Question Types

Cisco exams pose questions in a variety of formats, most of which are discussed here. As candidates progress toward the more advanced certifications, the difficulty of the exams is intensified, through both the subject matter and the question formats.

exam
ⓦatch

To pass these challenging exams, you may want to talk with other test takers to determine what is being tested and what to expect in terms of difficulty. The most helpful way to communicate with other CCNA hopefuls is the Cisco Network Professional Connection. With this bulletin-board system, you can ask questions from other members, including employees of Cisco. These discussions cover everything imaginable concerning Cisco networking equipment and certification. Go to https:// learningnetwork.cisco.com/index.jspa to learn how to access this source of a wealth of information. (Note that at the time of publication, this information was correct. Please contact Cisco directly for the most up-to-date information about Cisco's forums.)

True/False

The classic true/false question format is *not* used in the Cisco exams, for the obvious reason that a simple guess has a 50 percent chance of being correct. Instead, true/false questions are posed in multiple-choice format, requiring the candidate to identify the true or false statement from a group of selections.

Multiple Choice

Multiple choice is the primary format for questions in Cisco exams. These questions may be posed in a variety of ways.

Select the Correct Answer   This is the classic multiple-choice question, in which the candidate selects a single answer from a minimum of four choices. In addition to the question's wording, the choices are presented in a Windows radio button format, in which only one answer can be selected at a time. The question will instruct you to "Select the best answer" when you need to look for just one answer.

Select the Three Correct Answers   The multiple-answer version is similar to the single-choice version, but multiple answers must be provided. This is an all-or-nothing format; all the correct answers must be selected or the entire question is incorrect. In this format, the question specifies exactly how many answers must be selected. Choices are presented in a checkbox format, allowing more than one answer to be selected. In addition, the testing software prevents too many answers from being selected.

Select All That Apply   The open-ended version is the most difficult multiple-choice format, since the candidate does not know how many answers should be selected. As with the multiple-answer version, all the correct answers must be selected to gain credit for the question. If too many answers or not enough answers are selected, no credit is given. This format presents choices in a checkbox format, but the testing software does not advise the candidates whether they've selected the correct number of answers. Cisco's CCIE exams include questions like this. You won't see any questions like this on the ICND2 exam.

exam
Watch

Make it easy on yourself and find some "braindumps." These are notes about the exam from test takers, which indicate the most difficult concepts tested, what to look out for, and sometimes even what not to bother studying. Simply do a search for CCNA or ICND2 and browse the recent postings. Beware, however, of the person who posts a question reported to have been on the test and its answer. First, the question and its answer may be incorrect. Second, this is a violation of Cisco's confidentiality agreement, which you, as a candidate, must agree to prior to taking the exam. Giving out specific information regarding a test violates this agreement and could result in the revocation of your certification status.

Exhibits

Exhibits, usually showing a network diagram or a router configuration, accompany many exam questions. These exhibits are displayed in a separate window, which is opened by clicking the Exhibit button at the bottom of the screen.

Drag-and-Drop

Drag-and-drop questions list terms in one column and descriptions or definitions in another, where you have to click your mouse on a term, drag it, and drop it on the correct definition. With some questions, some terms or definitions might not be used; in others, a term might be used for multiple definitions.

Scenarios

While the normal line of questioning tests a candidate's "book knowledge," scenarios add a level of complexity. Rather than asking only technical questions, they apply the candidate's knowledge to real-world situations. Scenarios generally consist of one or two paragraphs and an exhibit that describes a company's needs or network configuration. This description is followed by a series of questions and problems that challenge the candidate's ability to address the situation. Scenario-based questions are commonly found in exams relating to network design, but they appear to some degree in each of the Cisco exams.

Simulations

The ICND2 exam will possibly include a handful of simulation questions. With a simulation question, you will be prompted to put a basic configuration on a Cisco router or switch. This will require you to access the command-line interface (CLI) of the router or switch, access the appropriate mode on the router or switch, supply a basic configuration, and possibly test the configuration. Some simulation questions will already have a preconfiguration on existing Cisco devices, with configuration errors. You will be required to find the configuration errors, fix them, and then test the corrections. While working with the router or switch simulator, you will have the context-sensitive help feature available to you. Before you actually start the exam at a VUE site, you are offered the chance to become more familiar with the look and feel of a simulator question. I highly recommend that you *not* skip this part, especially since the time you spend on this tutorial is *not* counted against you. For a demonstration of what the simulator is like, you can also visit https://learningnetwork.cisco.com/ and browse to the certification section to find the demo. This example is very similar to, but not exactly the same as, the simulator that you would see on the real exam. For additional simulation questions that are similar in concept to the actual exam, please be sure to investigate the McGraw-Hill Education Practice Tests for CCNA included in the digital resources that accompany this book.

Simlet

The CCNA- and Professional-level exams commonly have one simlet question. A simlet question is a multi-part question in which you are given a common scenario and must provide an answer for each question asked. Some simlets are three-part questions and some are six-part. Make sure you answer each of the simlets in the question before proceeding to the next question. Most simlets will require you to answer the questions by examining configurations on Cisco devices. The simlets will have you use the IOS CLI of one or more devices to answer the set of questions.

One easy technique to use in studying for certification exams is the 30-minutes-per-day effort. Simply study for a minimum of 30 minutes every day. It is a small but significant commitment. On a day when you just can't focus, give it at least 30 minutes. On a day when it flows completely for you, study longer. As long as you have more of the flow days, your chances of succeeding are high.

Studying Techniques

First and foremost, give yourself plenty of time to study. Networking is a complex field, and you can't expect to cram what you need to know into a single study session. It is a field best learned over time, by studying a subject and then applying your knowledge. Build yourself a study schedule and stick to it, but be reasonable about the pressure you put on yourself, especially if you're studying in addition to your regular duties at work.

Second, practice and experiment. In networking, you need more than knowledge; you also need understanding. You can't just memorize facts to be effective; you need to understand why events happen, how things work, and (most important) how and why they break.

The best way to gain deep understanding is to take your book knowledge to the lab. Try it out. Make it work. Change it a little. Break it. Fix it. Snoop around "under the hood." If you have access into a network analyzer, such as Wireshark, put it to use. You can gain amazing insight into the inner workings of a network by watching devices communicate with each other.

Unless you have a very understanding boss, don't experiment with router commands on a production router. A seemingly innocuous command can have a nasty side effect. If you don't have a lab, your local Cisco office or Cisco users' group may be able to help. Many training centers also allow students access to their lab equipment during off-hours. Many router and switch simulator products are also available on the market. The simulator included with the digital resources that accompany this book is a stripped-down version of Boson's NetSim simulator product. It can simulate many router and switch commands for various models of Cisco products. The version includes two 2600 series routers as well as three 2950 switches. It comes with a preset topology that includes Fast Ethernet, serial point-to-point connections, and Frame Relay. After activating the NetSim Learning Edition, if you want the full functionality of the simulator product, go to Boson .com | My Account | Special Offers for an upgrade offer that gives you a steep discount over buying the product at retail. By purchasing the full product, you have access to all of the commands within the product, as well as the capability to create your own topologies! For hands-on experience, this is a great bargain for the money that you would spend.

Another excellent way to study is through case studies. Case studies are articles or interactive discussions that offer real-world examples of how technology is applied to meet a need. These examples can serve to cement your understanding of a technique or technology by seeing it put to use. Interactive discussions offer added value because you can also pose questions of your own. User groups are an excellent source of examples, since the purpose of these groups is to share information and learn from each other's experiences.

The Cisco Networkers conference is not to be missed. Although renowned for its wild party and crazy antics, this conference offers a wealth of information. Held every year in cities around the world, it includes four to five days of technical seminars and presentations on a variety of subjects. As you might imagine, it's very popular. You have to register early to get the classes you want.

There is also the Cisco web site. This gem is loaded with collections of technical documents and white papers. As you progress to more advanced subjects, you will find great value in the large number of examples and reference materials available. But be warned: You need to do a lot of digging to find the really good stuff. Often you have to browse every document returned by the search engine to find exactly the one you need. This effort pays off. Most CCIEs I know have compiled six to ten binders of reference material from Cisco's site alone.

Scheduling Your Exam

The Cisco exams are scheduled by calling VUE directly or contacting the company online via its web site. For locations outside the United States, your local number can be found on VUE's web site at www.VUE.com. VUE representatives can schedule your exam, but they don't have information about the certification programs. Direct your questions about certifications to Cisco's education division at http://ciscocert.force.com/english.

Exams can be scheduled up to a year in advance, although this is really not necessary. Generally, scheduling a week or two ahead is sufficient to reserve the day and time you prefer. When you call to schedule, operators will search for testing centers in your area. For convenience, they can also tell which testing centers you've used before. You can also use VUE's online site, where you can easily search for the test centers closest to your address.

VUE accepts a variety of payment methods, with credit cards being the most convenient. When you pay by credit card, you can take tests the day after you call—provided, of course, that the testing center has room. VUE will e-mail you a receipt and confirmation of your testing date, which typically arrives the same day you schedule the exam. If you need to cancel or reschedule an exam, remember to call at least one day before your exam or you'll lose your test fee.

When you register for the exam, you will be asked for your Cisco testing ID number. This number is used to track your exam results back to Cisco. It's important that you use the same ID number each time you register, so that Cisco can follow your progress. Address information provided when you first register is also used by Cisco to ship certificates and other related material. If this is your first time taking a Cisco exam, VUE will assign you a unique ID number.

You will also be required to provide a valid e-mail address when registering. If you do not have an e-mail address that works, you will not be able to schedule the exam. Once you are registered, you will receive an e-mail notice containing your registration information for your scheduled exam. Examine it closely to make sure that it is correct.

In addition to the VUE testing sites, Cisco offers facilities for taking exams free of charge or at a greatly reduced rate at each Networkers conference in the United States. As you might imagine, this option is quite popular, so reserve your exam time as soon as you arrive at the conference.

Arriving at the Exam

As with any test, you'll be tempted to cram the night before. Resist that temptation. You should know the material by this point, and if you're too groggy in the morning, you won't remember what you studied anyway. Instead, get a good night's sleep.

Arrive early for your exam; this gives you time to relax and review key facts. Take the opportunity to review your notes. If you get burned out on studying, you can usually start your exam a few minutes early. On the other hand, I don't recommend arriving late. Your test could be canceled, or you might be left without enough time to complete the exam.

When you arrive at the testing center, you'll need to sign in with the exam administrator. You need to provide two forms of identification. Acceptable forms include government-issued IDs (for example, a passport or driver's license) and credit cards. One form of ID must include a photograph.

Aside from a brain full of facts, you don't need to bring anything else to the exam. In fact, your brain is about all you're allowed to take into the exam. All the tests are closed book, meaning that you don't get to bring any reference materials with you. You're also not allowed to take any notes out of the exam room. The test administrator will give you a small whiteboard and marker.

Calculators are not allowed, so be prepared to do any necessary math (such as hex-binary-decimal conversions or subnet masks) in your head or on the whiteboard.

Leave your pager and cell phone in your car—you are not allowed to take them into the actual testing room. Purses, books, and other materials must be left with the administrator before you enter. While you're in the exam room, it's important that you don't disturb other candidates; talking is not allowed during the exam.

In the exam room, the exam administrator logs you into your exam, and you have to verify that your name and exam number are correct. Currently Cisco also requires that a picture be taken of you, which is included in its database and printed on your exam results. If this is the first time you've taken a Cisco exam, you can select a brief tutorial for the exam software.

exam

ⓦatch   *You will also be asked to take a survey before the exam. You can skip the survey; however, since the survey doesn't count against your time limit,*   *I recommend that you do a brain-dump of information to your whiteboard and then quickly answer the survey.*

Before the test begins, you will be provided with facts about the exam, including the duration, the number of questions, and the score required for passing. Then the clock starts ticking, and the fun begins. Please note that Cisco does not officially publish the number of questions on its exams (typically 50 to 60) or the passing rate (typically between 800 and 850). Cisco changed this philosophy to allow it to dynamically adjust the number of questions and pass rates in order to create a harder or easier exam based on past scores of test takers. Typically, you'll have about 60 questions with about 75 to 90 minutes to complete the exam. But as I just mentioned, Cisco can change this at any time!

The testing software is Windows based, but you won't have access to the main desktop or to any of the accessories. The exam is presented in full screen, with a single question per screen. Navigation buttons allow you to move between questions. In the upper-right corner of the screen, counters show the number of questions and time remaining. Make sure you periodically look at the question you are on and the time remaining—you'll want to budget your time appropriately. Also remember that you'll probably need about 5 minutes to complete each of the two or three simulation questions. And once you answer a question and go to the next one, you cannot go back to previous questions! Also, some questions on the exam might be beta questions that are not actually graded; however, Cisco won't state this in the question, so make sure you answer every question.

The Grand Finale

When you're finished, the exam will automatically be graded. After what will seem like the longest 10 seconds of your life, the testing software will respond with your score. This is usually displayed as numbers showing the minimum passing score, your score, and a PASS/FAIL indicator. With some of the Cisco exams, the actual score is not displayed on the screen but only on the printed version of your test results.

If you're curious, you can review the statistics of your score at this time. Answers to specific questions are not presented; rather, questions are lumped into categories and results are tallied for each category. This detail is also provided on a report that has been automatically printed at the exam administrator's desk.

As you leave the exam room, you'll need to leave your whiteboard behind or return it to the administrator. In exchange, you'll receive a copy of the test report.

You should keep the test results in a safe place. Normally, the results are automatically transmitted to Cisco sometime during the same day you tested, but occasionally you might need the paper report to prove that you passed the exam.

Your company's personnel file is probably a good place to keep this report; the file tends to follow you everywhere, and it doesn't hurt to have favorable exam results turn up during a performance review.

Retesting

If you don't pass the exam, don't be discouraged—networking is complex stuff. Try to maintain a good attitude about the experience, and get ready to try again. Consider yourself a little more educated. You know the format of the test a little better, and the report shows which areas you need to strengthen.

If you bounce back quickly, you'll probably remember several of the questions you might have missed. This will help you focus your study efforts in the right area. Serious go-getters will reschedule the exam for five business days after the previous attempt, while the study material is still fresh in their minds—you must wait a minimum of five business days before taking the same exam again. And once you pass the exam, you can re-sit the exam only once a year.

A new CCNA certification is currently valid for three years. To recertify your CCNA, you can perform any of the following:

- Retake and pass the CCNA exam again.
- Pass any 642-level exam.
- Pass any CCIE written qualification exam.

Performing any of these actions currently recertifies your CCNA. However, Cisco can change the recertification process at any time. You can track your current certification status by going to www.cisco.com/go/certifications/login. If you haven't currently set up login credentials, you'll need to do this before logging into the certification site. You'll need to use your Cisco testing ID number to log in.

Ultimately, remember that Cisco certifications are valuable because they're hard to get. After all, if anyone could get one, what value would it have? In the end, it takes a good attitude and a lot of studying, but you can do it!

Part I

Cisco Catalyst Switches

1

Cisco IOS and Switch Security Review

T his book emphasizes the fundamental and important concepts of accessing, configuring, and managing Cisco routers and switches. These discussions assume that you have passed your Cisco CCENT exam and are familiar with placing a basic configuration on a Cisco router or switch. This chapter begins with a review of basic password security and remote-access protection by applying access control lists (ACLs) to virtual type terminals (VTYs). The remaining half of the chapter focuses on the port security feature supported by Cisco switches. Chapter 1 is a review of material covered on the CCENT exam; however, you will be tested on this material on the ICND2 exam as well. The remaining chapters in Part I focus specifically on Cisco switch features.

CERTIFICATION OBJECTIVE 1.01

Password and Access Protection

Each Cisco device supports several access modes. For CLI interaction, four modes are supported:

- **User EXEC**   Provides basic access to IOS with limited command availability (basically simple monitoring and troubleshooting commands)
- **Privileged EXEC**   Provides high-level management access to IOS, including all commands available at User EXEC mode
- **Configuration**   Allows configuration changes to be made to the device
- **ROMMON**   Loads a bootstrap program that allows for low-level diagnostic testing of the IOS device, performing the password recovery procedure, and performing an emergency upgrade

Of the four modes, the first three apply to IOS. While in ROMMON mode, IOS has not loaded and therefore packets are not moved between interfaces of the device. Both EXEC modes can be password-protected, allowing you to limit who can access your device to perform management, configuration, and troubleshooting tasks. The next two sections review password and VTY protection.

Passwords

The most common way of restricting physical access to IOS devices is to use some type of user authentication. For example, you can configure passwords to restrict access to the lines on IOS devices (User EXEC mode) as well as access to Privileged EXEC mode. Configuring passwords on Catalyst IOS switches, such as the 2950s and 2960s, is the same as configuring passwords on IOS routers. The following sections discuss the configuration of passwords on IOS devices.

User EXEC Password Protection

Controlling access to User EXEC mode on an IOS device is accomplished on a line-by-line basis: console, auxiliary, TTYs, and VTYs. Remember that not all devices support auxiliary ports, only routers support TTYs, and the number of VTYs an IOS device supports is product dependent, ranging from five VTYs (0–4) to almost a thousand.

To secure the console port, you must first go into the console's Line Subconfiguration mode with the **line console 0** command to configure the line password:

```
IOS(config)# line console 0
IOS(config-line)#  password console_password
```

The **0** in the first command specifies the console port. Lines and interfaces are numbered from 0 upward. Even though IOS devices have only a single console port, it is designated as 0 (this is true of most, but not all, Cisco products). Next, notice that the prompt on the second line changed. Once you are in Line Subconfiguration mode, you can use the **password** command to assign the console password. Passwords on IOS devices are *case sensitive*. Remember that the **password** command, when executed under **line console 0**, sets the User EXEC password for someone trying to access the IOS device from the console port only.

The auxiliary port is typically used as a backup console port or a remote-access port with a modem attached to it. The following code shows the syntax for setting up password authentication on the auxiliary port:

```
Router(config)# line aux 0
Router(config-line)# password console_password
Router(config-line)# exit
```

To set up a telnet password for your VTYs, use this configuration:

```
IOS(config)# line vty 0 15
IOS(config-line)# password telnet_password
IOS(config-line)# login
```

The **vty** parameter in this command refers to *virtual terminal*, a fancy name for telnet or SSH access. The 2950 and 2960 switches support up to 16 simultaneous VTY sessions, where each connection is internally tracked by a number: 0–15. Depending on the router model and IOS software version, this number might range from 5 (0–4) on up to almost 1000. You could assign a different password to each VTY, but then you wouldn't know which password to use when telnetting into an IOS device. However, IOS allows you to specify all 16 VTYs with the **line** command, simplifying your configuration, as in the preceding configuration: **line vty 0 15**. You need to specify the beginning and ending VTY numbers on the same line.

Once you are in Line Subconfiguration mode, use the **password** command to set your password. You also need to enter the **login** command to allow remote access to IOS—this tells IOS to use the password configured with the **password** command on the specified line.

---

e x a m

ⓦa t c h   *By default, only the first five VTYs (0–4) are enabled. On devices that support more VTYs, they must manually be enabled. When you remotely log into your IOS device using telnet and you see the message "Password required but none set," then you have not configured a password on the line with the* password *command and won't be able to log in until you configure it. Remember that you should secure your VTYs with a password and login process. A second option, applying an access control list (ACL), is discussed in the "VTYs and ACL Protection" section later in the chapter.*

If you only specify one number when configuring your VTYs, like the following, then you are only configuring *that* VTY:

```
IOS(config)# line vty 0
IOS(config-line)# password cisco123
IOS(config-line)# login
```

In this example, only the VTY 0 line is assigned a password and logins use the password on the line. If this was the only item you configured for your VTYs on a factory-default IOS device, then only one person could remotely access the IOS device using telnet or SSH via VTY 0.

Other ways of validating access are available, such as a local username database or through an external authentication server. (The configuration of an authentication server is beyond the scope of this book. For an in-depth discussion, see my book *Cisco Router Firewall Security* from Cisco Press.) A local username database is a database on the router that allows you to specify both a username and a password to restrict access to the lines on an IOS device. Using usernames and passwords is recommended over using only passwords on lines: the advantage of this approach is that each user can have his or her own password instead of sharing a password, providing for more accountability. The following commands illustrate the setup of a local username database and its use on VTYs:

Be familiar with this example, especially when performing this type of configuration on a factory-default IOS device.

```
IOS(config)# username name {secret | password} password
IOS(config)# line vty 0 15
IOS(config-line)# login local
```

The **username** command specifies the name and password for the user. The main difference between the **secret** and **password** parameters is that the **secret** parameter tells IOS to encrypt the password with an MD5 hash, and the **password** parameter doesn't (the password is stored in clear text). This is true of the Line Subconfiguration mode **password** command: it also is stored in clear text.

Note: The `login local` *command can be used on any of the lines on an IOS device to perform user authentication: console, auxiliary, VTYs, and TTYs. With user authentication, a username and password are prompted for authentication.*

Privileged EXEC Password Protection

Along with protecting access to the lines on an IOS device, you can also control access to Privileged EXEC mode by assigning a password to it. Two configuration options are shown here:

```
IOS(config)# enable password Privilege_EXEC_password
```

or

```
IOS(config)# enable secret Privilege_EXEC_password
```

Both of these commands configure the Privileged EXEC password. The main difference between the two, as with the **username** command, is that the **secret** parameter encrypts the Privileged EXEC password and the **password** parameter doesn't. If you configure both of these commands, the password configured with the **enable secret** command always takes precedence over the password configured with the **enable password** command. The **enable password** command is still supported by Cisco for backward-compatibility purposes.

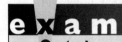

Without User EXEC and *Privileged EXEC authentication (passwords), you will not be able to* | *remotely access an IOS device via telnet or SSH, by default.*

Password Encryption

Passwords that are not encrypted can be encrypted by using the **service password-encryption** Global Configuration mode command. However, the **enable secret** command's encryption is *much* stronger than using the **service password-encryption** command to do the encryption.

on the

job

I recommend against using the enable password *command or the* username *command with the* password *parameter along with* service password-encryption, *since several easily accessible utilities on the Internet can be used to break this encryption: just do a search on "Cisco password cracker" using a search engine and you'll find a lot of them. And even with a password-cracking program such as Cain and Abel or L0phtCrack, given enough time, the MD5 hashed encryption using the secret keyword can also be broken. If someone steals your configuration file, you're vulnerable to an access attack. The best defense is protecting any access to your configuration file.*

Video

1.01. The digital resources that accompany this book include a multimedia demonstration of configuring passwords on an IOS device.

Restricting VTY Protocol Access

By default, all methods of access are allowed for the VTYs, including telnet and
SSH. Controlling the type of connection allowed on the VTYs is done with the
transport input (what protocol can be used to connect to the router)
and **transport output** (what protocol can be used to connect from the router)
commands:

```
IOS(config)# line vty line_# [line_#]
IOS(config-line)# transport input {all | telnet | ssh}
IOS(config-line)# transport output {all | telnet | ssh}
```

By default, all protocols are allowed.

In the following example, only the SSH protocol is allowed on the VTYs
(to or from the router):

```
Router(config)# line vty 0 15
Router(config-line)# transport input ssh
Router(config-line)# transport output ssh
```

VTYs and ACL Protection

ACLs, known for their ability to filter traffic as it either comes into or leaves an
interface, can also be used for other purposes, including restricting remote access
(VTY) to an IOS device, filtering routing
information, prioritizing traffic with queuing,
triggering phone calls with dial-on-demand
routing (DDR), changing the administrative
distance of routes, and specifying traffic
to be protected by an IPsec VPN, among

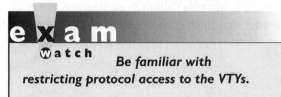

ACLs can be used for filtering of traffic through the IOS device as well as filtering remote-access traffic to IOS's VTY lines.

many others. The CCENT exam covers the introduction to ACLs. This chapter assumes that you have experience with creating and using ACLs. This section focuses on restricting telnet and SSH access to a Cisco IOS device by applying an ACL to the Cisco device's VTYs.

In addition to using standard IP ACLs to filter traffic as it enters and/or leaves an interface, you can use them to restrict VTY access (telnet and SSH) to your router. You might want to do this to allow only network administrators to access the CLI of your IOS device remotely. Setting this up is almost the same as setting up restricted access on an interface.

First, you need to create a standard ACL that has a list of **permit** statements that allow your corresponding network administrators remote access; include the IP addresses of their PCs in this list. When dealing with IP addresses in ACL statements, you can use *wildcard masks* to match on a range of addresses instead of manually entering every IP address that you want to match on.

Wildcard masks are used to match against bits in a packet. A 0 in a bit position means match, and a 1 means ignore. If you want to match against a subnet, invert the corresponding subnet mask. The trick is to subtract each octet in the subnet mask from 255, resulting in the wildcard mask. Some wildcard masks can be confusing, such as 0.0.1.255. For masks like this, it's sometimes easier to look at

them from a subnet mask perspective. In this example, the corresponding subnet mask would be 255.255.254.0. You can use a simple trick here by subtracting the wildcard mask from a local broadcast address (255.255.255.255) to come up with the correct wildcard mask. Don't be surprised if you have to use this trick for a handful of ACL questions on the exam.

Second, you need to activate your ACL. However, you will not do this on any of the router's interfaces. If you were to activate this ACL on an interface, it would allow any type of traffic from your administrators but drop *all* other traffic. When someone accesses your router via telnet or SSH, the router associates this connection with a VTY line. Therefore, you'll apply your standard ACL to the VTYs, like this:

```
Router(config)# line vty 0 4
Router(config-line)# access-class standard_ACL_# in|out
```

Remember that your router supports five telnets by default (0–4), and more on certain IOS devices. You can configure all VTYs simultaneously by specifying the beginning and ending line numbers after the **vty** parameter. If you don't apply the restriction to all of your VTYs, you are leaving a backdoor into your router, which might cause a security problem.

Also, notice the command used to apply the ACL to the line: **access-class**. This is different from activating an ACL on a router's interface. If you use the **in** parameter, you are restricting telnet and SSH access to the router itself. The **out** parameter is kind of unique. By using this parameter, you are restricting what destinations this router can telnet or SSH to when someone uses the **telnet**, **connect**, or **ssh** commands. This creates an exception to a standard ACL and has the router treat the address in the ACL statements as a destination address; it causes the router to compare this address to the address in the **telnet** command before allowing the user on the router to telnet to the specified destination.

Here's a simple example of using a standard ACL to filter telnet traffic to a router:

```
Router(config)# access-list 99 permit 192.168.1.0 0.0.0.255
Router(config)# line vty 0 4
Router(config-line)# access-class 99 in
```

In this example, only traffic from 192.168.1.0/24 is allowed to telnet or SSH into this router. Because of the implicit deny at the end of **access-list** 99, all other connections to this router (via the VTYs) will be dropped.

Video

1.02. The digital resources that accompany this book contain a multimedia demonstration of configuring a standard numbered ACL to restrict telnet access on a router.

CERTIFICATION OBJECTIVE 1.02

Port Security Feature

Port security is a switch feature that allows you to lock down Cisco IOS switch ports based on the MAC address or addresses associated with the interface, preventing unauthorized access to a LAN. For example, if MAC address 0001.001c.dddd is supposed to be off of fa0/1, but it is seen off of fa0/2, this

Port security and/or 802.1X can be used to lock down ports on a switch, preventing unauthorized access to your LAN network.

would be considered a security violation. Or, if more addresses are seen off the interface than you allow, this would also be considered a violation. As an administrator, you control what should happen when a violation occurs, be it generating a notification about the issue, dropping traffic for the MAC address that caused the violation, or completely disabling the port where the violation occurred.

The port security feature will not work on trunk ports (Chapter 2), switch port analyzer ports (SPANs), and EtherChannel ports (Chapter 3). However, it is compatible with 802.1X and voice VLANs (Chapter 2).

Port Security Configuration

Starting in IOS 12.1(6)EA2, Cisco standardized how port security is configured on its switches. The entire configuration is performed on an interface-by-interface basis by using the **switchport** commands:

```
switch(config)# interface fastethernet|gigabit 0/port_#
switch(config-if)# switchport mode access
switch(config-if)# switchport access vlan VLAN_#
switch(config-if)# switchport port-security
switch(config-if)# switchport port-security maximum value
switch(config-if)# switchport port-security violation
                   protect|restrict|shutdown
switch(config-if)# switchport port-security mac-address MAC_address
switch(config-if)# switchport port-security mac-address sticky
```

Be familiar with configuring port security with the `switchport port-security` *commands (enabling it, limiting the MAC addresses, violation* *mode, and sticky learning).* **You might even have to configure it as one of the simulation questions or examine the configuration in one of the simlet questions.**

First, you must enter the appropriate interface where you want to set up restricted security. The first command, **switchport mode access**, defines the interface as a host (access) port instead of a trunk port (trunking is explained in Chapter 2). The second command places the access port in a specific VLAN (also discussed in Chapter 2). The third command on the interface, **switchport port-security**, enables port security (it is disabled by default). The fourth command, **switchport port-security maximum**, specifies the maximum number of devices that can be associated with the interface. This defaults to 1 and can range from 1 to 132.

Set the maximum to 1 address for an interface to prevent spoofing of MAC addresses: only one MAC address is learned. Setting the maximum to 1 **prevents problems where a user might try to attach a hub or switch to the network to allow the connection of additional, possibly noncompliant, devices.**

The fifth command on the interface specifies what should occur if a security violation occurs—the MAC address is seen connected to a different port. Three options are possible:

- ■ **protect**   When the number of secure addresses reaches the maximum number allowed, any additionally learned addresses will be dropped. This applies only if you have enabled the sticky option, discussed following this list.
- ■ **restrict**   Causes the switch to generate a security violation alert.
- ■ **shutdown**   Causes the switch to generate an alert and to disable the interface. The only way to re-enable the interface is to use the **no shutdown** command. This is the default violation mode if you don't specify the mode.

If not specifically defined, the default port security violation mode is shutdown: the port is logically disabled for all traffic and a log message is generated (this includes the generation of an SNMP trap or a syslog message if these IOS features are enabled).

When an interface is disabled because of a violation with port security, you can reset the interface with this Configuration mode command: `errdisable recovery cause psecure-violation`.

The last two commands in the preceding code listing affect how the switch learns the secure MAC addresses on the interface. The first one has you specify the exact MAC address that is allowed to be associated with this interface—this is statically defining the MAC addresses allowed off of the port. The second command uses the sticky feature, which allows the switch to dynamically learn the MAC address(es) associated with the interface and convert these dynamic entries to static entries. The interface will learn MAC addresses only up to the maximum configured value for that interface. After you save your configuration (`copy running-config startup-config`), and when you reboot your switch, the sticky-learned addresses appear as statically secure addresses. Basically, sticky learning lets you avoid having to configure the MAC addresses associated with the interface.

If you don't statically define the MAC addresses or use sticky learning to learn them with port security, dynamic learning is used. Dynamic learning is similar to sticky learning in that the switch will learn the MAC addresses dynamically off of the interface up to the maximum defined; however, unlike sticky learning, these addresses are not saved: every time the switch boots up or the interface is reset, the MAC addresses are relearned for the interface.

Sticky and dynamic learning allow a switch to dynamically learn MAC addresses up to the maximum allowed for the interface. With dynamic learning, the MAC addresses are not saved as part of the running configuration; with sticky learning, the MAC addresses are saved as configuration commands in the running configuration. This is used as the most efficient way of learning the MAC addresses connected to the switch. Statically configuring a MAC address is typically used for network devices such as servers and routers. You can use static and either sticky or dynamic, but the switch will only allow MAC addresses up to the port security maximum that's configured (1, by default).

Port Security Verification

To verify your configuration, use the **show port-security interface** command:

```
switch# show port-security interface fa0/2
Port Security : Enabled
Port status : SecureUp
Violation mode : Restrict
Maximum MAC Addresses : 1
Total MAC Addresses : 1
Configured MAC Addresses : 1
Aging time : 0 mins
Aging type : Absolute
SecureStatic address aging : Disabled
Security Violation count : 0
```

In this example, you can see that port security is enabled, the violation mode is restrict, the maximum number of MAC addresses that can be connected to the port is 1, and one MAC address has to be statically configured for the port. At the bottom of the output, you can see that no security violations have occurred on the port.

e x a m
ⓦ a t c h

Be familiar with the `show port-security interface` *command. If the Port Security value is set to* `Disabled`, *then you must execute the* `show port-security` *command on the interface to enable it. Also be able to* *determine the number of MAC addresses configured (allowed). You can also use the* `show running-config` *command to verify the configuration of port security on a switch's interface.*

To see an overview configuration of port security on your switch, use the **show port-security** command:

```
switch# show port-security
Port     MaxSecureAddr  CurrentAddr  SecurityViolation  Security Action
         (Count)        (Count)      (Count)
--------------------------------------------------------------------------
Fa0/1       10             10            0                  Shutdown
Fa0/2        1              1            0                  Restrict
```

```
        .
        .
        .
----------------------------------------------------------------
Total Addresses in System :21
Max Addresses limit in System :6176
```

In this example, ten MAC addresses can be learned off of FA0/1, ten have been learned, and the violation mode is shutdown; but currently no violations have occurred on the port.

To see the MAC addresses statically defined or dynamically learned with port security, use the **show port-security address** command:

```
IOS# show port-security address
Secure Mac Address Table
----------------------------------------------------------------
Vlan  Mac Address     Type             Ports Remaining Age
                                             (mins)

----  --------------  ---------------- ----- -------------
1     0001.0001.0011  SecureDynamic    Fa0/1  15 (I)
1     0001.0001.0022  SecureDynamic    Fa0/1  15 (I)
1     0001.0001.1144  SecureConfigured Fa0/1  -
      .
      .
      .
----------------------------------------------------------------
Total Addresses in System :21
Max Addresses limit in System :6176
```

In this example, three MAC addresses are off of FA0/1, where the first two were learned dynamically and the last one was statically configured.

1.03. The digital resources that accompany this book include a multimedia demonstration of configuring and verifying port security on a switch.

CERTIFICATION SUMMARY

This chapter reviewed some of the IOS security features covered on the CCENT exam. You can protect access to your Cisco device by assigning User EXEC and Privileged EXEC passwords. Use the Line Subconfiguration mode **password** command and the **enable secret** or **enable password** command for the two respective levels. The **service password encryption** command encrypts clear-text passwords on an IOS device.

INSIDE THE EXAM

Password and Access Protection

One of the first things you would do in real life is secure your IOS device with passwords; you should expect to see some questions about how your VTYs are secured, including the differences between the `login` and `login local` parameters. Remember that passwords are *case sensitive* when configured.

Remember that you can use ACLs for things other than filtering of traffic through the IOS device, such as restricting VTY access to the device. Remember also that if you omit the wildcard mask in a standard ACL, it defaults to 0.0.0.0, a particular host—you might see a troubleshooting question related to this type of misconfiguration. Be able to troubleshoot problems based on ACL entries being placed in an incorrect order. Use the `access-class` command to restrict VTY access to an IOS device. Don't be surprised if you have to configure an actual ACL and activate it on a router's interface or VTY lines.

Port Security Feature

Even though this section was covered in the CCENT exam, don't be surprised to see questions on the ICND2 exam as well! Understand why port security is used, as well as the commands to configure it. Know why the maximum addresses for an interface is set to 1. Remember the three violation modes, as well as what they do. Be able to compare and contrast dynamic, sticky, and static learning and when each is used. And be able to configure this feature on a switch, since you might see it on a simulation question!

Standard ACLs can have numbers ranging from 1 to 99 and 1300 to 1999. To create a numbered ACL, use the `access-list` command. To filter telnet and SSH traffic to and from your IOS device, activate the standard IP ACL on your VTY lines with the `access-class` command.

Port security can be used to prevent unauthorized access to a LAN. Addresses can be learned dynamically (not saved), using sticky learning (saved), or statically configured. A violation occurs when more MAC addresses are off of an interface than are specified or when a MAC address is seen off of a different interface than expected. Violation modes are restrict, protect, and shutdown. Port security can be configured only on access (non-trunk) ports with the `switchport port-security` commands.

✓ TWO-MINUTE DRILL

Password and Access Protection

❑ Lines (access to User EXEC mode) can be secured with the **password** command. Access to Privileged EXEC mode can be secured with either the **enable password** or **enable secret** command; the former is unencrypted and the latter is strongly encrypted.

❑ Clear-text passwords can be encrypted with the **service password-encryption** command.

❑ Standard IP ACLs use numbers in the ranges 1–99 and 1300–1999.

❑ A wildcard mask is like an inverted subnet mask. A 0 in a bit position of the wildcard mask means the corresponding bit position in the condition's address must match that in the IP packet. A 1 in a bit position of the wildcard mask means there doesn't have to be a match.

❑ To invert a subnet mask into a wildcard mask, subtract each octet in the subnet mask from 255, which will result in the corresponding octet value for the wildcard mask.

❑ Standard ACLs can filter only on the source IP address. If you omit the wildcard mask, it defaults to 0.0.0.0. Use the **access-class** command to activate a standard ACL to restrict telnet access to a router.

Port Security Feature

❑ Port security is used to prevent unauthorized access to a LAN on access interfaces (non-trunk connections).

❑ The **switchport port-security** commands are used to configure port security.

❑ The defaults for port security are learning one MAC address on the interface with a violation mode of shutdown.

❑ Sticky learning allows a switch to dynamically learn which MAC addresses are associated with an interface, as well as save these in the running configuration of the switch.

SELF TEST

The following Self Test questions will help you measure your understanding of the material presented in this chapter. Read all the choices carefully, as there may be more than one correct answer. Choose all correct answers for each question.

Password and Access Protection

1. Enter the IOS command that will encrypt unencrypted passwords: _____.

2. Enter the wildcard mask value to match on every bit position in an address: _____.

3. Enter the wildcard mask value for the subnet mask of 255.255.248.0: _____.

4. Enter the standard IP ACL command to permit traffic from 192.168.1.0/24, using a list number of 10: _____.

5. Enter the IOS commands to activate ACL 99 inbound on the first five VTYs: _____.

Port Security Feature

6. Which switch feature is used to prevent unauthorized access to a LAN?
   A. Port security
   B. Port security and 802.1Q
   C. VTY passwords
   D. Enable password

7. Which of the following is *not* a default configuration for port security?
   A. 1 MAC address per interface
   B. Violation mode shutdown
   C. Sticky learning
   D. Disabled by default

8. What learning mode should you use to associate a server with a switch port when port security is enabled?
   A. Dynamic
   B. Automatic
   C. Sticky
   D. Static

SELF TEST ANSWERS

Password and Access Protection

1. ☑ The `service password-encryption` command will encrypt unencrypted passwords.

2. ☑ The value 0.0.0.0 is a wildcard mask that says to match on every bit position in an address.

3. ☑ The inverted subnet mask for 255.255.248.0 is 0.0.7.255. The trick is to subtract the subnet mask octets from 255.

4. ☑ `access-list 10 permit 192.168.1.0 0.0.0.255`

5. ☑ `line vty 0 4`
    `access-class 99 in`

Port Security Feature

6. ☑ **A.** Port security is used to prevent unauthorized access to a LAN.
   ☒ **B** is incorrect because 802.1Q is a VLAN trunking protocol. **C** and **D** are used to restrict access to the switch, not to the LAN for which the switch provides connectivity.

7. ☑ **C.** Dynamic, not sticky, learning is the default.
   ☒ **A**, **B**, and **D** are defaults and thus incorrect.

8. ☑ **D.** You should statically define MAC addresses of servers and routers when using port security.
   ☒ **A** and **C** are used for user ports. **B** is a nonexistent learning mode.

2

VLAN Review

Layer 2 devices, including bridges and switches, always propagate certain kinds of traffic in the broadcast domain: broadcasts, multicasts, and unknown destination traffic. This process affects every machine in the broadcast domain (layer 2 network). It affects the bandwidth of these devices' connections as well as their local processing. If you were using bridges, the only solution available to solve this problem would be to break up the broadcast domain into multiple broadcast domains and interconnect these domains with a router. With this approach, each new broadcast domain would be a new logical segment and would need a unique network number to differentiate it from the other layer 3 logical segments.

Unfortunately, this is a costly solution, since each broadcast domain, each logical segment, needs its own port on a router. The more broadcast domains that you have from bridges, the bigger the router required: an interface for each broadcast domain. As you will see in this chapter, switches also have the same problem with traffic that must be flooded. You will see, however, that switches have a unique solution to reduce the number of router ports required and thus the cost of the layer 3 device that you need to obtain: virtual LANs and trunking.

CERTIFICATION OBJECTIVE 2.01

VLAN Overview

A *virtual LAN* (VLAN) is a logical grouping of network devices in the same broadcast domain that can span multiple physical segments. The top part of Figure 2-1 shows an example of a simple VLAN, where every device is in both the same collision and broadcast domains. In this example, a hub is providing the connectivity, which represents to the devices connected to it, that the segment is a logical segment.

The bottom part of Figure 2-1 shows an example of a switch with four PCs connected to it. One major difference between the switch and the hub is that all devices connected to the hub are in the same collision domain, whereas in the switch example, each port of the switch is a separate collision domain. By default, all ports on a switch are in the same broadcast domain. In this example, however, the configuration of the switch places PC-E and PC-F in one broadcast domain (VLAN) and PC-G and PC-H in another broadcast domain.

FIGURE 2-1 VLAN examples

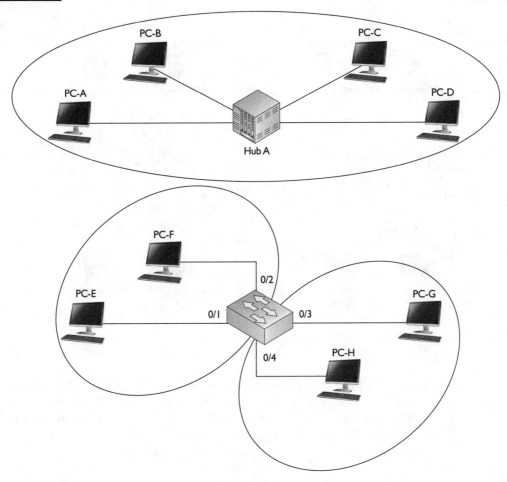

Switches are used to create VLANs, or separate broadcast domains. VLANs are not restricted to any physical boundary in the switched network, assuming that all the devices are interconnected via switches and that there are no intervening layer 3 devices. For example, a VLAN could be spread across multiple switches, or it could be contained in the same switch, as is shown in Figure 2-2. This example shows three VLANs. Notice that VLANs are not tied to any physical location: PC-A, PC-B, PC-E, and PC-F are in the same VLAN but are connected to different ports of different switches. However, a VLAN could be contained to one switch, as PC-C and PC-D are connected to SwitchA.

FIGURE 2-2 Physical switched topology using VLANs

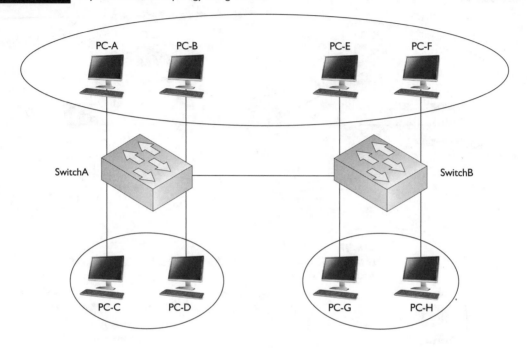

The switches in your network maintain the integrity of your VLANs. For example, if PC-A generates a broadcast, SwitchA and SwitchB will make sure that only other devices in that VLAN (PC-B, PC-E, and PC-F) will see the broadcast and that other devices will not, and that holds true even across switches, as is the case in Figure 2-2.

exam

ⓦatch   *A VLAN is a group of devices in the same broadcast domain or subnet. VLANs are good at logically separating/segmenting traffic between different groups of users. VLANs contain/ isolate broadcast traffic, where you need a router to move traffic between VLANs. VLANs create separate broadcast domains: they increase the number of broadcast domains, but decrease the size of the broadcast domains.*

Subnets and VLANs

Logically speaking, VLANs are also subnets. A subnet, or a network, is a contained broadcast domain. A broadcast that occurs in one subnet will not be forwarded, by default, to another subnet. Routers, or layer 3 devices, provide this boundary function. Each of these subnets requires a unique network number. And to move from one network number to another, you need a router. In the case of broadcast domains and switches, each of these separate broadcast domains is a separate VLAN; therefore, you still need a routing function to move traffic between different VLANs.

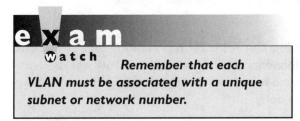

watch *Remember that each VLAN must be associated with a unique subnet or network number.*

From the user's perspective, the physical topology shown in Figure 2-2 would actually look like Figure 2-3. And from the user's perspective, the devices know that to reach another VLAN (subnet), they must forward their traffic to the default gateway address in their VLAN—the IP address on their router's interface.

FIGURE 2-3   Logical topology using VLANs

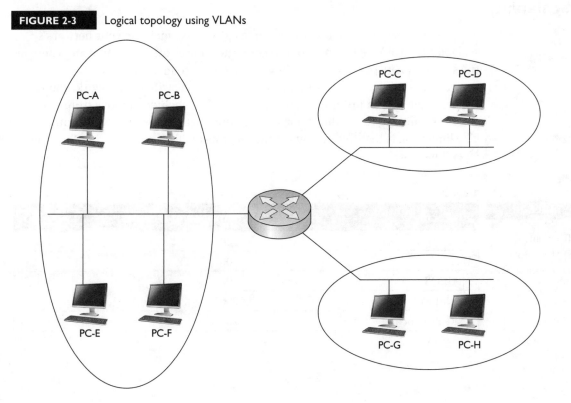

One advantage that switches have over bridges, though, is that in a switched VLAN network, assuming your routing function supports VLANs, the switch can handle multiple VLANs on a single port, and a router can route between these VLANs on the same single port. This special kind of connection is called a *trunk* and is discussed in more depth later in the "VLAN Connections" section. With a bridge, each VLAN must be placed on a separate port of a router, increasing the cost of your routing solution.

Cisco has recommendations as to the number of devices in a VLAN, which are shown in Table 2-1. Remember that these numbers are only recommendations from Cisco; however, they are backed by many years of designing and implementing networks.

on the **Ö**ob *Remember that the information listed in Table 2-1 represents recommendations only: every network and its components are unique. Each network has its own unique characteristics. I once saw a broadcast domain that had almost 1000 devices in it; it worked, but very poorly.*

Scalability

Through segmentation of broadcast domains, VLANs increase your network's scalability. Since VLANs are a logical construct, a user can be located anywhere in the switched network and still belong to the same broadcast domain. If you move a user from one switch to another switch in the same switched network, you can still keep the user in his or her original VLAN. This includes a move from one floor of a building to another floor, or from one part of the campus to another. The limitation is that the user, when moved, must still be connected to the same layer 2 network.

TABLE 2-1	Protocol	Number of Devices
Recommendations for Number of Devices in a VLAN	IP	500
	IPX	300
	NetBIOS	200
	AppleTalk	200
	Mixed protocols	200

VLANs provide for location independence in a switched network: many logical networks can use the same network infrastructure. This flexibility makes adds, changes, and moves of networking devices a simple process. It also allows you to group people together, perhaps according to their job function, which makes implementing your security policies easier. Logically separating people using VLANs provides additional security, since traffic must traverse a layer 3 device to go from one VLAN to another, where you can use an access control list to filter traffic. Broadcast storms can be mitigated by decreasing the number of broadcast domains, thus increasing the network's size.

VLANs and Traffic Types

Many network administrators use VLANs not only to separate different types of user traffic (commonly separated by job function), but also to separate it based on the type of traffic, placing network management, multicast, and voice over IP (VoIP) traffic into their own distinctive VLANs.

Network management traffic includes Simple Network Management Protocol (SNMP); Remote Monitoring (RMON); Spanning Tree Protocol (STP); Bridge Protocol Data Units (BPDUs), discussed in Chapter 3; Cisco Discovery Protocol (CDP) messages, discussed in Chapter 7; syslog messages, discussed in Chapter 8; Network Time Protocol (NTP) updates, discussed in Chapter 8; configuration backups of network devices, discussed in Chapter 7; and network device operating system upgrades, discussed in Chapter 7.

Multicast traffic is commonly used by video applications to transmit video streams intelligently from a server to one or more clients interested in seeing it, where UDP is used as a transport for the video stream. An example of a video solution that uses multicasts is Cisco's IP/TV server. Video traffic is delay sensitive—too much delay can be noticeable by the end user, where the actual video picture looks jumpy and jagged. By separating this traffic from other types through VLANs, and by setting up the necessary quality of service (QoS) for this VLAN traffic, you can help minimize or prevent delay issues.

VoIP traffic includes two kinds of traffic: signaling information sent from the VoIP phones to the VoIP gateway products, such as Cisco Unified Communications Manager (formerly called Cisco CallManager), and the actual voice conversations, which use UDP as a transport between VoIP phones and/or digital phones connected to VoIP PBXs. One issue with VoIP traffic is that it is delay-sensitive, so mixing this kind of traffic with other data types can cause performance issues that are very noticeable on voice connections; separating this traffic in its own VLAN and using QoS to ensure that this kind of traffic is given higher priority than other types is an important design consideration. Some Cisco Catalyst switches support a special type of VLAN, called a *voice VLAN*. With the voice VLAN feature, switches will automatically place a Cisco VoIP phone into the voice VLAN once the VoIP phone is plugged into the switch. The advantage of this approach is that you, as an administrator, no longer have to worry when a VoIP phone is added to the network about configuring the switch to place the phone into the correct VLAN.

e x a m

ⓦ a t c h   *Different data types, such as delay-sensitive voice or video (multicast), network management, and data application traffic, should be separated into different VLANs via connected switches to prevent problems in one data type from affecting others. QoS can be used to prioritize traffic types like VoIP and video to ensure that they receive the necessary bandwidth and are prioritized over other types of data traffic.*

VLAN Membership

A device's membership in a VLAN can be determined by one of three methods: static, dynamic, or voice. These methods affect how a switch will associate a port in its chassis with a particular VLAN. When you are dealing with static VLANs, you must manually assign a port on a switch to a VLAN using an *Interface Subconfiguration* mode command. VLANs configured in this way are typically called *port-based* VLANs.

With dynamic VLANs, the switch automatically assigns the port to a VLAN using information from the user device, such as its MAC address, IP address, or even directory information (a user or group name, for instance). The switch then consults a policy server, called a *VLAN membership policy server* (VMPS), which contains a mapping of device information to VLANs. One of the switches in your network must be configured as this server. Low-end Cisco switches cannot serve as a VMPS server switch, but other switches, such as the Catalyst 6500, can. In this situation, the low-end switches act as clients and use the 6500 to store the dynamic VLAN membership information.

Another option is to use 802.1X authentication, which is used to authenticate a device's access to a switch or wireless access point. The authentication credentials are stored on an authentication server. One policy you can assign the user account (associated with the authenticating device) on the authentication server is the VLAN to which the device belongs—the server can pass this to the layer 2 device, which, in turn, can associate the VLAN to the port with which the authenticated device is associated.

Dynamic VLANs have one main advantage over static VLANs: they support plug-and-play movability. For instance, if you move a PC from a port on one switch to a port on another switch and you are using dynamic VLANs, the new switch port will automatically be configured for the VLAN to which the user belongs. About the only time that you have to configure information with dynamic VLANs is if you hire an employee and the employee leaves the company or changes job functions.

If you are using static VLANs, not only will you have to configure the switch port manually with this updated information, but, if you move the user from one switch to another, you will also have to perform this manual configuration to reflect the user's new port. One advantage, though, that static VLANs have over dynamic VLANs is that the configuration process is easy and straightforward. Dynamic VLANs require a lot of initial preparation involving matching users to VLANs. (This book focuses exclusively on static VLANs, as dynamic VLANs are beyond the book's scope.)

Voice VLANs are unique. They are associated to ports that have VoIP phones attached. Some VoIP phones might have a multiport switch attached to them to allow other devices to connect to the switch via the phone. In this instance, the phone might tag frames to indicate which device is sending the traffic—phone or computer—so that the switch can then deal with the traffic correctly.

CERTIFICATION OBJECTIVE 2.02

VLAN Connections

When dealing with VLANs, switches support two types of switch ports: access links and trunks. When setting up your switches, you will need to know what type of connection an interface should use and configure it appropriately. As you will see, the configuration process for each type of interface is different. This section discusses the two types of connections.

Access Link Connections

An *access link* connection is a connection to a device that has a standardized Ethernet NIC that understands only standardized Ethernet frames—in other words, a normal NIC that understands IEEE 802.3 and Ethernet II frames. Access link connections can be associated only with a single VLAN (voice VLAN ports are an exception to this). This means that any device or devices connected to this port will be in the same broadcast domain.

For example, if ten users are connected to a hub, and you plug the hub into an access link interface on a switch, then all of these users will belong to the same VLAN that is associated with the switch port. If you wanted five users on the hub to belong to one VLAN and the other five to a different VLAN, you would need to purchase an additional hub and plug each hub into a different switch port. Then, on the switch, you would need to configure each of these ports with the correct VLAN identifier.

Trunk Connections

Unlike access link connections, *trunk* connections are capable of carrying traffic for multiple VLANs. To support trunking, the original Ethernet frame must be modified to carry VLAN information, commonly called a *VLAN identifier* or number. This ensures that the broadcast integrity is maintained. For instance, if a device from VLAN 1 has generated a broadcast and the connected switch has received it, when this switch forwards it to other switches, these switches need to know the VLAN origin so that they can forward this frame out only VLAN 1 ports and not other VLAN ports.

Cisco supports two Ethernet trunking methods:

- Cisco's proprietary InterSwitch Link (ISL) protocol for Ethernet
- IEEE's 802.1Q, commonly referred to as *dot1q* for Ethernet

Cisco's high-end switches, such as the Catalyst 6500s, support both types; however, Cisco's low-end switches support only 802.1Q: ISL is being phased out by Cisco. This book focuses on the use of the latter trunk method, dot1q.

Trunk Tagging

Trunking methods create the illusion that instead of a single physical connection between the two trunking devices, a separate logical connection exists for each VLAN between them. When trunking, the switch adds the source port's VLAN identifier to the frame so that the device (typically a switch) at the other end of the trunk understands what VLAN originated this frame, and the destination switch can make intelligent forwarding decisions on not just the destination MAC address, but also the source VLAN identifier.

Since information is added to the original Ethernet frame, normal NICs will not understand this information and will typically drop the frame. Therefore, you need to ensure that when you set up a trunk connection on a switch's interface, the device at the other end also supports the same trunking protocol and has it configured. If the device at the other end doesn't understand these modified frames or is not set up for trunking, it will, in most situations, drop them.

The modification of these frames, commonly called *tagging*, is done in hardware by application-specific integrated circuits (ASICs). ASICs are specialized processors. Since the tagging is done in hardware at faster-than-wire speeds, no latency is involved in the actual tagging process. And to ensure compatibility with access link devices, switches will strip off the tagging information and forward the original Ethernet frame to the device or devices connected to access link connections. From the user's perspective, the source generates a normal Ethernet frame and the destination receives this frame, which is an Ethernet 802.3 or II frame coming in and the same going out. In reality, this frame is tagged as it enters the switched infrastructure and sheds the tag as it exits the infrastructure: the process of tagging and untagging the frame is hidden from the users connected to access link ports.

Trunk-Capable Devices

Trunk links are common between certain types of devices, including switch-to-switch, switch-to-router, and switch-to-file server connections. Using a trunk link on a router is a great way of reducing your layer 3 infrastructure costs. For instance, in the old days of bridging, in order to route between different broadcast domains, you needed a *separate* physical router interface for each broadcast domain. So if you had two broadcast domains, you needed two router ports; if you had 20 broadcast domains, you needed 20 router ports. As you can see, the more broadcast domains you had with bridges, the more expensive the router would become.

Today, with the advent of VLANs and trunk connections, you can use a single port on a router to route between your multiple broadcast domains. If you had 2 or 20 broadcast domains, you could use just one port on the router to accomplish the routing between these different subnets. Of course, you would need a router and an interface that supported trunking. Not every Cisco router supports trunking; you would need at least a 1751 or higher router with the correct type of Ethernet interface. If your router didn't support trunking, you would need a separate router interface for each VLAN you had created to route between the VLANs. Therefore, if you have a lot of VLANs, it makes sense to economize and buy a router and the correct type of interface that supports trunking.

You can also buy specialized NICs for PCs or file servers that support trunking. For instance, suppose you want multiple VLANs to access a file server. You could use a normal NIC and set this up with an access link connection to a switch. Since this is an access link connection, the server could belong only to one VLAN. The users in the same VLAN, when accessing the server, would have all their traffic switched via layer 2 devices to reach it. Users in other VLANs, however, would require that their traffic be routed to this server via a router, since the file server is in a different broadcast domain.

e x a m

ⓦ a t c h   *If the same VLANs are on two connected switches, use a trunk connection between the switches to allow the associated VLANs on each side to communicate with each other. Trunk connections are commonly used on routers so that a router, via subinterfaces, can route between the VLANs. The configuration of trunking on a router's interface is discussed in Chapter 6. The trunking encapsulation, though, must match between the two trunking devices (such as using 802.1Q on both sides, or Cisco's proprietary ISL on both sides).*

If throughput is a big concern, you might want to buy a trunk NIC for the file server. Configuring this NIC is different from configuring a normal NIC on a file server. For each VLAN in which you want the file server to participate, you would create a virtual NIC, assign your VLAN identifier and layer 3 addressing to the virtual NIC for the specific VLAN, and then associate it with the physical NIC. Once you have created all of these logical NICs on your file server, you need to set up a trunk connection on the switch to the server. And once you have done this, members of VLANs in the switched network will be able to access the file server directly without going through a router. These trunk-capable NICs are common enough today that you might even see them in certain PCs, since these NICs are commonly used to support virtualization.

on the
(j)ob

A good example of a device that might need a trunk-capable NIC is a DHCP server, since it might need to assign IP addresses to users across multiple VLANs. If you don't have a trunk-capable NIC, but users are spread across multiple VLANs, you could use the IP helper feature on a Cisco router connected to the users' VLANs and have the router forward the DHCP broadcasts to the DHCP server located in a different VLAN. Another example of a device that might need a trunk-capable NIC is a server in a data center: this is commonly necessary to support the many virtual machines (VMs) running on the server.

Trunking Example

Figure 2-4 shows an example of a trunk connection between SwitchA and SwitchB in a network that has three VLANs. In this example, PC-A, PC-F, and PC-H belong to one VLAN; PC-B and PC-G belong to a second VLAN; and PC-C, PC-D, and PC-E belong to a third VLAN. The trunk between the two switches is also tagging VLAN information so that the remote switch understands the source VLAN of the originator.

Let's take a look at an example of the use of VLANs and the two different types of connections by using the network shown in Figure 2-5. In this example, PC-C generates a local broadcast. When SwitchA receives the broadcast, it examines the incoming port and knows that the source device is from the gray VLAN (the access link connections are marked with dots). Seeing this, the switch knows to forward this frame only out of ports that belong to the same VLAN: this includes access link connections with the same VLAN identifier and trunk connections. On this switch, one access link connection belongs to the same VLAN, PC-D, so the switch forwards the frame directly out this interface.

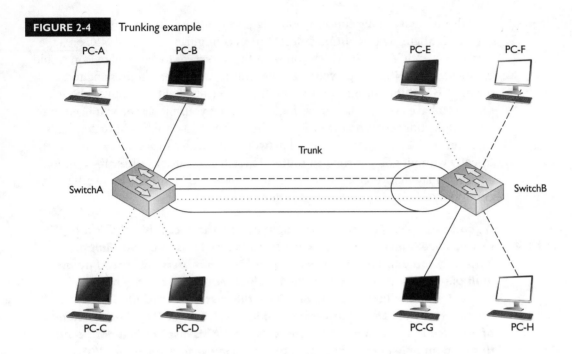

FIGURE 2-4   Trunking example

The trunk connection between SwitchA and SwitchB handles traffic for multiple VLANs. A VLAN tagging mechanism is required to differentiate the source of traffic when moving it between the switches. For instance, assume that no tagging mechanism took place between the switches. PC-C generates a broadcast frame, and SwitchA forwards it unaltered to PC-D and then SwitchB across the trunk. The problem with this process is that when SwitchB receives the original Ethernet frame, it has no idea what port or ports to forward the broadcast to, since it doesn't know the origin VLAN.

As shown in Figure 2-5, SwitchA tags the broadcast frame, adding the source VLAN to the original Ethernet frame (the broadcast frame is tagged). When SwitchB receives the frame, it examines the tag and knows that this is meant only for the VLAN to which PC-E belongs. Of course, since PC-E is connected via an access link connection, SwitchB first strips off the tagging and then forwards the original Ethernet frame to PC-E. This is necessary because PC-E has a standard NIC and doesn't understand VLAN tagging. Through this process, both switches maintained the integrity of the broadcast domain.

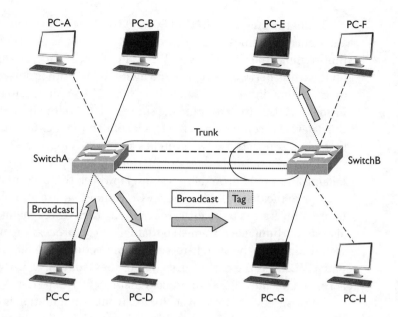

FIGURE 2-5

Broadcast traffic
example

802.1Q

ISL, which is Cisco proprietary, is being phased out in Cisco's products and being
replaced with IEEE's 802.1Q trunking standard, which was introduced in 1998. One
of the advantages provided by the IEEE standard is that it allows trunks between
different vendors' devices, whereas ISL is supported only on certain Cisco devices.
Therefore, you should be able to implement a multivendor trunking solution
without having to worry about whether or not a specific type of trunk connection is
or is not supported. The 2960 switches, as well as Cisco's higher-end switches such
as the 6500 series, support 802.1Q. Actually, the 2960 series of switches support *only*
802.1Q trunking—they don't support ISL. 802.1Q trunking is supported on switch
ports that are capable of either Fast or Gigabit Ethernet speeds.

   802.1Q trunks support two types of frames: tagged and untagged. An untagged
frame does not carry any VLAN identification information in it—basically, this
is a standard, unaltered Ethernet frame. The VLAN membership for the frame is
determined by the switch's port configuration: if the port is configured in VLAN 1,
the untagged frame belongs to VLAN 1. This VLAN is commonly called a *native*
VLAN. A tagged frame contains VLAN information, and only other 802.1Q-aware
devices on the trunk will be able to process this frame.

One of the unique aspects of 802.1Q trunking is that you can have *both* tagged and untagged frames on a trunk connection, such as that shown in Figure 2-6. In this example, the white VLAN (PC-A, PC-B, PC-E, and PC-F) uses tagged frames on the trunk between SwitchA and SwitchB. Any other device that is connected on this trunk line would need to have 802.1Q trunking enabled to see the tag inside the frame to determine the source VLAN of the frame. In this network, a third device is connected to the trunk connection: PC-G. This example assumes that a hub connects the two switches and the PC together.

PC-G has a normal Ethernet NIC and obviously wouldn't understand the tagging and would drop these frames. However, this presents a problem: PC-G belongs to the dark VLAN, where PC-C and PC-D are also members. Therefore, in order for frames to be forwarded among these three members, the trunk must also support untagged frames so that PC-G can process them. To set this up, you would configure the switch-to-switch connection as an 802.1Q trunk but set the native VLAN as the dark one, so that frames from this VLAN would go untagged across it and allow PC-G to process them.

One restriction placed on an 802.1Q trunk configuration is that it must be the *same* on both sides. In other words, if the dark VLAN is the native VLAN on one switch, the switch at the other end must have the native VLAN set to the dark

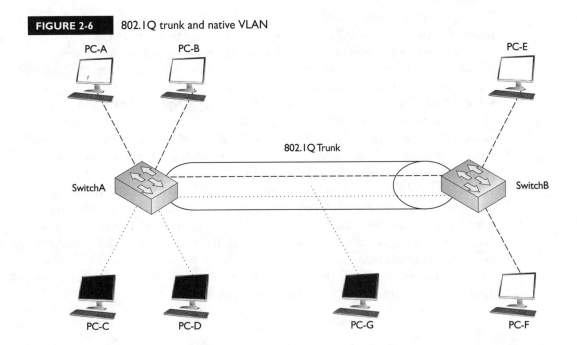

FIGURE 2-6   802.1Q trunk and native VLAN

VLAN. Likewise, if the white VLAN is having its frames tagged on one switch, the other switch must also be tagging the white VLAN frames with 802.1Q information.

With the 802.1Q tagging method, the original Ethernet frame is modified. A 4-byte field, called a *tag* field, is inserted into the header of the original Ethernet frame, and the original frame's FCS (checksum) is recomputed on the basis of this change. The first 2 bytes of the tag are the protocol identifier. For instance, an Ethernet type frame has a protocol identifier value of 0x8100, indicating that this is an Ethernet tagged frame. The next 3 bits are used to prioritize the frame, which is defined in the IEEE 802.1p standard. The fourth bit indicates if this is an encapsulated Token Ring frame (Cisco no longer sells Token Ring products), and the last 2 bits are used for the VLAN identifier (number).

Figure 2-7 shows the process that occurs when tagging an Ethernet frame by inserting the 802.1Q field into the Ethernet frame header. As you can see in this figure, step 1 is the normal, untagged Ethernet frame. Step 2 inserts the tag and recomputes a new FCS value. Below step 2 is a blow-up of the actual tag field. As you can see in this figure, the tag is inserted directly after the source and destination MAC addresses in the Ethernet header.

FIGURE 2-7

802.1Q framing process

Step 1

Destination MAC	Source MAC	Length or Type	Data	Original FCS

Step 2

Destination MAC	Source MAC	TAG	Length or Type	Data	New FCS

Type	Priority	Token Ring Encapsulation	VLAN ID

One advantage of using this tagging mechanism is that, since you are adding only 4 bytes, your frame size will not exceed 1518 bytes, and thus you could actually forward 802.1Q frames through the access link connections of switches, since these switches would forward the frame as a normal Ethernet frame.

CERTIFICATION OBJECTIVE 2.03

VLAN Trunk Protocol

The VLAN Trunk Protocol (VTP) is a proprietary Cisco protocol used to share VLAN configuration information between Cisco switches on trunk connections. VTP allows switches to share and synchronize their VLAN information, which ensures that your network has a consistent VLAN configuration.

Assume, for instance, that you have a network with two switches and you need to add a new VLAN. This could easily be accomplished by adding the VLAN manually on both switches. However, this process becomes more difficult and tedious if you have 30 switches. In this situation, you might make a mistake in configuring the new VLAN on one of the switches, giving it the wrong VLAN identifier, or you might forget to add the new VLAN to one of the 30 switches. VTP can take care of this issue. With VTP, you can add the VLAN on one switch and have this switch propagate the new VLAN, via VTP messages, to all of the other switches in your layer 2 network, causing them to add the new VLAN also.

This is also true if you modify a VLAN's configuration or delete a VLAN—VTP can verify that your VLAN configuration is consistent across all of your switches. VTP can even perform consistency checks with your VLANs to make sure that all the VLANs are configured identically. For instance, some of these components of a VLAN include the VLAN number, name, and type. If you have a VLAN number of 1 and a name of "admin" on one switch, but a name of "administrator" on a second switch for this VLAN, VTP can check for and fix these kinds of configuration mismatches.

VTP messages will propagate *only* across trunk connections, so you will need to set up trunking between your switches in order to share VLAN information via VTP. VTP messages are propagated as layer 2 multicast frames. Therefore, if a router separates two of your switches, the router will *not* forward the VTP messages from one of its interfaces to another.

In order for VTP to function correctly, you must associate your switch with a VTP domain. A *domain* is a group of switches that have the same VLAN information applied to them. Basically, a VTP domain is similar to an autonomous system, which some routing protocols use (autonomous systems and routing protocols are introduced in Chapter 4). A switch can belong only to a single domain. Domains are given names, and when switches generate VTP messages, they include the domain name in their messages. An incoming switch will not incorporate the VLAN changes in the received VTP message if the domain name in the message doesn't match the domain name configured on itself. In other words, a switch in one domain will ignore VTP messages from switches in other domains. The following sections cover the components and messages that VTP uses, as well as some of the advantages that it provides, such as pruning.

VTP Modes

When you are setting up VTP, you can choose from three different modes for your switch's configuration:

- Client
- Server
- Transparent

Table 2-2 shows the differences between these VTP modes.

TABLE 2-2		Server	Client	Transparent
Description of VTP Modes	Can add, modify, and delete VLANs	Yes	No	Yes
	Can generate VTP messages	Yes	No	No
	Can propagate VTP messages	Yes	Yes	Yes
	Can accept changes in a VTP message	Yes	Yes	No
	Default VTP mode	Yes	No	No
	Saves VLANs to NVRAM	Yes	No	Yes

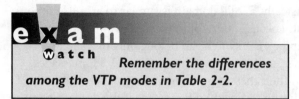

A switch configured in either VTP server or transparent mode can add, modify, and delete VLANs. The main difference between these modes is that the configuration changes made to a transparent switch affect only *that* switch and no other switch in the network. A VTP server switch, however, will make the change and then propagate a VTP message concerning the change on all of its trunk ports. If a server switch receives a VTP message, it will incorporate the update and forward the message out its remaining trunk ports. A transparent switch, on the other hand, ignores VTP messages—it will accept them on trunk ports and forward them out its remaining trunk ports, but it will not incorporate the changes in the VTP message in its local VLAN configuration. In this sense, transparent switches are like little islands, where changes on a transparent switch affect no one else but the transparent switch itself, and changes on other switches do not affect transparent switches.

A VTP client switch cannot make changes to its VLAN configuration itself—it requires a server switch to tell it about the VLAN changes. When a client switch receives a VTP message from a server switch, it incorporates the changes and then floods the VTP message out its remaining trunk ports.

Normally, you would set up one switch in server mode and all other switches in client mode. Then you would control who could make changes on the server switch. However, you should keep in mind that if you make a VLAN configuration mistake on the server switch, this mistake is *automatically propagated* to all the client switches in your network. Imagine that you accidentally deleted a VLAN on your server switch, and this VLAN had 500 devices in it. When this occurs, all the switches remove the VLAN from their configuration.

Given this problem, some administrators don't like to use VTP server and client modes; they prefer to configure all of their switches in transparent mode. The problem with transparent mode is that it isn't very scalable; if you need to add a VLAN to your network and your network has 20 switches, you would have to add the VLAN manually to each individual switch, which is a time-consuming process. Of course, the advantage of this approach is that if you make a mistake on a transparent switch, the problem is *not* propagated to other switches: it's localized.

You could also set up all of your switches in server mode, which is the default setting for VTP. As you can see, a wide range of VTP configuration options is available. You could even mix and match these options. Set up a couple of server switches, and have the remaining switches as clients, or set your switches initially as servers and clients, add all your VLANs on the server switch, allow the clients to acquire this information, and then change all the switches to transparent mode.

This process allows you to populate your switches' configurations easily with a consistent VLAN configuration during the setup process. Note that if you don't specify the VTP mode for your switch, it will default to *server*.

VTP Messages

If you use a client/server configuration for VTP, these switches can generate three types of VTP messages:

- Advertisement request
- Subset advertisement
- Summary advertisement

An *advertisement request* message is a VTP message a client generates to acquire VLAN information, to which a server will respond. When the server responds to a client's request, it generates a *subset advertisement*. A subset advertisement contains detailed VLAN configuration information, including the VLAN numbers, names, types, and other information. The client will then configure itself appropriately.

A *summary advertisement* is also generated by a switch in VTP server mode. Summary advertisements are generated every 5 minutes (300 seconds) by default, or when a configuration change takes place on the server switch. Unlike a subset advertisement, a summary advertisement contains only summarized VLAN information.

When a server switch generates a VTP advertisement, it can include the following information:

- The number and name of the VLAN
- The MTU size used by the VLAN
- The frame format used by the VLAN
- The Security Association ID (SAID) value for the VLAN (needed if it is an 802.10 VLAN, which is implemented in networks using FDDI)
- The configuration revision number
- The name of the VTP domain

This list includes a couple of important items that should be discussed further. Switches in either server or client mode will process VTP messages if they are in the same VTP domain; however, some restrictions are placed on whether the switch should incorporate the changes or not. For instance, one function of the VTP summary advertisements is to ensure that all of the switches have the most current changes. If you didn't make a change on a server switch in the 5-minute update interval, when the countdown timer expires, the server switch still sends out a summary advertisement with the same exact summary information. It makes no sense to have other switches, which have the most up-to-date information, incorporate the same information in their configuration.

To make this process more efficient, the *configuration revision number* is used to keep track of what server switch has the most recent changes. Initially, this number is set to zero (0). If you make a change on a server switch, it increments its revision number and advertises this to the other switches across its trunk links. When a client or server switch receives this information, it compares the revision number in the message to the last message it received. If the newly arrived message has a higher number, this server switch must have made changes. If the necessary VLAN information isn't in the VTP summary advertisement, all client and server switches will generate an advertisement request, and the server will respond with the details in a subset advertisement.

If a server switch receives a VTP message from another server, and the advertising server has a lower revision number, the receiving server switch will respond to the advertising server with a VTP message with its current configuration revision number. This will tell the advertising server switch that it doesn't have the most up-to-date VLAN information and should request it from the server that does. In this sense, the revision number used in a VTP message is somewhat similar to the sequence number used in TCP. Also, remember that transparent switches are not processing these VTP advertisements—they simply passively forward these messages to other switches on their trunk ports.

on the
() o b

IOS switches save the VLAN database and revision value in the vlan.dat file, not the startup-config file: server, transparent, and client mode switches. The `erase startup-config` *command will not delete this file. Therefore, it is possible that if you boot up a switch that has a higher revision number than an existing server switch in a domain, the switch's VLAN configuration could overwrite the existing VLAN information in the domain. You should delete the vlan.dat file on the switch before adding it to an existing network. This is done from Privileged EXEC mode with this command:* `delete vlan.dat`. *You must press* ENTER *twice after executing the command to confirm your option.*

VTP Pruning

VTP pruning is a Cisco feature that allows your switches dynamically to delete or add VLANs to a trunk, creating a more efficient switching network. By default, all VLANs are associated with a trunk connection. This means that if a device in *any* VLAN generates a broadcast, multicast, or an unknown unicast, the switch will flood this frame out all ports associated with the source VLAN port, including trunks. In many situations, this flooding is necessary, especially if the VLAN spans multiple switches. However, it doesn't make sense to flood a frame to a neighboring switch if that switch doesn't have any active ports in the source VLAN.

Trunking Without Pruning

Let's take a look at a simple example by examining Figure 2-8. In this example, VTP pruning is not enabled. PC-A, PC-B, PC-E, and PC-F are in the same VLAN. If PC-A generates a broadcast, SwitchA will forward this to the access link to which PC-B is connected as well as the trunk (since a trunk is a member of all VLANs, by default). This makes sense, since PC-E and PC-F, connected to SwitchB, are in the same VLAN.

Figure 2-8 shows a second VLAN with two members: PC-C and PC-D. If PC-C generates a local broadcast, SwitchA will obviously send to this to PC-D's port. What doesn't make sense is that SwitchA will flood this broadcast out its trunk port to SwitchB, considering that no devices on SwitchB are in this VLAN. This is an example of wasting bandwidth and resources. A single broadcast isn't a big problem; however, imagine this were a video multicast stream at 5 Mbps coming from PC-A. This network might experience throughput problems on the trunk, since a switch treats a multicast just like a broadcast—it floods it out all ports associated with the source port's VLAN.

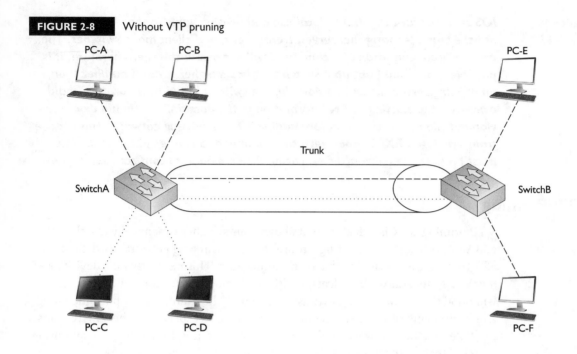

FIGURE 2-8 Without VTP pruning

You could use one of two methods to fix this problem: static VLAN pruning or dynamic VLAN pruning. With a static configuration, you would manually prune the inactive VLAN off the trunk on both switches, as shown in Figure 2-9. Notice that in this figure, the dark VLAN (indicated by dotted lines) has been pruned from the trunk. The problem with manual pruning is that if you add a dark VLAN member to SwitchB, you will have to log into both switches and manually add the pruned VLAN back to the trunk. This can become very confusing in a multiswitched network with multiple VLANs, where every VLAN is not necessarily active on every switch. It would be easy to accidentally prune a VLAN from a trunk that shouldn't have been pruned, thus creating connectivity problems.

Trunking with Pruning

The VTP pruning feature allows the switches to share additional VLAN information and allows them to prune inactive VLANs dynamically from trunk connections. In this instance, the switches share which VLANs are active. For example, SwitchA tells SwitchB that it has two active VLANs (the white one and the dark one). SwitchB, on the other hand, has only one active VLAN, and it shares this fact with SwitchA. Given the shared information, both SwitchA and

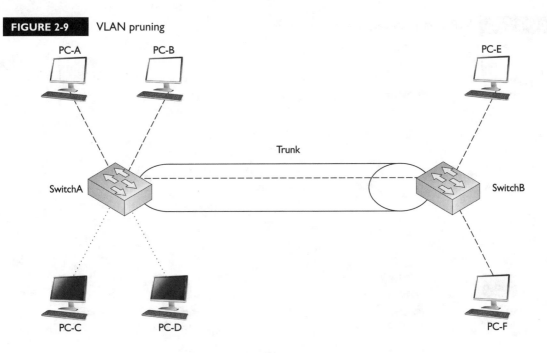

FIGURE 2-9 VLAN pruning

SwitchB realize that the dark VLAN is inactive across their trunk connection and therefore the dark VLAN should be dynamically removed from the trunk's configuration.

The nice thing about this feature is that if you happen to activate the dark VLAN on SwitchB by connecting a device to a port on the switch and assigning that port to the dark VLAN, SwitchB will notify SwitchA about the newly active VLAN, and both switches will dynamically add the VLAN back to the trunk's configuration. This will allow PC-C, PC-D, and the new device to send frames to each other, as is shown in Figure 2-10.

Only a VTP switch in server mode can enable VTP pruning, and the remaining switches in the domain must be either in VTP server or client mode. If you have transparent mode switches, you'll have to prune VLANs off their trunk links manually.

*e*x*a*m*

⊙*a*t*c*h *By default, all VLANs can traverse a trunk. VTP pruning is used on trunk connections to dynamically remove VLANs not active between the two switches. It must be enabled on a VTP server switch, and the other switches must be either servers or clients.*

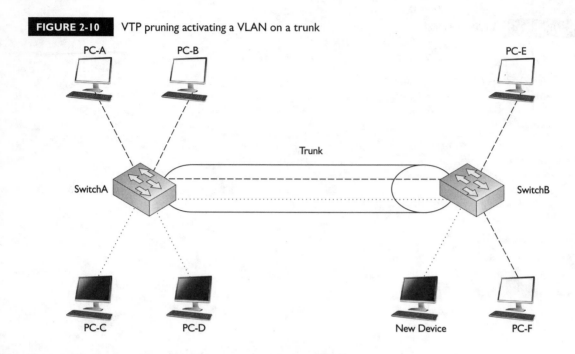

FIGURE 2-10   VTP pruning activating a VLAN on a trunk

VLAN Configuration

Unlike Cisco routers, every Cisco switch comes with a default configuration. For instance, some preconfigured VLANs are already on the switch, including VLAN 1. During the configuration, all VLAN commands refer to the VLAN number, even though you can configure an optional name for the VLAN. Every port on your switch, by default, is associated with VLAN 1. And all communications from the switch itself—VTP messages, Cisco Discovery Protocol (CDP) multicasts (discussed in Chapter 7), and other traffic the switch originates—occur in VLAN 1. Recall from your CCENT studies that the 2960's IP configuration is based on the VLAN interface for which you configure your IP address.

VLAN 1 is sometimes called the *management VLAN*, even though you can use a different VLAN. It is a common practice to put all of your management devices—switches, manageable hubs, and management stations—in their own

VLAN. If you decide to put your switch in a different VLAN than VLAN 1, it is recommended that you change this configuration on all your management devices so that you can more easily secure them, since other VLANs would have to go through a layer 3 device to access them; and on this layer 3 device, you can set up access control lists to filter unwanted traffic.

It's important that all your switches are in the same VLAN, since many of the switches' management protocols, such as CDP, VTP, and the Dynamic Trunk Protocol (DTP), which is discussed later in this chapter, occur within the switch's management VLAN. If one switch had its management VLAN set to 1 and another connected switch had it set to 2, the two switches would lose a lot of inter-functionality.

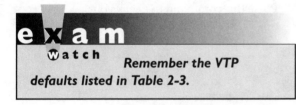

Remember the VTP defaults listed in Table 2-3.

Configuring VTP

One of the very first VLAN configuration tasks you'll perform on your switch is to set up VTP. Table 2-3 shows the default VTP configuration of the 2960 switches. The following sections cover the configuration of VTP on the two switches.

Your VTP configuration is done from *Global Configuration* mode on the 2960:

```
switch(config)# vtp domain VTP_domain_name
switch(config)# vtp mode server|client|transparent
switch(config)# vtp password VTP_password
switch(config)# vtp pruning
```

The **vtp domain** command defines the domain name for your switch. Remember that in order for switches to share VTP information, they must be in the same domain. Messages received from other domains are ignored. If you don't configure a domain name, the switch will learn this from a server advertisement.

TABLE 2-3	VTP Component	VTP Default Value
VTP Default Configuration Values	Domain name	None
	Mode	Server
	Password	None
	Pruning	Disabled
	Version	1

The rest of the commands in the configuration are optional. The second **vtp** command defines the VTP mode of the switch. If you don't configure this command, the default mode is **server**. You can configure a VTP MD5 password for your switches, which must match the password configured on every switch in the domain. Switches will use this password to verify VTP messages from other switches; if the created hashed values placed in VTP messages (generated by taking the VTP message and password and running it through MD5 to create the hash signature) can't be verified, the switches ignore the VTP messages. On the 2960 switches, pruning is disabled by default, but you can disable or enable it with the **vtp pruning** command. It is important to note that if pruning is enabled on a server switch, the server switch will propagate this to all other server and client switches in the same domain.

Once you are done configuring VTP, use this command to check your configuration:

```
switch# show vtp status
VTP Version : 1
Configuration Revision : 17
Maximum VLANs supported locally : 255
Number of existing VLANs : 7
VTP Operating Mode : Server
VTP Domain Name : dealgroup
VTP Pruning Mode : Enabled
VTP V2 Mode : Disabled
VTP Traps Generation : Disabled
MD5 digest : 0x95 0xAB 0x29 0x44 0x32 0xA1 0x2C 0x31
Configuration last modified by 0.0.0.0 at 3-1-03 15:18:37
Local updater ID is 192.168.1.4 on interface Vl1
    (lowest numbered VLAN interface found)
```

In this example, 17 configuration changes have occurred (examine the Configuration Revision field). The switch is operating in server mode in the *dealgroup* domain.

exam
ⓦatch   The vtp password command is used to authenticate VTP messages between switches. The show vtp status command will display the VTP mode in which the switch is operating, the configuration revision number, and the VTP domain to which the switch belongs.

The following command displays VTP statistics concerning VTP messages sent and received:

```
switch # show vtp counters
VTP statistics:
  Summary advertisements received : 12
  Subset advertisements received : 0
  Request advertisements received : 0
  Summary advertisements transmitted : 7
  Subset advertisements transmitted : 0
  Request advertisements transmitted : 0
  Number of config revision errors : 0
  Number of config digest errors : 0
  Number of V1 summary errors : 0
  .
  .
  .
```

In this example, you can see that the switch has sent and received VTP summary advertisements.

2.01. The digital resources that accompany this book contain a multimedia demonstration of configuring and verifying VTP on a switch.

Configuring Trunks

This section covers the setup of trunk connections on your switches using the 802.1Q trunking protocol. Before getting into the configuration, however, you should first be familiar with a protocol that is used to form a trunk between two devices: the Dynamic Trunk Protocol (DTP). One limitation of trunks is that they don't work with the port security and 802.1x authentication features; these features are used on access links.

Dynamic Trunk Protocol (DTP)

Cisco's proprietary trunking protocol is used on trunk connections to form trunks dynamically. DTP is used to form and verify a trunk connection dynamically between two Cisco switches. DTP supports five trunking modes, shown in Table 2-4.

If the trunk mode is set to *on* or *trunk* for an interface, this causes the interface to generate DTP messages on the interface and to tag frames on the interface, based on the trunk type (802.1Q on the 2960s). When set to *on*, the trunk

TABLE 2-4

DTP Modes and
Operation

DTP Mode	Generate DTP Messages	Default Frame Tagging
On or trunk	Yes	Yes
Desirable	Yes	No
Auto	No	No
Off	No	No
No-negotiate	No	Yes

interface always assumes the connection is a trunk, even if the remote end does not support trunking. Some of Cisco's switches use the term *trunk* instead of *on*, such as the 2960s.

If the trunk mode is set to *desirable*, the interface will generate DTP messages on the interface, but it will make the assumption that the other side is not trunk capable and will wait for a DTP reply message from the remote side. In this state, the interface starts as an access link connection. If the remote side sends a DTP message, and this message indicates that trunking is compatible between the two switches, a trunk will be formed and the switch will start tagging frames on the interface. If the other side does not support trunking, the interface will remain as an access link connection.

If the trunk mode is set to *auto*, the interface passively listens for DTP messages from the remote side and leaves the interface as an access link connection. If the interface receives a DTP message, and the message matches trunking capabilities of the interface, then the interface will change from an access link connection to a trunk connection and start tagging frames. This is the default DTP mode for a Cisco switch interface that is trunk capable.

If an interface is set to *no-negotiate*, the interface is set as a trunk connection and will automatically tag frames with VLAN information; however, the interface will not generate DTP messages: DTP is disabled. This mode is typically used when connecting trunk connections to non-Cisco devices that don't understand Cisco's proprietary trunking protocol and thus won't understand the contents of these messages.

If an interface is set to *off*, the interface is configured as an access link. No DTP messages are generated in this mode, nor are frames tagged.

Table 2-5 shows when switch connections will form a trunk. In this table, one side needs to be configured as either *on* or *desirable* and the other side as *on*, *desirable*, or *auto*, or both switches need to be configured as *no-negotiate*. Note that if you use the no-negotiate mode, trunking is formed but DTP is not used,

TABLE 2-5	Your Switch	Remote Switch
Forming Trunks	On	On, desirable, auto
	Desirable	On, desirable, auto
	Auto	On, desirable
	No-negotiate	No-negotiate

e x a m

ⓦatch   *Remember the DTP information in Tables 2-4 and 2-5 for the exam. The result of a successful DTP completion is the formation of an 802.1Q trunk. When using DTP autosensing, if the native VLAN doesn't match, a native VLAN mismatch error will occur.*

whereas if you use on, desirable, or auto, DTP is used. One advantage that DTP has over no-negotiate is that DTP checks for the trunk's characteristics: if they don't match on the two sides (for instance, as to the type of trunk or a mismatch with the native VLAN), then the trunk will not come up and the interfaces will remain as an access link connection. With no-negotiate, if the trunking characteristics don't match on the two sides, the trunk connection will probably fail.

Switch Trunk Configuration

Setting up a trunk on a 2960 is the same as on most of Cisco's IOS switches:

```
switch(config)# interface type slot_#/port_#
switch(config-if)# switchport mode trunk|dynamic desirable|
                          dynamic auto|nonegotiate
switch(config-if)# switchport trunk native vlan VLAN_#
```

All ports on a 2960 switch support trunking. Remember that the 2960 supports only 802.1Q trunking, so you must set up a trunk connection only to other 802.1Q trunking devices. If you want a trunk to be in an *on* state, use the **trunk** parameter. For a *desirable* DTP state, use **dynamic desirable**, and for an *auto* state, use **dynamic auto**. The default mode is auto. If you don't want to use DTP but still want to perform trunking, use the **nonegotiate** parameter. For 802.1Q trunks, the native VLAN is VLAN 1. You can change this with the **switchport trunk native vlan** command, but then you'll need to match up the native VLAN on all switches in the layer 2 network. If two interconnected switches have a different native VLAN on the connecting trunks, then traffic from one VLAN on one switch will end up in a different VLAN on the remote switch, which can create all kinds of problems.

After you have configured your trunk connection, you can use this command to verify it:

```
switch# show interfaces type 0/port_# switchport|trunk
```

Here's an example using the **switchport** parameter:

```
switch# show interface fastEthernet0/1 switchport
Name: Fa0/1
Switchport: Enabled
Administrative mode: trunk
Operational Mode: trunk
Administrative Trunking Encapsulation: dot1q
Operational Trunking Encapsulation: dot1q
Negotiation of Trunking: Disabled
Access Mode VLAN: 0 ((Inactive))
Trunking Native Mode VLAN: 1 (default)
Trunking VLANs Enabled: ALL
Trunking VLANs Active: 1,2
Pruning VLANs Enabled: 2-1001
Priority for untagged frames: 0
Override vlan tag priority: FALSE
Voice VLAN: none
```

In this example, `FA0/1`'s trunking mode is set to `trunk` (on), with the native VLAN set to 1. Here's an example using the **trunk** parameter:

```
switch# show interfaces trunk
Port    Mode      Encapsulation   Status      Native vlan
Fa0/1   on        802.1q          trunking    1
Port    Vlans allowed on trunk
Fa0/1   1-4094
Port    Vlans allowed and active in management domain
Fa0/1   1-2
Port    Vlans in spanning tree forwarding state and not pruned
Fa0/1   1-2
```

watch
Use the `show` | command to verify trunking. Be familiar
`interfaces switchport|trunk` | with the output of this command.

In this example, one interface is trunking—`fa0/1`: the trunking mode is on, the trunking protocol is 802.1Q, and the native VLAN is `1`.

watch
When executing the `show` `mac address-table` command, if you see multiple MAC addresses associated with a single interface, this can indicate that the interface is a trunk connection or that the | interface is an access link connection to another switch or hub. Switches typically have a separate MAC address table for each VLAN to simplify the lookup process for a MAC address on trunk connections.

Video

2.02. The digital resources that accompany this book contain a multimedia demonstration of configuring trunking on a switch.

EXERCISE 2-1

MHE Lab

Configuring Trunks on Your Switches

The last few sections dealt with setting up trunks on Cisco switches. You'll perform this lab using Boson's NetSim simulator. This exercise has you set up a trunk link between the two 2950 switches (2950-1 and 2950-2). You can find a picture of the network diagram for the NetSim simulator in the Introduction of this book. After starting up the simulator, click the Labs tab at the bottom left of the window. Click the McGraw-Hill Education tab (to the right of the Standard and Custom tabs) at the top left, and then double-click Exercise 2-1. This will load the lab configuration based on a simple configuration.

1. On the 2950-1 switch, set the trunk mode to trunk for the connection between the two 2950 switches and examine the status. Does the trunk come up?

Under the Lab Instructions tab, use the drop-down selector for Devices to choose 2950-1; or click the NetMap tab and double-click the 2950-1 device icon. Access Configuration mode: `enable` and `configure terminal`. Go into the interface: `interface fa0/1`. Set the trunk mode to trunk: `switchport mode trunk`. Exit Configuration mode: `end`. Use the `show interfaces trunk` command to verify the status. You might have to wait a few seconds, but the trunk should come up. If one side is set to *on* or *desirable* and the other is set to *on*, *desirable*, or *auto* (default), then the trunk should come up.

2. Save the configuration on the switch: `copy running-config startup-config`.

3. On the 2950-2 switch, set the trunk mode to trunk for the connection between the two 2950 switches and verify the trunking status of the interface.

   Under the Lab Instructions tab, use the drop-down selector for Devices to choose 2950-2; or click the NetMap tab and double-click the 2950-2 device icon. Access Configuration mode: `enable` and `configure terminal`. Go into the interface: `interface fa0/1`. Set the trunk mode to trunk: `switchport mode trunk`. Exit Configuration mode: `end`. Use the `show interfaces trunk` command to verify the status.

4. Save the configuration on the switch: `copy running-config startup-config`.

Now you should be more comfortable with setting up trunks on your switches. In the next section, you will be presented with setting up VLANs and associating interfaces to your VLANs.

Creating VLANs

This section covers how you can create VLANs on your switches and then statically assign access link connections (interfaces) to your newly created VLANs. Here are some guidelines to remember when creating VLANs:

■ The number of VLANs you can create is dependent on the switch model and IOS software.

- Some VLANs are preconfigured on every switch, including VLAN 1 and 1002–1005 (1002–1005 are used in Token Ring and FDDI networks only). These VLANs cannot be deleted!

- To add or delete VLANs, your switch must use either VTP server or transparent mode.

- VLAN names can be changed; VLAN numbers can't: you must delete a VLAN and re-add it in order to renumber it.

- All interfaces, by default, belong to VLAN 1.

- CDP, DTP, and VTP advertisements are sent in the native VLAN, which is VLAN 1, by default.

- Before deleting VLANs, reassign any ports from the current VLAN to another; if you don't, any ports from the deleted VLAN will be inoperable.

- Unknown destination MAC addresses are only flooded in the VLAN in which the source MAC address resides.

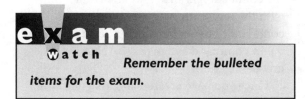

Remember the bulleted items for the exam.

Table 2-6 lists the VLAN capabilities of the 2960-X switches.

You can use two methods—an old one and a new one—to create VLANs on your 2960 switch. The old method requires you to go into the VLAN database in Privileged EXEC mode and create the VLAN (this is not covered in this book or the exam). The new method creates the VLAN from Configuration mode, like this:

```
switch(config)# vlan VLAN_#
switch(config-vlan)# name VLAN_name
```

When you execute the **vlan** command, you are taken into VLAN Subconfiguration mode, where you can enter your configuration parameters for the VLAN, such as its name. Use the **no** parameter in front of the **vlan** command to delete it.

TABLE 2-6	Switch Model	Software Revision	Number of VLANs
VLAN Capabilities of the 2960 Cisco Switches	2960	LAN Lite	64
	2960	LAN Base and IP Lite	1023

on the
ⓘob

Cisco recommends you use the newer method to create VLANs on your switches: the Global Configuration `vlan` command. Remember that your switch must be a VTP server or transparent switch to create or delete VLANs on it. Also, before you delete a VLAN, move all ports in the VLAN to a different one; otherwise, ports associated with a deleted VLAN will not be able to communicate with other ports until you either re-add the VLAN number back or move the ports to an existing VLAN. When this happens, the port LED(s) will be solid amber.

Once you have created your VLANs, you need to assign your VLANs to your switch's interfaces using the following configuration:

```
switch(config)# interface type 0/port_#
switch(config-if)# switchport mode access
switch(config-if)# switchport access vlan VLAN_#
```

exam

ⓦatch   *If you associate a nonexistent VLAN to a switch port with the `switchport access vlan` command, IOS will automatically create the VLAN.*

The first thing you must do is specify that the connection is an access link connection with the **switchport mode access** command. The **switchport access vlan** command assigns a VLAN to the access link connection.

Once you have created and assigned your VLANs, you can use various **show** commands to review and verify your configuration. The **show vlan** command displays the list of VLANs and which ports are assigned to them:

```
switch# show vlan
VLAN Name            Status    Ports
---- --------------- --------- ------------------------------
1    default         active    Fa0/1, Fa0/2, Fa0/3, Fa0/4
                               Fa0/5, Fa0/6, Fa0/7, Fa0/8
                               Fa0/9, Fa0/10, Fa0/11, Fa0/12
                               Fa0/13, Fa0/14, Fa0/15, Fa0/16
                               Fa0/17, Fa0/18, Fa0/19, Fa0/20
                               Fa0/21, Fa0/22, Fa0/23, Fa0/24
                               Gi0/1, Gi0/2
1002 fddi-default    act/unsup
 .
 .
 .
```

In this example, all the ports are assigned to VLAN 1. You can add the **brief** parameter to this command and it will not display the details for each VLAN at the bottom of the display. You can also use the **show interface switchport** command to see a specific interface's VLAN membership information. This command was shown earlier in the chapter in the "Switch Trunk Configuration" section.

2.03. The digital resources that accompany this book contain a multimedia demonstration of configuring VLANs on a switch.

Basic Troubleshooting of VLANs and Trunks

Now that you know how to set up a VLAN-based network, you will eventually run into a problem that is related to your VLAN configuration. You should check the following, in order, to determine the cause of the problem:

1. Check the status of your interface to determine whether it is a physical layer problem.
2. Check your switches' and routers' configuration to make sure nothing was added or changed.
3. Verify that your trunks are operational.
4. Verify that your VLANs are configured correctly and that the Spanning Tree Protocol (STP), discussed in Chapter 3, is functioning correctly.

The following sections cover some of the basic things that you should check whenever you experience switching problems.

Performance Problems

If you are experiencing slow performance or intermittent connection problems, you should first check the statistics on the interfaces of your switch with the **show interfaces** command. Are you seeing a high number of errors, such as collisions?

A few things can cause these problems. The most common is a mismatch in either the duplexing or the speed on a connection. Examine the settings on both sides of the connection. Also, make sure that you are using the correct cabling type: straight for a DTE-to-DCE connection and crossover for a DTE-to-DTE or DCE-to-DCE connection (as covered in your CCENT studies). And make sure that the cable does not exceed the maximum legal limit. Also, make sure that the connected IC is not experiencing a hardware problem or failure.

Local Connection Problems

If you are attempting to access the console port of a switch or router, and all you see is garbage in your terminal session, this could indicate an incorrect terminal setting. Usually the culprit is an incorrect baud rate. Some devices allow you to perform an operating system upgrade via the console port, and an administrator might change it to the highest possible value but forget to change it back to 9600 bps. If you suspect this, keep on changing your baud rate until you find the right speed.

If you are having problems accessing devices in the switched network, you can look at a few options. First, is the device you are trying to reach in the same VLAN? If so, make sure that you are using the correct IP addressing scheme in the VLAN and that the two devices trying to share information have their ports in the same VLAN. If the two devices are Cisco devices, you can use CDP to elicit some of this information, for instance, the IP address, by using the **show cdp** commands (discussed in Chapter 7). Is the switch learning about the devices in your network? You might want to examine your CAM tables and make sure that a port security violation is not causing your connectivity problem (see Chapter 1).

For VLAN information, use the **show** commands on your switches to check your VLAN configuration. Also, check the VLAN configuration on each switch and make sure the VLANs are configured with the same parameters by using the **show vlan** command. If the port LED is solid amber, your problem could be that the port's VLAN was deleted and the port wasn't reassigned. Other problems can also cause the port LED to turn amber, such as STP placing the port in a blocking state (Chapter 3) or port security has disabled the port because of a security violation (Chapter 1). Actually, if you see that a lot of port LEDs are amber, a deleted VLAN is likely the problem. Use the **show interface switchport** command to determine whether a deleted VLAN is the problem:

if you see that the VLAN assigned to the port is inactive, like this, then you've identified the culprit:

```
switch# show interface fastEthernet0/1 switchport
Name: Fa0/1
Switchport: Enabled
Administrative mode: static access
Operational Mode: static access
Administrative Trunking Encapsulation: dot1q
Operational Trunking Encapsulation: native
Negotiation of Trunking: Off
Access Mode VLAN: 5 (Inactive)
Trunking Native Mode VLAN: 1 (default)
  .
  .
  .
```

Notice that in this example VLAN 5 is inactive, indicating that the interface is assigned to the VLAN, but the VLAN was deleted, making the interface inoperable.

If you are using trunks between the switches, make sure that the trunks are configured correctly: **show interface trunk**. Make sure that the native VLAN number matches on both ends of the trunk: if they are mismatched, a trunk will not form.

Also, check VTP (if you are using it) by executing the **show vtp** commands. Make sure you have trunk connections between your switches, since VTP messages only traverse trunks. When using a server/client implementation, make sure that the domain name and, if using the password option, the password match among the VTP switches. Also, all switches must be running the same VTP version (by default, this is version 1).

Inter-VLAN Connection Problems

If you are having problems reaching devices in other VLANs, make sure that, first, you can ping the default gateway (router) that is your exit point from the VLAN. A common misconfiguration on a user's PC is a misconfigured default gateway. If you can't ping the default gateway, then go back to the preceding section and check local VLAN connectivity issues. If you can ping the gateway, check the router's configuration and its interface (Chapter 6). Also, make sure that the router has a route to the destination VLAN (**show ip route**). This is covered in Chapters 9, 10, and 11. If you do have a route to the destination, make sure the destination VLAN is configured correctly and that the default gateway in that VLAN can reach the destination device.

EXERCISE 2-2

Configuring VLANs on Your Switches

The last few sections dealt with the creation of VLANs and the assignment of interfaces to them. This lab builds upon this information and allows you to perform some of these configurations. You can find a picture of the network diagram for the simulator in the Introduction of this book. After starting up Boson's NetSim simulator, click the Lab Instructions tab. Next, double-click Exercise 2-2. This will load the lab configuration based on Exercise 2-1.

1. From the 2950-1, verify that you can ping Host-1 connected to fa0/3. Also ping Host-2 connected to 2950-1's fa0/4 interface.

2. Under the Lab Instructions tab, use the drop-down selector for Devices to choose 2950-1; or click the NetMap tab and double-click the 2950-1 device icon.

   Access the CLI of the 2950-1. Execute **ping 192.168.1.10** and **ping 192.168.1.11**. Both should be successful.

3. On the 2950-1, create VLAN 2. Then assign fa0/3 to VLAN 2 as an access link port. Examine your VLANs.

   Access Configuration mode: **enable** and **configure terminal**. Use the **vlan 2** command to create your VLAN. Go into the interface: **interface fastethernet0/3**. Assign the VLAN: **switchport mode access** and **switchport access vlan 2**. Exit out of Configuration mode: **exit** and **exit**.

4. View your VLANs on the 2950-1: **show vlan**. Make sure that all interfaces are in VLAN 1 except for fa0/3, which should be in VLAN 2.

5. From Host-1, ping Host-2 (192.168.1.11) connected to the 2950-1 switch. Is the ping successful?

   Under the Lab Instructions tab, use the drop-down selector for Devices to choose Host-1; or click the NetMap tab and double-click the Host-1 device icon. Execute **ping 192.168.1.11**. The ping should fail, since Host-2 is in VLAN 1, while Host-1 is in VLAN 2.

6. On the 2950-1 switch, move Host-2 to VLAN 2 and verify your configuration.

   Under the Lab Instructions tab, use the drop-down selector for Devices to choose 2950-1; or click the NetMap tab and double-click the 2950-1 device icon. On the 2950-1, go into the Host-2 interface: **configure terminal** and **interface fa0/4**. Assign the VLAN: **switchport** `mode access`, `switchport access vlan 2`, and `exit`. Exit out of Configuration mode: `exit` and `exit`.

7. View your VLANs: `show vlan`. Make sure that `fa0/3` and `fa0/4` are in VLAN 2.

8. From Host-1, ping Host-2 (192.168.1.11), which is connected to the 2950-1 switch. Is the ping successful? Can Host-1 ping the 2950-1 or 2950-2 switches?

   Under the Lab Instructions tab, use the drop-down selector for Devices to choose Host-1; or click the NetMap tab and double-click the Host-1 device icon. Execute `ping 192.168.1.11`. The ping should be successful, since all connections from Host-1 to Host-2 are in VLAN 2. Execute `ping 192.168.1.2` and `ping 192.168.1.3`. Both should fail, since both switches' IP addresses are in VLAN 1 and the hosts are in VLAN 2.

Now you should be more comfortable with configuring VLANs on your switches.

INSIDE THE EXAM

VLAN Overview

Interestingly, the information in this chapter is emphasized a bit more than that of other chapters on the CCNA exam. The exam focuses primarily on VLAN concepts and troubleshooting connectivity problems, but you might see a few questions on VLAN configurations. Understand what VLANs are, the benefits they provide, that they represent different subnets, and when they are used. Know that a router is needed to route between VLANs. Understand why VLANs are used to separate different kinds of traffic: data, voice, and video.

VLAN Connections

Understand the difference between an access link and a trunk and what each type can be connected to: switches, routers, and servers. Be familiar with 802.1Q, how it tags frames, and what the native VLAN is.

VLAN Trunk Protocol

Be *very* familiar with VTP, since it is probably the most emphasized topic in this chapter. Understand its function: consistent VLAN configuration. Be able to compare and contrast the VTP modes a

(Continued)

INSIDE THE EXAM

switch can operate in—server, client, and transparent—and what a switch will do with a VTP message based on the mode in which it is operating. Understand what the VTP password, domain, and configuration revision number are used for. Be familiar with how VTP pruning works.

VLAN Configuration

You should be familiar with the syntax of `vtp` commands, setting up a trunk port, and setting up an access link and assigning a

VLAN to it. Understand how DTP works and the modes that can be used to form a trunk. If you associate a nonexistent VLAN to a switch port with the `switchport access vlan` command, IOS will automatically create the VLAN. Be *very* familiar with the output of the `show vtp status`, `show interface switchport`, `show interface trunk`, and `show vlan` commands to identify how a switch is configured with VLAN information and to troubleshoot configuration problems.

CERTIFICATION SUMMARY

A VLAN is a group of devices in the same broadcast domain (subnet). To move among VLANs, you need a router. Static VLAN assignment to devices is also called port-based VLANs. An access link is a connection to a device that processes normal frames. Trunk connections modify frames to carry VLAN information. Ethernet trunking methods include ISL and 802.1Q. The 802.1Q method inserts a 4-byte field and recomputes the FCS for Ethernet frames; the 2960 switches support only 802.1Q.

VTP is a Cisco-proprietary protocol that transmits VLAN information across trunk ports. Switches must be in the same domain to share messages. There are three modes for VTP: client, server, and transparent. Server and transparent switches can add, change, and delete VLANs, but server switches advertise these changes. Clients can accept updates only from server switches. There are three VTP messages: advertisement request, subset advertisement, and summary advertisement. Servers generate summary advertisements every 5 minutes on trunk connections. The configuration revision number is used to determine which server switch has the most current VLAN information. VTP pruning is used to prune off VLANs that are not active between two switches, but it requires switches to be in server and/or client mode.

On the 2960, use the `vtp domain` command and `vtp server|client| transparent` commands to configure VTP. The default mode is server. To configure a VTP password, use the `vtp password` command.

DTP is a Cisco-proprietary trunking protocol. There are five modes: on (or trunk), off, desirable, auto, and no-negotiate. The on and desirable modes actively generate DTP messages; auto is the default. Use no-negotiate for non-Cisco switch connections. On the 2960, use the `switchport mode` command to set trunking and the `show interfaces switchport|trunk` command to verify it.

By default, all interfaces are in VLAN 1. On the 2960, use the `vlan` command in Global Configuration mode to create VLANs. Use the `switchport mode access` and `switchport access vlan` commands to associate an interface with a VLAN. The `show vlan` command displays your VLAN configuration.

✓ TWO-MINUTE DRILL

VLAN Overview

❑ A VLAN is a group of devices in the same broadcast domain that have the same network or subnet number. VLANs are not restricted to physical locations: users can be located anywhere in the switched network.

❑ Static, or port-based, VLAN membership is manually assigned by the administrator. Dynamic VLAN membership is determined by information from the user device, such as its MAC address or 802.1x authentication credentials.

VLAN Connections

❑ An access link is a connection to another device that supports standard Ethernet frames and supports only a single VLAN. A trunk is a connection that tags frames and allows multiple VLANs. Trunking is supported only on ports that are trunk capable: not all Ethernet ports support trunking.

❑ IEEE 802.1Q is a standardized trunking method. The 2960 supports only this method. The 802.1Q method inserts a VLAN tag in the middle of the frame and recomputes the frame's checksum. It supports a native VLAN—this is a VLAN that is not tagged on the trunk link. On Cisco switches, this defaults to VLAN 1.

VLAN Trunk Protocol

❑ VTP is used to share VLAN information to ensure that switches have a consistent VLAN configuration.

❑ VTP has three modes: server (allowed to make and accept changes, and propagates changes), transparent (allowed to make changes, ignores VTP messages), and client (accepts changes from servers and doesn't store this in NVRAM). The default mode is server.

❑ VTP messages are propagated only across trunks. For a switch to accept a VTP message, the domain name and optional password must match. There are three VTP messages: advertisement request (client or server request), subset advertisement (server response to an advertisement), and summary advertisement (server sends out every 5 minutes). The configuration revision number is used in the VTP message to determine whether it should be processed or not.

❑ VTP pruning allows for the dynamic addition and removal of VLANs on a trunk based on whether or not there are any active VLANs on a switch. Requires switches to be in server and/or client mode.

VLAN Configuration

❑ To configure VTP, use the `vtp domain` command to assign the domain, the `vtp mode` command to assign the mode, and `vtp password` to authenticate VTP messages. Use the `show vtp status` command to verify your VTP configuration.

❑ DTP is a Cisco-proprietary protocol that determines whether two interfaces on connected devices can become a trunk. There are five modes: on, desirable, auto-negotiate, off, and no-negotiate. If one side's mode is on, desirable, or auto and the other side's mode is on or desirable, a trunk will form. No-negotiate mode enables trunking but disables DTP.

❑ To enable trunking on a 2960's interface, use `switchport mode trunk`. To verify trunking, use the `show interfaces switchport|trunk` command.

❑ All ports on a switch are automatically placed in VLAN 1. To add a VLAN on a 2960, use the `vlan` command. To assign an interface to a VLAN, use `switchport mode access` and `switchport access vlan`. To view your VLANs and the ports assigned to them, use `show vlan`.

SELF TEST

The following Self Test questions will help you measure your understanding of the material presented in this chapter. Read all the choices carefully, as there may be more than one correct answer. Choose all correct answers for each question.

VLAN Overview

1. Which of the following is false concerning VLANs?
   A. A VLAN is a broadcast domain.
   B. A VLAN is a logical group of users.
   C. A VLAN is location dependent.
   D. A VLAN is a subnet.

2. Two groups of users are connected to a switch: sales and marketing. You are concerned about marketing and sales people seeing each other's traffic. What solutions would you use to prevent this? (Choose two answers.)
   A. VLANs
   B. Hubs
   C. MAC address filtering
   D. Router with ACLs

VLAN Connections

3. A connection that supports multiple VLANs is called a _____.

4. Which of the following is true concerning 802.1Q?
   A. It supports hub connections.
   B. It is not supported on the 2960 switches.
   C. The native VLAN is tagged.
   D. The original Ethernet frame is not modified.

VLAN Trunk Protocol

5. The _____ is a proprietary Cisco protocol used to share VLAN configuration information between Cisco switches on trunk connections.

6. Which VTP mode(s) will propagate VTP messages?
   A. Client and server
   B. Server
   C. Client, server, and transparent
   D. Transparent

7. You have a server switch with VLANs accounting, HR, and executives on one switch with a configuration revision value of 55 and another server switch with VLANs engineering, sales, and marketing with a configuration revision value of 57. Currently, the two switches are not connected together. You connect them together. What can happen? (Choose two answers.)
   A. If the domain names don't match, nothing occurs.
   B. If the domain names don't match, the VLANs on the higher revision switch are used and the other ones are deleted.
   C. If the domain names match, the engineering, sales, and marketing VLANs are deleted.
   D. If the domain names match, the accounting, HR, and executives VLANs are deleted.

VLAN Configuration

8. Enter the switch command to set the VTP mode to transparent mode: _____.

9. Which switch command enables trunking on a 2960 switch?
   A. `switchport mode trunk`
   B. `trunking on`
   C. `trunking enable`
   D. `switchport trunk on`

10. Which 2960 command assigns a VLAN to an interface?
   A. `vlan-membership static`
   B. `vlan`
   C. `switchport access vlan`
   D. `switchport mode access`

SELF TEST ANSWERS

1. ☑ **C.** VLANs are location *independent*, assuming the devices are connected via layer 2.
☒ **A, B,** and **D** are true, and thus incorrect answers.

2. ☑ **A** and **D.** When using switches to logically segregate traffic, use VLANs. To control access between them, use a router with ACLs.
☒ **B** is incorrect because hubs place people in the same broadcast domain. **C** is incorrect because filtering at layer 3 is more manageable than at layer 2.

3. ☑ A connection that supports multiple VLANS is called a *trunk*.

4. ☑ **A.** 802.1Q, because it supports a native VLAN, can use point-to-point and multipoint (hub) connections.
☒ **B** is incorrect, since the 2960 does support it. **C** is incorrect because the native VLAN is not tagged. **D** is incorrect because the original Ethernet frame is modified—a VLAN field is inserted and a new FCS is computed.

5. ☑ The *VLAN Trunk Protocol (VTP)* is a proprietary Cisco protocol used to share VLAN configuration information between Cisco switches on trunk connections.

6. ☑ **C.** Switches in all VTP modes will propagate VTP messages; however, only client and server switches will process these messages.
☒ **A** is incorrect because it doesn't include transparent. **B** is incorrect because it doesn't include client and transparent. **D** is incorrect because it doesn't include server and client.

7. ☑ **A** and **D.** If the domain names don't match, they ignore each other's VTP messages. If the domain names match, the switch with the highest revision number is used; the switch with the lowest revision number will have its VLANs deleted.
☒ **B** is incorrect because domain names must match for VTP messages to be processed. **C** is incorrect because the lower numbered revision switch will have its VLANs deleted.

8. ☑ `vtp transparent`

9. ☑ **A.** The `switchport mode trunk` command enables trunking on a 2960 switch.
☒ **B** enables trunking on a 1900 switch. **C** and **D** are nonexistent commands.

10. ☑ **C.** The `switchport access vlan` command assigns a VLAN to an interface on a 2960 switch.
☒ **A** is incorrect because `vlan-membership static` assigns a VLAN to an interface on a 1900. **B** is incorrect because `vlan` creates a VLAN. **D** is incorrect because `switchport mode access` sets the interface as an access link, versus a trunk, connection.

3

Switches and Redundancy

CERTIFICATION OBJECTIVES

T his chapter is the last chapter on layer 2 functions. Most larger networks implement redundancy in case of failures, whether it be multiple WAN connections, multiple paths in your layer 3 network, and/or multiple paths in your layer 2 network. This chapter focuses on layer 2 redundancy and the issues involved with layer 2 loops, including two features that are commonly used to solve these problems: the Spanning Tree Protocol (STP) and EtherChannels.

Layer 2 Redundancy

Cisco has developed a three-layer hierarchical model to help you design campus networks. Cisco uses this model to simplify designing, implementing, and managing large-scale networks. With traditional network designs, it was common practice to place the networking services at the center of the network and the users at the periphery. However, many things in networking have changed over the past decade, including advancements in applications, developments in graphical user interfaces (GUIs), the proliferation of multimedia applications, the explosion of the Internet, and fast-paced changes in your users' traffic patterns. Cisco's model was designed to accommodate these rapid changes.

Hierarchical Campus Design

Cisco's enterprise campus hierarchical model, shown in Figure 3-1, contains three layers: core, distribution, and access. A well-designed campus network typically follows this topology. The core layer, as its name suggests, is the backbone of the network. It provides a high-speed connection between the different distribution layer devices. Because of the need for high-speed connections, the core consists of high-speed *switches* and will not, typically, perform any type of packet or frame manipulations, such as filtering. Layer 2 or layer 3 switches (more commonly the latter) are used at the core with Gigabit connectivity, sometimes using EtherChannels (discussed at the end of the chapter). The traffic that traverses the core is typically intending to access enterprise corporate resources: connections to the Internet, WAN connections, and applications on servers in the campus server farm.

FIGURE 3-1

Cisco's
hierarchical
model

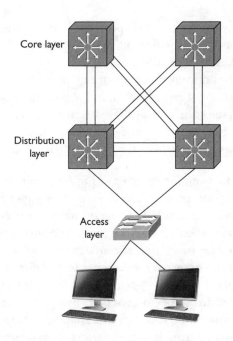

Core layer

Distribution
layer

Access
layer

on the
job

A layer 3 switch is basically a router that performs its switching using application-specific integrated circuits (ASICs) instead of a central CPU (ASICs are discussed in Chapter 4 and a bit later in this chapter). Some of Cisco's switches support this feature, from the Catalyst 3500s and higher, with the right IOS image.

Layer 3 switches are most commonly used at the distribution layer to connect the access layers to the core. Fast Ethernet, but more commonly Gigabit Ethernet, connections are used for this connectivity. For smaller networks, sometimes layer 2 switches are used. The responsibilities of the distribution layer include the following:

■ Containing broadcasts between the model layers via layer 3 separation, such as VLANs

■ Securing traffic between subnets using access control lists

■ Providing a hierarchy through layer 3 logical addressing and route summarization

■ Translating between different media types

Layer 3 separation is provided between the access layers and the core; however, between the distribution layer switches and the access layer switches, layer 2 is used, creating a layer 2 loop.

The bottom layer of the three-layer hierarchical model is the access layer. Actually, the access layer is at the periphery of your campus network, separated from the core layer by the distribution layer. The main function of the access layer is to provide the user's initial connection to your network. Typically, this connection is provided by a layer 2 switch or sometimes a wireless access point.

on the
()o b

Cisco has online design tools to help you choose the appropriate devices and uplink connections in your three-layer hierarchical network. In a basic design, you should not oversubscribe your access-to-distribution layer links by more than 20-to-1. Oversubscription occurs when too much traffic comes from your users' access connections and not enough bandwidth is available from the access layer switches to the distribution layer (oversubscription is discussed in more depth in Chapter 13). You should also not oversubscribe your distribution-to-core links by more than 4-to-1. However, every situation is unique when it comes to designing the appropriate solution. Rate limiting is commonly used to prevent users from oversubscribing and creating problems for other users or applications.

Layer 2 Issues

As you can see in Figure 3-1, a redundant design was implemented: two links exist from the access layer switch up to the distribution layer, with multiple layer 2 connections (in most cases, an EtherChannel) between the distribution layer switches. This redundancy commonly introduces layer 2 loops into a network design, which can create these layer 2 problems:

- Multiple frame copies
- Broadcast storms
- Mislearning MAC addresses

The following three sections will discuss these problems, using the simple example in Figure 3-2 to illustrate the issues these problems create.

Multiple Frame Copies and Broadcast Storms

Recall from your CCENT studies that a switch will flood three kinds of frames: broadcast, multicast, and unknown destination unicast frames. In the case of

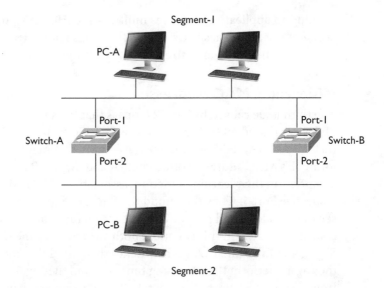

FIGURE 3-2

Simple layer 2
loop example

broadcast and multicast traffic, this can create serious performance issues with a layer 2 network that has loops. For example, imagine that PC-A in Figure 3-2 performs an ARP for PC-B's MAC address. Recall from Chapter 5 that Address Resolution Protocol (ARP) uses a broadcast mechanism to learn the MAC address that corresponds to a device's IP address. In Figure 3-2, both switches would receive this frame and flood it to Segment-2, since the frame is a broadcast.

The first problem this creates is that although PC-A generates one frame, Segment-2, along with PC-B, sees two frames. PC-B sees these as two distinct ARPs and will reply twice. On top of this, depending on the application receiving the traffic, PC-B might see multiple copies of the same frame as an error and reset its connection to the source of the transmissions, creating connectivity issues.

The bigger issue here, however, is that both switches, on their Segment-2 ports, would again see the flooded ARP request and flood it back to Segment-1. Basically, these broadcasts would continue to be flooded between the two segments, affecting all devices. Devices are affected since their NICs would be processing all of these broadcasts; as more devices generate ARPs and other types of broadcast frames, the bandwidth is eventually gobbled up by these broadcasts. In this scenario, the network will crash and the devices will run out of CPU cycles to process the broadcasts!

Recall from your CCENT studies that multicasts are only processed by NICs in which the user has an application running that needs to see the specific multicast traffic: It notifies the NIC about the multicast address or addresses to listen for and process. So a flood of multicasts won't affect the CPU cycles of devices not running an application that uses multicasting. However, multicasts still affect everyone's bandwidth, since switches flood this kind of traffic; if the multicasts are part of a high-speed video stream, this quickly gobbles up the bandwidth.

Mislearning MAC Addresses

The third issue caused by layer 2 loops is that the switches mislearn the location of devices (based on their MAC addresses). Going back to Figure 3-2, assume that PC-A's MAC address is 0000.01AA.AAAA. When PC-A generates an ARP for PC-B's MAC address, both Switch-A and Switch-B receive the ARP request and perform their learning function, associating PC-A's MAC address with their respective Port-1. They then flood the frame to Segment-2. Again, both switches see the broadcast and perform their learning function, associating PC-A with their respective Port-2. In this situation, both switches assume that PC-A moved from Segment-1 to Segment-2. Both switches then flood the frame to Segment-1, where they again perform their learning function, and they again think PC-A moved from Segment-2 back to Segment-1. This flip-flopping happens over and over as the two broadcasts circle around and around between the two segments.

One problem this can create is that if the timing is right and PC-B sends an ARP reply back to PC-A, both switches might have PC-A's MAC address associated with their respective Port-2. If this were true, both would assume PC-A was on Segment-2 and would drop and not forward the frame. Thus, PC-A wouldn't get the reply to its ARP request and then couldn't communicate with PC-B. Of course, PC-A could perform the ARP request again, but this would just make the problem worse, since now instead of two broadcasts circling around the loop, it would double to four!

show processes Command

The architecture of IOS devices varies; however, there are two common switching methods that involve handling of packets: process switching and Cisco Express Forwarding (CEF) switching. The latter is performed by application-specific integrated circuits (ASICs). ASICs are specialized processors that allow a device to perform a small set of instructions at very high speed. Similar to what a graphics process unit (GPU) does for graphics functions, ASICs, when used for networking functions, move traffic through a device. Depending on the Cisco product, it may have one or many ASICs. When processing traffic and determining where to forward it, the CPU will typically have to process the first packet in order to do a MAC address lookup in the CAM table on a switch or a destination IP address lookup in the routing table of a routing device. Once learned, this information can be stored in an ASIC's cache, and the ASIC can then use this information to process further frames or packets in the flow, reducing the burden on the CPU.

Besides building the ASIC caches, the CPU must perform other management protocols, like spanning tree information, routing protocol information, Cisco Discovery Protocol (CDP) frames, VLAN Trunk Protocol (VTP) frames, Dynamic Trunk Protocol (DTP) frames, etc., as well as normal traffic like broadcasts packets or unicast packets directed to one of its own IP addresses, like telnet, SNMP, SSH, and other management protocols. If too much management traffic needs to be processed by the CPU, this can quickly overwhelm an IOS device.

The **show processes** command displays the processes currently running on an IOS device. This information is useful in determining that the IOS device is running correctly and not overburdened. Here is an example of the command:

```
Switch# show processes
CPU utilization for five seconds: 21%/0%; one minute: 2%; five minutes: 2%
 PID QTy        PC Runtime(ms)  Invoked  uSecs    Stacks TTY Process
   1 Cwe 606E9FCC           0        1      0 5600/6000     0 Chunk Manager
   2 Csp 607180F0           0   121055      0 2608/3000     0 Load Meter
   3 M*         0           8       90     88 9772/12000    0 Exec
   4 Mwe 619CB674           0        1     023512/24000     0 EDDRI_MAIN
   5 Lst 606F6AA4       82064    61496   1334 5668/6000     0 Check heaps
   6 Cwe 606FD444           0      127      0 5588/6000     0 Pool Manager
   7 Lwe 6060B364           0        1      0 5764/6000     0 AAA_SERVER_DEADT
   8 Mst 6063212C           0        2      0 5564/6000     0 Timers
   9 Mwe 600109D4           0        2      0 5560/6000     0 Serial Backgroun
  10 Mwe 60234848           0        2      0 5564/6000     0 ATM Idle Timer
  11 Mwe 602B75F0           0        2      0 8564/9000     0 ATM AutoVC Perio
  12 Mwe 602B7054           0        2      0 5560/6000     0 ATM VC Auto Crea
  13 Mwe 606068B8           0        2      0 5552/6000     0 AAA high-capacit
  14 Msi 607BABA4      251264   605013    415 5628/6000     0 EnvMon
<-output omitted->
```

The first line of output is the most important, since it lists the CPU utilization of the IOS device. The example output below this varies between different IOS software images and modules installed.

You can qualify the **show processes** command with the **cpu** parameter, which breaks down the CPU utilization of the processes running on an IOS device. Here's an example:

```
Switch# show processes cpu
CPU utilization for five seconds: 38%/1%; one minute: 32%; five minutes: 32%
 PID Runtime(ms) Invoked    uSecs    5Sec    1Min    5Min TTY Process
   1           0      63        0   0.00%   0.00%   0.00%   0 Chunk Manager
   2          60   50074        1   0.00%   0.00%   0.00%   0 Load Meter
   3           0       1        0   0.00%   0.00%   0.00%   0 Deferred Events
<-output omitted->
  27         524  250268        2   0.00%   0.00%   0.00%   0 TTY Background
  28         816  254843        3   0.00%   0.00%   0.00%   0 Per-Second Jobs
  29      101100    5053    20007   0.00%   0.01%   0.00%   0 Per-minute Jobs
  30    26057260 26720902     975  12.07%  11.41%  11.36%   0 Cat4k Mgmt HiPri
  31    19482908 29413060     662  24.07%  19.32%  19.20%   0 Cat4k Mgmt LoPri
  32        4468  162748       27   0.00%   0.00%   0.00%   0 Galios Reschedul
  33           0       1        0   0.00%   0.00%   0.00%   0 IOS ACL Helper
  34           0       2        0   0.00%   0.00%   0.00%   0 NAM Manager
<-output omitted->
```

Five-second CPU utilization is expressed as $x\%/y\%$. The $x\%$ represents total CPU utilization, and $y\%$ represents the CPU that is spent at the interrupt level. When you troubleshoot Catalyst switches and Cisco routers, focus only on the total CPU utilization first, with the **show processes** command, and then use the **show processes cpu** command to determine which process or processes are creating the problem.

One of the common reasons for high CPU utilization is that the CPU is busy with the processing of packets for software-forwarded packets or control packets. Examples of software-forwarded packets are IPX or control packets, such as STP Bridge Protocol Data Units (BPDUs, discussed in the next section). A small number of these packets is typically sent to the CPU. However, a consistently excessive number of packets can indicate a configuration error or a network problem. You need to identify the cause of this event or events that lead to excessive packets being processed by the CPU to help troubleshoot the CPU utilization problems.

Some of the common reasons for high CPU utilization due to process-switched packets are

- A high number of spanning-tree port instances
- ICMP redirects; routing packets on the same interface
- IPX or AppleTalk routing
- Host learning (ARP or CAM table updates)

■ The `log` keyword used in ACL configurations (see Chapter 21)

■ Layer 2 forwarding loops

Other reasons for the switch of packets to the CPU are

■ MTU fragmentation. Be sure that all interfaces along the path of the packet have the same MTU.

■ ACL with TCP flags other than `established`.

■ IP version 6 (IPv6) routing. This is supported only via the software-switching path.

■ Generic Route Encapsulation (GRE). This is supported only via the software-switching path.

■ Excessive ARP and DHCP due to a large number of directly connected hosts.

■ Excessive SNMP polling by a legitimate or misconfigured host.

Many, many other issues can cause this problem; however, the most common cause of high CPU utilization on switches is the existence of layer 2 loops. The remainder of this chapter will focus on the Spanning Tree Protocol (STP) and how it can be used to deal with this issue.

CERTIFICATION OBJECTIVE 3.02

Spanning Tree Protocol

The main function of STP is to remove layer 2 loops from your topology, logically speaking. DEC, now a part of HP, originally developed STP. IEEE enhanced the initial implementation of STP, giving us the 802.1d standard. The two different implementations of STP, DEC and 802.1d, are not compatible with each other—you need to make sure that all of your devices support either one or the other. Additions were made to 802.1d, including Rapid STP (RSTP) and Multiple STP (MSTP). Based on these inclusions, the IEEE implementation today is referred to as 802.1D. All of Cisco's switches support IEEE's 802.1D protocol, which is enabled, by default, on their switches when sending out untagged frames (the native VLAN). If you have a mixed-vendor environment where some devices are running 802.1D and others are running DEC's STP, you might run into layer 2 looping problems.

> *Note: Typically IEEE uses a lowercase letter, like d, to indicate a draft or ongoing development state, and uses an uppercase letter, like D, to indicate a finalized standard. In this book, when 802.1d is mentioned, this specifies the original implementation of STP by IEEE, which excludes RSTP and MSTP. RSTP is covered later in the chapter, but MSTP is beyond the scope of this book.*

Bridge Protocol Data Units

For STP to function, the switches need to share information about themselves and their connections. What they share are Bridge Protocol Data Units (BPDUs), which are sent out as *multicast* frames to which only other layer 2 switches or bridges are listening. Switches will use BPDUs to learn the topology of the network: what switch is connected to other switches, and whether any layer 2 loops are based on this topology.

If any loops are found, the switches will logically disable a port or ports in the topology to ensure that there are no loops. Note that they don't actually shut down the ports, but they place the port or ports in a special disabled state for user traffic, as discussed later in the "Port States" section. Based on this port disabling process—in other words, from one device to any other device in the layer 2 network—only one path can be taken. If any changes occur in the layer 2 network—such as when a link goes down, a new link is added, a new switch is added, or a switch fails—the switches will share this information, causing the STP algorithm to be re-executed, and a new loop-free topology is then created.

By default, BPDUs are sent out every 2 seconds. This helps speed up convergence. *Convergence* is a term used in networking to describe the amount of time it takes to deal with changes and get the network back up and running. The shorter the time period to find and fix problems, the quicker your network is back online. Setting the BPDU advertisement time to 2 seconds allows changes to be quickly shared with all the other switches in the network, reducing the amount of time any disruption would create.

BPDUs contain a lot of information to help the switches determine the topology and any loops that result from that topology. For instance, each bridge has a unique identifier, called a *bridge* or *switch ID*. This is typically the priority of the switch and the MAC address of the switch itself. When switches advertise a BPDU, they place their switch ID in the BPDU so that a receiving switch can tell from which switch it is receiving topology information. The following sections cover the steps that occur while STP is being executed in a layer 2 network.

e x a m

Ⓦatch

Most bridges and switches use IEEE's 802.1d protocol to remove loops at layer 2 (data link layer) of the OSI Reference Model. BPDUs are used to share information, and they are sent out as multicasts every 2 seconds. The BPDU contains the switch's ID, made up of a priority value and the switch's MAC address.

Root Switch

The term *Spanning Tree Protocol* describes the process that is used to find and remove loops from a layer 2 network. The STP algorithm is similar to how link state routing protocols, such as Open Shortest Path First (OSPF), ensure that no layer 3 loops are created; of course, STP deals only with layer 2 loops (link state routing protocols are discussed in Chapters 4 and 10).

A spanning tree is first created. Basically, a spanning tree is an inverted tree. At the top of the tree is the root, or what is referred to in STP as the *root bridge* or *switch.* From the root switch, branches (physical Ethernet connections) extend and connect to other switches, and branches from these switches connect to other switches, and so on.

Take a look at the physical topology of a network, shown in Figure 3-3, to demonstrate a spanning tree. When STP is run, a logical tree structure is built, like that shown in Figure 3-4. As you can see from Figure 3-4, Switch-A is the root switch and is at the top of the tree. Underneath it are two branches connecting to Switch-B and Switch-C. These two switches are connected to Switch-E, creating

FIGURE 3-3

Physical layer 2 looped topology

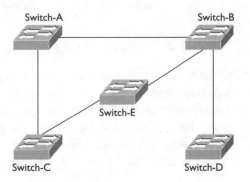

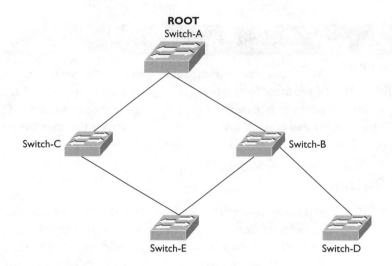

FIGURE 3-4

Logical layer 2
STP topology

a loop. Switch-B is also connected to Switch-D. At this point, STP is still running, and a loop still exists. As STP runs, the switches will determine, out of the four switches—Switch-A, Switch-B, Switch-C, and Switch-E—which port on these switches will be logically disabled in order to remove the loop. This ensures that from one device to any other device in the network, only one path will be used to connect the devices.

Actually, the very first step in STP is to elect the root switch. BPDUs are used for the election process. As mentioned earlier, when a device advertises a BPDU, the switch puts its switch ID in the BPDU. The switch ID is used to elect the root switch. The switch with the *lowest* switch ID is chosen as root. The switch ID is made up of two components:

- The switch's priority, which defaults to 32,768 on Cisco switches (2 bytes in length)
- The switch's MAC address (6 bytes in length)

With Cisco's switches, the default priority is 32,768, which is defined by IEEE 802.1d. Assuming that all your switches are Cisco switches and you don't change the default priority, the switch with the *lowest* MAC address will be chosen as the root switch. You can override the election process by changing the priority value assigned to a switch. If you want one switch to be the root, assign it a priority value that is lower than 32,768. Through the sharing of the BPDUs, the switches will figure out which switch has the lowest switch ID, and that switch is chosen as the root switch. Note that this election process is taking place almost simultaneously on each switch, where each switch will come up with the same result. In other words, the switch that has the lowest switch ID is not advertising to other switches that it has the lowest ID value and thus everyone else should be a non-root switch.

For Catalyst switches that implement VLANs (discussed in Chapter 2), the switches will have a different switch ID *per* VLAN, and a *separate* instance of STP *per* VLAN. Each VLAN has its own root switch (which can be the same switch for all VLANs, or different switches for each VLAN). And within each VLAN, STP will run and remove loops in that particular VLAN. Cisco calls this concept *per-VLAN STP* (PVST). This topic is discussed later in the "Per-VLAN STP Plus" section.

The election process of the root switch takes place each time a topology change occurs in the network, such as the root switch failing or the addition of a new switch. All the other switches in the layer 2 topology expect to see BPDUs from the root switch within the *maximum age time*, which defaults to 20 seconds. If the switches don't see a BPDU message from the root within this period, they assume that the root switch has failed and will begin a new election process to choose a new root switch.

Root Port

After the root switch is elected, every other switch in the network needs to choose a single port on itself that it will use to reach the root. This port is called the *root port*. For some switches, such as Switch-D in Figure 3-4, this is very easy—it has only one port it can use to access the switched topology. However, other switches, such as Switch-B, Switch-C, and Switch-E in Figure 3-4, might have two or more ports that they can use to reach the root switch. If multiple port choices are available, an intelligent method needs to be used to choose the best port. With STP, a few factors are taken into consideration when choosing a root port. It is important to note that the root switch itself will never have a root port—it's the root, so it doesn't need a port to reach itself!

Port Costs and Priorities

First, each port is assigned a cost, called a *port cost*. The lower the cost, the more preferable the port. The cost is an inverse reflection of the bandwidth of the port.

TABLE 3-1	Connection Type	New Cost Value	Old Cost Value
	10 Gbps	2	1
Port Costs for STP	1 Gbps	4	1
	100 Mbps	19	10
	10 Mbps	100	100

Two sets of costs exist for 802.1d's implementation of STP—one for the old method of calculation and one for the new, as is shown in Table 3-1. Cisco's discontinued Catalyst 1900 switch uses the old 802.1d port cost values, while Cisco's other Catalyst switches, including those currently sold today (such as the 2960 and 6500), use the newer cost values. Switches always prefer lower cost ports over higher cost ones. Each port also has a priority assigned to it, called a *port priority* value, which defaults to 32. Again, switches will prefer a lower priority value over a higher one.

One of the main reasons for replacing the old cost method with a newer one is the inherent weakness in the algorithm used to calculate the port cost: 1000 divided by the port speed. The assumption was that no port would have a speed greater than 1 Gbps (1000 Mbps). As you can see from today's Ethernet standards, 10 Gbps is making its way into corporate networks. With the old port cost method, 1 Gbps and 10 Gbps links were treated as having the same speed.

Path Costs

Path costs are calculated from the root switch. A path cost is basically the accumulated port costs from the root switch to other switches in the topology. When the root advertises BPDUs out its interfaces, the default path cost value in the BPDU frame is 0. When a connected switch receives this BPDU, it increments the path cost by the cost of its local incoming port. If the port was a Fast Ethernet port, then the path cost would be figured like this: 0 (the root's path cost) + 19 (the switch's port cost) = 19. This switch, when it advertises BPDUs to switches behind it, will include the updated path cost. As the BPDUs propagate further and further from the root switch, the accumulated path cost values become higher and higher.

e x a m

ⓦ **a t c h**   *Remember that path costs are incremented as a BPDU comes into a port, not when a BPDU is advertised out of a port.*

Root Port Selection

If a switch has two or more choices of paths to reach the root, it needs to choose one path and thus have one root port. A switch will go through the following STP steps when choosing a root port:

1. Choose the path with the *lowest* accumulated path cost to the root when it has a choice between two or more paths to reach the root.

2. If multiple paths to the root are available with the same accumulated path cost, the switch will choose the neighboring switch (that the switch would go through to reach the root) with the *lowest* switch ID value.

3. If multiple paths all go through the same neighboring switch, it will choose the local port with the lowest priority value.

4. If the priority values are the same between the ports, it will choose the physically lowest numbered port on the switch. For example, on a 2960, that would be FastEthernet 0/1 or Gigabit 0/1.

After going through this selection process, the switch will have one, and only one, port that will become its root port.

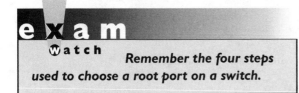

Designated Port

You now know that each switch has a single root port that it uses to reach the root switch. In addition to each switch having a root port, each segment has a single port that it uses to reach the root, and this port is called a *designated port*. For example, imagine that a segment has two switches connected to it. Either one or the other switch will forward traffic from this segment to the rest of the network.

The third step in running STP is to elect a designated port on a single switch for each segment in the network. The switch (and its port) that is chosen should have the best path to the root switch. Here are the steps taken by switches in determining which port on which switch will be chosen as the designated port for a particular LAN segment:

1. The connected switch on the segment with the lowest accumulated path cost to the root switch will be used.

2. If there is a tie in accumulated path costs between two switches, the switch with the lowest switch ID will be chosen.

3. If it happens that it is the same switch, but with two separate connections to the LAN segment, the switch port with the lowest priority is chosen.

4. If there is still a tie (the priorities of the ports on this switch are the same), the physically lowest numbered port on the switch is chosen.

After going through these steps for each segment, each segment will have a single designated port on a connected switch that it will use to reach the root switch. Sometimes the switch that contains the designated port is called a *designated switch*. This term is misleading, though, since it is a port on the switch that is responsible for forwarding traffic. A switch may be connected to two segments, but it may be the designated switch for only one of those segments; another switch may provide the designated port for the second segment.

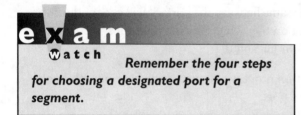

Remember the four steps for choosing a designated port for a segment.

Interestingly enough, *every* active port on the *root switch* is a designated port. This makes sense because the cost of the attached network segments to reach the root is *0*, the lowest accumulated cost value. In other words, each of these LAN segments is directly attached to the root switch, so in reality, it costs nothing for the segment to reach the root switch itself.

Port States

A port can be in one of five states when it is participating in STP:

- Blocking
- Listening
- Learning
- Forwarding
- Disabled

Of the five states, only the first four are used when the algorithm is running. The following sections cover these port states for STP.

Blocking

Ports will go into a *blocking* state under one of three conditions:

- During election of a root switch (for instance, when you turn on all the switches in a network)

■ When a switch receives a BPDU on a port that indicates a better path to the root switch than the port that the switch is currently using to reach the root

■ If a port is not a root port or a designated port

A port in a blocking state will remain there for 20 seconds by default (the maximum age timer). During this state, the port is listening to and processing only BPDUs on its interfaces. Any other frames that the switch receives on a blocked port are dropped. In a blocking state, the switch is attempting to figure out which port is going to be the root port, which ports on the switch need to be designated ports, and which ports will remain in a blocking state to break up any loops.

Listening

After the 20-second timer expires, a root port or a designated port will move to a *listening* state. Any other port will remain in a blocking state. During the listening state, the port is still listening for BPDUs and double-checking the layer 2 topology. Again, the only traffic that is being processed on a port in this state consists of BPDUs; all other traffic is dropped. A port will stay in this state for the length of the *forward delay timer*. The default for this value is 15 seconds.

Learning

From a listening state, a root and designated ports move into a *learning* state. During the learning state, the port is still listening for and processing BPDUs on the port; however, unlike while in the listening state, the port begins to process user frames. When processing user frames, the switch is examining the source addresses in the frames and updating its MAC or port address table, but the switch is still not forwarding these frames out destination ports. Ports stay in this state for the length of the forward delay time (which defaults to 15 seconds).

Forwarding

Finally, after the forward delay timer expires, ports that were in a learning state are placed in a *forwarding* state. In a forwarding state, the port will process BPDUs, update its MAC address table with frames that it receives, *and* forward user traffic through the port.

Disabled

The *disabled* state is a special port state. A port in a disabled state is not participating in STP. This could be because the port has been manually shut down by an administrator, manually removed from STP, disabled because of security issues, or rendered nonfunctional because of a lack of a physical layer signal (such as the patch cable being unplugged).

e x a m

w a t c h   *Four major port states are used in STP (802.1d): blocking (20 seconds), listening (15 seconds), learning (15 seconds), and forwarding. It can take 30 to 50 seconds for STP convergence to take place. STP must recalculate if a new root is discovered or a topology change occurs in the network (a new switch added or a change in the state of a port on a switch). In blocking and listening states, only BPDUs are processed. In a learning state, the MAC address table is being built. In a forwarding state, user frames are moved between ports. STP leaves ports in a blocking state to remove loops.*

Layer 2 Convergence

As you should have noticed in the last section, STP goes through a staged process, which *slows* down convergence. For switches, convergence occurs once STP has completed: a root switch is elected, root and designated ports have been chosen, the root and designated ports have been placed in a forwarding state, and all other ports have been placed in a blocking state.

If a port has to go through all four states, convergence takes 50 seconds: 20 seconds in blocking, 15 seconds in listening, and 15 seconds in learning. If a port doesn't have to go through the blocking state but starts at a listening state, convergence takes only 30 seconds. This typically occurs when the root port is still valid but another topology change has occurred. Remember that during this time period (until the port reaches a forwarding state), no user traffic is forwarded through the port. So, if a user was performing a telnet session and STP was being recalculated, the telnet session, from the user's perspective, would appear stalled or the connection would appear lost. Obviously, a user will notice this type of disruption.

e x a m

w a t c h   *STP convergence has occurred when all root and designated ports are in a forwarding state and all other ports are in a blocking state.*

PortFast Overview

The faster that convergence takes place, the less disruption it will cause for your users. You can reduce the two timers to speed up your convergence time, but this can create more problems if you aren't aware of what you are doing when you change them. For user ports, you can use the *PortFast* feature to speed up convergence. PortFast should be used only on ports that will not create layer 2 loops, such as ports connected to PCs, servers, and routers (sometimes referred to as a user, or edge, ports).

A port with PortFast enabled is always placed in a forwarding state—this is true even when STP is running and the root and designated ports are going through their different states. So, when STP is running, PortFast ports on the same switch can still forward traffic among themselves, limiting your STP disruption somewhat. However, if these devices wanted to talk to devices connected to other switches, they would have to wait until STP completed and the root and designated ports had moved into a forwarding state.

Ports connected to non-switch or non-bridge devices should be configured with PortFast, such as PCs, servers, and routers. However, make sure that you don't enable PortFast on a port connected to another layer 2 switch, since you might inadvertently be creating a layer 2 loop, which will create broadcast storms and mislearning of MAC addressing information.

PortFast Configuration

PortFast works with all versions of STP supported by Cisco switches. Configuring the PortFast feature is simple, and you can enable it globally or on an interface-by-interface basis. To enable it globally, use this command:

```
Switch(config)# spanning-tree portfast default
```

This command enables PortFast on all nontrunking ports on the switch.
To enable PortFast on an interface, use this configuration:

```
Switch(config)# interface type [slot_#/]port_#
Switch(config-if)# spanning-tree portfast [trunk]
```

The optional **trunk** parameter enables PortFast on trunk connections to nonswitch devices, such as a router or server with a trunk card.

3.01. The digital resources that accompany this book contain a multimedia demonstration of configuring PortFast.

BPDU Guard Feature

BPDU Guard is used on ports configured with the PortFast feature. In this instance, if a PortFast port receives a BPDU, the switch immediately disables the port. Remember that PortFast is used on nonswitch ports to keep them in a forwarding state: the assumption is that a PortFast port is not connected to a switch and therefore shouldn't be receiving BPDUs.

To enable BPDU Guard, use the following Global Configuration command:

```
Switch(config)# spanning-tree portfast bpduguard
```

Use the **show spanning-tree summary totals** command to verify your configuration:

```
Switch# show spanning-tree summary totals
Root bridge for: none.
PortFast BPDU Guard is enabled
UplinkFast is disabled
BackboneFast is disabled
Spanning tree default pathcost method used is short

Name                 Blocking Listening Learning Forwarding STP Active
-------------------- -------- --------- -------- ---------- ----------
  1 VLAN                   0         0        0          1          1
```

At the reception of BPDUs, the BPDU Guard operation disables the port that has PortFast configured. The BPDU Guard transitions the port into an *errdisable* state, and a message appears on the console. Here is an example of this message:

```
2001 May 23 18:13:12 %SPANTREE-2-RX_PORTFAST:Received BPDU on
PortFast enable port. Disabling 1/0/4
```

When a port has been placed in an error-disabled state, use the **errdisable recovery cause bpduguard** command to remove the error-disabled state:

```
Switch(config)# errdisable recovery cause bpduguard
```

Notice that you are in Global Configuration mode when executing this command.

Optionally, you can have the switch periodically do this by configuring the command with an interval, specified in seconds:

```
Switch(config)# errdisable recovery interval seconds
```

This automatically clears all errdisable states, including BPDU violations, on all ports every *x* seconds. However, if a BPDU violation occurs again, the port is placed back into an errdisable state.

Per-VLAN STP Plus

STP doesn't guarantee an optimized loop-free network. For instance, take a look at the network shown in Figure 3-5, which is an example of a network that is poorly designed. In this example, the network has two VLANs, and the root switch is Switch-8. The Xs are ports placed in a blocked state to remove any loops. If you look at this configuration for VLAN 2, it definitely isn't optimized. For instance, VLAN 2 devices on Switch-1, if they want to access VLAN 2 devices on Switch-4, have to go to Switches-2, -3, -6, -9, -8, and then -4. Likewise, VLAN 1 devices on either Switch-5 or Switch-7 that want to access VLAN 1 devices on Switch-4 must forward their traffic first to Switch-8 and then to Switch-4.

When one instance of STP is running, this is referred to as a *Common Spanning Tree* (CST). Cisco also supports a process called *Per-VLAN Spanning Tree Plus* (PVST+). With PVST+, *each* VLAN has its own instance of STP, with its own root switch, its own set of priorities, and its own set of BPDUs. In this scenario, the BPDUs have an additional field that is a component of the switch or bridge ID with these three subfields: switch priority, extended system ID, and switch's MAC address. The extended system ID is a new field and carries the VLAN ID (VID) for the instance of STP.

FIGURE 3-5

STP and VLANs

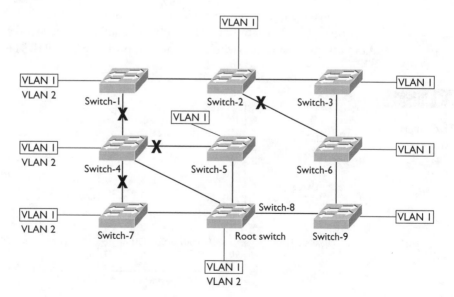

With the addition of this field, it is possible to have different priorities on switches in different VLANs; thus, you have the capability of having multiple root switches—one per VLAN. Each VLAN in PVST+, by default, will develop its own loop-free topology. Of course, PVST+, just like CST, doesn't create an optimized loop-free network; however, you can make STP changes in *each* VLAN to optimize traffic patterns for each separate VLAN. It is highly recommended that you tune STP for each VLAN to optimize it. Another advantage that PVST+ has is that if STP changes are occurring in one VLAN, they do not affect other instances of STP for other VLANs, making for a more stable topology. Given this, it is highly recommended that you implement VTP pruning to prune off VLANs from trunks of switches that are not using those VLANs. Pruning was discussed in Chapter 2.

The downside of PVST+ is that since each VLAN has its own instance of STP, more overhead is involved: more BPDUs and STP tables are required on each switch. Plus, it makes no sense to use PVST+ unless you tune it for your network, which means more work and monitoring on your part.

e x a m

⍵ a t c h *PVST+ supports one instance of STP per VLAN, allowing you to tune for the most optimal paths for each VLAN. CST supports one instance of STP for all VLANs.*

Simple STP Example

To help you get more familiar with the workings of 802.1d STP, take a look at an example of STP in action. Use the network shown in Figure 3-6 as a starting point and assume that these switches do not support Rapid STP (RSTP), discussed later

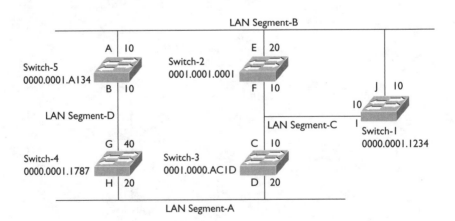

FIGURE 3-6

STP example network

in the chapter, but only 802.1d STP. I'll also assume that there is only one VLAN. The ports on each switch are labeled with a letter and a number. The letter is the port designator, and the number is the cost of the port as a BPDU enters the port.

Electing the Root Switch

The first thing that occurs once all these switches are booted up is the election of the root switch. The switches share BPDUs with one another to elect the root. In this example, all of the switches are using the default priority (32,768). Remember that the switch with the lowest switch ID is elected as root. Since all of the switches have the same priority, the switch with the lowest MAC address, which is Switch-1, is chosen as the root switch. Based on the election process, the new network topology looks like that shown in Figure 3-7.

Choosing Root Ports for Each Switch

After the root switch is elected, each nonroot switch must choose one of its ports that it will use to reach the root, called the *root port*. Let's take this one switch at a time so that you can see the decision process in detail. With Switch-1, which is the root switch, there are no root ports—if you recall, all ports on the root switch are designated ports.

 Switch-2 has two ports to use to reach the root: E and F. When Switch-1 generates its BPDUs on ports I and J, the original path cost is set to 0. As these BPDUs are received by other switches, the receiving switch increments the path cost by the cost of the port on which the BPDU was received. As the BPDU comes into port E, Switch-2 increments the path cost to 20 and for port F, a cost of 10.

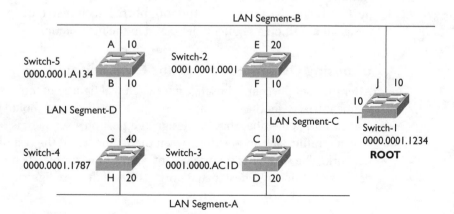

FIGURE 3-7

Root switch election

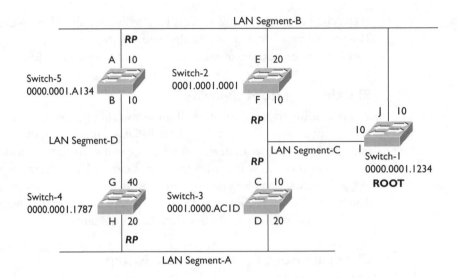

FIGURE 3-8

Root ports

The first check that Switch-2 makes is to compare the path costs. Port F has the best path cost and therefore is chosen as the root port, which is shown as *RP* in Figure 3-8. Switch-3 also has two paths to reach the root: via ports C and D. Port C's accumulated path cost is 10, while D's cost is 70. Therefore, port C is chosen as the root port. Switch-4 also has two ports to use to access the root: H and G. Port H has an accumulated path cost of 30, while G has a cost of 50, causing Switch-4 to choose port H as the root port. Switch-5's two ports, A and B, have accumulated path costs of 10 and 40, respectively, causing Switch-5 to choose Port A as the root port. Note that all the switches in the network are simultaneously running STP and figuring out for themselves who the root switch is and which port on themselves should be the root port. This is also true for choosing a designated port on a segment, discussed in the next section.

Choosing Designated Ports for Each Segment

After the root ports are chosen, each switch will figure out, on a segment-by-segment basis, whether its connected port to the segment should be a designated port or not. Remember that the designated port on a segment is responsible for moving traffic back and forth between the segment and the rest of the layer 2 network. The segments themselves, of course, are completely unaware of this process of choosing a designated port—the switches are figuring this out.

When choosing a designated port, the first thing that is examined is the accumulated path cost for the switch (connected to the segment) to reach the root. For two switches connected to the same segment, the switch with the lowest accumulated path cost will be the designated switch for that segment, and its port connected to that segment becomes a designated port.

Going back to our network example, let's start with the easiest segments: B and C. For Switch-1, the accumulated path cost for LAN Segment-B is 0, Switch-2 is 20, and Switch-5 is 10. Since the root switch (Switch-1) has the lowest accumulated path cost, its local port (J) becomes the designated port for LAN Segment-B. This process is also true for LAN Segment-C—the root switch has the lowest accumulated path cost (0), making port I on Switch-1 the designated port for LAN Segment-C.

LAN Segment-A has two choices: Switch-3's D port and Switch-4's H port. Switch-3 has the lower accumulated path cost: 10 versus Switch-4's 50. Therefore, Switch-3's D port becomes the designated port for LAN Segment-A.

LAN Segment-D also has two choices for a designated port: Switch-5's B port and Switch-4's G port. Switch-5 has an accumulated path cost of 10, and Switch-4 has a cost of 30. Therefore Switch-5's B port becomes the designated port for LAN Segment-D.

Figure 3-9 shows the updated STP topology for our network, where *DP* represents the designated ports for the LAN segments.

FIGURE 3-9

Root and designated ports

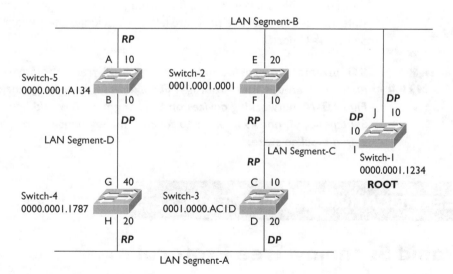

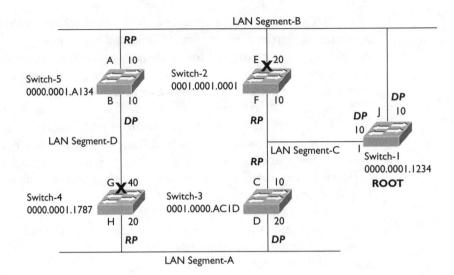

FIGURE 3-10

Ports in a
blocking state

Changing Port States

After the designated ports are chosen, the switches will move their root and designated ports through the various states—blocking, listening, learning, and forwarding—whereas any other ports will remain in a blocked state. Figure 3-10 shows the ports in a blocking state, designated by an X. Remember that on Switch-2, only Port F (the root port) is in a forwarding state: Port E will remain in a blocking state. In this example, two ports are left in a blocking state: Switch-2's E port and Switch-4's G port.

STP attempts to provide only a layer 2 loop-free topology—it does not guarantee an optimal topology! For example, in the network shown in Figure 3-10, networking devices on LAN Segment-A would have to go through Switches-3, -1, and -5 in order to reach LAN Segment-D, since Switch-4's G port is in a blocked state.

CERTIFICATION OBJECTIVE 3.03

Rapid Spanning Tree Protocol

The 802.1d standard was designed back when waiting for 30 to 50 seconds for layer 2 convergence wasn't a problem. However, in today's networks, this can cause serious performance problems for networks that use real-time applications, such as voice over IP (VoIP) or video. To overcome these issues, Cisco developed proprietary bridging features called PortFast (discussed earlier), UplinkFast, and BackboneFast. The problem with these features, however, is that they are proprietary to Cisco.

The Rapid Spanning Tree Protocol (RSTP) is an IEEE standard, defined in 802.1w, that is interoperable with 802.1d and an extension to it. With RSTP, there are only three port states:

- Discarding
- Learning
- Forwarding

A port in a discarding state is basically the grouping of 802.1d's blocking, listening, and disabled states. The following sections cover some of the enhancements included in RSTP.

> **e x a m**
> **ⓦ a t c h** *RSTP is backward compatible with 802.1d. RSTP is also compatible with Cisco's PVST+ in the native VLAN.*

Additional Port Roles

With RSTP, there is still a root switch and there are still root and designated ports performing the same roles as those in 802.1d. However, RSTP adds two more port types: *alternate* ports and *backup* ports. These two ports are similar to the ports in a blocking state in 802.1d. An alternate port is a port that has an alternative path or paths to the root but is currently in a discarding state. A backup port is a port on a segment that could be used to reach the root switch, but an active port is already designated for the segment. The best way to look at this is that an alternate port is a secondary, unused root port, and a backup port is a secondary, unused designated port. The third port role change in RSTP is that there is no longer a blocking state: this has been replaced by a *discarding* state. All ports are either in a forwarding or discarding state: the root ports and designated ports are in a forwarding state—all other ports are in a discarding state.

> **e x a m**
> **ⓦ a t c h** *New port states introduced in RSTP include alternate, backup, and discarding ports. All active ports in RSTP are either in a forwarding, learning, or discarding state. Once all ports are in a forwarding or discarding (blocking) state, RSTP has converged.*

Given these new port roles, RSTP calculates the final spanning tree topology the same way as 802.1d. Some of the nomenclature was changed and extended, and this is used to enhance convergence times, as you will see later in the "RSTP Convergence Features" section.

RSTP BPDUs

The 802.1w standard introduced a change with BPDUs. Some additional flags were added to the BPDUs, so that switches could share information about the role of the port the BPDU is exiting or leaving. This can help a neighboring switch converge faster when changes occur in the network.

In 802.1d, if a switch didn't see a root BPDU within the maximum age time (20 seconds), STP would run, a new root switch would be elected, and a new loop-free topology would be created. This is a time-consuming process. With 802.1w, if a BPDU is not received in three expected hello periods (6 seconds), STP information can be aged out instantly and the switch considers that its neighbor is lost and actions should be taken. This is different from 802.1d, where the switch had to miss the BPDUs from the root—here, if the switch misses three consecutive hellos from a neighbor, actions are immediately taken.

RSTP Convergence Features

The 802.1w standard includes new convergence features that are similar to Cisco's proprietary UplinkFast and BackboneFast features. The first feature, which is similar to Cisco's BackboneFast feature, allows a switch to accept *inferior BPDUs.*

Look at Figure 3-11 to understand the inferior BPDU feature. In this example, the root bridge is Switch-A. Both of the ports on Switch-B and Switch-C directly connected to the root are root ports. For the segment between Switch-B and Switch-C, Switch-B provides the designated port and Switch-C provides a backup port (a secondary way of reaching the root for the segment). Switch-B also knows that its designated port is an alternative port (a secondary way for the switch to reach the root), via Switch-C from Switch-C's BPDUs.

Following the example in Figure 3-11, the link between the root and Switch-B fails. Switch-B can detect this by either missing three hellos from the root port or detecting a physical layer failure. If you were running 802.1d, Switch-B would

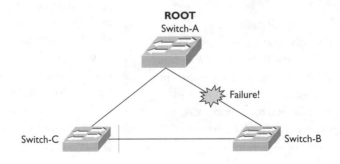

FIGURE 3-11

Accepting inferior BPDUs

see an inferior root BPDU (worse cost value) coming via Switch-C, and therefore all ports would have to go through blocking, listening, and learning states, which would take 50 seconds, by default, to converge. With the inferior BPDU feature, assuming that Switch-B knows that Switch-C has an alternate port for their directly connected segment, Switch-B can notify Switch-C to take its alternate port and change it to a designated port, and Switch-B will change its designated port to a root port. This process takes only a few seconds, if even that.

The second convergence feature introduced in 802.1w is *rapid transition*. Rapid transition includes two new components: edge ports and link types. An edge port is a port connected to a non–layer 2 device, such as a PC, server, or router. RSTP with rapid transition of edge ports to a forwarding state is the same as Cisco's proprietary PortFast. Changes in the state of these ports do not affect RSTP to cause a recalculation, and changes in other port types will keep these ports in a forwarding state.

Rapid transition can take place in RSTP only for edge ports and links that are point-to-point. The link type is automatically determined in terms of the duplexing of the connection. Switches make the assumption that if the port is configured for full-duplex between the two switches, the port can rapidly transition to a different state without having to wait for any timers to expire. If they are half-duplex, this feature won't work by default, but you can manually enable it for point-to-point half-duplex switch links.

Let's take a look at an example of rapid transition of point-to-point links by using the topology in Figure 3-12. The topology in Figure 3-12 is the same as that shown in Figure 3-11. In this example, however, the link between Switch-A (the root) and Switch-C fails. When this happens, Switch-C can no longer reach Switch-A on its root port. However, looking at the BPDUs it has been receiving from Switch-A and Switch-B, Switch-C knows that the root is reachable via Switch-B and that Switch-B provides the designated port (which is in a forwarding state) for the segment between Switch-B and Switch-C. Switch-C, knowing this, changes the state of the backup port

FIGURE 3-12

Rapid transition example

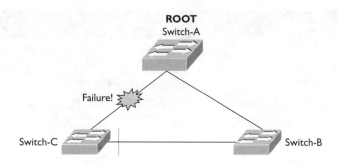

ROOT
Switch-A

Failure!

Switch-C

Switch-B

e x a m

ⓦatch   *RSTP converges much more rapidly than the original IEEE STP (802.1d) on point-to-point (P2P) links.*

e x a m

ⓦatch   *The* spanning-tree mode rapid-pvst *command enables RSTP on an IOS switch.*

to a root port and places it immediately into a forwarding state, notifying Switch-B of the change. This update typically takes less than a second, assuming that the failure of the segment between the root and Switch-C is a physical link failure, instead of three missed consecutive hello BPDUs.

RSTP Configuration

Cisco switches support three types of STP that incorporate VLAN, as displayed in Table 3-2. The default configuration on Cisco switches is a separate instance of STP per VLAN, one root switch for all the VLANs, and no load sharing.

This book focuses only on PVRST+, and briefly at that. To enable PVRST+, use the following command:

```
Switch(config)# spanning-tree mode rapid-pvst
```

Once enabled, you can view the STP on a per-VLAN basis with this command:

```
Switch# show spanning-tree vlan VLAN_# [detail]
```

Here's an example of this command:

```
Switch# show spanning-tree vlan 10
VLAN0010
Spanning tree enabled protocol rstp
Root ID Priority 32768
```

TABLE 3-2	STP	Description
STP Types	PVST+	802.1d per VLAN with Cisco-proprietary extensions (PortFast, UplinkFast, BackboneFast)
	PVRST+	802.1w (RSTP) per VLAN
	Multiservice Transport Platform (MSTP)	802.1s, referred to as multiple STP, combines Cisco's PVST+ with IEEE standards

```
This bridge is root
Hello Time 2 sec Max Age 20 sec Forward Delay 15 sec
Bridge ID Priority 32768 (priority 32768 sys-id-ext 10)
Address 0000.01c1.1111
Hello Time 2 sec Mag Age 20 sec Forward Delay 15 sec
Aging Time 300
Interface   Role   Sts   Cost   Pior.Nbr   Type
---------   ----   ---   ----   --------   ----
Fa0/1       Desg   FWD   19     128.1      P2p
Fa0/2       Desg   FWD   19     128.2      P2p
Fa0/3       Desg   FWD   19     128.3      P2p
.
.
.
```

e x a m

ⓦ a t c h   *Be familiar with the output of the* `show spanning-tree vlan` *and* `show spanning-tree interface` *commands.*

In this example, the switch is the root for VLAN 10 and RSTP is being used. Notice that all of its ports are designated ports (`Desg`) and are in a forwarding state (`FWD`)—if this were true for all active ports, then this switch would be the root switch, which indeed is the case here, as indicated by the fourth line of output (`This bridge is root`).

You can also verify STP on a per-port basis with the **show spanning-tree interface** command. Here's an example:

```
Switch# show spanning-tree interface fastethernet 1/0/5

Vlan        Role Sts Cost Prio.Nbr Type
--------    ---- --- ---- -------- ----
VLAN0001    Root FWD 19   128.1    P2P
VLAN0002    Altn DIS 19   128.2    P2P
VLAN0003    Root FWD 19   128.2    P2P
```

In this example, F1/0/5 is an alternate port in VLAN 2 either because it has a higher path cost to the root bridge, or there is a tie and this neighbor has a higher bridge ID.

o n   t h e
ⓘ o b   *To troubleshoot problems with PVRST+, use the* `debug spanning-tree pvst+` *command; to troubleshoot problems with ports changing state within STP, use* `debug spanning-tree switch` *state.*

PVST+ and RSTP Optimization

To understand the advantages offered by PVST+ and RSTP, examine Figure 3-13. This example shows two VLANs, numbered 1 and 2. The default behavior with Cisco's switches is that a single root switch is used for all VLANs, based on the switch with the lowest switch ID. In this instance, this is Switch-A. Notice that based on RSTP's calculation, Switch-C disabled its port to Switch-B for both its VLANs. The downside of this design is that of the two connections to the distribution layer, only one is being utilized on the access switch.

A better design is shown in Figure 3-13. However, to obtain this kind of topology, you must tune your network, making sure that Switch-A is the root for VLAN 1 and Switch-B is the root for VLAN 2. With this kind of design, you can actually utilize both of your uplink connections on your access layer switch up to the distribution layer switches. In Figure 3-14, VLAN 1 will use the left-hand uplink connection and VLAN 2 the right-hand uplink connection.

on the
Ⓘob

Based on the design in Figure 3-14, make sure the default gateway for VLAN 1 is Switch-A (assuming it's a layer 3 switch) and for VLAN 2 is Switch-B (assuming it's a layer 3 switch). If you don't configure it this way, but have the default gateway associated with Switch-A, VLAN 2's traffic will have to go from the access layer switch to Switch-B, and then across the EtherChannel to Switch-A before leaving the subnet. You can learn more about this in Cisco's CCNP Switching course.

FIGURE 3-13

PVST+ and RSTP nonoptimized

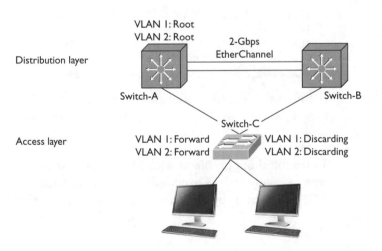

PVST+ and RSTP optimized

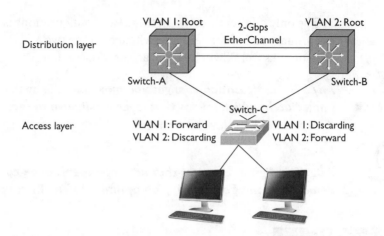

Remember that the topology in Figure 3-14 is created by you: you must manually change each switch's priority to create the desired topology. The commands to accomplish this include the following:

```
Switch(config)# spanning-tree vlan VLAN_# root primary
Switch(config)# spanning-tree vlan VLAN_# root secondary
Switch(config)# spanning-tree vlan VLAN_# priority priority_#
```

Remember that the default priority for a switch is 32,768. The first command changes the switch's priority to 4096 for the specified VLAN. The second command changes it to 8192 for the specified VLAN. The third allows you to customize the priority for the specified VLAN.

Based on the example in Figure 3-14, Switch-A's configuration would look like this:

```
Switch-A(config)# spanning-tree mode rapid-pvst
Switch-A(config)# spanning-tree vlan 1 root primary
Switch-A(config)# spanning-tree vlan 2 root secondary
```

Switch-B's configuration would look like this:

```
Switch-B(config)# spanning-tree mode rapid-pvst
Switch-B(config)# spanning-tree vlan 2 root primary
Switch-B(config)# spanning-tree vlan 1 root secondary
```

The only difference between these two configurations is that the priorities for the primary and secondary are switched on the two VLANs to allow for the use of both uplinks from Switch-C, the access layer switch.

Any STP configuration changes you make on your switches are effected immediately, which means that layer 2 will have to reconverge, causing a brief disruption in your layer 2 network.

3.02. The digital resources that accompany this book contain a multimedia demonstration of configuring an optimized PVRST+ topology.

EXERCISE 3-1

Examining STP Information on Your Switches

The last few sections dealt with the operation of STP. This lab builds upon this information and allows you to view STP in operation on switches. You can find a picture of the network diagram for the simulator in the Introduction of this book. After starting up Boson's NetSim simulator, click the Labs tab at the bottom left of the window. Click the McGraw-Hill Education tab (to the right of the Standard and Custom tabs) at the top left. Next, double-click Exercise 3-1. This will load the lab configuration based on Chapter 2.

1. From the 2950-1, verify that you can ping the Host-1 PC and the 2950-2 switch.

   Click the Lab Instructions tab and use the drop-down selector and choose 2950-1; or click the NetMap tab and double-click the 2950-1 device icon. Access the CLI of the 2950-1. Execute **ping 192.168.1.10** and **ping 192.168.1.3**. Both should be successful.

2. From Privileged EXEC mode, view the STP operation for VLAN 1: **show spanning-tree vlan 1**.

3. Compare the root ID and bridge ID at the top of the display: if they are the same, then this is the root switch, which means interfaces fa0/1 and fa0/2 (connected to 2950-2) should be in a forwarding state. If the IDs are different, then this is not the root switch and fa0/2 should be in a blocking state (BLK).

4. Click the Lab Instructions tab and use the drop-down selector and choose 2950-2; or click the NetMap tab and double-click the 2950-2 device icon. Access the CLI of the 2950-2. From the 2950-2, view the STP operation for VLAN 1.

5. From Privileged EXEC mode, view the STP operation for VLAN 1: **show spanning-tree vlan 1**. Examine the IDs and the fa0/1 and fa0/2 interfaces, as described in step 3.

Now you should be more comfortable with STP on your Catalyst IOS switches.

CERTIFICATION OBJECTIVE 3.04

EtherChannels

It is common to need higher bandwidth speeds for certain kinds of connections in your network, such as connections from the access layer to the distribution layer, between distribution layer switches, between distribution and core layer switches, and between certain servers or routers and their connected switches. For example, in Figures 3-1 and 3-14 you can see dual layer 2 connections between the two distribution layer switches as well as between the distribution and core layer switches. The problem with this type of design, however, is that it creates layer 2 loops; and with STP running, STP will ensure that only one path is active between two devices, limiting you to the bandwidth of one of possibly multiple connections.

EtherChannel Overview

An EtherChannel is a layer 2 solution that allows you to aggregate multiple layer 2 Ethernet-based connections between directly connected devices. Basically, an EtherChannel bundles together multiple Ethernet ports between devices, providing what appears to be a single logical interface. From STP's perspective, it sees the EtherChannel as a single logical connection between the connected devices, which means that you can actually use all of the individual connections, simultaneously, in the channel you've created.

EtherChannels provide these advantages:

■ **Redundancy** If one connection in the channel fails, you can use other connections in the channel.

■ **More bandwidth** Each connection can be used simultaneously to send frames.

■ **Simplified management** Configuration is done on the logical interface, not on each individual connection in the channel.

EtherChannel Restrictions

Interfaces in an EtherChannel must be configured identically: speed, duplexing, and VLAN settings (in the same VLAN if they are access ports, or the same trunk properties) must be the same. When setting up EtherChannels, you can use up to eight interfaces bundled together:

■ Up to eight Fast Ethernet connections, providing up to 800 Mbps

■ Up to eight Gigabit Ethernet connections, providing up to 8 Gbps

■ Up to eight 10-Gigabit Ethernet connections, providing up to 80 Gbps

When forming an EtherChannel, all ports must be configured for the same speed, trunk encapsulation type (access, 802.1Q, or ISL), and duplex setting.

Typically you can have a total of six EtherChannels on a switch, but this is larger on the higher-end IOS switches.

EtherChannel Operations

Channels can be formed dynamically between devices by using one of two protocols: Port Aggregation Protocol (PAgP) or Link Aggregation Control Protocol (LACP), compared in Table 3-3. Remember that ports participating in a channel must be configured identically.

TABLE 3-3	Protocols	Description
EtherChannel Protocols	PAgP	Proprietary to Cisco. It allows connected devices to group similarly configured ports dynamically into a single channel.
	LACP	Defined in the IEEE 802.1AX standard. Like PAgP, it learns from a connected device which ports between the two are identically configured and dynamically forms a channel between them.

Once a channel is formed, load balancing can be used by the connected devices to utilize all the ports in the channel. Load balancing is performed by reducing part of the binary addressing in the frame or packet to a numeric value and then associating the numeric value to one of the ports in the channel. Load balancing can use MAC or IP addresses, source or destination addresses, or both source and destination address pairs. With this fashion, you are guaranteed that all links in the channel will be utilized; however, you are not guaranteed that all the ports will be utilized the same.

For example, if you are load balancing based on source addresses, you are guaranteed that different source MAC addresses will use different ports in the channel. All traffic from a single-source MAC address, however, will always use the same port in the channel. Given this situation, if you have one device generating a lot of traffic, that link will possibly be utilized more than other links in the channel. In this situation, you might want to load balance based on destination or both source and destination addresses.

on the
job

To configure load balancing properly for a channel, you must understand the traffic patterns in your network. Once you understand your traffic patterns, you can get the most utilization out of your channel by choosing the correct load balancing type.

EtherChannel Configuration

As mentioned, you should make sure that all interfaces in the channel are configured identically (configuring interface properties was discussed in Chapter 10); otherwise, a channel might not form. Here is the configuration to set up an EtherChannel:

```
Switch(config)# interface type [slot_#/]port_#
Switch(config-if)# channel-group group_# mode mode
Switch(config-if)# port-channel load-balance {dst-ip | dst-mac |
                          src-dst-ip | src-dst-mac | src-ip | src-mac}
```

exam
watch   *If you want to treat this as a layer 3 interface on a router as an example and assign an IP address to it, the port channel must be designated as* `interface port-channel group_#`*.*

The *group_#* specifies the channel group to which the interface belongs, which can be from 1 to 6 (remember that you can have up to six EtherChannels on your switch). The *mode* can be one of those listed in Table 3-4. When using PAgP, one side needs to be configured as **desirable** and the other side as **desirable** or **auto**; or you can configure both sides to be **on**. When using LACP, one side needs to be **active** and the other side can be **active** or **passive**.

TABLE 3-4	Mode	Protocol	Description
EtherChannel Modes	`auto`	PAgP	Passively listens for PAgP queries from a Cisco device configured with either *desirable* or *on*. By default, the interface is not part of a channel.
	`desirable`	PAgP	Generates PAgP queries to form a channel, but by default, is not part of a channel.
	`on`	PAgP	Generates PAgP queries and assumes the port is part of a channel.
	`active`	LACP	Enables a channel if the other side responds to its LACP messages.
	`passive`	LACP	Passively listens for LACP messages to form a channel from an active port.

The **port-channel load-balance** command configures the type of load balancing you want to use on the channel. If you omit this command, it defaults to load balancing based on source MAC addresses (**src-mac**).

exam

ⓦatch   *If one side of a PAGP EtherChannel is set to* auto *for the mode, the other needs to be set to either* on *or* **desirable. The** active **and** passive **modes are only used to establish an EtherChannel using LACP.**

Here's a configuration of SwitchA forming an EtherChannel to SwitchB using PAgP:

```
SwitchA(config)# interface g1/0/1
SwitchA(config-if)# channel-group 1 mode auto
SwitchA(config-if)# exit
SwitchA(config)# interface g1/0/2
SwitchA(config-if)# channel-group 1 mode auto
SwitchA(config-if)# exit
```

Since the `auto` mode is used on SwitchA for PAgP, SwitchB must use either a mode of `on` or `desirable`, like this:

```
SwitchB(config)# interface g1/0/4
SwitchB(config-if)# channel-group 1 mode auto
SwitchB(config-if)# exit
SwitchB(config)# interface g1/0/5
SwitchB(config-if)# channel-group 1 mode auto
SwitchB(config-if)# exit
```

STP Troubleshooting

Troubleshooting problems created by loops can be a difficult task. This section covers some simple steps you can take to identify and fix layer 2 loop problems.

Loop Identification

One indication of a broadcast storm is very high CPU and port utilization on your switches. As mentioned at the beginning of the chapter, examine the switch's or switches' CPU utilization with the **show processes** and **show process cpu** commands. A constantly high CPU utilization could indicate a loop. To verify that it is a layer 2 loop causing the problem, capture and analyze traffic with a protocol analyzer to determine whether the same packet appears multiple times. This is typically done by connecting your protocol analyzer to a switch and using the Switch Port Analyzer (SPAN) feature on your switch, which copies frames from an interface or VLAN to the SPAN port. A good protocol analyzer should be able to see that a loop exists and notify you of this problem.

Once a loop is identified, to restore connectivity quickly, you should start disabling ports that are part of the loop; then diagnose the problem to determine whether a configuration issue on your part or the addition of a new layer 2 device is causing the problem. If you are having problems identifying what is causing the loop, turn on debug for STP (**debug spanning-tree events**).

Configuration Remedies

To simplify your troubleshooting process, disable as many features as necessary. For example, if you have EtherChannels enabled, disabling the channel will help determine whether the channel itself is not functioning correctly and possibly creating the layer 2 loop.

If you are not certain which switch is the root switch, log into the switch that logically should be the root and force it to become the root by changing its priority to 1 with the **spanning-tree vlan** *VLAN_#* **priority** command.

on the
job

A good step on your part should be to include the MAC addresses of each switch in your network topology diagram. Then, when troubleshooting loop problems, you'll find it much easier to determine whether a rogue switch was introduced into the topology that might be creating the loop.

Make sure that all your switches are running either 802.1d or 802.1w (RSTP), preferably the latter. Use the `show spanning-tree` command to verify this, as well as whether or not the switch is playing the role of root for a VLAN.

INSIDE THE EXAM

Layer 2 Redundancy

Cisco's exam focuses more on the concepts of this chapter than on the configuration. Be familiar with Cisco's three-layer hierarchy, since you might see it in illustrations on the exam. Understand the three issues with layer 2 loops (multiple frame copies, broadcast storms, and mislearning MAC addresses) and the problems these issues create.

Spanning Tree Protocol

Understand how STP works: how the root switch is elected, how root and designated ports are chosen, and the different states a port can be in. Don't be surprised if you are presented with a diagram and must choose answers dealing with these functions on the exam: Review the "Simple STP Example" section until you are comfortable with the STP terms and how the STP functions are derived. Remember that the switch ID is created from the switch's priority *and* MAC address. Be familiar with how long a port stays in a particular state for 802.1d STP. Understand when PortFast is best used and

the advantages that PVST+ provides when implementing VLANs.

Rapid Spanning Tree Protocol

Be familiar with the port states with RSTP: discarding, learning, and forwarding. Understand the difference between an alternate and a backup port. The configuration and tuning of RSTP is not emphasized on the exam.

EtherChannels

The configuration of EtherChannels is not emphasized on the exam; however, you need to understand what they are and when they are used.

STP Troubleshooting

Remember what symptoms you look for to identify a layer 2 loop. Be familiar with the configuration remedies in dealing with layer 2 loops.

CERTIFICATION SUMMARY

Bridges have three main functions: learn, forward, and remove loops. They learn by placing source MAC addresses and associated bridge ports in a port address or CAM table. They will flood traffic if the destination address is a multicast, broadcast, or unknown unicast destination. STP is used to remove layer 2 loops.

BPDUs are used by STP to learn about other neighboring switches. These are generated every 2 seconds as multicasts. When running STP, a root switch is elected—the one with the lowest switch or bridge ID. The switch ID is composed of a priority and the switch's MAC address. Each switch chooses a root port to reach the root switch—the one with the lowest accumulated path cost. Each segment has one port on one switch that becomes a designated port, which is used to forward traffic to and from the segment. This is typically the port on the switch with the lowest accumulated path cost. There are five port states: blocking (20 seconds), listening (15 seconds), learning (15 seconds), forwarding, and disabled. PortFast puts a port immediately into forwarding mode and should be used only on nonswitch ports. PVST+ has an instance of STP running per VLAN—this is proprietary to Cisco but standardized by IEEE with MSTP.

RSTP reduces convergence to a few seconds by having switches determine valid alternate root ports and backup designated ports that they can use when topology changes take place. PVST+ with RSTP is enabled with the `spanning-tree mode rapid-pvst` command.

EtherChannels bundle layer 2 connections between devices, creating a single logical port from STP's perspective. Load balancing can then be performed on the ports in the channel. PAgP or LACP is used to form the channel. No more than eight interfaces can be part of a channel.

If your CPU and/or port utilization is high, you might have a layer 2 loop. Typically, you should use a protocol analyzer and look for multiple copies of the same frame in your frame captures.

✓ TWO-MINUTE DRILL

Layer 2 Redundancy

❑ There are three layers to a campus design: access, distribution, and core.

❑ Redundancy in layer 2 networks can create loops that can cause multiple frame copies, broadcast storms, and/or mislearning MAC addresses.

Spanning Tree Protocol

❑ STP is defined in 802.1d. It removes loops from your network.

❑ The switch with the lowest switch ID (priority + MAC address) is elected as the root.

❑ Each switch chooses the best path to the root, and this port is called a root port. Each segment needs a switch port to access the rest of the network—this port is called a designated port.

❑ BPDUs are used to elect root switches and to share topology information. BPDUs are multicasts that are advertised every 2 seconds.

❑ There are five STP port states: blocking (only processing BPDUs—20 seconds), listening (only processing BPDUs—15 seconds), learning (processing BPDUs and building the CAM table—15 seconds), forwarding (processing BPDUs, building the CAM table, and forwarding user traffic), and disabled (the port is not enabled). Root and designated ports will eventually move into a forwarding state, which can take between 30 and 50 seconds.

❑ PortFast keeps a port in a forwarding state when STP is recalculating; it should *not* be used on switch-to-switch connections and thus could lead to inadvertent loops.

❑ PVST+ is proprietary to Cisco and allows for a separate STP instance per VLAN.

Rapid Spanning Tree Protocol

❑ RSTP has three port states: discarding, learning, and forwarding.

❑ RSTP supports two additional port types: alternate (secondary to a root port) and backup (secondary to a designated port).

EtherChannels

❑ From STP's perspective, an EtherChannel, which is a grouping of layer 2 physical connections between devices, is seen as a single logical connection.

❑ Ports must be configured identically in an EtherChannel. PAgP or LACP can be used to form a channel.

STP Troubleshooting

❑ Look for high CPU and/or port utilization as a symptom of a broadcast storm.

❑ Use a protocol analyzer and look for multiple frame copies to determine whether you have a loop.

SELF TEST

The following Self Test questions will help you measure your understanding of the material presented in this chapter. Read all the choices carefully, as there may be more than one correct answer. Choose all correct answers for each question.

Layer 2 Redundancy

1. Which of the following would not be a symptom of a layer 2 loop?
   A. Broadcast flooding
   B. Multiple frame copies
   C. Learning MAC addresses on incorrect ports
   D. None of these

Spanning Tree Protocol

2. The root switch is the one elected with the _____.
   A. lowest MAC address
   B. highest MAC address
   C. lowest switch ID
   D. highest switch ID

3. The switch port that is chosen to forward traffic for a segment is called a(n) _____.
   A. root port
   B. alternate port
   C. backup port
   D. designated port

4. Which is true concerning a port in a listening state? (Choose two answers.)
   A. It remains there for 15 seconds.
   B. It forwards BPDUs and builds the CAM table.
   C. It remains there for 20 seconds.
   D. It forwards BPDUs.

Rapid Spanning Tree Protocol

5. How many port states are there in RSTP?

A. 3

B. 4

C. 5

D. 6

6. What port role will be assigned to a port that has the second best path to the root switch?

A. Root

B. Designated

C. Alternate

D. Backup

7. Which command enables RSTP with PVRST+ on a switch?

A. `spanning-tree mode rapid-pvst`

B. `spanning-tree state rapid-pvst`

C. `stp state rapid-pvst`

D. `spanning-tree mode rtsp`

EtherChannels

8. Which of the following is true concerning EtherChannels?

A. You can have up to six ports in a channel.

B. You can have up to eight channels on a switch.

C. Ports must be configured identically to form a channel.

D. RSTP dynamically groups ports into a channel.

STP Troubleshooting

9. What symptom should you look for to determine whether you have a layer 2 loop?

A. High number of broadcast and/or multicast frames

B. High port utilization

C. User switch interfaces dropping and reconnecting

D. Port address tables not being updated

10. What tool would you use to determine whether you had a broadcast storm caused by a layer 2 loop?

A. `show interface` command

B. Protocol analyzer

C. `debug broadcast` command

D. `traceroute` command

SELF TEST ANSWERS

Layer 2 Redundancy

1. ☑ **A.** Switches flood broadcasts by default; seeing the *same* broadcast again and again could indicate a broadcast storm and a layer 2 loop.

   ☒ **B** and **C** are symptoms of a layer 2 loop. Since there is an incorrect answer, D is incorrect.

Spanning Tree Protocol

2. ☑ **C.** The switch with the lowest switch ID is elected as the root switch.

   ☒ **A** and **B** are incorrect because the decision is based on the switch ID, which includes the switch's priority and MAC address. **D** is incorrect because it is the lowest, not the highest, switch ID.

3. ☑ **D.** The switch port that is chosen to forward traffic for a segment is called a designated port.

   ☒ **A** is incorrect because the root port is the port that the switch uses to reach the root. **B,** the alternate port, is used in RSTP and is a secondary root port, and **C,** the backup port, is used in RSTP and is a secondary designated port.

4. ☑ **A** and **D.** In a listening state, the port processes and forwards BPDUs. A port stays in the listening state for 15 seconds.

   ☒ **B** occurs in the learning state. **C** is the time period for the blocking state.

Rapid Spanning Tree Protocol

5. ☑ **A.** There are three port states in RSTP: discarding, learning, and forwarding.

   ☒ Since there are only three states, **B, C,** and **D** are incorrect.

6. ☑ **C.** An alternate port has the second best path to the root switch.

   ☒ **A** is the best path to the root. **B** is the best path for a segment to the root. **D** is the second best path for a segment to the root.

7. ☑ **A.** The `spanning-tree mode rapid-pvst` command enables RSTP with PVST+ on a Catalyst switch.

   ☒ `state` is an invalid parameter, making **B** incorrect. **C** is an invalid command. **D** has an invalid `mode` parameter.

EtherChannels

8.   ☑   **C.** Ports must be configured identically to form a channel.
   ☒   **A** is incorrect because you can have up to eight ports in a channel. **B** is incorrect because the limit is six channels per switch. **D** rapidly converges STP: PAgP and LACP dynamically form channels.

STP Troubleshooting

9.   ☑   **B.** If you have a layer 2 loop, the switch's CPU and/or port utilization will be very high.
   ☒   **A** is true only if you are seeing duplicate broadcast/multicast frames, not just a high number of these. **C** would be indicative of a physical layer problem such as a cable issue. Port address tables would be constantly updated with correct and incorrect information, making **D** incorrect.

10.   ☑   **B.** When using a protocol analyzer to troubleshoot layer 2 loop problems, look for the same frame being repeated constantly.
   ☒   **A** will show an inordinate amount of statistical traffic on the interface, but it doesn't clarify it as broadcast or part of a loop. **C** is an invalid command. **D** is used to troubleshoot layer 3, not layer 2, problems.

Part II

Cisco Routers and LANs

4

Routers and Routing

The preceding part of the book focused on switches and protocols that function at layer 2. This part of the book moves up one layer in the OSI Reference Model to discuss layer 3, the network layer. Layer 3 devices are generically called *routers*. Routers basically have two functions:

- To find a layer 3 path to a destination network
- To move packets from one interface to another to get a packet to its destination

To accomplish the first function, a router will need to do the following:

- Learn about the routers to which it is connected to determine the networks that are reachable.
- Find locations of destination network numbers.
- Choose a *best* path to each destination.
- Maintain the most up-to-date routing information about how to reach destination networks.

ⓦatch *You should know the functions of routers: they learn about neighboring routers, find and choose the best paths to destinations, and maintain up-to-date reachability information.*

To accomplish the second function, a router will need to examine the destination IP address in an incoming IP packet, determine the network number of the destination, look in its routing table, and switch the packet to an outgoing interface.

As you will see in this chapter, the routing table contains a list of destination network numbers, the status of these networks, which interface the router should use to reach the destination, and which neighboring router the router should use if the destination is more than one hop away. This chapter introduces routing and the types of dynamic routing protocols: distance vector, link state, and hybrid protocols.

ⓦatch *Remember that routers must determine the network number of the destination in the destination field of the IP header and find the corresponding network in the routing table to route the packet.*

CERTIFICATION OBJECTIVE 4.01

Routing Introduction

Before a discussion of routers and routing protocols begins, you need a fundamental understanding of the types of routes that can exist on a router and how a router uses routes that it learns. The following sections discuss two learning methods (static and dynamic), how routers are grouped together (autonomous systems), and how routing protocols are weighed by the router when choosing a path between multiple routing protocols.

Types of Routes

A router can learn a route using one of two methods: *static* and *dynamic*. The following two sections discuss the two types.

Static Routes

A router can learn a static route in two ways: First, a router will look at its active interfaces, examine the addresses configured on the interfaces and determine the corresponding network numbers, and populate the routing table with this information. This is commonly called a *connected* or *directly connected* route. The second way that a router can learn a static route is for you to configure the route manually. For example, you might configure a static route for the destination network of 192.168.2.0/24 with a next-hop address of 192.168.1.2 (the neighbor to forward the traffic to). One special type of static route is called a *default route*, commonly called the *gateway of last resort*. If the specified destination is not listed in the routing table, the default route can be used to route the packet. A default route has an IP address of 0.0.0.0 and a subnet mask of 0.0.0.0, often represented as 0.0.0.0/0. Default routes are commonly used in small networks on a perimeter router pointing to the directly connected ISP router. The configuration of static and default routes is discussed in Chapter 9.

Dynamic Routes

A router learns dynamic routes by running a routing protocol. Routing protocols will learn about routes from other neighboring routers running the same routing protocol. Dynamic routing protocols share network numbers known by the router

TABLE 4-1	Routed Protocols	Routing Protocols
Routed and Routing Protocols	IP	RIP, IGRP, OSPF, EIGRP, BGP, IS-IS
	IPX	RIP, NLSP, EIGRP
	AppleTalk	RMTP, AURP, EIGRP

and reachability information concerning these networks. Through this sharing process, a router will eventually learn about all of the reachable network and subnet numbers in the network.

You should know that the terms *routing* protocol and *routed* protocol have two different meanings. A *routing* protocol learns about routes for a *routed* protocol. A routed protocol is a layer 3 protocol, such as Transmission Control Protocol/ Internet Protocol (TCP/IP) or Internetwork Packet Exchange (IPX). A routed protocol carries user traffic such as e-mail, file transfers, and web downloads. Table 4-1 shows some common routed protocols and the routing protocols that they use. This book focuses only on routing for IP traffic and covers the basics of the following dynamic IP routing protocols: Routing Information Protocol (RIP) v1 and v2 in Chapter 9, Open Shortest Path First (OSPF) in Chapter 10, and Enhanced Interior Gateway Routing Protocol (EIGRP) in Chapter 11.

e x a m

watch   *Remember the difference between a routed protocol and a routing protocol. Static routes typically are more secure than dynamic routes because you have complete control over what appears in the routing table when using static routes, whereas you have less control over what routing neighbors share with*   *dynamic routing. Static routes also have a lesser burden on a router over dynamic routing, since they don't have to process routing protocol messages. Static routes are commonly used on boundary routers: a default route pointing to the Internet and a summarized static route pointing to the internal network.*

Autonomous Systems

Some routing protocols understand the concept of an autonomous system, and some do not. An *autonomous system* (AS) is a group of networks under a single administrative control, which could be your company, a division within your company, or a group of companies. An *Interior Gateway Protocol* (IGP) refers to a routing protocol that handles routing within a single autonomous system. IGPs include RIP, EIGRP, OSPF, and Intermediate System-Intermediate System (IS-IS). An *Exterior Gateway Protocol* (EGP) handles routing between different autonomous systems. Today, only one EGP is active: the Border Gateway Protocol (BGP). BGP is used to route traffic across the Internet backbone between different autonomous systems.

Not every routing protocol understands the concept of an AS. An AS can provide distinct boundaries for a routing protocol, and thus provides some advantages. For instance, you can control how far a network number is propagated by routers. Plus, you can control what routes you will advertise to other autonomous systems and what routes you'll accept from these systems.

To distinguish one autonomous system from another, an AS can be assigned a unique number from 1 to 65,535. The Internet Assigned Numbers Authority (IANA) is responsible for assigning these numbers. Just like the public and private IP addresses defined in RFC 1918, there are public and private AS numbers. If you will be connected to the Internet backbone, are running BGP, and want to accept BGP routes from the Internet, you will need a public AS number. However, if you only need to break up your internal network into different systems, you can use private AS numbers. Routing protocols that understand the concept of an AS are EIGRP, OSPF, IS-IS, and BGP. RIP doesn't understand autonomous systems, while OSPF does; but OSPF doesn't require you to configure the AS number, whereas other protocols, such as EIGRP, do. Cisco's CCNP certification spends a lot of time discussing autonomous systems and routing between them. The CCNA exam focuses only on the basics of IGPs and routing within an AS.

Administrative Distance

As mentioned in the chapter introduction, each router needs to choose a *best* path to a destination. This process can become somewhat complicated if the router is receiving routing update information for a single network from multiple sources, such as connected, static, and IGP routing protocols, and must choose *one* of these sources as the best and place this choice in the router's routing table. As you will see in the next few sections, a router looks at two items when choosing a *best* path: administrative distance and routing metrics. The first item a router looks at is the administrative distance for a route source. Administrative distance is a Cisco-proprietary mechanism used to rank the IP routing protocols. As an example, if a router is running two IGPs, RIP and EIGRP, and is learning network 10.0.0.0/8 from both of these routing protocols, which one should the router pick and place in its routing table? Which one should the router *believe* more? Actually, the term *administrative distance* is somewhat misleading, since the term has nothing to do with measuring distance. The term *believability* better describes the process.

Administrative distance ranks the IP routing protocols, assigning a value, or weight, to each protocol. Distances can range from 0 to 255. A smaller distance is more believable by a router, with the best distance being 0 and the worst 255. Table 4-2 displays some of the default administrative distances Cisco has assigned to its IP routing protocols. Going back to the previous example of a router learning network 10.0.0.0/8 from RIP and EIGRP, since RIP has a value of 120 and EIGRP has a value of 90, which is a better (*lower*) administrative distance value, the router will use the EIGRP route.

e**x**a**m**

 ⓦatch   *Here are some important protocols to know and their administrative distances: connected (0), static (0 or 1), EIGRP (90), OSPF (110), and RIP (120). The*   *protocol with a lower distance is preferred over a protocol with a higher distance, where the most believable route is a directly connected one.*

TABLE 4-2	Administrative Distance	Route Type
Administrative Distance Values	0	Connected interface route
	0 or 1	Static route
	90	Internal EIGRP route (within the same AS)
	110	OSPF route
	120	RIPv1 and v2 route
	170	External EIGRP (from another AS)
	255	Unknown route (is considered an invalid route and will not be used)

Dynamic Routing Protocols

Unlike static routes that require manual configuration to tell the router where destination networks are, *dynamic routing protocols* learn about destination networks from neighboring routers through a sharing process. Dynamic routing protocols fall under one of three categories: distance vector, link state, and hybrid. Each of these routing protocol types takes a different approach in sharing routing information with neighboring routers and choosing the best path to a destination.

Because of the differences between the various routing protocol types, each has advantages and disadvantages. One choice you'll have to make will be which routing protocol you'll run on the routers in your network. You'll have to examine the following factors when choosing a routing protocol:

- Routing metrics used to choose paths
- How routing information is shared
- Convergence speed of the routing protocol
- How routers process routing information
- Overhead of the routing protocol

The following sections discuss these topics.

Routing Metrics

As mentioned in the "Administrative Distance" section, if your router has two types of routes, such as RIP and EIGRP, for the same network number, the router uses the administrative distance to choose the best one. However, a situation might arise where two paths to the destination network exist, and the *same* routing protocol, RIP, for instance, discovers these multiple paths to the destination network. If this is the case, a routing protocol will use a measurement called a *metric* to determine which path is the best path to place in the routing table.

Table 4-3 lists some common metrics, the IP routing protocols that use them, and brief descriptions of the metrics. As you can see from this table, some routing protocols use only a single metric. For instance, RIP uses hop count as a metric, and OSPF uses cost. Other routing protocols use multiple metric values to choose a best path to a destination. For instance, EIGRP can use bandwidth, delay, reliability,

	Metric	Routing Protocols	Description
TABLE 4-3	Bandwidth	EIGRP	The capacity of the links in Kbps (T1 = 1554)
Routing Protocol Metrics	Cost	OSPF	Measurement in the inverse of the bandwidth of the links
	Delay	EIGRP	Time it takes to reach the destination
	Hop count	RIP	How many layer 3 hops away from the destination
	Load	EIGRP	The path with the least utilization
	MTU	EIGRP	The path that supports the largest frame sizes
	Reliability	EIGRP	The path with the least amount of errors or downtime

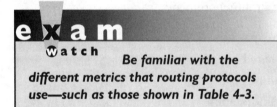

load, and maximum transmission unit (MTU) when choosing a best path to a destination.

Distance Vector Protocols

Of the three types of routing protocols—distance vector, link state, and hybrid—distance vector protocols are the simplest in their implementation. Distance vector routing protocols use distance (accumulated metric value) and direction (vector) to find paths to destinations. Most distance vector protocols use the Bellman-Ford algorithm (discussed shortly) for finding paths to destination networks. Sometimes these protocols are referred to as *routing by rumor*, since the routers learn routing information from directly connected neighbors, and these neighbors might have learned these networks from other neighboring routers. RIP is an example of a routing protocol that is a distance vector, and it is discussed in more depth in Chapter 9.

Advertising Updates

One of the mechanisms of a routing protocol is to share routing and reachability information with neighboring routers. Some protocols use local broadcasts to disseminate information, some use multicasts, and some use unicasts. Distance vector protocols originally used periodic local broadcasts with a destination IP address of 255.255.255.255 to share routing information. These protocols do this religiously, whether or not something has changed: Once their periodic timer expires, they broadcast their routing information to any devices connected to their interfaces. Note that distance vector protocols really don't care who listens to these updates, nor do they verify whether neighboring routers received the broadcast update.

Routers running distance vector protocols learn who their neighbors are by listening for routing broadcasts on their interfaces. No formal handshaking process or hello process occurs to discover who the neighboring routers are. Distance vector protocols assume that through the broadcast process, neighbors will be learned, and if a neighbor fails, the missed broadcasts from these neighbors will eventually be detected. And even if changes occur and your router misses an update from a neighbor, it is assumed that your router will learn about the change in the next broadcast update.

Processing Updates

When a distance vector protocol receives a routing update from a neighboring router, it performs these steps:

1. Increments the metrics of the incoming routes in the advertisement (for RIP, add 1 to the advertised hop count of the route).

2. Compares the network numbers in the routing update from the neighbor to what the router has in its routing table.

3. If the neighbor's information is better, places it in the routing table and removes the old entry.

4. If the neighbor's information is worse, ignores it.

5. If the neighbor's information is exactly the same as the entry already in the table, resets the timer for the entry in the routing table (in other words, the router already learned about this route from the same neighbor).

6. If the neighbor's information is a different path to a known destination network, but with the same metric as the existing network in the routing table, the router will add it to the routing table along with the old one. This assumes you have not exceeded the maximum number of equal-cost paths for this destination network number. In this situation, your router is learning about the same network number from two *different* neighbors, and both neighbors are advertising the network number with the same metric.

These six steps are generally referred to as the *Bellman-Ford algorithm*. As you can see from step 6, Cisco supports load balancing for equal-cost paths to a destination within a particular route type, such as RIP routes. Equal-cost load balancing allows a routing device to list a destination multiple times in the routing table, one for each path to the destination network, and use them simultaneously. The advantage of this approach is that if one path fails, convergence is instantaneous because the other paths are already in the routing table. Most vendors perform per-connection load balancing: all traffic for a particular connection is routed across the same path to reduce the likelihood of creating problems for the connection. Equal-cost load balancing is discussed in more depth in Chapters 10 and 11.

Since distance vector protocols are the simplest of the three protocol types, they are easy to set up and troubleshoot. They have very low overhead on the router, requiring few CPU cycles and memory to process updates: they receive an incoming update, increment the metrics, compare the results to the existing routes in the routing table, and update the routing table if necessary.

Link State Protocols

Link state protocols use an algorithm called the *Shortest Path First* (SPF) algorithm, invented by Edsger W. Dijkstra, to find the best path to a destination. Whereas distance vector protocols rely on *rumors* from other neighbors about remote routes, link state protocols will learn the complete topology of the network: which routers are connected to which networks. Because of the size of a network, this can create scalability problems. Therefore, link state protocols typically contain capabilities to limit the scope of their learning process, limiting a router's knowledge of the network topology to a smaller number of routers and routes.

Examples of link state protocols include OSPF and IS-IS. OSPF is covered in more depth in Chapter 10. IS-IS is an ISO link state protocol. It was originally developed by DEC as the DECnet Phase V routing protocol. It can route for both TCP/IP traffic and Connectionless Network Protocol (CLNP) and Connectionless Network Service (CLNS) traffic. IS-IS provides for more scalability than OSPF but is more complex to configure. Some ISPs use IS-IS as the routing protocol for their own networks.

Advertising Updates

Whereas distance vector protocols use local broadcasts to disseminate routing information, link state protocols use multicasts. A distance vector protocol will send out its routing table religiously on its periodic interval whether there are changes or not. Link state protocols are smarter. They multicast what is called a *link state advertisement* (LSA), which is a piece of routing information that contains who originated the advertisement and what the network number is.

LSAs are typically generated only when changes are made in the network, which is more resource-friendly to your network devices. In other words, periodic updates are rare occurrences. Whereas distance vector protocols use local broadcasts, which are processed by every machine on the segment, link state protocols use multicasts, which are processed only by other devices running the link state protocol. Plus, link state protocols send their updates reliably. A destination router, when receiving an LSA update, will respond to the source router with an acknowledgment. This process is different from distance vector protocols, which don't verify that a routing update was received from neighboring routers.

As a router learns routes from the LSAs of routers in the network, it builds a complete topology of the network—what routers are connected to other routers and what the network numbers are. This is stored in a local topological database. Whereas distance vector protocols are referred to as *routing by rumor*, link state protocols are referred to as *routing by propaganda*, since link state routers are learning which routers are sourcing (connected to) a network number. The LSAs gathered by a link state router are then stored in a local database, sometimes referred to as a *topology table*. Any time there is a change in the database, the router runs the SPF algorithm. The SPF algorithm builds an inverted tree, with the router itself at the top, and other routers and their connected network segments beneath it. This algorithm is somewhat similar to the STP algorithm that layer 2 devices use to remove loops. Depending on the tree structure and the metrics used, the link state router then populates the routing table with the best (shortest) paths to the networks in the SPF tree.

e x a m

⚠ a t c h *LSAs are flooded when a change occurs for a network. Upon receiving an LSA update, the local topology database is updated accordingly.*

Advantages of Link State Protocols

One of the advantages of link state protocols is that they use a hierarchical structure that helps limit the distance that an LSA travels. This reduces the likelihood that a change in the network will affect every router. This process is different from that of distance vector protocols, which use a flat topology. With distance vector protocols, a change in one part of the network will eventually affect every router in the network. Depending on the configuration of routers in a link state protocol, this is not necessarily true. For instance, OSPF uses areas to help contain changes; therefore, a change in one area won't necessarily affect other areas.

A second advantage of link state protocols is that they use multicasts to share routing information. Multicasts are sent to a group of devices, whereas broadcasts are sent to everyone. Only other routers running the link state protocol will process these LSA packets. Plus, link state routers send out only *incremental* updates. Incremental updates are updates sent out when a change occurs in the state of the network. This is much more advantageous than what distance vector protocols do: broadcast updates based on a periodic timer, which is typically either 30 or 60 seconds. Once all the link state routers are booted up and they learn the topology of the network, updates are typically sent out only when changes take place, which shouldn't be that often. The advantage of this process is that you are using your network's bandwidth and resources more efficiently than with distance vector protocols.

A third advantage that link state protocols have over distance vector protocols is that they support classless routing. Classless routing allows you to summarize a large group of contiguous routes into a smaller number of routes. This process is called *Variable-Length Subnet Masking* (VLSM) and *Classless Interdomain Routing* (CIDR). These concepts are discussed in depth in Chapter 5.

By summarizing routes, you are making the routing process more efficient. First, you are advertising a smaller number of routes. Second, in order for the summarized route to fail, all of the subnets or networks in the summarization must fail. As an example, you might have a WAN link that is *flapping*. A flapping route is going up and down, up and down, over and over again. This can create serious performance problems for link state protocols. When you perform summarization, if the specific route within a summarized route is flapping, this will not affect the status of the summarized route and thus won't affect many of the routers in your network. Third, by summarizing routes, you reduce the size of your router's routing link state database, which will reduce the number of CPU cycles required to run the SPF algorithm and update the routing table, as well as reduce your router's memory requirements for the routing protocol.

A fourth advantage of link state protocols is that with the use of the SPF algorithm, routing loops will not be included in the population of the routing table: by examining the inverted tree, loops can be easily detected and not included in a routing table. Routing loops can create problems with distance vector protocols, however—this problem is discussed in the "Distance Vector Protocol Problems and Solutions" section later in this chapter.

Disadvantages of Link State Protocols

Although link state protocols do have advantages, they have disadvantages as well. For instance, even though link state protocols can scale a network to a much larger size than distance vector protocols (assuming they've been addressed correctly to perform route summarization), link state protocols are more CPU- and memory-intensive. Link state protocols have to maintain more tables in memory: a neighbor table, a link state database, and a routing table. When changes take place in the network, the routers must update the link state database, run the SPF algorithm, build the SPF tree, and then rebuild the routing table, which requires a lot more CPU cycles than a distance vector protocol's approach: increment the metrics of incoming routes and compare this to the current routes in the routing table.

As an example, a flapping route in a link state network can affect the processing on many routers, especially if the change is occurring every 10 to 15 seconds. The advantage that distance vector protocols have is that the only time the routers have to perform a function is when they receive the periodic updates, and then processing these updates is router-friendly.

e**x**a m
watch
Link state protocols use the Shortest Path First (SPF) algorithm to choose the best path. Via link state updates, they learn the complete network topology by default. They send out triggered updates as changes occur. They are more CPU- and memory-intensive than distance vector protocols. However, they are more network-friendly in that they use multicasts to disseminate routing information and they only advertise changes. Plus, with route summarization and hierarchical routing, link state protocols can scale to very large network sizes. Disadvantages of link state protocols include the requirement for a hierarchical IP addressing scheme for optimal functionality and the high demand on router resources to run the link-state routing algorithm.

Hybrid Protocols

A *hybrid* protocol takes the advantages of both distance vector and link state protocols and merges them into a new protocol. Typically, hybrid protocols are based on a distance vector protocol but contain many of the features and advantages of link state protocols. Examples of hybrid protocols include RIPv2, EIGRP, and BGP. RIPv2 is covered in more depth in Chapter 9, and EIGRP is covered in Chapter 11. BGP is beyond the scope of this book, but is heavily emphasized in the CCNP certification.

As an example of a hybrid protocol's approach, Cisco's EIGRP reduces the CPU and memory overhead by acting like a distance vector protocol when it comes to processing routing updates; but instead of sending out periodic updates like a distance vector protocol, EIGRP sends out incremental, reliable updates via multicast messages, providing a more network- and router-friendly environment. EIGRP supports many other features of link state protocols, such as VLSM and route summarization.

BGP is also a hybrid protocol, drawing a lot of its functionality from distance vector protocols. It is based on a standard (RFC 1772) and is used as the de facto routing protocol to interconnect ISPs, and sometimes companies, on the Internet. Unlike most of the other protocols that use multicasts or broadcasts for dissemination, BGP sets up a TCP connection (port 179) to a neighboring peer and uses TCP to share connection information. Like EIGRP and OSPF, BGP supports route summarization. Unlike these protocols, BGP was meant to route between autonomous systems.

on the
Öob *It used to be that running a distance vector protocol such as RIP was sufficient for small to medium networks, given the overhead involved with link state protocols. With the advancement of hardware, distance vector protocols are not commonly used today, even in smaller networks; the most common dynamic IGP protocol is OSPF, with EIGRP a distant second. In small-office/home-office (SOHO) networks, static routes are the most common routing mechanism used.*

CERTIFICATION OBJECTIVE 4.03

Distance Vector Protocol Problems and Solutions

The remainder of this chapter focuses on the problems that pertain to distance vector routing protocols: they converge slowly and they are prone to routing (layer 3) loops. The next few sections cover these problems, as well as present solutions implemented by distance vector protocols to solve these problems.

Problem: Convergence

The term *convergence*, in routing parlance, refers to the time it takes for all of the routers to understand the current topology of the network. Link state protocols tend to converge very quickly, while distance vector protocols tend to converge slowly.

Convergence Example

To understand the issue that distance vector protocols have with convergence, let's look at an example. The network is shown in Figure 4-1. In this example, assume that the periodic timer for the distance vector protocol is set to 60 seconds. Also assume that the distance vector protocol is using hop count as a metric, and no special features are implemented in this example to solve convergence or routing loop problems.

This example has three routers, RouterA, RouterB, and RouterC, where these routers were just turned on. As you can see from the routers' routing tables, the only routes these routers initially know about are their directly connected routes, which they learn by examining the status of their interfaces, making sure that they are *up* and *up*; they then take the network numbers of these interfaces (learned from the configured IP address and subnet mask) and put this information in their routing tables. Currently, each router contains two routes in its routing table. Also notice the metric: these routes have a hop count of 0, since they are directly connected.

FIGURE 4-1   Convergence example after routers are turned on

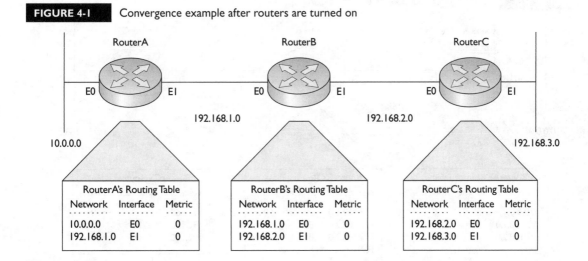

RouterA's Routing Table		
Network	Interface	Metric
10.0.0.0	E0	0
192.168.1.0	E1	0

RouterB's Routing Table		
Network	Interface	Metric
192.168.1.0	E0	0
192.168.2.0	E1	0

RouterC's Routing Table		
Network	Interface	Metric
192.168.2.0	E0	0
192.168.3.0	E1	0

Now that their interfaces are active and the routers have an initial routing table, they'll send out their first routing broadcast on these interfaces (they don't wait for their periodic timer in this instance, since the interfaces just went active). This broadcast contains the entries that they have in their routing tables. Assume that all routers are synchronized when they advertise their routing broadcasts, even though this would be highly unlikely in a production environment. This list shows which routers are advertising which routes on their active interfaces:

- **RouterA** Networks 10.0.0.0 and 192.168.1.0
- **RouterB** Networks 192.168.1.0 and 192.168.2.0
- **RouterC** Networks 192.168.2.0 and 192.168.3.0

After this first exchange of routing tables, each router will process its neighbors' received update and incorporate these changes, if necessary. Figure 4-2 displays the contents of the routing tables on the routers after this first exchange.

Let's break this process down one router at a time, starting with RouterA:

1. Receives networks 192.168.1.0 and 192.168.2.0 from RouterB and increments the metric by one hop for each route.

2. Compares the advertised routes from RouterB to what it has in its routing table.

3. Adds 192.168.2.0 because it is not in the routing table.

FIGURE 4-2   Convergence example after first routing update

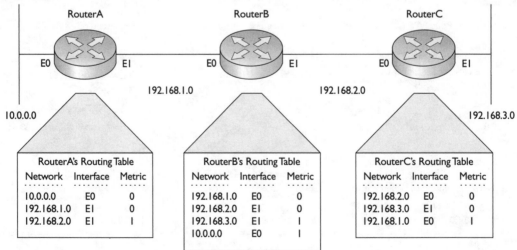

4. Ignores 192.168.1.0 from RouterB because RouterB has a hop count of 1, while the current routing table entry in the routing table has a hop count of 0.

Let's look at RouterC next:

1. Receives networks 192.168.1.0 and 192.168.2.0 from RouterB and increments the metric by one hop.
2. Compares the advertised routes from RouterB to what it has in its routing table.
3. Adds 192.168.1.0 because it is not in the routing table.
4. Ignores 192.168.2.0 from RouterB because RouterB has a hop count of 1 while the current routing table entry has a metric of 0.

RouterB is saved for last, since it presents a more complicated situation: it is receiving routes from both RouterA and RouterB. Here are the steps RouterB goes through:

1. Receives networks 10.0.0.0 and 192.168.1.0 from RouterA and 192.168.2.0 and 192.168.3.0 from RouterC and increments the metric by one hop.
2. Compares the advertised routes from RouterA and RouterC to what it has in its routing table.
3. Adds 10.0.0.0 and 192.168.3.0 because they are not currently in the routing table.
4. Ignores 192.168.1.0 and 192.168.2.0 from RouterA and RouterC, respectively, because RouterA and RouterC have a metric of 1 for these routes, while the current routing table entries have a metric of 0.

Looking at Figure 4-2, have the routers converged? Remember the definition of convergence: the routers understand the complete topology of the network. Given this definition, the routers have not yet converged. RouterA's routing table doesn't contain 192.168.3.0, and RouterC's routing table doesn't contain 10.0.0.0. Note, however, that RouterB has converged, but RouterA and RouterC still need additional routes.

After their periodic timers expire, the routers again generate local routing broadcast updates on each of their interfaces. Again, they broadcast their entire routing tables on these interfaces. Figure 4-3 shows the network after these routers process these new updates. The routers in this network go through the same process again when receiving the updates. Notice that RouterA's routing table now contains

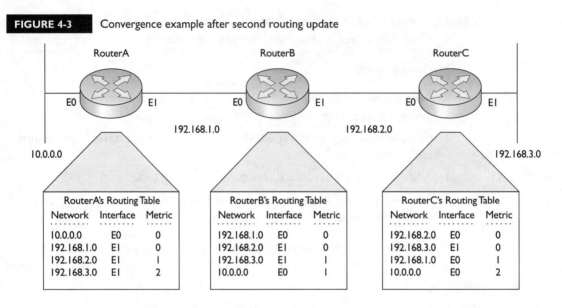

FIGURE 4-3   Convergence example after second routing update

192.168.3.0, with a hop count of 2, while RouterC's routing table contains 10.0.0.0, with a hop count of 2. Both of these routers learned these networks via RouterB. And since these networks have a hop count of 1 on RouterB, when the edge routers receive the routing table from RouterB, they increment the hop count to 2 for these network numbers.

Given the routing tables shown in Figure 4-3, the routers have fully converged. The problem is, however, that convergence took place only after two updates. The first update took place as soon as the interface was active, and the second update took place 60 seconds later. So in this example, it took more than 60 seconds for convergence to occur. You can imagine that if you have a few hundred routers in your network, it might take many minutes before your network converges and each router knows about all of the destinations that are reachable.

Let's use the same network, but assume that RouterA's E0 interface has failed and that RouterA has lost its connection to network 10.0.0.0, as shown in Figure 4-4. As you can see in this example, RouterA's routing table lists the network as unreachable. Unfortunately, RouterA cannot tell the rest of the network about the downed route until its periodic timer expires.

After the timer expires, RouterA advertises its routing table to RouterB, which is shown in Figure 4-5. After RouterB receives its update, it has converged. However, RouterC is still lacking this information about the updated topology and must wait for RouterB's periodic timer to expire in order to receive RouterB's updated routing table.

| FIGURE 4-4 | RouterA's E0 interface has failed. |

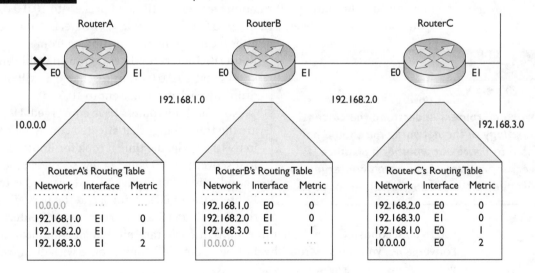

FIGURE 4-4   RouterA's E0 interface has failed.

RouterA   RouterB   RouterC

E0   E1   E0   E1   E0   E1

192.168.1.0   192.168.2.0

10.0.0.0   192.168.3.0

RouterA's Routing Table		
Network	Interface	Metric
10.0.0.0	...	...
192.168.1.0	E1	0
192.168.2.0	E1	1
192.168.3.0	E1	2

RouterB's Routing Table		
Network	Interface	Metric
192.168.1.0	E0	0
192.168.2.0	E1	0
192.168.3.0	E1	1
10.0.0.0	E0	1

RouterC's Routing Table		
Network	Interface	Metric
192.168.2.0	E0	0
192.168.3.0	E1	0
192.168.1.0	E0	1
10.0.0.0	E0	2

FIGURE 4-5   RouterB receives the updated information.

RouterA   RouterB   RouterC

E0   E1   E0   E1   E0   E1

192.168.1.0   192.168.2.0

10.0.0.0   192.168.3.0

RouterA's Routing Table		
Network	Interface	Metric
10.0.0.0	...	...
192.168.1.0	E1	0
192.168.2.0	E1	1
192.168.3.0	E1	2

RouterB's Routing Table		
Network	Interface	Metric
192.168.1.0	E0	0
192.168.2.0	E1	0
192.168.3.0	E1	1
10.0.0.0	...	...

RouterC's Routing Table		
Network	Interface	Metric
192.168.2.0	E0	0
192.168.3.0	E1	0
192.168.1.0	E0	1
10.0.0.0	E0	2

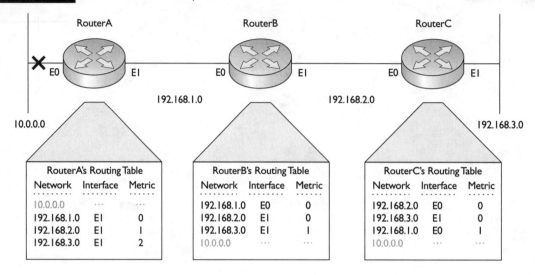

FIGURE 4-6 RouterC receives the updated information.

After RouterB's periodic timer has expired, it shares its routing table with RouterC, as is shown in Figure 4-6. Up to this point, RouterC assumed that it had the most up-to-date routing information and would still send packets to 10.0.0.0, since the routing table indicated that 10.0.0.0 was reachable via RouterB. However, after receiving the routing update from RouterB, RouterC updates its routing table and knows that 10.0.0.0 is not reachable; it will now drop any packets being sent to 10.0.0.0.

Now all three routers have converged. Here are the three things that affected convergence in this example: the time it took for RouterA to discover that E0 failed (a few seconds); the periodic timer on RouterA to advertise this to RouterB (up to 60 seconds); and the periodic timer on RouterB to advertise this to RouterC (up to 60 seconds). Given these three items, it could take more than 2 minutes to converge. As you can see from the past two examples, convergence with distance vector protocols is a slow process.

exam
ⓦatch *Convergence occurs when all routers understand the current topology of the network. You should be able to figure out whether a distance vector protocol has or hasn't converged by examining the routing tables on routers.*

Solution: Triggered Updates

Now that you understand some of the problems associated with convergence in distance vector protocols, consider one possible solution. Given the three things listed in the preceding paragraph that affected convergence with the unreachable network (10.0.0.0), the two things that slowed down convergence are related to periodic timers. You can actually use two solutions to speed convergence: change the periodic timer interval and/or use triggered updates.

The first solution is to change the periodic timer interval. For instance, in our example, the timer was set to 60 seconds. To speed up convergence, you might want to set the interval to 10 seconds. In this example, then, convergence would take only about 20 seconds. However, in today's networks, even waiting this amount of time creates network disruptions. Also, by setting the timer to 10 seconds, you are creating six times the amount of routing broadcast traffic, which is not very efficient.

The second solution is to implement triggered updates. Triggered updates complement periodic updates. The distance vector routing protocol would still generate periodic updates; however, whenever a change took place, the router would immediately generate an update without waiting for the periodic timer to expire. This can decrease convergence times, but it also creates a problem. If you had a flapping route, an update would be triggered each time the route changed state, which would create a lot of unnecessary broadcast traffic in your network and could cause a broadcast storm.

Problem: Routing Loops

The other main problem of distance vector protocols is that they are prone to routing loops. A *routing loop* is a layer 3 loop in the network. Basically, it is a disagreement about how a destination network should be reached.

Routing Loop Example

Let's take a look at a simple example of the kind of problems routing loops can create. Use the network shown in Figure 4-7. In this example, assume that RouterX was originally advertising 192.168.4.0 to RouterA, which passed this on to RouterB. RouterX, though, has failed and is no longer advertising 192.168.4.0. RouterA will eventually learn this by missing routing updates from RouterX. RouterA then incorporates

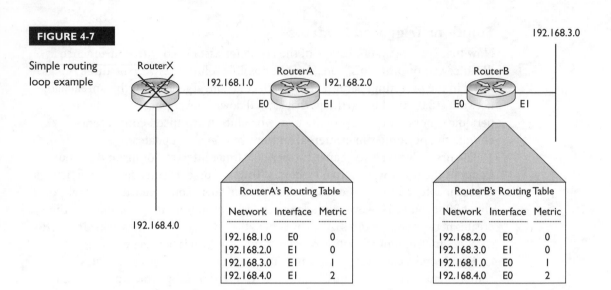

FIGURE 4-7

Simple routing loop example

the change into its routing table. RouterA must then wait for its periodic timer to expire before forwarding this update to RouterB. Before this happens, however, RouterB advertises its routing table to RouterA, which includes the 192.168.4.0 route, making it appear to RouterA that this network is reachable via RouterB. Since both RouterA and RouterB advertise 192.168.4.0 to each other, this creates confusion about how to reach 192.168.4.0, if it can even be reached (and in this case, it can't). In this example, RouterA thinks that to reach 192.168.4.0, it should send these packets to RouterB. RouterB, on the other hand, thinks that to reach 192.168.4.0, it should use RouterA. This is a very simple example of a routing loop. Typically, routing loops are created because of confusion in the network related to the deficiencies of using periodic timers.

Distance vector protocols use several mechanisms to deal with routing loop problems. However, these solutions slow down convergence. Link state and some hybrid protocols deal with routing loops better by using more intelligent methods that don't slow down convergence. The following sections cover the methods that a distance vector protocol might implement to solve routing loop problems.

Counting to Infinity Solution: Maximum Hop Count

One problem with a routing loop is called the *counting to infinity* symptom. When a routing loop occurs and a packet or packets are caught in the loop, they continuously circle around the loop, wasting bandwidth on the segments and CPU cycles on the routers that are processing these packets.

To prevent packets from circling around the loop forever, distance vector protocols typically place a hop count limit as to how far a packet is legally allowed to travel. As a packet travels from router to router, a router keeps track of the hops in the TTL field in the IP datagram header: for each hop a packet goes through, the packet's TTL field is decremented by 1. If this value reaches 0, the packet is dropped by the router that decremented the value from 1 to 0. (The function of the TTL field was covered in your CCENT studies.)

Placing a maximum hop count limitation on packets, however, doesn't solve routing loop problems—the loop still exists. This solution only prevents packets from getting stuck in the loop. Another issue with placing a hop count limit on packets is that, in some instances, the destination that the packet is trying to reach exceeds the maximum hop count allowed. A router doesn't distinguish between valid destinations and routing loop destinations when examining the TTL field; if the maximum is reached, then the packet is dropped.

RIP sets a hop count limit of 14. When a packet comes into an interface of a router, it decrements the TTL field, and if the hop count falls to 0, the router immediately drops the packet. If you have a destination that is beyond these limits, you can change the maximum hop count for your routing protocol; however, you should do this on every router in your network.

Solution: Split Horizon

Distance vector protocols implement a few solutions to deal with routing loops. *Split horizon* is used with small routing loops. Split horizon states that if a neighboring router sends a route to a router, the receiving router will *not* propagate this route back to the advertising router on the same interface.

Consider Figure 4-8 to see how split horizon functions. RouterA advertises 192.168.1.0 to RouterB out its E1 interface. Without split horizon in effect, RouterB could advertise this network right back to RouterA. Obviously, RouterA would ignore this, since the directly connected path is better than RouterB's advertised path. However, what would happen if RouterA's E0 interface failed

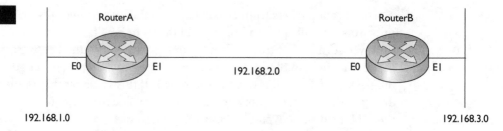

FIGURE 4-8

Split horizon example

192.168.1.0   192.168.2.0   192.168.3.0

and it received an update from RouterB stating that it had an *alternative* path to 192.168.1.0? In this situation, the network obviously has connectivity problems.

With split horizon, though, RouterB would never advertise 192.168.1.0 back to RouterA. Therefore, if RouterA's E0 interface would fail, both RouterA and RouterB would realize that there is no alternative path to reach this network until RouterA's E0 connection is fixed.

ⓦ a t c h *Split horizon prevents a router from advertising a route back out the same interface where the router originally learned the route.*

Solution: Route Poisoning and Hold-Down Timers

While split horizon is used to solve small routing loop problems, distance vector protocols use two mechanisms to deal with large routing loop problems: *route poisoning* and *hold-down timers*. Route poisoning is a derivative of split horizon. When a router detects that one of its connected routes has failed, the router will *poison* the route by assigning an infinite metric to it. In RIP, the route is assigned a hop count of 16 (15, by default, is the maximum), thus making it an *unreachable* network. When a router advertises a poisoned route to its neighbors, its neighbors break the rule of split horizon and send back to the originator the same poisoned route, called a *poison reverse*. This ensures that everyone received the original poisoned route update.

ⓦ a t c h *A poisoned route has an infinite metric assigned to it. A poison reverse causes the router to break the split horizon rule and advertise the poisoned route out all interfaces.*

In order to give the routers enough time to propagate the poisoned route and to ensure that no routing loops occur while propagation of the poisoned route occurs, the routers implement a *hold-down* mechanism. During this period, the routers will freeze the poisoned route in their routing tables for the period of the hold-down timer, which is typically three times the interval of the routing broadcast update.

When hold-down timers are used, a poisoned route will remain in the routing table until the timer expires. However, if a router with a poisoned route receives a routing update from a neighboring router with a metric that is the same or better than the original route, the router will abort the hold-down period, remove the poisoned route, and put the new route in its table. Also, if a router receives a worse route from a neighboring router, the router treats this as a suspect route and assumes that this route is probably part of a routing loop, ignoring the update. Of course, the worse metric route really might be a valid alternative path to the network; however, the function of hold-down timers and poisoning routes prohibits the use of this route until the hold period expires. While in a hold-down state, a poisoned route in the routing table will appear as *possibly down*.

One of the problems of using hold-down timers is that they cause the distance vector routing protocol to converge very slowly—if the hold-down period is 180 seconds, you can't use a valid alternative path with a worse metric until the hold-down period expires. Therefore, your users will lose their connections to this network for at least 3 minutes.

exam

watch   *Hold-down timers are used to keep the poisoned route in the routing table long enough so that the poisoned route has a chance to be propagated to all other routers in the network. One downside to hold-down timers is that they slow down convergence.*

Example of Route Poisoning and Hold-Down Timers

Understanding how poisoned routes and hold-down timers work can become complex. Let's take a look at an example to see how these two mechanisms work hand-in-hand to solve large routing loop problems. Use the network shown in Figure 4-9. In this example, assume the routers are running RIPv1.

In this example, RouterA's E0 interface fails, causing it to lose its connection to 192.168.1.0. Since RIPv1 doesn't use triggered updates, the routing protocol must wait for its periodic timer to expire before broadcasting its routing information to RouterB and RouterC. In RIPv1, the periodic update timer is set to 30 seconds. RouterA will poison the route (assign an infinite metric of 16 to 192.168.1.0) and send this to the other two routers when the periodic update timer expires.

When RouterB and RouterC receive the routing update with the poisoned route from RouterA, they will send back a poison reverse to RouterA. All routers will

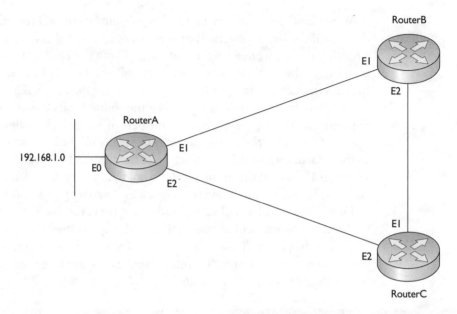

FIGURE 4-9

Route poisoning
and hold-down
timer example

freeze the poisoned route in their routing tables for the period of the hold-down timer. In RIPv1, this defaults to 180 seconds. RouterB and RouterC also advertise the poisoned route in their routing updates out any other active interfaces (once their periodic timers expire). As the propagation of the poisoned route is occurring, the routers that have already received it are counting down from their hold-down timer value.

If another router in the network advertises a worse path to 192.168.1.0 (this has to be a worse hop count than the route originally advertised from RouterA), the three routers shown in the network diagram won't use it, since they have frozen the poisoned route in their routing tables. The reason for this hold-down period is that someone else might be advertising 192.168.1.0, but it might not be a valid path. In other words, another router might be advertising reachability to 192.168.1.0, but it is assuming that this network is reachable via RouterA. In this situation, this rogue router hasn't received the poisoned route—the hold-down timer for the other routers, however, ensures that these rogue routers don't corrupt the routing tables by introducing incorrect or bad routing information, causing a routing loop.

During this process, if RouterA is able to fix its connection to 192.168.1.0, it will start advertising the reachability of the network to RouterB and RouterC. Since the metric RouterA is advertising is the same as the metric it had previously announced for this route, RouterB and RouterC will cancel their hold-down timers and replace the poisoned route with the new information.

INSIDE THE EXAM

Routing Introduction

Understand the basic functions of routers and routed and routing protocols. Knowing the terms in this chapter is very important: know what an autonomous system is, what administrative distance is, and what a metric is. Remember the administrative distances of the different IP routing protocols—be able to pick out what route will show up in the routing protocol based on multiple routing protocols learning the same route.

Dynamic Routing Protocols

Remember the metric components that routing protocols use. Be familiar with how distance vector protocols operate using the Bellman-Ford algorithm, and be able to compare distance

vector and link state protocol characteristics. Know how link state protocols operate through the use of LSAs and how they build a routing table.

Distance Vector Protocol Problems and Solutions

Understand the problems with distance vector protocols and the solutions employed to solve them. Understand how to find a routing loop by examining a routing table, and understand the solutions used to solve routing loop problems: counting to infinity, split horizon, hold-down timers, poisoned routes, and poisoned reverse. Be familiar with these terms and know what they mean.

CERTIFICATION SUMMARY

Routers find layer 3 paths to destination networks and switch packets from one interface to another to get the packets to their respective destinations. Routers learn about neighboring routers, find locations to destination locations, choose the best paths, and maintain up-to-date routing information. A routed protocol is a layer 3 protocol, such as IP or IPX. A routing protocol defines how to find destinations for a routed protocol, such as RIP or OSPF. Some routing protocols, such as EIGRP, use autonomous systems, which group networks under a single administrative control. Administrative distance is used by a Cisco router to choose among multiple routing protocols to put a destination in the routing table.

The routing protocol with the lowest administrative distance with a path to the destination is placed in the routing table.

There are two types of routing protocols: static and dynamic. When choosing a dynamic routing protocol, you should consider routing metrics, how routing information is shared, convergence time, how routing information is processed, and routing overhead. Routing metrics define the method used to calculate a cost to a destination. For instance, RIP uses hop count.

Distance vector protocols use broadcasts to share routing information and don't verify whether neighbors receive routing updates. They use the Bellman-Ford algorithm to process updates, which requires very little CPU processing and memory: They receive an update, increment the metrics, compare the results to the routing table, and update the routing table if necessary.

Link state protocols use the SPF algorithm to build the routing table, providing a loop-free topology. They use multicasts to share routing information incrementally and verify that neighbors received this information. Link state protocols support classless routing and allow you to summarize networking information in your routing table. The main downside of these protocols is that they require more CPU cycles and memory to process and store routing information. They are also prone to flapping route problems.

Hybrid protocols are based on the simplicity of a distance vector protocol but borrow from many features of link state protocols to make them more efficient and scalable. EIGRP and BGP are examples of hybrid protocols.

Distance vector protocols have problems with convergence and routing loops. Convergence is the amount of time it takes for all of the routers in the network to understand the current topology. Triggered updates can be used to speed up convergence. A routing loop is basically a disagreement about how to reach a particular network. Counting to infinity is resolved by placing a hop count limit to prevent packets from circling around the loop forever. Split horizon is used to prevent the creation of small routing loops: It prevents a router from advertising a route out the same interface from which the route was learned.

Route poisoning, poison reverse, and hold-down timers are used to prevent large routing loops. A route is poisoned if a network connected to a router goes down. Poison reverse has a router advertise a poisoned route out all interfaces, including the interface from which it was learned. Hold-down timers keep the poisoned route in the routing table to ensure the poisoned route is propagated to all routers before any (worse) alternative paths are chosen.

✔ TWO-MINUTE DRILL

Routing Introduction

❑ Routers learn about neighboring routers, find locations of destination networks, choose the best paths to each destination, and maintain routing tables.

❑ A static route is a manually configured route. A connected route is a network to which the router is directly connected on an interface.

❑ An autonomous system (AS) is a group of networks under a single administrative control, which could be your company, a division within your company, or a group of companies.

❑ Administrative distance is a Cisco-proprietary mechanism used to rank IP routing protocols, and it helps the router populate the routing table with the best paths to destinations. If you are running more than one routing protocol, administrative distance can determine which routing protocol to use when populating the routing table. The lower the administrative distance number, the more preferred the protocol.

Dynamic Routing Protocols

❑ Internally, a routing protocol will use a metric to choose a best path to reach a destination when more than one path exists to a destination within the same routing protocol.

❑ Distance vector protocols, such as RIPv1, use distance and direction to find paths to a destination and are referred to as routing by rumor. They generate periodic updates as broadcasts and build no formal relationships with other routers. They require little processing and memory, since they simply need to increment metrics and compare these to current networks in the routing table.

❑ Link state protocols, such as OSPF, use the SPF algorithm and understand the complete topology of the network (routing by propaganda). They multicast LSAs, which are specific routes, when changes occur in the network. The LSAs are stored in a link state database. These protocols converge fast, since they use incremental updates, but they require more memory and processing power. They also support a hierarchical structure and route summarization.

❏ Hybrid protocols, such as RIPv2 and EIGRP, take the advantages of both distance vector and link state protocols and merge them together.

Distance Vector Protocol Problems and Solutions

❏ Distance vector protocols converge slowly because of periodic updates. Some protocols overcome this by using triggered updates.

❏ Distance vector protocols are prone to routing loops. To solve this, they use these mechanisms: hop count limits, split horizon, poisoned routes, and hold-down timers.

❏ To prevent packets from circling around the loop forever, distance vector protocols typically place a hop count limit as to how far a packet is legally allowed to travel, referred to as maximum hop count or TTL.

❏ Split horizon states that if a neighboring router sends a route to a router, the receiving router will not propagate this route back to the advertising router on the same interface.

❏ With route poisoning, when a router detects that one of its connected routes has failed, the router will *poison* the route by assigning an infinite metric to it and advertising it to neighbors. When a router advertises a poisoned route to its neighbors, its neighbors break the rule of split horizon and send back to the originator the same poisoned route, called a *poison reverse*. In order to give the routers enough time to propagate the poisoned route and to ensure that no routing loops occur while propagation occurs, the routers implement a hold-down mechanism.

SELF TEST

The following Self Test questions will help you measure your understanding of the material presented in this chapter. Read all the choices carefully, as there may be more than one correct answer. Choose all correct answers for each question.

Routing Introduction

1. _____ is/are a routed protocol.
   A. RIP
   B. OSPF
   C. Both RIP and OSPF
   D. Neither RIP nor OSPF

2. A(n) _____ routes between different autonomous systems.
   A. BPG
   B. EGP
   C. IPP
   D. IGP

3. Your router is running RIP and OSPF, and both routing protocols are learning 192.168.1.0/24. Which routing protocol will your router use for this route?
   A. RIP
   B. OSPF

Dynamic Routing Protocols

4. A routing protocol will use a(n) _____ to determine which path is the best path.
   A. administrative distance
   B. metric
   C. hop count
   D. cost

5. Which type of routing protocol uses the Shortest Path First algorithm?
   A. Distance vector
   B. Link state
   C. Hybrid

6. Which is an example of a hybrid protocol?
   A. IS-IS
   B. EIGRP
   C. RIPv1
   D. OSPF

Distance Vector Protocol Problems and Solutions

7. What would you use to prevent a packet from traveling around a routing loop forever?
   A. Split horizon
   B. Poison reverse
   C. Hold-down timer
   D. TTL

8. _____ states that if a neighboring router sends a route to a router, the receiving router will not propagate this route back to the advertising router on the same interface.
   A. Split horizon
   B. Poison reverse
   C. Hold-down timer
   D. Hop count limit

9. How would you know that a route has been poisoned in the routing table?
   A. It has a metric of 0 assigned to it.
   B. It has an infinite metric assigned to it.
   C. It has an administrative distance of 0 assigned to it.
   D. It has an infinite administrative distance assigned to it.

10. You are 10 hops away from a destination network and intermediate routers are running RIP as a routing protocol. You ping a host in the destination network, but the ICMP message you receive back is "TTL expired in transit." What could cause this problem?
    A. A link is down between an intermediate router and the destination network.
    B. There is a mismatch in the administrative distances of RIP.
    C. A routing loop exists.
    D. The destination host has a physical layer problem.

SELF TEST ANSWERS

Routing Introduction

1.   ☑   **D.** RIP and OSPF are *routing* protocols, not *routed* protocols. Routed protocols are TCP/IP, IPX, AppleTalk, and so on.
     ☒   Answers **A, B,** and **C** are routing protocols, not routed protocols.

2.   ☑   **B.** An Exterior Gateway Protocol (EGP) routes between autonomous systems.
     ☒   **D** routes within an AS. **A** and **C** are nonexistent routing protocols.

3.   ☑   **B.** OSPF has a lower administrative distance of 110. The lower one is given preference.
     ☒   **A** is incorrect because it has a higher administrative distance of 120.

Dynamic Routing Protocols

4.   ☑   **B.** A routing protocol will use a metric to determine which path is the best path.
     ☒   **A** is incorrect because administrative distance is used to choose between different routing protocols, not within a routing protocol. Answers **C** and **D** are types of metrics.

5.   ☑   **B.** Link state protocols use the SPF algorithm, developed by Dijkstra, to choose the best path to a destination.
     ☒   **A** is incorrect because a distance vector uses distance and direction when choosing best paths. **C** is incorrect because hybrid protocols typically use methods based on distance vector protocols.

6.   ☑   **B.** EIGRP is a hybrid protocol, along with RIPv2.
     ☒   **A** and **D** are incorrect because IS-IS and OSPF are link state protocols. **C** is incorrect because RIPv1 is a distance vector protocol.

Distance Vector Protocol Problems and Solutions

7.   ☑   **D.** TTL, which implements a hop count limit, prevents an IP packet from traveling around a routing loop forever.
     ☒   **A** is incorrect because a split horizon is used to prevent small routing loops, preventing the advertisement of a route out the same interface it was learned on. **B** and **C** are used to prevent large routing loops: they allow network stabilization by waiting until every router learns about the downed route before accepting an alternative path.

8. ☑ **A.** Split horizon is used to prevent small routing loops, preventing the advertisement of a route out the same interface on which it was learned.

   ☒ **B** is incorrect because poison reverse assigns an infinite metric to the route, sends it to a neighboring router, and has the neighbor advertise this back to you. **C** is incorrect because a hold-down timer sets a timer that a poisoned route is held in the routing table. **D** is incorrect because a hop count limit is used to prevent a packet from traveling around a routing loop forever.

9. ☑ **B.** A poisoned route has an infinite metric assigned to it.

   ☒ **A** is incorrect because this would be a directly connected route. Administrative distance ranks different routing protocols, making **C** and **D** incorrect as well.

10. ☑ **C.** If you see a "TTL expired in transit" ICMP message, either the destination is more hops away than the routing protocol supports or a routing loop exists (RIP supports up to 15 hops).

    ☒ **A** and **D** are incorrect because you would receive a network or destination unreachable message from an intermediate router if these were true. **B** is incorrect because administrative distance is used to rank local routing protocols to choose which network is placed in a routing table when two routing protocols tell you about the same network.

5

VLSM

I n your CCENT studies you were introduced to IP addressing and subnetting, including such topics as classes of addresses, address components (network, host, and directed broadcast), and IP address planning. This chapter expands on the topic of IP addressing and introduces two new subjects: *Variable Length Subnet Masking* (VLSM) and route summarization. Because both of these topics expand upon the information you learned in your CCENT studies if you are still trying to grasp the mechanics of IP addressing, please re-examine your studies on IP addressing and practice some more before proceeding to this chapter. You'll need a solid understanding of subnetting to perform VLSM tasks and/or route summarization.

CERTIFICATION OBJECTIVE 5.01

VLSM

VLSM, originally defined in RFC 1812, allows you to apply *different* subnet masks to the *same* class address space. For instance, a good mask for point-to-point links is 255.255.255.252, which provides for two host addresses in each subnet. A good mask for a LAN connection might be 255.255.255.192, which provides for 62 host addresses for each network segment. Using a 255.255.255.252 mask for a LAN connection will not give you enough host addresses, and using a 255.255.255.192 mask on a point-to-point connection wastes addresses. One solution would be to divide the mask values in the middle to limit the waste of addresses, but this doesn't scale well. VLSM solves this problem by letting you use different subnet mask values on the *same* class address space. The following sections cover the advantages that VLSM provides, as well as how to use VLSM in your own network.

w a t c h   ***Remember that the best subnet mask for point-to-point links is 255.255.255.252 (/30).***

Features of VLSM

VLSM lets you have more than one mask for a given class of address, be it a Class A, B, or C network number. Classful protocols, such as Routing Information Protocol (RIP) v1, do not support VLSM. Deploying VLSM requires a routing protocol that is *classless*—Border Gateway Protocol (BGP), Enhanced Interior Gateway Routing

Protocol (EIGRP), Intermediate System-Intermediate System (IS-IS), Open Shortest Path First (OSPF), or RIPv2, for instance. VLSM provides two major advantages:

- Efficient use of addressing in large-scale networks
- Ability to perform route summarization, or route aggregation, to reduce the size of the routing tables in your routers

exam

🅦 **atch** *VLSM allows you to use more than one subnet mask for a given class address. Remember the two major advantages of VLSM: more efficient use of addresses, and route summarization/ aggregation.*

As these advantage points suggest, VLSM allows you to make more efficient use of IP addressing. Figure 5-1 shows a simple before-and-after example of using VLSM. In this example, a router at the corporate site (RouterA) has point-to-point WAN connections to the remote office routers (RouterB, RouterC, and RouterD). The LAN segments at these remote sites have about 50 devices (thus, the /26 mask). In the *before*

FIGURE 5-1 Using VLSM

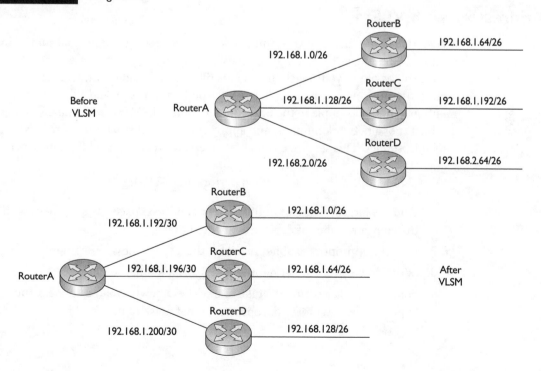

design, a single subnet mask is chosen—255.255.255.192—which allows 62 hosts per subnet. Because of the number of segments, two Class C networks are needed. On the WAN segments, this wastes a lot of addressing space, since you need only two host addresses on a point-to-point link.

The bottom part of Figure 5-1 shows a more efficient use of addressing by using VLSM. In this example, the three remote sites have a 255.255.255.192 mask, but the last subnet, 192.168.1.192/26, is assigned a *different* subnet mask. And these little subnetted subnets are then assigned to the point-to-point links of the WAN connections. Given the VLSM solution, only one Class C network is needed to assign addressing to this network. The second advantage of VLSM, route summarization, is discussed later in this chapter.

on the
(i)ob   *The way subnet zero should be used when performing VLSM is divided into two camps of people. Half prefer using subnet zero as the "subnetted subnet." This was a popular choice a while back when certain operating systems didn't necessarily support subnet zero, but network equipment, such as routers, could. The other half say that today it doesn't matter, since all modern TCP/IP stacks (even those for desktops, laptops, and mobile devices) support subnet 0.*

Addressing with VLSM

To use VLSM, you must be very familiar with IP addressing and normal subnetting, as discussed in the last chapter. If you have not yet fully grasped these concepts, VLSM will be out of your reach. If you are still uncomfortable with IP addressing and subnetting, review your CCNET studies on IP addressing and subnetting. As mentioned in the example in the preceding section, VLSM basically means taking a subnet (not a network number) and applying a different subnet mask to this, and only this, subnet. This section covers how to create an efficient addressing scheme using VLSM.

You should follow these steps when performing VLSM:

1. Find the largest segment in the network address space—the segment with the largest number of devices connected to it.

2. Find the appropriate subnet mask for the largest network segment.

3. Write down your subnet numbers to fit your subnet mask.

4. For your smaller segments, take one of these newly created subnets and apply a different, more appropriate, subnet mask to it.

5. Write down your newly subnetted subnets.

6. For even smaller segments, go back to step 4 and repeat this process.

Actually, you can take a subnetted subnet and subnet it again! With this process, you can come up with a very efficient addressing scheme to accommodate addressing needs in your network.

Here's an example: Assume that you have a Class C network (192.168.1.0/24) and three LAN segments—one with 120 hosts, one with 60 hosts, and one with 30 hosts. Assume that subnet 0 is valid. In steps 1 and 2, you find the largest segment and an appropriate subnet mask for it. This would be the segment with 120 hosts. To accommodate the 120 hosts, you would need a subnet mask of 192.168.1.0/25. If you recall from Chapter 6, a /25 subnet mask is 255.255.255.128 in decimal, and with a Class C network, this provides for two subnets with 126 host addresses each. In step 3, write down the newly created subnets: 192.168.1.0/25 and 192.168.1.128/25. You'll assign the first subnet to the large LAN segment. You now have two segments left: one with 60 hosts and one with 30 hosts. Again, start with the larger segment. Next, perform step 4. Which subnet mask is appropriate for 60 devices? If you guessed /26 (255.255.255.192), then you guessed correctly—this gives you 62 host addresses. Apply this subnet mask to the original *remaining* subnet. In step 5, you write down your newly created subnetted subnets by subnetting 192.168.1.128/25: 192.168.1.128/26 and 192.168.1.192/26. Then assign 192.168.1.128/26 to the segment with 60 devices.

This leaves you with one extra subnet. You could easily assign it to this segment, but this segment needs only 30 hosts and the mask has 62 hosts, which is not the most efficient mask. If you want, you can go back to step 4 and repeat the process for this subnet. The subnet mask /27 (255.255.255.224) is a subnet mask that results in 30 host addresses, resulting in two more smaller subnets from the original 192.168.1.192/26 subnet: 192.168.1.192/27 and 192.168.1.224/27. In this example, you have one extra subnet remaining that you could use for future growth! As you can see, with VLSM, you can be very efficient in your IP addressing design.

on the
Ｏｏｂ *You should leave room in each subnet for future growth. For instance, in the preceding example, using a mask of /27 on the 192.168.1.192 subnet creates two more subnets, each with 30 host addresses. If you use this address scheme and the 30-host segment grows, you'll have to go back and re-address a portion of your network, which is not fun.*

VLSM Example 1

Now that you understand the basics of performing VLSM, let's look at a more difficult example. Consider the network shown in Figure 5-2. In this example, you are given a Class C network: 192.168.2.0/24. You are tasked with using VLSM to accommodate the following requirements: Each remote site (total of seven sites) has no more than 30 hosts, and this isn't expected to grow in the future. The links between the central and remote routers are point-to-point connections.

You first need to be concerned with handling the largest segments, which are the remote sites with 30 hosts. To handle 30 hosts, you need a 225.255.255.224 (/27) subnet mask. This mask results in the following subnets: 192.168.2.0/27, 192.168.2.32/27, 192.168.2.64/27, 192.168.2.96/27, 192.168.2.128/27, 192.168.2.160/27, 192.168.2.192/27, and 192.168.2.224/27. Assume that subnet 0 is valid for this example.

FIGURE 5-2

VLSM example 1

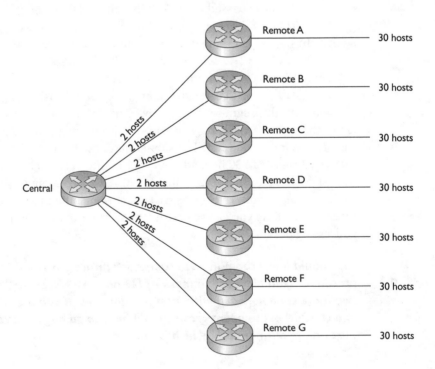

With a /27 mask, you have actually created eight subnets; however, you need only seven for the remote offices. This leaves you with one remaining subnet, but you still need to address the seven point-to-point links between the central and remote routers.

Assign the first seven subnets for the remote LAN segments, and use the last subnet (192.168.2.224/27) for VLSM and the point-to-point links. To accommodate the point-to-point links, use a 255.255.255.252 (/30) subnet mask, which results in the following subnetted subnets: 192.168.2.224/30, 192.168.2.228/30, 192.168.2.232/30, 192.168.2.236/30, 192.168.2.240/30, 192.168.2.244/30, 192.168.2.248/30, and 192.168.2.252/30.

With a /30 mask on the 192.168.2.224 subnet, you have created eight little subnets with two hosts each. You need only seven subnets for the point-to-point links, which leaves one small subnet remaining. Figure 5-3 shows the actual networking layout based on this example. Notice that this example used two subnet mask values, 255.255.255.224 and 255.255.255.252, with the same Class C network, 192.168.2.0/24.

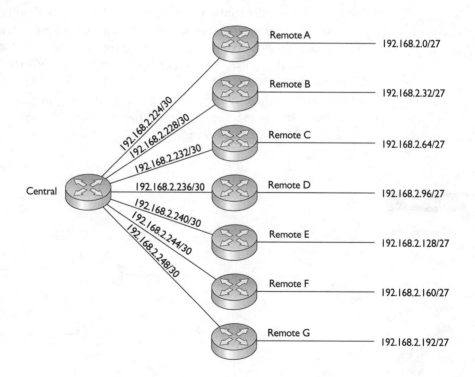

FIGURE 5-3

VLSM example 1 address design

VLSM Example 2

Here's another example, shown in Figure 5-4. You have been given a Class C network, 192.168.3.0/24, with the addressing requirements shown in the figure. You need to come up with a VLSM solution to accommodate all of the network segments with the single Class C network.

The first subnet of concern is the backbone router segment, since it is the largest: It requires 126 host addresses. Therefore, you will need to use a subnet mask that accommodates 126 hosts: 255.255.255.128 (/25). This subnet mask results in two subnets: 192.168.3.0/25 and 192.168.3.128/25. Assign the first subnet to the backbone router, leaving the second subnet for further subnetting with VLSM.

You next need to be concerned about the second largest subnet: the smaller router LAN segments. Each of these locations needs networks that will accommodate 30 host addresses. Take the remaining subnet (192.168.3.128/25) and apply a mask to it that will provide your remote site's addresses. The mask of 255.255.255.224 (/27) will do this for you, resulting in the following subnets: 192.168.3.128/27, 192.168.3.160/27, 192.168.3.192/27, and 192.168.3.224/27.

You now have four subnets, with 30 host addresses each. Assign the first three subnets to your smaller router LAN segments. Use the remaining subnet for your router-to-router connections. These links need six host addresses each. A 255.255.255.248 (/29) subnet mask will accommodate your addressing needs. Applying this to the fourth subnet results in the following smaller subnets: 192.168.3.224/29, 192.168.3.232/29, 192.168.3.240/29, and 192.168.3.248/29. You need only three of these subnets, leaving one for future growth. In all, this network design, shown in Figure 5-5, used three different subnet masks: 255.255.255.128, 255.255.255.224, and 255.255.255.248.

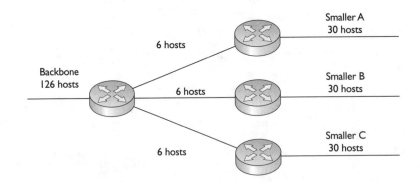

FIGURE 5-4

VLSM example 2

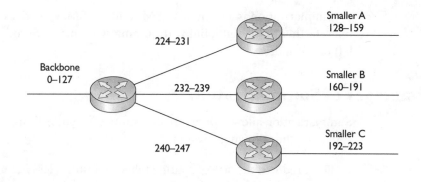

FIGURE 5-5

VLSM example 2
address design

Backbone
0–127

224–231

232–239

240–247

Smaller A
128–159

Smaller B
160–191

Smaller C
192–223

CERTIFICATION OBJECTIVE 5.02

Route Summarization

Route summarization is the ability to take a bunch of contiguous network numbers in your routing table and advertise these contiguous routes as a single summarized or aggregated route. VLSM allows you to summarize subnetted routes back to the class boundary. For instance, if you have 192.168.1.0/24 and have subnetted it to 192.168.1.0/26, giving you four networks, you could summarize these subnets in your routing table and advertise them as the Class C network number 192.168.1.0/24, as shown in Figure 5-6. In this example, the routing entries are reduced from four down to one in your routing updates. Notice in the preceding example that the same class network, 192.168.1.0, has two masks associated with it: 255.255.255.192 and 255.255.255.0.

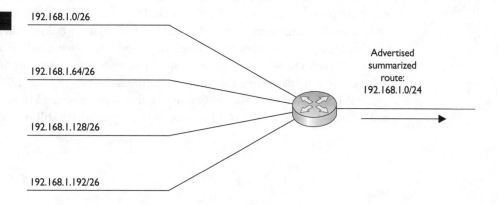

FIGURE 5-6

Simple route
summarization
example

192.168.1.0/26

192.168.1.64/26

192.168.1.128/26

192.168.1.192/26

Advertised
summarized
route:
192.168.1.0/24

Summarization is a form of VLSM. With VLSM, you are extending the subnet mask farther to the right, but with summarization, you're collapsing it back to the left of the address.

Advantages of Summarization

Summarization allows you to create a more efficient routing environment by providing the following advantages:

- It reduces the size of routing tables, requiring less memory and processing.
- It reduces the size of routing updates, requiring less bandwidth.
- It contains network problems such as routing flapping.

As you can see from the design shown in Figure 5-6, the size of the routing table update was reduced from four routes to one route, which requires less processing for any routers receiving this information. Thus, less bandwidth is required to advertise the update, and less memory and processing are required on the receiving routers to process the update.

Another advantage of route summarization is that it helps contain certain kinds of network problems. For example, assume that the device advertising the 192.168.1.64/26 subnet was going up and down, up and down, causing a condition called a flapping route. This condition obviously affects the connected router and any router that knows about this specific subnet: Every time the route goes up or down, other routers have to incorporate the change in their routing tables. However, routers that know only the summarized route are not affected by the subnet that is flapping. For these routers to be affected, all four subnets would have to fail, causing the router performing the summarization to stop advertising the summarized route.

This, obviously, is an advantage, but it does have a downside. Route summarization *hides* the complete picture of the network. This can cause routers to make bad assumptions. For instance, assume that 192.168.1.64/26 really is down but that routers in another part of the network are still receiving updates concerning the summarized route (192.168.1.0/24). From their perspective, since the router summarizing the route is still advertising this route, all addresses from 192.168.1.0 through 192.168.1.255 must be available. Obviously, this is not true, and thus other routers will still send traffic to 192.168.1.64/26, since they think it's still reachable.

You should be able to define route summarization: taking a bunch of contiguous network numbers in a routing table and reducing them to a smaller number of routing entries. Route summarization benefits include smaller routing tables and updates and containment of networking problems.

Classless Interdomain Routing

Classless Interdomain Routing (CIDR), specified in RFC 2050, is an extension to VLSM and route summarization. With VLSM, you can summarize subnets back to the Class A, B, or C network boundary. For example, if you have a Class C network 192.168.1.0/24 and subnet it with a 26-bit mask, you have created four subnets. Using VLSM and summarization, you can summarize these four subnets back to 192.168.1.0/24. CIDR takes this one step further and allows you to summarize a block of contiguous Class A, B, and/or C network numbers. This practice is commonly referred to as *supernetting*. Today's classless protocols support supernetting. However, it is most commonly configured by ISPs on the Internet who use BGP as a routing protocol.

Figure 5-7 shows an example of CIDR. In this example, a router is connected to four Class C networks: 192.168.0.0/24, 192.168.1.0/24, 192.168.2.0/24, and 192.168.3.0/24. The router is summarizing these routes into a single entry: 192.168.0.0/22. Table 5-1 illustrates the bits that are in common in this example.

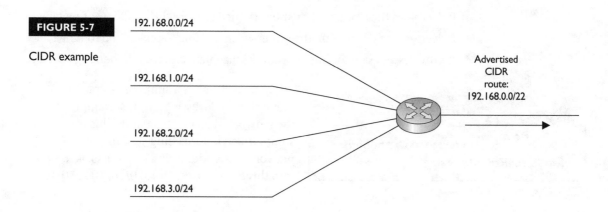

FIGURE 5-7

CIDR example

192.168.0.0/24

192.168.1.0/24

192.168.2.0/24

192.168.3.0/24

Advertised CIDR route: 192.168.0.0/22

TABLE 5-1	Third Octet Bits							
Common Bits in Summarization	192.168.0.0	0	0	0	0	0	0	0	0
	192.168.1.0	0	0	0	0	0	0	0	1
	192.168.2.0	0	0	0	0	0	0	1	0
	192.168.3.0	0	0	0	0	0	0	1	1
	Bits in Common								

e x a m

ⓦ a t c h   *CIDR is similar to VLSM, in that CIDR allows you to summarize multiple contiguous class networks together, like multiple Class C networks. This is also called supernetting.*

In the first 2 bytes, all bits in the four networks match (192.168). In the third octet, the first 6 bits match, totaling 22 bits. Notice the subnet mask for this summarization: 255.255.252.0. This mask, along with the beginning network, 192.168.0.0, includes addresses from 192.168.0.0 to 192.168.3.255, which are behind this router.

Hierarchical Addressing

To perform route summarization, you will need to set up your addressing in a hierarchical fashion. Hierarchical addressing provides the following benefits:

- It enables more efficient routing.
- It uses route summarization to decrease the size of routing tables.
- It decreases the amount of memory needed to store the smaller routing tables.
- It decreases the impact on the router when needing to rebuild the routing table.
- It provides a design to simplify your management and troubleshooting process.

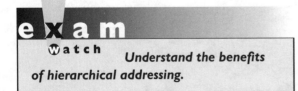

e x a m

ⓦ a t c h   *Understand the benefits of hierarchical addressing.*

Figure 5-8 shows a simple example of hierarchical addressing. In this example, the network is using 10.0.0.0/8. This is summarized before being sent to another network. This addressing space is broken up into three campuses: 10.1.0.0/16, 10.2.0.0/16,

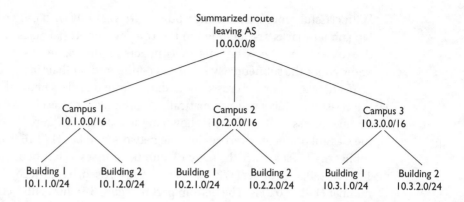

FIGURE 5-8

Simple hierarchical addressing example

and 10.3.0.0.16. Each of these sets of addresses is summarized when sharing routes between the campuses. Within each campus, the addressing is further broken up for the two buildings: 10.x.1.0/24, 10.x.2.0/24, and so on.

To implement a hierarchical addressing design and to take advantage of route summarization, you'll need a routing protocol that supports VLSM: BGP, EIGRP, IS-IS, OSPF, or RIPv2. When implementing route summarization, you'll need to consider the following:

■ The routing protocol must carry the subnet mask with the corresponding network entries it will be advertising.

■ Routing decisions must be made on the entire destination IP address.

■ To summarize routing entries, they must have the same highest order matching bits (see Table 5-1 as an example).

Routing and Subnet Masks

As mentioned in the preceding section, the routing protocol must carry the subnet mask with the corresponding network entries if you want to take advantage of route summarization. Otherwise, if you had more than one subnet mask applied to a class network number, the router wouldn't know which mask to use when routing a packet to a destination.

A good example of this problem is apparent in classful protocols, such as RIPv1, and how you lay out your IP addresses in your network.

With classful protocols, routing updates are sent out with only network entries: No subnet masks are included in the routing updates. The assumption is that the routers on other segments are connected to the same class network and thus know about the subnet mask since it is configured on their interfaces.

If a network number crosses boundaries from one class network to another, the classful protocol will automatically summarize it to the class address network number (Class A, B, or C), as is shown in the top part of Figure 5-9. As you can see, the classful protocol advertises just the network number (172.16.0.0) without any subnet mask. Plus, since the network number crosses a class boundary (172.16.0.0 to 192.168.1.0), the subnet (172.16.1.0) is not advertised, but instead, the class network number (172.16.0.0) is. The bottom part of Figure 5-9 shows how classless protocols react when crossing a class boundary (either by default or with configuration). Notice two things: The subnet mask is included in the routing update, and the routing update is *not* automatically summarized across the class boundary.

on the **!** **Job** *RIPv2 and EIGRP act as classful protocols by default and will, therefore, automatically summarize across network class boundaries; this can be manually disabled. You can also configure specific summarized routes. OSPF, on the other hand, acts as a classless protocol by default and will not automatically summarize any type of routing information; with OSPF, you must manually configure summarization.*

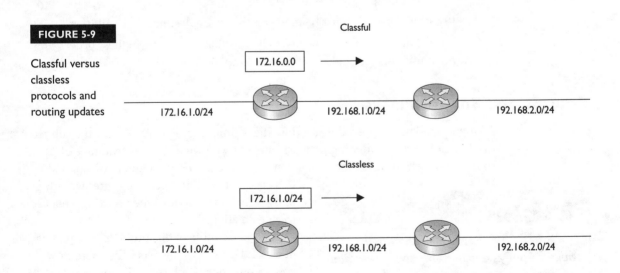

FIGURE 5-9

Classful versus classless protocols and routing updates

Given the routing behavior of classful routing protocols, certain addressing designs will create problems. Consider the network shown in the top part of Figure 5-10. With a classful protocol like RIPv1, the routers, when advertising networks across a class boundary, summarize the networks back to their class boundary. In this example, both RouterA and RouterB advertise 172.16.0.0—they don't advertise their specific subnets for 172.16.0.0. This creates a problem with RouterC, which receives two routes for 172.16.0.0. If RouterC wanted to reach 172.16.1.0/24, it really wouldn't know to which router (RouterA or RouterB) to send its packets.

Actually, it's a bit more complicated than this. For a basic RIP implementation, the last update received by RouterC would be placed in the route table, and the packet would be delivered out the interface to that router. However, half the time, it would go to RouterA, and the other half to RouterB, depending on when the route updates were received by RouterC. Were EIGRP used as a routing protocol, though, the metric might make one route better than another, and every packet would go to the one associated with the best metric.

This network design is referred to as a *discontiguous* subnet design—not all of the subnets are connected together. In this network, 172.16.1.0/24 and 172.16.2.0/24

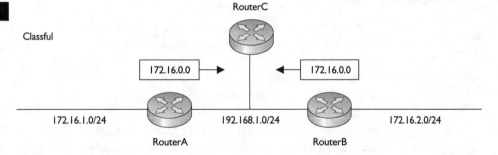

FIGURE 5-10

Discontiguous
subnets

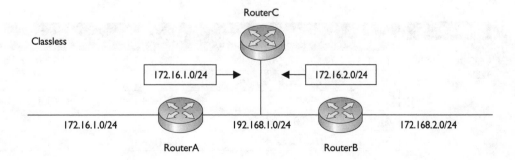

are not connected via another 172.16.0.0 subnet number. This creates routing problems for other routers not connected to the 172.16.0.0 network, and therefore, discontiguous subnet designs are not recommended with classful protocols.

Discontiguous subnets *are*, however, supported by *classless* protocols. As is shown in the bottom part of Figure 5-10, classless protocols include the subnet mask in the routing updates. In this example, RouterC knows exactly where 172.16.1.0/24 and 172.16.2.0/24 are located, since the mask is included in the routing updates.

Discontiguous subnets are not supported by classful protocols, but are supported by classless protocols. Classful protocols do not include the subnet mask when advertising network and subnet numbers.

However, discontiguous subnets are not recommended even with classless protocols, since they limit your ability to summarize routing information in the most efficient fashion. Routing protocols and how routing tables are built are covered in Chapters 4, 9, 10, and 11. For now, keep in mind the main point here: Classful routing protocols always advertise the classful network number across network boundaries.

The Routing Table

When implementing route summarization, you'll also need to consider that routing decisions made by a router must be made on the entire destination IP address in the IP packet header. The router always uses the longest matching prefix in the routing table to perform its routing decision. I'll use the routing table in Table 5-2 to illustrate a router's decision-making process.

A router receives an inbound packet on one of its interfaces and examines the destination IP address in the packet header: in this case, 172.16.17.65. The router then needs to examine its routing table and find the *best* match for this packet, and then it routes the packet out the corresponding interface to reach the destination.

TABLE 5-2	Entry	Network Destination	Next-Hop Address	Local Interface
Example Routing Table	1	172.16.17.66/32	172.16.1.1	E1
	2	172.16.17.64/24	172.16.2.1	E2
	3	172.16.17.0/24	172.16.3.1	E3
	4	172.16.0.0/16	172.16.2.1	E2
	5	0.0.0.0/0	172.16.4.1	E4

The router will basically sort the entries in the routing table by the most specific bits in a mask to the least number of bits when matching a destination address.

In the preceding routing table, entry 1 isn't a valid match since the mask for the entry indicates a *host* address (32-bit subnet mask). When comparing all 32 bits of 172.16.17.66 with all 32 bits of 172.16.17.65, no match is found. Typically, host address routes are placed in the routing table whenever you have moved a host from its native network segment to another, but, for logistical purposes, you cannot change the address on the host to correspond to its new segment. In other words, you need this host to retain its old IP address.

When comparing entry 2 in the routing table, the router is comparing the first 27 bits of 172.16.17.64 with the first 27 bits of 172.16.17.65, which *do* match. When comparing entry 3, the router compares the first 24 bits of 172.16.17.0 with the first 24 bits of 172.16.17.64, which *also* match. When comparing entry 4, the router compares the first 16 bits of 172.16.0.0 with the first 16 bits of 172.16.17.65, which also match.

When comparing entry 5, the router finds that the entry is a default route and matches any packet. Given this example, the first entry doesn't match, but the last four do match. The router needs to pick *one* entry and use it to route the packet to the destination. When picking an entry, the router uses the one that best matches—the one with the longest number of matching bits. Therefore, the router will use entry 2 in the routing table to route this packet to the corresponding destination.

Many vendors' routers, including Cisco, allow you to place the same destination more than once in the routing table when there are multiple paths to reach that destination. For example, RouterA might be able to reach 192.168.1.0/24 via RouterB and RouterC. In this situation, RouterA could have two entries for 192.168.1.0/24 in its routing table. When multiple paths to the same destination exist in the routing table, vendors load-share traffic by sending each connection via one path (load-sharing packets is not recommended, since it can cause problems with security devices like firewalls). So, for example, telnet traffic from HostA to HostB (in 192.168.1.0/24) would always be routed to the same next-hop neighbor, like RouterB.

Performing Summarization

As mentioned earlier, to summarize routing entries, they must have the same highest order matching bits. In other words, you can perform summarization when the network numbers in question fall within a range of a power-of-2 number—such as 2, 4, 8, 16, and so on—or within a range of a multiple of a power of 2. For example, assume a network number is 4, which is a power of 2. Valid multiples of this value would be 4, 8, 12, 16, and so on. So with network 4, you could include networks 4, 5, 6, and 7 with the correct summarization mask. The network boundary is based on the subnet mask.

For example, if you have a subnet mask of 255.255.255.240, you cannot start the summarization on a network number that is not a multiple of 16 (the number of addresses in a network accommodated by a mask of /28). For instance, 192.168.1.16/28 is a valid summarization for this mask, while 192.168.1.8/28 is not (it doesn't start on a multiple of 16). If the increment is not a power of 2 or a multiple of a power of 2, you can sometimes summarize the addresses into a set of smaller routes. The list of power-of-2 numbers in this case is 0, 2, 4, 8, 16, 32, 64, and 128. Also, when performing summarization, you want to make sure that *all* of the routes that are aggregated are associated with the router (or behind the router) that is advertising the summarized route.

Summarization and Powers of 2

When summarizing, however, remember that you can summarize routes only on a bit boundary (power of 2) or a multiple of a power-of-2 boundary. The trick to summarization is to look at your subnet mask options: 0, 128, 192, 224, 240, 248, 252, 254, and 255. Each of these masks covers a range of numbers, as is shown in Table 5-3. For instance, suppose you have a set of Class C subnets: 192.168.1.0/30 and 192.168.1.4/30. These networks contain a total of eight addresses and start on a power-of-2 boundary: 0. Therefore, you could summarize these as 192.168.1.0/29, which encompasses addresses from 192.168.1.0 through 192.168.1.7.

Let's take a look at another example. Say you have a set of Class C subnets: 192.168.1.64/26 and 192.168.1.128/26. Each of these networks has 64 addresses, for a total of 128 addresses. A mask value that accommodates 128 addresses in a Class C network is 255.255.255.128 (25 bits). However, this subnet mask poses a problem, since the bit value must be a power of 2 *and* start on a power-of-2 network boundary. With a 25-bit mask, there are only two network numbers: 192.168.1.0/25 and 192.168.1.128/25. The address 192.168.1.64/26 falls under the first network number, and the address 192.168.1.128/26 falls under the second one—so even though

TABLE 5-3	Mask Value	Range of Numbers	Number of Bits
Summarizing Network Numbers	0	256 numbers	0
	128	128 numbers	1
	192	64 numbers	2
	224	32 numbers	3
	240	16 numbers	4
	248	8 numbers	5
	252	4 numbers	6
	254	2 numbers	7
	255	1 number	8

the two networks are contiguous, they can't be summarized with a 25-bit mask (255.255.255.128). You could use a 24-bit mask (255.255.255.0); however, this includes a total of 256 addresses, not just the 128 addresses in question.

on the **Job**

You should summarize only for addresses that are connected to or behind your router. Otherwise, you could be propagating bad routing information— routes in another part of your network that your router is not connected to. In the just-mentioned example, if 192.168.1.0/26 and 192.168.1.192/26 were also behind your router, you could then summarize all four of these as 192.168.1.0/24.

All of this can be very confusing for someone just introduced to subnetting and summarization. Summarization is nothing more than listing all the routes and choosing the highest order bits that match to advertise, making sure to exclude those outside your coverage. Summarization usually gets difficult only when you have a poor addressing design in the first place—like the examples you might see on the ICND2 exam. In a nutshell, remember that you can create a summary route when the total number of addresses is a power of 2. If it is not a power of 2, you'll have to divide the addresses into smaller groups and summarize them separately. For the purposes of the ICND2 exam, simply do the following:

1. Write all possible subnet IDs from the existing diagram, including those outside the router's coverage.

2. Pick the highest order bits that match for only the routes you're summarizing. You will easily see in your bit chart which ones overlap (like that in Table 5-1).

3. Create as many summary routes as you can.
4. Advertise the single (leftover) routes separately.

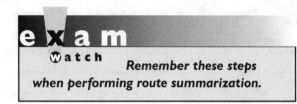

Remember these steps when performing route summarization.

Summarization Difficulties

The first two summarization examples were pretty simple. Let's look at a more complicated example to illustrate how difficult summarization can be if you don't lay out your addressing correctly in your network. In the network shown in Figure 5-11, Router A needs to summarize routes to which it and Routers B, C, and D are connected, realizing that other networks reside to the left of Router A. The goal is to have Router A advertise the least number of routes to routers to the networking cloud on the left. Remember that Router A should create summarizations only for the routes that it is connected to or that are behind it (Routers B, C, and D). Also, remember that these summarizations should either be a power of 2 or start on a power-of-2 networking boundary.

In this example, the first thing you want to do is put the routes that Router A knows about (those to its right) in numerical order: 192.168.5.64/28, 192.168.5.80/28, 192.168.5.96/28, 192.168.5.112/28, 192.168.5.192/28, and 192.168.5.208/28. Note that to the left of Router A reside other subnets of 192.168.5.0 that should not be included in the summarization. In this example, subnets 64, 80, 96, and 112 are contiguous, and if you use a 26-bit summarization mask, this would accommodate addresses from 64 through 127. These addresses are contiguous, and the summarization mask starts on a power-of-2 network boundary (address 64). To summarize subnets 192 and 208, you would need a 27-bit mask (255.255.255.224), which would include a block of 32 addresses: from 192 through 223.

FIGURE 5-11

Complex route summarization example

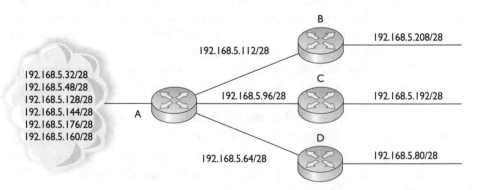

Router A can advertise the following summarized routes to the left network cloud:

- **192.168.5.64/26**   This covers addresses 64–127, which are to the right of Router A.
- **192.168.5.192/27**   This covers addresses 192–223, which are also to the right of Router A.

As you can see, the number of network entries Router A originally advertised was six network numbers. Through summarization, this was reduced to two summarized routes.

Understand the summarization examples in this section and practice summarization in the following **exercise to prepare for similar scenarios on the real exam.**

EXERCISE 5-1

Performing Route Summarization

The preceding sections dealt with route summarization and its advantages and disadvantages. This exercise will reinforce this material by having you look at an example network and come up with summarized routes for a router to reduce the number of routes it advertises to neighboring routers. You'll use the network shown in Figure 5-12. In this example, you need to summarize the routes to the right of Router A, making sure that these summarizations don't overlap any of the addresses in the network to the left of Router A. Please note that there is no guarantee that you can end up with one summary route or that any specific route can be summarized.

1. Write down your networks (to the right of Router A) in numerical order:

    Here are the networks that you want to summarize: 192.168.5.8/29, 192.168.5.16/29, 192.168.5.24/29, 192.168.5.32/29, 192.168.5.40/29, and 192.168.5.56/29.

2. Break up the networks into contiguous blocks of addresses, starting on a power-of-2 network boundary.

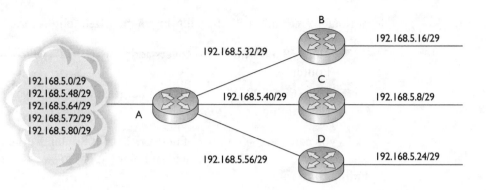

FIGURE 5-12

Summarization
exercise

Given that the subnet mask is 255.255.255.248 (29 bits), here are the blocks
of addresses:

- 192.168.5.8/29
- 192.168.5.16/29, 192.168.5.24/29
- 192.168.5.32/29, 192.168.5.40/29
- 192.168.5.56/29

Notice that even though subnets 8 and 16 are contiguous, a summarized mask
would have to include subnet 0, which is to the left of Router A. Remember
that the summarization must begin on a power-of-2 boundary (or multiple
of this) and must correspond to valid network numbers for this mask value.

3. Assign an appropriate *summarized* mask to each of the following contiguous
   blocks. For the given subnets, here is a list of those that can and can't be
   summarized, as well as the summarized masks:

   - **192.168.5.8/29**   Can't be summarized
   - **192.168.5.16/29, 192.168.5.24/29**   Can be summarized: 192.168.5.16/28
   - **192.168.5.32/29, 192.168.5.40/29**   Can be summarized: 192.168.5.32/28
   - **192.168.5.56/29**   Can't be summarized

   The subnet 192.168.5.8/29 can't be summarized, since when you shift 1 bit to
   the left in the subnet mask, this would include network 192.168.5.0/29, which
   is to the left of Router A. Remember that on a 28-bit mask, the networks
   increase in multiples of 16, starting at 0: 0, 16, 32, 48, 64, and so on. This is
   also true with 192.168.5.56. Shifting 1 bit to the left in the summarization
   would require the summarized route to start at 192.168.5.48. Now you should
   be more comfortable with route summarization.

EXERCISE 5-2

Verifying Route Summarization

In this exercise, you'll be given a summarized route and will have to determine whether a list of given addresses falls within this range. The summarized route is 194.1.128.0/18. Which of the following addresses fall in this range? 194.2.144.38, 194.1.1.150, 194.1.129.36, 194.1.191.88, or 194.1.64.31? You could approach this solution using one of two methods: Use the subnetting information shown in Table 5-1. The first method is shown in step 1, and the second in step 2. For the exam, use the method that is easier for you; however, using step 1 is the quicker of the two choices.

1. List the addresses in numerical order. Based on the subnet mask value, figure out the beginning address in the summarized route and the ending one. Choose the answers that fall between these.

    Here are the addresses in numerical order: 194.1.1.150, 194.1.64.31, 194.1.129.36, 194.1.191.88, and 194.2.144.38. The bit mask is /22; this is 255.255.192.0 in decimal. The summarization is occurring in the *third* octet, where the numbers are incrementing by 64 (256–192). This means the addresses range from 194.1.128.0 to 194.1.191.255. Therefore, the answers are 194.1.129.36 and 194.1.191.88.

2. Your second option is to create a table similar to Table 5-1. Break out the third octet of the summarized route, and do the same for the addresses in question. Compare them to determine whether they are included in the summarized route.

    You don't need to write down 194.2.144.38, since its second octet is different from the second octet in the summarized route. Table 5-4 has the binary breakout of the third octet of the summarized route and the remaining addresses shown. Notice that the first two addresses below the summarized route have the first 2 highest-order binary bits (based on the summarized subnet mask) being different, so they are not included in the summarized route; however, the last two addresses have the 2 highest order bits matching, so they are included in the summarized route.

TABLE 5-4

Exercise 5-2 Summarization Comparison

	Third Octet Bits							
194.1.128.0/18	1	0	0	0	0	0	0	0
194.1.1.150	0	0	0	0	0	0	0	1
194.1.64.31	0	1	0	0	0	0	0	0
194.1.129.36	1	0	0	0	0	0	0	1
194.1.191.255	1	0	1	1	1	1	1	1

INSIDE THE EXAM

VLSM

You will need to be very comfortable, not just with subnetting IP networks, but also with using VLSM to create efficient subnets. Remember the advantages of VLSM: efficient addressing, route summarization, and containment of layer 3 network problems. You need to know how to do VLSM, so remember the six steps: 1) find the largest segment; 2) choose a mask for this segment; 3) write down the network numbers; 4) take one of the subnets and apply a different mask to it; 5) write down the newly subnetted subnets; and 6) restart with step 4, if necessary. You will probably have to do something similar to this on the exam.

Route Summarization

Classless protocols, such as EIGRP, OSPF, RIPv2, IS-IS, and BGP, support VLSM and CIDR with route summarization. Classless protocols advertise network numbers and subnet masks in their routing updates. Remember the advantages of route summarization.

Understand the issues of discontiguous subnets and routing.

Routers make routing decisions based on all 32 bits of a destination IP address, looking for the most number of matching bits for a network number and mask in the routing table. Don't be surprised if you see a question on the exam that asks about what route in a routing table will be used to reach a destination. Equal-cost load sharing is supported by many vendors and allows a router to place multiple paths for a destination in the routing table and load-share connections across those routing paths.

Practice summarizing routes. Make sure you work through Exercises 5-1 and 5-2 and other exercises like them, since you might see questions similar to these on the exam. Remember that you are limited in time and can't afford to spend more than a minute or two on this process to answer such questions. Practice, practice, and more practice!

CERTIFICATION SUMMARY

VLSM allows you to apply more than one subnet mask to the same class address. VLSM's advantages include more efficient use of addressing and route summarization. Only classless protocols, such as RIPv2, EIGRP, OSPF, IS-IS, and BGP, support VLSM. To perform VLSM, find the segment with the largest number of devices. Find an appropriate mask for the segment and write down all of your network numbers using this subnet mask. Take one of these newly subnetted network numbers and apply a different subnet mask to it to create more, yet smaller, subnets.

Route summarization is the ability to take a group of contiguous network or subnet entries in your routing table and advertise these entries as a single summarized routing update. Through proper configuration of summarization, your routing table sizes will decrease, the number of advertised network numbers will decrease, and you'll be able to contain certain networking problems, especially flapping routes. CIDR is a special type of route summarization. VLSM allows you to summarize back only to the class boundary of the network: the Class A, B, or C network number. CIDR allows you to summarize a group of contiguous class network numbers.

Summarization can be achieved only by using a hierarchical addressing design in your network. Used with a proper address design, hierarchical addressing allows for more efficient routing: It decreases routing table sizes, the amount of memory for routing, and the number of processing cycles required, and simplifies routing troubleshooting. When implementing route summarization, note that the routing protocol must carry the subnet mask along with the routing entry: Only classless protocols allow this process. And since the mask is carried with the network number, discontiguous subnets are supported with classless protocols, but not classful ones. When the router makes routing decisions, it will use the entire destination IP address to make them.

When creating summarized entries, note that the network numbers being summarized must have the same highest-order matching bits. Remember that you can summarize routes only on a bit boundary, which is a power of 2, or a multiple of a power of 2. When summarizing, you need to know the ranges of addresses a mask value in an octet covers; for example, a subnet mask value of 192 covers 64 numbers.

✓ TWO-MINUTE DRILL

VLSM

❑ VLSM allows you to have different subnet masks applied to the same class address.

❑ Classless protocols, such as BGP, IS-IS, OSPF, and RIPv2, support VLSM.

❑ VLSM uses addressing more efficiently and allows you to configure route summarization.

❑ When setting up a network with VLSM, first find the largest segment. Then find an appropriate subnet mask for this network. Write down the subnet numbers according to this mask. For smaller segments, take one of the subnets and subnet it further, writing down your newly subnetted subnets.

Route Summarization

❑ Route summarization is the ability to take a bunch of contiguous network numbers in your routing table and advertise these contiguous routes as a single summarized route. The summarization must begin on a power-of-2 boundary (or a multiple of a power of 2).

❑ Summarization reduces the routing table size, reduces the bandwidth required for routing updates, and contains network problems. Proper summarization requires a hierarchical addressing design in your network.

❑ CIDR, commonly called supernetting, allows you to summarize routes to the left of the class boundary, such as a group of Class C networks.

❑ Routing protocols must carry the subnet mask with the network entry to perform route summarization. Routing decisions must be made on the entire destination IP address. Summarization requires that the routing entries have the same highest-order matching bits.

❑ Classful protocols have problems with discontiguous subnet masks; classless protocols do not.

SELF TEST

The following Self Test questions will help you measure your understanding of the material presented in this chapter. Read all the choices carefully, as there may be more than one correct answer. Choose all correct answers for each question.

VLSM

1. Which protocol supports VLSM?
   A. RIPv2
   B. IGRP
   C. RIP and IGRP
   D. None of these

2. You are given a Class C network, 192.168.1.0/24. You need one network with 120 hosts and two networks with 60 hosts. How many subnet masks do you need?
   A. 1
   B. 2
   C. 3
   D. 4

3. You are given a Class C network, 192.168.1.0/24. You need one network with 120 hosts and three networks with 60 hosts. What subnet mask values would you use?
   A. 255.255.255.128 and 255.255.255.192
   B. 255.255.255.128
   C. 255.255.255.192
   D. None of these

4. You are given a Class C network, 192.168.1.0/24. You need three networks with 60 hosts and two networks with 30 hosts. What are the subnet mask values you could use? (Choose two answers.)
   A. 255.255.255.128 and 255.255.255.192
   B. 255.255.255.224 and 255.255.255.240
   C. 255.255.255.192 and 255.255.255.224
   D. None of these

5. You are given this address space: 172.16.5.0/25. You need one network with 64 hosts and two with 30 hosts. What are the most specific subnet mask values to use?
   A. /25 and /26
   B. /26 and /27
   C. /27 and /28
   D. None of these

6. You are given a Class C network and you have four LAN segments with the following numbers of devices: 120, 60, 30, and 30. What subnet mask values would you use to accommodate these segments?
   A. /24, /25, and /26
   B. /25, /26, and /27
   C. /26, /27, and /28
   D. None of these

Route Summarization

7. VLSM allows you to summarize _____ back to the Class A, B, or C network boundary.
   A. subnets
   B. networks

8. Which of the following is not an advantage of route summarization?
   A. It requires less memory and processing.
   B. It supports smaller routing update sizes.
   C. It helps contain network problems such as flapping routes.
   D. It supports discontiguous subnets.

9. _____ allows you to create this summarization: 10.0.0.0/7.
   A. Subnetting
   B. CDR
   C. Supernetting
   D. VLSM

10. Which of the following are classless protocols?
    A. IGRP
    B. EIGRP
    C. IGRP and EIGRP
    D. Neither IGRP nor EIGRP

11. A routing protocol that supports route summarization must perform all except which of the following?

   A. Carry the subnet mask with the network entry.

   B. Make routing decisions based on the entire destination IP address.

   C. Summarize entries so that the same lowest-order bits match.

   D. None of these is correct.

12. You have the following two routes: 192.168.1.64/27 and 192.168.1.96/27. Enter the most specific summarized route for these two subnets: _____.

13. You have the following four routes: 192.168.1.32/30, 192.168.1.36/30, 192.168.1.40/30, and 192.168.1.44/30. Enter the most specific summarized route for these four subnets: _____.

SELF TEST ANSWERS

VLSM

1. ☑ **A.** RIPv2 supports VLSM (RIPv1 does not).
    ☒ **B** is classful and doesn't support VLSM. **C** includes a classful protocol. A is a correct answer, so **D** is incorrect.

2. ☑ **B.** You need two subnet masks: 255.255.255.128 (/25) and 255.255.255.192 (/26). This creates three networks, for instance, 192.168.1.0/25, 192.168.128/26, and 192.168.1.192/26.
    ☒ Therefore, answers **A, C,** and **D** are incorrect.

3. ☑ **D.** None of these answers is correct because this is impossible with a single Class C network. This is impossible because 120 hosts require a 255.255.255.128 mask, which is half a Class C network; 60 hosts require a 255.255.255.192 mask, but you need three of these, which is three-quarters of a Class C network.
    ☒ **A** is incorrect because it accommodates only the 120-host and two 60-host segments. **B** is incorrect because it accommodates only two subnets. **C** is incorrect because it accommodates the three 60-host segments, but not the 120-host segment.

4. ☑ **A and C.** Answer **A** creates one 126-host segment and two 62-host segments. Answer **C** creates three 62-host segments and two 30-host segments.
    ☒ **B** is incorrect because the second mask supports only 14 hosts. **D** is incorrect because A and C are correct answers.

5. ☑ **D.** None of these answers is correct. Sixty-four hosts require a 25-bit mask, and you are only given this to begin with—62 hosts would work with a 26-bit mask.
    ☒ **A, B,** and **C** don't support enough addresses.

6. ☑ **B.** A bit mask of 25 creates two networks: 0 and 128. If you take one of these subnets and apply a 26-bit mask, you have two more networks, such as 128 and 192. Taking one of these two subnets, applying a 27-bit mask creates two more subnets, such as 192 and 224.
    ☒ **A** and **C** don't support enough addresses to accommodate all four LAN segments. **D** is incorrect because B is the correct answer.

Route Summarization

7. ☑ **A.** VLSM allows you to summarize subnets back to the Class A, B, or C network boundary.
    ☒ **B** is a nonsubnetted address space and, therefore, is a Class A, B, or C network number and can't be summarized with VLSM, but it can be summarized with CIDR.

8. ☑ **D.** Discontiguous subnets are supported by classless protocols, but they are not an advantage of summarization. Actually, summarization is more difficult if you have discontiguous subnets.
☒ **A, B,** and **C** are advantages of route summarization.

9. ☑ **C.** Supernetting, or CIDR, supports summarization of contiguous blocks of Class A, B, or C networks.
☒ **A** is the opposite of summarization. **B** should be CIDR, not CDR. **D** is incorrect because VLSM allows you to summarize subnets, not networks.

10. ☑ **B.** EIGRP, as well as IS-IS, BGP, OSPF, and RIPv2, is a classless protocol.
☒ **A** is incorrect because IGRP is not a classless protocol. **C** is incorrect because the answer includes a classful protocol (IGRP). **D** is incorrect because B is the correct answer.

11. ☑ **C.** Summarized entries must have the same *highest*-order matching bits, not lowest.
☒ **A** and **B** are things a routing protocol supporting route summarization must perform. **D** is incorrect because answer C is correct.

12. ☑ **192.168.1.64/26**: This includes addresses from 192.168.1.64 through 192.168.1.127.

13. ☑ **192.168.1.32/28**: This includes addresses from 192.168.1.32 through 192.168.1.47.

6
Initial Router Configuration

This chapter builds upon the configuration concepts on the CCENT exam, covering some of the basic commands that you can use to access and configure a Cisco IOS router, which are, as you will see, much like those on the Catalyst IOS switches. The advantage this provides is that you don't have to learn a complete new command-line interface (CLI). The chapter first covers the components of the router and its bootup process, including the use of the *System Configuration Dialog* script: this prompts you for information about how you want to configure your router. You'll also learn about a new feature introduced in version 12.3T code, called *AutoSecure*. Finally, the chapter covers the commands used to create a very basic configuration on your IOS router, including setting up an interface for trunking.

CERTIFICATION OBJECTIVE 6.01

Router Hardware Components

Each IOS device has two main components: hardware and software. Almost every IOS-based router uses the same hardware and firmware components to assist during the bootup process, including the following: ROM (read-only memory), RAM (random access memory), flash, NVRAM (nonvolatile RAM), a configuration register, and physical lines and interfaces. All of these components can affect how the router boots up and finds and loads the operating system and its configuration file. The following sections cover these components in more depth.

Read-Only Memory (ROM)

The software in ROM cannot be changed unless you actually swap out the ROM chip on your router. ROM is nonvolatile—when you turn off your device, the contents of ROM are not erased. ROM contains the firmware necessary to boot up your router and typically has the following four components:

- **POST (power-on self test)** Performs tests on the router's hardware components.
- **Bootstrap program** Brings the router up and determines how the IOS image and configuration files will be found and loaded.

■ **ROM Monitor (*ROMMON* mode)** A mini–operating system that allows you to perform low-level testing and troubleshooting; for instance, ROMMON is used during the password recovery procedure. To abort the router's normal bootup procedure of loading IOS, use the CTRL-BREAK control sequence to enter ROMMON mode. The prompt in ROMMON mode is either > or rommon>, depending on the router model.

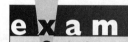

POST performs self-tests on the hardware. The bootstrap program brings the router up and finds an IOS image. ROMMON contains a mini–operating system used for low-level testing and debugging. The Mini-IOS is a stripped-down version of IOS used for emergency booting of a router and is referred to as RXBOOT mode. All of these components are stored in ROM.

Other Components

Your router contains other components that are used during the bootup process, including RAM, flash, NVRAM, the configuration register, and the physical lines and interfaces. The following paragraphs explain these components.

RAM is like the memory in your PC. On a router, RAM (in most cases) contains the running IOS image, the active configuration file, any tables (including routing, ARP, and other tables), and internal buffers for temporarily storing information such as interface input and output buffers and logging messages. IOS is responsible for managing memory. When you turn off your router, everything in RAM is erased.

Flash is a form of nonvolatile memory, like ROM, meaning that when you turn the router off, the information stored in flash is not lost. Routers store their IOS image in flash, but other information can also be stored here, such as a secondary configuration file. Note that some lower-end Cisco routers actually run IOS directly from flash (not RAM). Flash is slower than RAM, a fact that can create performance issues.

NVRAM is like flash in that its contents are not erased when you turn off your router. It is slightly different, though, in that it uses a battery to maintain the information when the Cisco device is turned off. Routers (and switches) use NVRAM to store their configuration files.

The *configuration register* is a special register in the router that determines many of its bootup and running options, including how the router finds the IOS image and its configuration file. The configuration uses a part of memory space in NVRAM. As you will see later in this chapter, you can manipulate this register to affect how your router boots up. You can also use the **boot** command to influence the location from which IOS and configuration file are loaded (discussed in the "Bootstrap Program" section later).

Every router has at least one line and one physical interface. *Lines*, or *ports*, are typically used for management access; the console and auxiliary lines are examples. *Interfaces* are used to move traffic

Flash is used to store the operating system, and NVRAM is used to store the configuration file. The configuration register is used to determine how the router will boot up.

through the router; they can include media types such as Ethernet, Fast Ethernet (FE), Gigabit Ethernet (GE), serial, and others. These interfaces can be used during the bootup process—you can have the bootstrap program load IOS from a remote Trivial File Transfer Protocol (TFTP) server (instead of flash), assuming that you have a sufficient IP configuration on your router.

CERTIFICATION OBJECTIVE 6.02

Router Bootup Process

A router typically goes through six steps when booting up:

1. The router loads and runs POST (located in ROM), testing its hardware components, including memory and interfaces.
2. The bootstrap program is loaded and executed.
3. The configuration register is checked to determine how to boot up (where to find the IOS image and configuration file).
4. The bootstrap program finds and loads an IOS image: Possible locations of IOS images include flash or a TFTP server.

w a t c h   ***Once POST completes***
and the bootstrap program is loaded, the
configuration is checked to determine
what to do next.

5. Once IOS is loaded, IOS attempts to find and load a configuration file, which is normally stored in NVRAM—if IOS cannot find a configuration file, it starts up the System Configuration Dialog.

6. After the configuration is loaded, you are presented with the CLI (remember that the first mode you are placed into is User EXEC mode).

If you are connected to the console line, you'll see the following output as your router boots up:

```
System Bootstrap, Version 11.0(10c), SOFTWARE
Copyright (c) 1986-1996 by cisco Systems
2500 processor with 6144 Kbytes of main memory

F3: 5593060+79544+421160 at 0x3000060

Cisco Internetwork Operating System Software
IOS (tm) 2500 Software (C2500-I-L), Version 12.0(5)
Copyright (c) 1986-1999 by cisco Systems, Inc.
Compiled Tue 15-Jun-99 19:49 by phanguye Image text-base:
0x0302EC70, data-base: 0x00001000 . . .
 .
 .
 .
cisco 2504 (68030) processor (revision N) with
     6144K/2048K bytes of memory.
Processor board ID 18086269, with hardware revision
     00000003
Bridging software.
X.25 software, Version 3.0.0.
Basic Rate ISDN software, Version 1.1.
2 Ethernet/IEEE 802.3 interface(s)
2 Serial network interface(s)
32K bytes of non-volatile configuration memory.
16384K bytes of processor board System flash (Read ONLY)

00:00:22: %LINK-3-UPDOWN: Interface Ethernet0, changed
     state to up
00:00:22: %LINK-3-UPDOWN: Interface Ethernet1, changed
     state to up
```

```
        .
        .
        .
Cisco Internetwork Operating System Software
IOS (tm) 2500 Software (C2500-I-L), Version 12.0(5)
Copyright (c) 1986-1999 by cisco Systems, Inc.
Compiled Tue 15-Jun-99 19:49 by phanguye

Press RETURN to get started!
```

6.01. The digital resources that accompany this book contain a multimedia demonstration of booting up a Cisco router.

You should notice a few things about this output. First, notice that the router is loading the bootstrap program—System Bootstrap, Version 11.0(10c)—and then the IOS image—IOS (tm) 2500 Software (C2500-I-L), Version 12.0(5). During the bootup process, you cannot see the actual POST process (unlike Catalyst switches). However, you will see information about the interfaces going up and/or down—this is where IOS is loading the configuration and bringing up those interfaces that you previously activated. Sometimes, if the router has a lot of interfaces, the Press RETURN to get started! message is mixed in with the interface messages. Once the display stops, just press ENTER to access User EXEC mode. This completes the bootup process of the router.

When a router boots up, it runs POST, loads the bootstrap program, finds and loads IOS, and loads its configuration file—in that order.

Bootstrap Program

As you saw in the bootup code example, the bootstrap program went out and found the IOS and loaded it. The bootstrap program goes through the following steps when trying to locate and load the IOS image:

1. Examine the configuration register value. This value is a set of four hexadecimal digits. The last digit affects the bootup process. If the last digit is between 0x2 and 0xF, then the router proceeds to the next step. Otherwise, the router uses the values shown in Table 6-1 to determine how it should proceed.

2. Examine the configuration file in NVRAM for **boot system** commands, which tell the bootstrap program where to find IOS. These commands are shown in the following paragraph.

3. If no **boot system** commands are found in the configuration file in NVRAM, use the first valid IOS image found in flash.

4. If there are no valid IOS images in flash, generate a TFTP local broadcast to locate a TFTP server (this is called a *netboot* and is not recommended because it is very slow and not very reliable for large IOS images).

5. If no TFTP server is found, load the Mini-IOS in ROM (RXBOOT mode).

6. If there is a Mini-IOS in ROM, then the Mini-IOS is loaded and you are taken into RXBOOT mode; otherwise, the router either retries finding an IOS image or loads ROMMON and goes into ROM Monitor mode.

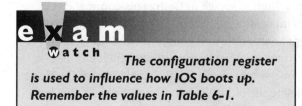

The configuration register is used to influence how IOS boots up. Remember the values in Table 6-1.

Table 6-1 contains the three common configuration register values in the fourth hex character of the configuration register that are used to influence the bootup process. The values in the configuration register are represented in *hexadecimal*, the register being 16 bits long.

For step 2 of the bootup process, here are the **boot system** commands that you can use to influence the order that the bootstrap program should use when trying to locate the IOS image:

```
Router(config)# boot system flash name_of_IOS_file_in_flash
Router(config)# boot system tftp IOS_image_name
                     IP_address_of_server
Router(config)# boot system rom
```

TABLE 6-1	Value in *Last* Digit	Bootup Process
Fourth Hex Character Configuration Register Values	0x0	Boot the router into ROMMON mode.
	0x1	Boot the router using the first IOS image in flash or the Mini-IOS in ROM (RXBOOT mode), if the latter exists.
	0x2–0xF	Boot the router using the default boot sequence.

6.02. *The digital resources that accompany this book contain a multimedia demonstration of using* `boot system` *commands on a router.*

on the **job**

The order in which you enter the `boot system` *commands is important, since the bootstrap program processes them in the order in which you configure them—once the program finds an IOS image, it does not process any more* `boot system` *commands in the configuration file. These commands are also supported on Catalyst IOS switches.*

The **boot system flash** command tells the bootstrap program to load the specified IOS filename in flash when booting up. Note that, by default, the bootstrap program loads the *first* valid IOS image in flash. This command tells the bootstrap program to load an image that's different from the first one. This might be necessary if you perform an upgrade and you have two IOS images in flash—the old one and the new one. By default, the old one still loads first (because it appears first in flash) unless you override this behavior with the **boot system flash** command or delete the old IOS flash image. You can also have the bootstrap program load IOS from a TFTP server—this is not recommended for large images, since the image is downloaded via the User Datagram Protocol (UDP), which is slow. And last, you can tell the bootstrap program to load the Mini-IOS in ROM with the **boot system rom** command. To remove any of these commands, just preface them with the **no** parameter.

exam

watch   *The* `boot system` *commands can be used to modify the default behavior of where the bootstrap program should load IOS. When the bootstrap program loads, it examines the configuration file stored in NVRAM for* `boot system` *commands. If they are found, the bootstrap program uses these commands to find IOS. If no* `boot system` *commands are found, the router uses the default behavior in finding and loading the IOS image (first image in flash, a broadcast to a TFTP server, and then IOS in ROM, if it exists). When the router is booting and you see the message* `boot: cannot open "flash:";`, *this indicates you misconfigured a* `boot system` *command and the corresponding IOS image filename in flash doesn't exist.*

System Configuration Dialog

When a router boots up, runs its hardware diagnostics, and loads IOS software, IOS then attempts to find a configuration file in NVRAM. If it can't find a configuration file to load, IOS then runs the System Configuration Dialog, commonly referred to as *Setup* mode, which is a script that prompts you for configuration information. The purpose of this script is to ask you questions that will allow you to set up a basic configuration on your router: It is not intended as a full-functioning configuration tool. In other words, the script doesn't have the ability to perform all the router's configuration tasks. Instead, it is used by novices who are not that comfortable with the IOS CLI. Once you become familiar with the CLI and many of the commands on the router, you'll probably never use this script again.

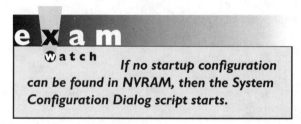

Running the System Configuration Dialog

As mentioned in the previous paragraph, one way to access the System Configuration Dialog is to boot up a router without a configuration in NVRAM. The second way is to use the **setup** Privileged EXEC mode command, shown here:

```
Router# setup
        --- System Configuration Dialog ---
Continue with configuration dialog? [yes/no]: yes
At any point you may enter a question mark '?' for help.
Use ctrl-c to abort configuration dialog at any prompt.
Default settings are in square brackets '[]'.

Basic management setup configures only enough connectivity
for management of the system, extended setup will ask you
to configure each interface on the system

First, would you like to see the current interface summary? [yes]:
Interface  IP-Address  OK? Method Status                Protocol
Ethernet0  unassigned  YES unset  administratively down down
Ethernet1  unassigned  YES unset  administratively down down
Serial0    unassigned  YES unset  administratively down down

Would you like to enter basic management setup? [yes/no]: no
Configuring global parameters:
    Enter hostname [Router]:
```

```
The enable secret is a password used to protect access to
privileged EXEC and configuration modes. This password, after
entered, becomes encrypted in the configuration.
Enter enable secret: dealgroup1
The enable password is used when you do not specify an
enable secret password, with some older software versions,
and some boot images.  Enter enable password: dealgroup2
The virtual terminal password is used to protect
access to the router over a network interface.
Enter virtual terminal password: cisco
Configure SNMP Network Management? [no]:
Configure LAT? [yes]: no
Configure AppleTalk? [no]:
Configure DECnet? [no]:
Configure IP? [yes]:
   Configure IGRP routing? [yes]: no
   Configure RIP routing? [no]:
 .
 .
 .

Configuring interface parameters:
Do you want to configure Ethernet0  interface? [no]: yes
  Configure IP on this interface? [no]: yes
    IP address for this interface: 172.15.1.1
    Subnet mask for this interface [255.255.0.0] : 255.255.255.0
    Class B network is 172.15.0.0, 24 subnet bits; mask is /24
Do you want to configure Serial0  interface? [no]:
 .
 .
 .

The following configuration command script was created:
hostname Router
enable secret 5 $1$/CCk$4r7zDwDNeqkxFO.kJxC3G0
enable password dealgroup2
line vty 0 4
 password cisco
 .
 .
 .

end

[0] Go to IOS command prompt without saving this config.
[1] Return back to the setup without saving this config.
[2] Save this configuration to nvram and exit.
Enter your selection [2]: 2
```

Information included in brackets ([ ]) indicates the default value—if you press ENTER, the value in the brackets is used. One problem with the script is that if you make a mistake, you can't go back to the preceding question. Instead, you must use the CTRL-C break sequence to abort the script and start over. The following sections break down the different components of the script.

on the
Ⓘob
The questions that the script asks you might differ from router to router, depending on the hardware model, the interfaces installed in it, and the software running on it.

Status and Global Configuration Information

At the beginning of the script, you are asked whether or not you want to continue. If you answer **yes** or **y**, the script will continue; otherwise, if you answer **no** or **n**, the script is aborted and you are returned to Privileged EXEC mode. The second thing that you are asked is if you want to see the status of the router's interfaces. If you answer **yes**, you'll see all of the interfaces on the router, the interfaces' IP addresses, and the status of the interfaces.

After the status information, you are taken into the actual configuration. The first part of the configuration deals with all configuration information for the router except for the interfaces, which is the second part. In this part of the configuration, you are asked for things like the Privileged EXEC password, VTY password (telnet and SSH), which network protocols you want to activate globally, and other global configuration information.

on the
Ⓘob
Note that you are prompted for two Privileged EXEC passwords in the script: enable secret and enable password. Even though you would normally configure only one, the script requires you to enter both and also requires that both passwords be different.

Protocol and Interface Configuration Information

After configuring the global information for the router, you are then led through questions about which interfaces you want to use and how they should be configured. The script is smart enough to ask only configuration questions based on how you answered the global questions. As an example, if you activate IP, the script asks you for each activated interface, if you want the interface to process IP, and, if yes, the IP addressing information for the interface.

TABLE 6-2	Option	Description
Options at the End of the System Configuration Dialog	0	Discard the script's configuration and return to Privileged EXEC mode.
	1	Return to the beginning of the script.
	2	Activate the script's configuration, save the configuration to NVRAM, and return to Privileged EXEC mode.

Exiting Setup Mode

After you answer all of the script's configuration questions, you are shown the router configuration the script created using your answers to the script's questions. Note that IOS hasn't yet activated the configuration file. Examine the configuration closely and then make one of the three choices shown in Table 6-2. Also, if you enter **1** as your option, when the script starts over again, the information that you previously entered appears in brackets and will be the default values when you press the ENTER key on an empty line.

6.03. The digital resources that accompany this book contain a multimedia demonstration of using the System Configuration Dialog on a Cisco router.

e x a m

ⓦ a t c h   *Remember that the System Configuration Dialog script is started when the router boots up and there is no configuration in NVRAM, or you use the* `setup` *command from Privileged EXEC mode. Also, know the three options at the end of the Setup dialog script. You can press* CTRL-C *to abort the script.*

Configuration Register

As mentioned in the preceding section, the configuration register is used by the bootstrap program to determine the location from which the IOS image and configuration file should be loaded. Once the router is booted up, you can view the configuration register value with the **show version** command:

```
Router> show version
Cisco IOS Software, 1841 Software (C1841-ADVIPSERVICESK9-M),
        Version 12.4(6)T7, RELEASE SOFTWARE (fc5)
```

```
Technical Support: http://www.cisco.com/techsupport
Copyright (c) 1986-2007 by Cisco Systems, Inc.
Compiled Thu 29-Mar-07 03:28 by khuie

ROM: System Bootstrap, Version 12.4(13r)T, RELEASE SOFTWARE (fc1)

Router1 uptime is 3 days, 22 hours, 5 minutes
System returned to ROM by reload at 19:06:33 UTC Fri Dec 7 2007
System image file is "flash:c1841-advipservicesk9-mz.124-6.T7.bin"
.
.
.
125K bytes of non-volatile configuration memory.
32768K bytes of processor board System flash (Read/Write)
Configuration register is 0x2102
```

You need to go to the very bottom of the display in order to view the register value.

Changing the Configuration Register from Configuration Mode

You can change the configuration register value from Configuration mode or from ROMMON mode. If you already have Privileged EXEC access to the router and want to change the register value, use this command:

```
Router(config)# config-register 0xhexadecimal_value
```

The register value is four hexadecimal digits, or 16 bits, in length. Each bit position in the register, though, indicates a function that the bootstrap program should take. Therefore, you should be very careful when configuring this value on your router.

Many sites on the Internet have downloadable configuration register utility programs for Cisco routers. Boson has a free one at this location: www.boson .com/FreeUtilities.html. With Boson's utility, you can select or deselect specific boot options, which will automatically generate the correct register value for you.

When entering the register value, you must always precede it with *0x*, indicating that this is a hexadecimal value. If you don't do so, the router assumes the value is decimal and *converts* it to hexadecimal. On Cisco routers, the default configuration register value is *0x2102*, which causes the router to use the default bootup process in finding and locating IOS images and configuration files. If you change this to *0x2142*, this tells the bootstrap program that, upon the next reboot, it should locate IOS using the default behavior, but *not* to load the configuration file in NVRAM; instead, you are taken directly into the System Configuration Dialog. This is the value that you will use to perform the password recovery procedure.

e x a m
watch

The default configuration register value is 0x2102, which causes a router to boot up using its default bootup process (look for `boot system` commands in the startup configuration, and if none are found, load the first IOS in flash, then load the default startup configuration file). You can see the configuration register value with the `show version` command.

If you've changed this value, you will see the existing value and the value the router will use upon rebooting. If the router boots up and doesn't have a configuration, but one exists in NVRAM, check the router's configuration register to see if it is set to 0x2142: this register setting causes IOS to ignore any configuration file in NVRAM when booting.

Changing the Configuration Register from ROM Monitor

Of course, one problem with the Configuration mode method of changing the register value is that you must gain access to Privileged EXEC mode first. This can be a problem if you don't know the passwords on the router. A second method, though, allows you to change the register value without having to log into the router. To use this method, you'll need console access to the router—you can't do this from the auxiliary line or from a VTY session. Next, you'll turn off the router and then turn it back on. As the router starts booting, you'll break into ROMMON mode with the router's break sequence. To break into the router, once you see the bootstrap program has loaded, you can, in most cases, use the CTRL-BREAK control sequence to break into ROMMON mode. Note that this control sequence may differ, depending on the terminal emulation program you are using on your PC.

Once in ROMMON mode, you can begin the process of changing the register value using one of two methods, depending on the router model that you have. Some of Cisco's routers, such as the 1900, 1800, and 2600 series, use the **confreg** command. This script asks you basic questions about the function and bootup process of the router. What's nice about the script is that you don't need to know the hexadecimal values for the configuration register, since the router will create them for you as you answer these questions. Here is an example of using this script:

```
rommon 5 > confreg
    Configuration Summary
enabled are:
load rom after netboot fails
console baud: 9600
boot: image specified by the boot system commands
     or default to: cisco2-C3600

do you wish to change the configuration? y/n  [n]:  y
enable  "diagnostic mode"? y/n  [n]:
enable  "use net in IP bcast address"? y/n  [n]:
disable "load rom after netboot fails"? y/n  [n]:
enable  "use all zero broadcast"? y/n  [n]:
enable  "break/abort has effect"? y/n  [n]:
enable  "ignore system config info"? y/n  [n]:
change console baud rate? y/n  [n]:
change the boot characteristics? y/n  [n]:

    Configuration Summary enabled are:
load rom after netboot fails
console baud: 9600
boot: image specified by the boot system commands
     or default to: cisco2-C3600
do you wish to change the configuration? y/n  [n]:  n
rommon 6 >
```

Video

6.04. The digital resources that accompany this book contain a multimedia demonstration of changing the configuration register in ROMMON mode (`confreg`) and using the IOS CLI `config-register` command on a router.

As a shortcut, you could also execute the following command from ROMMON mode: `confreg 0x2142`.

Just as in the System Configuration Dialog, any information in brackets ([ ]) represents default values. The first question that it asks is if you want to "change the configuration," which means change the register: answer **y** to continue. If you answer **y** to `ignore system config info`, the third hexadecimal digit becomes *4*, making a router's register value appear as *0x2142*. This option is used when you want to perform the password recovery procedure. The next-to-last question is `change the boot characteristics?`—this question, if you answer **y**, will repeat the questions again. Answer **n** to exit the script. If you make any changes, you are asked to save them (`do you wish to change the configuration?`)—answer **y** to save your new register value. Once you are done changing the register, reboot the router. On many routers, just type in the letter **i** or **b** in ROMMON mode to boot it up.

CERTIFICATION OBJECTIVE 6.03

Disabling Unused Services

The next two sections, "Manually Disabling Unused Services" and "AutoSecure" introduce some basic security for Cisco routers: disabling unnecessary services that may be running on your IOS router. Some services on Cisco devices might not be needed and therefore can be disabled. This increases security and reduces overhead on the Cisco device. The first subsection introduces how to disable services manually, which applies to both Cisco switches and Cisco routers, while the second subsection discusses how to run a script, called AutoSecure, to accomplish basically the same thing, although this is supported only on IOS routers.

Manually Disabling Unused Services

A quick way of seeing which TCP/IP ports are open on an IOS device is by using this command:

```
IOS# show control-plane host open-ports
Active internet connections (servers and established)
Prot    Local Address  Foreign Address  Service        State
  tcp            *:23             *:0    Telnet         LISTEN
  tcp            *:80             *:0    HTTP CORE       LISTEN
  udp            *:67             *:0    DHCPD Receive  LISTEN
```

Many services, whether they be TCP/IP or some other management service, might have been originally configured on the device but now either are no longer necessary, go against company policy, or present a security risk. These services should be removed from the IOS device's operation. One option of doing that is manually disabling the services. The following two sections discuss how to do this for global and interface services.

Global Commands

Here is a list of commands you might want to execute to disable unnecessary global processes or enable necessary global processes:

```
IOS(config)# no ip source-route
IOS(config)# no {service | ip finger}
IOS(config)# no service tcp-small-servers
IOS(config)# no service udp-small-servers
IOS(config)# no cdp run
IOS(config)# no ip bootp server
IOS(config)# no boot network
IOS(config)# no service config
IOS(config)# no ip domain-lookup
IOS(config)# service tcp-keepalives-in
IOS(config)# service tcp-keepalives-out
IOS(config)# no service dhcp
IOS(config)# ip host hostname IP_address
```

```
IOS(config)# no ip http server
IOS(config)# [no] service nagle
IOS(config)# no ftp-server enable
IOS(config)# no ftp-server write-enable
IOS(config)# no tftp-server flash:
IOS(config)# no ip identd
IOS(config)# no service pad
IOS(config)# no service password-recovery
```

You should disable the following processes/programs on your IOS device (these are global configurations):

■ **IP source routing**   Similar to Token Ring's source routing, where the source determines the path to reach a destination in IP.

■ **Finger**   Used to garner information about accounts on a machine. Finger is enabled by default on IOS routers. The **no service finger** command has been replaced by the **no ip finger** command.

■ **Small servers**   These are programs with port numbers less than 20, like Chargen, that can be used by hackers to hack into your router or create a DoS attack (in IOS 12.0 and later, these are disabled by default). For example, if the echo service is enabled, an attacker could send a fake DNS query with the source address of the DNS server and a destination of the router; when the router receives this, it responds back to the DNS server, which might allow the attacker to bypass any internal filters that would normally drop a UDP DNS query.

■ **CDP**   Proprietary Cisco protocol that is used to share basic hardware and software information with a connected Cisco device—this is enabled by default across all interfaces on an IOS device (discussed in Chapter 16).

■ **BootP**   Can be used by Cisco routers to acquire IOS images on BootP servers—this is enabled by default.

■ **Configuration auto-loading**   The **no service config** command disables the router from finding its configuration on a TFTP server; **no boot network** prevents the router from loading an IOS image from a TFTP server.

■ **DNS lookups**   Enabled by default and are sent to the 255.255.255.255 address. To globally disable DNS lookups, use the **no ip domain-lookup** command; manually define DNS servers with the **ip name-server** command.

- **TCP keepalives**   Should be enabled to verify if a session is still open and to prevent "orphaned" sessions. Sessions that are no longer in existence will be removed by the router.

- **DHCP**   Disable the DHCP server function of the router unless it's the only device that can supply IP addressing information to hosts (typically for branch offices). DHCP is discussed in Chapter 8.

- **HTTP server**   Routers can be managed via a web browser—disable this on a perimeter router and use HTTPS instead.

- **Nagle**   Handles TCP congestion by allowing multiple characters to be sent in the same segment, instead of different segments, like telnet.

- **FTP server**   Disable the FTP server and FTP upload functionality on the router (the router should not be an FTP server).

- **TFTP server**   Disable TFTP server functions on the router (the router should not be a TFTP server).

- **IdentD server**   Disable the identification server on the router.

- **X.25 PAD**   This is enabled by default on most Cisco routers and should be disabled if you are not using X.25.

- **Password recovery procedure**   Disable the ability to perform the password recovery procedure from ROMMON mode.

on the *Job*

Some of these commands are deprecated in the latest IOS versions, and some are specific to an IOS package.

Interface Commands

Here is a list of commands you might want to execute to disable unnecessary layer 3 interface processes, such as router interfaces, by default, or VLAN switch interfaces:

```
IOS(config)# interface type [slot_#/]port_#
IOS(config-if)# no ip proxy-arp
IOS(config-if)# no ip redirects
IOS(config-if)# no ip unreachables
IOS(config-if)# no ip mask-reply
IOS(config-if)# no mop enabled
IOS(config-if)# no cdp enable
IOS(config-if)# ntp disable
IOS(config-if)# no ip directed-broadcast
IOS(config-if)# no ip gratuitous-arps
IOS(config-if)# shutdown
```

You should disable the following processes/programs on your IOS device (these are interface configurations):

■ **Proxy ARP**   Used by routers to reply to a local ARP request for a remote device (in a different subnet).

■ **ICMP redirects**   Your router tells the source about an alternative path.

■ **ICMP unreachables**   Your router tells the source that the destination is unreachable—disable this, because you don't want hackers knowing if a device is not reachable, or just not there.

■ **ICMP mask replies**   Your router tells a querier what the subnet mask is (disabled by default).

■ **Route caching**   You want to force all traffic to go through ACLs and security instead of using an ASIC's cache (this should be used with caution, since you could overburden the device's CPU).

■ **MOP (Maintenance and Operation Protocol)**   Performs a similar function to TFTP in DecNET environments.

■ **CDP**   Proprietary Cisco protocol that is used to share basic hardware and software information with a connected Cisco device. Disable this on interfaces where you have non-Cisco devices or nontrusted devices.

■ **NTP**   If an interface is not expecting to receive NTP messages, disable NTP on that interface. If you are implementing NTP, make sure you're using NTP with authentication (discussed in Chapter 17).

■ **Directed broadcasts**   As of 12.0 and later, directed broadcasts are disabled by default.

■ **Gratuitous ARPs**   Most routers send out ARPs whenever a client connects and negotiates IP addressing information over a PPP link; a hacker can use this to execute an ARP poison attack, filling up the local ARP table.

■ **Interfaces**   IOS switches, by default, have all interfaces enabled. Cisco recommends disabling interfaces that are not in use.

AutoSecure

The problem with manually disabling unused services is that you have to manually configure individual commands. *AutoSecure* is an IOS feature originally introduced on the ISR series of Cisco routers, such as the 870s, 1800s, 2800s, and

3800s, that allows you to put a basic security configuration on your router by running a simple script. It was introduced in IOS 12.3 and 12.3T. It is a Privileged EXEC script similar to the System Configuration Dialog: where the latter creates a basic configuration for a router, AutoSecure focuses only on security functions for securing a router. Like the setup script, AutoSecure asks you basic questions about securing your router. It will automatically enable or disable specific services running on your router; set up a stateful firewall by configuring Context-Based Access Control (CBAC), which requires a security IOS image; configure access control lists; and perform other tasks.

To run the AutoSecure script, from Privileged EXEC mode, execute the **auto secure** command:

```
Router#  auto secure [management | forwarding] [no-interact]
```

You can run AutoSecure in two modes:

- **Interactive**   You are prompted for security information during the scripting process.
- **Noninteractive**   IOS performs all security functions based on a set of defaults from Cisco.

AutoSecure basically secures the router at two levels:

- Management plane (traffic destined to the router)
- Forwarding plane (traffic going through the router)

With no extra parameters with the **auto secure** command, the router will secure both the management and forwarding planes while asking you questions about the security process.

Here is an example of running the AutoSecure script:

```
Router# auto secure
              --- AutoSecure Configuration ---

*** AutoSecure configuration enhances the security of
the router, but it will not make it absolutely resistant
to all security attacks ***
AutoSecure will modify the configuration of your device.
All configuration changes will be shown. For a detailed
explanation of how the configuration changes enhance security
and any possible side effects, please refer to Cisco.com for
```

```
Autosecure documentation.
At any prompt you may enter '?' for help.
Use ctrl-c to abort this session at any prompt.

Gathering information about the router for AutoSecure

Is this router connected to internet? [no]: yes
Enter the number of interfaces facing the internet [1]: 1

Interface         IP-Address   OK? Method Status   Protocol
FastEthernet0/0   10.0.6.2     YES NVRAM  up          up
FastEthernet0/1   172.30.6.2   YES NVRAM  up          up
Enter the interface name that is facing the internet:
    FastEthernet0/1

Securing Management plane services...
Disabling service finger
Disabling service pad
Disabling udp & tcp small servers
Enabling service password encryption
Enabling service tcp-keepalives-in
Enabling service tcp-keepalives-out
Disabling the cdp protocol
.
.
.
Here is a sample Security Banner to be shown
at every access to device. Modify it to suit your
enterprise requirements.

Authorized Access only
  This system is the property of So-&-So-Enterprise.
  UNAUTHORIZED ACCESS TO THIS DEVICE IS PROHIBITED.
.
.
.
Enter the security banner {Put the banner between
k and k, where k is any character}:
$
Keep Out...This means you!
$
Enable secret is either not configured or
 is the same as enable password
Enter the new enable secret: cisco1234
Confirm the enable secret : cisco1234
```

```
Enter the new enable password: cisco5678
Confirm the enable password: cisco5678

Configuration of local user database
Enter the username: richard
Enter the password: mypassword123
Confirm the password: mypassword123
Configuring AAA local authentication
Configuring Console, Aux and VTY lines for
 local authentication, exec-timeout, and transport
Securing device against Login Attacks
Configure the following parameters
Blocking Period when Login Attack detected: 3
Maximum Login failures with the device: 3
Maximum time period for crossing the failed login attempts: 30
Configure SSH server? [yes]: yes
Enter the domain-name: richarddeal.com

Configuring interface specific AutoSecure services
Disabling the following ip services on all interfaces:
 no ip redirects
 no ip proxy-arp
 no ip unreachables
 no ip directed-broadcast
 no ip mask-reply
Disabling mop on Ethernet interfaces

Securing Forwarding plane services...
Enabling CEF (This might impact the memory requirements for
 your platform)
Enabling unicast rpf on all interfaces connected to internet

Configure CBAC Firewall feature? [yes/no]: yes

This is the configuration generated:
no service finger
no service pad
no service udp-small-servers
no service tcp-small-servers
service password-encryption
service tcp-keepalives-in
service tcp-keepalives-out
no cdp run
.
.
.
```

```
banner motd ^C
Keep Out...This means you!
^C
.
.
.
enable secret 5 $1$yc/V$99CEHvCR7KoZ/ZznqByyx0
enable password 7 045802150C2E1D1C5A
username richard password 7 083145560E0C1702
.
.
.
ip domain-name cisco.com
crypto key generate rsa general-keys modulus 1024
ip ssh time-out 60
ip ssh authentication-retries 2
line vty 0 15
 transport input ssh telnet
.
.
.
interface FastEthernet0/0
 no ip redirects
 no ip proxy-arp
 no ip unreachables
 no ip directed-broadcast
 no ip mask-reply
 no mop enabled
interface FastEthernet0/1
.
.
.
ip cef
interface FastEthernet0/1
 ip verify unicast source reachable-via rx allow-default 100
.
.
.
ip inspect name autosec_inspect ftp timeout 3600
ip inspect name autosec_inspect http timeout 3600
.
.
.
ip inspect name autosec_inspect udp timeout 15
ip inspect name autosec_inspect tcp timeout 3600
ip access-list extended autosec_firewall_acl
```

```
 permit udp any any eq bootpc
 deny ip any any
interface FastEthernet0/1
 ip inspect autosec_inspect out
 ip access-group autosec_firewall_acl in
end
Apply this configuration to running-config? [yes]: yes
Applying the config generated to running-config
The name for the keys will be: Router6.richarddeal.com
% The key modulus size is 1024 bits
% Generating 1024 bit RSA keys, keys will be non-
    exportable...[OK]
000018: *Oct  5 16:09:57.467 UTC: %AUTOSEC-1-MODIFIED:
       AutoSecure configuration has been Modified on this device
```

During any of the prompts, you can type **?** to bring up help, or press CTRL-C to abort the script. At the beginning of the script, you are asked if the router is connected to the Internet. If so, tell AutoSecure which interface (or interfaces) is connected to the Internet so that it can set up its security policies correctly. In the preceding example, Fast Ethernet0/1 is connected to the Internet.

6.05. The digital resources that accompany this book contain a multimedia demonstration of running AutoSecure.

At this point, global services for the Management plane are enabled or disabled. In this section, you are asked to create a login banner, where an example is provided. To start the banner, enter a delimiting character that won't show up in the text, such as ^ or #. When you type in this character the second time, this will end the banner. Authentication, authorization, and accounting (AAA) and SSH are then configured. Following this, AutoSecure disables certain services under all of the router's interfaces.

At this point, AutoSecure will enable Cisco Express Forwarding (CEF), enable Context-Based Access Control (CBAC), and create an ACL to block unwanted IP traffic. This finishes the script, and AutoSecure displays the configuration it will activate on the router. Press the ENTER key or enter **yes** to accept and activate the configuration.

Cisco recommends running the AutoSecure script after you run the System Configuration Dialog, but before you begin any other advanced configuration tasks from the CLI. If you don't run the System Configuration Dialog, put a basic configuration on your router, such as configuring and enabling the interfaces and configuring a routing protocol, and then run AutoSecure.

CERTIFICATION OBJECTIVE 6.04

Router Configuration

This chapter builds upon the basic IOS configuration commands covered in your CCENT studies, where you learned how to move around the CLI, change the name of the device, configure passwords, configure hardware characteristics for an interface, and enable an interface. This section discusses these fundamentals in addition to router-specific commands to use for a basic configuration.

Interface Configuration

This section on router configuration covers additional interface configurations, such as configuring assigning an IP address to an interface and changing the bandwidth metric. Following sections will discuss some **show** commands to verify your interface's configuration.

IP Addressing Information

You can use many commands on the router to set up your IP addressing information. One of the most commonly used commands is the command to assign an IP address to an interface; however, many more commands are used, including those for setting up DNS, restricting directed broadcasts, and performing other tasks. The following sections cover some of these configurations.

Unlike layer 2 switches (such as the 2960), which need only a single IP address for remote management, routers need a unique IP address on each interface that will route IP traffic. Actually, each interface on a router is a separate network or subnet, and therefore you need to plan your IP addressing appropriately and assign a network number to each router segment and then take an unused host address from the segment and configure it on the interface of the router. This address then becomes the default gateway for devices connected to that interface.

Let's look at a couple of examples of incorrectly and correctly assigning IP addresses to a router's interfaces. Figure 6-1 shows an invalid configuration example. In this example, only one network number is used: 192.168.1.0/24. Notice that *each* interface on the router has an address from this same network number. Actually, if you would try to configure this addressing scheme on a router, you would get an overlapping address error and be prevented from completing the addressing configuration.

FIGURE 6-1

Invalid addressing
configuration for
a router

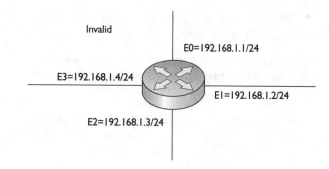

FIGURE 6-1

Invalid

E0=192.168.1.1/24

E3=192.168.1.4/24

E1=192.168.1.2/24

E2=192.168.1.3/24

Each interface needs a unique host address, as shown in Figure 6-2. Notice that in this example, each interface has an address from a *different* network number when compared to the other interfaces on the router. Which host address you choose for the router interface is up to personal preference. Many administrators use either the first or last host address in the network number for the router's interface, but any valid, unused host address from that network number can be used.

As you have probably already guessed, configuring an IP address on a router requires that you be in Interface Subconfiguration mode. Here is the syntax of this command:

```
Router(config)# interface type [slot_#/]port_#
Router(config-if)# ip address IP_address subnet_mask
```

This syntax, as you can see, is the same as that used for configuring an IP address on the 2960 switch (but under the VLAN interface). You can verify your IP addressing configuration with the **show interfaces** or **show ip interfaces** command, discussed later in this section.

Video

6.06. The digital resources that accompany this book contain a multimedia demonstration of configuring an IP address on an interface of a Cisco router.

FIGURE 6-2

Correct
addressing
configuration for
a router

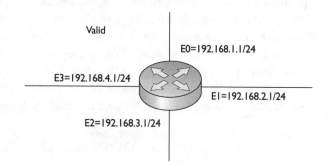

Valid

E0=192.168.1.1/24

E3=192.168.4.1/24

E1=192.168.2.1/24

E2=192.168.3.1/24

Using the example in Figure 6-2, the following would be the router's IP addressing configuration:

```
Router(config)# interface ethernet 0
Router(config-if)# ip address 192.168.1.1 255.255.255.0
Router(config-if)# no shutdown
Router(config-if)# exit
Router(config)# interface ethernet 1
Router(config-if)# ip address 192.168.2.1 255.255.255.0
Router(config-if)# no shutdown
. . .
```

exam
ⓦatch

If you omit the IP address on a router's interface, it will not process any IP traffic on that interface. If you misconfigured an IP address on a router's interface, use the `no ip address` command to remove it. Optionally, you can use the `ip address` command with the correct IP address and subnet mask to overwrite the existing IP address configuration on the interface. Also, you cannot have two different router interfaces with IP addresses in the subnet. For example, you cannot have an IP address of 192.168.1.1/24 on E0 and an IP address of 192.168.1.2/24 on E1—you'll receive an error message on the console when trying to configure the second address. Remember how to configure IP addressing on a router, since this might be part of a configuration or troubleshooting simulation question.

Bandwidth Parameter

All interfaces have a bandwidth value assigned to them. This is used by certain routing protocols, such as Open Shortest Path First (OSPF) and Enhanced Interior Gateway Routing Protocol (EIGRP), when making routing decisions. (Routing protocols are covered in Chapters 14, 18, 19, and 20.) For LAN-based interfaces, the speed of the interface becomes the bandwidth value, where the bandwidth is measured in kilobits per second (Kbps). However, on synchronous serial interfaces, the bandwidth defaults to 1554 Kbps, or the speed of a T1 link. This is true no matter what the physical clock rate is on the interface (you can change the serial link's clocked rate with the **clock rate** command). To change the bandwidth value for an interface, use the **bandwidth** Interface Subconfiguration mode command:

```
Router(config)# interface serial [slot_#/]port_#
Router(config-if)# bandwidth rate_in_Kbps
```

As an example, a serial interface clocked at 56,000 bps should have its bandwidth value changed to 56 Kbps, like this:

```
Router(config)# interface serial 0
Router(config-if)# bandwidth 56
```

watch Note that the `bandwidth` command does not change the clock rate on an interface: the `clock rate` command does this. The `bandwidth` command affects only routing protocols that use bandwidth as a metric.

The show ip interface Command

Common verification commands that you will use on a router are the **show interfaces** (discussed in Chapter 1) and **show ip interface** commands. The latter command displays the IP configuration of your router's interfaces, including its IP address and subnet mask:

```
Router> show ip interface [type [slot_#/]port_#]
```

Here is an abbreviated output of the **show ip interface** command:

```
Router# show ip interface
Ethernet1 is up, line protocol is up
  Internet address is 192.168.1.1/24
  Broadcast address is 255.255.255.255
  Address determined by setup command
  MTU is 1500 bytes
  Helper address is not set
  Directed broadcast forwarding is disabled
  Outgoing access list is not set
  Inbound  access list is 100
  .
  .
  .
```

watch Use the `show ip interface` command to determine whether an ACL is applied to an interface.

As you can see from this command, the status of the interface is shown, the IP address and mask are displayed, and direct broadcasts will be dropped if received on the interface. Any access list applied to the interface is also displayed.

An additional parameter to the preceding command, **brief**, will display a single-line description for each interface, as shown here:

```
Router# show ip interface brief
Interface   IP-Address  OK? Method Status                Protocol
Ethernet0   192.168.1.1 YES NVRAM  up                    up
Ethernet1   192.168.2.1 YES NVRAM  administratively down down
```

6.07. *The digital resources that accompany this book contain a multimedia demonstration of using the* `show ip interface` *command.*

This is an extremely useful command when you want to see a quick overview of all of the interfaces on the router, their IP addresses, and their statuses. This command also works on switches.

ⓦatch   *Use the* `show ip` `interface brief` *command to see a quick overview of the IP addresses on interfaces and their operational state.*

Subnet Zero Configuration

Starting with IOS 12.0, Cisco automatically allows you to use IP subnet zero networks—the first network number in a subnetted network. Prior to IOS 12.0, you were not, by default, allowed to use these subnets. However, if you needed extra networks, you could enable their use by configuring the **ip subnet-zero** command:

```
Router(config)# ip subnet-zero
```

In IOS 12.0 and later, this command will already be in the router's default configuration.

Static Host Configuration

As you are well aware, in the IP world, we typically don't type in an IP address to reach a destination. For example, if you want to reach Cisco's site, in your web browser address bar, you type *www.cisco.com* or *http://www.cisco.com*. Your web browser then resolves the host and domain names to an IP address. The router also supports hostnames for certain operations, such as ping and telnet (discussed in Chapter 7).

You can have your router resolve hostnames to IP addresses in two ways: static and dynamic (using DNS). You can create a static resolution table using this command:

```
Router(config)# ip host name_of_host [TCP_port_#]
                            IP_address_of_host [2nd_IP_address...]
```

You must first specify the name of the remote host. Optionally, you can specify a port number for the host—this defaults to 23 for telnet if you omit it. After this, you can list up to eight IP addresses for this host. The router will try to reach the host with the first address, and if that fails, it will try the second address, and so on. Use the **show hosts** command to examine your static entries, which are discussed following the next section.

DNS Resolution Configuration

If you have access to a DNS server or servers, you can have your router use these to resolve names to IP addresses. This is configured with the **ip name-server** command:

```
Router(config)# ip name-server IP_address_of_DNS_server
                            [2nd_server's_IP address ...]
```

You can list up to six DNS servers for the router to use with this command. Use the **show hosts** command to examine your static and dynamic entries. This command is discussed in the next section.

Many administrators don't like using DNS to resolve names to addresses on routers because of one nuisance feature on the router: Whenever you type a nonexistent command on the router, the router assumes you are trying to telnet to a device by that *name* and tries to resolve it to an IP address. This is annoying because either you have to wait for the DNS query to time out or you must execute the break sequence (CTRL-SHIFT-6).

on the job

One of the first things I typically configure on a router is the no ip domain-lookup *command so that when I mistype commands, I don't have to wait for the router to attempt to resolve the mistyped command to an IP address.*

You have another option, though, and that is to disable DNS lookups on the router with the following command:

```
Router(config)# no ip domain-lookup
```

6.08. The digital resources that accompany this book contain a multimedia demonstration of using and disabling name resolution on a Cisco router.

The show hosts Command

To view the static and dynamic DNS entries in your router's resolution table, use this command:

```
Router# show hosts
Default domain is CHECK.COM
Name/address lookup uses domain service
Name servers are 255.255.255.255
Host           Flag        Age   Type  Address(es)
a.check.com    (temp, OK)  1     IP    172.15.9.9
b.check.com    (temp, OK)  8     IP    172.15.1.1
f.check.com    (perm, OK)  0     IP    172.15.1.2
```

The first two entries in the table were learned via a DNS server (temp flag), whereas the last entry was configured statically on the router with the **ip host** command (perm flag).

EXERCISE 6-1

MHE Lab

Using IOS Features

The last few sections have covered how you configure basic IP addressing features on your Cisco router. You can perform the following exercises on a Cisco router to reinforce these skills. Use the router simulator included with the book, or you can use a real Cisco router. You can find a picture of the network diagram for the simulator in the Introduction to this book.

Access the simulator and click the Lab Instructions tab. Click the McGraw-Hill Education tab (to the right of the Standard and Custom tabs) at the top left. Double-click Exercise 6-1. This will load a basic configuration on devices in the network topology, including IP addresses on the Host PCs based on the simple configuration commands you learned during your CCENT studies.

1. Access the 2600-1 router. Click the Lab Instructions tab and use the drop-down selector and choose 2600-1; or click the NetMap tab and double-click the 2600-1 device icon.

2. Configure an IP address of 192.168.1.1/24 on fastethernet0/0 of the 2600-1 router and bring the interface up. Go to Privileged EXEC mode

and type these commands: `configure terminal`, `interface fastethernet0/0`, `ip address 192.168.1.1 255.255.255.0`, `no shutdown`, and `exit`.

3. Configure an IP address of 192.168.2.1/24 on the serial0 interface, set the clock rate to 64,000 bps, and enable the interface.

4. Configure serial0: `interface serial0`, `ip address 192.168.2.1 255.255.255.0`, `clock rate 64000`, `no shutdown`, and `exit`. Return to Privileged EXEC mode by typing `end`.

5. Save the configuration file on the router: `copy running-config startup-config`.

6. Test connectivity between the Host-1 PC and the 2600-1. Use the drop-down selector for Devices and select Host-1. Test the connection from Host-1 by pinging the 2600-1: `ping 192.168.1.1`. The ping should be successful.

7. Access the 2600-2 router: Click the Lab Instructions tab and use the drop-down selector and choose 2600-2; or click the NetMap tab and double-click the 2600-2 device icon.

8. Configure an IP address of 192.168.3.1/24 on fastethernet0/0 of the 2600-2 router and bring up the interface. Go to Privileged EXEC mode and type these commands: `configure terminal`, `interface fastethernet0/0`, `ip address 192.168.3.1 255.255.255.0`, `no shutdown`, and `exit`.

9. Configure an IP address of 192.168.2.2/24 on the serial0 interface and enable the interface. Configure serial0: `interface serial0`, `ip address 192.168.2.2 255.255.255.0`, `no shutdown`, and `exit`. Return to Privileged EXEC mode by typing `end`.

10. Save the configuration file on the router: `copy running-config startup-config`.

11. Test connectivity between the 2600-2 and 2600-1 routers: `ping 192.168.2.1`. The ping should be successful.

12. Test connectivity between the Host-3 PC and the 2600-2. Click the Lab Instructions tab and use the drop-down selector and choose Host-3; or click the NetMap tab and double-click the Host-3 device icon.. Test the connection from Host-3 by pinging the 2600-2: `ping 192.168.3.1`. The ping should be successful.

You should now be more familiar with configuring IP addressing information on a router.

CERTIFICATION OBJECTIVE 6.05

Router-on-a-Stick

Typically, we think of routing as traffic coming in one physical interface and leaving another physical interface. As you learned in Chapter 2, however, trunks can be used to support multiple VLANs, where each VLAN has a unique layer 3 network or subnet number. Certain router models and interface combinations, such as the 1800 series, support trunk connections. A *router-on-a-stick* is a router that has a single trunk connection to a switch and routes between the VLANs on this trunk connection. You could easily do this without a trunk (access-link connections), but each VLAN would require a separate access-link (physical) interface on the router, and this would increase the price of the router solution.

For instance, if you had five VLANs, and your router didn't support trunking, you would need five physical LAN interfaces on your router in order to route between the five VLANs. However, with a trunk connection, you can route between all five VLANs on a *single* interface. Because of cost and scalability, most administrators prefer using a router-on-a-stick approach to solve their routing problems in switched networks.

e x a m

ⓦ a t c h

A router-on-a-stick is a router that has a single trunk connection to a switch and routes between multiple VLANs on this trunk. Subinterfaces are used on the router to designate the VLAN with which they are associated. Each VLAN needs a different IP subnet configuration.

Subinterface Configuration

To set up a router-on-a-stick, you need to break up your router's physical interface into multiple logical interfaces, called *subinterfaces*. Cisco supports up to 1000 interfaces on a router, which includes both physical and logical interfaces. Once you create a subinterface, a router will treat this logical interface just like a physical interface: you can assign layer 3 addressing to it, enable, it, disable it, and do many other things.

To create a subinterface, use the following command:

```
Router(config)# interface type port_#.subinterface_#
                        [point|multipoint]
Router(config-subif)#
```

After entering the physical interface type and port identifier, follow this with a dot (.) and a subinterface number. The subinterface number can range from 0 to 4,294,967,295. The number that you use for the subinterface number is only for reference purposes within IOS, and the only requirement is that when creating a subinterface, you use a unique subinterface number. Many administrators prefer to use the VLAN number that the subinterface will handle for the subinterface number; however, this is not a requirement, and the two numbers are not related in any way.

At the end of the statement, you must specify the type of connection *if* the interface is of type serial; otherwise, you can omit it. The **point** parameter is used for point-to-point serial connections, and **multipoint** is used for multipoint connections (many devices connected to the interface). The **multipoint** parameter is used for connections that have more than one device connected to them (physically or logically). For a router-on-a-stick configuration, you can omit the connection type, since the default is **multipoint** for LAN interfaces.

Interface Encapsulation

Once you create a subinterface, you'll notice that your CLI prompt has changed and that you are now in Subinterface Configuration mode. If you are routing between VLANs, you'll need an interface that supports trunking. Some things are configured on the major interface, and some things are configured on the subinterface. Configurations such as duplexing and speed are done on the major (or physical) interface. Most other tasks are done on the subinterface (the logical interface), including to which VLAN the subinterface belongs and its IP addressing information.

6.09. The digital resources that accompany this book contain a multimedia demonstration of setting up a router-on-a-stick.

When setting up your subinterface for a router-on-a-stick, one thing that you must configure is the type of trunking—ISL or 802.1Q—and the VLAN with which the subinterface is associated, like this:

```
Router(config)# interface type port_#.subinterface_#
Router(config-subif)# encapsulation isl|dot1q VLAN_#
```

Use the **encapsulation** command to specify the trunk type and the VLAN associated with the subinterface. The VLAN number you specify here *must*

correspond to the correct VLAN number in your switched network. You must also set up a trunk connection on the switch for the port to which the router is connected. Once you do this, the switch will send tagged frames to the router, and the router, using your encapsulation, will understand how to read the tags. The router will be able to see from which VLAN the frame came and match it up with the appropriate subinterface that will process it. Remember that only a few of Cisco's switches today support ISL: all of them support 802.1Q, which is denoted with the `dot1q` parameter.

Router-on-a-Stick Example Configuration

Let's look at an example to see how a router-on-a-stick is configured. Figure 6-3 shows this configuration. Assume that this is a 3800 router, that the Fast Ethernet interface is the first interface in the first slot, and that the switch is using 802.1Q trunking on the connected interface.

FIGURE 6-3

Router-on-a-stick example

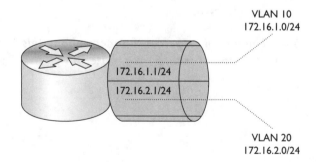

VLAN 10
172.16.1.0/24

172.16.1.1/24

172.16.2.1/24

VLAN 20
172.16.2.0/24

Here's the code example for this router:

```
Router(config)# interface fastethernet0/0
Router(config-if)# duplex full
Router(config-if)# no shutdown
Router(config-if)# exit
Router(config)# interface fastethernet0/0.1
Router(config-subif)# encapsulation dot1q 10
Router(config-subif)# ip address 172.15.1.1 255.255.255.0
Router(config-subif)# exit
Router(config)# interface fastethernet0/0.2
Router(config-subif)# encapsulation dot1q 20
Router(config-subif)# ip address 172.15.2.1 255.255.255.0
Router(config-subif)# exit
```

Notice in this example that the subinterface numbers in the **interface** command (1 and 2) do not match the VLAN numbers in the **encapsulation** command (10 and 20); remember that the subinterface numbers are used by IOS only to reference the particular subinterface and do not have to match any configuration on the subinterface.

on the
** job**

If you are configuring static routes and want to route traffic out of a particular subinterface, specify the major interface along with the subinterface number, such as `fastethernet0/0.2`*. Static routes are discussed in Chapter 9.*

INSIDE THE EXAM

Router Hardware Components

You should be familiar with the different hardware components, what they are used for, and how they affect the bootup process.

Router Bootup Process

You should be familiar with how the router boots up and finds its IOS and configuration file. Understand the use of the configuration

register, especially the difference between 0x2102 and 0x2142. Be able to interpret the configuration register value based on the last hexadecimal digit in the configuration register and how this affects the router's bootup process. Understand the use of the **boot system** commands and issues if you misconfigured

(Continued)

INSIDE THE EXAM

these commands. Use the `show version` command to verify these settings. Remember that the System Configuration Dialog will start automatically if the router boots up and can't find its configuration file in NVRAM. Be familiar with how the password recovery process is performed from ROMMON mode.

AutoSecure

Understand what the AutoSecure feature does in IOS.

Router Configuration

A router must have an IP address on its interface or it will not process any IP packets on the interface. You should be able to put a basic configuration on a router in a short time period. This includes assigning a hostname, configuring the Privileged EXEC and line passwords, creating a login banner, enabling interfaces, assigning a clock rate to a serial DCE interface, and assigning IP

addresses to interfaces. You might see a simulation question that has you do this on three to five routers, including turning on a routing protocol. You should be able to perform these basic tasks in less than three minutes on each router. Remember to test connectivity from a host in a subnet to the router's IP address connected to the subnet (the default gateway). Be able to interpret the output of the `show ip interface brief` command. Understand the use of the `ip subnet-zero` command.

Router-on-a-Stick

Understand how to configure a router-on-a-stick, especially how subinterfaces are created and how the `encapsulation` command associates a VLAN to the subinterface. Remember that the trunking protocol must match between the switch and the router: either 802.1Q or ISL. The IP address on the subinterface is the default gateway address for devices associated with that VLAN.

CERTIFICATION SUMMARY

The router contains the following components in ROM: POST, bootstrap program, and ROM Monitor (ROMMON). POST performs hardware tests. The bootstrap program finds and loads IOS. ROMMON provides basic access to the router to perform testing and troubleshooting.

The configuration register affects how the router boots up. By default, POST is run, the bootstrap program is loaded, the IOS image is located, and the configuration file is executed. You can change this by using **boot system** commands or by changing the configuration register value. The **show version** command displays the current register value and what it will be upon a reload. The default register value is typically 0x2102. For the password recovery, use 0x2142.

The router needs an IP address on each interface where it will be processing IP traffic. This is configured on an interface with the **ip address** command. Use the **show ip interface brief** command to view the status and configuration of your interfaces.

A router-on-a-stick uses a single trunk connection from a router to a switch to route among multiple VLANs. You must create a subinterface on your router for each VLAN. Each subinterface requires the **encapsulation isl|dot1q** command and a layer 3 address or addresses.

✓ # TWO-MINUTE DRILL

Router Hardware Components

❑ ROM stores the Mini-IOS, the bootstrap program, ROMMON, and POST.

❑ Flash stores IOS images.

❑ NVRAM stores the configuration files.

❑ RAM stores the active configuration, including tables and buffers.

Router Bootup Process

❑ The configuration register and **boot system** commands can be used to override the default router bootup behavior.

❑ Use the **show version** command to see the IOS version being used by the router as well as the register value.

❑ If the fourth hexadecimal character of the configuration register is 0x0, the router boots into ROMMON mode; if 0x1, the router boots the Mini-IOS or the first file in flash if a Mini-IOS doesn't exist; if 0x2–0xF, the router uses the default boot sequence. The default configuration register value is 0x2102. For the password recovery, it's 0x2142. Use the **config-register** IOS command to change this value.

❑ Here is the default bootup process: The bootstrap program examines the configuration register to determine how to boot up. If it is the default, the bootstrap program looks for **boot system** commands in the configuration file in NVRAM. If none are found, it looks for IOS in flash. If no files are found in flash, the bootstrap program generates a TFTP local broadcast to locate IOS. If no TFTP server is found, the bootstrap program loads the Mini-IOS in ROM. If there is no Mini-IOS in ROM, the bootstrap program loads ROMMON.

❑ The System Configuration Dialog (setup script) will run when the router boots up and there is no configuration file in NVRAM.

❑ Use the **confreg** command from ROMMON mode to change the configuration register to 0x2142 to perform the password recovery process.

AutoSecure

❑ AutoSecure puts a basic security configuration on a router, such as passwords, CBAC, ACLs, SSH, and other information. It is run from Privileged EXEC mode using the **auto secure** command.

Router Configuration

❑ IP addresses are configured on each interface of the router that will process IP packets with the **ip address** Interface Subconfiguration mode command. The **bandwidth** command changes the metric of the interface, which is used by some routing protocols.

❑ The **show ip interface brief** command displays a brief configuration and status of each interface on the router.

Router-on-a-Stick

❑ A router-on-a-stick is a router with a single trunk connection to a switch; a router routes between the VLANs on this trunk connection.

❑ To route between VLANs with a router-on-a-stick, use subinterfaces and specify the VLAN with the **encapsulation isl|dot1q** command on the subinterface.

SELF TEST

The following Self Test questions will help you measure your understanding of the material presented in this chapter. Read all the choices carefully, as there may be more than one correct answer. Choose all correct answers for each question.

Router Hardware Components

1. Which of the following are stored in ROM? (Choose two answers.)
   A. POST
   B. ROMMON
   C. Configuration file
   D. System recovery file

2. Which type of memory does not maintain its contents during a power-off state?
   A. NVRAM
   B. ROM
   C. RAM
   D. Flash

Router Bootup Process

3. Which router command would you use to view the configuration register value?
   A. `show register`
   B. `show interfaces`
   C. `show configuration`
   D. `show version`

4. Enter the router IOS Configuration mode command to change the configuration register so that it will not load the startup configuration file located in NVRAM: _____.

AutoSecure

5. When is AutoSecure run on a router?
   A. Manually from Privileged EXEC mode
   B. Manually from Configuration mode
   C. Automatically when the router boots up without a configuration
   D. Automatically when the router boots up without a configuration or manually from Privileged EXEC mode

Router Configuration

6. You need to configure an IP address on a router's serial interface (s0/0). Use the last host address in 192.168.1.128/30. The interface is a DCE, and you need to enable the interface. The speed of the connection is 64 Kbps. Set the bandwidth metric to match the speed of the interface. Enter the commands to accomplish this.

7. Enter the router Global Configuration mode command that will allow you to use the first address in the first subnet of a subnetted C class network: _____.

8. Examine this output:

```
Interface  IP-Address  OK? Method Status                Protocol
Ethernet0  192.168.1.1 YES NVRAM  up                    up
Ethernet1  192.168.2.1 YES NVRAM  administratively down down
```

Enter the router command that created this output: _____.

Router-on-a-Stick

9. When configuring a router-on-a-stick, the configuration is done on _____.
   A. physical interfaces
   B. major interfaces
   C. subinterfaces

10. Which router-on-a-stick command defines the VLAN for the interface?
   A. `vlan`
   B. `encapsulation`
   C. `trunk`
   D. `frame-type`

SELF TEST ANSWERS

Router Hardware Components

I. ☑ **A** and **B**. POST, ROMMON, the Mini-IOS, and the bootstrap program are in ROM.
☒ **C** is incorrect because the configuration file is stored in NVRAM, and **D** is a nonexistent file.

2. ☑ **C**. RAM contents are erased when you turn off the device.
☒ **A, B,** and **D** are incorrect; NVRAM, ROM, and flash maintain their contents when the device is turned off.

Router Bootup Process

3. ☑ **D**. Use the **show version** command to view the configuration register value.
☒ **A** is a nonexistent command. **B** is incorrect because **show interfaces** shows only interface statistics. **C** is the old command version for **show startup-config**.

4. ☑ Enter the **config-register 0x2142** command in Configuration mode to cause the router to boot up and not load the configuration file in NVRAM.

AutoSecure

5. ☑ **A**. AutoSecure can be run manually only from Privileged EXEC mode with the **auto secure** command.
☒ **B, C,** and **D** are incorrect.

Router Configuration

6. ☑ The router's configuration will look like this:

```
interface serial0/0
  ip address 192.168.1.130 255.255.255.252
  clock rate 64000
  bandwidth 64
  no shutdown
```

7. ☑ The `ip subnet-zero` command allows you to use the first and last subnet when configuring IP addresses on interfaces of your router.

8. ☑ `show ip interface brief`

Router-on-a-Stick

9. ☑ **C.** Trunking with a router-on-a-stick is done on subinterfaces.
☒ Hardware characteristics are configured on **A** (physical interfaces) when trunking, not VLANs. Sometimes the term in **B** (major interfaces) is used to refer to a physical interface.

10. ☑ **B.** Use the `encapsulation` command to specify the trunking encapsulation and the VLAN number for the subinterface.
☒ **A, C,** and **D** are nonexistent router commands.

7

IOS Device Management

T his chapter covers important IOS features that you can use to manage your IOS device. Many of these features are supported across all IOS devices, but some of them are supported on only certain devices. This chapter offers an in-depth discussion of configuration files. It also discusses how to upgrade your IOS device and remotely access it via Secure Shell (SSH). You can use many tools on your IOS device for troubleshooting connection problems, including the Cisco Discovery Protocol (CDP), ping, traceroute, telnet, and debug. These tools are discussed toward the end of the chapter.

CERTIFICATION OBJECTIVE 7.01

Router Configuration Files

You had a basic introduction to configuration files during your CCENT studies. Remember that a configuration file contains the commands used to configure an IOS device. Configuration files are typically located in one of three places: RAM, NVRAM, and/or an external server, such as a TFTP, FTP, HTTP, or Secure Copy (SCP) server. The configuration that the router is currently using is in RAM. You can back up, or save, this configuration either to NVRAM or to an external server.

As you may recall from your CCENT studies, the commands *related* to configuration files, even **show** commands, require you to be in Privileged EXEC mode. Also, the running configuration of an IOS device is not automatically saved to NVRAM—you must manually do this with the **copy running-config startup-config** command. The following sections show you how to manipulate your configuration files.

Saving Configuration Files

You can save your configuration from RAM to NVRAM with the **copy running-config startup-config** command. When you execute this command, whatever filename (the default is *startup-config*) you are copying to in NVRAM is completely overwritten. If you want to keep an old copy and a newer one in NVRAM, you'll need to specify a name other than startup-config. Note that the **copy** command has two parameters: The first parameter refers to where the source information is (what you want to copy it from), and the second parameter refers to where the destination is (where you want to copy it to).

You can copy your running-config or startup-config configuration file to flash, like this:

```
IOS# copy running-config flash:file_name
```

```
IOS# copy startup-config flash:file_name
```

This allows you to have multiple configuration files stored locally on your IOS device; however, when booting up, your IOS device, by default, will use the startup-config file in NVRAM to load its configuration.

on the **job** *It is not common practice to copy configuration files to flash, and for exam purposes, this is not where you back them up. However, I commonly do this when an FTP or TFTP server currently isn't reachable and I am too lazy to copy the configuration to the Windows Notepad application.*

You can also back up your configuration to an external server. This requires you to have the server software on a server or PC and IP configured correctly on your IOS device in order to access the server. The syntax looks like this on your IOS device:

```
IOS# copy running-config URL_location
```

For example, to back up your configuration file to a TFTP server, the configuration would look like this:

```
IOS# copy running-config tftp://192.168.1.10/mybackupfile.txt
```

The configuration is backed up to an ASCII text file. If you don't supply the full URL, just the protocol information, you'll be prompted for the additional information, like this:

```
IOS# copy running-config tftp
Address or name of remote host []? 192.168.1.10
Destination filename [router-confg]? mybackupfile.cfg
!!
781 bytes copied in 5.8 secs (156 bytes/sec)
IOS#
```

If the filename already exists on the server, the server *overwrites* the old file. After entering this information, you should see bang symbols (!) indicating the successful transfer of UDP segments to the TFTP server. If you see periods (.), this indicates an unsuccessful transfer. Plus, upon a successful transfer, you should also see how many bytes were copied to the server.

7.01. The digital resources that accompany this book contain a multimedia demonstration of backing up the configuration file of a router.

Restoring Configuration Files

There may be situations in which you have misconfigured your router or switch and want to take a saved configuration file and load it back into your Cisco device. You can do this by reversing the source and destination information in the **copy** command:

```
IOS# copy URL_location running-config
```

```
IOS# copy URL_location startup-config
```

Three variations of the **copy** command can restore your configuration. A TFTP server is used in this example for the first two options. Here is the first one:

```
IOS# copy tftp startup-config
Address or name of remote host []? 192.168.1.10
Source filename []? mybackupfile.cfg
Destination filename [startup-config]?
Accessing tftp://192.168.1.10/mybackupfile.cfg...
Loading mybackupfile.cfg from 192.168.1.10 (via Ethernet0): !
[OK - 781/1024 bytes]
[OK]
781 bytes copied in 11.216 secs (71 bytes/sec)
```

In this example, the configuration file is copied from a TFTP server to NVRAM (the startup-config file); if the file already exists in NVRAM, it will be overwritten. You can also restore your configuration from a TFTP server to active memory:

```
IOS# copy tftp running-config
```

7.02. The digital resources that accompany this book contain a multimedia demonstration of restoring the configuration file on a router.

There is one main difference between moving the configuration file from TFTP to NVRAM and moving it from TFTP to RAM. With the former method, the file in NVRAM is replaced with the one being copied; with the latter method, a *merge* process is used. During a merge process, IOS updates commands that are common to both places—the new file and in RAM. IOS also executes any new commands it finds in the uploaded configuration file and adds them to the running-config file. However, IOS does not delete any commands in RAM that it does not find in the uploaded configuration file. In other words, this is *not* a replacement process. As an example, assume that you have a configuration file on a TFTP server that has IPX and IP information in it, but your RAM configuration has IP and AppleTalk. In this example, the router updates the IP configuration, adds the IPX commands, but leaves the AppleTalk commands as they are.

This process is also true if you want to restore your configuration from NVRAM to RAM with this command (the third restore option):

```
IOS# copy startup-config running-config
```

If your backed-up configuration is in flash, use this syntax to restore it:

```
IOS# copy flash:file_name running-config|startup-config
```

e x a m

w a t c h   *The copy command backs up and restores configuration files:* copy running-config startup-config *and* copy running-config tftp *back up the configuration file. The* copy startup-config running-config *and* copy tftp running-config *or* copy tftp startup-config *commands restore the configuration file. The* erase startup-config *command deletes the configuration file.*

Creating and Deleting Configuration Files

Along with knowing how to back up and restore configuration files, you also need to know how to create and delete them. Actually, you already know how to create a basic configuration file by going into Configuration mode with the Privileged EXEC `configure terminal` command. When you are executing commands within this mode (whether by typing them or pasting them in), IOS is using a merge process (unless you use the **no** parameter for a command to delete or negate it).

Video

7.03. The digital resources that accompany this book contain a multimedia demonstration of deleting the NVRAM configuration file of a router.

You can also delete your configuration file in the startup-config file in NVRAM by using the following command:

```
IOS# erase startup-config
```

```
IOS# erase nvram
```

IOS 11.1 and earlier versions of this process, which are still supported, use the **write erase** command.

To verify the erasure, use the **show startup-config** command:

```
IOS# show startup-config
%% Non-volatile configuration memory is not present
```

Configuration File Nomenclature

Starting with IOS 12.0 and later, Cisco introduced command and naming nomenclatures that follow Cisco IOS File System (IFS) guidelines (what you are used to when entering a URL in a web browser address text box). Therefore, instead of entering a command and having a router prompt you for additional information, such as the IP address of a TFTP server as well as the filename, you can now put all of this information on a single command line. Commands that reference configuration files and IOS images contain prefixes in front of the file type, as shown in Table 7-1.

TABLE 7-1	Location	Description
File Locations	bootflash	Bootflash memory
	flash	Flash memory on the motherboard
	flh	Flash load helper log files
	ftp	FTP server
	nvram	Nonvolatile RAM (NVRAM)
	rcp	Remote Copy Protocol (RCP) server
	scp	Secure Copy (SCP) server—uses RCP through an SSH tunnel
	slot0	PCMCIA slot 0
	slot1	PCMCIA slot 1
	system	RAM
	tftp	TFTP server

Let's take a look at an example. For instance, say that you want to back up your router's configuration from RAM to NVRAM. With the new syntax, you could type in the following:

```
IOS# copy system:running-config nvram:startup-config
```

You don't always have to put in the type; for instance, in the preceding example, you could easily have entered this:

```
IOS# copy running-config startup-config
```

In many cases, IOS knows, based on the name of the file, which location you're referring to. For example, when you use *running-config*, IOS assumes you're referring to RAM, or **system:**, as the location.

To view the active configuration, you can use this command:

```
IOS# more system:running-config
```

If you want to delete a file in flash, such as a backed-up configuration file, use the following command:

```
IOS# delete flash:file_name
```

You'll be asked to verify whether you want to delete the file. You can also use this command to delete any file in flash.

on the job

The older style of entering configuration and IOS commands is still supported along with the new one. One command that I constantly use in production environments is the write memory *command, which can be abbreviated as* wr. *This performs the equivalent of the* copy running-config startup-config *command, but it requires only two keystrokes to perform! Please note, however, that the older command syntax is not supported on Cisco exams!*

Review of Configuration Files

It is important that you understand what action IOS will take when it is either backing up or restoring a configuration file to a particular location. Table 7-2 summarizes this information for the routers.

TABLE 7-2   Overview of IOS Process When Dealing with Configuration Files

Location (From)	Location (To)	Command	IOS Process
RAM	NVRAM	`copy running-config startup-config`	Overwrite
RAM	TFTP	`copy running-config tftp`	Overwrite
NVRAM	RAM	`copy startup-config running-config`	Merge
NVRAM	TFTP	`copy startup-config tftp`	Overwrite
TFTP	RAM	`copy tftp running-config`	Merge
TFTP	NVRAM	`copy tftp startup-config`	Overwrite
CLI	RAM	`configure terminal`	Merge

EXERCISE 7-1

MHE Lab

Manipulating Your Router's Configuration Files

The last few sections dealt with the router's configuration files and how you manipulate them. This exercise will help you reinforce your understanding of this material. You'll perform these steps on a 2600 router using Boson's NetSim simulator. You can find a picture of the network diagram for the simulator in the Introduction of this book. After starting up the simulator, click the Lab Navigator button. Next, double-click Exercise 7-1 and click the Load Lab button. This will load the lab configuration based on the exercises in Chapter 6.

1. Access the 2600-1 router.

   Click the Labs tab at the bottom left of the window. Click the McGraw-Hill Education tab (to the right of the Standard and Custom tabs) at the top left. Click the Lab Instructions tab and use the drop-down selector for Devices to choose 2600-1; or click the NetMap tab and double-click the 2600-1 device icon.

2. Access the 2600-1 router's Privileged EXEC mode and view the running configuration.

   Access Privileged EXEC mode: **enable**. Use the **show running-config** command.

3. Save your router's active configuration to NVRAM. Verify the copy.

    Use the `copy running-config startup-config` command. Verify the copy: `show startup-config`.

4. Change the hostname on the router to *different* and then reload the saved configuration from the NVRAM into RAM. What is the hostname once the restore has completed?

    Access Configuration mode (`configure terminal`) and use the `hostname different` command to change the router's name to *different*. Exit Configuration mode: `end`. Restore your configuration with `copy startup-config running-config`. Your prompt should change back to the previous name of the router (2600-1). (You might have to wait a few seconds for this to complete.)

5. Erase your router's saved configuration in NVRAM. Examine the configuration file in NVRAM. Save the active configuration file to NVRAM. Examine the configuration file in NVRAM.

    Use the `erase startup-config` command to erase your configuration in NVRAM. Press ENTER to confirm the erase. Use the `show startup-config` command to verify that the configuration file was deleted.

6. Save your configuration file in RAM to NVRAM. View the newly saved configuration file in NVRAM.

    Use the `copy running-config startup-config` command to save your configuration to NVRAM. Use the `show startup-config` command to verify that your router's configuration was backed up from RAM to NVRAM.

Now you should be more comfortable with manipulating a router's configuration files. In the next section, you will learn how you should deal with changes in your network.

CERTIFICATION OBJECTIVE 7.02

Changes in Your Network

When you decide to make changes to your network, including the addition or deletion of devices, you should always do some preparation work *before* you make the changes. Making changes can cause things to not function correctly, or not function at all, so you should always prepare beforehand. The following two sections cover the basics of handling changes.

Adding Devices

Before you add an IOS device to your network, you should gather the following information and perform the following tasks:

1. Decide which IP address you'll assign to the device for management purposes.
2. Configure the ports of the device, including the console and VTY ports.
3. Set up your passwords for User and Privileged EXEC access.
4. Assign the appropriate IP addresses to the device's interface(s).
5. Create a basic configuration on the device so that it can perform its job.

Changing Devices

You will constantly be making configuration changes to your network to enhance performance and security. *Before* you make any changes to your network, you should *always* back up your configuration files. Likewise, before you perform a software upgrade on your Cisco device, you should always back up the old IOS image.

You should check a few things before loading the new image on your IOS device. First, does the new image contain all of the features that your previous image had? Or at least the features that you need? Also, does your IOS device have enough flash *and* RAM to store and load the IOS image? You need to check these items before proceeding to load the new image.

At times, you may need to upgrade the hardware or add a new module to your Cisco device. Some devices require that you turn them off before doing the upgrade, while other devices can be left powered on. It is extremely important that you read the installation manual that comes with the hardware before performing the installation. If you install a hardware component into a device that requires that the device be turned off and the device is running, you could damage your new component or, worse, electrocute yourself.

on the !
Ọ o b

Remember that it is much easier to restore a backup copy than it is to re-create something from scratch. Also, whenever you make changes, always test the change to ensure that your Cisco device is performing as expected.

CERTIFICATION OBJECTIVE 7.03

IOS Image Files

The default location of IOS images is in flash. Some IOS devices have flash built into the motherboard, some use PCMCIA cards for storage, and some use a combination of both. At times, you will have to deal with the device's flash when you want to perform an upgrade, for instance. To view your files in flash, use the **show flash** command:

```
IOS# show flash
-#- --length-- -----date/time------ path
1             0 Sep 18 2007 15:42:20 +00:00 .Trashes
2          4096 Sep 18 2007 15:42:20 +00:00 ._.Trashes
3         12292 Sep 18 2007 15:55:12 +00:00 .DS_Store
4          1159 Sep 9 2007 18:01:42 +00:00 udp.phdf
5       4787200 Oct 3 2007 14:33:50 +00:00 sdm.tar
6          2679 Sep 9 2007 18:01:28 +00:00 ip.phdf
7        113152 Oct 3 2007 14:34:02 +00:00 home.tar
8          2227 Dec 4 2007 16:02:28 +00:00 pre_autosec.cfg
.
.
.
16     23787192 Sep 9 2007 17:45:30 +00:00
                        c1841-advipservicesk9-mz.124-6.T7.bin
.
.
.
31946752 bytes available (31922176 bytes used)
```

Use the show flash, *show* version, *or* dir *command to see how much flash memory is installed on your IOS device.*

In this example, you can see that a router's flash holds many files. Below the list of files, you can see how much flash is used (about 32MB), how much is available (about 32MB), and the total amount of flash on the router (64MB). You can also see how much flash you have installed on your IOS device with the **show version** command.

In addition to using the **show flash** command, you can use the **dir** command:

```
IOS# dir
Directory of flash:/
    1   drw-           0   Sep 18 2007 15:42:20 +00:00   .Trashes
    2   -rw-        4096   Sep 18 2007 15:42:20 +00:00   ._.Trashes
    .
    .
    .
   16   -rw-    23787192   Sep 9 2007 17:45:30 +00:00
                                    c1841-advipservicesk9-mz.124-6.T7.bin
63868928 bytes total (31946752 bytes free)
```

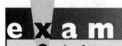

wa**t**c**h** *Know how to verify the amount of free space in flash.*

In this example, the amount of available flash is 31,946,752 bytes—you need to ensure that there is enough flash available before adding additional files to flash.

7.04. The digital resources that accompany this book contain a multimedia demonstration of viewing the contents of flash on a router.

Naming Conventions for IOS Images

Cisco has implemented a naming convention for its IOS images, allowing you to see the platform, software version, and features included in the image just by looking at the name of the image file. As an example, consider the image name from the preceding **show flash** command, *c1841-advipservicesk9-mz.124-6.T7.bin*, which is from a router. Here's an explanation of the nomenclature that Cisco uses for their IOS image names:

- *c1841* refers to the name of the platform on which the image will run. This is important because different router models have different processors, and an image compiled for one processor or router model will typically *not* run on a different model. Therefore, it is very important that you load the appropriate image on your device.

- *advipservicesk9* refers to the features included in this IOS version, commonly referred to as the *feature set*. In this example, IOS is the advanced IP services and *k9* refers to the inclusion of encryption support.

- *mz* or *z* means that the image is compressed and must be uncompressed before loading/running. If you see *l* (the letter *l*, not the number *1*) here, this indicates where the IOS image is run from. The *l* indicates that it is a relocatable image and that the image can be run from RAM. Remember that some images can run directly from flash, depending on the router model.

- *124-6.T7* indicates the software version number of IOS. In this instance, the version is 12.4(6)T7. Images names with *T* indicate new features, and those without *T* indicate the mainline (only bug fixes are made to it).

Finally, *.bin* at the end indicates that this is a binary image.

on the **Job** *The naming nomenclature discussed here applies to IOS images that are either included on your IOS device when you buy it from Cisco or applied when you download them from Cisco's web site. However, the name, in and of itself, has no bearing on the actual operation of IOS when it is loaded on your IOS device. For instance, you can download an image from Cisco and rename it poorperformance.bin, and this will have no impact on the IOS device's performance.*

Before Upgrading the IOS Image

This and the next section discuss how to upgrade and back up IOS software on your router. Before you upgrade IOS on your device, you should first back up the existing image to an external server, for two reasons. First, your flash might not be large enough to support two images—the old one and the new. If you load the new one and you experience problems with it, you'll probably want to load the old image back onto your device. Second, Cisco doesn't keep every software version available on its web site. Older versions of IOS are hard to locate, so if you are upgrading from an old version of IOS, I would highly recommend backing it up first.

Before you back up your IOS image to an external server, you should perform the following checks:

- Is the server reachable (test with the **ping** command)?
- Is there enough disk space on the server to hold the IOS image?
- Does the server support the file nomenclature that you want to use?
- Does the file have to exist on the server before you can perform the copy? (This is true with certain TFTP UNIX servers.)

Once you have performed these checks, you are ready to continue with the backup process.

Backing Up an IOS Image

To back up your IOS image, you'll use the **copy flash** *URL* command. Optionally, you can specify the name of the IOS in flash in the command line. The URL specifies a URL-style syntax and includes the protocol, such as TFTP, the IP address of the server, possibly the directory to put it in, and the name the image will be called on the server. Optionally, you can just specify the protocol in the URL, and you'll be prompted for the rest of the information, like this:

```
Router# copy flash tftp
Source filename []? c3640-js-mz.120-11
Address or name of remote host []? 192.168.1.10
Destination filename [c3640-js-mz.120-11]?
!!!!!!!!!!!!!!!!!!!!!!!!!!!!!!!!!!!!!!!!!!!!!!!!!!!!!!!!!!!!!!!!
.
.
.
6754416 bytes copied in 64.452 secs (105537 bytes/sec)
```

As the image is backed up, you should see a bunch of exclamation points filling up your screen (as shown here)—this indicates the successful copy of a packet. If you see a sequence of periods (.) instead, this indicates a failure. After a successful copy operation, you should see the number of bytes copied as well as how long it took. Compare the number of bytes copied to the file length in flash to verify that the copy was actually successful.

7.05. The digital resources that accompany this book contain a multimedia demonstration of backing up an IOS flash image on a router.

Loading an IOS Image

Before you upgrade IOS on your Cisco device, you first need to verify that your device meets the minimal hardware requirements:

- Does your router have the minimal amount of required RAM?
- Does your router have the minimal amount of required flash memory?

You can see the installed amount of RAM and flash with the **show version** command. Also remember to verify that your IOS device has enough free flash memory to add the device (**show flash** command or **dir** command); if not, you'll need to delete unneeded files to make room for the new image.

If you want to upgrade your IOS or load a previously saved IOS image, you'll need to place the IOS image on an external server and use the **copy** *URL* **flash** command. You'll be prompted for the same information you needed when you used the **copy flash tftp** command; however, the process that takes place after you enter your information is different. After you enter your information, IOS first verifies that the image exists on the TFTP server. If the file exists on the server, IOS then asks you if you want to erase flash. Answer **y** if you don't have enough space in flash for the older image(s) as well as the new one. If you answer **y**, flash is erased and reprogrammed; as this step proceeds, you will see a list of "e"s appear on the screen.

After flash is initialized, your router pulls the IOS image from the TFTP server. Just as in the copy operations with configuration files, a bunch of exclamation marks indicates successful copies, while periods indicate unsuccessful copies.

Here is an example of loading an IOS image into your router:

```
Router# copy tftp flash
Address or name of remote host []? 192.168.1.10
Source filename []? c3640-js-mz.120-7
Destination filename [c3640-js-mz.120-7]?
%Warning:There is a file already existing with this name
Do you want to over write? [confirm] y
Accessing tftp://192.168.1.1/c3640-js-mz.120-7...
Erase flash: before copying? [confirm] y
Erasing the flash filesystem will remove all files! Continue?
[confirm] y
Erasing device... eeeeeeeeeeeeeeeeeeeeeeeeeeeeeeeee ...erased
Erase of flash: complete
Loading c3640-js-mz.120-7 from 192.168.1.1 (via FastEthernet0/0):
!!!!!!!!!!!!!!!!!!!!!!!!!!!!!!!!!!!!!!!!!!!!!!!!!!!!!!!!!!!!!!!
.
.
.

[OK - 6754416/13508608 bytes]

Verifying checksum...  OK (0xCAF2)
6754416 bytes copied in 66.968 secs (102339 bytes/sec)
Router#
```

In this example, the router noticed that the name of the image that exists on the TFTP server is the same name that is in flash and verifies that you want to overwrite it. Also, notice that the router prompts you to erase flash—this is the default with IOS and will delete *all* files. Answer **n** if you don't want to completely erase flash.

After the router copies the IOS image to flash, you must reboot your router in order for it to use the new image. However, by default, the Cisco device loads the first valid IOS image in flash. To use a different one, you need to define this in your configuration with the **boot system** command (discussed in Chapter 6) and save this as part of the startup configuration file. The **boot system** commands are processed in order in the startup configuration file—if there is one there that is no longer needed, you should remove it with the corresponding **no boot system** command, followed by the old IOS image name. You can reboot your router in two ways: turn it off and back on, or use the Privileged EXEC **reload** command. The first method is a hard reboot, and the second one is a soft reboot.

7.06. The digital resources that accompany this book contain a multimedia demonstration of loading an IOS flash image on a router.

If you place an incorrect image on your router—for instance, a 3600 series image on a 2800 series router—the router will not boot up. You'll need to break into ROMMON mode and either do a TFTP boot or boot from the Mini-IOS in ROM (if this exists).

exam
watch
Use the `copy flash URL` command to back up the IOS image, and use the `copy URL flash` command to restore or upgrade the IOS. The `reload` command reboots the router. When doing an upgrade, if either the server is not reachable or you have misconfigured the IP address or filename, you'll get an error message on your CLI.

If you encounter a problem with accessing a remote server when performing the upgrade, you'll receive an error message. This could be because you configured the wrong IP address of the server in the **copy** command, or you entered a nonexistent IOS image name. Here's an example illustrating this problem:

```
Router# copy tftp://192.168.101.66/iosimage.bin flash
Destination filename [iosimage.bin]?
Accessing tftp://192.168.101.66/iosimage.bin...
%Error opening tftp://192.168.101.66/iosimage.bin (Timed out)
```

CERTIFICATION OBJECTIVE 7.04

Remote Access to Your IOS Device

In many instances, it might not be possible to be physically in front of your IOS device to manage it. You can optionally manage it remotely by accessing its CLI via telnet or SSH, or you can manage it with a GUI with a web browser. To access your IOS device's CLI remotely, you must first set up its virtual type terminals (VTYs), as discussed in Chapter 10. If you're accessing a layer 2 IOS switch, you'll need to assign an IP address to a VLAN interface; if you're accessing a router, you'll need to assign an IP address to one of its interfaces and enable it (discussed in Chapter 6). By default, only telnet is enabled on the router; this section will discuss how you enable SSH.

on the *One common solution for accessing a console remotely is to connect the*
job *console ports of your IOS devices to a terminal server and access them via the terminal server. You'll need to log into the terminal server first, either via its console line or remotely via SSH or telnet. From there, you can jump directly into an IOS device's console port to manage it. Many IOS routers support multiport async cards that can be used as this function: I commonly use Cisco routers for terminal servers.*

SSH vs. Telnet Access

One of the most common tools used by network administrators to manage their devices remotely is the telnet application. Telnet allows you access to the CLI of a device. However, the problem with telnet is that all information sent between you and the IOS device is sent in clear text, including your username and/or password. Since you don't want someone eavesdropping on your connection and seeing everything you do—logging in, viewing the operation of the device, and configuring the device—you want to protect yourself by encrypting the traffic.

The easiest way to accomplish this is to replace the use of telnet with SSH (Secure Shell). SSH uses RSA as an encryption algorithm to encrypt any data sent between you and your networking device. SSH is actually disabled, by default, on your IOS device.

e x a m
watch *Telnet sends traffic in clear text, making it susceptible to an eavesdropping attack. To secure remote access to your IOS device and prevent eavesdropping on the commands you're entering and the configurations you're viewing, use SSH as your remote-access* *terminal connection: SSH encrypts traffic. To prevent an access attack against your IOS device, you should combine SSH with filtering of management access to your device by using access control lists (which indicate what IP addresses can manage it).*

SSH Configuration

To set up SSH on your IOS device so that you can use an SSH client to access it, you'll need to configure the following:

- **A local username and password**   SSH requires both (the **username** command configures both).
- **A hostname and a domain name**   This information is required to label the RSA key pair on the IOS device (**hostname** and **ip domain-name** commands).
- **The SSH version to use**   The default is version 1, but the recommended version to use is 2 (**ip ssh version** command).
- **RSA public and private keys**   These are used to encrypt and decrypt the remote-access connection (**crypto key generate rsa** command).
- **Restricting VTY access**   By default, telnet is allowed on the VTYs— you should ensure that only SSH access is allowed (**login local** and **transport input** Line Subconfiguration commands).

7.07. The digital resources that accompany this book contain a multimedia demonstration of configuring SSH on an IOS device.

Here is an example configuration setting up SSH:

```
IOS(config)# username richard secret mypassword
IOS(config)# hostname alina
alina(config)# ip domain-name deal.com
alina(config)# ip ssh version 2
Please create RSA keys to enable SSH. alina(config)# crypto key generate rsa
The name for the keys will be: alina.deal.com
Choose the size of the key modulus in the range of 360 to 2048 for
    your General Purpose Keys. Choosing a key modulus greater than 512
    may take a few minutes. How many bits in the modulus [512]: 1024
% Generating 1024 bit RSA keys, keys will be non-exportable...[OK]
*Oct  5 16:48:23.455: %SSH-5-ENABLED: SSH 2.0 has been enabled
alina(config)# line vty 0 15
alina(config-line)# login local
alina(config-line)# transport input ssh
alina(config-line)# exit
```

e x a m

ⓦ a t c h *The transport input command on a line restricts remote-access connectivity to IOS based on the protocol/ application you specify.*

Notice in this example that when you execute the `crypto key generate rsa` command, you are prompted for the length of the RSA keys. The longer the keys, the more secure your connection will be, with 2048-bit keys being the strongest. Choosing a higher value, however, will take longer for the IOS device to generate. On IOS devices shipped today, this shouldn't take that long: it took me about 30 seconds to generate 2048-bit keys on an 1841 router.

Another item to point out about this configuration is the two commands on the VTYs. The `login local` command specifies the use of the local database (`username` command) for authentication: this causes the IOS device to prompt for both a username *and* password for authentication. Without the `local` parameter, the IOS device prompts only for a password, using the `password` command on the line to do the authentication (this process was discussed in Chapter 1). SSH requires the use of both usernames and passwords. The `transport input ssh` command restricts access to the VTYs to SSH use only; by default, all forms of remote access, including telnet, are allowed.

on the
ⓙob *If you will be using SSH to access your IOS device, you must use either a local username database, as described here, for your VTYs, or an authentication server (AAA). Also, I commonly use PuTTY as a console-access program (instead of HyperTerminal), telnet client, and SSH client. It's a great little program that does all these things, and it's free!*

CERTIFICATION OBJECTIVE 7.05

Basic Troubleshooting

This section focuses on troubleshooting tools that you can use on your routers and switches. One of your first troubleshooting tasks is to figure out in which layer of the OSI Reference Model things are not working. By narrowing down the problem to a specific layer, you've greatly reduced the amount of time that you'll need in order to fix the problem or problems.

When troubleshooting problems from user desktops, Cisco always recommends to start at the lowest layer and work your way up:

1. Verify the Ethernet cable connection.
2. Verify the operation of the NIC (`ipconfig`).
3. Verify the IP configuration of the NIC (`ipconfig`).
4. Verify the application information.

Cisco offers a wide variety of tools that you can also use. Table 7-3 has a list of the more common IOS commands and identifies at which layer of the OSI Reference Model each can be used in troubleshooting. The following sections cover most of these commands in more depth.

TABLE 7-3	OSI Reference Model Layer	Command
IOS Troubleshooting Commands	Layer 2	`show ip arp`
	Layer 2	`show interfaces`
	Layer 2	`show cdp neighbors`
	Layer 3	`ping`
	Layer 3	`traceroute`
	Layer 7	`telnet`
	Layers 2–7	`debug`

Local ARP Table

ARP is used to resolve layer 3 IP addresses to layer 2 MAC addresses. When a LAN device in a subnet needs to access resources beyond the subnet, it must forward its frames to the MAC address of the default gateway (router) and uses ARP for the resolution. The router builds a local ARP table when it receives traffic on an interface, keeping track of the IP-to-MAC address mappings. This can be viewed with the **show arp** command or **show ip arp** command:

```
IOS# show ip arp
Protocol  Address      Age (min)  Hardware Addr    Type   Interface
Internet  10.0.6.2         -       0007.0e46.4070   ARPA   FastEthernet0/0
Internet  172.30.6.2       -       0007.0e46.4071   ARPA   FastEthernet0/1
Internet  172.30.6.7       0       0050.5480.7e01   ARPA   FastEthernet0/1
```

A dash (-) in the (min) column means the address is local to the router; a time value indicates that the router learned the IP/MAC addressing mapping dynamically. The last entry in this example was dynamically learned within the last minute. If a particular MAC address isn't seen for a period of time, it is aged out of the ARP table. Likewise, when a frame matches an existing entry in the table, its aging time is reset to zero in the table. The Type column denotes the Ethernet encapsulation type (ARPA, SNAP, or SAP) used in the frame: TCP/IP uses ARPA for Ethernet.

The **show ip arp** command is important because if you see at least the router's own mappings in the table for its interfaces and that entries are being learned and updated in the table, then you have layer 2 connectivity on those interfaces.

7.08. The digital resources that accompany this book contain a multimedia demonstration of examining an ARP table on a router.

Cisco Discovery Protocol (CDP)

CDP is a Cisco proprietary data link layer protocol that was made available in version 10.3 of the router IOS. Many, but not all, Cisco devices support CDP, including Cisco routers and Catalyst switches. For those devices that support CDP, CDP is *enabled* by default. CDP messages received from one Cisco device, by default, are not forwarded to any other devices behind it. In other words, you can see CDP information about only other Cisco devices *directly* connected to your device. Most people misunderstand this, since CDP uses multicasts to disseminate its information. You would think that a Cisco switch would flood this kind of traffic; however, CDP is an exception to the rule in a network of Cisco devices.

CDP Information

CDP, as mentioned, works at the data link layer. However, since CDP uses a Subnetwork Access Protocol (SNAP) frame type, not every data link layer media type is supported. The media types that are supported are Ethernet, Token Ring, Fiber Distributed Data Interface (FDDI), Point-to-Point Protocol (PPP), High-Level Data Link Control (HDLC), Asynchronous Transfer Mode (ATM), and Frame Relay.

The information shared in a CDP packet about a Cisco device includes the following:

- Name of the device configured with the **hostname** command
- IOS software version
- Hardware capabilities, such as routing, switching, and/or bridging
- Hardware platform, such as 2800 or 2960
- The layer 3 address(es) of the device
- The interface on which the CDP update was generated

CDP Configuration

As mentioned in the last section, CDP is enabled on all Cisco CDP–capable devices when you receive your product from Cisco. On Cisco routers and switches, you can globally disable or enable CDP with this command:

```
IOS(config)# [no] cdp run
```

You can also enable or disable CDP on an interface-by-interface basis:

```
IOS(config)# interface type [slot_#/]port_#
IOS(config-if)# [no] cdp enable
```

Since CDP doesn't use many IOS resources (a small frame is generated once a minute), it is recommended that you keep it enabled unless your router is connected to the Internet or untrusted devices; then you should at least disable CDP on these interfaces. At a minimum, the information is only 80 bytes in length. Other, optional commands are related to CDP, such as changing the update and hold-down timers, but these commands are beyond the scope of this book.

CDP Status

To see the status of CDP on your Cisco device, use this command:

```
IOS# show cdp
Global CDP information:
Sending CDP packets every 60 seconds
Sending a holdtime value of 180 seconds
Sending CDPv2 advertisements is  enabled
```

As you can see from this output, CDP is enabled and generating updates every 60 seconds. The hold-down timer is 180 seconds. This timer determines how long a CDP neighbor's information is kept in the local CDP table without seeing a CDP update from that neighbor. These are the default timers for CDP.

You can also see the CDP configuration on an interface-by-interface basis by adding the **interface** parameter to the **show cdp** command:

```
IOS# show cdp interface
Serial0 is up, line protocol is up, encapsulation is HDLC
  Sending CDP packets every 60 seconds
  Holdtime is 180 seconds
Ethernet0 is up, line protocol is up, encapsulation is ARPA
  Sending CDP packets every 60 seconds
  Holdtime is 180 seconds
```

CDP Neighbors

To see a summarized list of the CDP neighbors to which your Cisco device is connected, use the **show cdp neighbors** command:

```
IOS# show cdp neighbors
Capability Codes: R - Router, T - Trans Bridge, B - Source Route
                  Bridge S - Switch, H - Host, I - IGMP,
                  r - Repeater

Device ID   Local Intrfce   Holdtme   Capability   Platform   Port ID
Router-A    Eth 0/0            176        R           2621      Fas 0/1
```

In this example, one device is connected with a device ID of *Router-A*, which is a 2621 router. If you see a MAC address for the device ID, this indicates that the connected Cisco device wasn't assigned a name with the **hostname** command. This update was received on ethernet0/0 on this device 4 seconds ago (hold-down timer of 176 seconds subtracted from the hold-down time of 180 seconds). The Port ID refers to the port at the remote side from which the device advertised the CDP message.

You can add the optional **detail** parameter to the preceding command to see the details concerning the connected Cisco device. You can also use the **show cdp entry *** command. Here is an example of a CDP detailed listing:

```
IOS# show cdp neighbor detail
-------------------------

Device ID: Router-A
Entry address(es):
  IP address: 192.168.1.1
Platform: cisco 2621,  Capabilities: Router
Interface: Ethernet0/0,  Port ID (outgoing port): FastEthernet0/1
Holdtime : 127 sec

Version :
Cisco Internetwork Operating System Software
IOS (tm) C2600 Software (C2600-IK9O3S3-M), Version 12.2(15)T9,
        RELEASE SOFTWARE (fc2)
TAC Support: http://www.cisco.com/tac Copyright (c) 1986-2003 by cisco Systems, Inc.
Compiled Sat 01-Nov-03 04:43 by ccai

advertisement version: 2
Duplex: half
.
.
.
```

In this example, you can see that the connected device is a 2621 series router running IOS 12.2(15)T9 and has an IP address of 192.168.1.1 configured on the connected interface.

To list the details of a specific neighbor, use this command:

```
IOS# show cdp entry neighbor's_name
```

The advantage of this approach over the approach in the preceding example is that this command lists only the specified neighbor's information. You can use an "*" as a wildcard to display all the neighbors. Here's an example of this command:

```
Router1# show cdp entry Router2
-------------------------------
Device ID: Router2
Entry address(es):
 IP address: 10.1.2.1
Platform: Cisco 2610, Capabilities: Router
Interface Serial0/0, Port ID (outgoing port): Serial0/1
Holdtime: 125 sec
.
.
.
```

In this example, Router2 has an IP address of 10.1.2.1 and Router1's serial0/1 interface is connected to Router2's serial0/0 interface.

Video

7.09. The digital resources that accompany this book contain a multimedia demonstration of using CDP on a router.

IOS devices support one additional CDP command, which allows you to view CDP traffic statistics:

```
IOS# show cdp traffic
Total packets output: 350, Input: 223
Hdr syntax: 0, Chksum error: 0, Encaps failed: 0
No memory: 0, Invalid: 0, Fragmented: 0
```

If you are receiving CDP traffic (Input parameter is incrementing with each execution of the command every minute), then the data link layer is functioning correctly.

exam

watch
CDP is enabled, by default, on all Cisco devices. CDP updates are generated as multicasts every 60 seconds with a hold-down period of 180 seconds for a missing neighbor. The `no cdp run` command globally disables CDP, while the `no cdp enable` command disables CDP on an interface (you should do this on a device's interface connected to the Internet or untrusted devices). Use `show cdp neighbors` to list your directly connected Cisco neighboring devices. Adding the `detail` parameter will display the layer 3 addressing, device model, software version, and other information configured on the neighbor. Be familiar with the output of the `show cdp` commands.

Layer 3 Connectivity Testing

As you saw in the preceding section, CDP can be very useful in determining whether the data link layer is working correctly with another directly connected Cisco device. You can even see the layer 3 address(es) configured on your neighboring device and use this for testing layer 3 connectivity. In addition to using CDP, you could use the `show interfaces` command for data link layer testing.

However, the main limitation of these two tools is that they don't test layer 3 problems. Cisco does offer tools for testing layer 3 connectivity, however. This section focuses on two of these commands: `ping` and `traceroute`. Both of these commands come in two versions: one for User EXEC mode and one for Privileged EXEC mode. The Privileged EXEC version provides additional options and parameters that can assist you in your troubleshooting process. The following sections cover these tools in more depth.

Using Ping

Ping (Packet Internet Groper) was originally developed for the IP protocol stack to test layer 3 connectivity. The Internet Control Message Protocol (ICMP) is used to implement ping. However, Cisco IOS has expanded the `ping` command to support other protocols, including Apollo, AppleTalk, CLNS, DECnet, IP, IPX, Vines, and XNS. Cisco uses ping to test layer 3 connectivity with other, non-IP protocols in a (typically) proprietary fashion. However, Cisco follows the standard when using `ping` to test IP connectivity. With each hop (routing device) a ping (or traceroute) packet traverses, that device decrements the time-to-live (TTL) field in the IP header. By default, ping and traceroute set the TTL to a value of 255. When the TTL is decremented to 0, the receiving device will drop the corresponding packet. For example, if a device sends a ping to a connected router, the device sets the TTL to 255. The receiving router would then decrement that by 1 upon receipt, resulting in a TTL of 254.

on the **job**

Ping was originally never intended to be an acronym. It was developed by Mike Muuss, who named it ping simply because it worked like sonar. Later on, David Mills created an acronym for it: Packet Internet Groper. Muuss was, apparently, not amused by the acronym.

Users can use the **ping** command from their Windows desktop to check for connectivity. Here are a couple of messages that indicate problems and possible reasons:

- **Destination host unreachable**   The router connected to the remote host cannot contact that host on the connected segment.
- **Destination network unreachable**   A router between the source and destination doesn't have a routing table entry that determines how to reach the destination (discussed in Chapter 9).

Simple ping Command   To execute a simple ping from either User mode or Privileged EXEC mode, enter the **ping** command on the CLI and follow it with the IP address or hostname of the destination:

```
IOS> ping destination_IP_address_or_host_name
```

Here is a simple example of using this command:

```
IOS> ping 192.168.1.10
Type escape sequence to abort.
Sending 5, 100-byte ICMP Echos to 192.168.1.10,
    timeout is 2 seconds:
!!!!!
Success rate is 100 percent (5/5),
    round-trip min/avg/max = 2/4/6 ms.
```

In this example, five test packets were sent to the destination and the destination responded to all five, as is shown by the exclamation marks (!). The default timeout to receive a response from the destination is 2 seconds—if a response is not received from the destination for a packet within this time period, a period (.) is displayed.

Table 7-4 shows examples of ping messages that you might see in displayed output. The bottom of the output shows the success rate—how many replies were received and the minimum, average, and maximum round-trip times for the ping packets sent (in milliseconds). This information can be used to detect whether a delay exists between you and the destination.

on the ⓙob
You might see a period (.) in the output for a couple of reasons: a response was received, but after the timeout period; or no response was seen at all. If a response was received, but after the timeout period, this might be because an ARP had to take place to learn the MAC address of a connected device or because of congestion—and this process could have occurred on multiple segments. Consider two examples: .!!!! and !!..!. If devices have to perform ARPs to get the MAC address of the next-hop device, you'll typically see the first example in your output. However, if your output looks like the second example, you're probably experiencing congestion or performance problems.

TABLE 7-4	Ping Output	Explanation
Output Codes for the ping Commands	.	A response was not received before the timeout period expired.
	!	A response was received within the timeout period.
	U	A remote router responded that the destination is unreachable—the network segment is reachable, but not the host.
	N	A remote router responded that the network is unreachable—the network cannot be found in the routing table.
	P	A remote device responded that the protocol is not supported.
	Q	Source quench, telling the source to slow its output.
	M	The ping packet needed to be fragmented, but a remote router couldn't perform fragmentation.
	A	The ping packet was filtered by a device with an access control list (administratively prohibited).
	?	The ping packet type is not understood by a remote device.
	&	The ping exceeded the maximum number of hops supported by the routing protocol (see Chapter 9).

Extended ping Command   IOS devices support an extended **ping** command, which can be executed only at Privileged EXEC mode.

To execute this command, just type **ping** by itself on the command line:

```
IOS# ping
 Protocol [ip]:
 Target IP address: 192.168.1.10
 Repeat count [5]:
 Datagram size [100]:
 Timeout in seconds [2]:
 Extended commands [n]: y
 Source address:
 Type of service [0]:
 Set DF bit in IP header? [no]:
 Data pattern [0xABCD]:
 Loose, Strict, Record, Timestamp, Verbose[none]:
 Number of hops [9]:
 Loose, Strict, Record, Timestamp, Verbose[RV]:
 Sweep range of sizes [n]:
Type escape sequence to abort.
Sending 5, 100-byte ICMP Echos to 192.168.1.10,
     timeout is 2 seconds:
 .
 .
 .
```

Video

7.10. The digital resources that accompany this book contain a multimedia demonstration of using the simple and extended ping *commands on a router.*

Following is an explanation of the parameters that might be required when you execute this command:

■ `Protocol`   The protocol to use for the ping (defaults to IP).

■ `Target IP address`   The IP address or hostname of the destination to test.

■ `Repeat count`   How many echo requests should be generated for the test (defaults to 5).

■ `Datagram size`   The size, in bytes, of the ping packet (defaults to 100).

■ `Timeout in seconds`   The amount of time to wait before indicating a timeout for the echo (defaults to 2 seconds). When seeing a mix of periods and bangs in the displayed output, increasing this value can help determine if you are experiencing congestion problems with a slow response time between your IOS device and the destination.

- Extended commands   Whether or not the remaining questions should also be asked (defaults to no).

- Source address   The IP address that should appear as the source address in the IP header (defaults to the IP address of the interface the ping will use to exit the IOS device).

- Type of service   The IP level for QoS (defaults to 0).

- Set DF bit in IP header?   Whether or not the ping can be fragmented when it reaches a segment that supports a smaller MTU size (the default is no—don't set this bit). Sometimes, a misconfigured MTU can cause performance problems. You can use this parameter to pinpoint the problem, since a device with a smaller MTU size will not be able to handle the larger packet.

- Data pattern   The data pattern that is placed in the ping. It is a hexadecimal four-digit (16-bit) number (defaults to 0xABCD) and is used to solve cable problems and crosstalk on cables.

- Loose, Strict, Record, Timestamp, Verbose   IP header options (defaults to none of these). The record parameter records the route that the ping took—this is somewhat similar to traceroute. If you choose record, you will be asked for the maximum number of hops that are allowed to be recorded by the ping (defaults to 9, and can range from 1 to 9).

- Sweep range of sizes   Send pings that vary in size. This is helpful when trying to troubleshoot a problem related to a segment that has a small MTU size (and you don't know what that number is). This defaults to n for no.

---

exam

watch
When troubleshooting PC problems, first determine whether the user can ping the loopback address of their PC: ping 127.0.0.1. If this fails, you know something is wrong with the TCP/IP protocol stack installation on the PC. Next, have the user try to ping the configured IP address. If this fails, you know that something is wrong with their IP address configuration. Next, have the user ping the default gateway. If this fails, either something is wrong with the configured default gateway address, the default gateway itself, the subnet mask value configured on the user's PC, or the layer 2 switch connecting them together (perhaps a mismatch in the VLAN on the router and PC interfaces of the switch).

Using Traceroute

One limitation of ping is that it will not tell you where, between you and the destination, layer 3 connectivity is broken. Traceroute, on the other hand, will list each router along the way, including the final destination. Therefore, if a layer 3 connection problem exists, traceroute will tell you at least where the problem begins. Like the **ping** command, **traceroute** has two versions: one for User EXEC mode and one for Privileged EXEC mode. The following two sections cover the two different versions.

Simple traceroute Command   The simple **traceroute** command, which works at both User and Privileged EXEC modes, has the following syntax:

```
IOS> traceroute destination_IP_address_or_host_name
```

Here is an example of this command:

```
IOS> traceroute 65.32.13.33
Type escape sequence to abort.
Tracing the route to 65.32.13.33
  1 10.98.240.1 20 msec 24 msec 16 msec
  2 65.32.15.254 16 msec 16 msec 12 msec
  3 65.32.13.33 12 msec 12 msec 12 msec
```

In this example, the destination was three hops away—each hop is listed on a separate line. For each destination, three tests are performed, where the round-trip time is displayed for each test. If you don't see a round-trip time, typically indicated by an asterisk ("*"), this indicates a possible problem or timeout in the response.

To break out of a ping or traceroute command, use the CTRL-SHIFT-6 break sequence. Also, instead of using the script to perform an extended ping or traceroute, you can execute by specifying all of the parameters on a single command line.

Table 7-5 shows other values that you might see instead of the round-trip time.
In certain cases, for a specific destination, you might see three asterisks (***) in the output; don't be alarmed if you see this, since it can occur for a variety of reasons: for instance, there may be an inconsistency in how the source and destination devices have implemented traceroute, or the destination may be configured not to reply to these messages. However, if you continually find the same destination repeated in the output with these reply messages, this indicates a layer 3 problem starting with either this device or the device preceding it.

| TABLE 7-5 | Traceroute Messages |

Traceroute Output	Explanation
*	Either the wait timer expired while waiting for a response or the device did not respond at all.
A	The trace packet was filtered by a remote device (administratively prohibited).
U	The port of the device is unreachable (the destination received the trace packet but discarded it).
H	The destination is unreachable (the destination segment was reachable, but not the host).
I	The user interrupted the traceroute process.
N	The network is unreachable (the destination segment was not reachable).
P	The protocol is unreachable (the device doesn't support traceroute).
Q	Source quench.
T	The trace packet exceeded the configured timeout value.
?	The device couldn't identify the specific trace type in the trace packet.

on the **Job**

If you have DNS lookups enabled on your IOS device (this is the `ip domain-lookup` command), IOS will attempt to resolve the IP address to a domain name before printing the output line for that device. If your traces seem to take a long time, this is usually the culprit. You can disable DNS lookups on your IOS device with the `no ip domain-lookup` command.

Extended traceroute Command The extended **traceroute** command is similar to the extended **ping** command and requires Privileged EXEC mode access to execute it:

```
IOS# traceroute
Protocol [ip]:
Target IP address: IP_address_of_the_destination
Source address:
Numeric display [n]:
Timeout in seconds [3]:
Probe count [3]:
Minimum Time to Live [1]:
Maximum Time to Live [30]:
```

```
Port number [33434]:
Loose, Strict, Record, Timestamp, Verbose [none]:
.
.
.
```

Some of these options are the same ones used by ping.

7.11. The digital resources that accompany this book contain a multimedia demonstration of using the simple and extended `traceroute` commands on a router.

Here is an explanation of the other options:

- `Numeric display` Turns off a DNS lookup for the names of the routers and the destination.
- `Time to Live` Specifies how many hops the trace is allowed to take.
- `Loose` Tells the router that the hops you specify must appear in the trace path, but other routers can appear as well.
- `Strict` Restricts the trace path only to those routers that you specify.
- `Record` Specifies the number of hops to leave room for in the trace packet.
- `Timestamp` Allows you to specify the amount of space to leave room for in the trace packet for timing information.
- `Verbose` Automatically selected whenever you choose any of the options from this question; it prints the entire contents of the trace packet.

One important item to point out about the **traceroute** command is that if more than one path exists to reach the destination, this command will test *each* path, which can take the trace process longer. And like the extended **ping** command, instead of using the script to perform the test, you can enter the command and all of its parameters on a single command line.

Layer 7 Connectivity Testing

The **ping** and **traceroute** commands can test only layer 3 connectivity. If you can reach a destination with either of these two commands, this indicates that layer 3 and below are functioning correctly. You can use other tools, such as telnet, to test the application layer. If you can telnet to a destination, then all seven layers of the OSI Reference Model are functioning correctly. As an example, if you can telnet to a machine but can't send an e-mail to it, then the problem is *not* a networking problem, but an application problem (with the e-mail program). Of course, if you are filtering traffic with an access control list, this could also be the culprit.

The `telnet` *command is used to test layer 7 (application layer) connectivity. To test telnet, the remote destination must have telnet configured and enabled. If the remote device is an IOS device, you must minimally configure the* `login` *and* `password` *commands on the VTYs (see Chapter 1).*

Using Telnet

If you've configured your Cisco devices correctly (with IP addressing and routing information and the appropriate commands on the VTYs), you should be able to telnet to them successfully. However, if you have followed the advice mentioned earlier in the "Remote Access to Your IOS Device" section, you might have to test connectivity with SSH instead. Cisco routers and switches support both incoming and outgoing telnet and SSH. This assumes you have set up the VTYs and configured your IP addressing correctly.

To open up a telnet session from your IOS device, you can use any of the following three methods:

```
IOS# name_of_the_destination | destination_IP_address
```

or

```
IOS# telnet name_of_the_destination | destination_IP_address
```

or

```
IOS# connect name_of_the_destination | destination_IP_address
```

All three of these methods work in the same manner: they all have IOS attempt to telnet the specified destination.

If you mistype a command name from the CLI, IOS assumes you're trying to use the first telnet method I've listed and attempts to resolve the name to an IP address using the local host table, a DNS server, or a DNS broadcast. To stop this behavior, configure the `no ip domain-lookup` command.

Suspending Telnet Sessions

If you are on an IOS device and telnet to a remote destination, you might want to go back to your IOS device. One way of doing this is to exit the remote device; however, you might just want to go back to your source Cisco device, make a quick adjustment, and then return to the remote device. Logging off and back onto the remote device is a hassle in this instance.

Cisco, however, has solved this problem by allowing you to *suspend* a telnet session, return to your original router or switch, do what you need to do, and then jump right back into your remote device—all without your having to log off and back onto the remote device. To suspend a telnet session, use the CTRL-SHIFT-6, X (hold down the CTRL, SHIFT, and 6 keys simultaneously, let go, and then press the X key) or CTRL-^ control sequence, depending on your keyboard.

On your source IOS, if you want to see the open telnet sessions that are currently suspended, use the **show sessions** command:

```
IOS# show sessions
Conn Host          Address      Byte   Idle    Conn Name
   1 10.1.1.1      10.1.1.1        0      1     10.1.1.1
*  2 10.1.1.2      10.1.1.2        0      2     10.1.1.2
```

This example shows two open telnet sessions. The one with the * preceding it is the default (last accessed) session. To resume the last session, all you have to do is press ENTER on an empty command line.

To resume a specific session, use this command:

```
IOS# resume connection_#
```

The connection number to enter is the number in the Conn column of the **show sessions** command. As a shortcut, you can just list the number of the connection without typing **resume**, and this will accomplish the same thing. If you are on the source router or switch and want to terminate a suspended telnet session without having to resume the telnet session and then log out of it, you can use this command:

```
IOS# disconnect connection_#
```

7.12. The digital resources that accompany this book contain a multimedia demonstration of using telnet on a router.

Verifying and Clearing Connections

If you are logged into an IOS device, you can view the other users that are also logged in with this command:

```
IOS# show users
     Line          User      Host(s)      Idle     Location
     0    con 0                            idle
     2    vty 0               idle         0        10.1.1.1
*    3    vty 1               idle         0        10.1.1.2
```

If you see an * in the first column, this indicates your current session. If you want to terminate someone's session, use the Privileged EXEC **clear line** command:

```
IOS# clear line line_#
```

The line number that you enter can be found in the Line column of the output of the **show users** command.

Debug Overview

One problem with using **show** commands is that they display only what is currently stored somewhere in the router's RAM, and this display is *static*. You have to re-execute the command to get a refreshed update. And **show** commands, unfortunately, do not always display detailed troubleshooting information. For instance, perhaps you want the router to tell you when a particular event occurs and display some of the packet contents of that event. The **show** commands cannot do this; however, **debug** commands can. One of the most powerful troubleshooting tools of IOS is the **debug** command, which enables you to view events and problems, in real time, on your Cisco device.

The **debug** commands, however, do have a drawback: Since the router has to examine and display many different things when this feature is enabled, the performance of IOS will suffer. As an example, if you want to see every IP packet that travels through a router, the router has to examine each packet, determine whether it is an IP packet, and then display the packet or partial packet contents on the screen. On a very busy router, this debug process can cause serious performance degradation. Therefore, you should be very careful about enabling a debug process on your router; you might want to wait till after hours or periods of lesser activity before using this tool.

on the job *You should never use the* debug all *command—this enables debugging for every process related to IOS features enabled on your router. In this situation, you'll see pages and pages of output messages on all kinds of things and, on a busy IOS device, probably crash it.*

Typically, you will use **debug** commands for detailed troubleshooting. For instance, you may have tried using **show** commands to discover the cause of a particular problem, but without any success. You should then turn to using a particular **debug** command to uncover the source of the problem. This command has many, many options and parameters—use context-sensitive help to view them. Many of the remaining chapters in this book will cover specific **debug** commands and their uses. To enable debug, you must be at Privileged EXEC mode. If you are not on the console when enabling debug, you'll also need to execute the Privileged EXEC **terminal monitor** command to actually see the debug output on your nonconsole line.

7.13. The digital resources that accompany this book contain a multimedia demonstration of using debug on a router.

Once you've fixed your problem or no longer need to see the debug output, you should always disable the debug process. You can disable it either by prefacing the **debug** command with the **no** parameter or executing one of the following two commands:

```
IOS# no debug all
```

or

```
IOS# undebug all
```

These two commands disable all running **debug** commands on your router. You can first use the **show debug** command to see which events or processes you have enabled.

If you want to see timestamps displayed in your debug output, enter the following command:

```
IOS(config)# service timestamps debug datetime msec
```

The **datetime** parameter displays the current date and time, while the **msec** parameter displays an additional timing parameter: milliseconds.

If you think your debug commands are causing performance problems, use the show processes cpu command (covered in Chapter 3) to check your CPU utilization for the device's various processes, including debug.

exam

watch *You can use the undebug   command to disable all debug functions.*
all command or the no debug all

EXERCISE 7-2

MHE Lab

Using the Router's Troubleshooting Tools

The last few sections dealt with the router's troubleshooting tools. This exercise will help you reinforce your understanding of this material. You'll perform these steps using Boson's NetSim simulator. You can find a picture of the network diagram for the simulator in the Introduction of this book. After starting up the simulator, click the LabNavigator button. Next, double-click Exercise 7-2 and click the Load Lab button.

1. Access the 2600-1 router in the simulator included with the media that accompanies this book. See what neighbors are directly connected to the router. What is the IP address of the 2600-2 router?

    Click the Labs tab at the bottom left of the window. Click the McGraw-Hill Education tab (to the right of the Standard and Custom tabs) at the top left. Click the Lab Instructions tab and use the drop-down selector for Devices to choose 2600-1; or click the NetMap tab and double-click the 2600-1 device icon. Use the **show cdp neighbors** command to view the 2600-1's neighbors—you may have to wait 60 seconds to see all the neighbors connected to this device (repeat the command as necessary). You should see one of the 2950 switches and the 2600-2 router. Use the **show cdp neighbors detail** command to view the 2600-2's address: it is 192.168.2.2.

2. Access the 2950-2 switch in the simulator. See what neighbors are directly connected to the router. Which neighbors do you see? What are their IP addresses?

   Click the Lab Instructions tab and use the drop-down selector for Devices to choose 2950-2; or click the NetMap tab and double-click the 2950-2 device icon. Use the **show cdp neighbors** command to view your neighbors. You should see the 2950-1 switch and 2600-1 router. You'll see the 2950-1 twice since there are two connections between these two switches. Add the **detail** parameter to the preceding command to see the neighbors' IP addresses.

You now should be more comfortable with some of the router's troubleshooting tools.

CERTIFICATION OBJECTIVE 7.06

Licensing

This section will focus on licensing on the Cisco ISR G2 routers. Licensing has become more and more common across many of Cisco platforms; even Cisco's switches are starting to support licensing of features and use.

Prior to Cisco IOS version 15 on Cisco routers, Cisco had up to 12 different image types for a particular device model and software version. To simplify this, Cisco now has only four image types:

- IP Base
- Data (MPLS and ATM)
- Unified Communications (VoIP and IP telephony)
- Security (Firewall, IPS, and VPNs)

You can use the **show license feature** command to view the technology package licenses and the feature licenses supported by your router. Here's an example of the use of this command:

```
Router# show license feature
Feature name    Enforcement Evaluation Subscription Enabled RightToUse
ipbasek9        no          no         no           yes     no
securityk9      yes         yes        no           yes     yes
uck9            yes         yes        no           yes     yes
datak9          yes         yes        no           no      yes
LI              yes         no         no           no      no
ios-ips-update  yes         yes        yes          no      yes
```

Licensing is enforced starting with Cisco ISR G2 routers (1900, 2900, and 3900 series). Licensing unlocks features in IOS code. Licenses come in two types:

■ **Evaluation**   This license is a temporary license that is only valid for a period of time, such as 60 days or 1 year.

■ **Permanent**   This license is valid for the life of the product.

Licenses are associated with two values from a Cisco ISR G2 router, referred to as a universal device identifier (UDI):

■ Product ID (platform type)

■ Serial number (found in ROM on the motherboard)

The importance of the UDI is that the license you obtain from Cisco is tied to this value. In other words, you can't take a license from one router and copy it to another router: the license is tied to the UDI value of your Cisco ISR G2 router. Here's an example of viewing the UDI information for license purposes on a 3925 ISR G2 router:

```
Router# show license udi

Device#   PID              SN              UDI

--------------------------------------------------------------------

*0        C3900-SPE100/K9  FHH13030044     C3900-SPE100/K9:FHH13030044
```

Use the **show license feature** command to view the package and feature licenses installed on your router.

Installing Licenses

Your router comes with an evaluation license, also known as a temporary license, for most packages and features supported on your router. If you want to try a new software package or feature, you can activate the evaluation license for that package or feature.

To install a permanent license, use the following Privileged EXEC command:

```
Router# license install URL-location
```

The license file is an XML file that you download from Cisco. Typically, you would place this in flash on the router, but you could pull it from a remote server via TFTP or FTP. Here's an example of installing a license on a 3950 router:

```
Router# license install flash0:uck9-C3900-SPE150_K9-FHH12250057.
xml
Installing licenses from "uck9-C3900-SPE150_K9-FHH12250057.xml"
Installing...Feature:uck9...Successful: Supported
1/1 licenses were successfully installed
0/1 licenses were existing licenses
0/1 licenses were failed to install
```

Once you've installed a license, it is not used until the router is rebooted. You can execute the **reload** command to do this.

To activate an evaluation license to try out technology packages, use this command:

```
Router(config)# license boot module module_name
                technology-package package_name
```

The *module_name* is the product model, like **c3900** for a 3950 router. The technology package name is one of the four packages. For example, the Security package parameter is **securityk9**. As with a permanent license, you must reboot the router for the license to take effect.

Licensing Verification

One of the first commands you can use to verify your licensing is the **show version** command. Here's an example based on the previous license installation example:

```
Router# show version
Cisco IOS Software, C3900 Software (C3900-UNIVERSALK9-M), Version
12.4(24.6)PI11k PI11 ENGINEERING WEEKLY BUILD, synced to V124_24_6_T9
```

```
.
.
.
Cisco C3945 (revision 1.0) with 2025472K/71680K bytes of memory.
Processor board ID FHH1226P01E
3 Gigabit Ethernet interfaces
4 Serial(sync/async) interfaces
2 ISDN Basic Rate interfaces
1 ATM interface
25 terminal lines
1 Virtual Private Network (VPN) Module
DRAM configuration is 72 bits wide with parity enabled.
255K bytes of non-volatile configuration memory.
2000880K bytes of ATA System CompactFlash 0 (Read/Write)
License Info:
License UDI:
----------------------------------------------------
Device#    PID                   SN
----------------------------------------------------
*0         C3900-SPE150/K9       FHH12250057
Technology Package License Information for Module:'c3900'
-----------------------------------------------------------------
Technology    Technology-package        Technology-package
              Current      Type         Next reboot
-----------------------------------------------------------------
ipbase        ipbasek9     Permanent    ipbasek9
security      None         None         None
uc            uck9         Permanent    uck9
data          None         None         None
```

Notice that in this example, the router has both an IP Base and Unified Communications (UC) permanent license installed.

You can also use the **show license** command to view the installed license, as shown in this example:

```
Router# show license
Index 1 Feature: ipbasek9
        Period left: Life time
        License Type: Permanent
        License State: Active, In Use
        License Count: Non-Counted
        License Priority: Medium
Index 2 Feature: securityk9
        Period left: 8 weeks, 3 days
        Period Used: 15  minute 38 second
        License Type: EvalRightToUse
        License State: Active, In Use
        License Count: Non-Counted
        License Priority: Low
```

```
Index 3 Feature: uck9
        Period left: Not Activated
        Period Used: 0  minute  0  second
        License Type: EvalRightToUse
        License State: Not in Use, EULA not accepted
        License Count: Non-Counted
        License Priority: None
  .
  .
  .
```

In this example, the IP Base package has a permanent license installed, the Security package has an activated evaluation license installed, and the Unified Communications package doesn't have a license installed.

Managing Licenses

This section will cover how to back up your license as well as how to uninstall a license. To back up a license, use the **license save** command:

```
Router# license save URL
```

You can save the license file to the local file system or a remote server. Here's an example of the use of this command:

```
Router# license save flash:/licenses.lic
license lines saved......to flash:licenses.lic
```

To uninstall (remove) a license from a router, you need to perform two actions:

1. Disable the technology package.
2. Clear the license.

To disable the technology package, use the **license boot module** command. Here's an example of disabling the Unified Communications package on a 3900 series router:

```
Router(config)# license boot module c3900 technology-package
                    uck9 disable
Router(config)# exit
Router# copy running-config startup-config
Router# reload
```

Once the router has rebooted, you need to clear the license with the **license clear** command. Here's an example:

```
Router# license clear uck9
*Jul  7 00:34:23.691: %SYS-5-CONFIG_I: Configured from console by console clear
uck9
Feature: uck9
    1    License Type: Permanent
         License State: Active, Not in Use
         License Addition: Exclusive
         License Count: Non-Counted
         Comment:
         Store Index: 15
         Store Name: Primary License Storage
Are you sure you want to clear? (yes/[no]): yes
*Jul  7 00:34:31.223: %LICENSE-6-REMOVE: Feature uck9 1.0 was removed
from this device.
UDI=C3900-SPE150/K9:FHH12250057; StoreIndex=15:Primary License Storage
```

Once done, you can re-enable the technology package:

```
Router(config)# no license boot module c3900 technology uck9 disable
Router(config)# exit
Router# reload
```

Upon rebooting, use the **show version** command to verify the license change.

INSIDE THE EXAM

Router Configuration Files

You should be intimately familiar with configuration files and when they are overwritten versus merged when using the **copy** command: re-examine Table 7-2 for an overview of this process.

Changes in Your Network

No Exam Watches are in this section: only practical knowledge you should always apply before making any changes on your IOS devices.

IOS Image Files

You should be familiar with the commands to verify the files located in flash, as well as what IOS image your device loaded from flash. You need to understand how to upgrade your IOS with the **copy** command and know what happens during the upgrade, as well as how to determine whether the upgrade failed.

(Continued)

INSIDE THE EXAM

Remote Access to Your IOS Device

You need to be able to compare telnet and SSH, and you should know how both are set up: review Chapter 10 for setting up your VTYs for telnet access. Understand the basic configuration to allow SSH access into your IOS device, as well as how to disable the use of telnet on the VTYs.

Basic Troubleshooting

You should be able to determine what router commands you can use to troubleshoot problems at the various OSI Reference Model layers. Know how CDP, including its timers, works and the kinds of information shared between directly connected Cisco devices. Be able to display the CDP tables on an IOS device and understand their output.

Know how to troubleshoot layer 3 problems with `ping` and `traceroute`, starting with testing of the TCP/IP protocol stack on a user's computer. Understand the different message responses you can

see when using the `ping` command and what they mean from a troubleshooting perspective.

You should know how to configure your VTYs to allow telnet access, and be able to determine whether or not this is set up correctly. Remember how to suspend a telnet from an IOS device, resume it, and display your open sessions. Know how to disable `debug` commands on your IOS device.

Licensing

Licenses come in two basic types: evaluation and permanent. Licenses are associated with the serial number of the IOS device and therefore cannot be moved to a different device, by default. The `license install` command installs new licenses. The `show version` and `show license` commands can be used to verify the licenses installed and activated on your IOS device.

CERTIFICATION SUMMARY

Use the **copy** commands to manipulate files, including configuration files and IOS images. Any time you copy something into RAM, IOS uses a merge process. For any other location, IOS uses an overwrite process. On IOS devices, use the **erase startup-config** command to delete the startup-config file in NVRAM. SSH should be used instead of telnet for remote terminal (CLI) access to the router, since SSH encrypts traffic between your desktop and an IOS device.

CDP is a Cisco-proprietary protocol that functions at the data link layer. Every 60 seconds, Cisco devices generate a multicast on each of their interfaces, containing basic information about themselves, including the device type, the version of software they're running, and their IP address(es). To disable CDP globally, use the **no cdp run** command. To see a list of your neighbors, use the **show cdp neighbors** command.

The **ping** and **traceroute** commands support an extended version at Privileged EXEC mode. If you want to suspend an active telnet session, use the CTRL-SHIFT-6, X control sequence. Pressing ENTER on a blank command line resumes the last suspended telnet session. Use the **resume** command to resume a telnet connection. Use the **show sessions** command to see your open telnet session. Use the **disconnect** command to disconnect a suspended telnet session. To disable debug on your IOS device, use **undebug all** or **no debug all**. Debug functions only at Privileged EXEC mode.

Starting in IOS version 15.0, the ISR G2 routers now require licenses to legally operate. Licenses are of two types: evaluation and permanent. To install a permanent license, use the **license install** command. To verify the licensing on your router, use the **show version** and **show license** commands.

✓ TWO-MINUTE DRILL

Router Configuration Files

❑ These commands perform a merge process: `copy startup-config running-config`, `copy tftp running-config`, and `configure terminal`. These commands perform an overwrite process: `copy running-config startup-config` and `copy running-config tftp`.

❑ IOS devices do not automatically save their configuration in RAM: you must execute the `copy running-config startup-config` command to save the active configuration file to NVRAM.

Changes in Your Network

❑ Always back up your configuration before making any changes to it—preferably to a remote server using SCP, which encrypts it.

IOS Image Files

❑ When upgrading your IOS, make sure you download the version of IOS from Cisco that contains the features that you purchased, and verify that your router has enough flash and RAM for the new image. Use the `copy URL flash` command to perform an IOS upgrade.

❑ Use the `reload` command to reboot your router.

Remote Access to Your IOS Device

❑ Use SSH for an encrypted remote-access terminal session to your router. The `transport input` command can be used to limit what management protocols are allowed on the VTYs.

Basic Troubleshooting

❑ For layer 2 troubleshooting, use the `show interfaces` command and `show cdp` command. For layer 3 troubleshooting, use `ping` and `traceroute`. For layer 7 troubleshooting, use `telnet`. For detailed troubleshooting, use `debug`.

❑ CDP is used to learn basic information about directly connected Cisco devices. It uses a SNAP frame format and generates a multicast every 60 seconds. It is enabled, by default, on a Cisco device.

❑ To execute an extended **ping** or **traceroute**, you must be at Privileged EXEC mode. **ping** tests only if the destination is reachable, while **traceroute** lists each layer 3 device along the way to the destination.

❑ To suspend a telnet session, use the CTRL-SHIFT-6, X or CTRL-∧ control sequence.

❑ The **debug** commands require Privileged EXEC access. To disable all **debug** commands, use **no debug all** or **undebug all**.

Licensing

❑ Use the **license install** command to install a new license. Use the **show version** and **show licenses** commands to view installed licenses.

SELF TEST

The following Self Test questions will help you measure your understanding of the material presented in this chapter. Read all the choices carefully, as there may be more than one correct answer. Choose all correct answers for each question.

Note: There are no practice questions for the "Changes in Your Network" section, since this information is provided for on-the-job practical usage.

Router Configuration Files

1. Which router commands perform an overwrite process? (Choose two answers.)
   A. `copy running-config startup-config`
   B. `copy startup-config running-config`
   C. `copy tftp running-config`
   D. `copy running-config tftp`

2. Enter the router command to delete your configuration file in NVRAM: _____.

3. You have executed the `show startup-config` command and see the following message: "%%Non-volatile configuration memory is not present." Which of the following answers are correct about these two things? (Choose two answers.)
   A. This command displays the running configuration in NVRAM.
   B. This command displays the saved configuration in NVRAM.
   C. This command displays the saved configuration in flash.
   D. The message indicates that flash needs to be reformatted.
   E. This message indicates that NVRAM needs to be reformatted.
   F. This message indicates that there is nothing stored in this memory location.

IOS Image Files

4. When backing up your IOS image from flash, which of the following will the `copy flash tftp` command prompt you for? (Choose three answers.)
   A. TFTP server IP address
   B. Verification to copy
   C. Source filename
   D. Destination filename

5. What IOS command will display the version of software your device is running?
   A. `show startup-config`
   B. `show flash`
   C. `show version`
   D. `dir` and `show version`

Remote Access to Your IOS Device

6. Enter the IOS configuration on the first five VTYs to allow only SSH access and to prompt for both a username and password for line authentication: _____.

7. Enter the IOS command that will create RSA public and private keys to encrypt and decrypt traffic for an SSH session: _____.

Basic Troubleshooting

8. Which of the following is true of CDP?
   A. The `show cdp neighbor` command displays what version of software the neighbor is running.
   B. The `no cdp run` command disables CDP on an interface.
   C. CDP sends out broadcasts every 60 seconds.
   D. CDP can be used to validate layer 2 connectivity.

9. Which router command would you use to test only layer 3 connectivity?
   A. `telnet`
   B. `show cdp traffic`
   C. `show interfaces`
   D. `traceroute`

10. How would you suspend a telnet session?
    A. CTRL-SHIFT-X, 6
    B. CTRL-SHIFT-6, X
    C. CTRL-6, X
    D. CTRL-C

Licensing

11. What IOS command is used to verify the installed licenses on a Cisco router?

A. `show installed-licenses`

B. `show flash:licenses`

C. `license view`

D. `show version`

SELF TEST ANSWERS

Router Configuration Files

1. ☑ **A** and **D.** Copying to any other place besides RAM (*running-config*) causes an overwrite.
    ☒ **B** and **C** are incorrect because copying to RAM is a merge process, not an overwrite process.

2. ☑ Use the `erase startup-config` command to delete your configuration file in NVRAM.

3. ☑ **B** and **F.** The `show startup-config` command displays a backed-up configuration in NVRAM. If no configuration is stored there, you see the "%%Non-volatile configuration memory is not present" message.
    ☒ **A** is incorrect because a saved configuration, not the running configuration, is found in NVRAM. **C** and **D** are incorrect because these commands show the configuration to flash, not NVRAM. You cannot reformat NVRAM; you can only copy over it or erase it, making **E** incorrect.

IOS Image Files

4. ☑ **A, C,** and **D.** When you use the `copy flash tftp` command, you are prompted for the TFTP server's IP address, the source filename of IOS in flash, and the name you want to call the IOS image on the TFTP server.
    ☒ **B** is incorrect because you are not prompted for a verification before the command is executed; however, you are prompted for this information if you are doing the reverse: upgrading the IOS device.

5. ☑ **C.** The `show version` command will display the current software version your IOS device is running.
    ☒ **B** is incorrect because `show flash` displays the saved configuration file in NVRAM. **B** and **D** (`dir` command) are incorrect because these commands display the files in flash, but not necessarily the IOS version currently running on the router.

Remote Access to Your IOS Device

6. ☑
```
line vty 0 4
    transport input ssh
    login local
```

7. ☑ `crypto key generate rsa`

Basic Troubleshooting

8. ☑ **D.** CDP can be used to validate that you have layer 2 connectivity with a connected device.
☒ **A** is incorrect because **show cdp neighbor** displays neighbors, but not their configuration, software version, or model number; you need the **detail** parameter for this information. **B** is incorrect because **no cdp run** disables CDP globally. **C** is incorrect because CDP uses multicasts, not broadcasts.

9. ☑ **D.** The **traceroute** command tests layer 3.
☒ **A** is incorrect because **telnet** tests layer 7. **B** and **C** are incorrect because **show cdp traffic** and **show interfaces** test layer 2.

10. ☑ **B.** Use CTRL-SHIFT-6, x to suspend a telnet session.
☒ **D** is incorrect because this break sequence is used to break out of the System Configuration Dialog. **A** and **C** are incorrect because these are nonexistent break sequences.

Licensing

11. ☑ **D.** Use the **show version** or **show licenses** command to display the licenses activated on an IOS device.
☒ **D** is incorrect because this break sequence is used to break out of the System Configuration Dialog. **A** and **C** are incorrect because these are nonexistent break sequences.

8

Management Protocols for Cisco Devices

This chapter introduces you to implementing some common management protocols and features on your router, including the Network Time Protocol (NTP), the Simple Network Management Protocol (SNMP), logging, and Cisco's proprietary NetFlow protocol.

Network Time Protocol

The date and time on your router are important for a multitude of reasons. The two most common ones are

- Logging of messages
- Using digital certificates for authentication

Obviously, having the correct timestamp on a log message will help you in forensics when examining logging messages regarding security. Digital certificates are used for authentication. One of the components validated on a device's certificate is if it is current: the certificate has beginning and ending dates and times on it. A peer that receives the certificate will compare its current time and make sure it falls between the beginning and ending dates and times on the certificate. As you can see, the date and time on your router are important. Two ways of setting time on your device are

- Manually configure the date and time
- Using the Network Time Protocol (NTP)

The following sections introduce you to NTP, as well as its configuration and verification on a Cisco IOS device.

NTP Overview

NTP is an open standard that allows you to synchronize your router's time with a centralized time server, where your device periodically polls the NTP server for the current date and time. NTP uses the User Datagram Protocol (UDP) on port 123. NTP can get the correct time for an internal or external server. The reliability of the server refers to its stratum level of clock source. The most accurate is an atomic clock, but most networks typically don't need that kind of precision and instead obtain time from a GPS source.

NTP has three basic methods of delivering time messages between the time server and the NTP client:

- **Broadcast**   The NTP server periodically announces the time using a broadcast message. This method assumes that all clients are in the local subnet.
- **Multicast**   The NTP server periodically announces the time using a multicast message. In most cases, multicast routing must be set up to disseminate the time across the network (multicast routing is beyond the scope of this book).
- **Unicast**   The NTP client periodically (commonly, every 10 minutes) queries the NTP server for the correct time.

on the
job

Most administrators will implement a multicast solution because it scales the best: the server sends out only one message, which, if multicast routing is configured correctly, will appear on all network segments that have NTP clients. The unicast approach is commonly used in smaller networks because it is easier to set up. This book will focus only on the NTP unicast method.

Cisco IOS devices support two versions of NTP:

- NTPv3/v4
- SNTP (Simple NTP)

NTPv3/v4 supports MD5 for authentication. A shared key is preconfigured on the time server and your networking device. This key is commonly referred to as a *pre-shared* key because it must exist on both devices before it can be used for authentication purposes. The time server hashes the current date and time message with the pre-shared key using MD5 and adds this signature to the time message. Your IOS device repeats this process with the received date and time and its locally configured pre-shared key and compares the two hash values, commonly referred to as a *message digest* or *digital signature,* to verify that the message is valid (the same key was used).

SNTP, as its name describes, is a simpler method of acquiring time. Unlike NTPv3, Cisco's IOS implementation of SNTP (as well as that of most vendors) doesn't support authentication of time messages. SNTP is not discussed in this book.

exam Watch

You should set up your own time server, commonly referred to as a local master clock (don't use one on the Internet, since they typically won't support authentication of messages), and implement MD5 authentication with NTPv3. SNTP is a simpler form of NTP that doesn't support any authentication, and therefore is not recommended for use in a production network.

NTP is a critical component for network management on networking devices, including logging and authentication functions. NTP makes sure that all your devices are synchronized with the same time source. However, NTP doesn't require authentication with a time source. In this instance, a hacker could send NTP packets to your devices, changing their time. The hacker can use this trick to confuse you during a time of an attack, or change the time to something outside that used by certificates, which will cause authentication failures for things like HTTPS or IPsec with certificates. There are three solutions to these problems: First, use NTPv3 or a VPN to the time source; second, use ACLs to filter timing information from only valid time sources; and third, set up your own master time source instead of using an untrusted one on the Internet.

NTP Configuration

IOS devices can be configured as NTP servers and/or clients. They are typically configured as time servers to relay time from a reliable local master clock. This section covers only the configuration of an NTP client on a Cisco device.

on the job

You shouldn't use an IOS device as a local master clock because IOS doesn't support a method of connecting to an externally reliable time source, such as GPS. However, many operating systems, like Windows and Linux, support NTP server applications that support external clock connections such as GPS.

Here is the router command to define NTP servers on an IOS device:

```
IOS(config)# ntp server IP_address [version number]
                    [key keyid] [source interface] [prefer]
```

You first need to define the IP address of the remote NTP server. If you don't specify the version number for NTP, it defaults to 3 (NTPv3). The optional **key** parameter references authentication information to be used to verify the server's or peer's timing communications: this must match what the server is using when NTPv3 authentication is performed (the use of the parameter is covered in the next paragraph). The **source** parameter specifies what IP address on the IOS device to use as the source address in the IP packet header when sending communications to the remote NTP server (note that you identify the layer 3 interface on the IOS device to reference the IP address to use). If you omit this parameter, it defaults to the address of the outgoing layer 3 interface. When you are entering multiple NTP servers, you can use the **prefer** parameter, which specifies that this NTP server is preferred over other servers for synchronization purposes; otherwise, the first server configured is the first one that the IOS device will query.

There are three commands you need to configure to set up authentication:

```
IOS(config)# ntp authenticate
IOS(config)# ntp authentication-key key_# md5 key_value
IOS(config)# ntp trusted-key key_#
```

The **ntp authenticate** command enables NTP authentication. The **ntp authentication-key** command defines a reference number for the key (*key_#*) as well as the authentication key (the same *key_#* and *key_value* must be configured on the remote NTP server). Last, the **ntp trusted-key** command specifies which NTP devices should be trusted with authentication, which prevents an accidental synchronization to a system that is not trusted. Notice that a reference number is used. This reference number must match that used in the **ntp authentication-key** command. By using a key number, you can create multiple keys, enabling you to update keys more easily and to have different keys for different peers.

Once you have defined authentication, you need to reference the key number in the corresponding **ntp server** command, which tells the IOS device which key to use when sending messages to specific peers.

NTP Verification

Once you have configured NTP on your IOS device, there are various **show** commands you can use to examine your configuration and troubleshoot problems. To see the current time on the router's software clock, use the **show clock** command.

There are two basic commands you'll use to examine NTP information:

■ `show ntp associations`
■ `show ntp status`

The first command displays associations with the NTP server(s). Here is an example of the **show ntp associations** command:

```
IOS> show ntp associations
  address          ref clock      st when  poll reach delay offset  disp
*~192.168.1.11  192.168.1.11     2   31    1024  377   4.1  -8.38   1.5
* master (synced), # master (unsynced), + selected, - candidate,
    ~ configured
```

The first set of leading characters displays synchronization information:

*	This router is synchronized to this peer.
#	This router is almost synchronized to this peer.
+	The peer has been selected for possible synchronization.
-	The peer is a candidate for synchronization.
~	The peer has been statically configured.

The `address` column lists the addresses of the NTP peer devices, while the `ref clock` column lists the addresses where peers in the `address` column are getting their time. The `st` column indicates the stratum level of the peer. The `when` column indicates the time since the last NTP message was received from this peer. The `poll` column indicates the polling interval, in seconds, this router is using to contact the specified peer. The `reach` column indicates the peer's reachability, in octal. The `delay` column displays the round-trip delay, in milliseconds, to the peer, and the `offset` column displays the relative time of the peer's clock to the local router's clock, in milliseconds.

The **show ntp status** command displays the status of NTP on the router. Here is an example of the **show ntp status** command:

```
IOS# show ntp status
Clock is synchronized, stratum 2, reference is 192.168.1.11
nominal freq is 250.0000 Hz, actual freq is 249.9990 Hz, precision is 2**19
reference time is AFE2525E.70597C87 (00:10:39.511 EDT Thu Jan 1 2004)
clock offset is 6.21 msec, root delay is 83.98 msec
root dispersion is 81.96 msec, peer dispersion is 2.02 msec
```

In this example, IOS is synchronized to the NTP server at 192.168.1.11, which provides a stratum level 2 service.

on the **!**Job

The NTP updates to time on a Cisco IOS device, like a router, are done in small incremental changes. Therefore, when you first boot up your IOS device, it might take quite a while before the router's software clock is completely synchronized with the NTP server. You can verify this from the output of the show ntp status *command. One way of speeding up the synchronization is to manually configure the clock on the router to be close to the time the NTP server is advertising. I would highly recommend this approach if your IOS device has a dead battery for its hardware clock and you need to reboot it. Once rebooted, manually set the time on the router to speed up the synchronization; however, the best solution would be to ensure the device is covered under Cisco's SmartNet Service maintenance and get a replacement for the device.*

NTP Configuration Example

Now that you have a basic understanding of NTP and its configuration, let's look at a simple example where a perimeter router needs to synchronize its time to an NTP server, shown in Figure 8-1. Here's the router's NTP client configuration:

```
Router(config)# ntp server 192.168.1.11 key 99 source ethernet0
Router(config)# ntp authenticate
Router(config)# ntp authentication-key 99 md5 55ab8972G
Router(config)# ntp trusted-key 99
Router(config)# interface ethernet1
Router(config-if)# ntp disable
Router(config)# interface ethernet2
Router(config-if)# ntp disable
```

In this example, the NTP server is 192.168.1.11, which is specified in the first command. The next three commands set up authentication and refer back to the first command with the key reference number of 99. Notice that the hash key is 55ab8912G, which must *also* be configured on the NTP server. Last, NTP is disabled on two interfaces that it doesn't expect to receive time messages from (this was discussed in Chapter 6 concerning the disabling of unused services). As you can see, setting up NTP is straightforward.

8.01. The digital resources that accompany this book contain a multimedia demonstration of configuring and verifying NTP on a Cisco router.

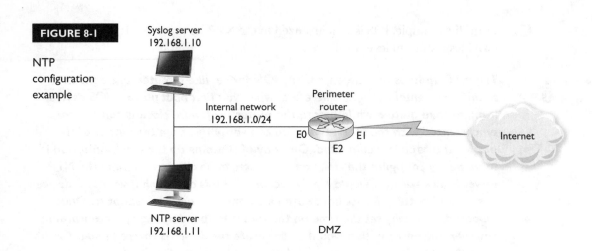

FIGURE 8-1

NTP
configuration
example

CERTIFICATION OBJECTIVE 8.02

Simple Network Management Protocol

Some management of network devices requires the use of the Simple Network Management Protocol (SNMP). SNMP is commonly used to remotely manage (configure and/or monitor) a remote networking device. The following sections briefly provide an overview of SNMP and its configuration.

SNMP Overview

SNMP is composed of three components:

■ **Network Management Station (NMS)**   This device accesses and manages agents and is sometimes referred to as the *manager*.

■ **Agent**   This is a device managed by an NMS.

■ **Management Information Base (MIB)**   This defines how information (configuration, operational, and statistical) is stored on an agent.

The interaction is between the NMS and the agent, which can involve two types of connections:

■ NMS sends "get" or "set" commands to the agent; get commands are used for retrieving MIB information, and set commands are used to change MIB information.

■ The agent sends "traps" or "informs" to the NMS, which are a form of log message, indicating an important condition on the device.

Information stored on an agent is located in an MIB. Each MIB is uniquely identified with an object identifier (OID). Get, send, and trap messages are based on the MIB information identified by a particular OID.

SNMP Versions

There are three main versions of SNMP: versions 1, 2c, and 3. SNMPv1 and v2c use community strings for security: read-only and read-write. The read-only community string is used to restrict the reading of MIB information, and the read-write community string is used to change MIB information. The main problem with community strings is that they are sent in clear text and thus are susceptible to eavesdropping attacks. SNMPv2c also added the support of inform requests, which allows for acknowledged notifications, and get bulk requests, which allows a management station to access multiple MIBs in one request.

SNMPv3 is an enhancement of SNMPv2c. Besides supporting the same MIB structure and gets, sets, and traps, SNMPv3 also supports authentication, message integrity, and payload encryption. Message integrity is used to ensure that SNMP messages have not been tampered with and are coming from a legitimate source; this is accomplished with the MD5 or SHA-1 HMAC functions (these are discussed in Chapter 12). Payload encryption is used so that a man-in-the-middle cannot examine the get, set, and trap command information. A man-in-the-middle is basically a device that sees traffic flowing between the source and destination. Encryption can be used to defeat man-in-the-middle attacks: the attacker can still see the packets, but the content is encrypted from eavesdropping. Encryption is accomplished with the DES, 3DES, or AES encryption algorithms.

Table 8-1 provides an overview of the security models and levels for the different SNMP versions.

SNMP Configuration

This section briefly introduces you to the configuration of SNMPv2c and SNMPv3 on IOS devices. Of the two, configuring SNMPv2c is simpler, but less secure.

With either version, the following commands define the location and contact information of the SNMP device:

```
IOS(config)# snmp-server location location_information
IOS(config)# snmp-server contact contact_name
```

The first command identifies the location of the device, like the building, floor, and wiring closet in which the Cisco device resides. The second command identifies the administrator contact information. Both of these can be pulled from the NMS.

TABLE 8-1   SNMP Security Models

SNMP Version	Level	Authentication	Encryption	What Happens
1	NoAuthNoPriv	Community string	No	Authenticates with a community string match
2c	NoAuthNoPriv	Community string	No	Authenticates with a community string match
3	NoAuthNoPriv	Username	No	Authenticates with a username
3	AuthNoPriv	MD5 or SHA	No	Provides MD5/SHA for authentication
3	AuthPriv	MD5 or SHA	DES, 3DES, or AES	Provides MD5/SHA for authentication and encryption via DES/3DES/AES

SNMPv2c Configuration

Here are the basic commands to set up SNMPv2c communications:

```
IOS(config)# snmp-server community string ro
IOS(config)# snmp-server community string rw
IOS(config)# snmp-server host NMS_IP_address traps string
IOS(config)# snmp-server enable traps
```

The first command defines the community string used to allow read-only access. The second command defines the community string for read-write access. Please note that the community string is sent in clear text in the SNMP packet to restrict access. The last two commands enable the sending of SNMP traps to an SNMP management station (you also have to match the community string on the IOS device to what the NMS has configured).

SNMPv3 Configuration

The configuration of SNMPv3 is much more complicated. Here's a list of commands involved in its setup:

```
IOS(config)# snmp-server view view_name oid_mib
             {included | excluded}
IOS(config)# snmp-server group group_name {v1 | v2c | v3}
             {auth | noauth | priv} [read read_view]
             [write write_view] [notify notify_view]
             [access-list ACL_ID]
IOS(config)# snmp-server user user_name group_name {v1 | v2c | v3}
             [auth {md5 | sha} auth_password] [priv {des |
             3des | aes {128 | 192 | 256}} encr_password]
             [access ACL_ID]
IOS(config)# snmp-server host host_name_or_IP [traps | informs]
             [version {1 | 2c | 3} [auth user_name]
IOS(config)# snmp-server enable traps
```

SNMP views (**snmp-server view**) control which OIDs can or can't be accessed. Using views is optional, but by default there's no restriction to accessing the OIDs if you have SNMP access to the IOS device.

Groups (**snmp-server group**) define the level of access. With groups, you can specify which version of SNMP is used; the required authentication type; which views can be accessed via gets, sets, and traps; and which NMS can access them (this is done via an access control list).

Users define the actual NMS. The authentication credentials define the HMAC signature function and key used to create signatures, and the privilege credentials define the encryption algorithm and key to use.

Here's a simple SNMPv3 configuration example:

```
IOS(config)# access-list 10 permit host 10.0.1.12
IOS(config)# snmp-server view myview interfaces included
IOS(config)# snmp-server group mygroup v3 priv read myview access 10
IOS(config)# snmp-server user myuser mygroup v3 auth sha a3fh95t11a
     priv aes 128 dkfjiewokd892a
IOS(config)# snmp-server host 10.0.1.12 traps version 3 auth myuser
IOS(config)# snmp-server enable traps
```

In this example, an SNMP view was created that includes the "interfaces" MIB/OID. An SNMP group for v3 was created, limiting the view to read access. The group references the view and the ACL to restrict SNMPv3 access. The SNMP user specifies the access credentials (protection) and references the group to use. The SNMP server is defined with traps being sent to the server, and the SNMP user configuration is referenced so the router knows the access method to enforce. Last, SNMP traps are enabled so the router can send events to the SNMP management station.

CERTIFICATION OBJECTIVE 8.03

Logging

An *event* is something that happens (someone logging in); an *incident* is an issue with what happened (an unauthorized login access was detected). Logging plays a key role in your management and security solution. Even though SNMP supports traps, the number of traps is limited: logging supports many more types and kinds of messages than do SNMP traps. Logging to a syslog server makes it easier to manage and keep a historical record of your logging information from a multitude of devices. Syslog uses UDP and runs on port 514. However, all logging information is sent in clear text, has no packet integrity checking, and is easy for a hacker to send false data to the syslog server. Therefore, it is highly recommended that you encrypt information between your networking devices and the syslog server, as well as set up a filter on the syslog server to accept only logging information from particular IP addresses.

By default, logging messages are sent to the router's console port; however, the following locations are also supported: terminal lines, internal memory buffer, SNMP traps, and a syslog server. Common destinations used by administrators are the logging buffer (RAM), the console terminal, and syslog servers. Syslog is the most common, since it allows you to easily centralize (aggregate) logging messages on a server. The advantage of using syslog is that messages can be stored on a hard drive on the syslog server instead of on the router itself, freeing up router resources. The following sections introduce you to logging as well as how to configure logging from the CLI.

Logging Messages

All of Cisco's log messages can contain the following information:

- **Timestamp**   The date and time of the occurrence (this is optional)
- **Log message name**   The name of the message
- **Severity level**   The severity level of the log message, embedded in the log name, like %SYS-5-CONFIG_I, where 5 is the severity level
- **Message text**   A very brief description of the event

Here's an example of a log message:

```
Nov 19 12:30:00 EST: %SYS-5-CONFIG_I: Configured from
     console by vty0 (10.0.11.11)
```

In this example, the timestamps have been enabled (they are disabled by default). This is followed by the category of logging (SYS indicates a system message), the severity level (5), and the subcategory (CONFIG indicates a change on the router). Last is the message text.

Logging Severity Levels

Table 8-2 summarizes the severity levels of log messages, as well as the importance of the severity levels.

TABLE 8-2		Logging Levels
Level	**Name**	**Description**
0	Emergency	The router is unusable (IOS can't load).
1	Alerts	The router needs immediate attention; for instance, the temperature is too high.
2	Critical	There is a critical condition; for instance, the router is running out of memory.
3	Errors	An error condition exists, such as an invalid memory size.
4	Warnings	A warning condition exists; for instance, a crypto operation failed.
5	Notifications	A normal event occurred; for instance, an interface changed state.
6	Informational	Informational message; for instance, a router dropped a packet because of an ACL filter.
7	Debug	Output of **debug** commands.

Logging Configuration

Here are the basic commands for setting up logging:

```
IOS(config)# logging [host] {hostname | IP_address}
IOS(config)# logging trap level_name_or_#
IOS(config)# logging console level_name_or_#
IOS(config)# logging buffered level_name_or_#
IOS(config)# logging monitor level_name_or_#
IOS(config)# logging facility facility_type
IOS(config)# logging source-interface interface_name
IOS(config)# logging on
```

ⓦatch   *The logging level indicates any message at that level or higher. For example, if you set the level to 3, messages from levels 1 to 3 would be logged. The default facility level is* local7.

The **logging host** command defines a syslog server to send log messages to. The **logging trap** command defines the severity level at which to log messages: this must specify the name or number of the level, shown in the first two columns of Table 8-2. The level indicates any message at that level or higher. For example, if you set the level to 3, messages from levels 1 to 3 would be logged. The **logging console** command defines the logging level for the console line; the

logging buffered command defines the logging leve~~~~~~~~~~~~~ges stored in the router's RAM; and the **logging monitor** c~~~~~~~~s the logging level for log messages sent to the router's other lines, ~~~~ VTYs.

The **logging facility** command is used to direct logging information to the appropriate file on the syslog server. The default is local7, but this can be changed. The facility type allows you to keep different log files for different devices on the same syslog server, making it easier to find log messages. The **logging source-interface** command specifies which interface on the router will be used to reach the syslog server—by default, the router will use its routing table to determine what interface, and thus what source IP address to use, when sending a log message. You might want to configure this command if the router has multiple interfaces it can use to reach the log server, and thus the possibility of multiple source IP addresses to use, but the syslog server is only allowing log messages from one of the router's IP addresses. Last, you must enable logging with the **logging on** command—this is not necessary for log messages sent to the console, which is enabled by default. Please note that there are many other parameters to the **logging** command, but the ones I've discussed are the most commonly configured parameters.

By default, Cisco IOS devices do not include the local timestamp (date and time) with the syslog messages sent to the syslog server: they rely on the server attaching its time to the message. To have the IOS device include its own local time, configure the following command:

```
IOS(config)# service timestamps {log | debug} datetime [msec]
```

You can add timestamps to log messages or the output of **debug** commands. The **msec** parameter specifies to include the current millisecond value in the router's timestamped log message.

Be familiar with the syntax of the service timestamps command.

Logging Verification

Use the **show logging** command to verify your configuration—if logging to the router's RAM (buffered) is enabled, you'll see these log messages at the bottom of the display:

```
IOS# show logging
   Syslog logging: enabled (0 messages dropped, 1 messages
            rate-limited, 0 flushes, 0 overruns, xml disabled,
            filtering disabled)
```

```
No Active Message Discriminator.
No Inactive Message Discriminator.
    Console logging: level debugging, 32 messages logged, xml
                disabled, filtering disabled
    Monitor logging: level debugging, 0 messages logged, xml
                disabled, filtering disabled
    Buffer logging:  level informational, 2 messages logged,
                 xml disabled, filtering disabled
    Logging Exception size (4096 bytes)
    Count and timestamp logging messages: disabled
    Persistent logging: disabled
No active filter modules.
ESM: 0 messages dropped
    Trap logging: level notifications, 27 message lines logged
        Logging to 10.0.0.1  (udp port 514,  audit disabled,
            authentication disabled, encryption disabled, link up),
            1 message lines logged,
            0 message lines rate-limited,
            0 message lines dropped-by-MD,
            xml disabled, sequence number disabled
            filtering disabled

Log Buffer (51200 bytes):
*Jan 29 16:39:25.991: %SYS-5-CONFIG_I: Configured from console by
    console
*Jan 29 16:39:26.991: %SYS-6-LOGGINGHOST_STARTSTOP: Logging to host
    10.0.0.1 port 514 started - CLI initiated
```

Logging CLI Example

I'll use the network shown in Figure 8-2 to illustrate how to set up a router to send log messages to a syslog server (10.0.0.1). Here's the configuration:

```
Router(config)# logging 10.0.0.1
Router(config)# logging trap 5
Router(config)# logging source-interface fa0/0
Router(config)# logging on
```

Notice that the router will only send log messages from level 5 and lower and that the router sources log messages from the FA0/0 interface.

8.02. The digital resources that accompany this book contain a multimedia demonstration of configuring and verifying syslogging on a Cisco router.

FIGURE 8-2

Logging example

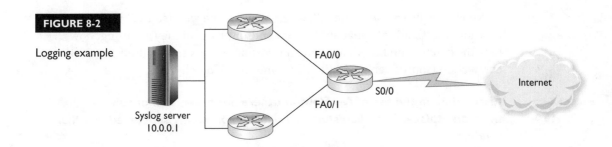

CERTIFICATION OBJECTIVE 8.04

NetFlow

NetFlow is a Cisco-proprietary technology to classify and identify traffic, as well as provide statistics for the traffic. Originally, it was meant for quality of service (QoS) and traffic management purposes, but it can be used to detect attacks by looking for anomalies in traffic sessions. Common uses for NetFlow include

- Network traffic accounting
- Usage-based network billing
- Network capacity and planning
- Security
- Denial of service (DoS) monitoring capabilities
- Network monitoring and troubleshooting

exam
ⓦatch

NetFlow allows administrators to identify applications causing network congestion, diagnose slow performance, and verify that an application receives the appropriate amount of bandwidth based on its class of service (CoS). Benefits include network, application, and user monitoring; network planning; and accounting/billing.

NetFlow is like a telephone bill, where you can see who (source) is connecting to whom (destination), what application and/or protocol they are using, how long the connection lasted, how much information was transmitted across the connection (source versus destination), and much, much more.

on the

Job

Cisco relies on the use of NetFlow, but there are other, similar solutions in the marketplace. The open standard sFlow is commonly supported by other vendors.

NetFlow Architecture

A *flow* is basically a session between two devices: the parameters associated with a connection involving information in the layer 3 and layer 4 header, as well as some other components, to identify a flow. A flow possibly contains the following information:

- Layer 3 protocol
- Source and destination IP addresses
- Source and destination port numbers
- CoS or type of service (ToS) information
- Input interface name
- Flow timestamp
- Next-hop IP address
- TCP flags

Minimally, a flow must contain a source IP address, a destination IP address, and an ingress interface. Cisco uses application-specific integrated circuits (ASICs) to capture the flow information. The technology used by the ASICs, Cisco Express Forwarding (CEF), implements many features to offload processing of the CPU to an interface or a card. The most common feature of CEF is to offload forwarding of the traffic from the CPU to the ASIC. Another function of CEF is to create flow information for NetFlow. Even though ASICs capture the flow information, the IOS device's CPU must be involved in forwarding the flow information to a NetFlow collector: this can be very CPU-intensive.

Some NetFlow information can be examined locally on the IOS device; however, to gather and examine NetFlow information over long periods of time, you need a NetFlow collector (basically a logging server that understands NetFlow flow information). The following are the versions supported by Cisco:

1	Original version of NetFlow
5	The standard and most common implementation
7	Specific to the 6500, 6800, and 7600 products
8	Reduces resource usage (summarized flow information)
9	Flexible file format to support additional fields and used for IPv6, multiprotocol label switching (MPLS), Border Gateway Protocol (BGP), and multicast

The most common implementation of NetFlow is version 5, but the most flexible is version 9. When sending NetFlow information to a collector, you must identify the version used on both the IOS device and collector so that they can understand the flow information. The NetFlow information is sent using UDP as a transport protocol. There are many, many products in the marketplace that can perform the function of a NetFlow collector. Cisco NetFlow Collector is a Cisco product that provides a GUI to examine flow information and statistics in a visual format, including bar charts, pie charts, and histograms, to name a few. One concern with a collector is the number of devices and amount of flow information the collector will receive: you can quickly overburden a collector if you send too much information to it.

NetFlow Configuration

To configure NetFlow, you must perform the following four tasks:

1. Enable data capturing on an interface: ingress is incoming and egress is outgoing.
2. Define the IP address and UDP port of the NetFlow collector.

3. Optionally identify the version of NetFlow to export the flow information.

4. Verify the NetFlow configuration, operation, and statistics.

Even though ASICs capture the flow information using CEF, the flow information must be stored in RAM. IOS allows you to define memory limits for NetFlow if you have limited memory on your IOS device. The default cache size depends on the particular Cisco product and platform.

The following commands show how to enable NetFlow from the CLI and how to export the information to a NetFlow collector:

```
IOS(config)# ip cef
IOS(config)# interface type number
IOS(config-if)# ip flow {ingress | egress}
IOS(config-if)# exit
IOS(config)# ip flow-export version {1 | 5 | 9}
IOS(config)# ip flow-export destination mgmt_IP UDP_port
```

NetFlow versions vary based on device and code. As of IOS 12.4, for example, routers only support versions 1, 5, and 9.

Flow monitors are NetFlow components that allow you to globally define NetFlow parameters, like the cache size and the number of unique flow records to collect. This configuration is then applied to a respective interface.

Most Cisco management stations, acting as collectors, listen on UDP port 9997, by default. Flow monitors are NetFlow components that allow you to globally define NetFlow parameters, like the cache size and the number of unique flow records to collect. This configuration is then applied to a respective interface (the configuration of flow monitors is beyond the scope of this book).

NetFlow Verification

There are two commands you can use to verify the NetFlow configuration on your IOS device. First verify that it is enabled on the respective interface:

```
IOS# show ip interface g1/0/1
 .
 .
 .
 Input features: Ingress-Netflow, MCI check
 Output features: Egress-NetFlow
```

To verify the NetFlow configuration and an overall status of the NetFlow operation, use the **show ip flow export** command:

```
Router# show ip flow export
Flow export v5 is enabled for main cache
  Exporting flows to 10.51.12.4 (9991)
  Exporting using source IP address 10.1.97.17
  Version 5 flow records
  11 flows exported in 8 udp datagrams
  0 flows failed due to lack of export packet
  0 export packets were sent up to process level
  .
  .
  .
```

In this example, 11 flows were exported to the NetFlow collector at 10.51.12.4.

To view a summary of the flow information captured by the IOS device, use the **show ip cache flow** command:

```
Router# show ip cache flow
IP packet size distribution (44027 total packets):
  1-32    64    96   128   160   192   224   256   288   320   352   384   416   448
 .119  .800  .000  .000  .000  .000  .000  .000  .000  .000  .000  .000  .000  .000
  480   512   544   576  1024  1536  2048  2560  3072  3584  4096  4608
 .000  .000  .000  .039  .000  .039  .000  .000  .000  .000  .000  .000
IP Flow Switching Cache, 278544 bytes
  51 active, 4045 inactive, 173 added
  84752 ager polls, 0 flow alloc failures
  Active flows timeout in 3 minutes
  Inactive flows timeout in 60 seconds
IP Sub Flow Cache, 25800 bytes
  153 active, 871 inactive, 451 added, 173 added to flow
  0 alloc failures, 0 force free
  1 chunk, 1 chunk added
  last clearing of statistics never
```

Protocol	Total Flows	Flows /Sec	Packets /Flow	Bytes /Pkt	Packets /Sec	Active(Sec) /Flow	Idle(Sec) /Flow
TCP-FTP	8	0.0	871	40	3.4	1394.5	0.4
TCP-FTPD	8	0.0	872	40	3.4	1394.9	0.1
TCP-WWW	4	0.0	871	40	1.7	1393.3	1.1
TCP-SMTP	4	0.0	871	40	1.7	1393.3	1.4
TCP-other	16	0.0	871	40	6.8	1393.3	1.1
UDP-other	72	0.0	1	53	0.0	0.0	15.4
ICMP	10	0.0	871	427	4.3	1394.6	0.3
Total:	122	0.0	357	117	21.6	571.3	9.4

```
SrcIf      SrcIPaddress    DstIf      DstIPaddress    Pr SrcP DstP Pkts
Et0/0.1    192.168.67.6    Et1/0.1*   172.16.10.200   01 0000 0C01    7
Et0/0.1    192.168.67.6    Et1/0.1    172.16.10.200   01 0000 0C01    7
Et0/0.1    172.16.6.1      Null       224.0.0.9       11 0208 0208    1
.
.
.
```

Using this command, you can see which protocols/applications use the highest volume of traffic and between which hosts these sessions occur.

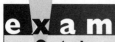

The `show ip cache flow` command visualizes the general NetFlow data captured by an IOS device.

8.03. The digital resources that accompany this book contain a multimedia demonstration of configuring and verifying NetFlow on a Cisco router.

INSIDE THE EXAM

Network Time Protocol

You should set up your own time server, commonly referred to as a local master clock (don't use one on the Internet, since they typically won't support authentication of messages), and implement MD5 authentication with NTPv3. SNTP is a simpler form of NTP that doesn't support any authentication, and therefore is not recommended for use in a production network.

Simple Network Management Protocol

The three components of SNMP are manager, agent, and MIBs. An SNMP trap/inform is an alert generated by an agent. SNMPv2c uses community strings and added the use of the inform and get bulk requests. SNMPv3 added message integrity, authentication, and encryption.

(Continued)

INSIDE THE EXAM

Logging

Common logging destinations used by administrators are the logging buffer (RAM), the console terminal, and syslog servers. The advantage of using syslog is that messages can be stored on a hard drive on the syslog server instead of on the router itself, freeing up router resources. Even though SNMP supports traps, the number of traps is limited: logging supports many more types and kinds of messages than SNMP traps. Syslog allows you to easily centralize (aggregate) logging messages on a server. The logging levels are emergency (0), alerts (1), critical (2), errors (3), warnings (4), notifications (5), informational (6), and debug (7). The logging level indicates any message at that level or higher. For example, if you set the level to 3, messages from levels 1 to 3 would be logged. The default facility level is `local7`. The **service timestamps** command adds the current date/time to logging and/or debug output.

NetFlow

NetFlow allows administrators to identify applications causing network congestion, diagnose slow performance, and verify that an application receives the appropriate amount of bandwidth based on its class of service (CoS). Benefits include network, application, and user monitoring; network planning; and accounting/billing. Minimally, a flow must contain a source IP address, a destination IP address, and an ingress interface. Traffic is considered in the same flow if the packets contain the same IP addressing, port numbers, and layer 3 protocol information. Sending flow information to a collector can be CPU-intensive. One concern with a collector is the number of devices and amount of flow information the collector will receive. Version 5 is the most common implementation of NetFlow. Flow monitors are NetFlow components that allow you to globally define NetFlow parameters, like the cache size and the number of unique flow records to collect. This configuration is then applied to a respective interface. The **show ip cache flow** command visualizes the general NetFlow data captured by an IOS device.

CERTIFICATION SUMMARY

The date and time on your router are important for logging of messages, digital certificates, and many other things. Common methods of accessing NTP information are via multicast messages from a server or unicast query messages from a client. NTPv3 supports authentication of messages using a digital signature created from MD5. It is recommended to set up your own local master time source.

SNMP is used to manage devices remotely. The three components of SNMP are the management station (NMS), the agent, and the MIBs. Get, send, and trap/inform messages are used between the NMS and the agent. SNMPv2c supports community strings for security, which are clear text. SNMPv3 supports message validation, authentication, and encryption of messages, and is thus more secure than SNMPv2c.

Logging is used to record events that occur on a device. Logging information can be viewed locally on a device or forwarded to a syslog server. The logging level of a message indicates its severity, where logging levels range from 0 (emergency) to 7 (debugging). Logging provides much more information than what is available with SNMP traps and informs. By default, logging is enabled for the console of IOS devices, but must be manually enabled for other destinations. Timestamps for logging and debug messages are disabled by default, but can be enabled with the `service timestamps` command.

NetFlow, a proprietary Cisco technology, captures information about flows that can be used for network traffic accounting, accounting/billing based on amount of traffic sent, network capacity planning, network monitoring, and many other network management functions. A flow is basically a session between two devices and must minimally contain a source IP address, a destination IP address, and an ingress interface. Cisco uses ASICs to capture the flow information. Cisco supports multiple versions of NetFlow, where version 5 is the most common. The `show ip cache flow command` displays a summary of the session flows, but to gather information historically, an external NetFlow collector is necessary.

✓ TWO-MINUTE DRILL

Network Time Protocol

❏ NTP has three methods of delivering time messages: broadcast, unicast, and multicast.

❏ NTPv3 supports authentication of messages using MD5 signatures.

❏ You should set up your own time server, commonly referred to as a local master clock, and implement MD5 authentication with NTPv3—don't use SNTP, because Cisco doesn't support authentication with it.

Simple Network Management Protocol

❏ The three components of SNMP are a manager, an agent, and MIBs.

❏ An SNMP trap/inform is an alert generated by an agent.

❏ SNMPv2c uses community strings and added the use of the inform and get bulk requests.

❏ SNMPv3 added message integrity, authentication, and encryption.

Logging

❏ Common logging destinations used by administrators are the logging buffer (RAM), the console terminal, and syslog servers. The advantage of using syslog is that messages can be stored on a hard drive on the syslog server instead of on the router itself, freeing up router resources. Syslog allows you to easily centralize (aggregate) logging messages on a server.

❏ Even though SNMP supports traps, the number of traps is limited: logging supports many more types and kinds of messages than SNMP traps.

❏ Logging levels are emergency (0), alerts (1), critical (2), errors (3), warnings (4), notifications (5), informational (6), and debug (7). The logging level indicates any message at that level or higher. For example, if you set the level to 3, messages from levels 1 to 3 would be logged.

❏ The default facility level is `local7`.

❏ The **`service timestamps`** command enables the addition of the local date, time, and, optionally, milliseconds to the logging or debug records.

NetFlow

❑ NetFlow allows administrators to identify applications causing network congestion, diagnose slow performance, and verify that an application receives the appropriate amount of bandwidth based on its class of service (CoS).

❑ NetFlow benefits include network, application, and user monitoring; network planning; and accounting/billing.

❑ Minimally, a flow must contain a source IP address, a destination IP address, and an ingress interface. Traffic is considered in the same flow if the packets contain the same IP addressing, port numbers, and layer 3 protocol information.

❑ Sending flow information to a collector can be CPU-intensive.

❑ One concern with a collector is the number of devices and amount of flow information the collector will receive.

❑ Flow monitors are NetFlow components that allow you to globally define NetFlow parameters, such as the cache size and the number of unique flow records to collect, which are then applied to a respective interface.

❑ The **show ip cache flow** command displays the general NetFlow data captured by an IOS device.

SELF TEST

The following Self Test questions will help you measure your understanding of the material presented in this chapter. Read all the choices carefully, as there may be more than one correct answer. Choose all correct answers for each question.

Network Time Protocol

1. SNTP uses which protocol to authenticate time messages?
   A. MD5
   B. SHA-1
   C. AES
   D. None

2. Which IOS command defines an NTP server?
   A. `ip ntp server`
   B. `ntp server`
   C. `ntp-server`
   D. `ip ntp-server`

Simple Network Management Protocol

3. Which of the following are components of SNMP? (Choose three answers.)
   A. Agent
   B. Manager
   C. NetFlow
   D. Syslog
   E. MIB

4. Which of the following are associated with SNMPv2c? (Choose two answers.)
   A. Community strings
   B. Encryption
   C. Informs
   D. Message validation
   E. Digital signatures

Logging

5. Enter the IOS command to enable logging to destinations other than the console: _____.

6. What are the common logging destinations used by administrators on Cisco devices? (Choose two answers.)
    A. TFTP server
    B. Terminal sessions
    C. Syslog servers
    D. RAM
    E. Flash

NetFlow

7. A NetFlow flow must minimally contain which items? (Choose two answers.)
    A. IP address
    B. Port numbers
    C. Ingress interface
    D. CoS

8. Version _____ is the most common implementation of NetFlow.

SELF TEST ANSWERS

Network Time Protocol

1. ☑ **D.** SNTP doesn't support authentication.
    ☒ **A** is incorrect because MD5 is used by NTPv3, not SNTP. **B** is incorrect because SHA-1, even though it creates digital signatures, isn't supported by SNTP or NTPv3. **C** is incorrect because AES is an encryption algorithm and neither SNTP nor NTPv3 supports it.

2. ☑ **B.** Use the `ntp server` command to define an NTP server.
    ☒ **A, C,** and **D** are incorrect because they are nonexistent IOS commands.

Simple Network Management Protocol

3. ☑ **A, B,** and **E.** The agent, the NMS (manager), and MIBs are the three components of SNMP.
    ☒ **C** and **D** are incorrect because they are not components of SNMP.

4. ☑ **A** and **C.** SNMPv2c uses community strings and added the use of the inform and get bulk requests.
    ☒ **B, D,** and **E** are incorrect because these are features of SNMPv3.

Logging

5. ☑ `logging on`

6. ☑ **C** and **D.** Common logging destinations used by administrators are the logging buffer (RAM), the console terminal, and syslog servers.
    ☒ **A** and **E** are incorrect because these are not supported destinations. **B** is incorrect because even though the console would be correct, VTY and TTY sessions would not be common.

NetFlow

7. ☑ **A** and **C.** Minimally, a flow must contain a source IP address, a destination IP address, and an ingress interface.
    ☒ **B** and **D** are incorrect because they are not necessary in order to define a flow.

8. ☑ **5.** Version 5 is the most common implementation of NetFlow.

Part III

Routing

9

Basic Routing

I n Chapter 4, you read about routing protocols, including the different types and their advantages and disadvantages. You performed a basic configuration of a router from the command-line interface (CLI) in Chapter 6. This chapter covers the basic configuration of static routes (IPv4 and IPv6) and distance vector protocols, specifically the IP Routing Information Protocol (RIP). The section on RIP focuses on the basics of this protocol; advanced configuration of RIP is beyond the scope of this book. However, by the end of the chapter, you'll be able to configure routers using static routes or a running RIP that will route traffic in a network between the router's interfaces. The end of the chapter focuses on different solutions for users finding redundant default gateways in case of failures.

CERTIFICATION OBJECTIVE 9.01

Static Routes

A *static route* is a manually configured route on your router. Static routes are typically used in smaller networks and when few networks or subnets exist, or with WAN links that have little available bandwidth. With a network that has hundreds of routes, static routes are not scalable, since you would have to configure each route and any redundant paths for that route on each router. This section covers the configuration of static routes and some of the issues associated with them. The first part focuses on IPv4 static routes and the second part focuses on IPv6 static routes—you'll be tested more thoroughly on IPv4 static routing, but should be familiar with IPv6 static routing as well.

e x a m

w a t c h *Dynamic routing protocols are preferred over static routes when many networks or subnets exist in a network, since the configuration of static routes would be prone to misconfiguration given the number of destinations. Static routes are typically used in small networks with few segments and little bandwidth, such as WAN links.*

IPv4 Static Route Configuration

To configure a static route for IP, use one of these two commands:

```
Router(config)# ip route destination_network_# [subnet_mask]
                IP_address_of_next_hop_neighbor
                [administrative_distance] [permanent]
```

or

```
Router(config)# ip route destination_network_# [subnet_mask]
                exit_interface_name
                [administrative_distance] [permanent]
```

The first parameter that you must specify is the destination network number. If you omit the subnet mask for the network number, it defaults to the Class A (255.0.0.0), B (255.255.0.0), or C (255.255.255.0) default subnet mask, depending on the network number of the destination.

After the subnet mask parameter, you can specify how to reach the destination network in one of two ways: you can tell the router the next-hop neighbor's IP address or the interface the router should exit to reach the destination network. You should use the former method if the link is a multi-access link (the link has more than two devices on it—three routers, for instance). You can use the latter method if it is a point-to-point link. In this instance, you must specify the *name* of the interface on the router, like so: **serial0**.

Optionally, you can change the administrative distance of a static route. If you omit this value, it will have one of two defaults, depending on the configuration of the previous parameter. If you specified the next-hop neighbor's IP address, then the administrative distance defaults to 1. If you specified the interface on the router it should use to reach the destination, the router treats the route as a connected route and assigns an administrative distance of 0 to it.

Note that you can create multiple static routes to the *same* destination. For instance, you might have primary and backup paths to the destination. For the primary path, use the default administrative distance value. For the backup path, use a number higher than this, such as 2. Once you have configured a backup path, the router will use the primary path, and if the interface on the router fails for the primary path, the router will use the backup route.

The **permanent** parameter will keep the static route in the routing table even when the interface the router uses for the static route fails. If you omit this parameter and the interface used by the static route fails, the router will remove this route from its routing table and attempt to find an alternative path to place in the routing table. You might want to use the **permanent** parameter if you never want packets to use another path to a destination, perhaps because of security reasons.

IPv4 Default Route Configuration

A *default route* is a special type of static route. Where a static route specifies a path a router should use to reach a specific destination, a default route specifies a path the router should use if it *doesn't know how to reach the destination.* Note that if a router does not have any path in its routing table telling it how to reach a destination and the router receives a packet destined for this network, the router will *drop* the packet. This is different from a switch, which will flood unknown destinations. Therefore, a default route can serve as a *catch-all*: if no path to the destination is specified, the router will use the default route to reach it.

To set up a default route, use the following syntax for a static route:

```
Router(config)# ip route 0.0.0.0 0.0.0.0
                IP_address_of_next_hop_neighbor
                [administrative_distance] [permanent]
```

or

```
Router(config)# ip route 0.0.0.0 0.0.0.0
                exit_interface_name
                [administrative_distance] [permanent]
```

The network number of 0.0.0.0/0 at first appears a bit strange. Recall from your ICND1 studies, however, that network 0.0.0.0 represents all networks, and a mask of all 0s in the bit position represents all hosts in the specified network. If the local interface associated with the static route is down, the static route will not be placed in the router's routing table. Note that if a destination router or network associated with the static route is not reachable, this will *not* affect the local static route.

Default Network Configuration

An alternative way to configure a default route is to define a default network. When you configure the **ip default-network** command, the router considers routes to that network for installation as the gateway of last resort on the router. This command is used when no other route exists in the routing table (connected, static, or dynamic). Use the **show ip route** command to verify if the default route has been set:

```
Router# show ip route
Codes: C - connected, S - static, I - IGRP, R - RIP, M - mobile,
       B - BGP, D - EIGRP, EX - EIGRP external, O - OSPF,
       IA - OSPF inter area, N1 - OSPF NSSA external type 1,
       N2 - OSPF NSSA external type 2, E1 - OSPF external type 1,
       E2 - OSPF external type 2, E - EGP, i - IS-IS, su - IS-IS summary,
       L1 - IS-IS level-1, L2 - IS-IS level-2, ia - IS-IS inter area,
       * - candidate default, U - per-user static route, o - ODR,
       P - periodic downloaded static route
Gateway of last resort is not set
     161.44.0.0/24 is subnetted, 1 subnets
C       161.44.192.0 is directly connected, Ethernet0
     131.108.0.0/24 is subnetted, 1 subnets
C       131.108.99.0 is directly connected, Serial0
S    198.10.1.0/24 [1/0] via 161.44.192.2
```

Between the code table at the top and the routes at the bottom is a line that says `Gateway of last resort is not set`. This is the default configuration. To define a gateway of last resort, use this command:

```
Router(config)# ip default-network network_number_to_use
```

The network number you define is the network the router should access as a last resort. Note that your routing table will need an entry indicating how to reach this default network, like a next-hop address. This is typically done via a static route.

Note the static route to 198.10.1.0 via 161.44.192.2 and that the gateway of last resort is not set in the previous example of the **show ip route** output. Next, configure a default network of 198.10.1.0:

```
Router(config)# ip default-network 198.10.1.0
```

When re-examining the routing table, it changes to this:

```
Router# show ip route
Codes: C - connected, S - static, I - IGRP, R - RIP, M - mobile,
       B - BGP, D - EIGRP, EX - EIGRP external, O - OSPF,
       IA - OSPF inter area, N1 - OSPF NSSA external type 1,
       N2 - OSPF NSSA external type 2, E1 - OSPF external type 1,
       E2 - OSPF external type 2, E - EGP, i - IS-IS, su - IS-IS summary,
       L1 - IS-IS level-1, L2 - IS-IS level-2, ia - IS-IS inter area,
       * - candidate default, U - per-user static route, o - ODR,
       P - periodic downloaded static route
Gateway of last resort is 161.44.192.2 to network 198.10.1.0
       161.44.0.0/24 is subnetted, 1 subnets
C         161.44.192.0 is directly connected, Ethernet0
       131.108.0.0/24 is subnetted, 1 subnets
C         131.108.99.0 is directly connected, Serial0
S*     198.10.1.0/24 [1/0] via 161.44.192.2
```

The gateway of last resort is now set as 161.44.192.2.

on the job *The ip default-gateway command and the ip default-network command function differently. The former is only used when the IOS device has IP routing disabled: when this is done, the ip default-gateway command defines the default router to use to exit the subnet. The ip route and ip default-network commands are used when the IOS device has IP routing enabled. Specific routes in the routing table are used, and if there is no match, then the default network is used.*

Default Routes and Distance Vector Protocols

A default route sometimes causes problems for certain routing protocols. A routing protocol can fall under two additional categories: *classful* and *classless*. Examples of classful protocols include RIPv1 and IGRP (no longer supported by Cisco). Examples of classless protocols include RIPv2, Open Shortest Path First (OSPF), Enhanced Interior Gateway Routing Protocol (EIGRP), Intermediate System-Intermediate System (IS-IS), and Border Gateway Protocol (BGP).

A classful routing protocol understands only class subnets. For instance, if you have 192.168.1.0/23 in a routing update, a classful routing protocol wouldn't understand it, since a Class C network requires 24 bits of network numbers. This can create problems with a default route, which has a /0 mask.

Also, when a classful router advertises a route out its interface, it does not include the subnet mask. For example, you might have 192.168.1.1/26 configured on your router's interface, and the router receives a routing update with 192.168.1.0. With a classful routing protocol, the router will comprehend subnet masks only for network numbers configured on its interfaces. In this example, the router assumes that for 192.168.1.0, the only valid mask is /26. Therefore, if the router sees 192.168.1.0/26 as the network number, but the network is really 192.168.1.0/27, a lot of routing confusion results.

Classless protocols, on the other hand, do not have any issues accepting routing updates with any bit value for a subnet mask. However, for classful protocols, you must configure the following command to accept nonconforming subnet masks, such as a default route:

```
Router(config)# ip classless
```

This command is also used to deal with *discontiguous* subnets in a network that is using a classful protocol: subnets separated by a different class network. For example, assume that you have networks 172.16.1.0/24, 172.16.2.0/24, and 172.16.3.0/24. However, a different class network, 192.168.1.0/24, sits between the first two Class B subnets and 172.16.3.0/24. In this situation, the router connected to 172.16.1.0/24 and 172.16.2.0/24, when it receives 172.16.0.0 from the side of the network connected to the discontiguous subnet, will *ignore* this routing entry.

Remember that when routes cross a class boundary in a classful protocol, the network number is sent as its classful number. Therefore, the router connected to 192.168.1.0/24 and 172.16.3.0/24, when it advertises updates across the 192.168.1.0/24 subnet, will advertise 172.16.0.0—not the actual subnet number. Since the router connected to 172.16.1.0/24 and 172.16.2.0/24 ignores the 172.16.0.0 routing information, it will not be able to reach 172.16.3.0. On top of this problem, even if you have a default route configured, since the router is connected to the 172.16.0.0 subnets, it assumes that 172.16.3.0 must also be connected; if it isn't in the routing table, then the route cannot be reached. This topic was discussed in Chapter 5.

By using the **ip classless** command, you are overriding this behavior; you're allowing your classful router to use a default route to reach discontiguous subnets. Not that this is a recommended design practice, but it does allow you to solve reachability problems for discontiguous subnets.

exam
Ⓦatch

Classful protocols, such as IP RIPv1, understand only classful subnets— you can apply only one subnet mask to a class address. Classless protocols, such as RIPv2, EIGRP, OSPF, and IS-IS, do not have this restriction. The ip classless *command allows a classful protocol to use a default route; omitting this command will cause the router to drop packets that don't match a specific destination network entry in the routing table.*

Static Route Verification and Troubleshooting

To verify the configuration of IPv4 static and default routes on your router, use the **show ip route** command:

```
Router# show ip route
Codes: C - connected, S - static, I - IGRP, R - RIP,
       M - mobile, B - BGP, D - EIGRP, EX - EIGRP external,
       O - OSPF, IA - OSPF inter area, N1 - OSPF NSSA
       external type 1, N2 - OSPF NSSA external type 2,
       E1 - OSPF external type 1, E2 - OSPF external type 2,
       E - EGP, i - IS-IS, L1 - IS-IS level-1, L2 - IS-IS level-2,
       * - candidate default, U - per-user static route, o - ODR,
       T - traffic engineered route
Gateway of last resort is 0.0.0.0 to network 0.0.0.0

     172.16.0.0/24 is subnetted, 3 subnets
C       172.16.1.0 is directly connected, Ethernet0
C       172.16.2.0 is directly connected, Serial0
S       172.16.3.0 is directly connected, Serial0
*S      0.0.0.0/0 is directly connected, Serial1
```

This command displays the IP routing table on your router and can contain directly connected subnets, static and default routes, and dynamically learned routes from a routing protocol. The top portion of the display for this command has a table of codes. These codes, which describe a type of route that may appear in the routing table, are shown in the first column at the bottom part of the display. In this example, there are two connected routes (C) and two static routes (S). The first static route is treated as a directly connected route, since it was created by specifying the interface to exit the router. The second static route is a default route—the asterisk (*) indicates the gateway of last resort: the path the router should use if no other specific path is available.

e x a m

ⓦatch *Be familiar with the output of the* show ip route *command and be able to determine, based on a router's configuration, what routes should appear in a router's routing table. By default,* *interfaces (including physical, VLAN, loopback, and subinterfaces) that are operational (up and up) will have their IPv4 networks automatically placed in the IOS's routing table with a code designation of C.*

Video *9.01. The digital resources that accompany this book contain a multimedia demonstration of setting up static routes on a router.*

EXERCISE 9-1

MHE Lab

Static Route Configuration

The past few sections have dealt with static routes and their configuration. This exercise will help you reinforce your understanding of this material. You'll perform this lab using Boson's NetSim simulator. In this exercise, you'll set static routes on the two routers (2600-1 and 2600-2). You can find a picture of the network diagram for Boson's NetSim simulator in the introduction of this book. After starting up the simulator, click the Labs tab at the bottom left of the window. Click the McGraw-Hill Education tab (to the right of the Standard and Custom tabs) at the top left. Next, double-click Exercise 9-1. This will load the lab configuration based on the exercises in Chapter 6.

1. Access the 2600-1 router. Click the Lab Instructions tab and use the drop-down selector for Devices to choose 2600-1; or click the NetMap tab and double-click the 2600-1 device icon.

2. On the 2600-1, verify that the fa0/0 and s0 interfaces are up. If they are not, bring them up. Examine the IP addresses configured on the 2600-1.

    Use the **show interfaces** command to verify your configuration. If fa0/0 and s0 are not up, go into the interfaces (fa0/0 and s0) and enable them using the **no shutdown** command. Use the **show interfaces** command to verify that the IP addresses you configured in Chapter 6 are still there.

3. Examine the routing table on the 2600-1.

    Use the **show ip route** command. You should have two connected networks: 192.168.1.0 connected to fa0/0 and 192.168.2.0 connected to s0.

4. Access the 2600-2 router. Click the Lab Instructions tab and use the drop-down selector for Devices to choose 2600-2; or click the NetMap tab and double-click the 2600-2 device icon.

5. On the 2600-2, verify that the fa0/0 and s0 interfaces are up. If not, bring them up. Examine the IP addresses configured on the 2600-2 and look at its routing table.

    On the 2600-2, use the **show interfaces** command to verify your configuration. If fa0/0 and s0 are not up, go into the interfaces (fa0/0 and s0) and enable them using the **no shutdown** command. Use the **show interfaces** command to verify that the IP addresses you configured in Chapter 6 are still there.

6. Examine the routing table on the 2600-2 router.

    Use the **show ip route** command. You should have two connected networks: 192.168.3.0 connected to fa0/0 and 192.168.2.0 connected to s0.

7. Test connectivity between Host-1 and the 2600-1.

    Click the Lab Instructions tab and use the drop-down selector for Devices to choose Host-1; or click the NetMap tab and double-click the Host-1 device icon. From Host-1, ping the 2600-1: **ping 192.168.1.1**. The ping should be successful.

8. Test connectivity between Host-3 and the 2600-2.

Click the Lab Instructions tab and use the drop-down selector for Devices to choose Host-3; or click the NetMap tab and double-click the Host-3 device icon. From Host-3, ping the 2600-2 router: `ping 192.168.3.1`. The ping should be successful.

9. Test connectivity between Host-3 and Host-1.

   From Host-3, ping Host-1: `ping 192.168.1.10`. The ping should fail: there is no route from the 2600-2 to this destination.

10. Look at the 2600-2's routing table: `show ip route`. It doesn't list 192.168.1.0/24.

11. On the 2600-2, configure a static route to 192.168.1.0/24, which is connected to the 2600-1.

    Click the Lab Instructions tab and use the drop-down selector for Devices to choose 2600-2; or click the NetMap tab and double-click the 2600-2 device icon. Configure a static route to reach 192.168.1.0/24 via the 2600-1 router. Configure the static route: `configure terminal`, `ip route 192.168.1.0 255.255.255.0 192.168.2.1`, and `end`.

12. View the routing table on the 2600-2 router.

    View the connected and static routes: `show ip route`. Make sure that 192.168.1.0/24 shows up in the routing table as a static route (`S`).

13. On the 2600-1, configure a static route to 192.168.3.0/24, which is connected to the 2600-2.

    Click the Lab Instructions tab and use the drop-down selector for Devices to choose 2600-1; or click the NetMap tab and double-click the 2600-1 device icon. Configure the static route: `configure terminal, ip route 192.168.3.0 255.255.255.0 192.168.2.2`, and `end`.

14. View the routing table on the 2600-1.

    View the connected and static routes: `show ip route`. Make sure that 192.168.3.0/24 shows up in the routing table as a static route (`S`).

15. From Host-3, ping the `fa0/0` interface of the 2600-1.

    Click the Lab Instructions tab and use the drop-down selector for Devices to choose Host-3; or click the NetMap tab and double-click the Host-3 device icon. Access Host-3 and ping the `fa0/0` interface of the 2600-1 router: `ping 192.168.1.1`. The ping should be successful.

16. From Host-3, ping Host-1.

    Ping Host-1: `ping 192.168.1.10`. The ping should be successful.

Now you should be more comfortable with configuring static routes.

EXERCISE 9-2

Basic IP and Routing Troubleshooting

This chapter has covered the basics of routers and routing. This exercise is a troubleshooting exercise and is different from the other exercises you have performed so far. In previous exercises, you were given a configuration task. In this exercise, the network is already configured; however, three problems exist in this network and you'll need to find and fix them to make it operate correctly. All of these problems deal with IP (layer 3) connectivity.

You'll perform this exercise using Boson's NetSim simulator. You can find a picture of the network diagram for Boson's NetSim simulator in the introduction of this book. The addressing scheme is the same. After starting up the simulator, click the Labs tab at the bottom left of the window. Click the McGraw-Hill Education tab (to the right of the Standard and Custom tabs) at the top left. Next, double-click Exercise 9-2. This will load the lab configuration based on the exercises in Chapters 6 and static routing (with problems, of course).

Let's start with your problem: Host-1 cannot ping Host-3. Your task is to find the three problems causing this and fix them. You should try this troubleshooting process on your own first; if you have problems, come back to the steps and solutions provided here.

1. Use ping to test connectivity from Host-1 to Host-3.

   Click the Lab Instructions tab and use the drop-down selector for Devices to choose Host-1; or click the NetMap tab and double-click the Host-1 device icon. On Host-1, ping Host-3: `ping 192.168.3.10`. Note that the ping fails.

2. Examine the IP configuration on Host-1.

   Execute `ipconfig /all`. Make sure the IP addressing information is correct: IP address of 192.168.1.10, subnet mask of 255.255.255.0, and default gateway address of 192.168.1.1.

3. Test connectivity from Host-1 to its default gateway by using ping.

   Ping the default gateway address: `ping 192.168.1.1`. The ping should be successful, indicating that at least layer 3 is functioning between Host-1 and the 2600-1.

4. Verify Host-3's IP configuration.

   Click the Lab Instructions tab and use the drop-down selector for Devices to choose Host-3; or click the NetMap tab and double-click the Host-3 device icon. Examine the IP configuration on Host-3 by executing `ipconfig /all`. Make sure the IP addressing information is correct: IP address of 192.168.3.10, subnet mask of 255.255.255.0, and default gateway address of 192.168.3.1.

5. Test connectivity from Host-3 to its default gateway by using ping.

   Ping the default gateway address: `ping 192.168.3.1`. The ping should fail, indicating that there is a problem between Host-3 and the 2600-2. In this example, assume layer 2 is functioning correctly; therefore, it must be a problem with the 2600-2.

6. Check the 2600-2's IP configuration.

   Click the Lab Instructions tab and use the drop-down selector for Devices to choose 2600-2; or click the NetMap tab and double-click the 2600-2 device icon. From the 2600-2, ping Host-3: `ping 192.168.3.10`. The ping should fail. Examine the interface on the 2600-2: `show interface fa0/0`. The interface is disabled, but it has the correct IP address: 192.168.3.1. Enable the interface: `configure terminal`, `interface fa0/0`, `no shutdown`, and **end**. The interface should come up. Retry the ping test: `ping 192.168.3.10`. The ping should be successful.

7. Access Host-1 and retry pinging Host-3.

   Click the Lab Instructions tab and use the drop-down selector for Devices to choose Host-1; or click the NetMap tab and double-click the Host-1 device icon. Test connectivity to Host-3: `ping 192.168.3.10`. The ping should still fail. So far, there is connectivity within 192.168.1.0 and 192.168.3.0, but there is still a problem between these two networks.

8. Check the interface statuses on the 2600-1 and verify connectivity to the 2600-2.

   Click the Lab Instructions tab and use the drop-down selector for Devices to choose 2600-1; or click the NetMap tab and double-click the 2600-1 device icon. Check the status of the interfaces: `show ip interface brief`. Notice that the fa0/0 and s0 interfaces are both up. Try pinging the 2600-2's s0 interface: `ping 192.168.2.2`. The ping fails. Examine CDP information that the 2600-1 has learned about the 2600-2: `show cdp entry 2600-2`. Notice that the 2600-2 has no IP address.

9. Fix the IP addressing problem on the 2600-2 and retest connectivity across the serial connection.

   Click the Lab Instructions tab and use the drop-down selector for Devices to choose 2600-2; or click the NetMap tab and double-click the 2600-2 device icon. Fix the IP address: `configure terminal`, `interface s0`, `ip address 192.168.2.2 255.255.255.0`, and `end`. Retest the connection to the 2600-1: `ping 192.168.2.1`. The ping should be successful.

10. Examine the routing table on the 2600-2 and verify that 192.168.1.0/24 shows up as a static route.

    Examine the routing table: `show ip route`. As you can see, 192.168.1.0 shows up as a static route and points to 192.168.2.1.

11. Access Host-3 and try connectivity between its default gateway and the 2600-1 router.

    Click the Lab Instructions tab and use the drop-down selector for Devices to choose Host-3; or click the NetMap tab and double-click the Host-3 device icon. Test the connection to the 2600-2: `ping 192.168.3.1`. The ping should be successful, considering you already tested it. Test connectivity to the 2600-1: `ping 192.168.2.1`. The ping should fail. This presents an interesting problem. Host-1 can ping the 2600-1. The 2600-1 can ping the 2600-2. Host-3 can ping the 2600-2. Therefore, on a hop-by-hop basis, you have IP connectivity. And the 2600-2 can even ping Host-1, indicating that some routing functioning is working.

12. Access the 2600-1 router and examine its routing table. Fix the problem.

    Click the Lab Instructions tab and use the drop-down selector for Devices to choose 2600-1; or click the NetMap tab and double-click the 2600-1 device icon. Examine the routing table: `show ip route`. Does the 2600-1 know how to reach 192.168.3.0/24? It does not. The 2600-2 router could ping Host-1 since the 2600-1 router is directly connected to these segments, but any traffic from the 2600-1 to 192.168.3.0/24 will fail since the router doesn't have a path. Add a static route to 192.168.3.0/24: `configure terminal`, `ip route 192.168.3.0 255.255.255.0 192.168.2.2`, and `end`. Test connectivity to Host-3: `ping 192.168.3.10`. The ping should be successful.

13. Now test connectivity between Host-1 and Host-3.

Click the Lab Instructions tab and use the drop-down selector for Devices to choose Host-1; or click the NetMap tab and double-click the Host-1 device icon. Test connectivity to Host-3: `ping 192.168.3.10`. The ping should be successful.

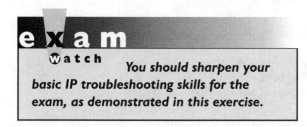

You should now feel comfortable troubleshooting routers that are using static routes for routing.

IPv6 Static Route Configuration

The fundamentals of IPv6 were covered previously during your CCENT studies. This and the next two chapters will focus on routing IPv6 traffic. This chapter will quickly review the configuration of IPv6 on an IOS device and introduce you to configuring IPv6 static routes.

Enabling IPv6 and Assigning Addresses

To use IPv6 on your router, you must, at a minimum, enable the protocol and assign IPv6 addresses to your interfaces, like this:

```
IOS(config)# ipv6 unicast-routing
IOS(config)# interface type [slot_#/]port_#
IOS(config-if)# ipv6 address ipv6_address_prefix/prefix_length
                      [eui-64]
```

The `ipv6 unicast-routing` command globally enables IPv6 and must be the first IPv6 command executed on the router. The `ipv6 address` command assigns the prefix, the length, and the use of EUI-64 to assign the interface ID. Optionally, you can omit the `eui-64` parameter and configure the entire IPv6 address.

To use stateless autoconfiguration, use the following configuration:

```
IOS(config)# interface type [slot_#/]port_#
IOS(config-if)# ipv6 address autoconfig [default]
```

If a default router is selected on this interface, the **default** parameter causes a default route to be installed using that default router. The **default** parameter can be specified only on one interface.

You can use the **show ipv6 interface** command to verify an interface's configuration. Here's an example configuration, with its verification:

```
IOS(config)# ipv6 unicast-routing
IOS(config)# interface fastethernet0/0
IOS(config-if)# ipv6 address 2001:1cc1:dddd:2::/64 eui-64
IOS(config-if)# end
Router# show ipv6 interface fastethernet0/0
FastEthernet0/0 is up, line protocol is up
  IPv6 is enabled, link-local address is FE80::207:EFF:FE46:4070
      [TEN]
  No Virtual link-local address(es):
  Global unicast address(es):
    2001:1CC1:DDDD:2:207:EFF:FE46:4070, subnet is
      2001:1CC1:DDDD:2::/64 [EUI/TEN]
  Joined group address(es):
    FF02::1
    FF02::2
  .
  .
  .
```

In this example, notice that the link-local address is FE80::207:EFF:FE46:4070. Also notice the global address: 2001:1CC1:DDDD:2:207:EFF:FE46:4070.

exam

ⓦatch   *You enable IPv6 with the ipv6 unicast-routing command— this enables forwarding of IPv6 packets. Once IPv6 is enabled, you must create IPv6* *addresses on the interfaces with the* ipv6 address ipv6_address_prefix/ prefix_length *command for IPv6 traffic to be processed on those interfaces.*

You can use the **ping** and **traceroute** commands to test connectivity with IPv6. Execute the command and immediately follow it with the IPv6 address you want to test. Here's an example:

```
IOS# ping 2001:DB8:D1A5:C800::5
Type escape sequence to abort.
Sending 5, 100-byte ICMP Echos to 2001:DB8:D1A5:C800::5, timeout
is
   2 seconds:
.!!!!
Success rate is 100 percent (5/5), round-trip min/avg/max =
0/0/4 ms
```

Remember that you can only test connectivity to link-local addresses in the same VLAN—however, you can test access to global addresses in the same or different VLANs.

*9.02. **The digital resources that accompany this book contain a multimedia demonstration of enabling IPv6 and configuring IPv6 on a router's interfaces.***

IPv6 Static Routing

Configuring an IPv6 static route is similar to configuring an IPv4 static route. Here is the syntax:

```
IOS(config)# ipv6 router prefix/bits IPv6_next_hop_address
```

The *prefix* is the network number you want to reach, with the corresponding number of bits of the network number. For a default route, use **::/0** as the prefix.

To view the IPv6 routes in the routing device's routing table, use the **show ipv6 route** command:

```
Router# show ipv6 route
IPv6 Routing Table - default - 19 entries
Codes:C - Connected, L - Local, S - Static, R - RIP, B - BGP
      U - Per-user Static route, I1 - ISIS L1, I2 - ISIS L2,
      IA - ISIS interarea, IS - ISIS summary, O - OSPF intra,
      OI - OSPF inter, OE1 - OSPF ext 1, OE2 - OSPF ext 2
IPv6 Routing Table - 8 entries
L   4000::2/128 [0/0]
    via ::, Ethernet1/0
C   4000::/64 [0/0]
    via ::, Ethernet1/0
```

```
LC  4001::1/128 [0/0]
     via ::, Loopback0
L   5000::2/128 [0/0]
     via ::, Serial6/0
C   5000::/64 [0/0]
     via ::, Serial6/0
S   5432::/48 [1/0]
     via 4000::1, Null
L   FE80::/10 [0/0]
     via ::, Null0
L   FF00::/8 [0/0]
     via ::, Null0
```

The formatting of the output is slightly different from that of the IPv4 routing table. Like the IPv4 routing table, a C indicates a directly connected route (network) and an S indicates a static route. The L is new—it's a host route. This is an IPv6 address of a host connected to that interface. Also notice that you can see the administrative distance and metric for each route ([X/Y]).

CERTIFICATION OBJECTIVE 9.02

Dynamic Routing Protocol Basics

Before learning how to configure a dynamic routing protocol such as RIP, consider some basic configuration tasks that are required no matter what dynamic routing protocol you are running. You need to perform two basic steps when setting up IP routing on your router:

- Enable the routing protocol.
- Assign IP addresses to your router's interfaces.

Note that the order of these tasks is not important. You already know how to configure an IP address on the router's interface: this was discussed in Chapter 6. The following sections cover the first bullet point in more depth.

Remember the two steps required to set up IP routing on a router.

The router Command

Enabling an IP routing protocol is a two-step process. First, you must go into Router Subconfiguration mode. This mode determines the routing protocol that you'll be running. Within this mode, you'll configure the characteristics of the routing protocol. To enter the routing protocol's configuration mode, use the following command:

```
Router(config)# router name_of_the_IP_routing_protocol
Router(config-router)#
```

The **router** command is used to access the routing protocol that you want to configure; it doesn't enable it. If you are not sure of the name of the routing protocol that you want to enable, use the context-sensitive help feature:

```
Router(config)# router ?
  bgp                    Border Gateway Protocol (BGP)
  eigrp                  Enhanced Interior Gateway Routing
                             Protocol (EIGRP)
  isis                   ISO IS-IS
  iso-igrp               IGRP for OSI networks
  mobile                 Mobile routes
  odr                    On Demand stub Routes
  ospf                   Open Shortest Path First (OSPF)
  rip                    Routing Information Protocol (RIP)
Router(config)#
```

As you can see from the context-sensitive help output, you have a lot of IP routing protocols at your disposal.

One important item to point out is that the `router` *command doesn't turn on the routing protocol. This process is done in the protocol's Router Subconfiguration mode, indicated by the* `(config-router)` *prompt.*

The network Command

Once in the routing protocol, you need to specify what interfaces are to participate in the routing process. By default, no interfaces participate in the routing process. To specify which interfaces will participate, use the **network** Router Subconfiguration mode command:

```
Router(config-router)# network IP_network_#
```

As soon as you enter a network number, the routing process becomes *active*. For distance vector protocols such as RIPv1, you need to enter only the Class A, B, or C network number or numbers that are associated with your interface or interfaces. In other words, if you have subnetted 192.168.1.0 with a subnet mask of 255.255.255.192 (/26) and you have subnets 192.168.1.0/26, 192.168.1.64/26, 192.168.1.128/26, and 192.168.1.192/26, you don't need to enter each specific subnet. Instead, just enter **192.168.1.0**, and this will accommodate all interfaces that are associated with this Class C network. If you specify a subnet, the router will *convert* it to the class address because RIP is a classful protocol.

Let's take a look at a simple example of the configuration, shown in Figure 9-1. This example focuses on the configuration of the **network** commands, assuming that the routing protocol is a classful protocol, such as RIPv1. In this example, the router is connected to a Class B network (172.16.0.0) and a Class C network (192.168.1.0), both of which are subnetted.

Assume that you forgot that you need to enter only the classful network numbers and you entered the subnetted values instead, like this:

```
Router(config-router)# network 172.16.1.0
Router(config-router)# network 172.16.2.0
Router(config-router)# network 192.168.1.64
Router(config-router)# network 192.168.1.128
```

When entering your **network** statements, you need to include any network that is associated with your router's interfaces; if you omit a network, your router will not include the omitted interface in the routing process. As you can see from the preceding example, all the subnets were included. Remember, however, that the router requires only that you enter the class addresses. If you were to execute

FIGURE 9-1

Simple network example

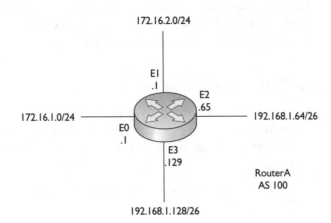

a **`show running-config`** command, you would not see the four networks just listed, but only the Class B and C network numbers. You shouldn't worry about this; it's just that you entered more commands than were necessary. In reality, you needed to enter only these two **network** commands:

```
Router(config-router)# network 172.16.0.0
Router(config-router)# network 192.168.1.0
```

Both ways of entering your statements are correct, but the latter is what the router will use if you type in all of the specific subnets.

Video

9.03. The digital resources that accompany this book contain a multimedia demonstration of an introduction to basic IP routing protocol configuration.

CERTIFICATION OBJECTIVE 9.03

RIP

IP RIP comes in two different versions: 1 and 2. Version 1 is a distance vector protocol and is defined in RFC 1058. Version 2 is an enhanced version of RIPv1 and is defined in RFCs 1721 and 1722. The CCNA exam now primarily focuses on version 2. However, you still need to know a few things about RIPv1, specifically its characteristics. This section covers the basics of configuring and troubleshooting your network using IP RIP.

RIP Operation

As you'll recall from Chapter 4, RIP is a distance vector protocol. RIP is an old protocol and therefore is very stable—in other words, Cisco doesn't do that much development on the protocol, unlike other, more advanced protocols. Therefore, you can feel safe that when you upgrade your IOS to a newer version, RIP will function the same way it did in the previous release. This section includes brief overviews of both versions of RIP.

RIPv1

RIPv1 uses local broadcasts to share routing information. These updates are periodic in nature, occurring, by default, every 30 seconds, with a hold-down period of 180 seconds. Both versions of RIP use *hop count* as a metric, which is not always the best metric to use. For instance, if you had two paths to reach a network, where one was a two-hop Ethernet connection and the other was a one-hop 64-Kbps WAN connection, RIP would use the slower 64-Kbps connection because it has a lesser accumulated hop-count metric. You have to remember this little tidbit when looking at how RIP will populate your router's routing table. To prevent packets from circling around a loop forever, both versions of RIP solve counting to infinity by placing a hop-count limit of 15 hops on packets. Any packet that reaches the 16th hop will be dropped.

And as mentioned in the previous section, RIPv1 is a *classful* protocol. This is important for configuring RIP and subnetting your IP addressing scheme: you can use only one subnet mask value for a given Class A, B, or C network. For instance, if you have a Class B network such as 172.16.0.0, you can subnet it with only one mask. As an example, you couldn't use 255.255.255.0 and 255.255.255.128 on 172.16.0.0—you can choose only one.

Another interesting feature is that RIP supports up to six equal-cost paths to a single destination, where all six paths can be placed in the routing table and the router can load-balance across them. The default is actually four paths, but this can be increased up to a maximum of six. Remember that an equal-cost path is where the metric for the multiple paths to a destination is the same. RIP will not load-balance across *unequal*-cost paths.

Figure 9-2 illustrates equal-cost-path load balancing. In this example, RouterA has two equal-cost paths to 10.0.0.0 (with a hop count of 1) via RouterB and RouterC. Putting both of these paths in RouterA's routing table offers two advantages:

■ The router can perform load balancing to 10.0.0.0, taking advantage of the bandwidth on both of these links.

■ Convergence is sped up if one of the paths fails. For example, if the connection between RouterA and RouterB fails, RouterA can still access network 10.0.0.0 via RouterC and has this information in its routing table; therefore, convergence is instantaneous.

For these two reasons, many routing protocols support parallel paths to a single destination. Some protocols, such as EIGRP, even support unequal-cost-path load balancing, which is discussed in Chapter 11.

FIGURE 9-2

Equal-cost-path load balancing

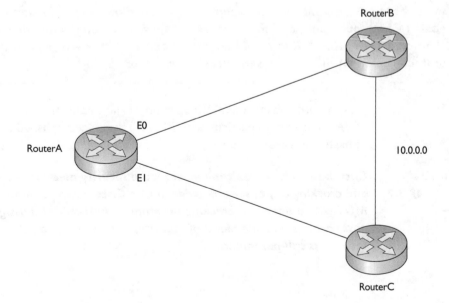

RIPv2

One thing you should keep in the back of your mind when dealing with RIPv2 is that it is based on RIPv1 and is, at heart, a distance vector protocol with routing enhancements built into it. Therefore, it is commonly called a *hybrid protocol*. You read about some of the characteristics that both versions of RIP have in common in the preceding section. This section focuses on the characteristics unique to RIPv2.

One major enhancement to RIPv2 pertains to how it deals with routing updates. Instead of using broadcasts, RIPv2 uses *multicasts*: updates are advertised to 224.0.0.9, which all RIPv2 routers will process. And to speed up convergence, RIPv2 supports *triggered* updates—when a change occurs, a RIPv2 router will immediately propagate its routing information to its connected neighbors.

A second major enhancement in RIPv2 is that it is a *classless* protocol. RIPv2 supports variable-length subnet masking (VLSM), which allows you to use more than one subnet mask for a given class network number. VLSM allows you to maximize the efficiency of your addressing design and summarize routing information to create very large, scalable networks. VLSM is discussed in Chapter 7.

As a third enhancement, RIPv2 supports authentication. You can restrict what routers you want to participate in RIPv2. This is accomplished using a clear-text or hashed password value.

RIP Configuration

As you will see in this section, configuring RIP is an easy and straightforward process. The basic configuration of RIP involves the following two commands:

```
Router(config)# router rip
Router(config-router)# network IP_network_#
```

ⓦatch *Use the* `router rip` *and* `network` *commands to configure RIP routing. Remember to put the class address (not the subnetted network number) in the* `network` *statement.*

As explained in the preceding section, RIPv1 is classful and RIPv2 is classless. However, whenever you configure *either* version of RIP, the **network** command assumes *classful*: You need to enter only the Class A, B, or C network number, not the subnets, as was discussed earlier in this chapter. If you refer back to Figure 9-1, the router's RIPv1 configuration would look like this:

```
Router(config)# router rip
Router(config-router)# network 172.16.0.0
Router(config-router)# network 192.168.1.0
```

9.04. The digital resources that accompany this book contain a multimedia demonstration of a basic RIP configuration on a router.

Specifying RIP Version 1 and 2

By default, the IOS *accepts* both RIPv1 and RIPv2 routing updates; however, it *generates* only RIPv1 updates. You can configure your router to

■ Accept and send RIPv1 only

■ Accept and send RIPv2 only

■ Use a combination of the two, depending on your interface configuration

To accomplish either of the first two items in the list, you need to set the version in your RIP configuration:

```
Router(config)# router rip
Router(config-router)# version 1|2
```

When you specify the appropriate version number, your RIP routing process will send and receive only the version packet type that you configured.

You can also control which version of RIP is running on an interface-by-interface basis. For instance, suppose a bunch of new routers at your site support both versions and a remote office understands only RIPv1. In this situation, you can configure your routers to generate RIPv2 updates on all their LAN interfaces, but for the remote-access connection at the corporate site, you could set the interface to run only RIPv1.

To control which version of RIP should handle generating updates on an interface, use the following configuration:

```
Router(config)# interface type [slot_#/]port_#
Router(config-router)# ip rip send {version 1 | version 2 |
                                     version 1 2}
```

With the `ip rip send` command, you can control which version of RIP the router should use on the specified interface when *generating* RIP updates. You can specify version 1 or 2, or you can specify both.

To control what version of RIP should be used when receiving RIP updates on a particular interface, use the following configuration:

```
Router(config)# interface type [slot_#/]port_#
Router(config-router)# ip rip receive {version 1 | version 2 |
                                        version 1 2}
```

Unless you need to run RIPv1 because of backward compatibility with an older router or host running RIP, you should use version 2 because of some of its enhancements over version 1, such as classless routing, multicasts, and triggered updates.

9.05. The digital resources that accompany this book contain a multimedia demonstration of RIPv2 configuration on a router.

Configuration Example

Let's use a simple network example, shown in Figure 9-3, to illustrate configuring RIPv2. Here's RouterA's configuration:

```
RouterA(config)# router rip
RouterA(config-router)# network 192.168.1.0
RouterA(config-router)# network 192.168.2.0
RouterA(config-router)# version 2
```

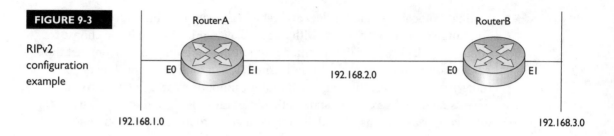

FIGURE 9-3

RIPv2
configuration
example

Here's RouterB's configuration:

```
RouterB(config)# router rip
RouterB(config-router)# network 192.168.2.0
RouterB(config-router)# network 192.168.3.0
RouterB(config-router)# version 2
```

As you can see, configuring RIPv2 is very easy.

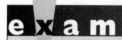

w a t c h   *Make sure you know how   set up a routing protocol, like RIPv2. You
to place a basic configuration on a router,   should also be familiar with verifying and
including IP addressing, as well as how to   troubleshooting your configuration.*

RIP Verification and Troubleshooting

Once you have configured IP RIP, a variety of commands are available to view and troubleshoot your RIP configuration and operation:

- `clear ip route`
- `show ip protocols`
- `show ip route`
- `debug ip rip`

The following sections cover these commands in more depth.

The clear ip route Command

The `clear ip route *` command is a Privileged EXEC mode command. This command clears and rebuilds the IP routing table. Any time you make a change to a routing protocol, you should clear and rebuild the routing table with this command. You can replace the asterisk (*) with a specific network number; if you choose to do so, this will only clear the specified route from the routing table. Note that the `clear` command clears only routes learned from a routing protocol (dynamic routes); static and directly connected routes cannot be cleared from the routing table using the `clear` command. Static routes must be cleared manually using the `no ip route` command, and directly connected routes are persistent and cannot be removed from the routing table unless the interface they are associated with is not operational.

The show ip protocols Command

The `show ip protocols` command displays all the IP routing protocols, including RIP, which you have configured and are running on your router. Here's an example of this command:

```
Router# show ip protocols
Routing Protocol is "rip"
  Sending updates every 30 seconds, next due in 5 seconds
  Invalid after 180 seconds, hold down 180, flushed after 240
  Outgoing update filter list for all interfaces is not set
  Incoming update filter list for all interfaces is not set
  Redistributing: rip
  Default version control: send version 2, receive version 2
    Interface        Send  Recv  Triggered RIP Key-chain
    Ethernet0        2     2
    Ethernet1        2     2
  Automatic network summarization is in effect
  Maximum path: 4   Routing for Networks:
    192.168.1.0
    192.168.2.0   Routing Information Sources:
    Gateway          Distance      Last Update
    192.168.2.2         120        00:00:22
    192.168.3.2         120        00:03:30
  Distance: (default is 120)
```

In this example, RIPv2 is running on the router. The routing update interval is 30 seconds, with the next update being sent in 5 seconds. You can see that two interfaces are participating: `Ethernet0` and `Ethernet1`. On these interfaces, RIPv2 is being used to generate and receive updates on these two interfaces. You can see the two networks specified with the **network** commands: 192.168.1.0 and 192.168.2.0. In this example, this router received an update 22 seconds ago from a neighboring router: 192.168.2.2. For the second gateway, 192.168.3.2, the router hasn't seen an update from it in 210 seconds. Given that the flush timer is 240 seconds, if the local router doesn't receive an update from 192.168.3.2 within 30 seconds, 192.168.3.2 and its associated routes are removed from the local router (flushed). And last, the default administrative distance of RIP is 120.

e x a m

ⓦatch *RIP advertises routes every 30 seconds. Its hold-down period is 180 seconds, and its flush period is 240 seconds. Be familiar with the output of the* `show ip protocols` *command: the version of RIP and when routes are flushed.*

Video

9.06. The digital resources that accompany this book contain a multimedia demonstration of the `show ip protocols` *command for RIP on a router.*

The show ip route Command

Your router keeps a list of the best paths to destinations in a routing table. A separate routing table is kept for each *routed* protocol. For instance, if you are running IP and IPX, your router will have two routing tables: one for each. However, if you are running two *routing* protocols for a single routed protocol, such as IP RIP and EIGRP, your router will have only one routing table for IP, with both sets of routes, possibly, in the same table.

To view the routing table, use the **show ip route** command. Here's an example of a RIPv2 router's table:

e x a m

ⓦatch *Remember the output of the* `show ip route` *command for the RIP routing protocol, including being able to identify the administrative distance and metric values.*

```
Router# show ip route
Codes: C - connected, S - static, I - IGRP, R - RIP,
       M - mobile, B - BGP, D - EIGRP, EX - EIGRP external,
       O - OSPF, IA - OSPF inter area, N1 - OSPF NSSA
       external type 1, N2 - OSPF NSSA external type 2,
       E1 - OSPF external type 1, E2 - OSPF external type 2,
       E - EGP, i - IS-IS, L1 - IS-IS level-1,
       L2 - IS-IS level-2, * - candidate default,
       U - per-user static route, o - ODR,
       T - traffic engineered route
```

```
Gateway of last resort is not set
     172.16.0.0/24 is subnetted, 2 subnets
C       172.16.1.0 is directly connected, Ethernet0
R       172.16.2.0 [120/1] via 172.16.1.2, 00:00:21, Ethernet0
     192.168.1.0/24 is subnetted, 2 subnets
C       192.168.1.0 is directly connected, Serial0
R     192.168.2.0/24 [120/2] via 192.168.1.2, 00:00:02, Serial2
```

In this example, you can see that two types of routes are in the routing table: R is for RIP and C is for a directly connected route. For the RIP entries, you can see two numbers in brackets: the administrative distance of the route and the metric. For instance, 172.16.2.0 has an administrative distance of 120 and a hop count of 1. Following this information is the neighboring RIP router that advertised the route (172.16.1.2), how long ago an update for this route was received from the neighbor (21 seconds), and on which interface this update was learned (Ethernet0).

9.07. The digital resources that accompany this book contain a multimedia demonstration of the `show ip route` *command for RIP on a router.*

The debug ip rip Command

Remember that the **show** commands show a static display of what the router knows, and they sometimes don't display enough information concerning a specific issue or problem. For instance, you might be looking at your routing table with the **show ip route** command and expect a certain RIP route to appear from a connected neighbor, but this network is not shown. Unfortunately, the **show ip route** command won't tell you why a route is or isn't in the routing table. However, you can resort to **debug** commands to assist you in your troubleshooting.

For more detailed troubleshooting of IP RIP problems, you can use the **debug ip rip** command, shown here:

```
Router# debug ip rip
RIP protocol debugging is on
Router#
00:12:16: RIP: received v1 update from 192.168.1.2 on Serial0
00:12:16:      192.168.2.0 in 1 hops
00:12:25: RIP: sending v1 update to 255.255.255.255 via Ethernet0
               172.16.1.1)
00:12:26:      network 192.168.1.0, metric 0
00:12:26:      network 192.168.2.0, metric 1
```

This command displays the routing updates sent and received on the router's interfaces. In this code example, the router received a V1 update from 192.168.1.2 on Serial0. This update contained one network, 192.168.2.0, indicating that this network is reachable from this and the advertising routers. After this update, you can see that your router generated a RIP update (local broadcast—255.255.255.255) on its Ethernet0 interface. This update contains two networks: 192.168.1.0 and 192.168.2.0. Also notice the metrics associated with these routes: 192.168.1.0 is connected to this router, while 192.168.2.0 is one hop away. When the neighboring router connected to Ethernet0 receives this update, it will increment the hop count by 1 for each route in the update.

exam
ⓦatch
Be familiar with the output of the debug ip rip *command to troubleshoot problems with RIP, such as a mismatch in the RIP versions. Remember* *that* debug *commands can create performance problems on routers and should be used only for troubleshooting and then disabled.*

If the two routers are running different RIP versions—v1 and v2—you'll see output like the following on your router when running the preceding **debug** command:

```
00:12:25: RIP: sending v1 update to 255.255.255.255
                       via Ethernet0 172.16.1.1)
00:12:26:      network 192.168.1.0, metric 0
00:12:26:      network 192.168.2.0, metric 1
00:12:32: RIP: ignored v2 packet from 192.168.2.1
                       (illegal version)
```

on the
ⓙo b
When using debug *commands, you must be at Privileged EXEC mode. To disable a specific* debug *command, negate it with the* no *parameter. To turn off debugging for all* debug *commands, use either the* undebug all *or* no debug all *command.*

Video

9.08. The digital resources that accompany this book contain a multimedia demonstration of the debug ip rip *command for RIP on a router.*

EXERCISE 9-3

Configuring RIP

The past few sections dealt with configuring RIP on a router. This exercise will help you reinforce your understanding of the material for setting up and troubleshooting RIP. You'll perform this lab using Boson's NetSim simulator. You can find a picture of the network diagram for Boson's NetSim simulator in the introduction of this book. In this exercise, you set IP RIPv1 on the two routers (2600-1 and 2600-2). After starting up the simulator, click the Labs tab at the bottom left of the window. Click the McGraw-Hill Education tab (to the right of the Standard and Custom tabs) at the top left. Next, double-click Exercise 9-3. This will load the lab configuration based on the exercises in Chapter 6.

1. On the 2600-1, verify that the `fa0/0` and `s0` interfaces are up. If not, bring them up. Click the Lab Instructions tab and use the drop-down selector for Devices to choose 2600-1; or click the NetMap tab and double-click the 2600-1 device icon. On the 2600-1, use the **show interfaces** command to verify your configuration. If `fa0/0` and `s0` are not up, go into the interfaces (`fa0/0` and `s0`) and enable them: **configure terminal**, **interface** type [slot_#/]port_#, **no shutdown**, and **end**.

2. Examine the IP addresses configured on the 2600-1.

   Use the **show ip interface brief** command to verify that the IP addresses you configured in Chapter 6 are still there.

3. Examine the routing table on the 2600-1.

   Use the **show ip route** command. You should have two connected networks: 192.168.1.0 connected to `fa0/0` and 192.168.2.0 connected to `s0`.

4. On the 2600-2, verify that the `fa0/0` and `s0` interfaces are up. If not, bring them up.

   Click the Lab Instructions tab and use the drop-down selector for Devices to choose 2600-2; or click the NetMap tab and double-click the 2600-2 device icon. On the 2600-2, use the **show interfaces** command to verify your configuration. If `fa0/0` and `s0` are not up, go into the interfaces (`fa0/0` and `s0`) and enable them: **configure terminal**, **interface** type port_#, **no shutdown**, and **end**. Use the **show interfaces** command to verify your interface configuration.

5. Examine the IP addresses configured on the 2600-2.

   Use the **show ip interface brief** command to verify that the IP addresses you configured in Chapter 6 are still there.

6. Examine the routing table on the 2600-2.

   Use the **show ip route** command. You should have two connected networks: 192.168.3.0 connected to fa0/0 and 192.168.2.0 connected to s0.

7. Test connectivity between Host-1 and the 2600-1.

   Click the Lab Instructions tab and use the drop-down selector for Devices to choose Host-1; or click the NetMap tab and double-click the Host-1 device icon. From Host-1, ping the 2600-1 router (the default gateway): **ping 192.168.1.1**. The ping should be successful.

8. Test connectivity between Host-3 and the 2600-2.

   Click the Lab Instructions tab and use the drop-down selector for Devices to choose Host-3; or click the NetMap tab and double-click the Host-3 device icon. From the Host-3, ping the 2600-2 router (the default gateway): **ping 192.168.3.1**. The ping should be successful.

9. Test connectivity between Host-3 and Host-1.

   From the Host-3, ping Host-1: **ping 192.168.1.10**. The ping should fail. Why? There is no route from the 2600-2 to this destination. (Look at the 2600-2's routing table: it doesn't list 192.168.1.0/24.)

10. Access the 2600-2 and examine the routing table to see why the ping failed.

    Click the Lab Instructions tab and use the drop-down selector for Devices to choose 2600-2; or click the NetMap tab and double-click the 2600-2 device icon. Examine the routing table: **show ip route**. Notice that it doesn't list 192.168.1.0/24, which explains why Host-3 can't reach Host-1.

11. Enable RIPv1 on the 2600-1 router.

    Click the Lab Instructions tab and use the drop-down selector for Devices to choose 2600-1; or click the NetMap tab and double-click the 2600-1 device icon. On the 2600-1, execute the following: **configure terminal, router rip, network 192.168.1.0, network 192.168.2.0**, and **end**.

12. Enable RIPv1 on the 2600-2 router.

    Click the Lab Instructions tab and use the drop-down selector for Devices to choose 2600-2; or click the NetMap tab and double-click the

2600-2 device icon. On the 2600-2, execute the following: `configure terminal`, `router rip`, `network 192.168.2.0`, `network 192.168.3.0`, and `end`.

13. On the 2600-1, verify the operation of RIP.

    Click the Lab Instructions tab and use the drop-down selector for Devices to choose 2600-1; or click the NetMap tab and double-click the 2600-1 device icon. Use the `show ip protocols` command to make sure that RIP is configured—check for the neighboring router's IP address. Use the `show ip route` command and look for the remote LAN network number as a RIP (R) entry in the routing table. On the 2600-1, you should see 192.168.3.0, which was learned from the 2600-2.

14. On the 2600-2, verify the operation of RIP.

    Click the Lab Instructions tab and use the drop-down selector for Devices to choose 2600-2; or click the NetMap tab and double-click the 2600-2 device icon. Use the `show ip protocols` command to make sure that RIP is configured—check for the neighboring router's IP address. Use the `show ip route` command and look for the remote LAN network number as a RIP (R) entry in the routing table. On the 2600-2, you should see 192.168.1.0, which was learned from the 2600-1.

15. On Host-1, test connectivity to Host-3.

    Click the Lab Instructions tab and use the drop-down selector for Devices to choose Host-1; or click the NetMap tab and double-click the Host-1 device icon. On Host-1, test connectivity: `ping 192.168.3.10`. The ping should be successful.

EXERCISE 9-4

MHE Lab

Basic RIP Troubleshooting

This exercise is a troubleshooting exercise and is similar to Exercise 9-3, in which you were given a configuration task to set up RIP. In this exercise, the network is already configured; however, three problems exist in this network and you'll need to find and fix them in order for the network to operate correctly. All of these problems deal with IP (layer 3) connectivity. You'll perform this exercise using

Boson's NetSim simulator. You can find a picture of the network diagram for Boson's NetSim simulator in the introduction of this book. The addressing scheme is the same as that configured in Chapter 6. After starting up the simulator, click the Labs tab at the bottom left of the window. Click the McGraw-Hill Education tab (to the right of the Standard and Custom tabs) at the top left. Next, double-click Exercise 9-4. This will load the lab configuration based on Chapter 6's exercises (with problems, of course).

Let's start with your problem: Host-1 cannot ping Host-3. Your task is to identify and fix the three issues. In this example, RIPv2 has been preconfigured on the routers. Try this troubleshooting process on your own first; if you have problems, come back to the steps and solutions provided here.

1. Use the ping tool to test connectivity from Host-1 to Host-3.

   Click the Lab Instructions tab and use the drop-down selector for Devices to choose Host-1; or click the NetMap tab and double-click the Host-1 device icon. On Host-1, ping Host-3: **ping 192.168.3.10**. Note that the ping fails.

2. Examine the IP configuration on Host-1.

   Execute **ipconfig /all**. Make sure the IP addressing information is correct: IP address of 192.168.1.10, subnet mask of 255.255.255.0, and default gateway address of 192.168.1.1.

3. Use the ping tool to test connectivity from Host-1 to its default gateway.

   Ping the default gateway address: **ping 192.168.1.1**. The ping should fail, indicating that at least layer 3 is not functioning between Host-1 and the 2600-1.

4. Check the 2600-1's IP configuration.

   Click the Lab Instructions tab and use the drop-down selector for Devices to choose 2600-1; or click the NetMap tab and double-click the 2600-1 device icon. From the 2600-1, ping Host-1: **ping 192.168.1.10**. The ping should fail. Examine the interface on the 2600-1: **show interface fa0/0**. The interface is enabled, but it has an incorrect IP address: 192.168.11.1. Fix the IP address: **configure terminal**, **interface fa0/0**, **ip address 192.168.1.1 255.255.255.0**, and **end**. Verify the IP address: **show interface fa0/0**.

5. Retest connectivity with ping.

Retry the ping test: **ping 192.168.1.10**. The ping should be successful. Save the configuration on the router: **copy running-config startup-config**.

6. Test connectivity from Host-1 to Host-3 with ping, as well as to the default gateway.

   Click the Lab Instructions tab and use the drop-down selector for Devices to choose Host-1; or click the NetMap tab and double-click the Host-1 device icon. On Host-1, ping Host-3: **ping 192.168.3.10**. Note that the ping still fails.

7. Examine Host-3's IP configuration.

   Click the Lab Instructions tab and use the drop-down selector for Devices to choose Host-3; or click the NetMap tab and double-click the Host-3 device icon. Examine the IP configuration on Host-3 by executing **ipconfig /all**. Make sure the IP addressing information is correct: IP address of 192.168.3.10, subnet mask of 255.255.255.0, and default gateway address of 192.168.3.1.

8. Test connectivity from Host-3 to its default gateway.

   Ping the default gateway address: **ping 192.168.3.1**. The ping should fail, indicating that there is a problem between Host-3 and the 2600-2. In this example, assume layer 2 is functioning correctly; therefore, it must be a problem with the 2600-2.

9. Check the interface statuses and IP configuration on the 2600-2.

   Click the Lab Instructions tab and use the drop-down selector for Devices to choose 2600-2; or click the NetMap tab and double-click the 2600-2 device icon. Check the status of the interfaces: **show interfaces**. Notice that fa0/0 is disabled, but s0 is enabled (*up* and *up*). Go into fa0/0 and enable it: **configure terminal**, **interface fa0/0**, **no shutdown**, and **end**. Verify the status of the fa0/0 interface: **show interface fa0/0**.

10. Verify connectivity from the 2600-2 to the 2600-1.

    Try pinging Host-3: **ping 192.168.3.10**. The ping should succeed. Try pinging the 2600-1's s0 interface: **ping 192.168.2.1**. The ping succeeds.

11. Verify RIP's configuration on the 2600-2.

Examine the RIP configuration: **show ip protocol**. You should see RIP as the routing protocol and networks 192.168.2.0 and 192.168.3.0 included. From the output, it looks like RIP is configured correctly on the 2600-2. Save the configuration on the router: **copy running-config startup-config**.

12. Test connectivity from the 2600-2 to Host-1. Examine the routing table.

    Test the connection to Host-1: **ping 192.168.1.10**. The ping should fail. This indicates a layer 3 problem between the 2600-2 router and Host-1.

13. View the routes in the 2600-2's routing table.

    Examine the routing table: **show ip route**. Notice that there are only two connected routes (192.168.2.0/24 and 192.168.1.0/24), but no RIP routes.

14. Access the 2600-1 router and examine RIP's configuration.

    Click the Lab Instructions tab and use the drop-down selector for Devices to choose 2600-1; or click the NetMap tab and double-click the 2600-1 device icon. Examine the routing table: **show ip protocol**. What networks are advertised by the 2600-1? You should see 192.168.1.0 and 192.168.11.0. Obviously, serial0's interface isn't included since 192.168.2.0 is not configured.

15. Fix the problem with the 2600-1's RIP configuration.

    Fix this configuration problem: **configure terminal**, **router rip**, **no network 192.168.11.0**, **network 192.168.1.0**, and **end**. Examine the routing protocol configuration: **show ip protocol**.

16. Test connectivity to Host-3 using ping.

    Test connectivity to Host-3: **ping 192.168.3.10**. The ping should be successful. Save the configuration on the router: **copy running-config startup-config**.

17. Now test connectivity between Host-1 and Host-3.

    Click the Lab Instructions tab and use the drop-down selector for Devices to choose Host-1; or click the NetMap tab and double-click the Host-1 device icon. Test connectivity to Host-3: **ping 192.168.3.10**. The ping should be successful.

Now you should be more comfortable with configuring IP RIP on your IOS router.

CERTIFICATION OBJECTIVE 9.04

Default Gateway Redundancy

The remainder of this chapter focuses on layer 3 redundancy issues. When you think of layer 3 redundancy, you're normally dealing with having multiple paths to a destination and using a dynamic routing protocol to find the best or alternative path. This section, however, deals with another type of layer 3 redundancy: default gateways and server load balancing. These are issues typically found at the access and distribution layers (see Chapter 3). I'll begin by talking about some of the issues of default gateway redundancy and some of the solutions that are available but don't work very well. The main part of this section deals with Cisco's Hot Standby Routing Protocol (HSRP), as well as other solutions, such as the Virtual Router Redundancy Protocol (VRRP) and Gateway Load Balancing Protocol (GLBP).

Problems of Traditional Default Gateway Redundancy Solutions

You can easily place two routing devices at the distribution layer of each switch block to provide redundancy for end stations to leave their VLAN. However, this might not provide a true fault-tolerant solution. This is especially true for situations in which end stations do not support a router discovery protocol to learn which routers they can use, or they can't be configured to use more than one default gateway address.

Proxy ARP Issues

Some end stations can use Proxy ARP to discover the IP address of the default gateway. In this situation, the end station dynamically acquires the IP address and MAC address of the default gateway and sends all its inter-VLAN traffic to this routing device. To begin, the end station doesn't know how to reach the destination and generates an ARP request for it. Obviously, if the destination is not in the same VLAN, no one responds and the end station assumes that the destination is not reachable. However, a Cisco router can proxy this ARP by sending back its own MAC address to the end station, and the end station can then use the router to send traffic out of the subnet. From the end station's perspective, it thinks it's sending traffic directly to the destination, but it's actually being relayed by the router. On Cisco IOS devices with routing enabled, Proxy ARP is enabled by default on the routing interfaces.

However, a problem arises when the default gateway fails. In this situation, the end station still sends its information to the failed default gateway, where the traffic is dropped. Sometimes a client re-performs the ARP after a lengthy period of time to verify the destination's (default gateway's) existence. (At this point, it will have discovered that the default gateway has failed, and then another routing device can perform the proxy.) However, in most implementations of ARP, the end station continues to use the same failed default gateway MAC address unless it is rebooted.

ICMP Router Discovery Protocol Issues

The ICMP Router Discovery Protocol (IRDP) is not a routing protocol like OSPF or RIP, but rather is an extension to ICMP that allows an end station to automatically discover the default gateways connected to the same VLAN. IRDP is covered in RFC 1256. In this environment, the routing devices periodically generate special multicast packets that announce the router's existence to the clients. This time period is usually between 5 and 10 minutes. Learned information usually has a maximum lifetime of 30 minutes on the client if no more IRDP messages are heard from the advertising routing device. The multicast packet includes the routing device's address and a lifetime value.

With IRDP, end stations can dynamically discover other routing devices when their primary default gateway fails. However, this might take up to 30 minutes, based on the lifetime value in the original multicast packet from the routing device. And even if you might consider using IRDP with your access layer devices, most end-station IP protocol stacks do not support IRDP.

Routing Protocol Issues

To overcome these two previous problems, you might be able to run a routing protocol on the end station, if the client supports this type of function. With IP, the only routing protocol that most end stations *might* support is RIP or OSPF. In RIP or OSPF, the end station could make intelligent decisions about which layer 3 routing device to use to access other subnets. However, the issue with RIP is that its convergence is very slow—it could take up to 180 seconds before an alternative routing device is chosen when the current primary routing device fails. With TCP sessions, this would cause a timeout. Because of this, as well as all the additional overhead that RIP creates, this solution is not very desirable for your end stations—and this assumes that your end stations and other network devices support a routing protocol such as RIP.

User Device Issues

In most campus environments, end stations are assigned a single IP address for the default gateway (which is usually done via DHCP). In this environment, if the routing device (default gateway) were to fail, the end station would lose its capability to access other networking devices outside of its VLAN. Unfortunately, there is no redundancy in this implementation because an end station can have only one default gateway address configured (whether it is assigned via DHCP or statically configured).

Hot Standby Routing Protocol

HSRP is a Cisco-proprietary protocol that provides a single definition of a default gateway on the end station and provides layer 3 redundancy for overcoming the issues of IRDP, Proxy ARP, and end-station routing protocols. Unlike the four previous solutions, HSRP is completely transparent to the end stations—you do not have to perform any additional configuration on the end stations themselves. HSRP allows Cisco routing devices to monitor each other's status, which provides a very quick failover when a primary default gateway fails. This is done by establishing HSRP groups.

With HSRP, a group of routing devices represents a single virtual default gateway. This virtual default gateway has a virtual IP address and a virtual MAC address. If the primary routing device fails, another routing device in the HSRP group takes over and processes the frames sent by the end stations to the virtual MAC address.

An advantage of HSRP groups is that different subnets (VLANs) can have different default gateways, thus providing load balancing. Also, within each HSRP group, there is a primary default gateway and the capability to use multiple routers to perform a backup function. You can have up to 256 standby groups per routing device, providing up to 255 default gateways. Routing devices can provide backup for multiple primary default gateways. Each standby group keeps track of the primary routing device that's currently forwarding traffic sent to the virtual MAC address. Note that only one routing device is actually forwarding traffic with HSRP.

Once nice feature of HSRP is that you can customize it based on the size of your network. For instance, if you have a VLAN with 1000 devices in it, you can set up two HSRP groups: one group for 500 devices and another group for the other 500 devices. You can then assign routing devices to each group. For example, if you had only two routing devices, you could have the first routing device be the active RP for group 1 but the standby for group 2, and vice versa for the second routing device. Through this process, you can have both of your routing devices forwarding traffic while still providing redundancy—if the active routing device in either group fails, the other routing device promotes itself to an active state.

HSRP Operation

As mentioned in the previous section, only one routing device actually forwards traffic for an HSRP group. Using a priority scheme, one routing device is elected as the forwarding router and the others perform as backups for a group. Each routing device has a default priority of 100, which you can manipulate. The routing device with the highest priority in the group is elected as the active router, and the other routing devices are placed in standby mode. The active routing device responds to any ARP packets from end stations and replies with the virtual MAC address of the group.

Each HSRP group must have a unique virtual IP address and a virtual MAC address, which means these numbers must be unique across different groups. This MAC address is 0000.0c07.ac*XX*. The 0000.0c is Cisco's vendor code. The 07-ac is HSRP's well-known address. The *XX* is the group number (in hexadecimal) for the HSRP group. Therefore, each HSRP group must have a unique number to ensure that the MAC address is unique in a VLAN.

---

e x a m

ⓦ a t c h   *The HSRP virtual MAC address begins with 0000.0c07.ac**XX**, where the last two digits represent the HSRP group number in hexadecimal. The active/master routing device for the VLAN is responsible for processing traffic sent to the virtual MAC and virtual IP addresses in the subnet/VLAN.*

With HSRP, the end stations would perform an ARP with the virtual IP address, requesting the virtual MAC address of the default gateway routing device. Note that in this setting, the end stations are completely unaware of the actual routing devices handling traffic destined for a virtual router. Even when the primary fails and the standby routing device starts handling traffic for the broadcast domain, the end stations still think they're talking to the same RP.

Types of Routing Devices   Every HSRP group contains routing devices that perform certain roles. Each HSRP group of routing devices contains the following types of routing devices:

- Virtual routing device
- Active routing device
- Standby routing device
- Other HSRP routing devices

The role of the virtual routing device is to provide a single RP that's always available to the end stations. It is not a real RP because the IP and MAC addresses of the virtual RP are not physically assigned to any one interface on any of the routing devices in the broadcast domain.

The role of the active and standby routing devices is based on the priority of the routing devices in the HSRP group. The routing device with the *highest* priority is elected as the active routing device, and the one with the second highest priority is elected as the standby routing device. If the priorities are the same, the IP address of the routing device is used as a tiebreaker. In this situation, the routing device with the *higher* IP address is elected for the role.

The active routing device is responsible for forwarding all traffic destined to the virtual routing device's MAC address. A second routing device is elected as a standby routing device. The standby routing device keeps tabs on the active routing device by looking for HSRP multicast messages, called *HSRP hellos*. The active routing device generates a hello every 3 seconds. If the standby routing device does not see any hellos from the active routing device for 10 seconds, the standby routing device promotes itself and begins performing the functions of the active routing device. Like the active routing device, the standby routing device also announces itself every 3 seconds so that if it fails, one of the other HSRP routers in the standby group can assume the standby routing device role.

The other routing devices in the HSRP group, if any exist, listen for the hello multicasts from the standby and active routing devices to ensure that they are performing their respective roles. When the active routing device fails, the view from the end stations' perspective is the same—they're still forwarding their frames to the virtual MAC address. When this happens, the standby routing device starts processing the frames sent to the virtual MAC address, and one of the other HSRP routers in the group is elected to the standby role.

Note: *If any end station uses a real MAC address of one of the routing devices in the broadcast domain, that specific routing device—whether it is active, standby, or another routing device—processes and forwards the frame.*

HSRP Multicast Messages   To determine which routing devices will become the active and standby routing devices, all the routing devices in the HSRP group initially send out HSRP multicast messages. These UDP messages, using port number 1985, are addressed to the all-router multicast address (224.0.0.1) with a Time-To-Live (TTL) value of 1. A TTL of 1 ensures that any multicast routing protocol that's running will not forward the message to a different subnet. The HSRP message contains the following information:

- HSRP version number.
- Op code message type:
  - **Hello messages**   These messages are used by the routing devices for the election process, as well as by the active and standby routing devices when they have been elected.
  - **Resign messages**   These messages are used by an RP when it wants to stop performing the function of the active RP.
  - **Coup messages**   These messages are used by an RP that wants to become the active RP.
- Current HSRP state (see the next section).
- Hello time interval of HSRP messages (defaults to 3 seconds)—that is, how often HSRP messages are generated.
- Hold-down time interval (defaults to 10 seconds)—the length of time that a hello message is considered valid.
- Priority of the RP—used to elect the active and standby routing devices.
- Standby group number (0–255).
- Authentication password, if configured.
- Virtual IP address of the HSRP group—the default gateway IP address that your end stations should use.

HSRP States   HSRP supports six different states. A routing device may go through all these states or only a few of them, depending on whether it becomes an active or standby routing device.

- Initial
- Learning
- Listening
- Speaking
- Standby
- Active

When the routing devices are enabled, they start in an *initial* state. Note that they have not begun the HSRP process in an initial state—only the routing devices themselves and their associated interfaces have been activated. In a learning state, a routing device listens for an active routing device. The routing device initially has no knowledge of any other HSRP routers. In this state, its purpose is to discover the current active and standby routing devices and the virtual IP address for the group.

After the routing device sees a multicast from the active/standby routing device, it learns about the virtual IP address. This is called the listening state. In this state, the routing device is neither the active nor standby routing device. If there's already a standby and active routing device, the listening routing device remains in this state and does not proceed to any of the next three states. The exception to this is if you've configured preemption. With preemption, a new routing device with a higher priority can usurp an existing active or standby routing device.

If the routing device enters the speaking state, it propagates multicast messages so that it can participate in the election process for the standby or active role. These hellos are sent out periodically so that other routing devices in the group know about everyone's existence. Note that for a routing device to enter this state, it must have the virtual IP address configured on it.

Based on the routing device's priority, it becomes either a standby or active routing device. In a standby state, the routing device is the next in line to assume the role of the active routing device if the active routing device fails. In an active state, the routing device is responsible for forwarding all traffic sent to the virtual MAC address of the broadcast domain. There can be only one active and one standby routing device. Both of these routing devices generate periodic hellos to other routing devices in the group to guarantee that end stations always have a default gateway that can forward their traffic if either of them fails.

It's important to point out that if you don't configure preemption, the first routing device that comes up takes on the active role and the second routing device takes on the standby role. Therefore, if you're setting up load balancing between routing devices so that certain routing devices handle traffic for certain VLANs and other routing devices handle traffic for other VLANs, you'll want to use preemption so that whenever a failed routing device comes back online, it resumes its former role.

HSRP Configuration

The configuration of HSRP is a simple process. The following sections discuss its configuration and how to optimize it for larger networks.

Basic Configuration   Only one command is necessary to enable HSRP. To do so, execute the following `standby` command on the routing device's interface. Use a subinterface for a trunk port and a VLAN interface for an internal routing device, like a layer 3 switch.

```
Router(config)# interface type [slot_#/]port_#
Router(config-if)# standby [group_#] ip IP_address
```

or

```
Switch(config)# interface vlan VLAN_#
Switch(config-if)# standby [group_#] ip IP_address
```

There are 256 HSRP groups supported per interface. After you execute the `standby` command on an active interface, the routing device enters the learning state. In this command, *group_#* is optional. If you omit it, it defaults to 0. Note that *group_#* is required if you have multiple standby groups. Remember that the IP address you specify in the `standby` command is not the actual IP address that's on the interface, but rather the virtual IP address. You need to take the virtual IP address and either hard-code it as the default gateway address on end stations or put it in your DHCP server configuration.

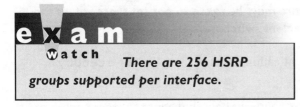

e x a m

ⓦ a t c h   *There are 256 HSRP groups supported per interface.*

To ensure that the end stations do not discover the real MAC address of the routing device's LAN interface, enabling HSRP disables ICMP redirects. You'll see the `no ip redirects` command appear on the routing device's interface.

Load Balancing   To influence which routing devices perform the active and standby roles, you can increase the routing device priorities. To do so, execute the following **standby** command on the routing device's interface:

```
IOS(config-if)# standby [group-number] priority new_priority
```

Remember that the higher the priority, the more likely it is that the routing device will become a standby or active routing device. The priority defaults to 100 but can be set from 0 to 255. To configure a routing device so that it can preempt the current standby or active routing device, use the **preempt** parameter:

```
IOS(config-if)# standby [group-number] preempt [delay delay_value]
```

The default delay is 0 seconds, which causes the routing device to immediately begin the preemption process. You can delay this by putting in a delay value from 0 to 3600 seconds (1 hour). The one problem with preemption is that it causes a slight disruption in traffic as the currently active routing device demotes itself and the new routing device promotes itself.

To modify the hello and hold-down times, execute the following **standby** command:

```
IOS(config-if)# standby [group_#] timers hello_time holddown_time
```

Here, *hello_time* defaults to 3 seconds and can range from 0 to 255 seconds. *holddown_time* defaults to 10 seconds and has the same range of valid values. Note that *holddown_time* should be at least three times greater than *hello_time* to ensure proper functioning of HSRP.

on the
job   *It is a common practice to adjust these timers to smaller values to speed up HSRP convergence. However, care must be taken to not set these values too small, which might cause inadvertent switchovers.*

If you want to configure authentication, execute the following **standby** command on the interface:

```
IOS(config-if)# standby [group-number] authentication password
```

The password can be up to eight characters; if omitted, the password defaults to *cisco*. The password needs to match on all HSRP routers in the same group.

Interface Tracking   In certain cases, it might be necessary for the active routing device to step down from its role and let another routing device assume the role. Consider the example shown in Figure 9-4. In this example, RP-B is the active RP for VLAN 20. If RP-B fails, RP-A notices this after missing the hello messages from RP-B. RP-A promotes itself and starts forwarding frames that are destined to the virtual MAC address.

Let's assume, however, that RP-B does not fail but instead its interface `vlan40` fails (connected to the core), as shown in Figure 9-5. Without HSRP running, RP-B would detect the failure and generate an ICMP redirect message to RP-A. This would allow RP-A to handle the redirected traffic. However, if RP-A and RP-B are participating in an HSRP group, ICMP redirects are disabled. This means that RP-B still functions as the active routing device and handles all traffic sent to the virtual MAC address. The problem that this causes is that after the layer 3 routing protocol has converged, the traffic still reaches its destination. However, to reach the destination, the traffic must pass through both RP-B *and* RP-A, thus introducing unnecessary latency.

FIGURE 9-4   HSRP example

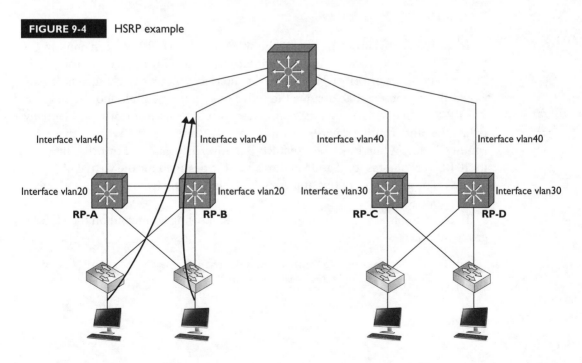

FIGURE 9-5 HSRP example without interface tracking

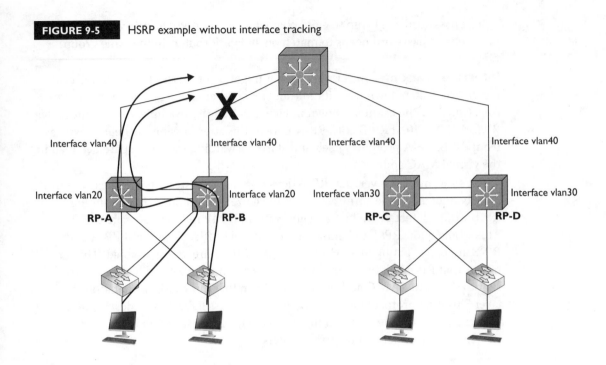

To overcome this problem and still be able to deploy HSRP, you can employ the HSRP interface tracking feature. Interface tracking allows the active routing device to lower its priority when one of the interfaces that it's tracking fails. This would allow another RP to assume the active role. In the example shown in Figure 9-5, RP-B, with interface tracking configured, would lower its priority—essentially telling the other routing devices that it no longer wants to serve as the active routing device. When RP-A sees that RP-B is advertising a lower priority than itself, RP-A promotes itself and handles all traffic destined for the virtual MAC address. The advantage of this approach is that the traffic from the user will only traverse one RP: RP-A.

To configure interface tracking, execute the following command on the HSRP group interface:

```
IOS(config-if)# standby [group_#] track interface_type interface_#
                        [decrement_value]
```

The **track** parameter is used to enter the interface that you want the HSRP RP to track. If this interface fails for whatever reason, the active routing device decrements its HSRP priority by the configured value. Note that *decrement_value* is optional and, if omitted, defaults to a decrement of 10 for the priority.

HSRP Verification

To verify the overall operation of HSRP, use the **show standby** command on the RP:

```
Switch# show standby
Vlan 1 - Group 1
  Local state is Active, priority 110, may preempt
  Hellotime 3 holdtime 10
  Next hello sent in 0:00:01
  Hot standby IP address is 172.16.10.1 configured
  Active router is local
  Standby router is 172.16.10.2 expires in 0:00:07
  Standby virtual mac address is 0000.0c07.ac01
Tracking interface states for 3 interfaces, 3 up:
  Up  Vlan1 Priority decrement: 10
```

In the preceding output, you can see that the active routing device is 172.16.10.1 and the standby RP is 172.16.10.2.

For a shorter description, add the **brief** parameter to the preceding command:

```
IOS# show standby brief
                           Active    Standby Group
Interface  Grp Prio P State  addr      addr    addr
Vlan1       1   100    Standby 172.17.10.2 local   172.16.10.254
```

In this example, this router, for VLAN 1, is in a standby state and the virtual IP address for the standby group is 172.16.10.254.

For additional troubleshooting, you can use the **debug standby** command from Privileged EXEC mode. This command displays all HSRP messages that have been sent and received by the RP.

9.09. The digital resources that accompany this book contain a multimedia demonstration of configuring and verifying HSRP on a router.

Other Protocols

This section will introduce two other protocols that you can use instead of HSRP:

- Virtual Router Redundancy Protocol (VRRP)
- Gateway Load Balancing Protocol (GLBP)

Virtual Router Redundancy Protocol

Virtual Router Redundancy Protocol (VRRP) performs a similar function as Cisco's proprietary HSRP. The one major downside to HSRP is that it is a proprietary protocol. VRRP, however, is an open standard and is defined in IETF's RFC 2338. Like HSRP, VRRP has end stations that use a virtual router for a default gateway. VRRP is supported for Ethernet media types, as well as in VLANs and MPLS VPNs.

on the job

HSRP and VRRP are very similar and accomplish the same goal: default gateway redundancy. HSRP is proprietary to Cisco, and VRRP is an open standard.

VRRP and HSRP are very similar protocols. One main difference between the two is that HSRP uses a virtual IP address for the default gateway, whereas VRRP can use either a virtual IP address or the interface address of the master router. If a virtual IP address is used, an election process takes place to choose a master router. The router with the highest priority is chosen as the master. All other routers are backup routers. If a real IP address is used, the router that has that address assigned to its interface must be the master router.

watch

VRRP object tracking ensures that the best VRRP router is selected as the master of the group based on priority and interface tracking.

VRRP is an IP protocol and has an IP protocol number of 112. The VRRP master router is responsible for generating VRRP multicast messages. It sends these messages to a multicast address of 224.0.0.18. The master typically generates these messages every second. If the master VRRP router fails, a backup VRRP router seamlessly processes the traffic sent to the master router's IP address. This process is referred to as object tracking: object tracking ensures that the best VRRP router is selected as the master of the group based on priority and interface tracking. VRRP supports preemption so that a failed master, after it has been repaired, can resume its role as master.

Note: *The configuration of VRRP is beyond the scope of this book.*

Gateway Load Balancing Protocol

The Gateway Load Balancing Protocol (GLBP) is a Cisco-proprietary protocol, like HSRP. One of the limitations of HSRP and VRRP is that only one router in the HSRP group is active and can forward traffic for the group—the rest of the routers sit idle. This is not an efficient process where one or more routing devices are not processing any traffic, nor are you taking advantage of the bandwidth of the connections that these other routing devices are connected to.

Cisco designed GLBP to rectify this issue. GLBP allows the dynamic assignment of a *group* of virtual addresses to end stations. With GLBP, up to four routing devices in the group can participate in the forwarding of traffic. Plus, if a GLBP routing device fails, fault detection occurs automatically and another GLBP routing device picks up the forwarding of packets for the failed routing device.

Here are some of the benefits of GLBP:

- Like HSRP, GLBP supports clear-text and MD5 password authentication between GLBP routing devices.
- GLBP supports up to 1024 virtual routers on a routing device.
- GLBP can load-balance traffic via four forwarding routing devices in a subnet or VLAN.

ⓦatch   **Be familiar with the benefits of GLBP.**

GLBP Operation   In GLBP, there are two types of routers: Active Virtual Gateway (AVG) and Active Virtual Forwarder (AVF). The AVG is the master gateway device and is responsible for assigning virtual MAC addresses to end stations when the end stations perform an ARP for the GLBP default gateway address. Basically, the AVG is responsible for address management in the GLBP group.

ⓦatch   **The AVG is responsible for processing the ARP request for the virtual IP address(es).**

An AVF is a routing device that forwards traffic for a GLBP group. The AVG is also an AVF. Basically, up to four routing devices configured in the same GLBP group are AVFs.

I'll use Figure 9-6 to give a basic illustration of how GLBP works. In this example, RP-A

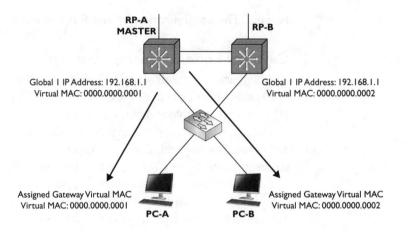

FIGURE 9-6

GLBP operation

is the master (AVG). When PC-A sends an ARP request for the default gateway MAC address, the AVG is responsible for responding back with a virtual MAC address to the end station. In this example, it responded back with its own virtual MAC address. PC-B then ARPs for the same gateway address. RP-A responds back with a virtual MAC address. Based on the load-balancing algorithm used by GLBP, RP-A responds back with a different virtual MAC address (RP-B's). Load balancing is discussed in the next section. As you can see from this example, both RP-A and RP-B are forwarding traffic for the same VLAN.

GLBP also supports interface tracking. With interface tracking, if a tracked interface on an AVF fails, the AVF demotes itself and has another AVF pick up the processing associated with this failed interface. This process is similar to HSRP's interface tracking feature.

> ### e x a m
> ### ⓦ a t c h
> *An active virtual gateway (AVG) will reply with up to four possible virtual MAC addresses of the active virtual forwarders (AVFs) for the subnet/VLAN.*

Load Balancing with GLBP   Multiple RPs can be used to forward traffic with GLBP to perform load balancing. GLBP supports three methods of load balancing:

- Round-robin
- Weighted
- Host-dependent

The default method of load balancing is round-robin. With round-robin load balancing, the AVG assigns a different AVF default gateway address to each client.

If you have two routing devices and six clients, three clients will use the AVG and three will use the AVF.

With weighted load balancing, a weighting factor is used to determine which AVF's address the AVG routing device assigns to an end station. This enables you to tune GLBP so that a certain amount of hosts use one routing device rather than another if there is a difference in processing power between the routing devices.

With host-based load balancing, a host is assigned the same virtual gateway address each time. However, if the routing device associated with this address fails, another routing device within GLBP can pick up the processing so that redundancy is provided.

Note: *The configuration of GLBP is beyond the scope of this book.*

INSIDE THE EXAM

Static Routes

Be familiar with when static routes are used versus a dynamic routing protocol. Understand the syntax of the `ip route` command and the default values, if omitted. Know how to configure a default route. Be able to find misconfigured static routes in a router's configuration. Know how to read the output of the `show ip route` command and to find the administrative distance and metric values of dynamic routing protocols in this output. If the local interface associated with the static route is down, the static route will not be placed in the router's routing table. Note that if a destination router or network associated with the static route is not reachable, this will *not* affect the local static route. Remember that you must first execute the `ipv6 unicast-routing` command to enable IPv6. Know the command to create an EUI-64 address for a router's interface: `ipv6 address`.

Dynamic Routing Protocol Basics

Remember the two things that need to happen to enable routing on a router: enabling the routing protocol by assigning networks to it, and activating interfaces by enabling and assigning addresses to them. Don't be surprised if you see a simulation question on the exam for which you have to configure or troubleshoot a dynamic routing protocol—RIPv2, OSPF, or EIGRP—on multiple routers.

(Continued)

INSIDE THE EXAM

RIP

Understand the differences between RIPv1 and RIPv2 and be able to compare and contrast these protocols. Be able to configure RIPv2 successfully on a router. Understand the output of the **show ip protocols** and **debug ip rip** commands to troubleshoot routing and connectivity problems. Understand the problems **debug** commands can create on a router and how to disable **debug**.

Default Gateway Redundancy

The HSRP active/master routing device for the VLAN is responsible for processing traffic sent to the virtual MAC and virtual IP addresses in the subnet/VLAN. The HSRP virtual MAC address begins with 0000.0c07 .ac*XX*, where the last two digits represent the HSRP group number in hexadecimal. The default hello timer is 3 seconds and the dead interval timer is 10 seconds. Up to 255 HSRP groups are supported per interface. VRRP object tracking ensures that the best VRRP router is selected as the master of the group based on priority and interface tracking. In GLBP, an active virtual gateway (AVG) will reply with up to four possible virtual MAC addresses of the active virtual forwarders (AVFs) for the subnet/VLAN. The AVG is responsible for processing the ARP request for the virtual IP address(es). Like HSRP, GLBP supports clear-text and MD5 password authentication between GLBP routing devices. GLBP supports up to 1024 virtual routers on a routing device. GLBP can load-balance traffic via four forwarding routing devices in a subnet or VLAN.

CERTIFICATION SUMMARY

Two types of routing protocols can be used to define or learn destination networks: static and dynamic. To create a static route, use the **ip route** command. For a default route, use 0.0.0.0/0 as the network number and subnet mask. To view your router's routing table, use the **show ip route** command. You must first execute the **ipv6 unicast-routing** command to enable IPv6. An address must be assigned to each interface, typically using the EUI-64 method, for it to process IPv6 packets.

When setting up IP routing, you must enable the routing protocol and configure IP routing on your router's interfaces. The **router** command takes you into the routing process, while the **network** command specifies what interfaces will participate in the routing process. Use the `ip address` command to assign IP addresses to your router's interfaces.

RIPv1 generates local broadcasts every 30 seconds to share routing information, with a hold-down period of 180 seconds. Hop count is used as the metric for choosing paths. RIP can load-balance across six equal-cost paths to a single destination. RIPv2 uses multicasts instead of broadcasts and also supports VLSM for hierarchical routing and route summarization. RIPv2, to speed up convergence, uses triggered updates. Use the `router rip` command to go into the routing process and use the `network` command to specify your connected networks. When specifying your connected networks, specify only the Class A, B, or C network number (not subnet numbers), since RIPv1 is classful: even though RIPv2 is classless, configure it as a classful protocol. Use the `version` command to enable RIPv2. The `debug ip rip` command will display the actual routing contents that your router advertises in its updates or receives in neighbors' updates.

The `show ip protocols` command displays information about the IP routing protocols currently configured and running on your router. It shows metric information, administrative distances, neighboring routers, and routes that are being advertised. The `show ip route` command displays the IP routing information currently being used by your router. An R in the left-hand column indicates an RIP route.

HSRP is a Cisco-proprietary protocol that provides default gateway redundancy and is invisible to the end stations in the VLAN. A single virtual IP and MAC address is used per group. An active routing device, elected by the routing device with the highest priority (or IP address, if a tie occurs), forwards traffic. A standby routing device monitors the active routing device. There are six stages an HSRP might go through: initial, learning, listening, speaking, standby, and active. A routing device goes into a speaking state when an election occurs, or if it is the active or standby routing device. The active routing device can tell the rest of the routing devices about the virtual addresses. To enable HSRP, use the `standby ip` command on a routing device's interface. HSRP supports both preemption and interface tracking.

VRRP is an open standard for default gateway redundancy. VRRP has a master and backup routing devices. Either a virtual IP address or a real IP address (of the master) is used.

GLBP is an enhanced version of HSRP. It allows for up to four routing devices to forward traffic from the group. Routing devices are grouped together, and each group is assigned one or more virtual addresses. The AVG is responsible for address management, whereas the AVFs forward traffic—the AVG can also be an AVF. GLBP supports three types of load balancing: round-robin (default), weighted, and host-dependent.

✔ TWO-MINUTE DRILL

Static Routes

❑ Use the `ip route` command to configure a static route.

❑ After the subnet mask parameter, you have two ways of specifying how to reach the destination network: you can tell the router either the next-hop neighbor's IP address or the interface the router should exit to reach the destination network. The former has an administrative distance of 1 and the latter, 0 (a directly connected route).

❑ The `ipv6 unicast-routing` command globally enables IPv6 and must be the first IPv6 command executed on the router. The `ipv6 address` command assigns the prefix, the length, and the use of EUI-64 to assign the interface ID.

Dynamic Routing Protocol Basics

❑ To set up IP on your router, you need to enable the routing protocol and assign IP addresses to your router's interfaces.

❑ Use the `router` and `network` commands to enable routing. With classful protocols, use the class address in the `network` command.

RIP

❑ RIP uses hop count as a metric and has a hop-count limit of 15. IP RIP supports up to six equal-cost paths to a single destination.

❑ RIPv1 sends out periodic routing updates as broadcasts every 30 seconds. The hold-down timer is 180 seconds. It is a classful protocol.

❑ RIPv2 uses triggered updates and sends its updates out as multicasts. It is a classless protocol and supports VLSM and route summarization. Optionally, RIPv2 updates can be authenticated.

❑ Use the `router rip` and `network` commands to set up RIP. Use the `version` command to hard-code the version. Use the following commands for troubleshooting: `show ip protocols`, `show ip route`, and `debug ip rip`.

❑ After making a change to an IP routing protocol, use the `clear ip route *` command to clear the IP routing table and rebuild it.

Default Gateway Redundancy

❑ To enable HSRP, use the **standby ip** command on a routing device's interface.

❑ HSRP is proprietary, and VRRP is an open standard. Both accomplish the same thing: default gateway redundancy within a VLAN.

❑ HSRP uses a virtual address as the default gateway address; VRRP supports the use of a physical or virtual address.

❑ GLBP, which is proprietary to Cisco and based on HSRP, allows more than one active routing device in a subnet.

SELF TEST

The following Self Test questions will help you measure your understanding of the material presented in this chapter. Read all the choices carefully, as there may be more than one correct answer. Choose all correct answers for each question.

Static Routes

1. Enter the command to set up a static route to 192.168.1.0/24, where the next-hop address is 192.168.2.2: _____.

2. What subnet mask would you use to set up a default route?
   A. 0.0.0.0
   B. 255.255.255.255
   C. Depends on the type of network number
   D. None of these answers

3. What is the default administrative distance of a static route where the next hop specified is the IP address of a neighboring router?
   A. 0
   B. 1
   C. 90
   D. 120

4. Which IPv6 command must first be entered on a Cisco router?
   A. `router ipv6-unicast`
   B. `ipv6 address`
   C. `ipv6 unicast-routing`
   D. `ipv6 support enable`

Dynamic Routing Protocol Basics

5. You have a distance vector protocol such as RIP. You've entered the RIP process by executing `router rip`. On one of your router's interfaces, you have the following IP address: 192.168.1.65 255.255.255.192. Enter the command to include this interface in the RIP routing process: _____.

RIP

6. RIP generates routing updates every _____ seconds.
   A. 15
   B. 30

C. 60

D. 90

7. RIP has a hold-down period of _____ seconds.
    A. 60
    B. 120
    C. 180
    D. 280

8. RIP has a maximum hop count of _____ hops.
    A. 10
    B. 15
    C. 16
    D. 100

9. RIP supports load balancing for up to _____ _____ paths.
    A. Six, unequal-cost
    B. Four, unequal-cost
    C. Four, equal-cost
    D. Six, equal-cost

10. Which of the following is true concerning RIPv2?
    A. It uses triggered updates.
    B. It uses broadcasts.
    C. It is classful.
    D. It doesn't support route summarization.

11. Enter the router command used to view which routing protocols are active on your router, as well as their characteristics and configuration: _____.

Default Gateway Redundancy

12. Which of the following is a valid virtual MAC address for an HSRP group?
    A. 0000.6e00.0014
    B. 0000.0c07.ac18
    C. 0000.ac07.0c0a
    D. 0000.0cac.0c0f

SELF TEST ANSWERS

Static Routes

1. ☑ `ip route 192.168.1.0 255.255.255.0 192.168.2.2`

2. ☑ **A.** A default route is set up with an IP address and mask of 0.0.0.0 0.0.0.0.
   ☒ **B** is incorrect because this number indicates that the complete IP address is a network number, commonly called a host route. **C** is incorrect because the network number would use a standard subnet mask based on the network you're trying to reach: 0.0.0.0 as a subnet mask indicates all hosts. And since there is a correct answer, **D** is incorrect.

3. ☑ **B.** The default administrative distance of a static route pointing to a neighbor's IP address is 1.
   ☒ **A** is incorrect because 0 is the value of a static route with an interface or a connected route. **C** is incorrect because 90 is EIGRP's administrative distance, and **D**, 120, is RIP's administrative distance.

4. ☑ **C.** The `ipv6 unicast-routing` command globally enables IPv6 and must be the first IPv6 command executed on the router.
   ☒ **A** and **D** are invalid commands. **B** assigns an IPv6 address to an interface.

Dynamic Routing Protocol Basics

5. ☑ `network 192.168.1.0`. Remember that RIPv1 is classful.

RIP

6. ☑ **B.** RIP generates routing updates every 30 seconds.
   ☒ **A, C,** and **D** are invalid update intervals.

7. ☑ **C.** RIP has a hold-down period of 180 seconds.
   ☒ **A, B,** and **D** are invalid hold-down periods.

8. ☑ **B.** RIP has a maximum hop count of 15 hops.
   ☒ **A, C,** and **D** are invalid maximum hop-count values.

9. ☑ **D.** RIP supports load balancing for up to six equal-cost paths.
   ☒ **A** and **B** are invalid because RIP doesn't support unequal-cost paths. **C** is incorrect because four is the default, but six is the maximum.

10. ☑ **A.** RIPv2 supports triggered updates.

    ☒ **B** is incorrect because RIPv2 uses multicasts. **C** is incorrect because RIPv2 is classless. **D** is incorrect because RIPv2 supports VLSM and route summarization.

11. ☑ To view the IP routing protocols running on your router, use `show ip protocols`.

Default Gateway Redundancy

12. ☑ **B.** HSRP virtual MAC addresses begin with 0000.0c07.ac.

    ☒ **A**, **C**, and **D** are incorrect because the MAC addresses don't begin with 0000.0c07.ac.

10

OSPF Routing

T he Open Shortest Path First (OSPF) protocol is a link state protocol that handles routing for IP traffic. Version 2 of OSPF, which is explained in RFC 2328, is an open standard, such as Routing Information Protocol (RIP) vI and RIPv2. Chapter 4 offered a brief introduction to link state protocols. As you will see in this chapter, OSPF draws heavily on the concepts described in Chapter 4, but it also has some unique features of its own. Besides covering the characteristics of OSPF, you'll be presented with enough information to undertake a basic routing configuration using OSPF. A more thorough discussion is covered in Cisco's CCNP certification.

CERTIFICATION OBJECTIVE 10.01

OSPF Overview

OSPF was created in the mid-1980s to overcome many of the deficiencies and scalability problems that RIP had in large enterprise networks. Because it is based on an open standard, OSPF is very popular in many corporate networks today and has many advantages, including these:

- It will run on most routers, since it is based on an open standard.
- It uses the SPF algorithm, developed by Edsger Dijkstra, to provide a loop-free topology.
- It provides fast convergence with triggered, incremental updates via link state advertisements (LSAs).
- It is a classless protocol and allows for a hierarchical design with VLSM and route summarization, thus reducing routing overhead.
- It contains a two-layer hierarchy to contain problems within an area and to reduce routing overhead.
- It has an intelligent metric (cost), which is the inverse of the bandwidth of an interface.
- It allows you to extensively control routing update information through summarization and filtering.

Given its advantages, OSPF does have its share of disadvantages:

■ It requires more memory to hold the adjacency (list of OSPF neighbors), topology (a link state database containing all of the routers and their routes/links), and routing tables.

■ It requires extra CPU processing to run the SPF algorithm, which is especially true when you first turn on your routers and they are initially building the adjacency and topology tables.

■ For large networks, it requires careful design to break up the network into an appropriate hierarchical design by separating routers into different *areas*.

■ It is more complex to configure and more difficult to troubleshoot than distance vector protocols.

Knowing the advantages and disadvantages of any routing protocol is useful when it comes to picking a protocol. Typically, OSPF is used in large enterprise networks that have either a mixed routing vendor environment or a policy that requires an open standard for a routing protocol, which gives a company flexibility when it needs to replace any of its existing routers.

Remember the advantages and disadvantages of OSPF: it's an open standard, it supports a hierarchical design using areas, it converges quickly, and it uses cost as a metric.

Typically, when you start having more than 50 routers, Cisco recommends you use a more advanced routing protocol such as OSPF or EIGRP. In a mixed-vendor environment there is basically one choice between these two: OSPF.

Hierarchical Design: Areas

To provide scalability for very large networks, OSPF supports two important concepts: autonomous systems and areas. Autonomous systems (ASs) were discussed in Chapter 4. Within an AS, *areas* are used to provide hierarchical routing. An area is a group of contiguous networks. Basically, areas are used to control when and how much routing information is shared across your network. In flat network designs, such as those that use IP RIP, if a change occurs on one router (perhaps a flapping route problem), it affects *every* router in the entire network.

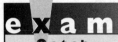

watch *Remember that OSPF supports a two-layer hierarchy: the backbone (area 0 or 0.0.0.0) and areas connected to the backbone.*

With a correctly designed hierarchical network, these changes can be contained within a single area.

OSPF implements a two-layer hierarchy: the backbone and areas off the backbone, as shown in Figure 10-1. This network includes a backbone and three areas connected to the backbone. Each area is given a unique number that is 32 bits in length. The area number can be represented by a single decimal number, such as 1, or in a dotted-decimal format, such as *0.0.0.1*. Area 0 is a special area and represents the top-level hierarchy of the OSPF network, commonly called the *backbone*. Through a correct IP addressing design, you should be able to summarize routing information between areas. By summarizing your routing information, perhaps one summarized route for each area, you are reducing the amount of information that routers need to know about. For instance, each area in Figure 10-1 is assigned a separate Class B network number.

FIGURE 10-1 OSPF hierarchical design

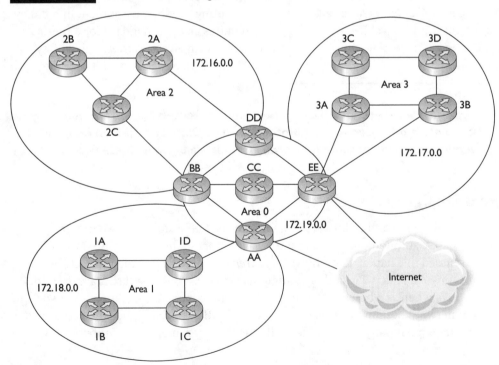

Through summarization on the border routers between areas, other areas would not need to see all the Class B subnets—only the summarized network numbers for each respective area (the Class B network numbers themselves).

The backbone (area 0) in OSPF is required and non-0 areas (like areas 1, 2, 3, etc.) must be connected to the backbone. The preferred connection is a physical connection; however, OSPF supports a feature called virtual links *that allows an area to be logically connected to the backbone. A discussion of virtual links is beyond the scope of this book.*

Area 2, for instance, doesn't need to see all of the subnets of area 1's 172.18.0.0 network number, since only two paths exist out of area 2 to the backbone. Area 2, however, needs to see all of its internal subnets to create optimized routing tables to reach its own internal networks within area 2. Therefore, in a correctly designed OSPF network, each area should contain specific routes only for its own areas and summarized routes to reach other areas. By performing this summarization, the routers have a smaller topology database (they know only about links in their own area and the summarized routes) and their routing tables are smaller (they know only about their own area's routes and the summarized routes). Through a correct hierarchical design, you can scale OSPF to very large sizes. Chapter 5 discussed route summarization.

Note that the ICND2 and CCNA exams focus on only single-area designs, and the material throughout the rest of the sections of this chapter covers only single-area concepts. The CCNP-level material, however, spends a lot of time on both single- *and* multi-area designs. Designing a multi-area OSPF network can become very complicated and requires a lot of networking knowledge and skill.

An excellent resource for OSPF, called the "OSPF Design Guide," can be found free on Cisco's web site: www.cisco.com/c/en/us/support/docs/ip/open-shortest-path-first-ospf/7039-1.html. It covers both single- and multi-area designs in great depth.

Metric Structure

Unlike RIP, which uses hop count as a metric, OSPF uses cost. Cost is actually the inverse of the bandwidth of a link: the faster the speed of the connection, the lower the cost. The most preferred path is the one with the lowest accumulated cost value. By using cost as a metric, OSPF will choose more intelligent paths than

RIP (metrics are discussed in more depth in the "OSPF Metric Values" section later in the chapter).

Remember that on synchronous serial links, no matter what the clock rate of the physical link is, the bandwidth always defaults to 1544 Kbps. You'll want to code this correctly with the **bandwidth** Interface Subconfiguration mode command (discussed in Chapter 6). This is important if you have multiple synchronous serial paths to a destination, especially if they have different clock rates. OSPF supports load balancing of up to 16 equal-cost paths to a single destination; however, only four equal-cost paths are used by default. Remember that if you don't configure the bandwidth metric correctly on your serial interfaces, your router might accidentally include paths with different clock rates, which can cause load-balancing issues.

exam
☔atch   *OSPF uses cost as a metric, which is the inverse of the bandwidth of a link.*

For example, if you have one serial connection clocked at 1544 Kbps and another clocked at 256 Kbps and you don't change the bandwidth values, OSPF will see *both* connections as 1544 Kbps and attempt to use both when reaching a single destination across these links. This is because the default bandwidth on a serial link is 1544, no matter what the clock speed of the interface is. This can create throughput problems when the router is performing load balancing—half of the connections will go down one link and half down the other, creating congestion problems for the 256-Kbps connection. Therefore, remember that you should change bandwidth of the interface with the **bandwidth** command (covered in Chapter 6).

CERTIFICATION OBJECTIVE 10.02

OSPF Operation

As mentioned, OSPF is a link state protocol like that generically described in Chapter 4. However, each link state protocol, such as OSPF and IS-IS, has its own unique features and characteristics. This section introduces you to how OSPF operates in a single-area design.

Router Identities

Each router in an OSPF network needs a unique ID—this must be unique not just within an area, but within the entire OSPF network. The ID is used to provide a unique identity to the OSPF router. The ID is included in any OSPF messages the router generates that other OSPF routers will process. The router ID is chosen according to one of the following criteria:

■ The highest IP address on the router's active loopback interfaces is used (this is a logical interface on a router).

■ If no loopback interface exists with an IP address, the highest IP address on its active interfaces is used when the router boots up.

on the **ⓙob**

Loopbacks typically have a host mask (/32). Cisco supports other masks for loopback interfaces, but many vendors restrict you to a /32 mask.

The router ID is used by the router to announce itself to the other OSPF routers in the network. This ID must be unique. If no loopback interfaces are configured,

ⓦatch   *Remember how a router acquires its router ID for OSPF: the active loopback with the highest IP address or the active physical interface with the highest IP address.*

the router will use the highest IP address from one of its active physical interfaces. Optionally you can manually define the router ID, always ensuring what it will be no matter what interfaces exist on the router.

If no active interface exists, the OSPF process will not start and therefore you will not have any OSPF routes in your routing table. It is highly recommended, therefore, that you use a loopback interface because it is always up and thus the router can obtain a router ID and start OSPF.

Finding Neighbors

An OSPF router learns about its OSPF neighbors and builds its adjacency and topology tables by sharing link state advertisements (LSAs), which exist in different types. When learning about the neighbors to which a router is connected, as well as keeping tabs on known neighbors, OSPF routers will generate LSA hello messages every 10 seconds. When a neighbor is discovered and an adjacency is formed with the neighbor, a router expects to see hello messages from the neighbor. If a neighbor's hello is not seen within the dead interval time, which defaults to 40 seconds, the neighbor is declared dead. When this occurs, the router will advertise this information, via an LSA message, to other neighboring OSPF routers.

Whereas RIP accepts routing updates from just about any other RIP router (unless RIPv2 with authentication is configured), OSPF has some rules concerning if and how routing information should be shared. First, before a router will accept any routing information from another OSPF router, the routers must build an *adjacency* between them on their connected interfaces. When this adjacency is built, the two routers on the connected interfaces are called *neighbors*, indicating a special relationship between the two. In order for two routers to become neighbors, the following must match on each router:

- The area number
- The hello and dead interval timers on their connected interfaces
- The OSPF password (optional), if it is configured
- The area stub flag, indicating the type of area; a stub is used to contain OSPF messages and routing information, which is beyond the scope of this book
- MTU sizes on the connected interfaces

If these items do not match, the routers will not form an adjacency and will ignore each other's routing information.

Let's assume that you turned on all your routers simultaneously on a segment. In this case, the OSPF routers will go through three states, called the *exchange process*, in determining whether they will become neighbors:

1. **Down state** The routers have not exchanged any OSPF information with any other router.

2. **Init state**   A destination router receives a new router's hello and adds it to its neighbor list (assuming that values in the preceding bullet points match). Note that communication is only unidirectional at this point.

3. **Two-way state**   The new router receives a unidirectional reply (from the destination router) to its initial hello packet and adds the destination router to its neighbor database.

Once the routers have entered a *two-way* state, they are considered neighbors. At this point, an election process takes place to elect the designated router (DR) and the backup designated router (BDR) on the segment.

Designated and Backup Designated Routers

An OSPF router will not form adjacencies to just any router. Instead, a client/ server design is implemented in OSPF on *each* broadcast segment. For each multi-access broadcast segment, such as Ethernet, there is a DR and a BDR, as well as other OSPF routers, called *DROTHERs*. As an example, if you have ten VLANs in your switched area, you'll have ten DRs and ten BDRs. The one exception of a segment not having these two routers is on a WAN point-to-point link.

When an OSPF router comes up, it forms adjacencies with the DR and the BDR on each multi-access segment to which it is connected; if it is connected to three segments, it will form three sets of adjacencies. Any exchange of routing information is between these DR/BDR routers and the other OSPF neighbors on a segment (and vice versa). An OSPF router talks to a DR using the IP multicast address 224.0.0.6. The DR and the BDR talk to all OSPF routers using the 224.0.0.5 multicast IP address.

The OSPF router with the highest priority becomes the DR for the segment. If there is a tie, the router with the highest *router ID* (not IP address on the segment) will become the DR. By default, all routers have a priority of *1* (priorities can range from 0 to 255—it's an 8-bit value). If the DR fails, the BDR is promoted to DR and another router is elected as the BDR. Figure 10-2 shows an example of the election process, where router E is elected as the DR and router B is elected as the BDR. Note that in this example, each router has the default priority, 1; therefore, router E is chosen as the DR since it has the highest router ID, and router B is chosen as the BDR because it has the second highest router ID. If a router has a priority of 0, it will never become the DR or BDR.

on the
ⓘob

The DR and BDR priority is changed on an interface-by-interface basis and is configured with the `ip ospf priority` *command within the Interface Subconfiguration mode. Once the DR and BDR are elected, they maintain these roles even if other routers form adjacencies with them that have higher priorities: an election or re-election will occur only if no DR or BDR exists.*

exam
ⓦatch

The router with the highest priority (or highest router ID) becomes the DR—note that it is not the highest IP address on the link. This process is true for multi-access segments, but not point-to-point links, where DRs/BDRs are not used. Setting the priority to 0 means the router will never become the DR or BDR.

FIGURE 10-2

DR and BDR election process

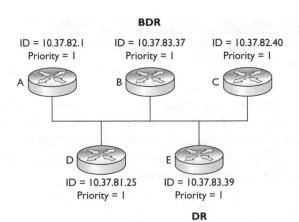

Sharing Routing Information

After electing the DR/BDR pair, the routers continue to generate hellos to maintain communication. This is considered an *exstart* state, in which the OSPF routers are ready to share link state information. The process the routers go through is called an *exchange protocol*, and is outlined here:

1. **Exstart state**   The DR and BDR form adjacencies with the other OSPF routers on the segment. Then, within each adjacency, the router with the highest router ID becomes the master and starts the exchange process first (shares its link state information). Note that the DR is not necessarily the master for the exchange process. The remaining router in the adjacency will be the slave.

2. **Exchange state**   The master starts sharing link state information first with the slave. These are called *database description packets* (DBDs), also referred to as DDPs. The DBDs contain the link state type, the ID of the advertising router, the cost of the advertised link, and the sequence number of the link. The slave responds back with an LSACK—an acknowledgment to the DBD from the master. The slave then compares the DBD's information with its own.

3. **Loading state**   If the master has more up-to-date information than the slave, the slave will respond to the master's original DBD with a link state request (LSR). The master will then send a link state update (LSU) with the detailed information of the links to the slave. The slave will then incorporate this into its local link state database. Again, the slave will generate an LSACK to the master to acknowledge the fact that it received the LSU. If a slave has more up-to-date information, it will repeat the exchange and loading states.

4. **Full state**   Once the master and the slave are synchronized, they are considered to be in a full state.

To summarize these four steps, OSPF routers share a type of LSA message in order to disclose information about available routes; basically, an LSA update message contains a link and a state, as well as other information. A *link* is the router interface on which the update was generated (a connected route). The *state* is a description of this interface, including the IP address configured on it and the relationship this router has with its neighboring router. However, OSPF routers will not share this information with just any OSPF router—just between themselves and the DR/BDR on a segment.

OSPF uses incremental updates after entering a full state. This means that whenever changes take place, only the change is shared with the DR, which will then share this information with other routers on the segment. Figure 10-3 shows an example of this. In this example, Network Z, connected to router C, goes down. Router C sends a multicast to the DR and the BDR (with a destination multicast address of 224.0.0.6), telling them about this change. Once the DR and the BDR incorporate the change internally, the DR then tells the other routes on the segment (via a multicast message sent to 224.0.0.5, which is all OSPF routers)

FIGURE 10-3

LSA update process

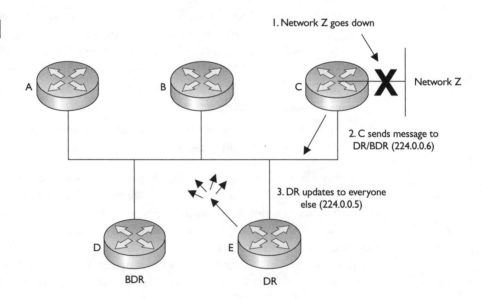

1. Network Z goes down

Network Z

2. C sends message to DR/BDR (224.0.0.6)

3. DR updates to everyone else (224.0.0.5)

BDR

DR

about the change concerning Network Z. Any router receiving the update will then share this update to the DRs of other segments to which they are connected.

Note that the communications between OSPF routers is connection oriented, even though multicasts are used. For example, if a router tells a DR about a change, the DR acknowledges this new piece of information with the source of the communication. Likewise, when the DR shares this information with the other routers on the segment, the DR expects acknowledgments from each of these neighbors. Remember that when an OSPF router exchanges updates with another, the process requires an acknowledgment: this ensures that a router or routers have received the update.

The exception to the incremental update process is that the DR floods its database every 30 minutes to ensure that all of the routers on the segment have the most up-to-date link state information. It does this with a destination address of 224.0.0.5 (all OSPF routers on the segment).

Each LSA message has a type associated with it. This book focuses on the following three, which are the ones found within a single area:

- **LSA Type 1 (Router LSA)**   These are generated by every router for each link that belongs to an area. They are flooded only inside of the area to which they belong. The Link ID of this LSA is the Router ID of the router that generated it.
- **LSA Type 2 (Network LSA)**   These are generated by the DR and describe the routers that are connected to that segment. They are sent inside the area for which the network segment belongs. The Link ID is the interface IP address of the designated router, which describes that particular segment.
- **LSA Type 5 (External LSA)**   Autonomous system external LSAs are generated by autonomous system boundary routers (ASBRs) and contain routes to networks that are external to the current AS. The Link ID is a network number advertised in the LSA.

In summary, the first two LSA types represent links within the local area and the last LSA type represents links from a different autonomous system. These LSA types are placed in a local database on the routing device. Other LSA types exist, but are beyond the scope of this book.

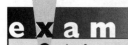

ℰxam

ⓦatch   *The advantage of a single area design is that it reduces the number of LSA types used with OSPF and removes the need for OSPF virtual links.*

When building the routing table using link state information, an OSPF router can keep up to 16 paths to a single destination in its routing table. The only restriction is that the paths must have the same accumulated cost metric.

e x a m

ⓦatch

A two-way state indicates that two OSPF routers are neighbors. A full state indicates the completion of sharing of links between routers. In order to build and maintain the OSPF database, hello (establish neighbors) and LSA (routing information) messages are used.

CERTIFICATION OBJECTIVE 10.03

OSPF Configuration

Configuring OSPF is slightly *different* from configuring RIP. When configuring OSPF, use the following syntax:

```
Router(config)# router ospf process_ID
Router(config-router)# network IP_address wildcard_mask
                               area area_#
```

The `process_ID` is locally significant and is used to differentiate between OSPF processes running on the same router. It can be any number from 1 to 65,535. Your router might be a boundary router between two OSPF autonomous systems, and to differentiate them on your router, you'll give them unique process IDs. Note that these numbers do *not* need to match between different routers and that they have nothing to do with autonomous system numbers. You would need to use different process numbers if your routing device was connected to two different OSPF networks: you would need a different, locally unique process number for each OSPF network. Each OSPF process will have its own OSPF database identified by the process ID. (How to configure two OSPF processes on the same router is beyond the scope of this book.)

When configuring the OSPF routing process, you must specify a process ID (identifier). This uniquely identifies an instance of the OSPF database on the router and is only locally significant: it doesn't have to match on each router in the AS. It can be any number from 1 to 65,535. Different process numbers are used to identify different OSPF networks a routing *device is connected to. The* `network 0.0.0.0 255.255.255.255 area 0` *command will include all interfaces in area 0. The* `network 10.10.2.16 0.0.0.15 area 0` *command will include all interfaces in area 0 that fall within 10.10.2.16 through 10.10.2.31. Each OSPF process will have its own OSPF database identified by the process ID.*

When specifying what interfaces go into an OSPF area, use the **network** command. As you can see in the preceding code listing, the syntax of this command is different from that of RIP's configuration, where you specify only a class address. OSPF is classless. With this command, you can be very specific about what interface belongs to a particular area. The syntax of this command lists an IP address or network number, followed by a *wildcard mask*, which is different from a subnet mask. A wildcard mask tells the router the interesting component of the address—in other words, what part of the address it should match on. This mask is also used with access lists.

A wildcard mask is 32 bits in length. A 0 in a bit position means there must be a match, and a 1 in a bit position means the router doesn't care. Actually, a wildcard mask is an *inverted* subnet mask, with the 1s and 0s switched. Using a wildcard mask, you can be very specific about which interfaces belong to which areas. The last part of the command tells the router to which area these addresses on the router belong.

Unlike in RIP, the `network` *statement allows you to specify an IP address and a wildcard mask, which is an inverted subnet mask. You must also specify to which area this address or addresses will belong:* `network` `network_#` `wildcard_mask` **area** `area_#`. *A trick* *of converting a subnet mask to a wildcard mask is to subtract the subnet mask from 255.255.255.255; the result will be the corresponding wildcard mask. You'll need to be able to look at a wildcard mask in an OSPF* `network` *command and determine which interface or interfaces it includes.*

Let's look at some code examples to see how the wildcard mask works. Use the router shown in Figure 10-4 as an illustration.

```
Router(config)# router ospf 1
Router(config-router)# network 10.1.1.1 0.0.0.0 area 0
Router(config-router)# network 10.1.2.1 0.0.0.0 area 0
Router(config-router)# network 172.16.1.1 0.0.0.0 area 0
Router(config-router)# network 172.16.2.1 0.0.0.0 area 0
```

In this example, the interfaces with addresses of 10.1.1.1, 10.1.2.1, 172.16.1.1, and 172.16.1.1 all are associated with area 0. A wildcard mask of 0.0.0.0 says that there must be an exact match against the address on the router's interface in order to place it in area 0.

Here's another example that accomplishes the same thing:

```
Router(config)# router ospf 1
Router(config-router)# network 10.0.0.0 0.255.255.255 area 0
Router(config-router)# network 172.16.0.0 0.0.255.255 area 0
```

In this example, interfaces beginning with an address of 10 or 172.16 are to be included in area 0. Or, if all the interfaces on your router belonged to the same area, you could use this configuration:

```
Router(config)# router ospf 1
Router(config-router)# network 0.0.0.0 255.255.255.255 area 0
```

In this example, all interfaces are placed in area 0. As you can see, OSPF is very flexible in allowing you to specify which interface or interfaces will participate in OSPF and to which area they will belong.

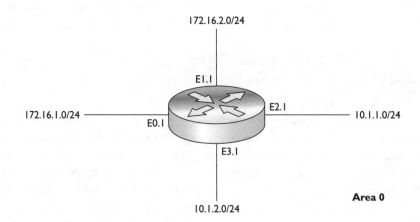

FIGURE 10-4

OSPF network
configuration
example

10.01. *The digital resources that accompany this book contain a multimedia demonstration of configuring OSPF on a router.*

Loopback Interfaces

A *loopback interface* is a logical, virtual interface on a router. By default, the router doesn't have any loopback interfaces, but they can be easily created. All IOS platforms support loopback interfaces, and you can create as many of these interfaces as you need. These interfaces are treated as physical interfaces on a router: you can assign addressing information to them, include their network numbers in routing updates, and even terminate IP connections on them, such as telnet and SSH.

exam

ⓦatch
A loopback interface is a logical interface that always remains up. Use the `interface loopback` *command to create it. Using a loopback interface as a routing protocol's router ID creates stability for the routing protocol since the loopback interface is always up, by default. If two or more loopback interfaces exist, the one with the highest IP address will be the one that is chosen for the OSPF router ID, by default.*

Here are some reasons you might want to create a loopback interface:

- To assign a router ID to an OSPF router
- To use for testing purposes, since this interface is always up
- To terminate special connections, such as GRE tunnels or IPsec connections, since this interface is always up

on the
ⓘob
The router ID for OSPF is chosen when the OSPF routing process is started. This occurs when you execute the `router ospf` *command manually or when the router's configuration is loaded when booting up. Therefore, if you create a loopback interface after enabling OSPF, the loopback won't be used as the router ID; however, if you reboot the router, the loopback interface will be used, by default. Therefore, I recommend that you create your loopback interface and assign an IP address to it first and then enable OSPF to eliminate any confusion about what your router's router ID is.*

To create a loopback interface, use the following command:

```
Router(config)# interface loopback port_#
Router(config-if)# ip address IP_address subnet_mask
```

As you can see, creating a loopback interface is easy. You can specify port numbers from 0 to 2147483647. The number you use is only locally significant. Once you enter the loopback interface, you can execute almost any interface command on it; for instance, you can assign it an IP address with the **ip address** command.

on the job *10.02. The digital resources that accompany this book contain a multimedia demonstration of creating a loopback interface on a router.*

Default Route Propagation

On your perimeter OSPF router connected to the ISP, you typically have a default route pointing to the ISP. To take this route and redistribute it into your OSPF process, basically making your perimeter router an ASBR, use the following configuration:

```
Router(config)# ip route 0.0.0.0 0.0.0.0
                          ISP_interface_or_IP_address
Router(config)# router ospf process_ID
Router(config-router)# default-information originate
```

exam
watch *Use the `default-information originate` command to inject a default route into an OSPF routing process. Make sure your default route doesn't point to your internal network, but your ISP's network; otherwise, you'll be creating a routing loop.*

OSPF Metric Values

You can affect the cost metric that OSPF uses in picking the best-cost routes for the routing table in two ways. First, remember that the cost metric is the inverse of the accumulated bandwidth values of routers' interfaces. The default measurement that Cisco uses in calculating the cost metric is $cost = 10^8/(interface\ bandwidth)$. 10^8 represents 100 Mbps. You can also affect the value of the cost by changing the 10^8 value with the **auto-cost reference-bandwidth** command.

Table 10-1 contains some default costs for different interface types.

To change the cost of an interface manually, use the following configuration:

```
Router(config)# interface type [slot_#/]port_#
Router(config-if)# ip ospf cost cost_value
```

Notice that the cost is assigned within an interface. This value can range from 1 to 65,535. Note that each vendor might use a different calculation to come up with a cost value.

on the
ⓘob   *It is very important that the costs for a link match for every router on a given segment. Mismatched cost values on a segment can cause routers to run the SPF algorithm continually, greatly affecting the routers' performance.*

Normally, you won't be changing the default cost values on an interface. However, since OSPF uses the inverse of bandwidth as a metric and serial interfaces default to a bandwidth of 1544 Kbps, you will definitely want to match the bandwidth metric on the serial interface to its real clock rate. To configure the bandwidth on your router's interfaces, use the following command:

```
Router(config) interface type [slot_#/]port_#
Router(config-if)# bandwidth speed_in_Kbps
```

TABLE 10-1

Default OSPF Costs for Different IOS Interfaces

Cost Value	Interface Type
1785	56-Kbps serial line
1652	64-Kbps serial line
64	T1
10	Ethernet
1	Fast Ethernet

As an example, if the clock rate were 64,000, you would use the following command to configure the bandwidth correctly: **bandwidth 64**. Note that the speed is in *Kbps* for the **bandwidth** command. For example, assume you configured the bandwidth with this: **bandwidth 64000**. By doing this, the router would assume the bandwidth metric of the interface is 64 Mbps, not Kbps.

By default, the router will place up to four equal-cost OSPF paths to a destination in the router's routing table. This can be increased up to 16 equal-cost paths with the following configuration:

```
Router(config)# router ospf process_ID
Router(config-router)# maximum-paths #_of_max_paths
```

10.03. The digital resources that accompany this book contain a multimedia demonstration of changing OSPF metrics on a router.

---

e x a m

ⓦatch   The bandwidth command should be used on synchronous serial interfaces to match the bandwidth metric to the clocked rate of the interface. Changing the bandwidth associated to an interface with the bandwidth command, or changing the OSPF cost for an interface with the ip ospf cost command, will change the costs for routes associated with the interface. Synchronous serial interfaces, no matter what they are clocked at, default to a bandwidth metric of 1544 Kbps. The default number of maximum paths is four.

OSPF Authentication

OSPF supports authentication of neighbors and routing updates. This is used to prevent rogue OSPF routers from injecting bad or misleading routing information into your topological databases. Authentication can be done with a clear-text password or a digital signature created with the MD5 algorithm. Of the two, the latter is the more secure: clear-text passwords can be seen by an eavesdropper between two OSPF neighbors. When using MD5, to prevent a replay attack where the same information is always sent to a neighbor, such as a hello message, a non-decreasing sequence number is included in the message to ensure that the message and the signature are unique. The authentication information is placed in every LSA and validated before being accepted by an OSPF router. To become neighbors, the keying information—clear-text password or key for the MD5 algorithm—must match on the two peers.

Remember that if the password/key values on two OSPF neighbors don't match, an adjacency will not occur. Of the two methods, using MD5 is definitely much more secure than a clear-text password.

Configuring authentication is a two-step process: specifying the password/key to use and enabling authentication. The configuration of the key is done on an interface-by-interface basis, which means that every neighboring OSPF router off of the same interface must use the password/key. Here's the command to configure the password/key value:

```
Router(config)# interface type [slot_#/]port_#
Router(config-if)# ip ospf authentication-key password
```

Starting in Cisco IOS 12.4, any password greater than eight characters is truncated to eight characters by the router. The password is stored in clear text in the router's configuration. To encrypt it, use the **service password-encryption** command.

Next, you must specify whether the password is sent in clear text or used by MD5 to create a digital signature. This can be done on the interface or on an area-by-area basis. To specify the interface method, use this configuration:

```
Router(config)# interface type [slot_#/]port_#
Router(config-if)# ip ospf authentication [message-digest]
```

If you omit the **message-digest** parameter, the key is sent as a clear-text password. Your other option is to configure the use of the password/key for an area with which the router is associated:

```
Router(config)# router ospf process_ID
Router(config-router)# area area_# authentication
                              [message-digest]
```

If you omit the **message-digest** parameter, the key is sent as a clear-text password.

Of the two approaches, the latter is the older method: the interface method (former method) was added in IOS 12.0 and is the preferred approach.

10.04. The digital resources that accompany this book contain a multimedia demonstration of setting up OSPF MD5 authentication on a router.

CERTIFICATION OBJECTIVE 10.04

OSPF Troubleshooting

Once you have configured OSPF, the following commands are available to view and troubleshoot your OSPF configuration and operation:

- `show ip protocols`
- `show ip route`
- `show ip ospf`
- `show ip ospf database`
- `show ip ospf interface`
- `show ip ospf neighbor`
- `debug ip ospf adj`
- `debug ip ospf events`
- `debug ip ospf packet`

The following sections cover these commands.

The show ip protocols Command

The `show ip protocols` command displays all of the IP routing protocols that you have configured and that are running on your router. Here's an example of this command with OSPF:

```
Router# show ip protocols
Routing Protocol is "ospf 1"
  Outgoing update filter list for all interfaces is not set
 Incoming update filter list for all interfaces is not set
  Router ID 192.168.100.1
  Number of areas in this router is 1. 1 normal 0 stub 0 nssa
  Maximum path: 4
  Routing for Networks:
    0.0.0.0 255.255.255.255 area 0
  Routing Information Sources:
    Gateway         Distance      Last Update
    192.168.1.100       110       00:00:24
    192.168.100.1       110       00:00:24
  Distance: (default is 110)
```

ⓦ **a t c h** *Remember that the default administrative distance of OSPF is 110.*

In this example, the router's ID is 192.168.100.1. All interfaces are participating in OSPF (0.0.0.0 255.255.255.255) and are in area 0. There are two OSPF routers in this network: 192.168.1.100 (another router) and 192.168.100.1 (this router). Notice that the default administrative distance is 110.

Video

10.05. The digital resources that accompany this book contain a multimedia demonstration of using the `show ip protocols` **command on an OSPF router.**

The show ip route Command

Your router keeps a list of the best IP paths to destinations in a routing table. To view the routing table, use the **show ip route** command:

```
Router# show ip route
Codes: C - connected, S - static, I - IGRP, R - RIP,
       M - mobile, B - BGP, D - EIGRP, EX - EIGRP external,
       O - OSPF, IA - OSPF inter area, N1 - OSPF NSSA
       external type 1, N2 - OSPF NSSA external type 2,
       E1 - OSPF external type 1, E2 - OSPF external type 2,
       E - EGP, i - IS-IS, L1 - IS-IS level-1,
       L2 - IS-IS level-2, * - candidate default,
       U - per-user static route, o - ODR,
       T - traffic engineered route
Gateway of last resort is not set
       10.0.0.0/24 is subnetted, 1 subnets
O        10.0.1.0 [110/65] via 192.168.1.100, 00:04:18, Serial0
C      192.168.1.0/24 is directly connected, Serial0
C      192.168.100.0/24 is directly connected, Ethernet0
```

ⓦ **a t c h** *OSPF routes show up as an* O *in the output of the* `show ip route` *command. Remember the two numbers in* *brackets ([]): administrative distance and cost (when dealing with an OSPF route).*

In this example, there is one OSPF route (O): 10.0.1.0. This route has an administrative distance of 110, a metric cost of 65, and can be reached via neighbor 192.168.1.100.

10.06. The digital resources that accompany this book contain a multimedia demonstration of using the `show ip route` command on an OSPF router.

The show ip ospf Command

To view an overview of your router's OSPF configuration, use the **show ip ospf** command:

```
Router# show ip ospf
  Routing Process "ospf 1" with ID 10.1.1.1 and Domain ID
10.1.1.1
  Supports only single TOS(TOS0) routes
  Supports opaque LSA
  SPF schedule delay 5 secs, Hold time between two SPFs 10 secs
  Minimum LSA interval 5 secs. Minimum LSA arrival 1 secs
  LSA group pacing timer 100 secs
  Interface flood pacing timer 55 msecs
  Retransmission pacing timer 100 msecs
  Number of external LSA 0. Checksum Sum 0x0
  Number of opaque AS LSA 0. Checksum Sum 0x0
  Number of DCbitless external and opaque AS LSA 0
  Number of DoNotAge external and opaque AS LSA 0
  Number of areas in this router is 1. 1 normal 0 stub 0 nssa
  External flood list length 0
     Area BACKBONE(0)
        Number of interfaces in this area is 2
        Area has message digest authentication
        SPF algorithm executed 4 times
        Area ranges are
        Number of LSA 4. Checksum Sum 0x29BEB
        Number of opaque link LSA 0. Checksum Sum 0x0
        Number of DCbitless LSA 3
        Number of indication LSA 0
        Number of DoNotAge LSA 0
        Flood list length 0
```

This command shows the OSPF timer configurations and other statistics, including the number of times the SPF algorithm is run in an area.

10.07. The digital resources that accompany this book contain a multimedia demonstration of using the `show ip ospf` command on an OSPF router.

The show ip ospf database Command

To display lists of information related to the OSPF database for a specific routing device, including the collection of OSPF link states, use the **show ip ospf database** command. Here's an example:

```
Router# show ip ospf database
OSPF Router with ID(192.168.1.11) (Process ID 1)
            Router Link States(Area 0)
  Link ID        ADV Router      Age      Seq#        Checksum Link count
  192.168.1.8    192.168.1.8     1381     0x8000010D   0xEF60   2
  192.168.1.11   192.168.1.11    1460     0x800002FE   0xEB3D   4
  192.168.1.12   192.168.1.12    2027     0x80000090   0x875D   3
  192.168.1.27   192.168.1.27    1323     0x800001D6   0x12CC   3
            Net Link States(Area 0)
  Link ID        ADV Router      Age      Seq#        Checksum
  172.16.1.27    192.168.1.27    1323     0x8000005B   0xA8EE
  172.17.1.11    192.168.1.11    1461     0x8000005B   0x7AC
```

In the two sections, the Router Link States section indicates the LSA type 1 messages and the Net Link States section indicates the LSA type 2 messages. The Link ID column represents the router ID number. The ADV Router column represents the router ID of the advertising routing device. The Age column represents how old the link state information is. The Seq# column is used to detect old or duplicate LSAs from OSPF neighbors. The Link count column represents the number of interfaces detected for a routing device. The Checksum column is the checksum of the update to ensure reliability.

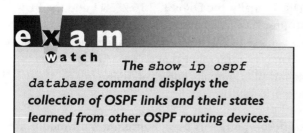

ⓦatch   *The show ip ospf database command displays the collection of OSPF links and their states learned from other OSPF routing devices.*

The show ip ospf interface Command

On an interface-by-interface basis, your OSPF router keeps track of what area an interface belongs to and what neighbors, if any, are connected to the interface. To view this information, use the **show ip ospf interface** command:

```
Router# show ip ospf interface
Ethernet 1 is up, line protocol is up
Internet Address 172.16.255.1/24, Area 0
Process ID 100, Router ID 172.16.255.1, Network Type BROADCAST,
Cost: 10
```

```
Transmit Delay is 1 sec, State DROTHER, Priority 1
Designated Router id 172.16.255.11, Interface address 172.16.255.11
Backup Designated router id 172.16.255.10, Interface addr
172.16.255.10
Timer intervals configured, Hello 10, Dead 40, Wait 40, Retransmit 5
Hello due in 0:00:03
Neighbor Count is 3, Adjacent neighbor count is 2
   Adjacent with neighbor 172.16.255.10  (Backup Designated Router)
   Adjacent with neighbor 172.16.255.11  (Designated Router)
```

e x a m

ⓦatch

The `show ip ospf interface` command displays your router's ID, the ID of the DR and BDR, the hello timer (10 seconds), the dead interval (40 seconds), the number of neighbors, and the number of adjacencies. Remember that the hello and dead interval time values must match to become a neighbor with another OSPF router.

In this example, the router ID is 172.16.255.1. Its state is DROTHER, which means that it is *not* the DR or BDR. Actually, the DR is 172.16.255.11 and the BDR is 172.16.255.10 (these are their router IDs). Also notice that the hello and dead interval timers are at their default values: 10 and 40 seconds, respectively. A total of three neighbors have two adjacencies—remember that adjacencies are built only between routers and the DR and BDR, not all routers on the segment.

Video

10.08. The digital resources that accompany this book contain a multimedia demonstration of using the `show ip ospf interface` command on an OSPF router.

The show ip ospf neighbor Command

To see all of your router's OSPF neighbors, use the **show ip ospf neighbor** command:

```
Router# show ip ospf neighbor
     ID          Pri   State        Dead Time     Address          Interface
  172.16.255.11   1    FULL/DR       0:00:31     172.16.255.11      Ethernet0
  172.16.255.10   1    FULL/BDR      0:00:33     172.16.255.10      Ethernet0
```

```
172.16.255.9    1    2WAY/DROTHER   0:00:35    172.16.255.9    Ethernet0
172.16.254.2    1    FULL/DR        0:00:39    172.16.254.2    Serial0.1
```

In this example, three routers are connected to `Ethernet0`: 172.16.255.11 is a DR, 172.16.255.10 is a BDR, and 172.16.255.9 is another OSPF router (DROTHER). Notice that for the DR and the BDR, the state is *full*, which is to be expected, since this router and the DR/BDR share routing information with each other. The DROTHER router is in a *two-way* state, which indicates that the router is a neighbor, but this router and the DROTHER router will not share routing information directly with each other since the other router is *not* a DR or BDR. Optionally, you can add the ID of the neighbor to the **show ip ospf neighbor** command to get more information about a particular neighbor.

e x a m

ⓦatch   *Remember that the show ip ospf neighbor command lists all of the router's OSPF neighbors, their OSPF states, their router IDs, and which interface the neighbors are connected to.*

on the
ⓙob   *If the MTU sizes are different on the OSPF routers' interfaces, they will not become neighbors; verify the MTU size on each neighbor with the show interfaces or show ip interfaces command.*

▶ **Video**

10.09. The digital resources that accompany this book contain a multimedia demonstration of using the show ip ospf neighbor command on an OSPF router.

The debug ip ospf adj Command

For more detailed troubleshooting, you can use **debug** commands. If you want to view the adjacency process that a router builds to other routers, use the **debug ip ospf adj** command:

```
Router# debug ip ospf adj
172.16.255.11 on Ethernet0, state 2WAY
OSPF: end of Wait on interface Ethernet0
OSPF: DR/BDR election on Ethernet0
OSPF: Elect BDR 172.16.255.10
```

```
OSPF: Elect DR 172.16.255.11
      DR: 172.16.255.11 (Id) BDR: 172.16.255.10 (Id)
OSPF: Send DBD to 172.16.255.11 on Ethernet0
      seq 0x10DB opt 0x2 flag 0x7 len 32
OSPF: Build router LSA for area 0, router ID 172.16.255.11
```

In this example, you can see the election process for the DR and BDR and the sharing of links (DBDs) with the DR.

If two routers have misconfigured the authentication type for OSPF, such as clear-text passwords on one and MD5 on the other, you'll see the following with the previous **debug** command:

```
OSPF: Rcv pkt from 192.168.1.1, Serial1/0:
Mismatch Authentication type. Input packet specified
                      type 0, we use type 1
```

However, if you have mismatched the passwords (keys) on the two OSPF routers, you'll see something like this:

```
OSPF: Rcv pkt from 192.168.1.1, Serial1/0 :
Mismatch Authentication Key - Clear Text
```

10.10. The digital resources that accompany this book contain a multimedia demonstration of using the debug ip ospf adj *command on an OSPF router.*

The debug ip ospf events Command

If you want to view OSPF events on your router, use the **debug ip ospf events** command:

```
Router# debug ip ospf events
4d02h: OSPF: Rcv hello from 192.168.1.100 area 0 from Serial0 192.168.1.100
4d02h: OSPF: End of hello processing
```

ⓦatch *Be familiar with these debug commands and the reasons that can cause two routers not to become neighbors.*

In this example, the router received a hello packet from 192.168.1.00, which is connected to Serial0. You might see the following kinds of information as well:

- Hello intervals that do not match for routers on a segment

■ Dead intervals that do not match for routers on a segment

■ Mismatched subnet masks for OSPF routers on a segment

10.11. The digital resources that accompany this book contain a multimedia demonstration of using the `debug ip ospf events` command on an OSPF router.

The debug ip ospf packet Command

If you want to view OSPF packet contents of LSAs, use the **debug ip ospf packet** command:

```
Router# debug ip ospf packet
4d02h: OSPF: rcv. v:2 t:1 l:48 rid:192.168.1.100
      aid:0.0.0.0 chk:15E4 aut:0 auk: from Serial0
```

Table 10-2 explains the values shown in this command.

10.12. The digital resources that accompany this book contain a multimedia demonstration of using the `debug ip ospf packet` command on an OSPF router.

TABLE 10-2	Field Value	Explanation
Debug Field Explanations for debug ip ospf packet	Aid:	OSPF area ID number
	Auk:	OSPF authentication key used for neighbor authentication
	Aut:	Type of OSPF authentication (0–none, 1–simple password, 2–MD5 hashing)
	Keyid:	MD5 key value if this authentication mechanism is enabled
	L:	Length of the packet
	Rid:	OSPF router ID
	Seq:	Sequence number
	T:	OSPF packet type (1–hello, 2–data description, 3–link state request, 4–link state update, 5–link state acknowledgment
	V:	OSPF version number

EXERCISE 10-1

Configuring OSPF

The last few sections dealt with configuring OSPF on a router. This exercise will help you reinforce your understanding of this material for setting up and troubleshooting OSPF. You'll perform this lab using Boson's NetSim simulator. You can find a picture of the network diagram for Boson's NetSim simulator in the introduction of this book. In this exercise, you'll set up OSPF on the two routers (2600-1 and 2600-2). After starting up the simulator, click the Labs tab at the bottom left of the window. Click the McGraw-Hill Education tab (to the right of the Standard and Custom tabs) at the top left. Next, double-click Exercise 10-1. This will load the lab configuration based on the exercises in Chapter 6.

1. On the 2600-1, verify that the `fa0/0` and `s0` interfaces are up. If not, bring them up. Examine the IP addresses configured on the 2600-1 and look at its routing table.

   Click the Lab Instructions tab and use the drop-down selector for Devices to choose 2600-1; or click the NetMap tab and double-click the 2600-1 device icon. On the 2600-1, use the **show interfaces** command to verify your configuration. If `fa0/0` and `s0` are not up, go into the interfaces (`fa0/0` and `s0`) and enable them: **configure terminal**, **interface** *type* *port*, **no shutdown**, **end**, and **show interfaces**. Use the **show ip route** command. You should have two connected networks: 192.168.1.0 connected to `fa0/0` and 192.168.2.0 connected to `s0`.

2. On the 2600-2, verify that the `fa0/0` and `s0` interfaces are up. If not, bring them up. Examine the IP addresses configured on the 2600-2 and look at its routing table.

   Click the Lab Instructions tab and use the drop-down selector for Devices to choose 2600-2; or click the NetMap tab and double-click the 2600-2 device icon. On the 2600-2, verify that the `fa0/0` and `s0` interfaces are up. If not, bring them up: **configure terminal**, **interface** *type* *port*, **no shutdown**, **end**, and **show interfaces**. Use the **show interfaces** command to verify that the IP addresses you configured in Chapter 6 are still there. Use the **show ip route** command. You should have two connected networks: 192.168.3.0 connected to `fa0/0` and 192.168.2.0 connected to `s0`.

3. Test connectivity between Host-1 and the 2600-1.

   Click the Lab Instructions tab and use the drop-down selector for Devices to choose Host-1; or click the NetMap tab and double-click the Host-1 device icon. From Host-1, ping the 2600-1: `ping 192.168.1.1`. The ping should be successful.

4. Test connectivity between Host-3 and the 2600-2.

   Click the Lab Instructions tab and use the drop-down selector for Devices to choose Host-3; or click the NetMap tab and double-click the Host-3 device icon. From Host-3, ping the 2600-2 router: `ping 192.168.3.1`. The ping should be successful.

5. Test connectivity between Host-3 and Host-1.

   From Host-3, ping Host 1: `ping 192.168.1.10`. The ping should fail: there is no route from the 2600-2 to this destination (look at the 2600-2's routing table; it doesn't list 192.168.1.0/24).

6. Enable OSPF on the 2600-1 router, using a process ID of 1, and put all interfaces in area 0.

   Click the Lab Instructions tab and use the drop-down selector for Devices to choose 2600-1; or click the NetMap tab and double-click the 2600-1 device icon. On the 2600-1 router, configure the following: `configure terminal`, `router ospf 1`, `network 0.0.0.0 255.255.255.255 area 0`, and `end`.

7. Enable OSPF on the 2600-2 router, using a process ID of 1, and put all interfaces in area 0.

   Click the Lab Instructions tab and use the drop-down selector for Devices to choose 2600-2; or click the NetMap tab and double-click the 2600-2 device icon. On the 2600-2 router, configure the following: `configure terminal`, `router ospf 1`, `network 0.0.0.0 255.255.255.255 area 0`, and `end`.

8. On the 2600-2, verify the operation of OSPF. Is either router a DR or BDR on the WAN link?

   Use the `show ip protocols` command to make sure that OSPF is configured—check for the neighboring router's update. Use the `show ip route` command and look for the remote LAN network number as an OSPF (O) entry in the routing table. Use the `show ip ospf neighbor` command to view your neighboring router. Neither should be a DR or BDR on the serial link, since point-to-point connections don't use DRs and BDRs.

9. On the 2600-1, verify the operation of OSPF.

   Click the Lab Instructions tab and use the drop-down selector for Devices to choose 2600-1; or click the NetMap tab and double-click the 2600-1 device icon. Use the `show ip protocols` command to make sure that OSPF is configured—check for the neighboring router's update. Use the `show ip route` command and look for the remote LAN network number as an OSPF (O) entry in the routing table. Use the `show ip ospf neighbor` command to view your neighboring router.

10. On Host-1, test connectivity to Host-3.

    Click the Lab Instructions tab and use the drop-down selector and choose Host-1; or click the NetMap tab and double-click the Host-1 device icon. On Host-1, execute this: `ping 192.168.3.10`. The ping should be successful.

EXERCISE 10-2

Troubleshooting OSPF

This exercise will help introduce you to an already configured network, but with some configuration issues that are preventing OSPF connectivity. You'll perform this lab using Boson's NetSim simulator. You can find a picture of the network diagram for Boson's NetSim simulator in the introduction of this book. After starting up the simulator, click the Labs tab at the bottom left of the window. Click the McGraw-Hill Education tab (to the right of the Standard and Custom tabs) at the top left. Next, double-click Exercise 10-2. This will load the lab configuration based on the exercises in Chapter 6 (with problems in the configurations, of course).

Let's start with the problem: Host-1 cannot ping Host-3. Your task is to figure out the multiple problems and fix them. In this example, OSPF has been preconfigured on the routers. Try this troubleshooting process on your own first; if you have problems, come back to the following steps and solutions provided here.

1. Test connectivity from Host-1 to Host-3 with ping, as well as from Host-1 to its default gateway.

   Click the Lab Instructions tab and use the drop-down selector for Devices to choose Host-1; or click the NetMap tab and double-click the Host-1 device icon. On Host-1, ping Host-3: `ping 192.168.3.10`. Note that the ping fails. Ping the default gateway address: `ping 192.168.1.1`. The ping should fail, indicating that at least layer 3 is not functioning between Host-1 and the 2600-1. Examine the IP configuration on Host-1 by executing **ipconfig**. Make sure the IP addressing information is correct: IP address of 192.168.1.10, subnet mask of 255.255.255.0, and default gateway address of 192.168.1.1. Notice that the IP address is 192.168.100.10. Change this address to 192.168.1.10. Change the IP address by executing **ipconfig /ip 192.168.1.10 255.255.255.0**. Try pinging the 2600-1 again: **ping 192.168.1.1**. The ping should succeed. On Host-1, ping Host-3: **ping 192.168.3.10**. Note that the ping still fails.

2. Test connectivity from Host-3 to its default gateway.

   Click the Lab Instructions tab and use the drop-down selector for Devices to choose Host-3; or click the NetMap tab and double-click the Host-3 device icon. Examine the IP configuration on Host-3 by executing **ipconfig /all**. Make sure the IP addressing information is correct: IP address of 192.168.3.10, subnet mask of 255.255.255.0, and default gateway address of 192.168.3.1. Ping the default gateway address: **ping 192.168.3.1**. The ping should fail, indicating that there is a problem between Host-3 and the 2600-2. In this example, assume layer 2 is functioning correctly; therefore, it must be a problem with the 2600-2.

3. Check the interface statuses and IP configuration on the 2600-2.

   Click the Lab Instructions tab and use the drop-down selector for Devices to choose 2600-2; or click the NetMap tab and double-click the 2600-2 device icon. Check the status of the interfaces: **show interfaces**. Notice that fa0/0 has the wrong IP address (192.168.30.1) and is disabled. Go into fa0/0, fix the IP address, and enable it: **configure terminal, interface fa0/0, ip address 192.168.3.1, no shutdown**, and **end**. Verify the status of the fa0/0 interface: **show interface fa0/0**. Try pinging Host-3: **ping 192.168.3.10**. The ping should succeed.

4. Verify connectivity from the 2600-2 to the 2600-1.

   Try pinging the 2600-1's serial1/0 interface: **ping 192.168.2.1**. The ping succeeds.

5. Verify OSPF's configuration on the 2600-2.

   Examine the 2600-2's OSPF configuration: **show ip protocol**. You should see OSPF as the routing protocol and networks 192.168.2.0 and 192.168.3.0 included (0.0.0.0 255.255.255.255). From this output, it looks like OSPF is configured correctly on the 2600-2.

6. Save the configuration on the 2600-2: `copy running-config startup-config`.

7. Test connectivity from the 2600-2 to Host-1. Examine the routing table.

   From the 2600-2 router, test the connection to Host-1: `ping 192.168.1.10`. The ping should fail. This indicates a layer 3 problem between the 2600-2 and Host-1. Examine the routing table: `show ip route`. Notice that there are only two connected routes (192.168.2.0/24 and 192.168.1.0/24), but no OSPF routes.

8. Access the 2600-1 router and examine OSPF's configuration. Fix the problem.

   Click the Lab Instructions tab and use the drop-down selector for Devices to choose 2600-1; or click the NetMap tab and double-click the 2600-1 device icon. Examine the routing table: `show ip protocol`. What networks are advertised by the 2600-1? You should see 192.168.100.0 and 192.168.2.0. Obviously, `fa0/0`'s interface isn't included since 192.168.1.0 is not configured. Fix this configuration problem: `configure terminal`, `router ospf 1`, `no network 192.168.100.0 0.0.0.255 area 0`, `network 192.168.1.0 0.0.0.255 area 0`, and `end`. Test connectivity to Host-3: `ping 192.168.3.10`. The ping should be successful. Save the configuration on the router: `copy running-config startup-config`.

9. Examine the routing table on the 2600-2. Test connectivity from the 2600-2 to Host-1.

   Click the Lab Instructions tab and use the drop-down selector for Devices to choose 2600-2; or click the NetMap tab and double-click the 2600-2 device icon. Examine the routing table: `show ip route`. Notice that there are only two connected routes (192.168.2.0/24 and 192.168.1.0/24) and one OSPF route (192.168.1.0/24). From the 2600-2 router, test the connection to Host-1: `ping 192.168.1.10`. The ping should succeed.

10. Now test connectivity between Host-1 and Host-3.

    Click the Lab Instructions tab and use the drop-down selector for Devices to choose Host-1; or click the NetMap tab and double-click the Host-1 device icon. Test connectivity to Host-3: `ping 192.168.3.10`. The ping should be successful.

Now you should be more comfortable with configuring and troubleshooting OSPF.

CERTIFICATION OBJECTIVE 10.05

OSPFv3 for IPv6

IPv6 supports both static and dynamic routing protocols. Cisco's IOS IPv6 supports these routing protocols: static, RIPng, OSPFv3, IS-IS for IPv6, MP-BGP4, and EIGRP for IPv6. This book covers only an introduction to static, RIPng, and OSPFv3 routing; the other dynamic routing protocols are covered in more depth in Cisco's CCNP curriculum and certification.

OSPFv3 has been enhanced with many features, making it just as scalable as other Interior Gateway Protocols. The protocol number for OSPFv3 is 89. Here are some of the enhancements:

- The OSPFv3 process requires a router ID, just as in OSPFv2 (IPv4). This is a 32-bit number that must statically be configured; it cannot be acquired by an IPv4 address on the routing device, since you might not even be using IPv4 on the routing device.

- When forming adjacencies, the routers use their link-local addresses as their source. The link-local addresses are what appear in the link state database and routing table for next-hop addresses.

- Because link-local addresses are used, conflicting global addresses on the interfaces will not prevent adjacencies from being formed: in other words, the global addressing structure has been abstracted from the interface. In OSPFv2 this would cause routers to fail building an adjacency, but doesn't cause a problem in OSPFv3.

- Any router within an area can perform summarization or filtering. This was one of the biggest weaknesses of OSPFv2 compared to EIGRP. In OSPFv2, only ABRs and ASBRs could do summarization or filtering, whereas an EIGRP router could do this. This greatly limited the scalability of OSPFv2. OSPFv3 no longer has this issue.

Enabling OSPFv3 for IPv6 is a little bit different than enabling OSPFv2 for IPv4. The following sections briefly introduce you to a basic OSPFv3 configuration and verification.

OSPFv3 Global Configuration

As in OSPFv2, in OSPFv3 you enable a process globally and can perform certain functions within the process, like assigning the router ID and defining the areas:

```
IOS(config)# ipv6 router process_ID
IOS(config-router)# router-id router_ID
IOS(config-router)# area area_number
```

The process ID, as in OSPFv2, uniquely identifies the OSPF process locally running on the routing device (it is locally significant and is not shared with other OSPFv3 routing devices). The router ID is a 32-bit number typically represented using a dotted-decimal format. The area number is also a 32-bit number, which can be represented by a decimal (12) or a dotted-decimal (0.0.0.12) format. Here's a simple example:

```
IOS(config)# ipv6 unicast-routing
IOS(config)# ipv6 router process_ID
IOS(config-router)# router-id router_ID
IOS(config-router)# area area_number
```

on the
() o b

Typically when creating router IDs, I use the first digit to represent the area that the router is in. For ABRs, the first number would be 0 and the second number (and possibly the third number) would represent an area the device is located within. The last octet I reserve for the identity of the router within the area. For example, if I had a backbone router with all its interfaces within area 0, its router ID might be 0.0.0.1. If I had an ABR connected to area 1, its router ID might be 0.1.0.5. This helps me quickly identify who the router is and what its role is. You must hard-code the router ID in OSPFv3, and it's optional in OSPFv2. However, even in OSPFv2, I sometimes use this method for certain customers.

OSPFv3 Interface Configuration

Once you set up the global properties for OSPFv3, you must place interfaces into the local process. Unlike OSPFv2, where you used the **network** command within the OSPFv2 routing process configuration, IPv6's configuration is like RIPng, where you perform the configuration under an interface:

```
IOS(config)# interface type [slot_#/]port_#
IOS(config-if)# ipv6 ospf process_ID area area_number
```

Simple OSPFv3 Configuration Example

Here's an example configuration placing two interfaces in area 0:

```
IOS(config)# ipv6 unicast-routing
IOS(config)# ipv6 router ospfv3 1
IOS(config-router)# router-id 0.0.0.1
IOS(config-router)# area 0
IOS(config-router)# exit
IOS(config)# interface g1/0/1
IOS(config-if)# ipv6 ospf 1 area 0
IOS(config-if)# exit
IOS(config)# interface g1/0/2
IOS(config-if)# ipv6 ospf 1 area 0
IOS(config-if)# exit
```

As you can see, the configuration is fairly simple. Remember that your Cisco device does not need a global IPv6 address on an interface in order to participate in OSPFv3—only a link-local address, which it will automatically acquire, assuming IPv6 is globally enabled and the interface is enabled.

OSPFv3 Verification

Once you've configured OSPFv3, you can verify the operation of OSPFv3 by using **show** commands similar to those used in OSPFv2. To display general information about OSPFv3 routing processes, use the **show ipv6 ospf** command. Here's an example:

```
IOS# show ipv6 ospf
Routing Process "ospfv3 1" with ID 10.10.10.1
 SPF schedule delay 5 secs, Hold time between two SPFs 10 secs
 Minimum LSA interval 5 secs. Minimum LSA arrival 1 secs
 LSA group pacing timer 240 secs
 Interface flood pacing timer 33 msecs
 Retransmission pacing timer 66 msecs
 Number of external LSA 0. Checksum Sum 0x000000
 Number of areas in this device is 1. 1 normal 0 stub 0 nssa
    Area BACKBONE(0)
        Number of interfaces in this area is 2
        MD5 Authentication, SPI 1000
        SPF algorithm executed 2 times
        Number of LSA 5. Checksum Sum 0x02A005
        Number of DCbitless LSA 0
        Number of indication LSA 0
        Number of DoNotAge LSA 0
        Flood list length 0
```

In this example, the router's ID is 10.10.10.1 and two interfaces are connected to area 0.

To display IPv6 neighbor discovery (ND) cache information (the actual neighbors), use the **show ipv6 neighbors** command. Here's an example:

```
Router# show ipv6 ospf neighbors
Neighbor ID  Pri  State     Dead Time  Interface ID  Interface
172.16.4.4   1    FULL/  -  00:00:31   14            Serial1/0/1
172.16.3.3   1    FULL/BDR  00:00:30   3             FastEthernet0/0
172.16.5.5   1    FULL/  -  00:00:33   13            Serial1/0/2
```

Use the **show ipv6 route** command to view the routing table. To view only the OSPF routes, add the **ospf** parameter: **show ipv6 route ospf**.

INSIDE THE EXAM

OSPF Overview

Remember that OSPF is an open-standard protocol and either it or EIGRP should be used when dealing with large layer 3 networks: it supports hierarchical routing (two layers—backbone and others) and uses cost as an intelligent metric.

OSPF Operation

Be able to determine an OSPF router's ID based on the interfaces that are active and the loopbacks, if any, that are configured. Understand how OSPF routers form a neighbor relationship and know the components that must match between them. Remember the differences between a two-way state and a full state. Know how LSAs are disseminated and the multicast addresses used for transmitting LSAs. Know the differences between DRs, BDRs, and DROTHERs and when DRs and BDRs are used: broadcast and multi-access segments. Be familiar with how DRs and BDRs are elected and be able to choose which routers will perform which role based on output of router **show** commands and example network illustrations.

OSPF Configuration

Be familiar with the basic configuration of OSPF on Cisco routers: you might have to set

(Continued)

INSIDE THE EXAM

up and/or troubleshoot a basic configuration of OSPF on *multiple* routers (perhaps three to five routers) in a simulation question. Be able to define a process ID. The process ID is locally significant and can range from 1 to 65,535. You need a different process number for each OSPF instance (different autonomous system) a routing device is connected to. Remember that a wildcard mask is used to associate an interface or interfaces with an area in the **network** command. Understand why loopback interfaces are typically configured for OSPF. Be familiar with metrics of OSPF routes and the load-balancing process the routing protocol uses.

OSPF Troubleshooting

Expect questions on OSPF configurations that have problems and be able to pinpoint the problem or problems. Be very familiar

with the various **show** and **debug** commands for OSPF. Know how to read the routing table and pick out OSPF routes and their associated costs. Understand the output of the **show** and **debug** commands and be able to pinpoint problems related to failed neighbor relationships: mismatched timers, incorrect authentication, and mismatched subnets.

OSPFv3 for IPv6

You should be able to compare and contrast OSPF with IPv4 and IPv6. Remember that you must first execute the **ipv6 unicast-routing** command to enable IPv6. Know the command to create an EUI-64 address for a router's interface: **ipv6 address**. Remember how to enable OSPFv3: **ipv6 router ospfv3** *process_ID* (global) and **ipv6 ospf** *process_ID* **area** *area_number* (interface).

CERTIFICATION SUMMARY

OSPF is an open-standard routing protocol for IP, which uses cost as a metric. It uses the Dijkstra algorithm (SPF) to provide a loop-free routing topology and uses incremental updates with route summarization support. OSPF is hierarchical, supporting two layers: backbone (area 0) and areas connected to the backbone. Its downside is that OSPF requires more memory and CPU processes than distance vector protocols, and it is more difficult to configure and troubleshoot.

Each OSPF router has a router ID, which is either the highest IP address on a loopback interface or the highest IP address on an active interface. LSAs are used to develop neighbor relationships and are sent as multicasts every 10 seconds. For

LAN segments, a DR and a BDR are elected (highest router ID) to disseminate routing information. Routers use 224.0.0.6 to send information to the DR/BDR. OSPF is connection oriented in that any routing information sent to another router requires a responding ACK. When DRs share routing information to their neighbors, the multicast address used is 224.0.0.5.

Configuring OSPF requires you to specify a process ID, which is locally significant to the router. When configuring the **network** command, you specify an IP address or network number, a wildcard mask (inverted subnet mask), and a number for the area to which the address or network belongs. The **show ip ospf interface** command displays OSPF information about the router's ID, the DR and BDR, and timer information. The **show ip ospf neighbor** command displays your router's neighbors as well as their OSPF states.

You must first execute the **ipv6 unicast-routing** command to enable IPv6. An address must be assigned to each interface, typically using the EUI-64 method, for it to process IPv6 packets. Like RIPng, OSPFv3 and EIGRP must be configured globally and then enabled on a per-interface basis. In the OSPFv3 global configuration, you define the router ID and the area numbers; you then associate the interfaces to the areas for an OSPF process.

✔ TWO-MINUTE DRILL

OSPF Overview

❑ OSPF is an open-standard, link state protocol. It's classless and supports hierarchical routing and route summarization. It uses cost as a metric, which is the inverse of the bandwidth of a link.

❑ OSPF requires more memory and faster processors to handle its additional information.

OSPF Operation

❑ Each OSPF router has an ID, which is either the highest IP address on a loopback interface, if one exists, or the highest IP address on an active interface.

❑ Routers use LSAs to learn the topology of the network. To share information with another router, the routers must be neighbors: their area numbers and types, timers, and passwords must match.

❑ DRs and BDRs assist in sharing topology information. Traffic sent to a DR/BDR pair is multicast to 224.0.0.6. Traffic sent to all routers on a segment has a destination address of 224.0.0.5. Hello messages are sent out every 10 seconds, with a dead interval timer of 40 seconds. The DR sends a periodic update every 30 minutes.

OSPF Configuration

❑ You must give the OSPF routing process a process ID, which is locally significant to the router. You use a wildcard mask when specifying which interfaces are in which areas and are participating in OSPF: **network** *IP_address wildcard_mask* **area** *area_#*.

❑ Loopback interfaces are always active unless manually disabled and are used to give an OSPF router an ID.

❑ The **bandwidth** command is used to derive a cost value for an interface metric; it should be configured on serial interfaces since the bandwidth defaults to 1544 Kbps on these.

❑ By default, OSPF load-balances across four equal-cost paths to a destination.

OSPF Troubleshooting

❑ The administrative distance for OSPF is 110.

❑ The **show ip ospf interface**, **show ip ospf database**, **show ip ospf neighbor**, **debug ip ospf adj**, and **debug ip ospf events** commands can be used to troubleshoot neighbor relationship problems.

OSPFv3 for IPv6

❑ The **ipv6 unicast-routing** command globally enables IPv6 and must be the first IPv6 command executed on the router.

❑ The **ipv6 router ospf** *process_ID* command takes you into the OSPFv3 routing process, and the **router-id** and **area** commands define the router's ID and the areas the router is connected to. The **ipv6 ospf** *process_ID* **area** *area_number* command associates an interface to a particular OSPF routing process and area. The **show ipv6 route** command displays the IPv6 routes in the IPv6 routing table.

SELF TEST

The following Self Test questions will help you measure your understanding of the material presented in this chapter. Read all the choices carefully, as there may be more than one correct answer. Choose all correct answers for each question.

OSPF Overview

1. Which of the following is false concerning OSPF?
   A. It provides a loop-free topology.
   B. It is a classful protocol and allows for a hierarchical design.
   C. It requires more memory and processing cycles than distance vector protocols.
   D. It is complex to configure and difficult to troubleshoot.

2. OSPF uses _____ as a metric.
   A. bandwidth
   B. delay
   C. cost
   D. hop count

OSPF Operation

3. An OSPF's router ID is based on _____.
   A. the lowest IP address on its loopback interface, if configured, or the lowest IP address on its active interfaces
   B. the highest IP address on its loopback interface, if configured, or the highest IP address on its active interfaces
   C. the highest IP address on its active interfaces, if configured, or the highest IP address on its loopback interfaces
   D. the lowest IP address on its active interfaces, if configured, or the lowest IP address on its loopback interfaces

4. OSPF hellos are sent every _____ seconds on a multi-access medium.
   A. 5
   B. 10
   C. 15
   D. 40

5.   Which of the following is true concerning OSPF?

    A.   Setting an interface priority to 0 causes a router to become a DR on that interface.

    B.   If the dead interval timer doesn't match between two OSPF routers, they will not become neighbors.

    C.   DRs are elected on broadcast, multi-access, and point-to-point segments.

    D.   Routers use a multicast address of 224.0.0.5 to send LSAs to the DR/BDR.

OSPF Configuration

6.   The OSPF process ID is _____.

    A.   locally significant and is the router ID

    B.   globally significant and must match on every router

    C.   locally significant

    D.   an AS number

7.   Enter the OSPF command to include all of its interfaces in area 0: _____.

OSPF Troubleshooting

8.   When examining routes in the routing table, enter the code used to represent OSPF routes: _____.

9.   Which of the following can you not see from the `show ip ospf interface` command?

    A.   Process and router ID of you and the neighboring OSPF routers

    B.   Hello and dead interval timers

    C.   Priority of your router

    D.   Cost of the interface

10.   Two OSPF routers cannot form a neighbor relationship. Which of the following would not cause this problem?

    A.   Hello and dead intervals don't match.

    B.   MTU sizes don't match.

    C.   Subnet masks don't match.

    D.   Router IDs don't match.

OSPFv3 for IPv6

11. Which IPv6 command must first be entered on a Cisco router?
    A. `router ipv6-unicast`
    B. `ipv6 address`
    C. `ipv6 unicast-routing`
    D. `ipv6 support enable`

SELF TEST ANSWERS

OSPF Overview

1. ☑ **B.** OSPF is a classless, not a classful, protocol.
    ☒ **A**, **C**, and **D** are true concerning OSPF.

2. ☑ **C.** OSPF uses cost as a metric.
    ☒ **A**, bandwidth, is used to compute the cost, where cost is the inverse of the bandwidth. **B** is incorrect because delay is used by EIGRP. **D** is incorrect because hop count is used by RIP.

OSPF Operation

3. ☑ **B.** An OSPF's router ID is based on the highest IP address on its loopback interface, if configured, or the highest IP address on its active interfaces.
    ☒ **A** is incorrect because it specifies the lowest IP address. **C** is incorrect because the loopback is used first, if configured. **D** is incorrect because the loopback is checked first.

4. ☑ **B.** OSPF hellos are sent every 10 seconds.
    ☒ **A** and **C** are incorrect timers. **D** is incorrect because 40 is the dead interval timer.

5. ☑ **B.** The hello and dead interval timers, the area number, the OSPF router, the area type, and the MTU sizes must match on a segment for routers to form a neighbor relationship.
    ☒ **A** is incorrect because an interface priority of 0 will cause a router never to become a DR/BDR. **C** is incorrect because point-to-point segments don't use DRs/BDRs. **D** is incorrect because 224.0.0.6 is used when sending LSAs to the DR/BDR.

OSPF Configuration

6. ☑ **C.** The OSPF process ID is locally significant.
    ☒ **A** is incorrect, because the router ID is based on the highest IP address of a loopback or active interface. **B** is incorrect, because it is locally significant. **D** is incorrect, because OSPF requires a process ID to be configured, not an autonomous system number.

7. ☑ `network 0.0.0.0 255.255.255.255 area 0`.

OSPF Troubleshooting

8. ☑ The code used to represent OSPF routes is O. The letter O is used to represent OSPF routes in an IP routing table.

9. ☑ **A.** You can see the router IDs of the other routers off an interface, but not their process IDs, which are locally significant.

    ☒ **B, C,** and **D** can be viewed and are therefore incorrect answers.

10. ☑ **D.** Router IDs in an AS must be unique and cannot match.

    ☒ **A, B,** and **C** must match, as well as the area type, to form a neighbor relationship.

OSPFv3 for IPv6

11. ☑ **C.** The `ipv6 unicast-routing` command globally enables IPv6 and must be the first IPv6 command executed on the router.

    ☒ **A** and **D** are invalid commands. **B** assigns an IPv6 address to an interface.

11
EIGRP Routing

CERTIFICATION OBJECTIVES

I n Chapter 9, you were introduced to the configuration of Routing Information Protocol (RIPv1 and v2), a distance vector routing protocol, and in Chapter 10, you learned about the configuration of Open Shortest Path First (OSPF), a link state protocol. This chapter focuses on Cisco's proprietary routing protocol for TCP/IP: the Enhanced Interior Gateway Routing Protocol (EIGRP). EIGRP is a hybrid protocol; fundamentally, it is a distance vector protocol with many link state protocol advantages built into it. This chapter covers only the basic operation and configuration of EIGRP. A more thorough discussion is covered in Cisco's CCNP-level courses and exams.

CERTIFICATION OBJECTIVE 11.01

EIGRP Overview

EIGRP is a Cisco-proprietary routing protocol for TCP/IP. It's actually based on Cisco's proprietary IGRP routing protocol, with many enhancements built into it. Because it has its roots in IGRP, the configuration is similar to IGRP; however, it has many link state characteristics that were added to it to allow EIGRP to scale to enterprise network sizes. These characteristics include the following:

- Fast convergence
- Loop-free topology
- Variable Length Subnet Masking (VLSM) and route summarization
- Multicast and incremental updates
- Multiple *routed* protocols

The following sections cover some of the characteristics of EIGRP, its operation, and its configuration.

As of Cisco IOS release 12.3, Cisco no longer supports its older sibling, IGRP; EIGRP is still supported and widely deployed, however.

EIGRP has the following characteristics:

- Uses multicast addresses to disseminate routing information
- Offers load balancing across six paths to a destination (equal or unequal metrics)

- Supports an intelligent and complex metric structure
- Has fast convergence (triggered updates when changes occur and saves neighbors' routing tables locally)
- Has little network overhead, since it uses incremental updates

Metrics and Interoperability

Like its older cousin IGRP, EIGRP uses the same metric structure, based on these components: bandwidth, delay, reliability, load, and maximum transmission unit (MTU). By default, only *bandwidth* and *delay* are used in the metric computation and the other values are turned off; however, you can manually enable these values in the metric algorithm.

One interesting point about the IGRP and EIGRP routing protocols is that if you have some routers in your network running IGRP and others running EIGRP, and both sets have the same autonomous system number configured, routing information will *automatically* be shared between the two. This makes it easy to migrate from IGRP to EIGRP. When sharing routes between the two routing protocols, the routers have to perform a conversion concerning the metrics. Even though both protocols use the same metric components, they store them in different size values: EIGRP uses a 32-bit metric, while IGRP uses a 24-bit metric. When integrating the two protocols together, EIGRP routes are divided by 256 to fit a 24-bit metric structure when passed to IGRP, and IGRP routes are multiplied by 256 to fit a 32-bit metric structure when passed to EIGRP.

Routing Tables and Updates

EIGRP uses the Diffusing Update Algorithm (DUAL) to update the local routing table. This algorithm enables very fast convergence by storing a neighbor's routing information in a local topology table. If a primary route in the routing table fails, DUAL can take a backup route from the topology table (a neighbor's routing table) and place this into the routing table without necessarily having to talk to other EIGRP neighboring routers to find an alternative path to the destination.

EIGRP supports both automatic and manual summarization. Remember that EIGRP is, at heart, a distance vector protocol, and therefore it will automatically summarize routes across Class A, B, and C network boundaries, as was discussed in Chapter 5. You can also manually summarize within a class network at your discretion. Configuration of summarization is beyond the scope of this book, but it is covered in depth in Cisco's CCNP-level material.

One really unique feature of EIGRP is that it supports three routed protocols: IP (IPv4 and IPv6), Internetwork Packet Exchange (IPX), and AppleTalk. In other words, EIGRP can route for all three of these protocols simultaneously. If you are running these routed protocols in your environment, EIGRP is a perfect fit. You need to run only one routing protocol for all three instead of running a separate routing protocol for each, definitely reducing your routing overhead.

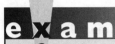

EIGRP supports route summarization and routing for IPv4, IPv6, IPX, and AppleTalk. The DUAL algorithm is used to build a loop-free routing topology.

CERTIFICATION OBJECTIVE 11.02

EIGRP Operation

Unlike most distance vector routing protocols, EIGRP learns a partial topology of the network beyond its directly connected neighbor. Like OSPF, EIGRP uses hello packets to discover and maintain neighbor relationships (stored in a neighbor table) and to share routing information (stored in the topology and routing tables). EIGRP uses the multicast address of 224.0.0.10 for the destination in its hello packets. EIGRP generates hello packets every 5 seconds on LAN, point-to-point, and multipoint connections faster than T1/E1 speeds. Otherwise, hellos are generated every 60 seconds. The dead interval period is three times the hello interval.

EIGRP supports multicast and incremental updates. Hello packets are generated every 5 seconds on LAN interfaces as multicasts (224.0.0.10). Hellos are used to maintain the EIGRP neighbor and the EIGRP topology tables in RAM.

Building Neighbor Relationships

For EIGRP routers to become neighbors, the following information must match in their hello packets:

- The autonomous system (AS) number
- The K-values (these enable/disable the different metric components used in the DUAL algorithm)

Unlike OSPF, the hello and hold-down timers on the two routers do *not* need to match in order for the routers to become neighbors.

When two routers determine whether they will become neighbors, they go through the following process:

1. The first router generates a hello with its configuration information.
2. If the configuration information matches (AS number and K-values), the second router responds with an *update* message with its local topology information.
3. The first router responds with an ACK message, acknowledging the receipt of the second router's *update* message.
4. The first router then sends its topology to the second router via an *update* message.
5. The second router responds with an ACK.

At this point, the two routers have converged. This process differs from that of OSPF, where routing information is disseminated via a designated router. With EIGRP, any router can share routing information with any other router. As you can see from the preceding steps, EIGRP, like OSPF, is connection oriented: certain EIGRP messages sent by a router will cause it to expect an acknowledgment (ACK) from the destination(s). Here are the message types for which an EIGRP router expects an ACK back:

- **Update**   Contains a routing update
- **Query**   Asks a neighboring router to validate routing information
- **Reply**   Responds to a query message

ⓦatch *EIGRP has five message types: hello, update, query, reply, and acknowledgment.*

If an EIGRP router doesn't receive an ACK from these three packet types, the router will try a total of 16 times to resend the information. After this, the router declares the neighbor dead. When a router sends a hello packet, however, no corresponding ACK is expected in return.

Choosing Routes

EIGRP can use the following metric components when choosing a route: bandwidth, delay, reliability, load, and MTU. By default, however, only bandwidth and delay are activated (the MTU size, however, is exchanged between the peers, even though it's not used by default). Bandwidth and delay are the K1 and K3 values.

on the
ⓙob *Because bandwidth is used in EIGRP's metric computation, it is important that you match up this value correctly with the speed of your serial interfaces. Cisco assumes that a serial interface is connected to a T1 connection, so if this is incorrect, use the* bandwidth *command to correct it (discussed in Chapter 4). Remember to put the bandwidth value in Kbps.*

ⓦatch *Be familiar with the terms in Table 11-1.*

Table 11-1 explains important terms used by EIGRP.

EIGRP uses a less complicated approach than OSPF when choosing best-path routes to a destination and is thus less CPU intensive; however, it does have more overhead than a distance vector protocol, such as RIPv2. EIGRP routers keep topology information in a *topology table.* The topology table contains the routes that neighbors are advertising, the advertised distances (metrics) of the neighbor for these routers, and the feasible distances of this router to reach these network destinations. A *successor route* is a path in the topology table that has the best metric (feasible distance) compared to all the other alternative paths to the same network destination. A *feasible successor* is a valid backup route to the successor route.

ⓦatch *Successor routes are stored in the IP routing and EIGRP topology tables. A feasible successor is a valid backup route that can be used if the successor route is no longer valid.*

TABLE 11-1	Important EIGRP Terms

Term	Definition
Neighbor table	Contains a list of the EIGRP neighbors and is similar to the adjacencies that are built in OSPF between the designated router/backup DR and the other routers on a segment. Each routed protocol (IP, IPX, and AppleTalk) for EIGRP has its own neighbor table.
Topology table	Similar to OSPF's database, contains a list of all destinations and paths the EIGRP router learned—it is basically a compilation of the neighboring routers' routing tables. A separate topology table exists for each routed protocol.
Successor	The best path to reach a destination within the topology table.
Feasible successor	The best backup path to reach a destination within the topology table—multiple successors can be feasible for a particular destination.
Routing table	This is all of the *successor* routes from the topology table. There is a separate routing table for each routed protocol.
Advertised distance	The distance (metric) that a neighboring router is advertising for a specific route.
Feasible distance	The distance (metric) that your router has computed to reach a specific route: the advertised distance from the neighboring router plus the local router's interface metric.

Not just any route can be chosen as a feasible successor. For a route to be considered a feasible successor in the topology table, the neighbor router's advertised distance must be *less than* that of the original route's feasible distance. If a successor route in the routing table fails and a feasible successor exists in the topology table, the EIGRP router goes into a *passive* state—it immediately takes the feasible successor route from the topology table and puts it in the routing table, converging almost instantaneously. If the EIGRP router does not have a feasible successor in the topology table, it will go into an *active* state and generate a query packet for the route in question. This query is sent to the neighbor or neighbors that originally advertised this route.

The concern that EIGRP has with nonfeasible successor routes is that the path these routers are advertising might be part of a routing loop. EIGRP goes into an active state for these paths to verify this by double-checking with these neighbors. The neighbors will verify the information that they have in their topology table and reply to the requester with the appropriate information concerning these alternative paths. The terms *passive* and *active* can be misleading—passive means that a valid alternative route exists and can be immediately used in the routing table without contacting any of the advertising neighbors, while active indicates that an alternative path exists but might or might not be valid.

e x a m

ⓦatch　　*When a successor route is no longer available and no feasible successor route exists in the topology table, a multicast EIGRP query is sent to all other neighbors advertising the same route to determine whether they have a valid path (successor route) to the destination network.*

CERTIFICATION OBJECTIVE 11.03

EIGRP Configuration

Setting up EIGRP is almost as simple as configuring RIPv2:

```
Router(config)# router eigrp autonomous_system_#
Router(config-router)# network IP_network_# [subnet_mask]
```

As you can see from these commands, enabling EIGRP is straightforward: you need to enter an autonomous system (AS) number and **network** statements for interfaces that will participate in EIGRP. The AS number must match that of the neighboring routers, or the adjacency process will fail. Note that the network numbers you specify are *classful* network numbers, even though EIGRP is *classless*. Optionally, you can qualify the network number with a subnet mask value, including only certain subnets of a class address in the EIGRP AS.

e x a m

ⓦatch　　*You must specify the AS number when configuring EIGRP. The AS number must match that of the neighboring routers, or the adjacency process will fail. Even though EIGRP is classless, by default you configure it as a classful protocol when specifying your network numbers with the* network *command. For example,* network 172.16.0.0 *would include the interfaces associated with subnets 172.16.1.0/24 and 172.16.100.0/24.*

EIGRP Configuration Example

Let's look at a simple example, shown in Figure 11-1, to help illustrate how to configure EIGRP on a router.

Here's the routing configuration of the router for Figure 11-1:

```
IOS(config)# router eigrp 200
IOS(config-router)# network 172.16.0.0
IOS(config-router)# network 10.0.0.0
```

This router has four interfaces: 172.16.1.1/24, 172.16.2.1/24, 10.1.1.1/24, and 10.1.2.1/24. Remember that when configuring your **network** commands, put in only the Class A, B, or C network numbers, or qualify them with a subnet mask. In the preceding example, the Class B and A network numbers were entered, activating EIGRP routing on all four interfaces.

11.01. The digital resources that accompany this book contain a multimedia demonstration of configuring EIGRP on a router.

You could also have been more specific with your **network** statements by including the subnet mask value to include specific interfaces in the EIGRP AS, like this:

```
IOS(config)# router eigrp 200
IOS(config-router)# network 172.16.1.0 255.255.255.0
IOS(config-router)# network 172.16.2.0 255.255.255.0
IOS(config-router)# network 10.1.1.0 255.255.255.0
IOS(config-router)# network 10.1.2.0 255.255.255.0
```

FIGURE 11-1

EIGRP network example

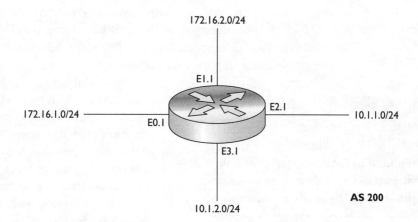

on the !ob *Either of these two approaches will work in the example in Figure 11-1; however, in practice, I recommend using the latter, especially in situations where your router might be running more than one routing protocol, such as EIGRP and OSPF, and you want only certain subnets of a class address included in each routing protocol. Also, the EIGRP routing process supports a* shutdown *command, which allows you to disable EIGRP without having to remove its configuration. You can use the* no shutdown *command in the EIGRP routing process to re-enable it.*

Other EIGRP Commands

You should be aware of three other configurations when enabling EIGRP: load balancing, summarization, and authentication of routing updates.

Load Balancing

EIGRP supports load balancing across six paths to the same destination. By default, EIGRP will do only equal-cost load balancing. With equal-cost load balancing, EIGRP will only use successor routers that have the same metric value. However, you can enable *unequal*-cost load balancing of EIGRP routes by using the **variance** and **traffic-share** Router Subconfiguration mode commands.

To enable unequal-cost paths for EIGRP, use the **variance** Router Subconfiguration mode command:

```
IOS(config)# router eigrp autonomous_system_#
IOS(config-router)# variance multiplier
```

The *multiplier* value is a positive integer. By default, the variance is equal to one. To use an unequal-cost path (less preferred), the router multiplies the best metric path (feasible distance) by the multiplier value; if the less preferred path's metric (advertised distance) is less than this value, the router will include it in the routing table along with the best metric path.

The multiplier can range from 1 to 128. The default is 1, which means the EIGRP router will use only the best metric path(s). If you increase the multiplier, the router will use any route that has a metric less than the best metric route multiplied by the variance value. Care must be taken, however, to ensure that you do not set a variance value too high; otherwise, routing loops may accidentally be created.

exam ⓦatch *Use the* variance *command to load-balance across unequal-cost paths. The default is to place only equal-cost paths in the routing table.*

e x a m

ⓦ a t c h   *Be able to correctly compute additional successor routes added to the routing table by using a variance multiplier.*

To illustrate how this is used, examine Table 11-2. In this example, three neighbors are advertising the same route, 192.168.1.0/24, to your router. By default, RouterB has the best feasible distance and is thus used in your router's routing table as a successor route. If you set the variance to 2, then RouterC's alternative path could also be included in the routing table along with RouterB's successor route: RouterC's FD (60) is less than 2 times RouterB's FD (40). In other words, 60 < 2 × 40 (or 80). RouterD's path is not used since its FD is greater than 2 times RouterB's FD.

When load balancing, the router will do the process intelligently. In other words, if you have two WAN links (64 Kbps and 128 Kbps) included in the routing table to reach a single destination, it makes no sense to send half of the traffic down the 64-Kbps link and the other half down the 128-Kbps link. In this situation, you would probably saturate your slower-speed 64-Kbps link. EIGRP, instead, will load-balance traffic in proportion to the inverse of the metric for the path. So, given this example, about one-third of the traffic would be sent down the 64-Kbps link and two-thirds down the 128-Kbps link.

You can override this behavior with the **traffic-share** Router Subconfiguration mode command:

```
IOS(config)# router eigrp autonomous_system_#
IOS(config-router)# traffic-share balanced
```

or

```
IOS(config-router)# traffic-share min across-interfaces
```

The first command provides the default behavior for load balancing, as was explained in the preceding paragraph. The **min** parameter has the router put the unequal-cost paths in the router's routing table; however, the router won't use these routes unless the best metric route fails. This is used when you don't want to

TABLE 11-2
Example EIGRP Topology Table for Variance Computation

Network Number	Neighboring Router	Feasible Distance (FD)	Advertised Distance (AD)
192.168.1.0/24	RouterB	40	20
	RouterC	60	20
	RouterD	85	35

use the worse connections, which perhaps are slower connections such as dial-up, but you still want to take advantage of fast convergence: when the primary path fails, the secondary path is already in the routing table.

Note that by using the variance feature, you can introduce additional paths to a destination in your IP routing table. By doing this, when one path fails, you already have a backup path in the routing table, so convergence is instantaneous. If you want your router to use only the best path, but you want to put the alternative paths in the routing table, use the `traffic-share min across-interfaces` command.

When testing load balancing from a router, be careful to not use ping or traceroute since these packets are process switched instead of fast switched or CEF switched, which can produce confusing results in the load-balancing tests: each possible path is tested. Instead, preferably, perform the test from any other device behind the load-balancing router.

Summarization

EIGRP automatically summarizes routes on a class boundary (shown in the top part of Figure 11-2). For example, if a router is connected to subnets in 172.16.0.0/16 and a separate network, such as 192.168.1.0/24, then EIGRP

FIGURE 11-2

Discontiguous
subnets

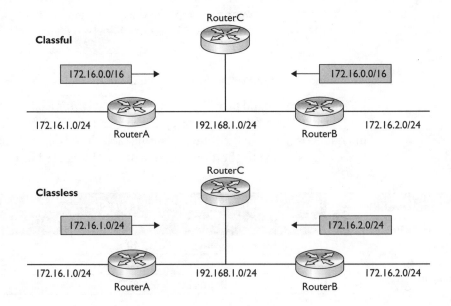

will send the 172.16.0.0/16 route out the 192.168.1.0/24 interface (instead of the specific subnets of 172.16.0.0/16). If your network is split into two parts, 172.16.1.0/24 and 172.16.2.0/24, but is connected by 192.168.1.0/24, this would cause reachability problems, since the two sides would advertise 172.16.0.0/16 at the network boundary. This problem was discussed in Chapter 5.

To turn off automatic summarization for an AS, use the following configuration:

```
IOS(config)# router eigrp autonomous_system_#
IOS(config-router)# no auto-summary
```

exam

⚙️atch *Use the* no *auto-summary command on an EIGRP router when you have discontiguous subnets of a class address with the EIGRP routing process.*

By turning off automatic summarization, you are turning the EIGRP process into a classless protocol, like that shown in the bottom of Figure 11-2. Manual summarization of routes using EIGRP is beyond the scope of this book.

Neighbor Authentication

EIGRP supports authentication of routing updates from neighboring peers using the Message Digest 5 (MD5) algorithm. Using MD5 to authenticate routing updates ensures that your routers accept updates only from authorized routers and prevents unsupported routers from injecting bad routing updates into your routing process.

Setting up EIGRP authentication is a three-step process: enabling EIGRP, defining a key to use for MD5 authentication, and enabling authentication. Enabling EIGRP was discussed earlier. This section will focus on the latter two steps.

To define the keys used for MD5 authentication, use the following configuration:

```
IOS(config)# key chain name_of_key_chain
IOS(config-keychain)# key key_number
IOS(config-keychain-key)# key-string key_value
IOS(config-keychain-key)# accept-lifetime start_time
                {infinite | end_time | duration seconds}
IOS(config-keychain-key)# send-lifetime start_time
                {infinite | end_time | duration seconds}
```

The **key chain** command specifies the name of the key chain information to use, commonly referred to as a *key ring*; the name is locally significant and takes you into a subcommand mode. The **key** subcommand mode command specifies the number of the key, which must match on all routers on the segment using the authentication key; this command takes you into a second subcommand mode. The **key-string** command specifies the actual authentication key, which can be up to 16 characters in length. Each key can have a separate lifetime value, allowing different keys to be used at different times; however, if you use this approach, it's recommended that you use the Network Time Protocol (NTP) to synchronize the date and time on your routers. The **accept-lifetime** command specifies when you'll accept the key value, and the **send-lifetime** command specifies when you'll use this key to create authenticated EIGRP routing updates. If you don't specify either set of time values, the default to the current time is valid indefinitely.

To enable authentication, you set up your EIGRP configuration on an interface:

```
IOS(config)# interface type number
IOS(config-if)# ip authentication mode eigrp AS_# md5
IOS(config-if)# ip authentication key-chain
                eigrp AS_# key_chain_name
```

As you can see from this configuration, you must enable authentication for the EIGRP AS number and then specify the name of the key chain you'll use. Note that since you are referencing a key chain, you can have different keys being used for different interfaces; however, all routers in the same subnet need to use the same keying information.

Let's look at a simple example of two routers' configurations using authentication. Both routers are connected to the same Ethernet segment and/or VLAN. Here's RouterA's configuration:

```
RouterA(config)# key chain RouterAchain
RouterA(config-keychain)# key 1
RouterA(config-keychain-key)# key-string 0123456789
Router(config)# interface fastethernet 0/0
Router(config-if)# ip authentication mode eigrp 100 md5
Router(config-if)# ip authentication key-chain eigrp 100
                RouterAchain
```

Here's RouterB's configuration:

```
RouterB(config)# key chain RouterBchain
RouterB(config-keychain)# key 1
RouterB(config-keychain-key)# key-string 0123456789
RouterB(config)# interface fastethernet 1/0
Router(config-if)# ip authentication mode eigrp 100 md5
Router(config-if)# ip authentication key-chain eigrp 100
                RouterBchain
```

CERTIFICATION OBJECTIVE 11.04

EIGRP Troubleshooting

Following are some of the common commands you'll use when viewing and troubleshooting EIGRP on your router:

- `show ip protocols`
- `show ip route`
- `show ip eigrp neighbors`
- `show ip eigrp topology`
- `show ip eigrp interfaces`
- `show ip eigrp traffic`
- `debug ip eigrp`
- `debug eigrp packets`

The following sections cover these commands.

The show ip protocols Command

You can use the **show ip protocols** command to display the IP routing protocols that have been configured and are running on your router. Here is an example of this command for EIGRP:

```
IOS# show ip protocols
Routing Protocol is "eigrp 200"
  Outgoing update filter list for all interfaces is not set
  Incoming update filter list for all interfaces is not set
  Default networks flagged in outgoing updates
  Default networks accepted from incoming updates
  EIGRP metric weight K1=1, K2=0, K3=1, K4=0, K5=0
  EIGRP maximum hopcount 100
  EIGRP maximum metric variance 1
  Redistributing: eigrp 200
  Automatic network summarization is in effect
  Automatic address summarization:
    10.0.0.0/8 for Serial0
  Maximum path: 4
  Routing for Networks:
```

```
          10.0.0.0
          192.168.4.0
     Routing Information Sources:
          Gateway         Distance         Last Update
          (this router)         90         00:00:08
          192.168.4.101         90         00:00:06
     Distance: internal 90 external 170
```

In this command, you can see that the AS is 200 and the variance is 1 (only equal-cost load balancing). The K1 and K3 metrics are enabled, which means that only bandwidth and delay are used by the DUAL algorithm when computing a metric. Two **network** statements are configured: 10.0.0.0 and 192.168.4.0. There is one neighboring router, 192.168.4.101. The administrative distance of internal EIGRP (routers in the same AS number) is 90.

11.02. The digital resources that accompany this book contain a multimedia demonstration of the `show ip protocols` *command for EIGRP on a router.*

The show ip route Command

To view the EIGRP routes in your router's routing table, use the **show ip route** command:

```
IOS# show ip route
Codes: C - connected, S - static, I - IGRP, R - RIP,
       M - mobile, B - BGP, D - EIGRP, EX - EIGRP external,
       O - OSPF, IA - OSPF inter area, N1 - OSPF NSSA
       external type 1, N2 - OSPF NSSA external type 2,
       E1 - OSPF external type 1, E2 - OSPF external type 2,
       E - EGP, i - IS-IS, L1 - IS-IS level-1,
       L2 - IS-IS level-2, * - candidate default,
       U - per-user static route, o - ODR,
       T - traffic engineered route
Gateway of last resort is not set
     10.0.0.0/8 is variably subnetted, 2 subnets, 2 masks
C       10.0.4.0/24 is directly connected, FastEthernet0
D    192.168.100.0/24 [90/2195456] via 192.168.4.101, 00:00:08, Serial0
D    192.168.101.0/24 [90/2195837] via 192.168.3.1, 00:00:05, Ethernet0
                      [90/2195837] via 192.168.3.2, 00:00:03, Ethernet0
C    192.168.4.0/24 is directly connected, Serial0
```

11.03. The digital resources that accompany this book contain a multimedia demonstration of the `show ip route` command for EIGRP on a router.

At the bottom of the display, a D in the first column refers to an EIGRP route. In this example, there is one EIGRP route that was learned from 192.168.4.101. For an EIGRP route, you'll see two sets of values in brackets ([]). The first value indicates the administrative distance of the route (90) and the second the feasible distance of the router (the metric). Following this you can see the peer with which the route is associated, how long ago an update was received concerning this route or neighbor, and which local interface on the router to use to reach the neighbor. Notice that for network 192.168.101.0/24 there are two successor routes with the same metric, which means the router will load-balance traffic across these two paths to this destination.

A *D in the routing table indicates an EIGRP route. EIGRP has a default administrative distance of 90.*

If you are not seeing EIGRP routes in the routing table for a peer, check the following on your router:

- Make sure the interface is operational and that you don't have a layer 2 or layer 3 problem: **show interfaces**.
- Make sure you have EIGRP neighbors with the **show ip eigrp neighbors** command.
- Make sure the correct K-values are enabled on both EIGRP routers, the **network** commands are configured correctly, and that both routers are in the same EIGRP AS: use the **show ip protocols** command to verify this.

To view only the EIGRP routes in the routing table, use the `show ip route eigrp` command. The `show ip route` command displays routes for all routing protocols: connected, static, and dynamic protocols.

The show ip eigrp neighbors Command

To view the list of EIGRP neighbors that your router has learned, use the **show ip eigrp neighbors** command:

```
IOS# show ip eigrp neighbors
IP-EIGRP neighbors for process 200
Address          Interface  Hold  Uptime    SRTT  RTO   Q    Seq
                            (sec)           (ms)        Cnt  Num
192.168.4.101 Se0           13    00:02:10  610   3660  0    4
```

This example has one neighbor (192.168.4.101). Table 11-3 explains the output of this command.

on the
job

If you see a log message on your router about your router and a neighboring EIGRP router "not on a common subnet," then you have misconfigured the IP addressing on either your router or the peer router (they're in different subnets).

Video

11.04. The digital resources that accompany this book contain a multimedia demonstration of the show ip eigrp neighbors *command for EIGRP on a router.*

exam
watch

The show ip eigrp neighbors command is used to display EIGRP routers that have adjacencies to your router, their IP addresses, the retransmit intervals, and their queue counts. If you are not seeing a neighbor, make sure that your network commands in the EIGRP routing process include the interface your neighbor is connected to.

TABLE 11-3   Fields from the show ip eigrp neighbors Command

Field	Description
Process	AS number of the EIGRP routing process for the neighbor; if your router is running more than one AS, you'll see different sections of neighbors, each listed under a different AS number
Address	IP address of the EIGRP neighbor
Interface	Your router's interface on which you are receiving the neighbor's hellos
Hold	The remaining time left before you declare your neighbor dead when you are not seeing hello messages from the neighbor
Uptime	Length of time that you have known your neighbor
SRTT (smooth round-trip time)	The measured amount of time, in milliseconds, that it takes for your router to send EIGRP information to a neighbor and to get an ACK back
RTO	The amount of time, in milliseconds, that your router will wait before resending an EIGRP packet from the transmission queue to a neighbor
Q Cnt	The number of update/query/reply packets that you have queued up, ready to be sent to the neighbor
Seq Num	The sequence number of the update/query/reply packet that your neighbor last sent

The show ip eigrp topology Command

To see the list of successors and feasible successors, as well as other types of EIGRP routes learned from EIGRP neighbors, use the **show ip eigrp topology** command:

```
IOS# show ip eigrp topology
IP-EIGRP Topology Table for AS(200)/ID(192.168.4.100)

Codes: P - Passive, A - Active, U - Update, Q - Query,
       R - Reply,r - Reply status
P 10.10.10.0 255.255.255.0, 2 successors, FD is 0
        via 10.10.1.1    (46251776/46226176), Ethernet0
        via 10.10.2.1    (46251776/46226176), Ethernet1
        via 10.10.1.3    (46277376/46251776), Ethernet0
```

11.05. The digital resources that accompany this book contain a multimedia demonstration of the `show ip eigrp topology` *command for EIGRP on a router.*

When a route is listed for a neighbor, you'll see two values in parentheses. The first value is the feasible distance (the metric value for your router to reach the destination), while the second value is the advertised distance (the metric value the neighbor is advertising). In this example, you can see two successor routes (the first two), but no feasible successor routes (FD is 0). Also notice that 10.10.10.0 is in a passive state (P), since it has two successor routes. Remember that for there to be a feasible successor, the advertised distance of the route has to be less than (not less than or equal to) the current successor route. In this case, the third route's advertised distance is the same as the two successor routes, so it's not a feasible successor. In addition to seeing a passive code (P), other codes you can see are active (A—where EIGRP is computing possible paths to a destination), update (U—where an update was sent to the destination), query (Q—where a query was sent to the destination), reply (R—where a reply packet was sent to a destination), and reply status (r—where the router sent a query and is waiting for a reply).

exam

ⓦatch *The topology table displays all routes/paths to each destination. Be able to pick out successor and feasible successor routes from the output of the* `show ip eigrp topology` *command.*

The show ip eigrp interfaces Command

To see information about the interfaces on which EIGRP is enabled, use the following command:

```
IOS# show ip eigrp interfaces
IP EIGRP interfaces for process 100
                Xmit Queue  Mean  Pacing Time  Multicast  Pending
 Int  Peers  Un/Reliable   SRTT  Un/Reliable  Flow Timer  Routes
 Et0/0  1        0/0        337      0/10          0          0
 Se1/0  1        0/0         10      1/63         103         0
```

Optionally, you can qualify the output by specifying an interface after the **interfaces** parameter. Table 11-4 explains the information found in the preceding output. In this example, EIGRP is enabled for Ethernet0/0 and Serial1/0 in AS 100, and one EIGRP peer is off of each interface.

The show ip eigrp traffic Command

To see information about traffic statistics for EIGRP, use the following command:

```
IOS# show ip eigrp traffic
IP-EIGRP Traffic Statistics for process 200
  Hellos sent/received: 274/139
  Updates sent/received: 3/4
```

TABLE 11-4   Fields from the show ip eigrp interfaces Command

Field	Description
Int	Interface on which the EIGRP process is enabled
Peers	Number of EIGRP peers in the AS seen off of the associated interface
Xmit Queue Un/Reliable	Number of EIGRP packets remaining queued up in the Unreliable and Reliable queues
Mean SRTT	Average smooth round-trip time (SRTT) in milliseconds between all neighbors off of the interface
Pacing Time Un/Reliable	Number of milliseconds the router waits after transmitting Unreliable and Reliable EIGRP packets
Multicast Flow Timer	Number of milliseconds to wait for an acknowledgment of a sent EIGRP multicast packet before transmitting another multicast packet
Pending Routes	Number of EIGRP routes in packets waiting to be sent from the transmit queue on the specified interface

```
Queries sent/received: 1/0
Replies sent/received: 0/1
Acks sent/received: 4/3
Input queue high water mark 1, 0 drops
SIA-Queries sent/received: 0/0
SIA-Replies sent/received: 0/0
```

As you can see from this output, the router is sending and receiving hellos and updates and is sharing information with neighboring EIGRP routers.

11.06. The digital resources that accompany this book contain a multimedia demonstration of the `show ip eigrp traffic` *command for EIGRP on a router.*

The debug ip eigrp Command

To troubleshoot EIGRP routing problems, you can use **debug** commands. The following command displays EIGRP events (other parameters are available for this command):

```
IOS# debug ip eigrp
IP-EIGRP: 10.0.4.0/24 - don't advertise out Serial0
IP-EIGRP: 192.168.4.0/24 - do advertise out Serial0
IP-EIGRP: 10.0.0.0/8 - do advertise out Serial0
IP-EIGRP: Int 10.0.0.0/8 metric 28160 - 25600 2560
IP-EIGRP: Processing incoming UPDATE packet
IP-EIGRP: Int 192.168.100.0/24 M 2195456 - 1657856
          537600 SM 281600 - 56000 25600
IP-EIGRP: 192.168.100.0/24 routing table not updated
IP-EIGRP: 10.0.4.0/24 - don't advertise out Serial0
IP-EIGRP: 192.168.4.0/24 - do advertise out Serial0
IP-EIGRP: 10.0.0.0/8 - do advertise out Serial0
IP-EIGRP: Int 10.0.0.0/8 metric 28160 - 25600 2560
IP-EIGRP: Processing incoming UPDATE packet
IP-EIGRP: Int 10.0.0.0/8 M 4294967295 - 1657856
          4294967295 SM 4294967295 - 1657856 4294967295
```

In this example, I disabled and re-enabled Serial0. As you can see, it is advertising 192.168.4.0 to its neighbor connected to this interface.

11.07. The digital resources that accompany this book contain a multimedia demonstration of the `debug ip eigrp` *command for EIGRP on a router.*

The debug eigrp packets Command

If you see an EIGRP neighbor as a peer and/or see EIGRP routing updates from the peer in the routing table, the two peers are using matching keys for authentication. If you don't see a router as a neighbor (**show ip eigrp neighbors**) when you expect to see a peer as a neighbor, this could indicate an authentication problem. When using the **debug eigrp packets** command and you see "authentication mismatch" and "dropping peer, invalid authentication" messages, then the two peers have an authentication configuration problem:

```
IOS# debug eigrp packets
EIGRP Packets debugging is on
    (UPDATE, REQUEST, QUERY, REPLY, HELLO, IPXSAP, PROBE,
     ACK, STUB, SIAQUERY, SIAREPLY)
EIGRP: pkt key id = 2, authentication mismatch
EIGRP: Serial0/1: ignored packet from 192.168.1.2,
    opcode = 5 (invalid authentication)
EIGRP: Dropping peer, invalid authentication
EIGRP: Sending HELLO on Serial0/1
AS 100, Flags 0x0, Seq 0/0 idbQ 0/0 iidbQ un/rely 0/0
%DUAL-5-NBRCHANGE: IP-EIGRP(0) 100: Neighbor 192.168.1.2
 (Serial0/1) is down: Auth failure
```

Make sure the lifetime values match between peer routers so that when changing from one key to another, the right key value is used to authenticate the routing updates successfully—this is a common misconfiguration that causes authentication to fail.

If you see a "Mismatched adjacency values" or "K-Value mismatch" message in the preceding **debug** command output, it could be caused by a mismatch in the AS number or a mismatch in the K-values enabled on the two EIGRP routers.

11.08. The digital resources that accompany this book contain a multimedia demonstration of the debug eigrp packets *command for EIGRP on a router.*

CERTIFICATION OBJECTIVE 11.05

EIGRP for IPv6

EIGRP has been updated to support IPv6 routing, formally referred to as EIGRP for IPv6. EIGRP for IPv6 is a stand-alone process and not part of the EIGRP for IPv4 configuration. It supports the same features as its older EIGRP implementation for IPv4: DUAL algorithm, rich metric structure, load balancing, and many others.

The scalability features found in EIGRP for IPv4, neighbor discovery, the DUAL algorithm, metrics, load balancing, multicast, and incremental updates, are also found in EIGRP for IPv6. Like EIGRP for IPv4, EIGRP for IPv6 uses hello packets to discover and become neighbors with other local EIGRP for IPv6 routers. Also like EIGRP for IPv4, EIGRP for IPv6 uses multicasts, but the FF02::A IPv6 multicast link-local address is used. This section provides a cursory introduction to the configuration of EIGRP for IPv6.

EIGRP for IPv6 Global Configuration

Here are the basic global commands to enable EIGRP for IPv6:

```
IOS(config)# ipv6 unicast-routing
IOS(config)# ipv6 router eigrp autonomous_system
IOS(config-rtr)# eigrp router-id router_ID
IOS(config-rtr)# [no] shutdown
```

The first command enables IPv6 on the routing devices. The second command specifies the autonomous system that the routing device is associated with. As with EIGRP for IPv4, the autonomous system number must match between two routers or they will not form a neighbor relationship.

The **eigrp router-id** command defines the router's 32-bit ID. You can represent this as a decimal or dotted-decimal number, like 10.1.1.1. The **shutdown** command disables or enables the EIGRP process. Depending on IOS version, the default can vary.

e x a m

ⓦatch *Enable the EIGRP routing process for IPv6 with the* `no shutdown` *command.*

EIGRP for IPv6 Interface Configuration

Once you set up the global properties for EIGRP for IPv6, you must place interfaces into the local process. Unlike EIGRP for IPv4, where you use the **network** command within the EIGRP routing process configuration, IPv6's configuration is like RIPng and OSPFv3, where you perform the configuration under an interface:

```
IOS(config)# interface type [slot_#/]port_#
IOS(config-if)# ipv6 eigrp autonomous_system
```

EIGRP for IPv6 Simple Configuration

Here's an example configuration placing two interfaces in autonomous system 100:

```
IOS(config)# ipv6 unicast-routing
IOS(config)# ipv6 router eigrp 100
IOS(config-router)# eigrp router-id 100.1.1.1
IOS(config-router)# no shutdown
IOS(config)# interface g1/0/1
IOS(config-if)# ipv6 eigrp 100
IOS(config-if)# exit
IOS(config)# interface g1/0/2
IOS(config-if)# ipv6 eigrp 100
IOS(config-if)# exit
```

As you can see, the configuration is fairly simple and very similar to OSPFv3's configuration. Remember that your Cisco device does not need a global IPv6 address on an interface in order to participate in EIGRP for IPv6—only a link-local address, which it will automatically acquire, assuming IPv6 is globally enabled and the interface is enabled.

EIGRP for IPv6 Verification

To verify the neighbor relationships for EIGRP for IPv6, use the **show ipv6 eigrp neighbors** command:

```
IOS# show ipv6 eigrp neighbors
IPv6-EIGRP neighbors for AS (100)
H Address
Intf   Hold   Uptime    SRTT   RTO   Q   Seq
                        (sec)  (ms)           Cnt  Num
0 Link-local address:  Et0/0  14    00:00:13  11  200  0   2
FE80::A8BB:CCFF:FE00:200
```

In this example, there is one neighbor connected to interface E0/0 in autonomous system 100.

To display entries in the EIGRP IPv6 topology table, use the **show ipv6 eigrp topology** command:

```
IOS# show ipv6 eigrp topology
IPv6-EIGRP Topology Table for AS(1)/ID(2001:0DB8:10::/64)
Codes: P - Passive, A - Active, U - Update, Q - Query, R - Reply,
r - reply Status, s - sia Status
```

```
P 2001:0DB8:3::/64, 1 successors, FD is 281600
    via Connected, Ethernet1/0
```

In this example there is one successor route in the topology table.

To view the EIGRP routes in the routing table, use the `show ipv6 route eigrp` command. Like in IPv4, EIGRP for IPv6 routes are denoted by a D. The output of all these `show` commands is very similar to the IPv4 corresponding commands.

INSIDE THE EXAM

EIGRP Overview

Remember that EIGRP is proprietary to Cisco, and remember the components it uses in its metric structure and the routing protocols it supports.

EIGRP Operation

Be familiar with the operation of EIGRP, including how neighbor adjacencies are built using multicast hello messages and how this information is maintained in local neighbor and topology tables. Be familiar with the EIGRP message types and how they are used. Memorize and understand the terms used in Table 11-1.

EIGRP Configuration

Know the basic commands in enabling EIGRP: `router eigrp` and `network`. Be able to detect misconfigured EIGRP routing processes on routers by looking for misconfigured `network` commands or

AS numbers. Be able to pick out successor routes, feasible successor routes, and successor routers created by using the `variance` command from the topology table. Remember when the `no auto-summary` command is used for EIGRP.

EIGRP Troubleshooting

Expect a few questions on troubleshooting EIGRP problems. You should be able to understand and interpret the output of the various `show` commands for EIGRP to find problems with an EIGRP configuration.

EIGRP for IPv6

Remember how to enable EIGRP for IPv6: `ipv6 router eigrp` *autonomous_ system* and `no shutdown` (global) and `ipv6 eigrp` *autonomous_system* (interface).

CERTIFICATION SUMMARY

Cisco's proprietary EIGRP routing protocol is based on IGRP. Enhancements of EIGRP include fast convergence, a loop-free topology, route summarization, multicast and incremental updates, and routing for IP, IPX, and AppleTalk. Hellos are sent every 5 seconds as multicasts to develop and maintain a neighbor relationship. EIGRP's metrics are bandwidth, delay, reliability, load, and MTU.

The DUAL algorithm is used to provide a loop-free topology. This algorithm provides fast convergence by storing a neighbor's routing information locally in a topology table. The best path is called a successor route, and any valid alternative paths are called feasible successors. The advertised distance is a neighbor's metric to reach a destination, while the feasible distance is your router's metric to reach the same destination. There are five EIGRP messages: hello, update, query, reply, and acknowledgment.

Enabling EIGRP is simple: you must specify an AS number with the **router** command and you enter connected network numbers with the **network** command. The **show ip eigrp neighbors** command displays adjacent neighbors and issues with building an adjacency with other EIGRP routers. The **show ip eigrp topology** command shows the topology table the DUAL algorithm uses to build the routing table. EIGRP routes show up as D in the IP routing table.

You must first execute the **ipv6 unicast-routing** command to enable IPv6. An address must be assigned to each interface, typically using the EUI-64 method, for it to process IPv6 packets. Like RIPng and OSPFv3, EIGRP must be configured globally and then enabled on a per-interface basis. For EIGRP for IPv6, the global configuration requires the configuration of an autonomous system number and, possibly, bringing up the routing process with the **no shutdown** command.

TWO-MINUTE DRILL

EIGRP Overview

❏ EIGRP, which is based on IGRP, is a hybrid protocol with many link state protocol characteristics: it supports fast convergence, provides a loop-free topology, supports route summarization and VLSM, and uses multicasts and incremental updates.

❏ EIGRP uses bandwidth and delay, by default, in its metric computation, but it can also use reliability, load, and MTU.

EIGRP Operation

❏ EIGRP sends hello multicasts (224.0.0.10) out every 5 seconds on its interfaces. To form a neighbor relationship, EIGRP routers must have matching AS numbers and K-values.

❏ EIGRP uses the DUAL algorithm to maintain the topology table and update the routing table. A successor route is the route with the best path to the destination. A feasible successor route is a valid backup route (not part of a routing loop). The advertised distance is the distance for a neighbor to reach a destination network, and the feasible distance is the distance for this router to reach the same network.

❏ EIGRP maintains separate neighbor, topology, and routing tables for each routed protocol.

EIGRP Configuration

❏ Configuring EIGRP requires an AS number. Remember to use classful network numbers in your **network** statements or include a subnet mask value to qualify the network number.

❏ Use the **variance** command to include other nonsuccessor EIGRP routes in your routing table.

❏ Use the **no auto-summary** command when you have discontiguous subnets for a classful address in your EIGRP network.

EIGRP Troubleshooting

❑ To verify your EIGRP configuration, use the following commands: **show ip protocols**, **show ip eigrp neighbors**, **show ip eigrp topology**, and **show ip eigrp traffic**.

EIGRP for IPv6

❑ The **ipv6 unicast-routing** command globally enables IPv6 and must be the first IPv6 command executed on the router.

❑ The **ipv6 router eigrp** *autonomous* command takes you into the EIGRP for IPv6 routing process, and the **no shutdown** command enables the EIGRP for IPv6 process (this is required in certain versions of IOS). The **ipv6 eigrp** *autonomous_system* command associates an interface to a particular EIGRP for IPv6 autonomous system.

SELF TEST

The following Self Test questions will help you measure your understanding of the material presented in this chapter. Read all the choices carefully, as there may be more than one correct answer. Choose all correct answers for each question.

EIGRP Overview

1. EIGRP will route for _____.
   A. IP
   B. IP and IPX
   C. IP and AppleTalk
   D. IP, IPX, and AppleTalk

2. EIGRP uses the _____ algorithm to update its routing table.
   A. Bellman-Ford
   B. Dijkstra
   C. DUAL
   D. Integrated

EIGRP Operation

3. EIGRP generates hellos every _____ seconds on LAN segments.
   A. 5
   B. 10
   C. 15
   D. 30

4. A(n) _____ route is the best path to reach a destination within the EIGRP topology and routing tables.
   A. Successor
   B. Feasible successor
   C. Advertised distance
   D. Feasible distance

5. When a successor route is no longer available and no feasible successor route exists in the topology table, a _____ is sent to all other neighbors advertising the same route to determine whether they have a valid path to the destination network.
   A. multicast active message
   B. broadcast query message
   C. multicast reply message
   D. multicast query message

EIGRP Configuration

6. Enter the EIGRP command or commands to include the interfaces with 192.168.1.1/26, 192.168.1.65/26, and 192.168.1.129/26 in the routing process: _____.

7. Enter the EIGRP command to advertise specific subnets, instead of advertising summarized classful routes, across a class boundary: _____.

EIGRP Troubleshooting

8. When examining the IP routing table, an EIGRP route will be shown as what letter?
   A. I
   B. R
   C. O
   D. D

9. Enter the EIGRP command to view only the successor routes: _____.

10. Enter the EIGRP command to view both the successor and feasible successor routes: _____.

EIGRP for IPv6

11. Enter the EIGRP command to enable the EIGRP routing process for IPv6: _____.

SELF TEST ANSWERS

EIGRP Overview

1. ☑ **D.** EIGRP supports three routed protocols: IP, IPX, and AppleTalk.
☒ **A** is incorrect because it omits IPX and AppleTalk. **B** is incorrect because it omits AppleTalk. **C** is incorrect because it omits IPX.

2. ☑ **C.** EIGRP uses the DUAL algorithm to update its routing table.
☒ **A** is incorrect because Bellman-Ford is used by the distance vector protocols.
B is incorrect because Dijkstra is used by link state protocols. **D** is a nonexistent routing algorithm.

EIGRP Operation

3. ☑ **A.** EIGRP generates hellos every 5 seconds.
☒ **B, C,** and **D** are incorrect hello periods.

4. ☑ **A.** A successor route is the best path to reach a destination within the topology table.
☒ **B** is incorrect because a feasible successor is a valid backup route. **C**, advertised distance, refers to a neighbor's distance to a route. **D**, feasible distance, refers to a router's distance to a route.

5. ☑ **D.** A multicast query message is sent to neighbors to determine whether a nonfeasible successor route to a destination is valid.
☒ **A** is incorrect because this is the state the route is in, not the message sent. **B** is incorrect because EIGRP uses multicasts, not broadcasts. **C** is incorrect because a reply message is in response to a query.

EIGRP Configuration

6. ☑ `network 192.168.1.0`

7. ☑ `no auto-summary`

EIGRP Troubleshooting

8. ☑ **D.** A D in the routing table indicates an EIGRP route.
☒ **A** is incorrect because an I indicates an IGRP route. **B** is incorrect because an R indicates a RIP route. **C** is incorrect because an O is an OSPF route.

9. ☑ `show ip route`. Successor routes are populated in the router's IP routing table.

10. ☑ `show ip eigrp topology`

EIGRP for IPv6

11. ☑ `no shutdown`

Part IV

Cisco Routers and WANs

12

WAN
Introduction

Τ he preceding few chapters introduced you to configuring advanced IP features on your Cisco router. This chapter introduces you to wide area networking (WAN) concepts and some basic point-to-point configurations, including High-Level Data Link Control (HDLC) and Point-to-Point Protocol (PPP). This chapter also introduces the use of virtual private networks (VPNs) in a WAN, briefly covering the most popular VPN implementations, IPsec and SSL. New to this exam is the Generic Route Encapsulation (GRE) protocol, which is introduced at the end of this chapter.

CERTIFICATION OBJECTIVE 12.01

Wide Area Networking Overview

Typically, LAN connections are used within a company and WAN connections allow you to connect to remote locations or sites. With a WAN, you don't own the infrastructure for WAN connections—another company, such as a telephone company or cable provider, provides the infrastructure. WAN connections are usually slower than LAN connections. A derivative of WAN solutions is the metropolitan area network (MAN). MANs sometimes use high-speed LAN connections in a small geographic area between different companies or divisions within a company. MANs are becoming more and more popular in large cities and even provide connections over a LAN medium, such as Ethernet.

Equipment and Components

WAN connections are made up of many types of equipment and components. Figure 12-1 shows some of the WAN terms used for these, and Table 12-1 shows the terms and definitions. As you may recall from your CCENT studies, data communications equipment (DCE) terminates a connection between two sites and provides clocking and synchronization for that connection; it connects to data termination equipment (DTE). The DCE category includes equipment such as channel service units/data service units (CSU/DSUs), Network Terminator Type 1 (NT1), and cable and analog modems. A DTE is an end-user device, such as a router or PC, which connects to the WAN via the DCE. In some circumstances, the function of the DCE might be built into the DTE's physical interface. For instance, certain Cisco routers can be purchased with built-in NT1s or CSU/DSUs in their WAN interfaces. Or you might have a laptop with a built-in analog modem.

FIGURE 12-1

WAN terms

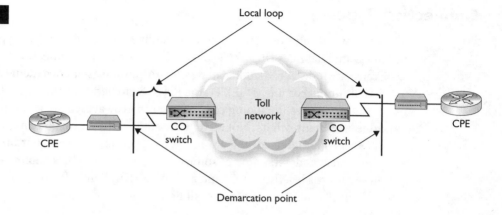

TABLE 12-1 WAN Terms and Definitions

Term	Definition
Customer premises equipment (CPE)	Your network's equipment, which includes the DCE (modem, NT1, CSU/DSU) and your DTE (router, access server).
Demarcation point	Where the responsibility of the carrier is passed on to you; this could be inside or outside your local facility; note that this is a *logical* boundary, not necessarily a physical boundary.
Local loop	The connection from the carrier's switching equipment to the demarcation point.
Central office (CO) switch	The carrier's switch within the toll network.
Toll network	The carrier's internal infrastructure for transporting your data.

Connection Types

Many WAN solutions are available, including the following: analog modems and Integrated Services Digital Network (ISDN) for dialup connections, Asynchronous Transfer Mode (ATM), dedicated point-to-point leased lines (dedicated circuits), digital subscriber line (DSL), Frame Relay, Switched Multi-megabit Data Services (SMDS), wireless (including cellular, laser microwave, radio, and satellite), X.25, cable, and many others. Not all of these solutions are available in every area, and not every solution is ideal for your needs. Therefore, one of your first tasks is to gain a basic understanding of some of these services. This chapter covers some of these services briefly, and Chapter 13 focuses on Frame Relay.

Typically, WAN connections fall under one of four categories:

- Leased lines, such as dedicated circuits or connections
- Circuit-switched connections, such as analog modem and digital ISDN dialup connections
- Packet-switched connections, such as Frame Relay and X.25
- Cell-switched connections, such as ATM and SMDS

The following sections introduce you to these four connection types.

e x a m

ⓦ a t c h   *WANs primarily operate at the physical and data link layers. Even though you might see Ethernet used for*   *some WAN connections, Cisco considers it a LAN technology.*

Leased-Line Connections

A leased-line connection is basically a dedicated circuit connection between two sites. It simulates a single cable connection between the local and remote sites. Leased lines are best suited when both of these conditions hold:

- The distance between the two sites is small, making the leased-line connection cost effective.
- A constant amount of traffic occurs between two sites and you need to guarantee bandwidth for certain applications.

Even though leased lines can provide guaranteed bandwidth and minimal delay for connections, other available solutions, such as ATM, can provide the same features. The main disadvantage of leased lines is their cost—they are typically the most expensive WAN solution. Another disadvantage is that each connection to a site requires a separate interface on your router. For example, if you had a central office router that needed access to four remote sites, the central office router would need four WAN interfaces for terminating the four leased lines. With Frame Relay and ATM, you could use one WAN interface to provide the same connectivity.

Leased lines use synchronous serial connections, with their data rates ranging from 2400 bps all the way up to 45 Mbps, in what is referred to as a *DS3* connection. A synchronous serial connection allows you to send and receive information simultaneously without having to wait for any signal from the remote side. Nor does a synchronous connection need to indicate when it is beginning to send something or the end of a transmission. These two things, plus how clocking is done, are the three major differences between synchronous and asynchronous connections—asynchronous connections are typically used for dialup connections, such as modems.

If you purchase a leased line, you will need the following equipment:

- **DTE**   A router with a synchronous serial interface: this provides the data link framing and terminates the WAN connection.

- **DCE**   A CSU/DSU to terminate the carrier's leased-line connection: this provides the clocking and synchronization for the connection.

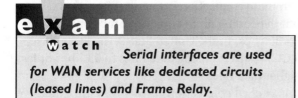

Figure 12-2 shows an example of the equipment required for a leased-line connection. The CSU/DSU is responsible for handling the physical layer framing, clocking, and synchronization of the connection. Common data link layer protocols you can use for dedicated connections include PPP and HDLC.

Circuit-Switched Connections

Circuit-switched connections are dialup connections, like those that are used by a PC with a modem when dialing up an ISP. Circuit-switched connections include the following types:

- **Asynchronous serial connections**   These include analog modem dialup connections and the standard telephone system, which is commonly referred to as Plain Old Telephone Service (POTS) by the telephone carriers.

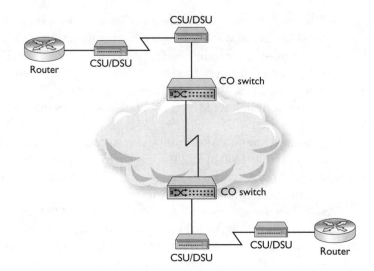

FIGURE 12-2

Leased-line
example

- **Synchronous serial connections** These include digital ISDN Basic Rate Interface (BRI) and Primary Rate Interface (PRI) dialup connections; they provide guaranteed bandwidth.

Asynchronous serial connections are the cheapest form of WAN services but are also the slowest and most unreliable of the services. For instance, every time you make a connection using an analog modem, there is no guarantee of the connection rate you'll get. With these connections, the top connection rate in the United States is 53 Kbps, but depending on the quality of the connection, you might get something as low as 300 bps. In the United States, the Federal Communications Commission (FCC) restricts analog data rates to 53 Kbps or less. Other countries might support higher data rates.

The main problem with circuit-switched connections is that they are expensive if you need to make connections over long distances, with a per-minute charge that varies depending on the destination: the more data you have to send, the more time it will take, and the more money it will cost. Therefore, asynchronous circuit-switched connections are typically used for home office and low-speed backup connections, as well as temporary low-speed connections for additional boosts in bandwidth when your primary link becomes congested or when it fails.

With leased lines, as soon as the circuit is installed and you have configured your DTE, the line remains up unless there is a problem with the carrier's network or the DTE or DCE equipment. This is different from circuit-switched connections, which are temporary—you make a phone call to the remote DTE, and when the line comes up, you transmit your data. Once you are done transmitting your data, the phone connection is terminated.

If you will be using a circuit-switched analog connection, you'll need this equipment:

- **DTE** A router with an asynchronous serial interface
- **DCE** A modem

If you will be using a circuit-switched digital connection, you'll need this equipment:

- **DTE** A router with an ISDN interface
- **DCE** An NT1 for a BRI or a CSU/DSU for a PRI

Figure 12-3 shows an example of an analog circuit-switched connection. With this connection, you'll typically use PPP or HDLC for the encapsulation: SLIP is rarely used since it lacks authentication and supports only IP as a transport protocol.

Packet-Switched Connections

With leased lines and circuit-switched connections, a physical circuit is used to make the connection between the two sites. With a leased line, the same circuit path is always used. With circuit-switched connections, the circuit path is built every time a phone call is made, making it highly probable that the same circuit path will not be used for every phone call.

FIGURE 12-3

Analog circuit-switched connection

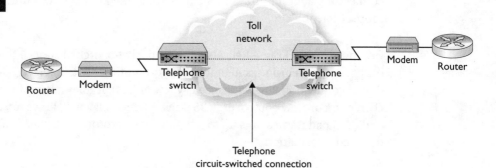

Packet-switched connections use logical circuits to make connections between two sites. These logical circuits are referred to as *virtual circuits* (VCs). One advantage that a logical circuit has over a physical one is that a logical circuit is not tied to any particular physical circuit. Instead, a logical circuit is built across any available physical connection. Another advantage of logical circuits is that you can build multiple logical circuits over the same physical circuit. Therefore, with a single physical connection to a carrier, you can connect to multiple sites. This is not possible with leased lines: for each location to which you want to connect, you need a *separate* physical circuit, making the cost of the solution much higher than one that uses logical circuits. Technologies that use packet switching and logical circuits include ATM, Frame Relay, SMDS, and X.25. From a cost perspective, packet-switched solutions fall somewhere between circuit-switched solutions and leased lines.

on the
job

Both Frame Relay and ATM are in regression in their usage in the marketplace. The advent of cable modems, DSL, fiber to the home, and other technologies have drastically cut into the deployment of Frame Relay and ATM. X.25 usage is very uncommon today because of the proliferation of reliable digital circuits.

X.25   The oldest of these four technologies is X.25, which is an ITU-T standard. X.25 is a network layer protocol that runs across both synchronous and asynchronous physical circuits, providing a lot of flexibility for your connection options. X.25 was actually developed to run across an unreliable medium. It provides error detection *and* correction, as well as flow control, at both the data link layer (by Link Access Procedure, Balanced [LAPB]) and the network layer (by X.25). In this sense, it performs a function similar to what TCP, at the transport layer, provides for IP. Because of its overhead, X.25 is best delegated to asynchronous, unreliable connections. If you have a synchronous digital connection, another protocol, such as Frame Relay or ATM, is much more efficient.

Frame Relay   Frame Relay is a digital packet-switched service that can run only across synchronous digital connections at the data link layer. Because it uses digital connections (which have very few errors), it does not perform any error correction or flow control as X.25 does. Frame Relay will, however, detect errors and drop bad frames. It is up to a higher layer protocol, such as TCP, to resend the dropped information.

If you are setting up a Frame Relay connection, you'll need the following equipment:

- **DTE**   A router with a synchronous serial interface
- **DCE**   A CSU/DSU to connect to the carrier

Figure 12-4 shows an example of a Frame Relay connection. In this example, the router needs only a single physical connection to the carrier to connect to multiple sites: this is accomplished via virtual circuits (VCs). Frame Relay supports speeds from fractional T1 or E1 connections (56–64 Kbps) up to a DS3 (45 Mbps). Frame Relay is discussed in more detail in Chapter 13.

ATM   ATM is also a packet-switched technology that uses digital circuits. Unlike Frame Relay and X.25, however, this service uses fixed-length (53-byte) packets, called *cells*, to transmit information. Therefore, this service is commonly called a cell-switched service. It has an advantage over Frame Relay in that it can provide guaranteed throughput and minimal delay for a multitude of services, including voice, video, and data. However, it does cost more than Frame Relay services. ATM (sort of an enhanced Frame Relay) can offer a connection-guaranteed bandwidth, limited delay, limited number of errors, quality of service (QoS), and more. Frame Relay can provide some minimal guarantees to connections, but not to the degree of precision that ATM can. Whereas Frame Relay is limited to 45-Mbps connections, ATM can scale to very high speeds: OC-192 (SONET), for instance, affords about 10 Gbps of bandwidth.

FIGURE 12-4

Frame Relay packet-switched connection

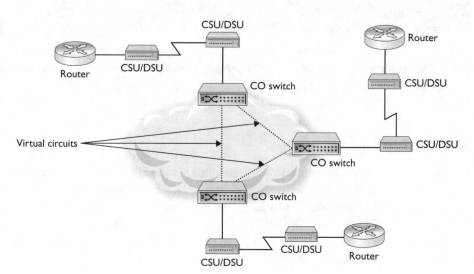

WAN Interfaces on Cisco Routers

Cisco supports a wide variety of serial cables for its serial router interfaces. Some of the cable types supported for synchronous serial interfaces are EIA/TIA-232, EIA/TIA-449, EIA/TIA-530, V.35, and X.21. The end that connects to the DCE device is defined by these standards. However, the end that connects to the Cisco router is proprietary in nature. Cisco's cables have two different end connectors that connect to a router's serial interfaces:

- **DB-60** Has 60 pins
- **DB-26** Has 26 pins and is flat, like a USB cable

Note that these connectors are for synchronous serial connections. Cisco has other cable types, typically with RJ-45 connectors, for asynchronous connections.

WAN Cabling

In WAN connections, your router is the DTE and the equipment to which it attaches, such as a modem, CSU/DSU, or an NT1, is a DCE. The DCE is responsible for providing the clocking and synchronization of the physical layer connection. The cabling discussed in this section applies only to DTE-to-DCE connections. The cabling used for the WAN connection is dependent on the technology and speed of access that you are using.

TABLE 12-2	Cable Standards	HDLC	PPP	Frame Relay	HSSI
WAN Cable Types	EIA/TIA-232	Yes	Yes	Yes	No
	EIA/TIA-449	Yes	Yes	Yes	No
	EIA/TIA-612/613	No	No	No	Yes
	X.21	Yes	Yes	Yes	No
	V.24	Yes	Yes	Yes	No
	V.35	Yes	Yes	Yes	No

Table 12-2 lists the connectors/cables and when they are used. Each cable has two ends: one connects to the DCE and the other to the DTE. The DCE endpoint is defined in the Cable Standards column in Table 12-2. However, the DTE end is proprietary to Cisco.

e x a m

ⓦatch *Be familiar with the data link encapsulation types listed in Table 12-3, such as HDLC, PPP, and LAPB (Frame Relay).*

Encapsulation Methods

Many different methods are available for encapsulating data for serial connections. Table 12-3 shows the most common ones. The following sections cover HDLC and PPP in more depth.

TABLE 12-3	Common Encapsulation Methods

Protocol	Explanation
High-Level Data Link Control (HDLC)	Based on ISO standards, it is used with synchronous and asynchronous connections.
Synchronous Data Link Control Protocol (SDLC)	Used in IBM SNA environments, it has been replaced by HDLC.
Link Access Procedure Balanced (LAPB)	Used in X.25, it has extensive error detection and correction.
Link Access Procedure D Channel (LAPD)	It is used by ISDN to signal call setup and teardown of phone connections.
Link Access Procedure Frame mode bearer services (LAPF)	It is used in Frame Relay between a DTE and a DCE and is similar to LAPD.
Point-to-Point Protocol (PPP)	Based on RFC standards, PPP is the most common encapsulation used for dialup and dedicated circuits. It provides for authentication, handling multiple protocols, compression, multilink, and error detection.

Serial Interface Review

This section provides a quick review of interfaces, focusing on serial interfaces used for WAN connectivity. You should be familiar with this information based on your CCENT studies, but you could be tested on this again for the ICND2 exam.

Serial Interface Configuration

When connecting a serial cable to the serial interface of a router, clocking is typically provided by an external device, such as a modem or a CSU/DSU. The router is the DTE and the external device is the DCE, where the DCE provides the clocking.

In some cases, however, you might connect two routers back to back using the routers' serial interfaces. For instance, if you are building your own lab to practice CCNA commands, you'll more than likely connect the routers back to back to reduce equipment costs. In this situation, each router, by default, is a DTE. Since clocking is required for the interface to be enabled, one of the two routers will have to perform the function of an external DCE. This is accomplished by using the **clock rate** Interface Subconfiguration mode command on the serial interface:

```
Router(config)# interface serial [slot_#/]port_#
Router(config-if)# clock rate rate_in_bits_per_second
```

When entering the clock rate, you can't choose any arbitrary value: this is dependent on the type of cable you are using and the type of interface it's connected to. Use context-sensitive help to find out which clock rates your serial interface supports. Here are some possible values: 1200, 2400, 4800, 9600, 19200, 38400, 56000, 72000, 125000, 148000, 500000, 800000, 1000000, 1300000, 2000000, and 4000000.

Note that that you can't choose an arbitrary router in the back-to-back connection to be the DCE—this is based on how the two routers are cabled. One end of the cable is physically the DTE, and the other is the DCE. Some cables are marked and some are not, depending on where they were purchased. If you are not sure which router has the DTE end of the cable and which has the DCE end, you can determine this with the **show controller** command:

```
Router> show controller serial [slot_#/]port_#
```

This is one of the few commands in which you *cannot* concatenate the type and the port number—you must separate them by a space. Here is an example of the use of this command:

```
Router> show controller serial 0
HD unit 0, idb = 0x121C04, driver structure at 0x127078
buffer size 1524 HD unit 0, DTE V.35 serial cable attached
 .
 .
 .
```

Notice that the second line of this example holds two important pieces of information: the connection type (DTE) and the type of cable (V.35).

Here is an example of an interface connected to the end of a DCE cable:

```
Router> show controller serial 0
HD unit 0, idb = 0x1BA16C, driver structure at 0x1C04E0
buffer size 1524  HD unit 0, V.35 DCE cable, clockrate 64000
 .
 .
 .
```

In this example, the clocking has already been configured: 64,000 bps (bits per second).

12.01. The digital resources that accompany this book include a multimedia demonstration of setting the clocking on a serial interface on a Cisco router.

Viewing Interface Information

One of the most common commands that you will use on an IOS device is the **show interfaces** command. This command allows you to see the status and configuration of your interfaces, as well as some statistical information. Here is the syntax of this command:

```
Router> show interfaces [type [slot_#/]port_#]
```

If you don't specify an interface, the IOS device displays all of its interfaces—those enabled as well as those disabled. Here is an example of the output of this command on a router:

```
Router# show interfaces e0
Ethernet 0 is up, line protocol is up
  Hardware is MCI Ethernet, address is 0000.0c00.1234
                              (bia 0000.0c00.1234)
  Internet address is 172.16.16.2, subnet mask is 255.255.255.252
  MTU 1500 bytes, BW 10000 Kbit, DLY 100000 usec, rely 255/255,
                  load 1/255
  Encapsulation ARPA, loopback not set, keepalive set (10 sec)
  ARP type: ARPA, ARP Timeout 4:00:00
  Last input 0:00:00, output 0:00:00, output hang never
  Last clearing of "show interface" counters 0:00:00
  Output queue 0/40, 0 drops; input queue 0/75, 0 drops
  Five minute input rate 0 bits/sec, 0 packets/sec
  Five minute output rate 4000 bits/sec, 8 packets/sec
     2240375 packets input, 887359872 bytes, 0 no buffer
     Received 722137 broadcasts, 0 runts, 0 giants
     0 input errors, 0 CRC, 0 frame, 0 overrun, 0 ignored, 0 abort
     10137586 packets output, 897215078 bytes, 0 underruns
     4 output errors, 1037 collisions, 3 interface resets,
                     0 restarts
```

Troubleshooting Interface Problems

One of the first things that you want to examine in this display is the status of the interface: Ethernet0 is up, line protocol is up. The first up refers to the status of the physical layer, and the second up refers to the status of the data link layer. Here are the possible values for the physical layer status:

- ■ **Up** The device is sensing a physical layer signal on the interface.
- ■ **Down** The device is not sensing a physical layer signal on the interface, a condition that can arise if the attached device is turned off, there is no cable attached, or you are using the wrong type of cable.
- ■ **Administratively down** You used the **shutdown** command to disable the interface.

Here are the possible values for the data link layer status:

■ **Up** The data link layer is operational.

■ **Down** The data link layer is not operational, a condition that can be caused by missed keepalives on a serial link, no clocking, an incorrect encapsulation type, or a disabled physical layer.

---

e x a m

ⓦ**a t c h** *If the interface status is "up and up," the interface is operational; if it is "up and down," it signals a problem with the data link layer (layer 2). For a serial interface, this could be caused by a CSU/ DSU not providing clocking to the interface; likewise, if there is a mismatch in the encapsulation type for the two endpoints of the serial connection, the status will be "up and down." If the interface status is "down and down," there is a physical layer* *problem (layer 1). If the interface status is "administratively down and down," the interface was disabled with the* shutdown *command. The "Hardware is" refers to the physical (layer 1) properties of the interface, and the "Encapsulation" refers to the data link (layer 2) properties of the interface. If the hardware type for an interface says "LANCE," then the interface is a Fast Ethernet interface (on older routers and switches).*

The second line of output from the **show interfaces** command has the hardware interface type (in this example, it's an Ethernet controller). This is followed by the MAC address on the interface. The third line has the IP address and subnet mask configured on the interface (you won't see this on a layer 2 switch's interface). The fourth line has the MTU Ethernet frame size as well as the routing protocol metrics. (These metrics are discussed in depth in Chapters 4, 9, 10, and 11, which discuss routing protocols.) Notice the BW parameter in this line. Referred to as the *bandwidth* of the link, this is used by some routing protocols, such as Open Shortest Path First (OSPF) and Enhanced Interior Gateway Routing Protocol (EIGRP), when making routing decisions. For Ethernet, this is 10,000 Kbps. The line after this refers to the layer 2 encapsulation (frame) type used; with Ethernet, this can be ARPA (used with TCP/IP), Subnetwork Access Protocol (SNAP), or SAP.

e x a m

ⓦ**a t c h** *Be familiar with the output of the* show interfaces *command. The MTU size indicates the maximum packet size (not frame or segment).*

Table 12-4 explains some of the elements that you may see with the **show interfaces** command. Note that depending

TABLE 12-4 Explanation of the Elements in the `show interfaces` Command

Element	Description
Address	The MAC address of the interface; BIA (burnt-in address) is the MAC address burnt into the Ethernet controller—this can be overridden with the Interface `mac-address` command.
Last input/output	The last time a packet was received on or sent out of the interface—can be used to determine whether the interface is operating or not.
Last clearing	Indicates the last time the `clear counters` command was executed on the interface.
Output queue	Indicates the number of packets waiting to be sent out the interface—the number after the slash (/) is the maximum size of the queue and then the number of packets dropped because the queue was full.
Input queue	Indicates the number of packets received on the interface and waiting to be processed—the number after the slash (/) is the maximum size of the queue and then the number of packets dropped because the queue was full.
No buffers (input)	Number of received packets dropped because the input buffer was filled up.
Runts (input)	Number of packets received that were less than the minimum for the encapsulation type (64 bytes for Ethernet).
Giants (input)	Number of packets received that were greater than the maximum allowed size (1518 bytes for Ethernet).
Input errors	The total number of input errors received on the interface.
CRC (input)	Indicates packets received that had checksum errors.
Frame (input)	Indicates the number of packets received that had both CRC errors and cases where the length of the frame was not on a byte boundary.
Overruns (input)	Number of times the inbound packet rate exceeded the capabilities of the interface to process the traffic.
Ignored (input)	Number of inbound packets that were dropped because of the lack of input buffer space.
Aborts (input)	Number of received packets that were aborted.
Collisions (output)	Number of times the interface tried transmitting a packet, but a collision occurred—this should be less than 0.1% of total traffic leaving the interface.
Interface resets (output)	Number of times the interface changed state by going down and then coming back up.
Restarts (output)	Number of times the controller was reset because of errors—use the `show controllers` command to troubleshoot this problem.

on the kind of IOS device and type of interface, the output displayed in the **show interfaces** command may differ slightly.

In the following example, notice that there are a lot of input and CRC errors for the fa0/0 switchport:

```
IOS# show interfaces fa0/0
FastEthernet 0/1 is up, line protocol is up (connected)
   Hardware is MCI Ethernet, address is 0000.0c00.1234
   MTU 1500 bytes, BW 10000 Kbit, DLY 100000 usec, rely 255/255,
                    load 1/255
   Encapsulation ARPA, loopback not set, keepalive set (10 sec)
   Full-duplex, 100Mbps, media type is 10/100BaseTx
   input flow-control is off, output flow-control is unsupported
   Last input 0:00:00, output 0:00:00, output hang never
   Last clearing of "show interface" counters 0:00:00
   Output queue 0/40, 0 drops; input queue 0/75, 0 drops
   Five minute input rate 354000 bits/sec, 335 packets/sec
   Five minute output rate 357000 bits/sec, 328 packets/sec
     12375 packets input, 1900414 bytes, 0 no buffer
      Received 1133 broadcasts (0 multicasts)
      0 runts, 0 giants, 0 throttles
      735 input errors, 731 CRC, 0 frame, 0 overrun, 0 ignored, 0 abort
      .
      .
      .
```

Notice that the fa0/0 interface is configured for full-duplex 100 Mbps. If autosensing of the speed/duplex was used (which is the default), then the word `auto` would appear in the duplexing line. The culprit is probably a duplex mismatch on the other end.

CERTIFICATION OBJECTIVE 12.02

HDLC

Based on ISO standards, the HDLC protocol can be used with synchronous and asynchronous connections and defines the frame type and interaction between two devices at the data link layer. The following sections cover how Cisco implements HDLC and how it is configured on a router's serial interface.

Frame Type

Cisco's implementation of HDLC is based on ISO's standards, but Cisco has made a change in the frame format, making it proprietary. In other words, Cisco's HDLC will work only if the remote end also supports Cisco's HDLC. Figure 12-5 shows examples of some WAN frame formats, including ISO's HDLC, Cisco's HDLC, and PPP. Notice that the main difference between ISO's HDLC and Cisco's frame format is that Cisco has a proprietary field: *Type*. One of the problems with ISO's HDLC is that it does not define how to carry multiple protocols across a single link, as does Cisco's HDLC with the Type field. Therefore, ISO's HDLC is typically used on serial links where there is only a single protocol to transport. The *default* encapsulation on Cisco's synchronous serial interfaces is HDLC. Actually, Cisco supports only its own implementation of HDLC, not ISO's implementation.

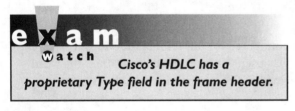

e x a m

ⓦatch *Cisco's HDLC has a proprietary Type field in the frame header.*

FIGURE 12-5

WAN frame types

ISO's HDLC

Flag	Address	Control	Data	FCS	Flag

Cisco's HDLC

Flag	Address	Control	Type	Data	FCS	Flag

PPP

Flag	Address	Control	Protocol	Data	FCS	Flag

Configuring HDLC

As mentioned in the preceding section, the default encapsulation on Cisco's synchronous serial interfaces is HDLC. You need to use the following configuration only if you changed the data link layer protocol to something else and then need to set it back to HDLC:

```
Router(config)# interface serial [slot_#/]port_#
Router(config-if)# encapsulation hdlc
```

Notice that you must be in the serial interface (Interface Subconfiguration mode) to change its data link layer encapsulation. If you had a different encapsulation configured on the serial interface, executing this command would set the frame format to Cisco's HDLC. Note that the other side must be set to Cisco's HDLC or the data link layer will fail on the interface (the interface will be "up, line protocol is down").

---

e x a m

ⓦatch *HDLC is the default encapsulation on synchronous serial interfaces of Cisco routers. Use the* show interfaces *command to see the encapsulation type. Use the* encapsulation hdlc *command to change the serial interface's encapsulation* *to Cisco's HDLC. Note that if one router is a Cisco router and the other a non-Cisco router when using HDLC, the interface will show as "up, line protocol is down." This would also be true if one side was using PPP and the other HDLC or if a DCE was not providing any clocking to the router (DTE).*

After you have configured HDLC, use the **show interfaces** command to view the data link layer encapsulation:

```
Router# show interfaces serial 1
Serial1 is up, line protocol is up
  Hardware is MCI Serial
  Internet address is 192.168.2.2 255.255.255.0
  MTU 1500 bytes, BW 1544 Kbit, DLY 20000 usec, rely 255/255, load 1/255
  Encapsulation HDLC, loopback not set, keepalive set (10 sec)
  Last input 0:00:02, output 0:00:00, output hang never
  .
  .
  .
```

Notice in this example that the physical and data link layers are up and that the encapsulation is set to Cisco's HDLC (Encapsulation HDLC).

on the

ob

Remember that the `encapsulation hdlc` *command is the default on a serial interface and is thus not displayed with the* `show running-config` *command. Use the* `show interfaces` *command to view the encapsulation type on a serial interface. Notice (from the* `show interfaces` *output) that HDLC sends keepalives and expects responses back (the default keepalive timer is 10 seconds). If no responses to the keepalives are seen, the interface will show as "up, line protocol is down."*

> *12.02. The digital resources that accompany this book contain a multimedia demonstration of configuring HDLC on a router.*

CERTIFICATION OBJECTIVE 12.03

PPP

Whereas Cisco's HDLC is a proprietary protocol, PPP is based on an open standard defined in RFCs 1332, 1661, and 2153. Like HDLC, PPP is a layer 2 protocol and works with asynchronous and synchronous serial connections as well as High-Speed Serial Interfaces (HSSI) and ISDN interfaces (BRI and PRI). The following sections offer an overview of PPP and how to configure it, including authentication.

exam

ⓦatch   *HDLC on Cisco routers is proprietary and can be used only on a point-to-point connection between two Cisco routers. When connecting Cisco and non-Cisco routers on point-to-point connections, PPP should be used since* *it is an open standard. HDLC, PPP, and Frame Relay are layer 2 protocols. PPP is supported on both synchronous and asynchronous circuits, whereas the others are only supported for synchronous circuits.*

PPP Components

PPP has many more features than HDLC. Like HDLC, PPP defines a frame type and how two PPP devices communicate with each other, including the multiplexing of network and data link layer protocols across the same link. However, PPP also does the following:

- Performs dynamic configuration of links
- Allows for authentication
- Compresses packet headers
- Tests the quality of links
- Performs error detection and correction
- Allows multiple PPP physical connections to be bound together as a single logical connection (referred to as *multilink*), creating the ability to load-balance across multiple links

PPP supports handling multiple encapsulated protocols, authentication, compression, multilink, *and error detection/correction, and can be used over synchronous and asynchronous circuits.*

PPP has three main components:

- Frame format (encapsulation)
- Link Control Protocol (LCP)
- Network Control Protocol (NCP)

Each of these three components plays an important role in the setup, configuration, and transfer of information across a PPP connection. The following sections cover these components.

Frame Format

The first component of PPP is the frame format, or encapsulation method, it uses. The frame format defines how network layer packets are encapsulated in a PPP frame, as well as the format of the PPP frame. PPP is typically used for serial WAN connections because of its open-standard character. It works on asynchronous (modem) and synchronous (ISDN, point-to-point, and HSSI) connections. If you are dialing up to your ISP, you'll be using PPP. PPP's frame format is based on ISO's HDLC, as you can see in Figure 12-5. The main difference is that the PPP frame has a Protocol field, which defines the protocol of the network layer data that is encapsulated.

LCP and NCP

The second and third components of PPP are LCP and NCP. LCP is responsible for establishing, configuring, authenticating, and testing a PPP connection. It handles all of the up-front work in setting up a connection. Here are some of the things that LCP will negotiate when setting up a PPP connection:

- Authentication method used (PPP Authentication Procedure [PAP] or Challenge-Handshake Authentication Protocol [CHAP]), if any
- Compression algorithm used (Stacker or Predictor), if any
- Callback phone number to use, if defined
- Multilink: other physical connections to use, if configured

LCP and NCP go through three steps to establish a PPP connection:

1. Link establishment (LCP)
2. Authentication (LCP)
3. Protocol negotiation (NCP)

The first step is the link establishment phase. In this step, LCP negotiates the PPP parameters that are to be used for the connection, which may include the authentication method and compression algorithms. If authentication has been configured, the authentication type is negotiated. This can be either PAP or CHAP. These are discussed later in the "PPP Authentication" section. If authentication is configured and there is a match on the authentication type on both sides, authentication is performed in the second step. If this is successful, NCP, in the third step, will negotiate the upper layer protocols, which can include protocols such as IP and IPX as well as data link layer protocols (bridged traffic, such as Ethernet, and Cisco's CDP) that will be transmitted across the PPP link. Once LCP and NCP perform their negotiation and the connection has been authenticated (if this has been defined), the data link layer will come up (the status of a router's interface will be "up, line protocol is up").

Once a connection is enabled, LCP uses error detection to monitor dropped data on the connection as well as loops at the data link layer. The Quality and Magic Numbers protocol is used by LCP to ensure that the connection remains reliable.

e x a m
w a t c h

LCP is responsible for negotiating and maintaining a PPP connection, including any optional

authentication. NCP is responsible for negotiating upper layer protocols that will be carried across the PPP connection.

Configuring PPP

The configuration of PPP is almost as simple as that of HDLC. To specify that PPP is to be used on a WAN interface, use the following configuration:

```
Router(config)# interface type [slot_#]port_#
Router(config-if)# encapsulation ppp
```

e x a m
w a t c h

The encapsulation ppp command can be applied only to asynchronous or synchronous serial

interfaces on a router, and thus PPP's authentication is applicable only on serial interfaces.

As you can see, you need to specify the **ppp** parameter in the **encapsulation** Interface Subconfiguration mode command. With the exception of authentication, other PPP options are not discussed in this book.

Video

12.03. The digital resources that accompany this book contain a multimedia demonstration of configuring PPP on a router.

Troubleshooting PPP

Once you have configured PPP on your router's interface, you can verify the status of the interface with the **show interfaces** command:

```
Router# show interfaces serial 0
Serial0 is up, line protocol is up
  Hardware is MCI Serial
  Internet address is 192.168.1.2 255.255.255.0
  MTU 1500 bytes, BW 1544 Kbit, DLY 20000 usec, rely 255/255, load 1/255
  Encapsulation PPP, loopback not set, keepalive set (10 sec)
  lcp state = OPEN
  ncp ccp state = NOT NEGOTIATED    ncp ipcp state = OPEN
  ncp osicp state = NOT NEGOTIATED   ncp ipxcp state = NOT NEGOTIATED
  ncp xnscp state = NOT NEGOTIATED   ncp vinescp state = NOT NEGOTIATED
  ncp deccp state = NOT NEGOTIATED   ncp bridgecp state = NOT NEGOTIATED
  ncp atalkcp state = NOT NEGOTIATED  ncp lex state = NOT NEGOTIATED
  ncp cdp state = OPEN
  .
  .
  .
```

In the fifth line of output, you can see that the encapsulation is set to PPP. Below this is the status of LCP (lcp state = OPEN). An OPEN state indicates that LCP has successfully negotiated its parameters and brought up the data link layer. The statuses of the protocols by NCP follow. In this example, only two protocols are running across this PPP connection: IP (ncp ipcp state = OPEN) and CDP (ncp cdp state = OPEN).

exam

ⓦatch   *If one side is configured for PPP and the other side is configured with a different encapsulation type (such as HDLC), the interface status will be "up, line protocol is down." If the physical and data link layers are "up, line protocol is up" and*   *you don't have layer 3 connectivity, there is probably a problem with the IP addressing on the two peers: you're using the wrong address when doing a ping or the addresses on the two peers are in the wrong subnets.*

If you are having problems with the data link layer coming up when you've configured PPP, you can use the following **debug** command to troubleshoot the connection:

```
Router# debug ppp negotiation
PPP protocol negotiation debugging is on
Router# configure terminal
Enter configuration commands, one per line.  End with CNTL/Z.
Router(config)# interface serial 0
Router(config-if)# no shutdown
%LINK-3-UPDOWN: Interface Serial0, changed state to up
ppp: sending CONFREQ, type = 5 (CI_MAGICNUMBER), value = 4FEFE5
PPP Serial0: received config for type = 0x5 (MAGICNUMBER) value = 0x561036 acked
PPP Serial0: state = ACKSENT fsm_rconfack(0xC021): rcvd id 0x2
ppp: config ACK received, type = 5 (CI_MAGICNUMBER), value = 4FEFE5
ipcp: sending CONFREQ, type = 3 (CI_ADDRESS), Address = 192.168.2.1
ppp Serial0: Negotiate IP address: her address 192.168.2.2 (ACK)
ppp: ipcp_reqci: returning CONFACK.
ppp: cdp_reqci: returning CONFACK
PPP Serial0: state = ACKSENT fsm_rconfack(0x8021): rcvd id 0x2
ipcp: config ACK received, type = 3 (CI_ADDRESS), Address = 192.168.2.1
PPP Serial0: state = ACKSENT fsm_rconfack(0x8207): rcvd id 0x2
ppp: cdp_reqci: received CONFACK
%LINEPROTO-5-UPDOWN: Line protocol on Interface Serial0, changed state to up
```

In this example, **debug** was first enabled and then the serial interface was enabled. Notice that the two connected routers go through a negotiation process. They first verify their IP addresses, 192.168.2.1 and 192.168.2.2, to make sure they are not the same address, and then they negotiate the protocols (ipcp_reqci and cdp_reqci). In this example, IP and CDP are negotiated and the data link layer comes up after the successful negotiation.

---

e x a m

ⓦ a t c h *Use the encapsulation ppp command to change a serial interface's encapsulation to PPP. When you look at the output of the show interfaces command, any protocol listed as OPEN has been negotiated correctly. If you are having problems with the LCP negotiation, use the debug ppp negotiation command.*

12.04. The digital resources that accompany this book contain a multimedia demonstration of troubleshooting PPP on a router.

PPP Authentication

PPP, unlike HDLC, supports device authentication. Two methods can be used to implement authentication: PAP and CHAP. Both of these authentication methods are defined in RFC 1334; RFC 1994 replaces the CHAP component of RFC 1334. The authentication process is performed (by LCP) before the network and data link layer protocols are negotiated for the PPP connection by NCP. If the authentication fails, the data link layer will not come up. Authentication is optional and adds very little overhead to the connection. As you will see in the following sections, the setup and troubleshooting of PAP and CHAP are easy.

PAP

Of the two PPP authentication protocols, PAP is the simplest but the least secure. During the authentication phase, PAP goes through a two-way handshake process. In this process, the source sends its username (or hostname) and password, in clear text, to the destination. The destination compares this information to a list of locally stored usernames and passwords. If it finds a match, the destination sends back an *accept* message. If it doesn't find a match, it sends back a *reject* message. The top part of Figure 12-6 shows an example of PAP authentication.

FIGURE 12-6

PAP and CHAP
authentication

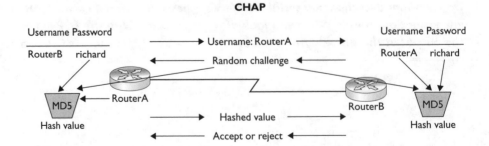

The configuration of PAP is straightforward. First, you need to determine which side will be the client side (sends the username and password) and which will be the server side (validates the username and password). To configure PAP for a PPP client, use this configuration:

```
Router(config)# interface type [slot_#]port_#
Router(config-if)# encapsulation ppp
Router(config-if)# ppp pap sent-username your_hostname
                       password password
```

The first thing you must do on the router's interface is to define the encapsulation type as PPP. Second, you must specify that PAP will be used for authentication and provide the username and password that will be used to perform the authentication on the server side. This is accomplished with the **ppp pap sent-username** command.

To configure the server side of a PPP PAP connection, use the following configuration:

```
Router(config)# hostname your_router's_hostname
Router(config)# username remote_hostname
                       password matching_password
Router(config)# interface type [slot_#/]port_#
Router(config-if)# encapsulation ppp
Router(config-if)# ppp authentication pap
```

The first thing you must do is give your router a unique hostname. Second, you must list the remote hostnames and passwords these remote hosts will use when authenticating to your router. This is accomplished with the **username** command. Please note that the password you configure on this side must match the password on the remote side (it's case sensitive). On your router's WAN interface, you need to enable PPP with the **encapsulation ppp** command. Then you can specify PAP authentication with the **ppp authentication pap** command.

The preceding client and server code listings perform a one-way authentication— the client authenticates to the server and not vice versa. If you want to perform two-way authentication, where each side must authenticate to the other side, configure both devices as PAP servers and clients.

12.05. The digital resources that accompany this book contain a multimedia demonstration of configuring PPP authentication using PAP on a router.

CHAP

One main problem with PAP is that it sends the username and password across the connection in clear text. If someone is tapping into the connection and eavesdropping on the PPP communication, she will see the actual password that is being used, making it an insecure authentication method. CHAP, on the other hand, uses a one-way hash function based on the Message Digest 5 (MD5) hashing algorithm to hash the password. This hashed value is then sent across the wire. In this situation, the actual password is never sent. Anyone tapping the wire will not be able to reverse the hash to come up with the original password. This is why MD5 is referred to as a one-way function—it cannot be reverse-engineered.

CHAP uses a three-way handshake process to perform authentication. The bottom part of Figure 12-6 shows the CHAP authentication process. First, the source sends its username (not its password) to the destination. The destination sends back a challenge, which is a random value generated by the destination. The challenge contains the following information:

- **Packet identifier** Set to 01 for a challenge, 02 for the reply to a challenge, 03 for allowing the PPP connection, and 04 for denying the connection
- **ID** A local sequence number assigned by the challenger to distinguish among multiple authentication processes
- **Random number** The random value used in the MD5 hash function
- **Router name** The name of the challenging router (the server), which is used by the source to find the appropriate password to use for authentication

e x a m

ⓦ a t c h *CHAP uses a three-way handshake. Authentication is periodically performed. Authentication commonly fails because administrators either don't match up the usernames and passwords (`username` command) on the two endpoints or don't match up the authentication protocol (`ppp authentication` command).*

Both sides then take the source's username, the matching password, and the challenge and run them through the MD5 hashing function. The source then takes the result of this function and sends it to the destination. The destination compares this value to the hashed output that it generated—if the two values match, the password used by the source must have been the same as that which was used by the destination, and thus the destination will permit the connection. This authentication process is performed periodically.

The following configuration shows how to set up two-way CHAP authentication:

```
Router(config)# hostname your_router's_hostname
Router(config)# username remote_hostname
                         password matching_password
Router(config)# interface type [slot_#/]port_#
Router(config-if)# encapsulation ppp
Router(config-if)# ppp authentication chap
```

Notice that this is the same configuration used with server-side PAP, with the exception of the omission of the sent username. The only difference is that the **chap** parameter is specified in the **ppp authentication** command.

12.06. The digital resources that accompany this book contain a multimedia demonstration of configuring PPP authentication using CHAP on a router.

Actually, here is the full syntax of the **ppp authentication** command:

```
Router(config-if)# ppp authentication {chap | pap | ms-chap}
                         [chap |pap | ms-chap]
```

Be familiar with the ppp authentication *command and that a primary and fallback authentication method can be specified.*

If you specify **pap chap** or **chap pap**, the router will negotiate both authentication parameters in the order that you specified them. For example, if you configure **chap pap**, your router will first try to negotiate CHAP; if this fails, then it will negotiate PAP.

Microsoft has its own implementation of CHAP, which is not compatible with the RFC version of CHAP. Therefore, if you are connecting to a Microsoft device, choose ms-chap *for your authentication parameter.*

Troubleshooting Authentication

To determine whether authentication was successful, use the **show interfaces** command:

```
Router# show interfaces serial 0
Serial0 is up, line protocol is down
  Hardware is MCI Serial
```

```
Internet address is 192.168.1.2 255.255.255.0
MTU 1500 bytes, BW 1544 Kbit, DLY 20000 usec, rely 254/255, load 1/255
Encapsulation PPP, loopback not set, keepalive set (10 sec)
lcp state = ACKRCVD
ncp ccp state = NOT NEGOTIATED    ncp ipcp state = CLOSED
ncp osicp state = NOT NEGOTIATED    ncp ipxcp state = NOT NEGOTIATED
ncp xnscp state = NOT NEGOTIATED    ncp vinescp state = NOT NEGOTIATED
ncp deccp state = NOT NEGOTIATED    ncp bridgecp state = NOT NEGOTIATED
ncp atalkcp state = NOT NEGOTIATED    ncp lex state = NOT NEGOTIATED
ncp cdp state = CLOSED
```

Notice the lcp state in this example: it's not OPEN. Also, notice the states for IP and CDP: CLOSED. These things indicate that something is wrong with the LCP setup process, causing the data link layer to fail ("up, line protocol is down"). In this example, the CHAP passwords on the two routers didn't match.

12.07. The digital resources that accompany this book contain a multimedia demonstration of troubleshooting PPP authentication on a router.

Of course, looking at the preceding output, you don't really know that this was an authentication problem. To determine this, use the **debug ppp authentication** command. Here's an example of the use of this command with two-way CHAP authentication:

```
RouterA# debug ppp authentication
%LINK-3-UPDOWN: Interface Serial0, changed state to up
Se0 PPP: Treating connection as a dedicated line
Se0 PPP: Phase is AUTHENTICATING, by both
Se0 CHAP: O CHALLENGE id 2 len 28 from "RouterA"
Se0 CHAP: I CHALLENGE id 3 len 28 from "RouterB"
Se0 CHAP: O RESPONSE id 3 len 28 from "RouterA"
Se0 CHAP: I RESPONSE id 2 len 28 from "RouterB"
Se0 CHAP: O SUCCESS id 2 len 4
Se0 CHAP: I SUCCESS id 3 len 4
%LINEPROTO-5-UPDOWN: Line protocol on Interface Serial0, changed state to up
```

In this example, notice that both routers—RouterA and RouterB—are using CHAP for authentication. Both routers send a CHALLENGE, and both receive a corresponding RESPONSE. Notice the I and O following Se0 CHAP:, which indicate the direction of the CHAP message: I is for inbound and O is for outbound. Following this is the status of the hashed passwords: SUCCESS. And, last, you can see the data link layer coming up for the serial interface.

Here's an example of a router using PAP with two-way authentication:

```
RouterA# debug ppp authentication
%LINK-3-UPDOWN: Interface Serial0, changed state to up
Se0 PPP: Treating connection as a dedicated line
Se0 PPP: Phase is AUTHENTICATING, by both
Se0 PAP: O AUTH-REQ id 2 len 18 from "RouterA"
Se0 PAP: I AUTH-REQ id 3 len 18 from "RouterB"
Se0 PAP: Authenticating peer RouterB
Se0 PAP: O AUTH-ACK id 2 len 5
Se0 PAP: I AUTH-ACK id 3 len 5
%LINEPROTO-5-UPDOWN: Line protocol on Interface Serial0, changed state to up
```

In this example, notice that the authentication messages are different. The AUTH-REQ shows the server requesting the authentication from a router, and the AUTH-ACK acknowledges the successful password matching by a router. Notice that since both routers are requesting authentication, both routers are set up in server mode for PAP.

exam

watch

Unlike HDLC, PPP supports authentication. PAP authentication sends the username and password across the wire in clear text. CHAP doesn't send the password in clear text—instead, a hashed value from the MD5 algorithm is sent. Use the ppp authentication command to specify which PPP authentication method to use. The username command allows you to build a local authentication table, which lists the remote names and passwords to use for authentication. The debug ppp authentication command can help you troubleshoot PPP problems—be familiar with the output of this command.

EXERCISE 12-1

Configuring PPP

The last few sections dealt with the configuration of PPP on IOS routers. This exercise will help you reinforce your understanding of this material by configuring PPP and authentication. You'll perform this lab using Boson's NetSim simulator. You can find a picture of the network diagram for Boson's NetSim simulator in the introduction of this book. After starting the simulator, click the Labs tab at the bottom left of the window. Click the McGraw-Hill Education tab (to the right of the Standard and Custom tabs) at the top left. Next, double-click Exercise 12-1. This will load the lab configuration based on the exercises in Chapter 6.

1. Check network connectivity between the two routers.

   Click the Lab Instructions tab and use the drop-down selector for Devices to choose 2600-1; or click the NetMap tab and double-click the 2600-1 device icon. From the 2600-1 router, verify the status of the serial interface: **show interface s0**. Make sure the encapsulation is HDLC. From the 2600-1 router, ping the 2600-2: **ping 192.168.2.2**. The ping should be successful.

2. On the 2600-1 router, set up PPP as the encapsulation on the serial0 interface.

   Click the Lab Instructions tab and use the drop-down selector for Devices to choose 2600-1; or click the NetMap tab and double-click the 2600-1 device icon. On the 2600-1, enter the serial interface: **configure terminal** and **interface serial0**. Set up PPP as the data link frame type: **encapsulation ppp** and **end**.

3. Verify the status of the serial0 interface.

   View the status of the interface: **show interface serial0**. The physical layer should be *up* and the data link layer should be *down*—the 2600-2 still has HDLC configured. Also, examine the output of the **show** command to verify that the encapsulation is PPP.

4. On the 2600-2 router, set up PPP as the encapsulation on the serial0 interface.

   Click the Lab Instructions tab and use the drop-down selector for Devices to choose 2600-2; or click the NetMap tab and double-click the 2600-2 device icon. On the 2600-2, enter the serial interface: `configure terminal` and `interface serial0`. Set up PPP as the data link frame type: `encapsulation ppp` and `end`.

5. Verify the status of the `serial0` interface.

   View the status of the interface: `show interface serial0`. The physical and data link layers should be *up* (this should also be true on the 2600-1 router). Also check to make sure the encapsulation is PPP.

6. Test connectivity by pinging the 2600-1's `serial0` interface.

   Test connectivity: `ping 192.168.2.1`. The ping should be successful.

7. Set up PPP CHAP authentication on the 2600-1. Use a password of *richard*. Test the authentication.

   Click the Lab Instructions tab and use the drop-down selector for Devices to choose 2600-1; or click the NetMap tab and double-click the 2600-1 device icon. Access Configuration mode: `configure terminal`. On the 2600-1, set up your username and password: `username 2600-2 password richard`. Enter the serial interface: `interface serial0`. Set the authentication to CHAP: `ppp authentication chap`. Shut down the interface: `shutdown`. Bring the interface back up: `no shutdown`. Exit Configuration mode: `end`.

8. Examine the status of the `serial0` interface.

   Examine the status of the interface: `show interface serial0`. The data link layer should be down, and the LCP should be ACKRCVD. Please note that you don't really need to bring the interface down and back up, because after a period of time, LCP will notice that authentication configuration and will perform it.

9. Set up PPP CHAP authentication on the 2600-2. Use a password of *richard*. Test the authentication. Test the connection.

   Click the Lab Instructions tab and use the drop-down selector for Devices to choose 2600-2; or click the NetMap tab and double-click the 2600-2 device icon. Access Configuration mode: `configure terminal`. On the 2600-2, set up your username and password: `username 2600-1 password richard`. Enter the serial interface: `interface serial0`. Set the authentication to CHAP: `ppp authentication chap`. Shut down the interface: `shutdown`. Bring the interface back up: `no shutdown`. Exit Configuration mode: `end`.

10. Examine the status of the serial0 interface.

    Examine the status of the interface: **show interface serial0**. The data link layer should come up and the LCP should be OPEN. IP and CDP should be the two protocols in an OPEN state.

11. Test connectivity to the 2600-1.

    Ping the 2600-1: **ping 192.168.2.1**. The ping should be successful.

EXERCISE 12-2

Basic PPP Troubleshooting

This exercise is a troubleshooting exercise and is different from Exercise 12-1. In that exercise, you set up a PPP CHAP connection between the 2600-2 and 2600-1 routers. In this exercise, the network is already configured; however, there are three problems in this network you'll need to find and fix in order for it to operate correctly. All of these problems deal with connectivity between the 2600-2 and 2600-1 routers. You'll perform this exercise using Boson's NetSim simulator. You can find a picture of the network diagram for Boson's NetSim simulator in the introduction of this book. The addressing scheme is the same. After starting up the simulator, click the Labs tab at the bottom left of the window. Click the McGraw-Hill Education tab (to the right of the Standard and Custom tabs) at the top left. Next, double-click Exercise 12-2. This will load the lab with a PPP configuration on your routers.

Let's start with your problem: The PPP data link layer between the 2600-2 and 2600-1 won't come up. Your task is to figure out and fix three problems. Try this troubleshooting process on your own first; if you have problems, come back to the steps and solutions provided here.

1. Examine the status of the serial interface on the 2600-1.

    Click the Lab Instructions tab and use the drop-down selector for Devices to choose 2600-1; or click the NetMap tab and double-click the 2600-1 device icon. Examine serial0: **show interfaces serial0**. Note that the interface is up and the line protocol is down. This indicates a physical or data link layer problem.

2. Check the status of serial0 on the 2600-2.

Click the Lab Instructions tab and use the drop-down selector for Devices to choose 2600-2; or click the NetMap tab and double-click the 2600-2 device icon. Examine the status of the interface: **show interfaces serial0**. Notice that the interface is administratively down. Activate the interface: **configure terminal**, **interface serial0**, **no shutdown**, and **end**. Wait a few seconds and examine the status of the interface: **show interfaces serial0**. Notice that the status of the interface is up and down, indicating that there is a problem with the data link layer. Notice that the encapsulation, though, is set to PPP.

3. Check the 2600-1's serial encapsulation and the rest of its configuration.

    Click the Lab Instructions tab and use the drop-down selector for Devices to choose 2600-1; or click the NetMap tab and double-click the 2600-1 device icon. Examine the status of the interface: **show interfaces serial0**. Notice that the status of the interface is up and down, indicating that there is a problem with the data link layer. Notice that the encapsulation, though, is set to PPP. Since both sides are set to PPP, there must be an authentication problem. Examine the 2600-1's active configuration: **show running-config**. CHAP is configured for authentication on serial0. Notice, though, that the **username** has the 2600-1's, and not the 2600-2's. Fix this by doing the following: **configure terminal**, **no username 2600-1 password cisco**, **username 2600-2 password cisco**, and **end**. Re-examine the router's configuration: **show running-config**. Examine the status of the interface: **show interfaces serial0**. The data link layer is still down, so there must be a problem on the 2600-2 router.

4. Access the 2600-2 router and determine the PPP problem.

    Click the Lab Instructions tab and use the drop-down selector for Devices to choose 2600-2; or click the NetMap tab and double-click the 2600-2 device icon. Examine the active configuration: **show running-config**. The **username** command is correct, with the 2600-1's hostname and a password of *cisco*. However, there is a problem with the PPP authentication method on the serial interface: CHAP is missing. Fix this problem: **configure terminal**, **interface serial0**, and **ppp authentication chap**. Bounce the interface: **shutdown**, **no shutdown**, and **end**. Re-examine the router's configuration: **show running-config**. Wait a few seconds and examine the status of the interface: **`show interfaces serial0`**. The data link layer should now be up and line protocol is up.

5. Now test connectivity between the 2600-2 and 2600-1.

   Test connectivity to the 2600-1: **`ping 192.168.2.1`**. The ping should be successful. If you want to allow connectivity for all devices, you'll need to add a static route on both the 2600-2 (to reach 192.168.1.0/24) and the 2600-1 (to reach 192.168.3.0/24).

Now you should be more comfortable with configuring PPP on a router.

CERTIFICATION OBJECTIVE 12.04

Virtual Private Networks

One WAN solution becoming more common today is virtual private networks, commonly called VPNs. The *network* part of the term refers to the use of a public network, such as the Internet, to implement the WAN solution. The *virtual* part of the term hides the public network from the internal network components, such as users and services. This is similar to using virtual circuits (VCs) to connect remote locations, such as a corporate office, remote access users and SOHOs, branch and regional offices, and business partners, as shown in Figure 12-7. Actually, a VPN is similar to a Frame Relay network; however, a VPN uses a public network for its connectivity and Frame Relay uses a private one. The *private* part of the term specifies that the traffic should remain private—not viewable by eavesdroppers in the network. This is accomplished using encryption to keep the data confidential.

Many VPN technologies exist, such as IPsec, Point-to-Point Tunneling Protocol (PPTP), Layer 2 Transport Protocol (L2TP), SSL, and others; however, this chapter serves as a quick introduction to VPNs. A detailed introduction to VPNs—the different types and the technologies they use, how they work, how to configure them on Cisco devices, and how to troubleshoot them—is covered extensively in my book *The Complete Cisco VPN Configuration Guide* (Cisco Press, 2005).

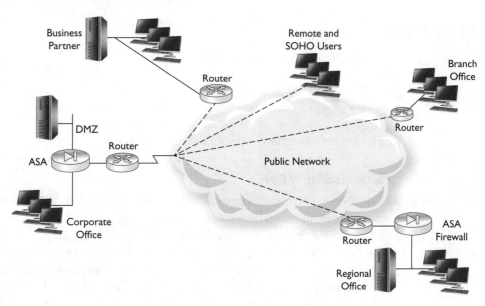

FIGURE 12-7

Network using a VPN

Intranet: Same company sites
Extranet: Third-party and business partners
Remote Access: Users and SOHOs
Business Partner
Remote and SOHO Users
Branch Office
Router
Router
DMZ
Router
ASA
Public Network
Corporate Office
Router
ASA Firewall
Regional Office

Benefits

VPNs provide four main benefits over setting up a private WAN network, such as those used by Frame Relay, point-to-point circuits, and ATM:

- **Security** Security is provided through data encryption to protect confidentiality, data integrity checking to validate packets, and authentication to prevent unauthorized access.
- **Cost** Public networks, such as the Internet, can be used instead of building a private WAN infrastructure, greatly reducing a company's WAN infrastructure cost.
- **Bandwidth** Inexpensive high-bandwidth connections, such as DSL and cable, can be used to interconnect offices to allow for fast and secure access to corporate resources.

exam watch *Be familiar with the benefits of VPN solutions.*

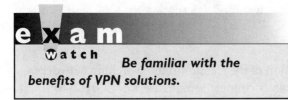

■ **Scalability** Companies can easily add large numbers of users and offices without building a significant WAN infrastructure.

VPN Types

VPNs fall under two implementation types:

■ Site-to-site VPNs
■ Remote-access VPNs

The following sections will expand on these types.

Site-to-Site VPNs

Site-to-site VPNs, sometimes called *LAN-to-LAN* or *L2L* VPNs, connect two locations or sites together, basically extending a classical WAN design. Two intermediate devices, commonly called *VPN gateways*, protect the traffic between the two LANs. This type of VPN tunnels packets between the locations: the original IP packet from one LAN is encrypted by one gateway, forwarded to the destination gateway, and then decrypted and forwarded to the local LAN at its end to the destination. From the perspective of the real source and destination, the VPN is *virtual*—they don't even know their traffic is being protected between the two VPN gateways. The most common site-to-site protocol used to protect traffic is IPsec. Routers are commonly used as the VPN gateway device, though other devices can be used, such as firewalls. Cisco products that support IPsec L2L VPNs include IOS routers and the ASA security appliances. Because of scalability features such as dynamic multipoint VPNs (DMVPNs), Cisco routers are the preferred choice for IPsec L2L gateways.

L2Ls come in two flavors: *intranet* and *extranet*. An intranet L2L basically connects two offices of the same company together, such as a corporate office and a regional or branch office. An extranet is an L2L VPN that connects two different companies together, such as a corporate office and another company that is a business partner. Address translation is commonly required here because the two companies might be using the same private address space.

Remote-Access VPNs

Remote-access VPNs are an extension of the classic circuit-switching networks, such as POTS and ISDN. They securely connect remote users or SOHOs to a corporate or branch office. With a remote-access VPN, the VPN provides a virtualization process, making it appear that the remote-access user or office is physically connected to the corporate office network. Common protocols used for remote-access VPNs include IPsec, SSL, PPTP, and L2TP. Cisco supports all four of these protocols; however, most of Cisco's development effort is based on IPsec and SSL. These are discussed in the next two sections.

Easy VPN   Cisco's IPsec remote-access solution is called *Easy VPN*. Easy VPN is a design approach Cisco took to make it easy to deploy, scale to a large number of users, and centralize policy configurations. Easy VPN involves two components:

- Easy VPN Server
- Easy VPN Remote or Client

The Easy VPN Server centralizes the policy configurations for the Easy VPN Remotes and provides access to corporate resources. All of your IPsec remote-access policies are configured on the Servers and pushed down to the Remotes, which implement the policies. This makes it easy to change policies, since they need to be changed only on a small number of Servers, not on any of the Remotes. Easy VPN Server products that Cisco supports include the ASA security appliances and Cisco IOS routers. Since the concentrators are end-of-life, the recommended platform for Easy VPN Servers is the ASA security appliances.

The Easy VPN Remote allows the user or users to access corporate resources securely via the Easy VPN Server. Very little configuration is required on the Remote to bring up a tunnel—another reason the term *easy* is used to describe this solution. Easy VPN Remotes include the following products from Cisco: the Cisco VPN Client (CVC), which runs on Windows, OS X, Solaris, and Linux (is currently end-of-sale [EOS]), and AnyConnect Secure Mobility Client; the Certicom and Movian clients (run on mobile devices); and hardware clients such as the ASA 5505 and small-end routers such as the ISR 800 through the 3900 series routers. Easy VPN allows users to use their applications as they would without having a VPN in place; the downside of Easy VPN is that special software must be installed on user desktops, laptops, or mobile devices or a hardware client must be deployed.

WebVPN Unlike IPsec, which is an open standard, SSL VPNs, even though they use SSL as their protection protocol, are implemented differently by each vendor, making them proprietary. SSL VPNs are one of the newest VPNs in the marketplace today. Cisco's SSL VPN solution is called WebVPN and provides three secure connection methods: clientless, thin client, and network client mode. The clientless and thin client implementations use a normal web browser, with JavaScript installed, to provide the VPN solution. The main advantage of this is that no special software has to be installed on a user's desktop—they use the web browser that is already there! The downside of this is that the applications must be either web based or a supported handful of non–web-based applications, such as telnet. The AnyConnect Mobility client provides network layer protection and allows users to use their day-to-day applications without any modifications. And on the VPN gateway side, setting up the gateways, changing their policies, and adding new users to them are easy tasks. However, they are not as scalable or as secure as using IPsec.

on the job

It is not uncommon to see a company use both Easy VPN and WebVPN: Easy VPN is used for situations in which hardware clients are used at SOHOs or when users are using company computers, such as laptops, where it is acceptable to install the Cisco VPN Client. WebVPN is commonly used when it is not possible to install Easy VPN client software, such as for business partners accessing your network or employees using airport Internet kiosks when they are traveling.

IPsec

IPsec, short for IP Security, is an open standard defined across quite a few different RFCs. IPsec functions at the network layer and protects IP packets. IPsec can be used for L2L VPNs as well as remote-access VPNs. Compared to all other VPN solutions, using IPsec is the most secure and widely used solution today, but also the most difficult to set up and troubleshoot. The next two sections briefly cover the services IPsec offers and the protocols it uses to provide for protection.

IPsec Services

IPsec provides four main services:

- **Authentication** Verifying the identity of remote peers; digital signatures are used to provide identity verification via pre-shared keys or digital certificates.

- **Confidentiality**   Guaranteeing that no intermediate device can decipher the contents of the payload in a packet; encryption is used to "hide" the real data.

- **Integrity**   Guaranteeing that the contents of a packet have not been tampered with (changed) by an intermediate device; a derivative of hashing functions, called HMAC functions, is used to verify the source of every packet and check if the packet was tampered with or not (HMAC is defined later in the "Integrity: HMAC Functions" section).

- **Anti-replay protection**   Verifying that each packet is unique and not duplicated; ensuring that copies of a valid packet are not used to create a denial of service attack; protected sequence numbers are used to detect duplicate packets and drop them.

IPsec Components

The following sections discuss the components of IPsec, including keys, encryption algorithms, HMAC functions, and protocols. The following information provides only a brief introduction to these components.

Confidentiality: Keys and Encryption   A *key* is a term used in security to protect information. Just as you would use a password to protect a user account, or a PIN to protect your ATM card, a key in the data world is used to protect your information. Keys can be used in two ways: to perform encryption and decryption and to provide authentication and integrity of your transmission. Typically, the longer the key, the more difficult it is for a man-in-the-middle (MTM) attack to break the encryption process by doing reverse-engineering to discover the key.

Two methods are used for implementing keying solutions: symmetric keys and asymmetric keys. With symmetric keys, the same key is used to protect your information. Because it uses the same key for both encryption and de-encryption, the algorithm used is much simpler and thus the protection process is very fast; therefore, symmetric keys are commonly used for encrypting large amounts of data. However, the problem with symmetric keys is that somehow the keys need to be shared between the two peers. There are two methods of accomplishing this securely:

- *Pre-share the keys out-of-band.* This is not very scalable if you need to manage hundreds of keys.
- *Share the keys across a secure connection.* The Diffie-Hellman (DH) protocol accomplishes this for IPsec.

Examples of symmetric encryption algorithms supported by IPsec include Data Encryption Standard (DES), Triple DES (3DES), and Advanced Encryption Standard (AES), which are 128-bit, 192-bit, and 256-bit, respectively. Of the three, AES is the most secure. Cisco's IOS routers and ASAs support modular cards to perform these types of encryption in hardware at very high speeds.

When using asymmetric keys, two keys are generated for a unidirectional communication: one is kept by the source (private key), and the other is given to the destination (public key). When the destination wants to send something to the source, it uses the source's public key to encrypt the information, and then, when the source receives the data, the source uses its corresponding private key to decrypt it. Since only the corresponding private key can decrypt the information, the private key is never shared. And because communication is a two-way process, the destination will also have to generate two keys and share its public key with the original source. Asymmetric keys are much more secure than symmetric keys; however, the former is much, much slower when protecting information—about 1500 times slower than symmetric key algorithms. Therefore, asymmetric keys are usually used either to share symmetric keys or to perform authentication of a peer.

DH and RSA are two examples of asymmetric keying algorithms. IPsec uses DH to share keys (a key exchange protocol) and RSA to authenticate VPN peers. Within IPsec, DH supports 368-, 768-, 1024-, and 1536-bit keys. RSA supports key sizes from 512 bits to 2048 bits (up to eight times longer than AES-256).

Integrity: HMAC Functions   Hashing functions are used to verify whether information was changed. Hashed message authentication code (HMAC) functions are a derivative of hashing functions and are used specifically for security functions: they take a variable-length input and a symmetric key and run these through the

HMAC function, resulting in a fixed-length output. The fixed-length output is commonly called a *digital signature*. IPsec supports two HMAC functions:

- Message Digest 5 (MD5)
- Secure Hashing Algorithm version 1 (SHA-1)

MD5 is defined in RFC 1321 and creates a 128-bit digital signature. MD5 is used in many other protocols, including PPP's CHAP and authentication of routing updates in RIPv2, EIGRP, OSPF, BGP, and others. SHA-1 is defined in RFC 2404 and creates a longer signature of 160 bits in length. Of the two, SHA-1 is more secure, but slower.

In IPsec, HMAC functions are used to validate that a packet is coming from a trusted source (packet authentication) and that the packet hasn't been tampered with (packet integrity). The source takes information from the packet being sent, along with the symmetric key, and runs it through the HMAC function, creating a digital signature. The signature is then added to the original packet and sent to the destination. The destination repeats the process: it takes the original packet input along with the same symmetric key, and should be able to generate the same signature that was sent in the packet. If the signature generated is the same, then the packet must come from someone who knows the symmetric key and knows that the packet hasn't been tampered with; if the computed signature is not the same, then the packet is dropped since either the signature in it is a fake or the packet was tampered with between the source and destination.

Authentication: Peer Validation   Another important component of any VPN solution, including IPsec, is validating the peer's identity through some form of authentication. IPsec supports two forms of authentication: device and user (commonly called extended authentication, or XAUTH for short). L2L sessions support only device authentication, while remote-access sessions support both. Device authentication supports two methods of validating a peer:

- **Pre-shared keys (PSKs)**   PSKs require that a pre-shared symmetric key be configured on each VPN peer. This key is then used, along with identity information from the peer, to generate a signature. The remote end can then validate the signature using the same PSK.
- **RSA signatures**   RSA signatures use asymmetric keys for authentication. Hashes of signatures (created with a private key) are placed on digital certificates generated by a central certificate authority (CA). The signatures can then be validated with the associated public key.

Of the two, PSK is the easier to implement; however, certificates using RSA signatures are a much more scalable solution.

IPsec Protocols

IPsec is actually a group of standards, protocols, and technologies that work together to build a secure session, commonly called a *tunnel*, to a remote peer. An IPsec tunnel comprises three connections: one management connection and two unidirectional data connections. The tunnel is built across two phases. The management connection is built during Phase 1 and is used to share IPsec-related information between the two peers. The two data connections are built during Phase 2 and are used to transmit user traffic. All three connections are protected. Here is a brief description of these protocols used to build a tunnel:

- ■ **ISAKMP**   The *Internet Security Association and Key Management Protocol* is used to build and maintain the tunnel; it defines the format of the management payload, specifies the mechanics of a key exchange protocol for the encryption algorithms and HMAC functions, negotiates how the tunnel will be built between the two devices, and authenticates the remote device.

- ■ **IKE**   The *Internet Key Exchange Protocol* is responsible for generating and managing keys used for encryption algorithms and HMAC functions. Actually, it is a combination of ISAKMP and IKE working together that secures the tunnel between two devices: they use UDP as a transport and connect on port 500.

- ■ **DH**   The *Diffie-Hellman* process is used to securely exchange the encryption and HMAC keys that will be used to secure the management and data connections.

- ■ **AH**   The *Authentication Header* protocol is used only to confirm the origination and validity of data packets (on the data connections) received from a peer; it accomplishes this by using HMAC functions, where the signature created is based on almost the entire IP packet. Its two main disadvantages are that it breaks if it goes through any type of address translation device and it does not support encryption.

- ■ **ESP**   The *Encapsulation Security Payload* protocol is used to provide packet confidentiality and authentication. It provides confidentiality through encryption and provides packet authentication through an HMAC

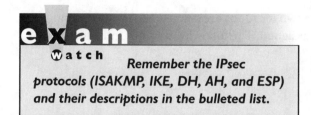

watch *Remember the IPsec protocols (ISAKMP, IKE, DH, AH, and ESP) and their descriptions in the bulleted list.*

function. Because it supports encryption, it is the protocol that companies use to protect the data connections; however, its downside is that its signature process does not protect the outer IP header and thus cannot detect packet tampering in the header, whereas AH can. ESP's other main advantage is that it can work through address translation devices doing NAT without any changes, but it requires an encapsulation in a UDP packet to work through a PAT or firewall device. This part of the IPsec standard is called NAT Transparency or Traversal, or NAT-T for short.

CERTIFICATION OBJECTIVE 12.05

Generic Route Encapsulation Tunnels

A unicast Generic Route Encapsulation (GRE) point-to-point tunnel is a logical connection between two routers that is used to carry all types of IP and non-IP traffic. GRE tunnels are commonly used with IPsec site-to-site VPN solutions to provide for scalability and flexibility. Originally developed by Cisco and then standardized in RFCs 1701 and 1702, GRE provides a logical connection (subnet) between two routers across either a private or public network. See Figure 12-8 for

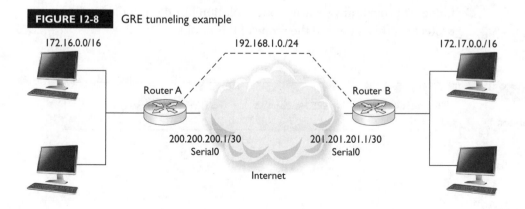

FIGURE 12-8 GRE tunneling example

an example. In this example, the two locations are connected via a GRE tunnel with the 192.168.1.0/24 subnet assigned. The following sections introduce you to GRE and its configuration.

GRE Overview

To provide the logical connection between devices, Cisco IOS uses a logical tunnel interface. When "tunneling" packets, information is added to the original data (either a packet or a frame) to indicate that GRE is being used and to specify the destination GRE device to forward it to. Figure 12-9 illustrates the encapsulation process. The GRE header that is added is an additional 24 bytes, which doesn't include the outer IP header's length. Cisco supports the encapsulation of either layer 3 packets (such as IPv4 or IPv6, IPX, and so forth) or layer 2 frames (bridging traffic).

Using Figure 12-8 as an example, the 192.168.1.0/24 subnet provides the logical connection. From the 172.16.0.0/16 and 172.17.0.0/16 networks' perspective, the Internet appears as a single logical hop connecting the two networks. When traffic flows between them, the IP packets are encapsulated using GRE. For example, if traffic is flowing from 172.16.1.1 to 172.17.1.1, when the packets reach RouterA, it adds a GRE header to them and then an outer IP header, where the source address is itself (200.200.200.1) and the destination is RouterB (201.201.201.1). RouterA and RouterB then tunnel the traffic between the two networks.

GRE has these characteristics:

- It can transport any layer 3 protocol or bridged traffic.
- It is stateless: it does not provide any flow control or acknowledgement process.
- It doesn't provide any security (but a solution like IPsec could be used to protect it—this is beyond the scope of this book).

FIGURE 12-9

GRE encapsulation process

Transport IP Header	GRE Header	IP Packet or Frame

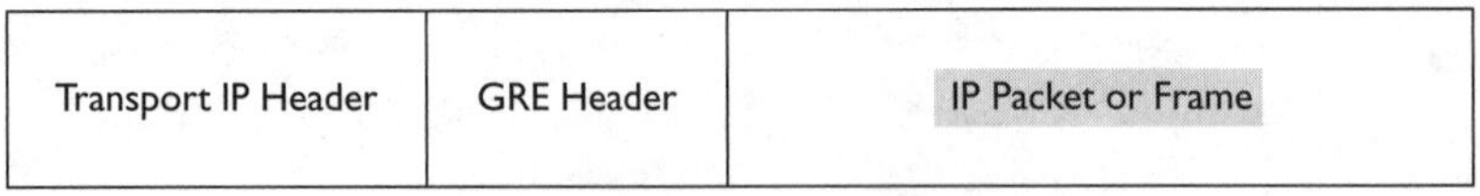

GRE Configuration and Verification

To implement a GRE solution, you need to perform the following:

- Create a tunnel interface
- Specify the GRE tunnel mode (optional)
- Specify the source and destination routers of the logical tunnel
- Configure IP addressing for the tunnel interface
- Enable routing (static or dynamic) so that the routers know what networks are reachable across the tunnel

GRE Command Syntax

Creating a tunnel interface and its properties is easy, as shown in the following configuration:

```
Router(config)# interface tunnel interface_#
Router(config-if)# tunnel mode gre ip
Router(config-if)# tunnel source interface_name_or_local_IP_addr
Router(config-if)# tunnel destination reachable_IP_addr_of_peer
Router(config-if)# ip address IP_addr subnet_mask
```

The tunnel interface number is an unused tunnel interface number on the router, where 0 is the lowest number. Identifying an encapsulation protocol (**tunnel mode**) is optional: if not defined, it defaults to a GRE point-to-point interface. Other encapsulation methods are available, but are beyond the scope of this book. You must specify the source of the tunnel (**tunnel source** command), which is either an IP address of the public interface of the local router or the name of the interface that has this IP address assigned. The tunnel destination is the reachable IP address of the destination router (**tunnel destination** command). The IP addresses must be reachable by the two routers; if the routers are connected to the Internet, then the addresses must be public IP addresses. The two peers need to have unique IP addresses in the same subnet. In Figure 12-8, this would be an address in the 192.168.1.0/24 subnet.

on the
ĵ o b

Since these are point-to-point connections, I recommend that you use a /30 mask to conserve addressing, since a /30 mask provides for just two host addresses.

GRE Configuration Example

Again referring to Figure 12-8, here is RouterA's configuration for the GRE tunnel:

```
RouterA(config)# interface tunnel 0
RouterA(config-if)# tunnel source serial0
RouterA(config-if)# tunnel destination 201.201.201.1
RouterA(config-if)# ip address 192.168.1.1 255.255.255.0
```

Here is RouterB's configuration:

```
RouterB(config)# interface tunnel 0
RouterB(config-if)# tunnel source serial0
RouterB(config-if)# tunnel destination 200.200.200.1
RouterB(config-if)# ip address 192.168.1.2 255.255.255.0
```

Notice that both routers have a unique IP address on the tunnel interface: RouterA has 192.168.1.1 and RouterB has 192.168.1.2. In order to reach destinations on both sides of the tunnel, you could configure either static routing or a dynamic routing protocol. Here is an example static route you could configure for RouterA:

```
RouterA(config)# ip route 172.17.0.0 255.255.0.0 192.168.1.2
```

Notice that in this example, the next-hop address is the GRE interface address of RouterB. If you are configuring a dynamic routing protocol, like OSPF or EIGRP, your network command would need to include the GRE subnet (192.168.1.0/24). Your routing table would then include the GRE tunnel interface (`tunnel0` in our example) and a next-hop address of 192.168.1.2 to use to reach the remote subnet.

GRE Verification

The GRE interface you created is treated just like every other interface on the router. You can use the **show interfaces** command to verify its operation, like this:

```
RouterA# show interfaces
Tunnel0 is up, line protocol is up
  Hardware is Tunnel
  Internet address is 192.168.1.1/24
  MTU 17916 byes, BW 100 Kbit/sec, DLY 50000 usec,
    reliability 255/255, txload 1/255, rxload 1/255
  Encapsulation TUNNEL, loopback not set
  Keepalive not set
  Tunnel source 200.200.200.1, destination 201.201.201.1
  Tunnel protocol/transport: GRE/IP
```

If both sides' tunnel source and destination IP addresses are reachable, then the line protocol will be *up*, as is the case in this example.

INSIDE THE EXAM

Wide Area Networking Overview

Remember that WANs operate at the physical and data link layers. You should be familiar with what DCE and DTE are, what their main functions are, and examples of these kinds of devices. WAN services that use VCs, such as Frame Relay and ATM, are used to connect multiple locations together using a single WAN interface. Be able to compare and contrast different data link layer encapsulation types, such as HDLC and PPP, as shown in Table 12-2. Serial interfaces are used for synchronous connections. You should be very familiar with the output of the **show interfaces** command and be able to decipher the status of the physical and data link layers of an interface. Don't be surprised to see two or three questions related to interface problems or statuses on the exam.

HDLC

Remember that Cisco's implementation of HDLC is proprietary: the frame header has a proprietary Type field. Know how to troubleshoot problems with HDLC interfaces: mismatch in encapsulation types, Cisco and non-Cisco devices, misconfigured IP addressing, and missed keepalive responses—this statement also applies to the section on configuring PPP.

Remember that when you execute the **show running-config** command, if no **encapsulation** command is displayed in the configuration for a synchronous serial interface, the default encapsulation is HDLC.

PPP

PPP should be used in a mixed-vendor environment. Know the services PPP provides: authentication via CHAP and PAP, support for multiple encapsulated protocols, compression, multilink, error detection/correction, and support for synchronous and asynchronous circuits. Be able to explain what LCP and NCP do within PPP and the differences between PAP and CHAP authentication. As with HDLC, know how to troubleshoot PPP connections by examining the status of the LCP state with the **show interfaces** command, and be able to identify problems with misconfigured PAP or CHAP authentication by examining a router's configuration with the **show running-config** command.

Virtual Private Networks

VPNs are not currently emphasized on the exam; however, you might be asked a general question about when VPNs are most

(Continued)

INSIDE THE EXAM

recommended, the different kinds of VPNs Cisco offers, and some of the basic terms used by a VPN, such as IPsec.

Generic Route Encapsulation Tunnels

A unicast GRE point-to-point tunnel is a logical connection between two routers that is used to carry all types of IP and non-IP traffic. It is stateless: it does not provide any flow control or acknowledgement process and also does not provide any security. The `tunnel source` and `tunnel destination` commands are required, and a layer 3 address needs to be assigned from the same subnet.

CERTIFICATION SUMMARY

The CPE is your WAN equipment. The demarcation point is the point where the carrier's responsibility for the circuit ends. The local loop is the connection from the demarcation point to the carrier's WAN switching equipment. There are four main WAN connection categories. Leased lines include dedicated circuits, which are useful for short connections where you have constant traffic and need guaranteed bandwidth. Circuit-switched connections provide dialup capabilities, as are needed for analog modems and ISDN. These connections are mostly used for backup of primary connections and for an additional bandwidth boost. Packet-switched connections include Frame Relay and X.25. They are used to connect multiple sites together at a reasonable cost. If you need guaranteed bandwidth or need to carry multiple services, cell-switched services, such as ATM, provide a better solution.

Switch interfaces are enabled by default, but router interfaces need to be enabled with the `no shutdown` command. For DCE serial interfaces, routers need a clock rate applied with the `clock rate` command. Use the `show interfaces` command to view the status and configuration of your interfaces.

Cisco synchronous serial interfaces support DB-60 and DB-26 connectors. The default encapsulation on these interfaces is Cisco's HDLC. Cisco's HDLC and ISO's HDLC are not compatible with each other. Use the `encapsulation hdlc` command to change an interface's encapsulation to Cisco's HDLC. The `show interfaces` command displays the data link layer encapsulation for a serial interface.

PPP is one of the most commonly used data link encapsulations for serial interfaces. It is an open standard. It defines three things: frame type, LCP, and NCP. When building a PPP connection, LCP takes place first, then authentication, and last NCP. LCP is responsible for negotiating parameters and setting up and maintaining connections, which include authentication, compression, link quality, error detection, multiplexing network layer protocols, and multilink. NCP handles the negotiation of the upper layer protocols that the PPP connection will transport. To set up PPP as an encapsulation type on your serial interface, use the **encapsulation ppp** command. Use the **debug ppp negotiation** command to troubleshoot LCP and NCP problems.

There are two forms of PPP authentication: PAP and CHAP. PAP sends the password across the wire in clear text, while CHAP sends a hashed output value from the MD5 hash algorithm—the password is not sent across the connection. PAP goes through a two-way handshake, while CHAP goes through a three-way handshake. Authentication is optional but can be configured with the **ppp authentication** {**chap** | **pap** | **ms-chap**} Interface Subconfiguration mode command. To build a local authentication table with usernames and passwords, use the **username** command. If you have authentication problems, troubleshoot them with the **debug ppp authentication** command.

VPNs are becoming a common and inexpensive solution for providing protected connectivity across a public network. VPN implementation types include site to site and remote access. The most common VPN implementations are IPsec and SSL. Cisco's remote access VPNs include Easy VPN for IPsec and WebVPN for SSL. Easy VPN has two components: Server and Remote. The Server centralizes policy configurations. Cisco supports both hardware and software Remote devices. IPsec is an open standard for implementing site-to-site and remote-access VPNs. It provides authentication, confidentiality, integrity, and anti-replay protection. Protocols used to implement IPsec include ISAKMP, IKE, DH, AH, and ESP.

GRE is a non-secure way of interconnecting different networks across an intermediate network. Since GRE does not provide security, it is commonly protected using another protocol, like IPsec, when traversing a public network. Creating a GRE tunnel interface requires the following commands: **interface tunnel**, **tunnel source**, and **tunnel destination**. If routing IP traffic across the GRE tunnel, then both sides need a unique IP address in the same subnet assigned to their respective tunnel interfaces.

TWO-MINUTE DRILL

Wide Area Networking Overview

❑ DCEs provide synchronization and clocking on a serial connection. Examples of DCEs include modems, NT1s, and CSU/DSUs (T1 lines).

❑ Leased lines are dedicated circuits. Circuit-switched connections use analog modems or ISDN for dialup connections. Packet-switched services, such as ATM, Frame Relay, and X.25, use VCs for transmitting data. Of these, leased lines are the most costly. Packet-switched services are used when you need to connect a router to multiple destinations but the router has only a single serial interface.

❑ The `no shutdown` command enables an interface; interfaces on switches are enabled by default, but router interfaces are disabled. The `clock rate` command specifies the speed of a DCE serial interface on a router and is required when connecting two serial interfaces back to back without using external clocking devices such as CSU/DSUs. Use the `show controller` command to verify whether or not the serial interface is a DTE or DCE.

HDLC

❑ ISO's HDLC and Cisco's HDLC are not compatible. Cisco's frame format has a proprietary Type field that allows for the transport of multiple protocols. Cisco's HDLC is the default encapsulation on synchronous serial interfaces and is not displayed with the `show running-config` command.

❑ To configure this frame format on an interface, use this command: `encapsulation hdlc`. Use the `show interfaces` command to verify your encapsulation and to troubleshoot problems when the data link layer is down.

PPP

❑ PPP is an open standard that provides dynamic configuration of links, authentication, error detection, compression, and multiple links.

❑ LCP sets up, configures, and transfers information across a PPP connection. NCP negotiates the data link and network protocols that will be transported across this link. The PPP frame format is based on ISO's HDLC.

❑ Use this interface command to specify PPP: `encapsulation ppp`. Use the `show interfaces` command to view the PPP status. OPEN indicates successful negotiation, and CLOSED indicates a problem. Use the `debug ppp negotiation` command for detailed troubleshooting of LCP and NCP.

❑ PAP uses a two-way handshake and sends the password across in clear text. CHAP uses a three-way handshake and sends a hashed value, which is created by MD5 by inputting a challenge, the hostname, and the password.

❑ To set up authentication, use the `ppp authentication chap|pap` command. Use the `debug ppp authentication` command to troubleshoot. CHALLENGE, RESPONSE, and SUCCESS messages are from CHAP, and AUTH-REQ and AUTH-ACK are from PAP.

Virtual Private Networks

❑ VPNs provide protection connections between different networks (L2L) and networks and users (remote access).

❑ Cisco's two main remote-access technologies are IPsec with Easy VPN and SSL with WebVPN.

❑ IPsec provides peer authentication via pre-shared keys or certificates (RSA signatures), confidentiality via encryption, packet integrity via HMAC functions, and anti-replay protection via unique sequence numbers in packets.

Generic Route Encapsulation Tunnels

❑ GRE provides a logical connection between two routers.

❑ GRE can transport any layer 3 protocol or bridged traffic.

❑ GRE doesn't provide any security.

❑ Configuring a tunnel interface requires the remote sides be reachable; in a public network, this would require both sides to have public addresses on their interfaces connected to the Internet.

❑ Creating a GRE tunnel interface requires the following commands: `interface tunnel`, `tunnel source`, and `tunnel destination`.

SELF TEST

The following Self Test questions will help you measure your understanding of the material presented in this chapter. Read all the choices carefully, as there may be more than one correct answer. Choose all correct answers for each question.

Wide Area Networking Overview

1. Which device provides clocking and synchronization on a synchronous serial interface on a router connected to a DTE cable?
   A. The router itself
   B. Modem
   C. CSU/DSU
   D. Carrier switch

2. At what layer or layers does a WAN typically operate at within the OSI Reference Model?
   A. Physical only
   B. Data link only
   C. Physical and data link
   D. Physical, data link, and network

3. You examine your interfaces, and the `Ethernet 0` interface status says `Ethernet 0 is up, line protocol is down`. What does this indicate?
   A. A physical layer problem
   B. A data link layer problem
   C. A network layer problem
   D. There is no problem.

HDLC

4. Which frame field is different between ISO HDLC and Cisco's HDLC?
   A. Address
   B. Control
   C. Flag
   D. Type

5. The default encapsulation on a synchronous serial interface is _____.
   A. HDLC
   B. PPP
   C. neither HDLC nor PPP
   D. auto-sensed on synchronous serial interfaces

PPP

6. PPP can do all of the following except _____.
   A. authentication
   B. compression
   C. quality of service
   D. All answers are correct.

7. _____ negotiates the data link and network layer protocols that will traverse a PPP connection.
   A. LCP
   B. NCP
   C. CDP
   D. PAP

8. When you have configured PPP on an interface and use the `show interfaces` command, what state indicates the successful negotiation of a network layer protocol?
   A. ACK
   B. CHALLENGE
   C. CLOSED
   D. OPEN

9. Which of the following is false concerning CHAP?
   A. It sends an encrypted password.
   B. It sends a challenge.
   C. It is more secure than PAP.
   D. It uses a three-way handshake.

Virtual Private Networks

10. Which VPN technology implements confidentiality?
    A. MD5
    B. AES
    C. DH
    D. IKE

11. What are the two components of Easy VPN?
    A. Server
    B. Gateway
    C. Host
    D. Remote

Generic Route Encapsulation Tunnels

12. Which of the following is an optional command when creating a GRE tunnel on a Cisco router?
    A. `interface tunnel`
    B. `tunnel mode gre ip`
    C. `tunnel source`
    D. `tunnel destination`

SELF TEST ANSWERS

Wide Area Networking Overview

1. ☑ **C.** CSU/DSUs are used to terminate synchronous digital circuits and provide DCE services such as clocking and synchronization.

    ☒ **A** is incorrect because a router can provide clocking only when connected to the DCE end of the cable. **B** is incorrect because a modem is used for asynchronous services, and **D** is incorrect because it is a DTE and doesn't provide clocking/synchronization.

2. ☑ **C.** WANs primarily operate at the physical and data link layers.

    ☒ Therefore **A**, **B**, and **D** are incorrect.

3. ☑ **B.** The line protocol is down refers to a problem in the data link layer.

    ☒ **A** is incorrect because the physical layer is up. **C** is incorrect because the status refers only to the physical and data link layers. Since there is a correct answer, **D** is incorrect.

HDLC

4. ☑ **D.** The Type field is unique between the Cisco HDLC frame format and ISO's HDLC.

    ☒ **A**, **B**, and **C** are incorrect because they are in both frame formats.

5. ☑ **A.** HDLC is the default encapsulation on synchronous serial interfaces.

    ☒ **B** is incorrect because PPP is not the default on any type of a serial interface. **C** is incorrect because HDLC is the default. **D** is incorrect because no auto-sensing feature is supported on serial interfaces for the encapsulation method to use.

PPP

6. ☑ **C.** PPP does error detection and correction, but not quality of service.

    ☒ **A** and **B** are supported by PPP, and since answer C is correct, **D** is incorrect.

7. ☑ **B.** NCP negotiates the data link and network layer protocols that will traverse a PPP connection.

    ☒ **A** is incorrect because LCP sets up and monitors the PPP connection. **C** is incorrect because CDP is a proprietary Cisco protocol that allows Cisco devices to share some basic information. **D** is incorrect because PAP performs authentication for PPP.

8. ☑ **D.** OPEN indicates a successful negotiation of a network layer protocol in the **show interfaces** output.

    ☒ **A** is a nonexistent state. **B** shows up as a message type in the output of the **debug ppp authentication** command. **C** indicates an unsuccessful negotiation.

9. ☑ **A.** CHAP doesn't send the encrypted password—it sends a hashed value created from the MD5 algorithm.

   ☒ **B, C,** and **D** are true concerning CHAP.

Virtual Private Networks

10. ☑ **B.** Confidentiality is provided by encryption algorithms such as DES, 3DES, and AES.

    ☒ **A** is incorrect because MD5 is an HMAC function, which provides for packet integrity; **C** is incorrect because DH is used to exchange keys for encryption and HMAC functions; **D** is incorrect because IKE is used to create and manage keys on a VPN device.

11. ☑ **A and D.** The two components of Easy VPN are Server and Remote (sometimes called Client).

    ☒ **B** and **C**, Gateway and Host, are nonexistent terms in Easy VPN.

Generic Route Encapsulation Tunnels

12. ☑ **B.** The encapsulation configuration is optional with GRE—it defaults to GRE point-to-point.

    ☒ **A, C,** and **D** are required commands and therefore incorrect answers.

13

Frame Relay

C hapter 12 introduced you to wide area networking and point-to-point connections using High-Level Data Link Control (HDLC) and Point-to-Point Protocol (PPP) for a data link layer encapsulation. These protocols are common with leased lines and circuit-switched connections. This chapter introduces you to the second WAN topic: Frame Relay. Frame Relay is a data link layer packet-switching protocol that uses digital circuits to transmit data and thus is virtually error-free. Therefore, it performs only error detection—it leaves error correction to an upper layer protocol, such as TCP or the application itself.

Frame Relay is actually a group of separate standards, including those from ITU-T and ANSI. Interestingly enough, Frame Relay defines only the interaction between the Frame Relay customer premises equipment (CPE) and the Frame Relay carrier switch. The connection across the carrier's network is *not* defined by the Frame Relay standards. Most carriers, however, use Asynchronous Transfer Mode (ATM) as a transport to move Frame Relay frames between different sites.

CERTIFICATION OBJECTIVE 13.01

Virtual Circuits

Frame Relay is connection-oriented: a layer 2 connection must be established before information can be sent to a remote device. The connections used by Frame Relay are provided by virtual circuits (VCs). A VC is a logical connection between two devices; therefore, many VCs can exist on the same physical interface. The advantage that VCs have over leased lines is that they can provide full connectivity (fully meshed) at a much lower price. VCs are also full-duplex: you can simultaneously send and receive on the same VC. Other packet- and cell-switching technologies, such as ATM and X.25, also use VCs. Most of the information covered in this section concerning VCs is true of Frame Relay as well as these other technologies.

Fully Meshed Design

As mentioned, VCs are more cost-effective than leased lines because they reduce the number of physical connections required to fully mesh your network, but still allow a fully meshed topology. Let's assume you have two choices for connecting four WAN devices together: leased lines and VCs. The top part of Figure 13-1 shows an example of connecting these devices using leased lines. Notice that to fully mesh this network (every device is connected to every other device), six leased lines are required, including three serial interfaces on each router.

To figure out the number of connections required, you can use the following formula: $(N \times (N - 1)) / 2$. In this formula, N is the number of devices you are connecting together. In our example, this is four devices, resulting in $(4 \times (4 - 1)) / 2 = 6$ leased lines. The more devices that you have, the more leased lines you need, as well as additional serial interfaces on each router. For instance, if you have 10 routers you want to fully mesh, you would need a total of 9 serial interfaces on each router and a total of 45 leased lines! If you were thinking of using a smaller end router, such as a 2600, this would be unrealistic. Therefore, you would need a

FIGURE 13-1   Leased lines and VCs

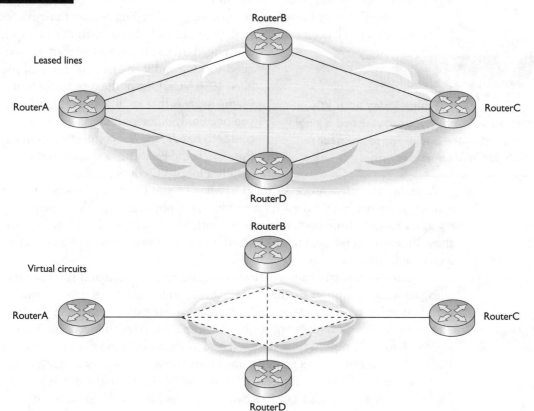

larger router, such as a 3900 or 7300, to handle all of these dedicated circuits. Imagine that you had 100 routers and you wanted to fully mesh them: you would need 99 serial interfaces on each router and 4950 leased lines! Not even a 7700 router can handle this!

Advantages of VCs

As you can see from the preceding section, leased lines have scalability problems. Frame Relay overcomes them by using virtual circuits. With VCs, you can have multiple logical circuits on the same physical connection, as is shown in the bottom part of Figure 13-1. When you use VCs, your router needs only a single serial interface connecting to the carrier. Across this physical interface, you'll use logical VCs to connect to your remote sites.

You can use the same formula described in the preceding section to figure out how many VCs you'll need to fully mesh your network. In our 4-router example,

you'd need 6 VCs. If you had 10 routers, you'd need 45 VCs; and if you had 100 routers, you'd need 4950 VCs. One of the nice features of Frame Relay is that in all of these situations, you need only *one* serial interface on each router to handle the VC connections. Given this, you could easily use a smaller router to handle a lot of VC connections.

Actually, VCs use a process similar to what T1 and E1 leased lines use in sending information. With a T1, for instance, the physical layer T1 frame is broken up into 24 logical time slots, or channels, with 64 Kbps of bandwidth each. Each of these time slots is referred to as a DS0, the smallest fixed amount of bandwidth in a channelized connection.

For example, you can have a carrier configure your T1 so that if you have six sites you want to connect to, the carrier can separate these time slots so that a certain number of time slots are redirected to each remote site, as is shown in Figure 13-2. In this example, the T1 has been split into five connections: Time slots 1–4 go to RemoteA, time slots 5–12 go to RemoteB, time slots 13–20 go to RemoteC, time slots 21–23 go to RemoteD, and time slot 24 goes to Remote E.

As you can see from the figure, this is somewhat similar to the use of VCs. However, breaking up a T1's or E1's time slots does have disadvantages. For

FIGURE 13-2   Leased lines and time slots

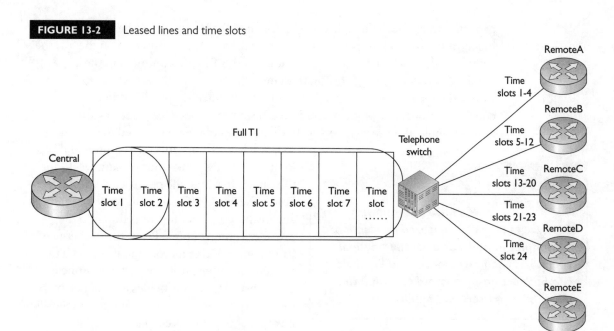

instance, assume that the connection from the central site needs to send a constant rate of 128 Kbps of data to RemoteE. You'll notice that the T1 was broken up and only one DS0, time slot 24, was assigned to this connection. Each DS0 has only 64 Kbps' worth of bandwidth. Therefore, unfortunately, this connection will become congested until traffic slows down to a data rate below 64 Kbps. With this type of configuration, it is difficult to reconfigure the time slots of the T1, because you must also have the carrier involved. If your data rates change to remote sites, you'll need to reconfigure the time slots on your side to reflect the change, as well as have the carrier reconfigure its side. With this process, adapting to data rate changes is a very slow and inflexible process. Even for slight data rate changes to remote sites—say, for example, a spike of 128 Kbps to RemoteE—there will be a brief period of congestion. This is true *even if* the other time slots are empty—remember that these time slots are configured to have their traffic sent to a specific destination and only that destination.

Frame Relay, using VCs, has an advantage over leased lines in this regard. VCs are *not* associated with any particular time slots on the channelized T1 connection. With Frame Relay, any time slot can be used to send traffic. This means that each VC to a destination has the potential to use the full bandwidth of the T1, which provides much more flexibility. For example, if the RemoteE site has a brief bump in its traffic from 64 Kbps to 128 Kbps, and there is free bandwidth on the T1, the central router can use the free bandwidth on the T1 to accommodate the extra bandwidth required to get traffic to RemoteE.

Another advantage of Frame Relay is that it is much simpler to add new connections once the physical circuit has been provisioned. Consider Figure 13-2 as an example. If these were leased-line connections and you wanted to set up a separate leased line between RemoteA and RemoteB, it might take four to eight weeks for the carrier to install the new leased line! With Frame Relay and VCs, since these two routers already have a physical connection into the provider running Frame Relay, the carrier needs to add only a VC to its configuration to tie the two sites together—this can easily be done in a day or two. This fact provides a lot of flexibility to meet your network's requirements, especially if your traffic patterns change over time.

VCs have the following advantages over a channelized connection: it's simpler to add VCs once the physical circuit has been provisioned, and bandwidth can be more easily allotted to match the needs of your users and applications.

Types of VCs

There are two types of VCs: *permanent* VCs (PVCs) and *switched* or *semi-permanent* VCs (SVCs). A PVC is similar to a leased line: it is configured up front by the carrier and remains up as long as a physical circuit path exists from the source to the destination. SVCs are similar to telephone circuit-switched connections: whenever you need to send data to a connection, an SVC is dynamically built and then torn down once your data has been sent. PVCs are typically used when you have data that is constantly being sent to a particular site, while SVCs are used when data is sent periodically. Cisco routers support both types of VCs; however, this book focuses on the configuration of PVCs for Frame Relay.

PVCs

A PVC is similar to a leased line, which is why it is referred to as a *permanent* VC. PVCs must be configured or dynamically learned on each router and built on the carrier's switches before you can send any data. One disadvantage of PVCs is that they require a lot of manual configuration up front to establish the VC. Another disadvantage is that they aren't very flexible: if the PVC fails, there is no dynamic rebuilding of the PVC around the failure. However, once you have a PVC configured, it will always be available, barring any failures between the source and destination. One advantage that PVCs have over SVCs is that SVCs must be set up when you have data to send, a fact that introduces a small amount of delay before traffic can be sent to the destination.

SVCs

SVCs are similar to making a telephone call. For example, when you make a telephone call in the United States, you need to dial a 7-, 10-, or 11-digit telephone number. This number is processed by the carrier's telephone switch, which uses its telephone routing table to bring up a circuit to the destination phone number. Once the circuit is built, the phone rings at the remote site, the destination person answers the phone, and *then* you can begin talking. Once you are done talking, you hang up the phone. This causes the carrier switch to tear down the circuit-switched connection.

SVCs use a similar process. Each SVC device is assigned a unique address, similar to a telephone number. To reach a destination device using an SVC, you'll need to know the destination device's address. In WAN environments, this is typically configured manually on your SVC device. Once your device knows the destination's address, it can forward the address to the carrier's SVC switch. The SVC switch then finds a path to the destination and builds a VC to it. Once the VC is built, the source and destination are notified about this, and both can start sending data across it. Once the source and destination are done sending data, they can signal their connected carrier switch to tear the connection down. An example of this process is ATM, where the layer 2 addresses are called Network Service Access Point (NSAP) addresses. These are similar to Ethernet's MAC addresses or Frame Relay's Data Link Connection Identifier (DLCI) addresses.

One advantage of SVCs is that they are temporary. Therefore, since you are using the SVC only part of the time, the cost of the SVC is less than that of a PVC, since a PVC, even if you are not sending data across it, has to be sustained in the carrier's network.

The problem with SVCs, however, is that the more you use them, the more they cost. Compare this to making a long-distance telephone call where you are being billed for each minute—the more minutes you talk, the more expensive the connection becomes. At some point in time, it will be actually cheaper to use a fixed PVC instead of a dynamic SVC. SVCs are actually good for backup purposes—you might have a primary PVC to a site that costs X dollars a month and a backup SVC that costs you money only if you use it, and then that cost is based on how much you use it—perhaps based on the number of minutes used or the amount of traffic sent. If your primary PVC fails, the SVC is used only until the primary PVC is restored.

To determine whether you should be using an SVC or PVC, you'll need to weigh in factors such as the amount of use and the cost of a PVC versus that of an SVC given this level of use. Another advantage of SVCs is that they are adaptable to changes in the network—if there is a failure of a physical link in the carrier's network, the SVC can be rebuilt across a redundant physical link inside the carrier's network.

The main disadvantages of SVCs are the initial setup and troubleshooting efforts associated with them as well as the time they take to establish. For example, to establish an SVC, you'll need to build a manual resolution table for each network layer protocol that is used between your router and the remote router. If you are running IP, IPX, and AppleTalk, you'll need to configure all three of these entries in your resolution table. Basically, your resolution table maps the remote router's network layer address to its SVC address. Depending on the number of protocols that you are running and the number of sites to which you are connecting, this process can take a lot of time. And when you experience problems with SVCs, they become more difficult to troubleshoot because of the extra configuration involved on your side as well as the layer 2 routing table used on the carrier's side. Setting up PVCs is actually much easier. Plus, each time an SVC doesn't exist to a remote site, your router has to establish one, and it has to wait for the carrier switch to complete this process before your router can start sending its information to the destination.

on the
() o b
Even though Frame Relay is a much more cost-effective solution than a dedicated circuit, it is slowly being replaced by other options, such as VPNs using the Internet via DSL and cable modem connections. However, for delay-sensitive traffic such as voice and video, a private network such as Frame Relay or ATM is used; even so, these two private network technologies are being supplanted by multiprotocol label switching (MPLS) across Ethernet or ATM in carrier networks.

Supported Serial Connections

A typical Frame Relay connection looks similar to Figure 13-3. As you can see in this example, serial cables connect from the router to the CSU/DSU and from the carrier switch to the CSU/DSU. The serial cables that you can use include the following: EIA/TIA-232, EIA/TIA-449, EIA/TIA-530, V.35, and X.25. The connection between the two CSU/DSUs is a channelized connection; it can be

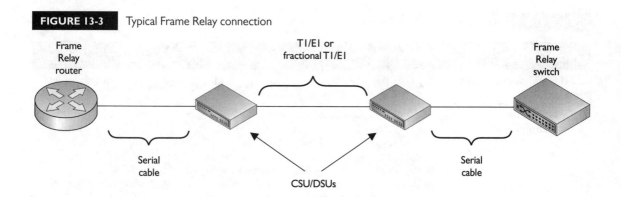

FIGURE 13-3   Typical Frame Relay connection

a fractional T1/E1 that has a single or multiple time slots, a full T1/E1 (a T1 has 24 time slots and an E1 has 30 usable time slots), or a DS3 (a T3 is clocked at 45 Mbps and an E3 is clocked at 34 Mbps).

CERTIFICATION OBJECTIVE 13.02

Frame Relay Terms

When compared to HDLC and PPP, Frame Relay is much more complex in operation, and many more terms are used to describe its components and operation. Table 13-1 contains an overview of these terms. Only the configuration of LMI is discussed in this book—the configuration of other parameters, such as B_C and B_E, is beyond the scope of this book. The proceeding sections describe the operation of Frame Relay and cover these terms in more depth.

Remember the terms in Table 13-1. LMI is a keepalive mechanism used between the DTE and DCE to ensure that both are operational and VCs are not inadvertently deleted or disabled by either side.

TABLE 13-1   Common Frame Relay Terms

Term	Definition
LMI (local management interface)	This defines how the DTE (the router or other Frame Relay device) interacts with the DCE (the Frame Relay switch).
DLCI (Data Link Connection Identifier)	This value is used to uniquely identify each VC on a physical interface: it's the address of the VC. Using DLCIs, you can multiplex traffic for multiple destinations on a single physical interface. DLCIs are locally significant and can change on a segment-by-segment basis. In other words, the DLCI that your router uses to get to a remote destination might be *45*, but the destination might be using *54* to return the traffic—and yet it's the *same* VC. The Frame Relay switch will do a translation between the DLCIs when it is switching frames between segments. DLCIs are layer 2 addresses: This is similar to the use of MAC addresses in Ethernet networks.
Access rate	This is the speed of the physical connection (such as a T1) between your router and the Frame Relay switch.
CIR (committed information rate)	This is the average data rate, measured over a fixed period of time, that the carrier guarantees for a VC.
B_C (committed burst rate)	This is the average data rate (over a period of a smaller fixed time than the CIR) that a provider guarantees for a VC; in other words, it implies a smaller time period but a higher average than the CIR to allow for small bursts in traffic.
B_E (excessive burst rate)	This is the fastest data rate at which the provider will ever service the VC. Some carriers allow you to set this value to match the access rate.
DE (discard eligibility)	This is used to mark a frame as low priority. You can do this manually, or the carrier will do this for a frame that is nonconforming to your traffic contract (exceeding CIR/B_C values).
Oversubscription	When you add up all of the CIRs of your VCs on an interface, they exceed the access rate of the interface: you are betting that all of your VCs will not run, simultaneously, at their traffic-contracted rates.
FECN (forward explicit congestion notification)	This value in the Frame Relay frame header is set by the carrier switch (typically) to indicate congestion inside the carrier network to the destination device at the end of the VC; the carrier may be doing this to your traffic as it is on its way to its destination.
BECN (backward explicit congestion notification)	This value is set by the destination DTE (Frame Relay device) in the header of the Frame Relay frame to indicate congestion (from the source to the destination) to the source of the Frame Relay frames (the source DTE, the router). Sometimes, the carrier switches can generate BECN frames in the backward direction to the source to speed up the congestion notification process. The source can then adapt its rate on the VC appropriately.

LMI

LMI is used only locally, between the Frame Relay DTE (a router) and the Frame Relay DCE (a carrier switch), as is shown in Figure 13-4. In other words, LMI information originating on one Frame Relay DTE will *not* be propagated across the carrier network to a remote Frame Relay DTE: it is processed only between the Frame Relay DTEs and DCEs, which is why the term *local* is used in LMI. LMI is used for management purposes and allows two directly connected devices to share information about the status of VCs, as well as their configuration.

Three different standards are defined for LMI and its interaction with a Frame Relay DTE and DCE:

■ ANSI's Annex D standard, T1.617.

■ ITU-T's Q.933 Annex A standard.

■ The *Gang of Four,* for the four companies that developed it: Cisco, DEC, StrataCom, and NorTel (Northern Telecom). This standard is commonly referred to as Cisco's LMI.

FIGURE 13-4   LMI example

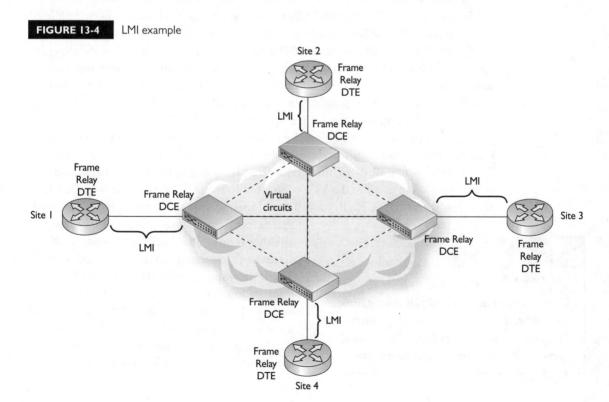

Because LMI is locally significant, each Frame Relay DTE in your network does not have to use the same LMI type. For example, Site 1 and Site 2, shown in Figure 13-4, might have a PVC connecting them together. The Site 1 router might be using ANSI for an LMI type, and the Site 2 router might be using the Q.933 LMI type. Even though they have a PVC connecting them, the LMI process is local and can therefore be different. Actually, the LMI type is typically dependent on the carrier and the switch that it is using. Most carrier switches support all three types, but some carrier switches don't. Likewise, those that do support all three might have standardized on a particular type. Cisco routers support all three LMI standards.

LMI's Functions

The main function of LMI is to allow the Frame Relay DTE and DCE to exchange status information about the VCs and themselves. To implement this function, the Frame Relay DTE sends an LMI *status enquiry* (query) message periodically to the attached Frame Relay DCE. Assuming that the DCE is turned on and the DCE is configured with the same LMI type, the DCE responds with a *status reply* message. These messages serve as a *keepalive* function, allowing the two devices to determine each other's state. Basically, the DTE is asking the switch "are you there?" and the switch responds "yes, I am." By default, only the DTE originates these keepalives and only the DCE responds.

After so many status enquiries, the Frame Relay DTE generates a special query message called a *full status update*. In this message, the DTE is asking the DCE for a full status update of all information that is related to the DTE. This includes such information as all of the VCs connected to the DTE, their addresses (DLCIs), their configurations (CIR, B_C, and B_E), and their statuses. For example, let's assume that Site 1 from Figure 13-4 has a PVC to all other remote sites and that it sends a full status update message to its connected DCE. The DCE responds with the following PVC information: Site 1 → Site 2, Site 1 → Site 3, and Site 1 → Site 4. Notice that the DCE switch does *not* respond with these VCs: Site 2 → Site 3, Site 3 → Site 4, and Site 2 → Site 4, since these VCs are not local to this DTE.

TABLE 13-2	LMI Type	DLCI #
LMI Addresses	ANSI Annex D	0
	ITU-T Q.933 Annex A	0
	Gang of Four (Cisco)	1023

LMI Standards

For the LMI communication to occur between the DTE and the DCE, the LMI information must use a VC. In order for the DTE and DCE to know that the Frame Relay frame contains LMI information, a reserved VC is used to share LMI

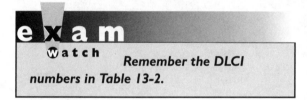

information. The LMI type that you are using will determine the DLCI address that is used in the communication. Table 13-2 shows the DLCI addresses assigned to the three LMI types. DLCIs are discussed in more depth in the following section.

Remember the DLCI numbers in Table 13-2.

DLCIs

Each VC has a unique *local* address, called a DLCI. This means that as a VC traverses various segments in a WAN, the DLCI numbers can be *different* for each segment. The carrier switches take care of converting a DLCI number from one segment to the corresponding DLCI number used on the next segment.

DLCI Example

Figure 13-5 shows an example of how DLCIs are used. This example shows three routers and three carrier switches. RouterA has a PVC to RouterB, and RouterA has another PVC to RouterC. Let's take a closer look at the PVC between RouterA and RouterB. Starting from RouterA, the PVC traverses three physical links:

- RouterA → Switch 1 (DLCI 200)
- Switch 1 → Switch 2 (DLCI 200)
- Switch 2 → RouterB (DLCI 201)

Note that DLCIs are locally significant: they need to be unique only on a segment-by-segment basis and do *not* need to be unique across the entire Frame

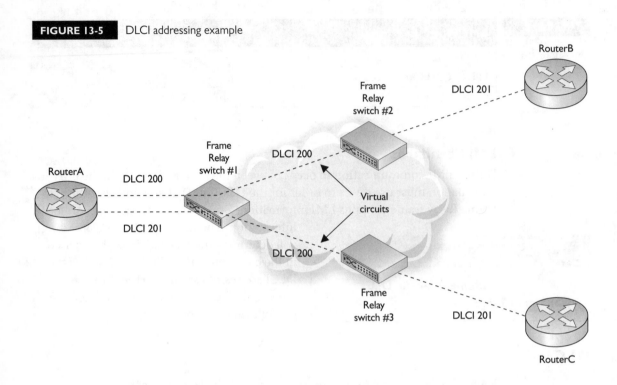

FIGURE 13-5   DLCI addressing example

Relay network. This is similar to the use of MAC addresses in Ethernet. Given this statement, the DLCI number can change from segment to segment, and it is up to the carrier switch to change the DLCI in the frame header to the appropriate DLCI value for the next segment. This fact can be seen in Figure 13-5, where the DTE segments have different DLCI values (200 and 201), but we're still dealing with the same PVC. Likewise, the DLCI numbers of 200 and 201 are used elsewhere in the network. What is important are the DLCI numbers on the *same* segment. For instance, RouterA has two PVCs to two different destinations. On the RouterA → Switch 1 connection, each of these PVCs needs a unique address value (200 and 201); however, these values do not have to be the same for each segment to the destination.

This can become confusing unless you look at the DLCI addressing from a device's and segment's perspective. As an example, if RouterA wants to send data to RouterB, it encapsulates it in a Frame Relay frame and puts a DLCI address of 200 in the header. When Switch 1 receives the frame, it looks at the DLCI address *and* the interface on which it was received and compares these to its DLCI switching table. When it finds a match, the switch takes the DLCI number for the next segment (found in the same table entry), substitutes it into the frame header, and forwards the frame to the next device. In this case, the DLCI number remains the same (200). When Switch 2 receives the frame from Switch 1, it performs the same process and realizes it needs to forward the frame to RouterB, but before doing this, it must change the DLCI number to 201 in the frame header. When RouterB receives the frame, it also examines the DLCI address in the frame header. When it sees 201 as the address, RouterB knows that the frame originated from RouterA.

This process, at first, seems confusing. However, to make it easier, look at it from the router's perspective:

- When RouterA wants to reach RouterB, RouterA uses DLCI 200.
- When RouterB wants to reach RouterA, RouterB uses DLCI 201.
- When RouterC wants to reach RouterA, RouterC uses DLCI 201.

When the carrier creates a PVC for you between two sites, it assigns the DLCI number that you should use at each site to reach the other site. Certain DLCI numbers are reserved for management and control purposes, such as LMI's 0 and 1023 values. Reserved DLCIs are 0–15 and 1008–1023. DLCI numbers from 16–1007 are used for data connections.

DLCIs are locally significant: Your router uses a local DLCI number in the Frame Relay frame header to indicate the destination peer to which *the frame is to be forwarded. The carrier's switches take care of mapping DLCI numbers for a VC between DTEs and DCEs.*

Network and Service Interworking

As mentioned earlier in this chapter, Frame Relay is implemented between the Frame Relay DTE and the Frame Relay DCE. How the frame is carried across the Frame Relay carrier's network is not specified. In almost all situations, ATM is used as the layer 2 transport. ATM, like Frame Relay, uses VCs. ATM, however, uses a different nomenclature in assigning an address to a VC. In ATM, two identifiers are assigned to a VC: a virtual path identifier (VPI) and a virtual channel identifier (VCI). These two numbers serve the same purpose that a DLCI serves in Frame Relay. Like DLCIs, the VPI/VCI value is locally significant.

Two standards, FRF.5 and FRF.8, define how the frame and address conversion takes place between Frame Relay and ATM:

- **FRF.5 (Networking Interworking)** The two DTEs are Frame Relay and the carrier uses ATM as a transport.
- **FRF.8 (Service Interworking)** One DTE is a Frame Relay device and the other is an ATM device, and the carrier uses ATM as a transport.

Figure 13-6 shows an example of these two standards. FRF.5 defines how two Frame Relay devices can send frames back and forth across an ATM backbone, as is shown between RouterA and RouterB. With FRF.5, the Frame Relay frame is received by the connected switch. The switch figures out which ATM VC is to be used to get the information to the destination and *encapsulates* the Frame Relay frame into an ATM frame, which is then chunked up into ATM cells. When the ATM cells are received by the destination carrier switch, the switch reassembles the ATM cells back into an ATM frame, extracts the Frame Relay frame that was encapsulated, and then looks up the DLCI in its switching table. When switching the frame to the next segment, if the local DLCI number is different, the switch changes the DLCI in the header and recomputes the cyclic redundancy check (CRC).

FIGURE 13-6   Network and service interworking example

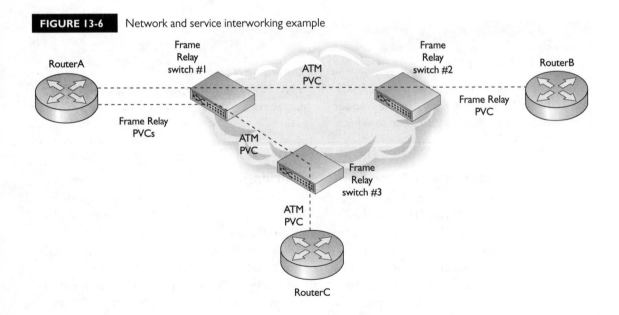

The connection between RouterA and RouterC is an example of an FRF.8 connection. With FRF.8, one DTE is using Frame Relay and the other DTE is using ATM. The carrier uses ATM to transport the information between the two DTEs. For example, in Figure 13-6, RouterA sends a Frame Relay frame to RouterC. The carrier's switch *converts* the Frame Relay frame into an ATM frame, which is different from what FRF.5 does. The switch then segments the ATM frame into cells and assigns the correct VPI/VCI address to the cells to get to the remote ATM switch. In this example, RouterA thinks it's talking to another Frame Relay device (RouterC). RouterC, on the other hand, thinks it's talking to an ATM device (RouterA).

VC Data Rates

Each data VC has a few parameters associated with it that affect its data rate and throughput. These values include the following: CIR (committed information rate), B_C (committed burst rate), B_E (excessive burst rate), and access rate. This section covers these four values and how the Frame Relay switch uses them to enforce the traffic contract for the VC.

CIR is the average contracted rate of a VC measured over a period of time. This is the guaranteed rate that the carrier is giving to you, barring any major outages the carrier might experience in its network.

Two burst rates allow you to go above the CIR limit temporarily, assuming the provider has enough bandwidth in its network to support this temporary burst. B_C allows you to burst up to a higher average than CIR for a VC, but the time period of the burst is smaller than the time period over which CIR is measured. If you send information above the CIR but below the B_C value, the carrier will permit the frame into its network.

The B_E value indicates the maximum rate you are allowed to send into the carrier on a VC. Any frames that exceed this value are dropped. If you send traffic at a rate between B_C and B_E, the carrier switch marks the frames as discard eligible, using the 1-bit Discard Eligible (DE) field in the Frame Relay frame header. By marking this bit, the carrier is saying that the frame is allowed in the network; however, as soon as the carrier experiences congestion, these are the first frames that are dropped. From the carrier's perspective, frames sent at a rate between B_C and B_E are bending the rules but will be allowed if enough bandwidth is available for them.

It is important to point out that *each* VC has its own CIR, B_C, and B_E values. However, depending on the carrier's implementation of Frame Relay, or how you purchase the VCs, the B_C and B_E values might not be used. In some instances, the B_E value defaults to the access rate—the speed of the physical connection from the

Frame Relay DTE to the Frame Relay DCE. This could be a fractional T1 running at, say, 256 Kbps, or a full T1 (1.544 Mbps).

No matter how many VCs you have, or what their combined CIR values are, you are always limited to the access rate—you can't exceed the speed of the physical connection. It is a common practice to oversubscribe the speed of the physical connection: this occurs when the total CIR of all VCs exceeds the access rate. Basically, you're betting that all VCs will not simultaneously run at their CIRs, but that most will run below their CIR values at any given time, requiring a lower speed connection to the carrier. A Frame Relay setup incurs two basic costs: the cost of each physical connection to the Frame Relay switch and the cost of each VC, which is usually dependent on its rate parameters.

Figure 13-7 shows an example of how these Frame Relay traffic parameters affect the data rate of a VC. The graph shows a linear progression of frames leaving a router's interface on a VC. As you can see from this figure, as long as the data rate of the VC is below the CIR/B_C values, the Frame Relay switch allows the frames

FIGURE 13-7   VC traffic parameters

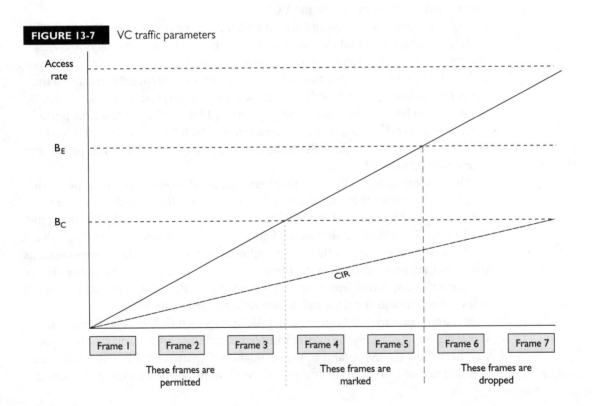

into the Frame Relay network. However, those frames (4 and 5) that exceed the B_C value will have their DE bits set, which allows the carrier to drop these frames in times of internal congestion. Also, any frames that exceed B_E are dropped: in this example, Frames 6 and 7 are dropped.

Some carriers don't support B_C and B_E. Instead, they mark all frames that exceed the CIR as discard eligible. This means that you can send all your frames into the carrier network at the access rate speed and the carrier will permit them in (after marking the DE bit). All of these options and implementations can make it confusing when you're trying to find the right Frame Relay solution for your network. For example, one carrier might sell you a CIR of 0 Kbps, which causes the carrier to permit all your traffic into the network but marks all of the frames as discard eligible. Assuming the carrier experiences no congestion problems, you're getting great service. Of course, if the carrier is constantly experiencing congestion, you are getting very poor service, since some or most of your frames are dropped.

If you need a guaranteed rate for a VC or VCs, you can obtain this from most carriers, but this costs more money than a CIR of 0 Kbps for a VC. The more bandwidth you require, the more expensive the circuit, since the carrier must reserve this bandwidth inside its network to accommodate your traffic rate needs. And what makes this whole process complex is looking at the traffic rates for all your connections and trying to get the best value for your money. Some network administrators oversubscribe their access rates, expecting that not all VCs will simultaneously send traffic at their CIR traffic rates. How Frame Relay operates and how your traffic behaves can make it difficult to pick the right Frame Relay service for your network.

Congestion Control

In the preceding section, you were shown how the different traffic parameters for a VC affect how traffic enters the carrier's network. Once this is accomplished, these values have no effect on traffic as it traverses the carrier's network to your remote site. Of course, this poses problems in a carrier's network—what if the carrier experiences congestion and begins dropping frames? It would be nice for the carrier to indicate to your Frame Relay DTEs that there is congestion and to have your devices slow the rates of their VCs before the carrier begins dropping your frames. Remember that Frame Relay has no retransmit option—if a frame is dropped because it has a field checksum sequence (FCS) error or experiences congestion, it is up to the actual source device that *created* the data to resend it.

To handle this problem, Frame Relay has a standard mechanism to signify and adapt to congestion problems in a Frame Relay carrier's network. Every Frame Relay frame header has two fields that are used to indicate congestion: FECN and BECN. Figure 13-8 shows an example of how FECN and BECN are used. As RouterA sends its information into the carrier network, the carrier network experiences congestion. For the VCs that experience congestion, the carrier marks the FECN bit in the frame header as these frames are heading *to* RouterB. Once the frames arrive at RouterB and RouterB sees the FECN bit set in the Frame Relay frame header, RouterB can send a Frame Relay frame in the reverse direction on the VC, marking the BECN bit in the header of the frame. With some vendors' carrier switches, to speed up the congestion notification process, the carrier switch actually generates a BECN frame in the reverse direction of the VC, back to the source, to indicate congestion issues. Once RouterA receives the BECN frames, it can then begin to slow down the data rate on the VC.

One of the main drawbacks of using the FECN/BECN method of congestion notification is that it is not a very efficient form of flow control. For example, the carrier might begin to mark the FECN bit in frames as they are headed to the destination to indicate a congestion problem. As the destination is responding to the source with BECN frames, the congestion disappears. When the source receives the BECN frames, it begins to slow down even though the congestion problem no longer exists.

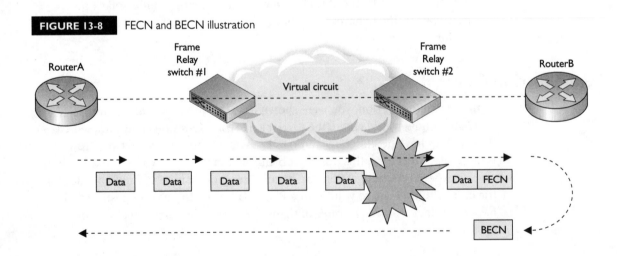

FIGURE 13-8   FECN and BECN illustration

watch *FECN is used to indicate congestion as frames go from the source to the destination. BECN is used by the destination (and sent to the source) to indicate that there is congestion from the source to the destination.*

On top of this, there is no way of notifying the source or destination how much congestion exists—the source might begin slowing down the VC too slowly or too quickly without any decent feedback about how much to slow down. Because of these issues, many companies have opted to use ATM. ATM also supports flow control, but its implementation is more sophisticated than Frame Relay and allows VCs to adapt to congestion in a real-time fashion.

CERTIFICATION OBJECTIVE 13.03

Frame Relay Configuration

The remainder of this chapter focuses on the different ways of configuring Frame Relay on your router. Like the other WAN encapsulations, PPP and HDLC, Frame Relay's configuration is done on your router's serial interface.

Encapsulation Configuration

To set the data link layer encapsulation type to Frame Relay, use this configuration:

```
Router(config)# interface serial [slot_#/]port_#
Router(config-if)# encapsulation frame-relay [cisco|ietf]
```

Notice that the **encapsulation** command has options for two different frame types. The frame type you configure on your router must match the frame type configured on the Frame Relay DTEs at the remote side of your VCs. The default is **cisco** if you don't specify the encapsulation type. This frame type is proprietary to Cisco equipment. In most instances, you'll use the standardized frame type (**ietf**). IETF has defined a standardized Frame Relay frame type in RFC 1490, which is interoperable with all vendors' Frame Relay equipment.

on the **job**   *Most Frame Relay providers use IETF as the data link layer frame type.*

Once you have configured your frame type, use the **show interfaces** command to verify your frame type configuration:

```
Router# show interfaces serial 1/0
Serial 1/0 is up, line protocol is up
   Hardware is MCI Serial
   Internet address is 172.16.2.1, subnet mask is 255.255.255.0
   MTU 1500 bytes, BW 256 Kbit, DLY 20000 usec, rely 255/255, load 1/255
   Encapsulation FRAME-RELAY, loopback not set, keepalive set
   LMI DLCI    0, LMI sent 1107, LMI stat recvd 1107
   LMI type is ANSI Annex D
   .
   .
   .
```

Notice that the encapsulation type has been changed to FRAME-RELAY in this example.

13.01. The digital resources that accompany this book contain a multimedia demonstration of changing the encapsulation type to Frame Relay on a router.

e x a m

ⓦatch *The encapsulation frame-relay command has two encapsulation types: cisco and ietf. The default is cisco. ietf is used for vendor interoperability. If you are connecting a Cisco router, via Frame Relay,* *to a non-Cisco router and the data link layer is down, the culprit is probably the encapsulation type, assuming you are receiving LMIs from the switch. In this instance, set the encapsulation type to ietf.*

LMI Configuration

Once you have set the encapsulation on your serial interface, you need to define the LMI type that is used to communicate information between your router and the carrier's switch: remember that LMI is a local process. What you configure on your router doesn't have to match what is on the remote routers: What has to match is what your carrier is using on its switch (the DTE to DCE connection).

Use this configuration to configure the LMI type:

```
Router(config)# interface serial [slot_#/]port_#
Router(config-if)# frame-relay lmi-type {ansi | cisco | q933a}
```

Note that the LMI type is specific to the entire interface, not to a VC. Table 13-3 maps the LMI parameters to the corresponding LMI standard.

Starting with IOS 11.2, Cisco routers can autosense the LMI type that is configured on the carrier's switch. With this feature, the router sends a status enquiry for each of the three LMI types to the carrier's switch, one at a time, and waits to see which one the switch will respond to. The router keeps on doing this until the switch responds to one of them. If you are not getting a response from the carrier, it is most likely that the carrier forgot to turn on and configure LMI on its switch. Remember that a Cisco router generates an LMI status enquiry message every 10 seconds. On the sixth message, the router sends a full status update query. Since Cisco routers can autosense the LMI type used by the carrier, it is not necessary to hard-code it.

Video

13.02. The digital resources that accompany this book contain a multimedia demonstration configuring the LMI type on a router.

Troubleshooting LMI

If you are experiencing LMI problems with your connection to the carrier's switch, you can use three commands to assist you in the troubleshooting process:

- `show interfaces`
- `show frame-relay lmi`
- `debug frame-relay lmi`

The following sections cover each of these commands in detail.

TABLE 13-3	Parameter	Standard
LMI Parameters	`ansi`	ANSI's Annex D standard, T1.617
	`cisco`	The Gang of Four
	`q933a`	ITU-T's Q.933 Annex A standard

The show interfaces Command

Besides showing you the encapsulation type of an interface, the **show interfaces** command also displays the LMI type that is being used as well as some LMI statistics, as is shown here:

```
Router# show interfaces serial 0
Serial 0 is up, line protocol is up
    Hardware is MCI Serial
    Internet address is 172.16.2.1, subnet mask is 255.255.255.0
    MTU 1500 bytes, BW 256 Kbit, DLY 20000 usec, rely 255/255, load 1/255
    Encapsulation FRAME-RELAY, loopback not set, keepalive set
    LMI DLCI    0, LMI sent 1107, LMI stat recvd 1107
    LMI type is ANSI Annex D
    .
    .
    .
```

ⓦatch *Be familiar with the output of the* show interfaces *command in determining whether the frame relay encapsulation has been configured.*

Notice the two lines below the encapsulation. The first line shows the DLCI number used by LMI (0) as well as the number of status enquiries sent and received. If you re-execute the **show interfaces** command every 10 seconds, both of these values should be incrementing. The second line shows the actual LMI type used (ANSI Annex D).

The show frame-relay lmi Command

If you want to see more detailed statistics regarding LMI than what the **show interfaces** command displays, you can use the **show frame-relay lmi** command, shown here:

```
Router# show frame-relay lmi
LMI Statistics for interface Serial0
                        (Frame Relay DTE) LMI TYPE = ANSI
    Invalid Unnumbered info 0        Invalid Prot Disc 0
    Invalid dummy Call Ref 0         Invalid Msg Type 0
    Invalid Status Message 0         Invalid Lock Shift 0
    Invalid Information ID 0         Invalid Report IE Len 0
    Invalid Report Request 0        Invalid Keep IE Len 0
    Num Status Enq. Sent 12          Num Status msgs Rcvd 12
    Num Update Status Rcvd 2         Num Status Timeouts 2
```

on the ⓞⓙob *If you see the* Num Status Timeouts *increasing, but the* Num Status msgs Rcvd *is not increasing, this probably indicates that the provider forgot to enable LMI on its switch's interface.*

With this command, you can see both valid and invalid messages. If the Invalid field values are incrementing, this can indicate a mismatch in the LMI configuration: you have one LMI type configured and the switch has another type configured. The last two lines of the output refer to the status enquiries that the router generates. The Num Status Enq Sent field is the number of enquiries your router has sent to the switch. The Num Status msgs Rcvd field is the number of replies that the switch has sent upon receiving your router's enquiries. The Num Update Status Rcvd are the number of full status update messages the switch has sent. The Num Status Timeouts indicates the number of times your router sent an enquiry and did *not* receive a response.

13.03. The digital resources that accompany this book contain a multimedia demonstration of the show frame-relay lmi command on a router.

The debug frame-relay lmi Command

For more detailed troubleshooting of LMI, you can use the **debug frame-relay lmi** command. This command shows the actual LMI messages being sent and received by your router.

Here's an example of the output of this command:

```
Router# debug frame-relay lmi
Serial1/0 (in): Status, myseq 290
RT IE 1, length 1, type 0
RT IE 3, length 2, yourseq 107, my seq 290
PVC IE 0x7, length 0x6, dlci 112, status 0x2 bw 0
Serial1/0 (out): StEnq, myseq 291, yourseq 107, DTE up
Datagramstart = 0x1959DF4, datagramsize = 13
FR encap = 0xFCF10309
00 75 01 01 01 03 02 D7 D4
```

In this output, the router, on `Serial1/0`, first receives a status reply from the switch to the two hundred ninetieth LMI status enquiry the router sent—this is the very first line of the debug output. Following this on the fifth line is the router's two hundred ninety-first status enquiry (`StEnq`) being sent to the switch.

13.04. The digital resources that accompany this book contain a multimedia demonstration of the `debug frame-relay lmi` *command on a router.*

PVC Configuration

The preceding two sections showed you how to configure the interaction between your router (DTE) and the carrier's switch (DCE). This section expands upon this and shows you how to send data between two Frame Relay DTEs. As mentioned earlier in the chapter, to send data to another DTE, a VC must first be established. This can be a PVC or an SVC. The CCNA and ICND2 exams focus on PVCs, so the topic is restricted to the configuration of PVCs in this book.

One of the first issues that you'll have to deal with is the router, which, by default, doesn't know what PVCs to use and which device is off of which PVC. Remember that PVCs are given unique locally significant addresses called DLCIs. Somehow the router has to learn the DLCI numbers and the layer 3 address that is at the remote end of the VC (this is similar to the problem of how devices with IP addresses need to talk to each other across Ethernet, which uses MAC addresses). With TCP/IP, the Address Resolution Protocol (ARP) is used to solve this problem. Two methods are available to resolve this issue in Frame Relay: manual and dynamic resolution. These resolutions map the layer 3 address of the remote Frame Relay DTE to the local DLCI number your router uses to reach this DTE. The following sections cover the configuration of both of these resolution types.

Manual Resolution

If you are using manual resolution to resolve layer 3 remote addresses to local DLCI numbers, use the following configuration:

```
Router(config)# interface serial [slot_#/]port_#
Router(config-if)# frame-relay map protocol_name
                        destination_address local_dlci_#
                        [broadcast] [ietf | cisco]
```

The **frame-relay map** command defines the manual resolution process. The *protocol_name* parameter specifies the layer 3 protocol that you are resolving: IP, IPX, or AppleTalk, for instance. If you are running two protocols between yourself and the remote DTE, such as IP and IPX, you will need a separate **frame-relay map** command for each protocol and destination mapping. Following the name of the protocol is the *remote* DTE's layer 3 address (*destination_address*), such as its IP address. Following the layer 3 address is the *local* DLCI number *your* router should use in order to reach the remote DTE. These are the only three required parameters.

The other two parameters, the **broadcast** parameter and the frame type parameter, are optional. By default, local broadcasts and multicasts do not go across a manually resolved PVC. Therefore, if you are running Routing Information Protocol (RIPv2), Open Shortest Path First (OSPF), or Enhanced Interior Gateway Routing Protocol (EIGRP) as a routing protocol, the routing updates these protocols generate will not go across the PVC unless you configure the **broadcast** parameter. If you don't want broadcast traffic going across a VC, then don't configure this parameter. If this is the case, then you'll need to configure static routes on both Frame Relay DTEs.

The beginning of this section described how to change the encapsulation type for Frame Relay frames with the **encapsulation frame-relay** command. This command allows you to specify one of two frame types: **ietf** or **cisco**, with **cisco** being the default. The problem with this command is that it specifies the same encapsulation on every VC for the specified interface. When doing manual resolution, you can specify the encapsulation for *each* VC separately. If you omit this on your manual mapping statement, the encapsulation defaults to that encapsulation type on the serial interface.

e x a m

ⓦatch Use the `frame-relay map` command to configure manual resolution of local PVCs to use to reach remote destinations. By default, broadcasts do not go across a manually resolved VC unless you use the `broadcast` parameter—this allows routing protocols such as RIP, EIGRP, and OSPF to work across the manually resolved VC.

Let's look at an example, shown in Figure 13-9, to illustrate how to set up manual resolution for a PVC configuration. Here's the configuration for RouterA:

```
RouterA(config)# interface serial 0
RouterA(config-if)# encapsulation frame-relay ietf
RouterA(config-if)# frame-relay lmi-type q933a
RouterA(config-if)# ip address 192.168.2.1 255.255.255.0
RouterA(config-if)# frame-relay map ip 192.168.2.2 103 broadcast
```

FIGURE 13-9   PVC manual resolution example

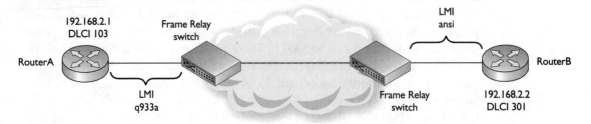

Here's the configuration for RouterB:

```
RouterB(config)# interface serial 0
RouterB(config-if)# encapsulation frame-relay ietf
RouterB(config-if)# frame-relay lmi-type ansi
RouterB(config-if)# ip address 192.168.2.2 255.255.255.0
RouterB(config-if)# frame-relay map ip 192.168.2.1 301 broadcast
```

First, notice that the two routers are using *different* LMI types at each end. This is okay, since LMI is used only between the Frame Relay DTE and DCE devices. Second, notice that the DLCI numbers are different at each end. Again, remember that DLCI numbers are locally significant and do not have to be the same on all segments the VC traverses: the carrier will assign these values for you and send you the correct mappings to use for the DLCIs.

13.05. The digital resources that accompany this book contain a multimedia demonstration of configuring manual resolution for a PVC on a router.

on the job

One common problem of setting up manual resolution is that it is very common for administrators to configure the wrong DLCI for the VC. For example, in the configuration shown for Figure 13-9, some administrators forget that DLCIs are locally significant and configure DLCI 301 on RouterA and DLCI 103 on RouterB. When troubleshooting this problem, examine the status of the VC with the `show frame-relay pvc` *or* `show frame-relay map` *command, looking for a "deleted" status for the VC. These* `show` *commands are discussed in the next section.*

Dynamic Resolution

Instead of using manual resolution for your PVCs, you can use *dynamic* resolution. Dynamic resolution uses a feature called *Inverse ARP*. This is something like a reverse ARP in TCP/IP. Inverse ARP allows devices to automatically discover the layer 3 protocols and addresses that are used on each VC.

Inverse ARP occurs every 60 seconds on VCs that are not manually configured, and it occurs only on VCs that are in an *active* state. Recall from the LMI section that the state of the VCs is learned from the full status update message. For example, once the physical layer for the interface comes up, your router starts sending its LMI enquiries every 10 seconds. On the sixth one, it sends a full status message, which requests the statuses of the VCs that the switch directs to this router's interface. In this example, it will take at least a minute before the router learns of the status of the VC.

Once the router sees an active status for a VC, it *then* does an Inverse ARP on the VC if it is not already manually resolved with a `frame-relay map` command. This frame contains the layer 3 protocol and protocol address used by the router. When the frame arrives at the remote DTE, the device takes the protocol, layer 3 address, and *local* DLCI number in the frame header and puts them in its VC resolution table. The remote DTEs do the same thing. Within a short period of time, your router will know the layer 3 addresses at the end of each of its dynamically learned VCs. Once the router knows who is at the other end of the VC, your router can begin transmitting data to the remote DTE.

e x a m

ⓦ a t c h   *Inverse ARP allows a router to send a Frame Relay frame across a VC with its layer 3 addressing information. The destination can then use this, along with* *the incoming DLCI number, to reach the advertiser. Inverse ARP basically resolves a known local DLCI number to a layer 3 address, like IP.*

e x a m

ⓦ a t c h   *Remember the VC statuses in Table 13-4.*

VC Status   You already know about one of the three states for a VC: active. Table 13-4 shows all three basic statuses for a VC. For Inverse ARP to take place, the VC must have an active status.

TABLE 13-4	Status	Description
VC Statuses	Active	The VC between both Frame Relay DTEs is up and operational.
	Inactive	The VC between your Frame Relay DTE and DCE is up and operational, but something is wrong with the connection between your connected Frame Relay switch and the *destination* DTE.
	Deleted	You are not receiving any LMI messages from the Frame Relay switch for a local VC.

Disadvantages of Dynamic Resolution   Even though dynamic resolution requires no configuration on your router in order to work, it does have some disadvantages. First, one of the main problems of dynamic resolution is that in order for you to send data across the VC, you must wait until you learn the status of the VC and wait for the Inverse ARP to occur. This process can sometimes take more than 60 seconds, even if the data link layer is operational and the VC is in place. The advantage of manually resolved PVCs is that as soon as the data link layer is up, your router can immediately begin to send traffic to the destination router. Assuming that the Frame Relay switch replies to your router's first LMI enquiry, this can be less than a second before your router can begin transmitting information to the destination DTE. So even though the manual resolution process requires you to configure all of the manual resolution entries, many network administrators choose to do this so that data can begin to traverse the VCs as soon as the physical and data link layers are "up and line protocol is up."

The second disadvantage of dynamic resolution is that in some instances, with equipment from multiple vendors, you might experience problems with how different vendors implement Inverse ARP. In this case, the dynamic resolution fails and you must resort to configuring manual resolution with the `frame-relay map` command. This might even be true between Cisco routers. I have experienced problems with routers running very old and new versions of IOS trying to perform Inverse ARP between them and failing. You could either use manual resolution or upgrade IOS on the older routers.

The third problem with dynamic resolution is that Inverse ARP works only with the following protocols: AppleTalk, DECnet, TCP/IP, IPX, Vines, and XNS. If you use another protocol, you will need to configure manual resolution commands to solve your resolution problem.

Configuring Inverse ARP   By default, Inverse ARP is already *enabled* on your Cisco router. You can disable it or re-enable it with the following configuration:

```
Router(config)# interface serial [slot_#/]port_#
Router(config-if)# [no] frame-relay inverse-arp
                        [protocol_name] [DLCI_#]
```

Without any options, the **frame-relay inverse-arp** command enables Inverse ARP for all VCs on the router's serial interface. You can selectively disable Inverse ARP for a particular protocol or VC (DLCI #). Use the **clear frame-relay-inarp** command to clear the Inverse ARP resolution table. To see the Inverse ARP statistics, use this command:

```
Router# show frame-relay traffic
Frame Relay statistics:
ARP requests sent 14, ARP replies sent 0
ARP request recvd 0, ARP replies recvd 10
```

Dynamic Resolution Example   Previously, you saw how to set up manual resolution for the VC connection shown in Figure 13-9. Using the same network, this example implements dynamic resolution to illustrate how this is set up on your router. In this example, assume that your router is autosensing the LMI type. Here's the configuration for RouterA:

```
Router(config)# interface serial 0
Router(config-if)# encapsulation frame-relay ietf
Router(config-if)# ip address 192.168.2.1 255.255.255.0
```

Here's the configuration for RouterB:

```
Router(config)# interface serial 0
Router(config-if)# encapsulation frame-relay ietf
Router(config-if)# ip address 192.168.2.2 255.255.255.0
```

With autosensing of the LMI type, you don't need to configure the LMI type on the interface. And since you are using dynamic resolution with Inverse ARP, which is enabled by default, you don't need any additional configuration on your router's serial interface. As you can see from these code examples, the only thing you have to configure is the encapsulation type on the interface, making the setup of Frame Relay a simple and straightforward process.

13.06. The digital resources that accompany this book contain a multimedia demonstration of configuring dynamic resolution for a PVC on a router.

PVC Status Verification

To see all of the Frame Relay PVCs terminated at your router, as well as their statistics, use the **show frame-relay pvc** command. Optionally, you can look at just one PVC by following this command with the local DLCI number, as shown in this example:

```
Router# show frame-relay pvc 100
PVC Statistics for interface Serial0
                         (Frame Relay DTE) DLCI = 100,
     DLCI USAGE = LOCAL, PVC STATUS = ACTIVE, INTERFACE = Serial0
      input pkts 15         output pkts 26        in bytes 508
      out bytes 638         dropped pkts 1        in FECN pkts 0
      in BECN pkts 0        out FECN pkts 0       out BECN pkts 0
      in DE pkts 0          out DE pkts 0
      out bcast pkts 0      out bcast bytes 0
      pvc create time 00:22:01, last time pvc status
              changed 00:05:37
```

In this example, PVC 100's status is ACTIVE, which indicates that the PVC is operational between the two Frame Relay DTEs. You can also see traffic statistics for the PVC. In this example, 15 packets were received and 26 packets were transmitted on this PVC.

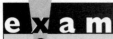

e x a m

ⓦatch
Use the `show frame-relay pvc` command to view the statuses of your VCs. If you see an ACTIVE state, this indicates that the VC is operational from this DTE (such as a Cisco router) to the destination DTE. If your router is receiving BECNs, in the output of this command, this indicates congestion in the forward direction from you to your remote Frame Relay peer.

To see the VC resolution table, which maps layer 3 addresses to local DLCI numbers, use the **show frame-relay map** command:

```
Router# show frame-relay map
Serial0 (up): ip 192.168.2.2 dlci 32(0x20, 0x1C80), dynamic,
                    Broadcast, CISCO, status defined, active
```

In this output, one PVC has a local DLCI of 32. At the end of this PVC is a router with an IP address of 192.168.2.2. Notice that this information was learned via Inverse ARP (dynamic), local broadcasts and multicasts are allowed, the default frame type is CISCO, and the status of the VC is active. If you had configured manual resolution for this connection, the entry would have listed static instead of dynamic. Also, if the frame type was based on RFC 1490, the frame type would have been listed as IETF.

13.07. The digital resources that accompany this book contain a multimedia demonstration of using the show frame-relay pvc command.

If you manually map the layer 3 addresses to DLCIs, and assign a nonexistent DLCI to the resolution, your output will look like this:

```
Router# show frame-relay map
Serial0 (up): ip 192.168.2.2 dlci 32(0x20, 0x1C80), static,
                              Broadcast, CISCO, status defined, deleted
```

Notice that in this example the DLCI has been manually mapped (static) and the status is deleted.

exam
ⓦatch
Use the show frame-relay map command to view the manual or Inverse ARP mappings of layer 3 addresses to local DLCIs; those learned dynamically via Inverse ARP will have the keyword dynamic associated with the VC. If you statically map the layer 3 address to a DLCI and the status of the DLCI is deleted, then you probably misconfigured the DLCI number to one that doesn't exist on the Frame Relay switch. With this command, you can see the LMI type, local DLCI number, the remote layer 3 IP address, and the status of the VC. The word "Broadcast" indicates that broadcasts and multicasts used by various protocols, like RIP, OSPF, and EIGRP, can function on the VC.

13.08. The digital resources that accompany this book contain a multimedia demonstration of using the show frame-relay map command on a router.

EXERCISE 13-1

Configuring Frame Relay

The preceding few sections dealt with the configuration of Frame Relay on a physical serial interface. This exercise will help you reinforce your understanding of this material by configuring a simple Frame Relay connection. Inverse ARP will be used to resolve the addresses for the VC. The DLCI number on both sides is 100. You'll perform this lab using Boson's NetSim simulator. You can find a picture of the network diagram for Boson's NetSim simulator in the Introduction of this book. After starting up the simulator, click the Labs tab at the bottom left of the window. Click the McGraw-Hill Education tab (to the right of the Standard and Custom tabs) at the top left. Next, double-click Exercise 13-1. This will load the lab configuration based on the exercises in Chapter 6.

1. On the 2600-1 router, disable `serial0`—this is the dedicated point-to-point connection—so that you can set up Frame Relay.

   Click the Lab Instructions tab and use the drop-down selector for Devices to choose 2600-1; or click the NetMap tab and double-click the 2600-1 device icon. Execute the following: **configure terminal**, **interface serial0**, **shutdown**, and **end**. Use the **show interfaces** command to check the status of the interfaces. At this point, only the `fa0/0` interface on the 2600-1 should be enabled.

2. On the 2600-2 router, disable `serial0`—this is the dedicated point-to-point connection— so that you can set up Frame Relay.

   Click the Lab Instructions tab and use the drop-down selector for Devices to choose 2600-2; or click the NetMap tab and double-click the 2600-2 device icon. Execute the following: **configure terminal**, **interface serial0**, **shutdown**, and **end**. Use the **show interfaces** command to check the status of the interfaces. At this point, only the `fa0/0` interface on the 2600-2 should be enabled.

3. Enable Frame Relay on the 2600-1. Enable the `serial1` interface. Use the Cisco frame type for Frame Relay. Set the LMI type to ITU-T. Assign the IP address.

   Click the Lab Instructions tab and use the drop-down selector for Devices to choose 2600-1; or click the NetMap tab and double-click the 2600-1 device icon. Enable the Frame Relay interface: **configure terminal**, `interface serial1`, and `no shutdown`. Set the encapsulation and frame type: `encapsulation frame-relay`. Set the LMI type: `frame-relay lmi-type q933a`. Assign the IP address on the interface: `ip address 192.168.10.1 255.255.255.0`. Exit Configuration mode: `end`.

4. Verify the operational state of the interface as well as LMI.

    Use the `show interfaces` command to verify that the interface is up and up and that LMI is functioning. Use the `show frame-relay lmi` command to make sure the router is sending and receiving LMI information.

5. Enable Frame Relay on the 2600-2. Enable the `serial1` interface. Use the Cisco frame type for Frame Relay. Set the LMI type to ITU-T. Assign the IP address. Verify the operation of LMI.

    Click the Lab Instructions tab and use the drop-down selector for Devices to choose 2600-2; or click the NetMap tab and double-click the 2600-2 device icon. From the 2600-2 router, enable the interface: `configure terminal`, `interface serial1`, and `no shutdown`. Set the encapsulation and frame type: `encapsulation frame-relay`. Set the LMI type: `frame-relay lmi-type q933a`. Assign the IP address on the interface: `ip address 192.168.10.2 255.255.255.0`. Exit Configuration mode: `end`.

6. Verify the operational state of the interface as well as LMI.

    Use the `show interfaces` command to verify that the interface is up and up and that LMI is functioning. Use the `show frame-relay lmi` command to make sure the router is sending and receiving LMI information.

7. Verify your PVC configuration and status on the 2600-2.

    View the resolution entry: `show frame-relay map`. View the PVC: `show frame-relay pvc`. The status of the VC should be ACTIVE.

8. Verify your PVC configuration and status on the 2600-1.

    Click the Lab Instructions tab and use the drop-down selector for Devices to choose 2600-1; or click the NetMap tab and double-click the 2600-1 device icon. View the resolution entry: `show frame-relay map`. View the PVC: `show frame-relay pvc`. The status of the VC should be ACTIVE.

9. Ping the 2600-2's Frame Relay interface address.

    Test connectivity: `ping 192.168.10.2`. The ping should be successful.

10. On the 2600-1 router, set up a static route to the 2600-2's remote network. View the routing table.

On the 2600-1, set up the static route to reach 192.168.3.0/24: `configure terminal` and `ip route 192.168.3.0 255.255.255.0 192.168.10.2`. Exit Configuration mode: `end`. View the routing table and look for the static route: `show ip route`.

11. On the 2600-2 router, set up a static route to the 2600-1's remote network. View the routing table.

Click the Lab Instructions tab and use the drop-down selector for Devices to choose 2600-2; or click the NetMap tab and double-click the 2600-2 device icon. On the 2600-2, set up the static route to reach 192.168.3.0/24: `configure terminal` and `ip route 192.168.1.0 255.255.255.0 192.168.10.1`. Exit Configuration mode: `end`. View the routing table and look for the static route: `show ip route`.

12. From Host-1, test the connection to Host-3.

Click the Lab Instructions tab and use the drop-down selector for Devices to choose Host-1; or click the NetMap tab and double-click the Host-1 device icon. On Host-1, ping Host-3: `ping 192.168.3.10`. The ping should be successful.

You should now be more familiar with setting up a basic manually resolved Frame Relay connection to a remote site.

CERTIFICATION OBJECTIVE 13.04

Non-Broadcast Multi-Access Environments

Non-broadcast multi-access (NBMA) is a term used to describe WAN networks that use VCs for connectivity. In a broadcast medium in LAN environments such as Ethernet, every device on a segment or VLAN is in the same broadcast domain—when a device generates a broadcast, every other device in the broadcast domain will see the segment, as is shown in the top part of Figure 13-10. As you can see in this example, RouterA generates one broadcast and the other two routers, RouterB and RouterC, receive it. With WAN networks that use VCs, each device is connected to another device via a point-to-point VC—only two devices can be connected to a VC. This poses a problem with NBMA environments.

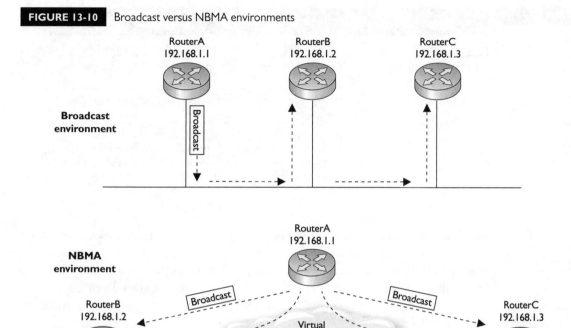

FIGURE 13-10   Broadcast versus NBMA environments

An NBMA environment is an environment that allows access by multiple devices but doesn't support a traditional broadcast environment such as Ethernet. Frame Relay is an example of an NBMA network.

Topology Types

Before reading more about the issues of NBMA environments, consider some of the topologies you can use to connect your devices using VCs. Table 13-5 contains the terms used to describe these various topologies. The bottom part of Figure 13-10 shows an example of a fully meshed network. In such a network, it is easy to emulate a

TABLE 13-5	Topology	Description
NBMA Topology Types	Fully meshed	Your router has VC connections to every other router.
	Partially meshed	Your router has VC connections to some, but not all, of the other routers.
	Point-to-point	Your router has a VC connection on only one other router (this is used to emulate leased lines/dedicated circuit connections).
	Star	Your router has VC connections to some, but not all, of the other routers. This is sometimes called a *hub-and-spoke* topology, where the routers are partially meshed. Each remote site router has a connection to the central site router.

broadcast environment. In this environment, your router *replicates* the local broadcast across every VC in the subnet on that interface. For example, in Figure 13-10, when RouterA wants to send a local broadcast, it sends it across the two VCs to RouterB and RouterC. In a fully meshed environment, every device receives the original broadcast frame. This process is also true if RouterB or RouterC generates a broadcast in this example.

Split Horizon Issues

The main problem of NBMA environments arises when the network is *partially* meshed for a *subnet*. This can create problems with routing protocols that support split horizon. Recall from Chapter 4 that distance vector protocols, such as RIP, use split horizon to prevent routing loops. Split horizon states that if routing information is learned on an interface, this routing information will not be propagated out the same interface.

This is an issue with partially meshed networks that use VCs. For instance, two routers may be in the same subnet but not have a VC between them. With partially meshed networks, this can create routing issues. Look at Figure 13-11 to see the problem. This figure shows a network in which RouterA has a VC to the other three routers, but these three routers must go through RouterA to reach the other routers (a hub-and-spoke/star topology). The assumption here is that all of the routers are in the same subnet and the three VCs terminated at RouterA are going into the same serial interface.

Let's look at this from a routing perspective, assuming that these routers are running RIPv2. RouterB, RouterC, and RouterD have no issues—they have

FIGURE 13-11   NBMA and split horizon issues

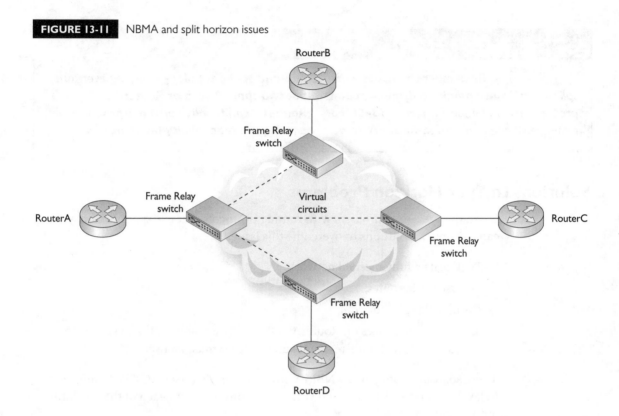

only one VC apiece and can send and receive their routing updates on their VCs. However, RouterA has a problem disseminating routing information from RouterB, RouterC, or RouterD to the other routers in the subnet.

For example, assume that RouterB generates a routing update. Since RouterB doesn't have a VC to RouterC and RouterD, it forwards the update to RouterA, in hopes that RouterA will forward this to the other two routers in the subnet. However, when RouterA receives the routing update from RouterB, RouterA can't forward this to RouterC and RouterD because of split horizon. Even though these two routers are off of different VCs than RouterB, they are off of the *same* physical interface. Therefore, by default, any routing information from these remote routers will not be propagated by RouterA to the other remote counterparts.

Figure 13-11 shows a prime example of an NBMA environment. Even though it is possible to reach every router in the subnet, even if it takes an extra hop, in the WAN network, broadcasts (and multicasts) don't function correctly.

Solutions to Split Horizon Problems

Given the preceding problem with routing protocols that use split horizon, you can use several solutions to overcome this issue:

■ Create a fully meshed network.

■ Use static routes.

■ Disable split horizon.

■ Use subinterfaces on RouterA and associate a single VC and subnet to each subinterface. (Point-to-point subinterfaces must be used.)

These solutions apply to any NBMA environment that uses VCs, including Frame Relay, X.25, and ATM. The following paragraphs deal with each of these solutions individually.

As to the first solution, if you fully mesh your WAN network, you don't have to deal with split horizon problems with distance vector protocols: every router has a VC to every other router in the WAN. Therefore, when any router generates a routing update broadcast, the broadcast is replicated across every VC to all of the destination routers. The main problem with this solution is that to fully mesh your WAN network, you have to purchase a lot of VCs. In many cases, this doesn't make financial sense. For instance, in Figure 13-11, if most of the traffic is from RouterB, RouterC, and RouterD to RouterA, it makes no sense to pay extra money just to replicate the routing updates to the three nonconnected routers.

The second solution has you configure static routes on RouterB, RouterC, and RouterD to solve your routing problems. This works fine if the number of networks and subnets these routers are connected to is small. But if these are major regional sites, with hundreds of networks behind these routers, then setting up static routes becomes a monumental task. Not only does it take a lot of time to configure all of these routes, but you must also test and troubleshoot them, making this solution not scalable.

The third solution has you disable split horizon on RouterA. Some layer 3 protocols allow you to disable split horizon, and some don't. And if the routing protocol allows you to disable split horizon, it is an all-or-nothing proposition. In other words, Cisco doesn't let you enable or disable split horizon on an interface-by-interface basis. This can create problems if RouterA has multiple LAN connections. By disabling split horizon in this situation, you are allowing RouterB, RouterC, and RouterD to learn each other's routes, but you may be creating routing loops on the LAN side of RouterA.

Subinterfaces

The fourth solution is the *preferred* method for solving split horizon and routing problems in NBMA environments. Recall from Chapter 6 that a subinterface is a logical interface associated with a single physical interface. A physical interface can support many subinterfaces. Cisco routers treat subinterfaces just as they do physical interfaces. You can shut down a physical interface, shutting down all of its associated subinterfaces, or you can shut down a single subinterface while keeping the remaining subinterfaces operational.

When using subinterfaces in a Frame Relay environment, you basically configure two commands on the physical (or major) interface:

- `encapsulation frame-relay`
- `frame-relay lmi-type`

All other configuration commands should be placed under the appropriate *subinterface.*

Overcoming Split Horizon Issues

By using subinterfaces and placing each subinterface in a *separate* subnet, you make it possible for routing information received on one subinterface to be propagated to other subinterfaces on the same physical interface. Figure 13-12 shows an example of how subinterfaces can be used to overcome split horizon issues in a partially meshed NBMA environment. In this example, you create a separate subinterface on RouterA for each destination. Since RouterA is using a separate *subinterface* for each of these connections, a different subnet is used for each router-to-router VC. With this setup, if RouterB sent a routing update to RouterA, it would be processed on one subinterface and the routing information could be broadcast out the other two subinterfaces. This process allows you to overcome the split horizon problem.

on the *The main problem with the subinterface solution, however, is that for each*
(j) o b *subinterface on RouterA, you need a separate network or subnet number.*
Therefore, it is highly recommended that you use a 255.255.255.252 subnet
mask (/30), which allows for two host addresses per subnet, conserving
addresses.

FIGURE 13-12   Subinterfaces and split horizon

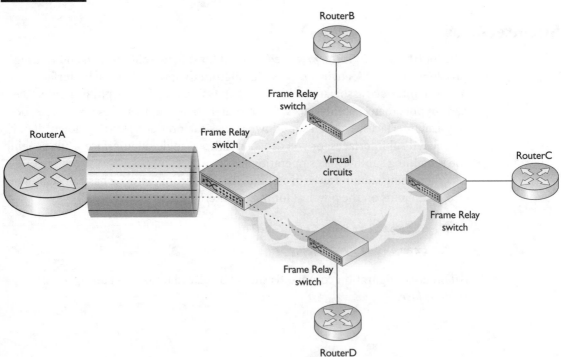

Subinterface Types

As was described in Chapter 6, two types of subinterfaces exist: point-to-point and multipoint. Multipoint subinterfaces (subinterfaces with many VCs terminated on them) are good for fully meshed networks. If the WAN is fully meshed, the devices can be placed in the same subnet and thus require only one network number to address your devices. However, multipoint subinterfaces don't work well in partially meshed network designs. In this situation, they have problems with routing protocols that use split horizon.

on the *If you are concerned about the addressing needs required of point-to-point*
job *subinterfaces, you can use the `ip unnumbered` Interface Subconfiguration mode command. This command borrows an IP address from another active interface on the router without your having to assign a different subnet to the connection. Most network administrators shy away from this command because it has its own set of issues, which are beyond the scope of this book.*

Point-to-point subinterfaces work best in partially meshed environments or in environments in which you need to simulate a leased-line connection. Point-to-point subinterfaces are used to overcome routing protocols that use split horizon. But like multipoint subinterfaces, point-to-point subinterfaces have their fair share of problems. In the biggest problem, each point-to-point subinterface requires a separate network or subnet number. If you have 200 subinterfaces on your serial interface, then you need 200 subnets to accommodate your addressing needs.

Creating Subinterfaces

13.09. The digital resources that accompany this book contain a multimedia demonstration of creating subinterfaces on a router.

To create a subinterface, use the following syntax:

```
Router(config)# interface serial [slot_#/]port_#.subinterface_#
                          {point-to-point | multipoint}
Router(config-subif)#
```

Subinterface numbers can range from 1 to well over 100 million. What number you choose as the subinterface number doesn't matter; it needs to be unique only among all of the subinterfaces for a given physical interface. The router uses this number to differentiate the subinterfaces for each physical interface. Once you create a subinterface, notice that the prompt changed from `Router(config)#` to `Router(config-subif)#`.

on the
①ob

Once you create a subinterface, you can delete it by prefacing the `interface` command with the `no` parameter. However, once you delete the subinterface, the subinterface still exists in the router's memory. To completely remove the subinterface, you need to save your configuration and reboot your router. Also, if you want to change the subinterface type from multipoint to point-to-point or vice versa, you must delete the subinterface, save your configuration, and reboot your router.

Configuring Frame Relay with Subinterfaces

When you are configuring Frame Relay with subinterfaces, you must associate your DLCI or DLCIs with each subinterface by using the **frame-relay interface-dlci** command:

```
Router(config)# interface serial [slot_#/]port_#.subinterface_#
                          {point-to-point | multipoint}
Router(config-subif)# frame-relay interface-dlci local_DLCI_#
```

If you have a point-to-point subinterface, you can assign only one VC, and thus one DLCI, to it. If it is a multipoint subinterface, you can assign multiple DLCIs to it. When creating your subinterfaces, it is a common practice to match the subinterface number with the DLCI number; however, remember that these two numbers have nothing in common and can be different. Also, make sure that you assign your layer 3 addressing to the subinterface and *not* the physical (main) interface. The frame type and LMI type are, however, configured on the physical interface.

The **frame-relay interface-dlci** command uses dynamic resolution with Inverse ARP. If you can't use Inverse ARP, or don't want to, then use the **frame-relay map** command on the subinterface to perform manual resolution, like this:

```
Router(config)# interface serial [slot_#/]port_#.subinterface_#
                          {point-to-point | multipoint}
```

```
Router(config-if)# frame-relay map protocol_name
                        destination_address local_dlci_#
                        [broadcast] [ietf | cisco]
```

Example Configuration with Multipoint Subinterfaces

This section offers an example of using multipoint subinterfaces on a router to set up Frame Relay connections. Use the network shown in Figure 13-13. In this example, assume that LMI is being autosensed and a single multipoint subinterface is used on RouterA.

Here's the configuration for RouterA:

```
RouterA(config)# interface serial 0
RouterA(config-if)# encapsulation frame-relay ietf
RouterA(config-if)# no shutdown
RouterA(config-if)# exit
RouterA(config)# interface serial0.1 multipoint
RouterA(config-subif)# ip address 192.168.1.1 255.255.255.0
RouterA(config-subif)# frame-relay interface-dlci 101
RouterA(config-subif)# frame-relay interface-dlci 102
```

FIGURE 13-13

Multipoint subinterface example

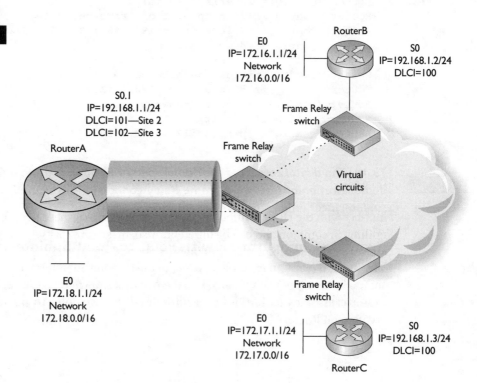

Since this is a partially meshed network and you are terminating two VCs on the same subinterface, you need to do one of the following to solve split horizon issues: disable split horizon on RouterA or configure static routes on RouterB and RouterC.

This example configures static routes. Here's the configuration for RouterB:

```
RouterB(config)# interface serial 0
RouterB(config-if)# encapsulation frame-relay ietf
RouterB(config-if)# ip address 192.168.1.2 255.255.255.0
RouterB(config-if)# no shutdown
RouterB(config-if)# exit
RouterB(config)# interface ethernet 0
RouterB(config-if)# ip address 172.16.1.1 255.255.255.0
RouterB(config-if)# no shutdown
RouterB(config-if)# exit
RouterB(config)# ip route 172.17.0.0 255.255.0.0 192.168.1.1
```

Notice in this example that you did not need to configure the DLCI number on the physical interface, since the router will learn this from the full status update via LMI. Also notice the static route on RouterB, which allows it to reach RouterC's network.

Here's the configuration for RouterC:

```
RouterC(config)# interface serial 0
RouterC(config-if)# encapsulation frame-relay ietf
RouterC(config-if)# ip address 192.168.1.3 255.255.255.0
RouterC(config-if)# no shutdown
RouterC(config-if)# exit
RouterC(config)# interface ethernet 0
RouterC(config-if)# ip address 172.17.1.1 255.255.255.0
RouterC(config-if)# no shutdown
RouterC(config-if)# exit
RouterC(config)# ip route 172.16.0.0 255.255.0.0 192.168.1.1
```

13.10. The digital resources that accompany this book contain a multimedia demonstration of setting up Frame Relay connections using multipoint subinterfaces on a router.

Example Configuration with Point-to-Point Subinterfaces

This section offers an example of using point-to-point subinterfaces on a router to set up Frame Relay connections. Use the network shown in Figure 13-14. In this example, assume that LMI is being autosensed and two point-to-point subinterfaces are used on RouterA.

FIGURE 13-14

Point-to-point
subinterface
example

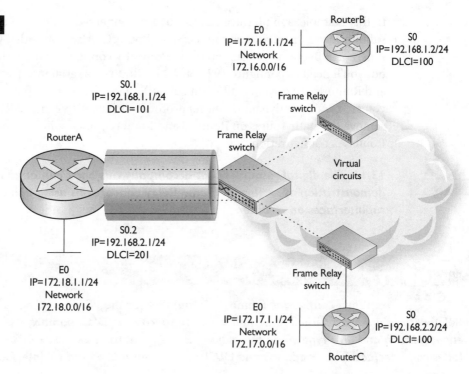

The configurations on RouterB and RouterC are the same as before, with the exception that the static routes are not needed, since point-to-point subinterfaces are being used on RouterA and RouterC will need a different IP address because of the two subnets (instead of one). The biggest difference is the configuration on RouterA, shown here:

```
RouterA(config)# interface serial 0
RouterA(config-if)# encapsulation frame-relay ietf
RouterA(config-if)# no shutdown
RouterA(config-if)# exit
RouterA(config)# interface serial0.1 point-to-point
RouterA(config-subif)# ip address 192.168.1.1 255.255.255.0
RouterA(config-subif)# frame-relay interface-dlci 101
RouterA(config-subif)# exit
RouterA(config)# interface serial0.2 point-to-point
RouterA(config-subif)# frame-relay interface-dlci 201
RouterA(config-subif)# ip address 192.168.2.1 255.255.255.0
```

In this example, subinterface `serial0.1` is connected to RouterB and subinterface `serial0.2` is connected to RouterC. Also notice that there is a different subnet on each subinterface. RouterB's configuration doesn't change, but you'll need to configure 192.168.2.2 on RouterC's serial interface (RouterB and RouterC are now in a different subnet). One other item to point out is that if you are running a dynamic routing protocol such as RIPv2 or EIGRP, you could remove the static routes on RouterB and RouterC, since split horizon is solved by RouterA's configuration.

Video

13.11. The digital resources that accompany this book contain a multimedia demonstration of setting up Frame Relay connections using point-to-point subinterfaces on a router.

exam
ⓦatch

When configuring Frame Relay with subinterfaces, the Frame Relay encapsulation and LMI type go on the major (physical) interface. The IP address and DLCI number for the VC go on the subinterface. To specify the DLCI number, use the `frame-relay interface-dlci` or `frame-relay map` command on the subinterface.

EXERCISE 13-2

MHE Lab

Configuring Frame Relay with Subinterfaces

The preceding few sections dealt with the configuration of Frame Relay using subinterfaces. This exercise will help you reinforce your understanding of this material by configuring a simple Frame Relay point-to-point connection. This exercise builds upon Exercise 13-1, moving the configuration from that exercise and placing it on a point-to-point subinterface. Also, Inverse ARP is used to perform the resolution. You'll perform this lab using Boson's NetSim simulator. You can find a picture of the network diagram for Boson's NetSim simulator in the Introduction of this book. This exercise has you first set up two routers (2600-1 and 2600-2) and verify network connectivity. Following this, you'll configure your

ACL. After starting up the simulator, click the Labs tab at the bottom left of the window. Click the McGraw-Hill Education tab (to the right of the Standard and Custom tabs) at the top left. Next, double-click Exercise 13-2. This will load the lab configuration based on Exercise 13-1.

1. Remove the IP address on the physical interface of the 2600-1.

   Click the Lab Instructions tab and use the drop-down selector for Devices to choose 2600-1; or click the NetMap tab and double-click the 2600-1 device icon. Remove the IP address on the interface: **configure terminal**, **interface serial1**, and **no ip address 192.168.10.1 255.255.255.0**. Exit Configuration mode: **end**.

2. Verify your changes on the 2600-1.

   Use the **show interface serial1** command to verify the removal of the IP address and that the interface is up and up and that LMI is functioning. Use the **show frame-relay lmi** command to make sure the router is still sending and receiving LMI information.

3. Remove the IP address on the physical interface of the 2600-2.

   Click the Lab Instructions tab and use the drop-down selector for Devices to choose 2600-2; or click the NetMap tab and double-click the 2600-2 device icon. From the 2600-2 router, remove the IP address on the interface: **configure terminal**, **interface serial1**, and **no ip address 192.168.10.2 255.255.255.0**. Exit Configuration mode: **end**.

4. Verify your changes on the 2600-2.

   Use the **show interface serial1** command to verify the removal of the IP address and that the interface is up and up and that LMI is functioning. Use the **show frame-relay lmi** command to make sure the router is still sending and receiving LMI information.

5. Create a point-to-point subinterface on the 2600-1 router with a subinterface number of 100. Assign the DLCI to the subinterface. The DLCI number used locally is 100. Assign the IP address to the subinterface.

   Click the Lab Instructions tab and use the drop-down selector for Devices to choose 2600-1; or click the NetMap tab and double-click the 2600-1 device icon. Create the subinterface: **configure terminal** and **interface** serial 1.100 point-to-point. Assign the DLCI: `frame-relay interface-dlci 100`. Assign the IP address: `ip address 192.168.10.1 255.255.255.0`. Exit Configuration mode: `end`.

6. Verify the PVC's configuration on the 2600-1.

   View the PVC: `show frame-relay pvc`.

7. Create a point-to-point subinterface on the 2600-2 router with a subinterface number of 100. Assign the DLCI to the subinterface. The DLCI number used locally is 100. Assign the IP address to the subinterface.

   Click the Lab Instructions tab and use the drop-down selector for Devices to choose 2600-2; or click the NetMap tab and double-click the 2600-2 device icon. On the 2600-2, create the subinterface: `configure terminal`, `interface serial 1.100 point-to-point`. Assign the DLCI: `frame-relay interface-dlci 100`. Assign the IP address: `ip address 192.168.10.2 255.255.255.0`. Exit Configuration mode: `end`.

8. Verify the PVC's configuration on the 2600-2.

   View the PVC: `show frame-relay pvc`.

9. On the 2600-1, test the connection to the 2600-2. Verify the router's routing table.

   Click the Lab Instructions tab and use the drop-down selector for Devices to choose 2600-1; or click the NetMap tab and double-click the 2600-1 device icon. On the 2600-1 router, ping the 2600-2's Frame Relay interface: `ping 192.168.10.2`. The ping should be successful. If it isn't, wait 1 minute and try again—the Inverse ARP might be taking place.

10. From Host-1, test the connection to Host-3.

    Click the Lab Instructions tab and use the drop-down selector for Devices to choose Host-1; or click the NetMap tab and double-click the Host-1 device icon. On Host-1, ping Host-3: `ping 192.168.3.10`. The ping should be successful.

Now you should be more familiar with configuring Frame Relay with subinterfaces.

INSIDE THE EXAM

Virtual Circuits

You should be very familiar with the terms used in Frame Relay, some of the basic configuration commands, and how to interpret the output of the various **show** commands to troubleshoot problems. VCs are a much cheaper solution than using dedicated lines/circuits and are more easily provisioned after the initial line is installed to the carrier's switch.

Frame Relay Terms

You should be very familiar with the terms listed in Table 13-1, including the use of LMI and FECNs and BECNs. Remember that periodically a full status update is received from the carrier switch, containing a list of the VCs, their configurations, and their statuses. You should know how DLCIs are used to reach destinations and that they are locally significant: study Figure 13-5 and the discussion in the "DLCI Example" section.

Frame Relay Configuration

Remember the two encapsulation types for a Frame Relay frame: Cisco and IETF. IETF is used in a multivendor environment. If you don't configure the LMI type, Cisco routers will autosense it. The **show interfaces** and **show frame-relay lmi** commands will indicate whether you are sending status enquiries and receiving replies from the carrier switch. Know how to resolve layer 3 addresses to local DLCIs with the **frame-relay map** command and how to get routing updates across the VC with the **broadcast** parameter. Know how to troubleshoot misconfigured manually resolved VCs. Be familiar with how Inverse ARP works and be able to identify VCs dynamically resolved with the **show frame-relay pvc** command. Know the three states of a VC—inactive, active, and deleted—and how they can be used to troubleshoot problems with a VC.

Non-Broadcast Multi-Access Environments

Be familiar with the problems associated with connectivity and routing across an NBMA network and how to solve split horizon problems. The recommended solution is subinterfaces, where a single VC and subnet is associated with each subinterface. Know how to associate a DLCI to a subinterface with the **frame-relay interface-dlci** command.

CERTIFICATION SUMMARY

Frame Relay uses VCs for connectivity. A VC is a logical connection between devices. There are two types of VCs: PVCs, which are similar to a leased line, and SVCs, which are similar to circuit-switched calls. VCs have advantages over leased lines in that once a physical connection is provisioned, it is easy to add VCs as well as allocate bandwidth for users or applications by using VCs. If you want to fully mesh your Frame Relay routers, use this formula to figure out the number of required connections: $(N \times (N - 1)) / 2$.

LMI defines how a Frame Relay DTE (router) interacts with a Frame Relay DCE (carrier switch). There are three types of LMI: Gang of Four, ANSI Annex D, and ITU-T Q.933 Annex A. LMI is local to the two devices (router and Frame Relay switch) and is never forwarded to another device. By default, DTEs originate LMI messages. Cisco routers generate LMI messages every 10 seconds, with a full status update occurring every sixth message. Each VC is given an address, called a DLCI. DLCIs are also locally significant and can change on a segment-by-segment basis. Carrier switches remap DLCI numbers in the Frame Relay header if a DLCI addressing change occurs from one segment to another. Carriers use two methods for transporting Frame Relay frames across their network.

Many parameters can be used to control the rate of traffic and congestion for a VC. CIR is the guaranteed average rate of a VC. B_C is a higher supported average rate, but measured over a shorter period than CIR. If frames exceed this rate, they are marked as discard eligible and are the first frames dropped by the carrier when the carrier experiences congestion problems. B_E is the maximum rate at which the carrier will service the VC; any data sent above this rate is dropped. Oversubscription occurs when the combined CIRs of all of your VCs exceeds your access rate (physical line rate). You are betting that not all VCs will simultaneously run at their CIRs. FECN and BECN are used to indicate congestion from the source to the destination DTE.

There are two Frame Relay encapsulations: Cisco's and IETF's. Use the **encapsulation frame-relay** command to specify the encapsulation type. Cisco routers can autosense the LMI type. To hard-code the LMI type, use the **frame-relay lmi-type** command. The **show interfaces** and **show frame-relay lmi** commands show the number of LMI messages sent and received.

You can perform layer 3 to DLCI resolution in your configuration in two ways: manually and dynamically. To specify a manually resolved VC, use the **frame-relay map** command. Inverse ARP, which occurs every 60 seconds, allows you to dynamically learn the layer 3 addresses from each VC. Inverse ARP requires the VC to be in an active state, which indicates the VC is functioning between the two DTEs. If the VC is in an inactive state, the VC is functioning between the DTE and DCE, but there is a problem between the local DCE and the remote DTE. If the VC is in a deleted state, there is a problem with the VC between the local DTE and the local DCE. Use the `show frame-relay map` command to see your resolutions and the `show frame-relay pvc` command to view your PVCs.

NBMA environments have problems with distance vector routing protocols and split horizon when the network is partially meshed. To overcome split horizon, you can use any of the following solutions: fully mesh the network, use static routes, disable split horizon, or use subinterfaces. The recommended approach is to use subinterfaces. When you are configuring Frame Relay for subinterfaces, the encapsulation type and LMI type go on the main physical interface. All layer 3 addressing and the DLCI number for the VC (`frame-relay interface-dlci`) are configured on the subinterface.

TWO-MINUTE DRILL

Virtual Circuits

❑ Use this formula to figure out the number of connections required to fully mesh a network: $(N \times (N - 1)) / 2$.

❑ VCs are not tied to any particular time slots on a channelized connection and are much easier to add or change than leased lines.

❑ A PVC is similar to a leased line and is always up. An SVC is similar to a telephone circuit-switched connection and is brought up when you have data to send and is torn down when you are finished transmitting data. PVCs are best used if you have delay-sensitive information or you are constantly sending data. SVCs are used when you occasionally need to send information or for backup purposes.

Frame Relay Terms

❑ LMI defines how the Frame Relay DTE and DCE interact and is locally significant. There are three implementations of LMI: ITU-T Annex A, ANSI Annex D, and the Gang of Four. Cisco routers autosense LMI. By default, Cisco routers send out LMI queries every 10 seconds, with a full status update every sixth query.

❑ DLCIs are used to locally identity a VC—they are the address of the VC. Since this number has only local significance, it can change on a hop-by-hop basis.

❑ Congestion experienced as frames go to a destination will have the FECN bit set. The destination will then send a frame—with the BECN bit set—back to the source, indicating congestion.

Frame Relay Configuration

❑ The `encapsulation frame-relay` command specifies the encapsulation type. There are two frame types: `cisco` and `ietf`; `cisco` is the default, but `ietf` is an open standard and is used in a multi-vendor environment.

❏ Use the `frame-relay lmi-type` command to hard-code the LMI type. Cisco routers can autosense the LMI type. Use these commands to troubleshoot LMI: `show interfaces`, `show frame-relay lmi`, and `debug frame-relay lmi`.

❏ To configure a manually resolved PVC, use the `frame-relay map` command. If you omit the `broadcast` parameter, local broadcasts and multicasts won't traverse the VC. Inverse ARP is used for dynamic resolution. This occurs on a VC after the full status update is received and the VC is not already manually resolved.

❏ There are three statuses of VCs: active (the VC is up and operational between the two DTEs), inactive (the connection is functioning at least between the DTE and DCE), and deleted (the local DTE/DCE connection is not functioning). To view a PVC, use the `show frame-relay pvc` command. To see the resolution entries, use the `show frame-relay map` command.

Non-Broadcast Multi-Access Environments

❏ Partially meshed networks have VC connections to some, but not all, routers. A star (hub-and-spoke) topology is partially meshed. Partially meshed networks with VCs have problems with split horizon, which can be overcome by using one of the following solutions: use a fully meshed network, use static routes, disable split horizon, or use subinterfaces.

❏ When using subinterfaces, the physical interface has the encapsulation and LMI type configured on it. Everything else is configured on the subinterface. When you delete a subinterface, save your configuration and reboot the router to remove it from RAM. Point-to-point subinterfaces should be used to solve split horizon problems.

❏ Use the `frame-relay interface-dlci` command to associate a VC to a particular subinterface.

SELF TEST

The following Self Test questions will help you measure your understanding of the material presented in this chapter. Read all the choices carefully, as there may be more than one correct answer. Choose all correct answers for each question.

Virtual Circuits

1. You have a total of five routers. _____ dedicated circuits are required to fully mesh the network, where every router needs _____ interfaces.
   A. 5, 5
   B. 8, 4
   C. 10, 5
   D. 10, 4

Frame Relay Terms

2. _____ defines how the Frame Relay DTE and DCE interact with each other.
   A. DLCI
   B. CIR
   C. LMI
   D. PMI

3. The address of a Frame Relay VC is called a _____.
   A. data link layer connection identifier
   B. data layer connection index
   C. data link connection index
   D. data link connection identifier

4. When a carrier experiences congestion, it marks the _____ bit in the header of the Frame Relay frame.
   A. CIR
   B. DE
   C. BECN
   D. FECN

Frame Relay Configuration

5. Cisco routers generate LMI enquiries every _____ seconds and a full status update every _____ seconds.

   A. 10, 60

   B. 10, 6

   C. 60, 300

   D. 15, 60

6. Enter the router command to have the serial interface use a frame encapsulation type compatible with a non-Cisco router: _____.

7. When using the `show interfaces` command, which Frame Relay information can you not see?

   A. The DLCI number used for LMI

   B. The number of LMIs sent and received

   C. Statuses of PVCs

   D. The LMI type

8. Which Frame Relay command is used to manually resolve layer 3 addresses to DLCIs?

   A. `frame-relay interface-dlci`

   B. `frame-relay map`

   C. `frame-relay resolve`

   D. `frame-relay lmi-type`

9. If you see a VC with an inactive status, this indicates which of the following?

   A. The connection between both Frame Relay DTEs is up and operational.

   B. The connection between your Frame Relay DTE and DCE is up and operational, but something is wrong with the connection between your connected Frame Relay switch and the destination DTE.

   C. You are not receiving any LMI messages from the Frame Relay switch.

Non-Broadcast Multi-Access Environments

10. _____ topologies in NBMA environments do not have problems with split horizon.

   A. Partially meshed

   B. Fully meshed

   C. Hub-and-spoke

   D. Star

11. Enter the router command to associate DLCI 500 within a subinterface: _____.

SELF TEST ANSWERS

Virtual Circuits

1. ☑ **D.** Use the $(N \times (N - 1) / 2)$ formula for the number of circuits. You need a total of 10 circuits and 4 interfaces on each router.

   ☒ **A** has the wrong number of circuits and interfaces. **B** has the wrong number of circuits. **C** has the wrong number of interfaces.

Frame Relay Terms

2. ☑ **C.** The local management interface (LMI) defines how the Frame Relay DTE and DCE interact with each other.

   ☒ **A** is incorrect because DLCI defines the local address of a VC. **B** is incorrect because CIR defines the average traffic rate for a VC. **D** is incorrect because PMI is a nonexistent acronym in this context.

3. ☑ **D.** The address of a Frame Relay VC is called a data link connection identifier (DLCI).

   ☒ **A** and **B** include the term *layer* and are therefore incorrect. **B** and **C** use the term *index* and are therefore incorrect.

4. ☑ **D.** When a carrier experiences congestion, it marks the FECN bit in the header of the Frame Relay frame.

   ☒ **A** is incorrect because CIR specifies the average rate of a VC. **B** is incorrect because DE is used to mark frames that exceed their allowable rate. **C** is incorrect because BECN is marked by the destination device to indicate congestion and is sent to the source device.

Frame Relay Configuration

5. ☑ **A.** Cisco routers generate LMI enquiries every 10 seconds and a full status update every 60 seconds.

   ☒ **B** specifies the wrong update interval for the full update message. **C** has wrong values for both timers. **D** has a wrong value for the status enquiry timer.

6. ☑ `encapsulation frame-relay ietf`

7. ☑ **C.** When using the `show interfaces` command, you cannot see the statuses of the PVCs—you need to use the `show frame-relay pvc` command.

   ☒ **A**, **B**, and **D** can be seen in the output of this command.

8. ☑ **B.** The `frame-relay map` command is used to manually resolve layer 3 addresses to DLCIs.

   ☒ **A** is incorrect because `frame-relay interface-dlci` associates a DLCI to a subinterface. **C** is a nonexistent command. **D** is incorrect because `frame-relay lmi-type` hard-codes the LMI type for the physical serial interface.

9. ☑ **B.** If you see a VC with an inactive status, this indicates that the connection between your Frame Relay DTE and DCE is up and operational, but something is wrong with the connection between your connected Frame Relay switch and the destination DTE.

   ☒ **A** indicates an active VC. **C** indicates a deleted VC.

Non-Broadcast Multi-Access Environments

10. ☑ **B.** Fully meshed topologies in NBMA environments do not have problems with split horizon.

    ☒ **A, C,** and **D** are incorrect because these topologies have problems with split horizon.

11. ☑ `frame-relay interface-dlci 500`

Part V

Appendixes

A

Exam Readiness
Checklist:
ICND 200-101

Exam Readiness Checklist

Official Objective	Study Guide Coverage	Ch#	Beginner	Intermediate	Advanced
LAN Switching Technologies (21%)					
Identify enhanced switching technologies (RSTP, PVSTP, and EtherChannels)	Switches and Redundancy	3			
Determine the technology and media access control method for Ethernet networks	IOS and Switch Security Review VLAN Review	1 2			
Identify basic switching concepts and the operation of Cisco switches	IOS and Switch Security Review VLAN Review	1 2			
IP Routing Technologies (26%)					
Describe the boot process of Cisco IOS routers	Initial Router Configuration	6			
Configure and verify the operation status of a serial interface	IOS and Switch Security Review WAN Introduction	1 12			
Manage Cisco IOS files, including boot preferences, Cisco IOS images, and licensing	iOS Device Management	7			
Differentiate methods of routing and routing protocols, including administrative distance, split horizon, metric, and next hop	Cisco Routers and LANs Basic Routing	4 9			
Configure and verify OSPF (multi-area), including neighbor adjacencies, OSPF states, configuring OSPFv2, configuring OSPFv3, configuring router IDs, and understanding LSA types and purpose	VLSM OSPF Routing	5 10			
Configure and verify EIGRP (single AS), including understanding feasible distance, feasible successor, administrative distance, metric component, router IDs, auto-summary, path selection, and equal- and unequal-cost load balancing	VLSM EIGRP Routing	5 11			

Exam Readiness Checklist

Official Objective	Study Guide Coverage	Ch#	Beginner	Intermediate	Advanced
Passive interfaces	OSPF Routing EIGRP Routing	10 11			
IP Services (6%)					
Recognize high availability, including VRRP, HSRP, and GLBP	Basic Routing	9			
Configure and verify syslog	Management Protocols for Cisco Devices	8			
Describe SNMPv2 and SNMPv3	Management Protocols for Cisco Devices	8			
Troubleshooting (32%)					
Identify and correct common network problems	IOS and Switch Security Review VLAN Review Initial Router Configuration iOS Device Management Basic Routing	1 2 6 7 9			
Utilize NetFlow data	Management Protocols for Cisco Devices	8			
Troubleshoot and resolve spanning tree operation issues (verify root switch, verify priority, verify spanning tree mode, and verify port states)	Switches and Redundancy	3			
Troubleshoot and resolve routing issues (verify routing is enabled, routing table is correct, and correct path selection)	Initial Router Configuration iOS Device Management Basic Routing OSPF Routing EIGRP Routing	6 7 9 10 11			
Troubleshoot and resolve OSPF problems (verify neighbor adjacencies, hello and dead timers, OSPF area, interface MTU, network types, neighbor states, and OSPF topology table)	OSPF Routing	10			
Troubleshoot and resolve EIGRP problems (verify neighbor adjacencies, AS number, load balancing, and split horizon)	EIGRP Routing	11			

Exam Readiness Checklist

Official Objective	Study Guide Coverage	Ch#	Beginner	Intermediate	Advanced
Troubleshoot and resolve inter-VLAN problems (verify connectivity, encapsulation, subnet, native VLAN, and port mode trunk status)	VLAN Review Initial Router Configuration	2 6			
Troubleshoot and resolve WAN implementation issues, including serial interfaces, frame relay, and PPP	WAN Introduction Frame Relay	12 13			
Monitor NetFlow statistics	Management Protocols for Cisco Devices	8			
Troubleshoot EtherChannel problems	Switches and Redundancy	3			
WAN Technologies (15%)					
Identify WAN technologies, including metro Ethernet, vsat, cellular 3g/4g, MPLS, T1/E1, ISDN, DSL, Frame Relay, cable, and VPN	WAN Introduction	12			
Configure and verify a basic WAN serial connection	WAN Introduction	12			
Configure and verify a PPP connection between two Cisco routers	WAN Introduction	12			
Configure and verify Frame Relay on Cisco routers	Frame Relay	13			
Implement and troubleshoot PPPoE	WAN Introduction	12			

B

About the CD-ROM

The CD-ROM included with this book comes complete with unique electronic practice exam questions written by McGraw-Hill Education authors and delivered by the Boson Exam Environment (BEE); the Boson NetSim Limited Edition (LE) with practice labs written by McGraw-Hill Education authors; Boson Software utilities; video training from the author; a PDF glossary for the book; and a PDF copy of the book for studying on the go.

The software must be installed to access the Boson NetSim LE, the BEE, and the Boson Software utilities.

System Requirements

The system requirements for the Boson NetSim LE and the BEE are as follows:

- **Supported Operating Systems**   Windows 8, Windows 7, Windows Vista, Windows XP
- **NET Framework**   Microsoft .NET Framework Version 4.0
- **Processor**   1-GHz Pentium processor or equivalent (Minimum); 3-GHz Pentium processor or equivalent (Recommended)
- **RAM**   512MB (Minimum); 2GB (Recommended)
- **Hard Disk**   A minimum of 250MB of available space
- **Display**   1024×768, 256 colors (Minimum); 1024×768 high color, 32-bit (Recommended)
- Active Internet connection

The PDF files require Adobe Acrobat, Adobe Reader, or Adobe Digital Editions to view.

Installing and Running the Boson NetSim LE and BEE

If your computer CD-ROM drive is configured to auto run, the CD-ROM should automatically start upon inserting the disc. If the auto run feature did not launch the CD-ROM, browse to the CD-ROM and double-click the Setup icon. From the opening screen, you may install the Boson NetSim LE or the BEE by clicking the Install NetSim LE or the Install BEE links and following the steps on the Boson download page.

For information about technical support related to the content of the practice exam, see "McGraw-Hill Education Content Support" at the end of this appendix. Information about customer support for the Boson Software included on the CD-ROM is also given at the end of the appendix.

Boson NetSim LE

The Boson NetSim LE is a restricted version of the Boson NetSim. Boson NetSim is an interactive network simulator that allows you to simulate a wide variety of tasks as if you are working on a real network. Once you have installed the NetSim LE, you may access it quickly through Start | Programs | Boson Software.

Register the Boson NetSim LE

The first time the simulator runs, it requires registration. Enter your Boson account information along with the activation code found on the inside flap of the envelope that contained the CD-ROM. If you do not have a valid boson .com account, you will have to create one when installing the NetSim LE. Once registration is complete, the software will load. To load any of the labs found in this book, select one of them from the McGraw-Hill Education tab of the Lab Navigator and click the Load Lab button.

BEE and Practice Exams

The BEE is a software-based delivery platform for the electronic practice exams. The electronic practice exams are created to help you review material covered on the CCNA ICND2 certification exam. To assist you in your studies, you have the option to customize your test-taking environment by selecting the number of questions, the type of questions, and the time allowed. The BEE allows you to review questions by topic and also provides the option to take an exam in study mode, which includes references and answers. This practice exam has been written by McGraw-Hill Education authors, is delivered by the BEE, and is available by purchasing this McGraw-Hill Education book.

Installing and Running the BEE

To access your practice exam, install the BEE. Then, use the Exam Wizard to activate the practice exam using the activation code from the back of the book. Note that an active Internet connection is required for the initial activation, download, and use of the practice exam content.

Accessing Your Practice Exam

Follow these steps to access the practice exam on the CD-ROM:

1. Install the Exam Engine by clicking the link from the CD-ROM menu and following the instructions on the Boson download page.
2. The first time you run the software, the Exam Wizard should start and will guide you through the process of activating and downloading the exam.

If the wizard does not automatically start, choose the Exam Wizard option or use the Unlock An Exam option, available through Exam Tools.

Using the Exam Wizard

1. Select the Activate A Purchased Exam option.
2. Enter your activation key (located on the inside flap of the envelope containing the CD-ROM).
3. Select the exam(s) you want to download.

Using the Unlock An Exam Tool

1. Select Unlock An Exam.
2. Enter your e-mail address, password, and activation key (located on the inside flap of the envelope containing the CD-ROM).
3. Select the My New Exams tab.
4. Select the exam(s) you want to download.
5. Click the Download Exam or Download All button.

Video Training from the Author

Video clips provide detailed examples in audio video format direct from the author of the book. You can access the videos directly from the Video table of contents by clicking the Author Video Index link on the main page.

Glossary

A bonus glossary of key terms from the book has been included for your review in PDF format.

PDF Copy of the Book

The entire contents of the book are provided as a PDF on the CD-ROM. This file is viewable on your computer and many portable devices.

- **To view the PDF on a computer**, Adobe Acrobat, Adobe Reader, or Adobe Digital Editions is required. A link to Adobe's web site, where you can download and install Adobe Reader, has been included on the CD-ROM.

Note: *For more information on Adobe Reader and to check for the most recent version of the software, visit Adobe's web site at www.adobe.com and search for the free Adobe Reader or look for Adobe Reader on the product page. Adobe Digital Editions can also be downloaded from the Adobe web site.*

- **To view the PDF on a portable device**, copy the PDF file to your computer from the CD-ROM, and then copy the file to your portable device using a USB or other connection. Adobe offers a mobile version of Adobe Reader, the Adobe Reader mobile app, which currently supports iOS and Android. For customers using Adobe Digital Editions and an iPad, you may have to download and install a separate reader program on your device. The Adobe web site has a list of recommended applications, and McGraw-Hill Education recommends the Bluefire Reader.

Help

Individual help features are available through the Boson NetSim LE and the BEE. Review the Boson NetSim LE User's Guide for details on registration and how-to directions on completing the practice labs.

Removal of the Software Installation(s)

For best results for removal of Windows programs, choose Start | Programs | Control Panel | Add/Remove Programs to remove the NetSim (LE) or the Boson Exam Engine software.

McGraw-Hill Education Content Support

For questions regarding the PDF copy of the book, e-mail **techsolutions@mhedu .com** or visit **http://mhp.softwareassist.com**.

For questions regarding book content, content of the practice exam, videos, or additional study materials, e-mail **customer.service@mheducation.com**. For customers outside the United States, e-mail **international_cs@mheducation. com**.

Boson Software Technical Support

For technical problems with the Boson NetSim LE (installation, operation, and removal installations) and the Boson Exam Engine, and for questions regarding the Boson activation, e-mail **support@boson.com**, or visit **www.boson.com**, or follow the help instructions in the help features included with the Boson NetSim LE or BEE.

INDEX

E

S

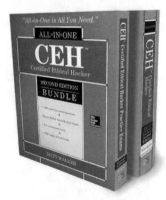

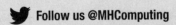